The handbook of communication skills

The Handbook of Communication Skills is recognised as one of the core texts in the field of communication. This thoroughly revised and updated third edition arrives at a time of considerable growing interest in this area, with recent research showing the importance of communication skills for success in many walks of life. The book's core principle, that interpersonal communication can be conceptualised as a form of skilled activity, is examined in detail and a comprehensive transactional model of skilled communication presented, which takes into account current conceptual and research perspectives.

This book provides a comprehensive analysis of research, theory and practice in the key skill areas of communication, such as non-verbal communication, persuasion, leadership, assertiveness, self-disclosure, listening and negotiation. Each chapter is written by a recognised authority in that particular specialism, among them world leaders in their particular fields. In the 10 years since the last edition, a large volume of research has been published and the text has been comprehensively updated by reviewing this wealth of data. In addition, a new chapter on persuasion has been added – one of the areas of most rapid growth in social psychology and communication.

The Handbook of Communication Skills represents the most significant single contribution to the literature in this domain. It will be of continued interest to researchers and students in psychology and communication, as well as in a variety of other contexts, from vocational courses in health, business and education, to many others such as nurses and social workers whose day-to-day work is dependent on effective interpersonal skills.

Owen Hargie is Professor of Communication at the University of Ulster, Adjunct Professor at the Norwegian University of Science and Technology and Associate Professor at the University of Chester. He is a Chartered Member, Registered Practitioner, and Associate Fellow of the British Psychological Society, and a member of the International Communication Association. His special areas of interest are in the study of interpersonal, health, cross-community and organisational communication. He has published 15 books and over 100 book chapters and journal articles.

The handbook of communication skills

Third edition

Edited by Owen Hargie

Routledge
Taylor & Francis Group

LONDON AND NEW YORK

First edition published 1986
by Croom Helm
Reprinted 1989, 1991 (twice), 1993 by
Routledge

Second edition published 1997
by Routledge
Reprinted 1997 and 2000

Third edition published 2006
by Routledge
27 Church Road, Hove, East Sussex
BN3 2FA

Simultaneously published in the USA
and Canada
by Routledge
270 Madison Avenue, New York,
NY 10016

*Routledge is an imprint of the Taylor
& Francis Group, an informa business*

© 2006 Routledge

Typeset in Century Old Style by
RefineCatch Limited, Bungay, Suffolk
Printed and bound in Great Britain by
TJ International Ltd, Padstow,
Cornwall
Cover design by
Hannah Armstrong

This publication has been produced
with paper manufactured to strict
environmental standards and with
pulp derived from sustainable forests.

*British Library Cataloguing in
Publication Data*
A catalogue record for this book is
available from the British Library

*Library of Congress Cataloging-in-
Publication Data*
Handbook of communication skills /
[edited by] Owen D.W. Hargie. – 3rd ed.
     p. cm.
   Includes bibliographical references
and index.
     ISBN 0-415-35910-4 (hardcover) –
     ISBN 0-415-35911-2 (pbk.)
1. Interpersonal communication.
2. Communication – Psychological
aspects.   3 Interviewing.
I. Hargie, Owen.
BF637.C45H284   2006
302 – dc22   2005028329

ISBN13: 978-0-415-35910-8 (hbk)
ISBN13: 978-0-415-35911-5 (pbk)

ISBN10: 0-415-35910-4 (hbk)
ISBN10: 0-415-35911-2 (pbk)

In memory of my old friend, Sean Hill

Contents

CONTENTS

List of contributors

James C. Baxter is Professor Emeritus of Psychology at the University of Houston.

Robert N. Bostrom is Professor Emeritus in the Department of Communication at the University of Kentucky, Lexington.

George Brown is Professor and Senior Tutor in the Centre for Medical Education, University of Nottingham.

Len Cairns is Associate Professor and Associate Dean (Development) in the Faculty of Education at Monash University, Victoria, Australia.

David Dickson is Senior Lecturer in the School of Communication, University of Ulster, Jordanstown.

Kathryn Dindia is Professor in the Department of Communication at the University of Wisconsin, Milwaukee.

Daniel Druckman is Vernon M. and Minnie I. Lynch Professor of Conflict Resolution at George Mason University, Fairfax, Virginia.

Steve Duck is Daniel and Amy Starch Distinguished Research Chair at the University of Iowa.

Megan K. Foley is a Presidential Graduate Fellow in Communication Studies at the University of Iowa.

Hugh Foot is Professor of Psychology at the University of Strathclyde, Glasgow.

Randall A. Gordon is Professor of Psychology at the University of Minnesota, Duluth.

Owen Hargie is Professor of Communication at the University of Ulster, Jordanstown.

Allen E. Ivey is Distinguished University Professor (Emeritus), University of Massachusetts, Amherst, and Professor, University of South Florida, Tampa.

May McCreaddie is Senior Lecturer [Research] in the School of Health, Nursing and Midwifery, University of Paisley.

Amina Memon is Professor of Forensic Psychology at the University of Aberdeen.

Rob Millar is Lecturer in the School of Psychology at the University of Ulster, Magee Campus.

Ian E. Morley is Senior Lecturer in the Department of Psychology at the University of Warwick.

Daniel J. O'Keefe is Professor of Communication Studies at Northwestern University.

Richard F. Rakos is Professor of Psychology at Cleveland State University, Cleveland.

Sandra A. Rigazio-DiGilio is Professor in the School of Family Studies/Marriage and Family Therapy Program, University of Connecticut, Storrs.

Richard M. Rozelle is Professor Emeritus of Psychology at the University of Houston.

Charles H. Tardy is Professor and Chair of Speech Communication at the University of Southern Mississippi.

Dennis Tourish is Professor of Management in Aberdeen Business School at the Robert Gordon University, Scotland.

Anne Tracey is Lecturer in the School of Psychology, University of Ulster, Magee Campus.

Arjaan Wit is Assistant Professor of Social and Organisational Psychology at Leiden University, The Netherlands.

Editorial introduction

EW AREAS OF ACADEMIC study have attracted so much attention as that of interpersonal communication. In recent years there
has been a deluge of research studies in this field. The reasons for this
were aptly summarised by Wiemann (2003, p. ix): 'Our ability to create
and sustain our social world depends in large measure on how well we
communicate. People's social skills are crucial to their well-being – individually and collectively. The importance of understanding skilled
behavior in all its complexities cannot be overstated.' Studies have
shown a clear and positive relationship between effective interpersonal
skills and a range of benefits such as greater happiness in life, resilience
to stress and psychosocial problems, and enhanced academic and professional achievements (Hargie & Dickson, 2004). Indeed, to the question
of why we should study this area, Stewart, Zediker and Witteborn
(2005, p. 70) answered, 'There's a direct link between the quality of your
communication and the quality of your life.'

In relation to the professional domain, as society developed and
became more complex, the need evolved for a greater number of what
Ellis (1980) termed 'interpersonal professionals' who spend a large part
of their working lives in face-to-face interaction with others. Such professionals include doctors, teachers, speech therapists, physiotherapists,
occupational therapists, social workers, psychologists, nurses, careers
advisers, counsellors and business executives, to name but a few. Historically, the training of many of these professionals focused almost
entirely upon the acquisition of specialised knowledge. More recently,
however, the centrality of interpersonal communication in their work
has been recognised and catered for in training. As noted by Greene and
Burleson (2003, p. xiii), 'In light of the importance of communication

skills, it is hardly surprising that they have been a continuing object of study by scholars and researchers from numerous disciplines.'

Competence in most types of professions involves the effective implementation of three main sets of skills.

1   *Cognitive skills.* This relates to the knowledge base of the profession, that which characterises it and sets it apart from others. Barristers must have knowledge of existing legal structures, doctors need to understand human anatomy, and so on.

2   *Technical skills.* These are the specialised practical and manipulative techniques essential to the profession. Thus, a surgeon must be able to utilise a scalpel skilfully, a nurse has to be able to dress a wound, and a surveyor needs to know how to use a theodolite.

3   *Communication skills.* Here, the professional must have the ability to interact effectively with clients and other professionals.

Traditionally, the education and training of most professional groups placed emphasis upon the former two sets of skills at the expense of interpersonal skills. This is somewhat surprising, given that it has long been recognised that the ability to communicate effectively is essential for success in many walks of life (McCroskey, 1984). The oldest extant essay, written *circa* 3000 BC, consisted of advice to Kagemni, the eldest son of Pharaoh Huni, on how to speak effectively in public. Likewise, the oldest book, the *Precepts* written in Egypt by Ptah-Hotep about 2675 BC, is a treatise on effective communication. It can thus be argued that scholarship in the field of communication has been ongoing for some 5000 years.

In the last edition of this book it was pointed out that the study of communication had been neglected in the education and training of many professional groups. In the intervening decade, much has changed. Communication as a social science discipline has developed at a very rapid pace. There has been a huge growth in communication research and theory, as evidenced by the number of journals and books now devoted to this discipline. This has been paralleled by a concomitant large increase in the number of students undertaking undergraduate and postgraduate degree programmes in this field. A significant proportion of this work has been at the interpersonal level, including the study of professional interaction. Given the importance of effective communication, it is reasonable to expect that professionals should have knowledge of, and expertise in, communication skills. Therefore, it is hardly surprising that in the past few years increasing attention has been devoted to the study of such skills in professional contexts. Almost without exception, those involved in the training of professionals now recognise the necessity for neophytes to become competent communicators.

Increasing attention has also been devoted to the entire spectrum of socially skilled interaction. The fairly obvious observation that some individuals are more socially skilled than others has led to carefully formulated and systematic investigations into the nature and functions of social skills. There are three discrete contexts within which such investigations have taken place.

1   *Developmental.* Here the concern is with the development of skilled behaviour in

children; with how, and at what stages, children acquire, refine and extend their repertoire of social skills.

2   *Remedial.* In this context, the focus of attention is upon those individuals who, for whatever reason, fail to develop an adequate repertoire of social skills. Investigators are interested in attempting to determine the nature and causes of social inadequacy, and in ascertaining to what extent deficits can be remediated.

3   *Specialised.* Here, attention is devoted to the study of interpersonal skills in professional encounters. Most professions necessitate interaction of a specialised nature either with clients or with other professionals. Therefore, it is important to chart the types of communication skills that are effective in specific professional situations.

It is with the latter context that this book is concerned. Research into specialised social skills has developed rapidly, and the decade since the publication of the second edition of this handbook has witnessed a vast amount of investigation. This text now brings together much of this research to provide a comprehensive study of those communication skill areas central to effective interpersonal functioning in a range of professional contexts.

Although it is difficult to sectionalise communication, for the purpose of analysis the book is divided into four main sections. Part I sets the book in context by providing a theoretical framework for the study of communication as a form of skilled activity. The concept of communication as skilled performance is examined (Chapter 1), and an operational model of interpersonal communication as skill is fully delineated (Chapter 2). Part II then focuses upon nine core communication skills, namely, non-verbal communication, questioning, reinforcement, reflecting, explaining, self-disclosure, listening, humour and laughter, and persuasion. These are included as 'core' skills, as they occur to a greater or lesser degree in most interactions. While these skills are not entirely mutually exclusive (for example, aspects of non-verbal communication are relevant to all of the other chapters), each chapter deals with a discrete and important component of communication.

In Part III, the focus moves to an analysis of interpersonal communication in four specialised and widely researched contexts. These are broader areas of communication, involving a combination of the skills included in Part II. This section incorporates an examination of central dimensions inherent in situations where assertion and confrontation are required (Chapter 12), a synopsis of factors that impinge upon the individual working in a task group (Chapter 13), negotiating and bargaining encounters (Chapter 14), and pivotal elements inherent in the development, maintenance and dissolution of relationships (Chapter 15).

Part IV is then devoted to the study of four interviewing contexts. The importance of interviewing was succinctly summarised by Millar et al. (1992, p. 183): 'The interview is a ubiquitous activity. Everyone will have had the experience of being interviewed at one time or another, and an increasing number of people are required to play the role of interviewer in a professional capacity. For this latter group, a knowledge of the nature of interviewing can make an important contribution to effective practice.' This is an apt justification for the inclusion of this section. While it is beyond the scope of the present text to include chapters on all types of interview, the main forms of interview relevant to most professionals are included, namely, the employment interview (Chapter 16), the helping interview (Chapter 17), the appraisal interview (Chapter 18) and the cognitive interview (Chapter 19). The final chapter then provides an overview bringing together the main issues arising from the study of communication skills and relates these to the context of training (Chapter 20).

The information about interpersonal communication provided in this book should be regarded as providing resource material. How these resources are applied will depend upon the personality of the reader and the situation in which any interaction occurs. It is impossible to legislate in advance for every possible social context, and decisions about what approach could best be employed can be made only in the light of all the available background information. As such, this book certainly does not provide a preordained set of responses for given situations. Rather, it offers a selection of communication perspectives that facilitate the interactive process. In this way, it proffers valuable information that can be used to reflect upon, refine and extend one's own personal style and pattern of interaction.

Thus, this text provides reviews of research, theory and practice pertaining to a range of key skills and dimensions of communication. At the same time, it should be realised that the coverage of interpersonal skills is not intended to be exhaustive, since there are specialised skills relevant to particular contexts (such as 'breaking bad news' in the medical sphere) that could not be covered in a text of this nature. Furthermore, research in the field of social interaction is progressing rapidly, and it is anticipated that other general skills will be identified as our knowledge of this area increases. Finally, although the aspects contained in this book are presented separately, in practice they overlap, are interdependent and often complement one another. However, for the purposes of analysis and evaluation, it is valuable to identify separately those elements of communication which seem to 'hang together', and thereby attempt to understand and make sense of what is a complex field of study.

REFERENCES

Ellis, R. (1980). Simulated social skill training for the interpersonal professions. In W. Singleton, P. Spurgeon & R. Stammers (Eds), *The analysis of social skill*. New York: Plenum.

Greene, J. & Burleson, B. (2003). Preface. In J. Greene & B. Burleson (Eds), *Handbook of communication and social interaction skills*. Mahwah, NJ: Lawrence Erlbaum.

Hargie, O. & Dickson, D. (2004). *Skilled interpersonal communication: research, theory and practice*. London: Routledge.

McCroskey, J. (1984). Communicative competence: the elusive construct. In R. Bostrom (Ed.), *Competence in communication: a multidisciplinary approach*. Beverly Hills, CA: Sage.

Millar, R., Crute, V. & Hargie, O. (1992). *Professional interviewing*. London: Routledge.

Stewart, J., Zediker, K. & Witteborn, S. (2005). *Together. Communicating interpersonally: a social construction approach*, 6th edn. Los Angeles, CA: Roxbury.

Wiemann, J. (2003). Foreword. In J. Greene & B. Burleson (Eds), *Handbook of communication and social interaction skills*. Mahwah, NJ: Lawrence Erlbaum.

Part I

Communication skill in theory and practice

Chapter 1

Skill in theory: Communication as skilled performance

Owen Hargie

A NY ANALYSIS OF INTERPERSONAL communication is inevit-ably fraught with difficulties. The interpersonal process is complex, ever-changing, and directly affected by a large number of interrelated factors. This means that in order to make sense of, and systematically investigate, social encounters, some form of interpretive framework is usually employed. In fact, numerous alternative frameworks have been developed for this purpose. For example, interpersonal encounters have been conceptualised variously as:

- a form of joint economic activity or social exchange in which both sides seek rewards and try to minimise costs, which may be in the form of money, services, goods, status, or affection (Sletta, 1992)
- transactional episodes during which individuals play roles akin to acting as either parent, adult, or child, and respond to others at one of these three levels (Hargaden & Sills, 2002)
- a type of dramatic performance composed of major scenes, in which everyone has a role to play with expected lines, some have more prominent roles than others, the actors behave differently 'front stage' as opposed to 'back-stage', there are various 'props' in the form of furniture and fittings, there is a storyline, and all of this changes from one 'production' to the next (Hare & Blumberg, 1988).

These are just three of the approaches that have been developed as templates for the interpretation of interpersonal communication. In this chapter and in Chapter 2, another such approach will be presented, namely, the perspective that social behaviour can be conceptualised as a form of skilled performance, and that it is therefore meaningful to compare socially skilled behaviour (such as interviewing or negotiating) with motor skill behaviour (such as playing tennis or operating a machine). In further pursuit of this analogy, it is argued that the models and methods successfully employed for over 100 years in the study of motor skill can usefully be applied to interpersonal skill. The validity of this comparison, and the accompanying implications for the study of social behaviour, will be investigated.

This chapter is concerned with an examination of the nature of skill, and in particular with the perspective that interpersonal communication can be viewed as a form of skill. In order to evaluate this perspective, it is necessary to relate the history of the study of interpersonal skill directly to the study of motor skill, since it was from the latter source that the concept of communication as skill eventually emerged. The extent to which this analogy can be pursued is then discussed, together with an analysis of the nature of social skill per se. Overall, therefore, this chapter provides a reference point for the entire book, by delineating the nature and defining features of interpersonal skill.

MOTOR SKILLS

The study of perceptual-motor skill has a long and rich tradition within psychology. Such skills, which involve coordinated physical movements of the body, are widely employed in human performance, and they include, for example, eating, dressing, walking, writing, riding a bicycle, and playing golf. Welford (1968) traced the scientific study of motor skill back to 1820, when the astronomer Bessel examined differences between individuals in a task that involved the recording of star-transit times. However, direct psychological interest in the nature of motor skill really began with explorations by Bryan and Harter (1897) into the learning of Morse code, followed by studies on movement by Woodworth (1899), and investigations by Book (1908) into the learning of typewriting skills. Since this early research, the literature on perceptual-motor skill has become voluminous, and indeed this area remains an important focus of study.

Numerous definitions of 'motor skill' have been put forward. Marteniuk (1976, p. 13) stated that 'a perceptual-motor skill refers to those activities involved in moving the body or body parts to accomplish a specified objective', while Kerr (1982, p. 5), in similar vein, iterated that 'a motor skill is any muscular activity which is directed to a specific objective'. These definitions emphasise the goal-directed nature of skilled behaviour, which is regarded as intentional, rather than chance or unintentional. As Whiting (1975, p. 4) pointed out: 'Whatever processes may be involved in *human* skill learning and performance, the concern is with *intentional* attempts to carry out motor acts, which will bring about predetermined results.'

A further distinction has been made between innate behaviour, such as breathing and coughing, and learned behaviour. For behaviour to be regarded as skilled, it must have been learned. This feature is highlighted by a number of theorists. Thus, 'motor skill' was defined by Knapp (1963, p. 4) as 'the learned ability to bring about predetermined results with maximum certainty', while Magill (1989, p. 7) noted that skills 'all have in common the property that each needs to be learned in order to be properly executed'.

Other aspects were covered by Cratty (1964, p. 10), who described motor skill as 'reasonably complex motor performance ... [denoting] ... that some learning has taken place and that a smoothing or integration of behavior has resulted'. Skilled behaviour is therefore more complex than instinctive or reflexive movements, and consists of an integrated hierarchy of smaller component behaviours, each of which contributes in part to the overall act. In this respect, Summers (1989, p. 49) viewed skilled performance as requiring 'the organization of highly refined patterns of movements in relation to some specific goal'. Two remaining features of skill were emphasised by Proctor and Dutta (1995, p. 18), namely, the role of practice and the ease of operation: 'Skill is goal-directed, well-organized behavior that is acquired through practice and performed with economy of effort.'

As these definitions indicate, while there are commonalities, theorists tend to emphasise different features, so that Irion (1966, p. 2), in tracing the history of this research, concluded: 'The field of motor skills does not suffer from a lack of variety of approach. Indeed, the approaches and methods are so extremely various that there is some difficulty in defining, in a sensible way, what the field of motor skills is.' Robb (1972, p. 1), in discussing the acquisition of motor skill, reached a similar conclusion, stating: 'The problems associated with how one acquires skill are numerous and complex. For that matter, the term *skill* is itself an illusive and confusing word.'

However, Welford (1958, p. 17) summarised the study of this field as being encapsulated in the question: 'When we look at a man working, by what criteria in his performance can we tell whether he is skilled and competent or clumsy and ignorant?' In other words, his basic distinction was between skilled and unskilled behaviour (although, in fact, these two concepts represent opposite ends of a continuum of skilled performance, with individuals being more or less skilled in relation to one another). In his investigations of the nature of skill, Welford (1958) identified the following three main characteristics.

1   They consist of an organised, coordinated activity in relation to an object or a situation and, therefore, involve a whole chain of sensory, central, and motor mechanisms, which underlie performance.
2   They are learnt, in that the understanding of the event or performance is built up gradually with repeated experience.
3   They are serial in nature, involving the ordering and coordination of many different processes or actions in sequence. Thus, the skill of driving involves a pre-set repertoire of behaviours, which must be carried out in temporal sequence (put gear into neutral, switch on ignition, and so on).

INTERPERSONAL SKILLS

Given the vast amount of attention devoted to the analysis and evaluation of motor skill performance, it is rather surprising that it was some considerable time before psychologists began to investigate seriously the nature of social skill. Welford (1980) attributed the growth of interest in this field to the initial work of Crossman. In a report on the effects of automation on management and social relations in industry, Crossman (1960) noted that a crucial feature in the work of the operator of an automatic plant was the ability to use social skills to communicate with co-workers. He also noted that no real efforts had yet been made to identify or analyse these skills. Crossman subsequently contacted Michael Argyle, a social psychologist at the University of Oxford, and together they carried out a study of social skill, explicitly designed to investigate the similarities between man–machine and man–man interactions. In this way, the first parallels were drawn between motor and social skills.

In 1967, Fitts and Posner, in their discussion of technical skills, emphasised that social skills were also important. In the same year, Argyle and Kendon published a paper in which they related the features of motor skill, as identified by Welford, directly to the analysis of social skill. They proposed a definition of skill as comprising 'an organized, coordinated activity, in relation to an object or a situation, that involves a chain of sensory, central and motor mechanisms. One of its main characteristics is that the performance, or stream of action, is continuously under the control of the sensory input ... [and] ... the outcomes of actions are continuously matched against some criterion of achievement or degree of approach to a goal' (Argyle & Kendon, 1967, p. 56). While recognising some of the important differences between motor and social performance, they argued that this definition could be applied in large part to the study of social skill.

The intervening years since the publication of Argyle and Kendon's paper have witnessed an explosion of interest in the nature, function, delineation, and content of socially skilled performance. However, quite often researchers and theorists in this area have been working in differing contexts, with little cross-fertilisation between those involved in clinical, professional, and developmental settings. The result has been a plethora of different approaches to the analysis and evaluation of interpersonal skill. Therefore, it is useful to examine the current degree of consensus as to what exactly is meant by the term 'social skill'.

In one sense, this is a term that is widely employed and generally comprehended, since it has already been used in this chapter and presumably understood by the reader. Indeed, the terms 'communication skill', 'social skill', and 'interpersonal skill' have entered the lexicon of everyday use. For example, many job advertisements stipulate that applicants should have high levels of social, or communication, skill. In this global sense, social skills can be defined as the skills employed when communicating at an interpersonal level with other people. This definition is not very illuminating, however, since it describes what these skills are *used for* rather than what they *are*. It is rather like defining a bicycle as something that gets you from one place to another. As illustrated in the next section, attempts to provide a more technical, insightful definition of social skill are manifold.

DEFINITIONS OF INTERPERSONAL SKILL

In reviewing this field, Phillips (1978) concluded that a person was socially skilled according to 'The extent to which he or she can communicate with others, in a manner that fulfils one's rights, requirements, satisfactions, or obligations to a reasonable degree without damaging the other person's similar rights, satisfactions or obligations, and hopefully shares these rights, etc. with others in free and open exchange' (p. 13). This definition emphasised the macroelements of social encounters, in terms of reciprocation between participants, and focused upon the outcome of behaviour rather than the skills per se (although Phillips also noted that knowing how to behave in a range of situations was part of social skill). A similar approach was adopted by Combs and Slaby (1977, p. 162), who defined social skill as 'the ability to interact with others in a given social context in specific ways that are socially acceptable or valued and at the same time personally beneficial, mutually beneficial, or beneficial primarily to others'.

Although again highlighting outcome, this definition differed from that of Phillips in that it is less clear about to whom the skilled performance should be of benefit. Both definitions view social skill as an ability, which the individual may possess to a greater or lesser extent. Kelly, Fincham and Beach (2003, p. 724) linked ability to performance when they pointed out that 'Communication skills refer to the ability to realize communicative goals while behaving in a socially appropriate manner.' A similar focus has been emphasised by other theorists. Spence (1980) encompassed both the outcome or goals of social interaction and the behaviour of the interactors when she defined social skills as 'those components of social behaviour which are necessary to ensure that individuals achieve their desired outcome from a social interaction' (p. 9). In like vein, Kelly (1982, p. 3) stated: 'Social skills can essentially be viewed as behavioral pathways or avenues to an individual's goals.' Ellis (1980, p. 79) combined the goal-directed nature and the interactive component when he pointed out: 'By social skills I refer to sequences of individual behaviour which are integrated in some way with the behaviour of one or more others and which measure up to some pre-determined criterion or criteria.' More specific aspects of situational features were noted by Cartledge and Milburn (1980, p. 7), who viewed social skills as 'behaviors that are emitted in response to environmental events presented by another person or persons (for example, cues, demands, or other communications) and are followed by positive environmental responses'.

Several theorists have restricted their definitions to the behavioural domain. Rinn and Markle (1979) conceived of social skill as a repertoire of verbal and non-verbal behaviours, as did Wilkinson and Canter (1982, p. 3), who stated that 'Verbal and nonverbal behaviour are therefore the means by which people communicate with others and they constitute the basic elements of social skill.' Curran (1979), in discussing definitional problems, actually argued that the construct of social skill should be limited to motoric behaviour. He based his argument on the fact that the behavioural domain is still being charted and that this task should be completed before expanding the analysis into other domains. However, this emphasis on behaviourism would not be acceptable to many of those involved in research, theory, and practice in social skills who regard other aspects of human performance (such as cognition and emotion) as being important, both in determining behaviour and understanding the communication process.

A final defining feature was recognised by Becker, Heimberg and Bellack (1987, p. 9), who highlighted that 'To perform skillfully, the individual must be able to identify the emotions or intent expressed by the other person and make sophisticated judgments about the form and timing of the appropriate response.' Thus, the skilled individual needs to take cognisance of the others involved in the encounter. This involves perceptual acumen and perspective-taking ability, together with a capacity to mesh one's responses meaningfully, and at apposite moments, with those of others.

An evaluation of these definitions reveals a remarkable similarity with the position relating to motor skill, in that there are common elements, but no uniform agreement about the exact nature of interpersonal skill. One problem here is that any detailed study of higher-order skill will involve a long process. There is a well established '10-year rule' in relation to the learning of complex skill routines, in that the highest level of performance in any field is only attained after 10 years of concerted practice and training (e.g. Bryan & Harter 1899; Ericsson, 1996a). Top chess players, Olympic athletes, international soccer players, celebrated musicians, etc., will all have engaged in at least a decade of intensive practice. It is very probable that the 10-year rule also applies to complex social skills (negotiating, teaching, counselling, etc.). This makes analysis and synthesis problematic. While there has been study of how various types of motor skill performance change over time (Ericsson, 1996b), there is a paucity of such research in relation to interpersonal skill.

In the interpersonal domain, Spitzberg and Dillard (2002, p. 89) concluded that 'what constitutes skill, even in well-defined contexts, is difficult to specify'. Phillips (1980, p. 160) aptly summed up the state of affairs that still pertains: 'The simple facts about all social skills definitions are these: they are ubiquitous, varied, often simple, located in the social/interpersonal exchange, are the stuff out of which temporal and/or long-range social interactions are made, underlie and exemplify normative social behaviour and, in their absence, are what we loosely call psychopathology.' It is also useful to consider the rationale provided by Segrin and Givertz (2003, p. 136) in relation to this issue:

> A clear, comprehensive, and widely accepted definition of social skills may never come to fruition. Social skills are complex and, at least to some extent, influenced by person and situation. Trying to define social skills in a sentence is like trying to define some complex motor skill, such as being a good baseball player, in one sentence. There are many components to these skills.

However, Furnham (1983) argued that the lack of consensus in skills definitions was not a major problem, pointing out that while there also exists no agreed-upon definition of psychology, this has not retarded the development of the discipline. Indeed, progress in all areas is a cycle in which initially less precise terms are sharpened and redefined in the light of empirical enquiry. In addition, social interaction is such a dynamic, complex process, involving a labyrinth of impinging variables, that an understanding of even a small part of the process can be difficult to achieve. In their detailed examination of the area, Matthews, Davies, Westerman and Stammers (2000, p. 139) concluded: 'Understanding skilled performance is difficult, because of the complexity of skilled action. . . . Some skills are simply too complex to capture with a manageable model, although we may be able to model critical aspects of them.' Skilled performance is not a unitary activity. There is a large variety of different types of skill, some of which involve basic activities that are simple to execute, while others incorporate a range of intricate subelements, making them much more complicated to master (Holding, 1989).

It is hardly surprising therefore that differing definitions of what constitutes social skill have proliferated within the literature. Any definition must, of necessity, be a simplification of what is an intricate, multifarious, and multifaceted process. This is not to say that definitions are without value: at the very least, they set parameters as to what should be included in the study of social skill and, therefore, act as a template for legitimate investigation in this field. Moreover, while definitions vary in emphasis, the defining features of skill can be charted. Thus, Michelson, Sugai, Wood and Kazdin (1983) identified six main elements as being central to the concept of social skills; namely, that they:

1   are learned
2   are composed of specific verbal and non-verbal behaviours
3   entail appropriate initiations and responses
4   maximise available rewards from others
5   require appropriate timing and control of specific behaviours
6   are influenced by prevailing contextual factors.

Given the above parameters, the definition adopted in this book is that social skill involves *a process in which the individual implements a set of goal-directed, inter-related, situationally appropriate social behaviours, which are learned and controlled.* This definition emphasises six main features.

PROCESS

While behaviour is a key aspect of skill, it is in turn shaped by a range of other features. As such, motoric behaviour represents the overt part of an overall process in which the individual pursues goals, devises implementation plans and strategies, continually monitors the environment, considers the position of others involved in the encounter, responds appropriately in that situation, estimates the likelihood of goal success, and adjusts future behaviour accordingly (the operationalisation of these process elements of skilled performance will be discussed in more detail in Chapter 2). In this way, interaction is a transactional process in which each person's response is guided and shaped by the responses of others. In fact, a common analogy is made between interacting and dancing (Adler, Rosenfeld & Proctor, 2001; Clampitt, 2001). Both are carried out for a wide variety of reasons, some of which overlap. Thus, one may dance or interact to express oneself, to impress others, to help to develop a relationship, to pass the time, to seduce a partner, and so on. Interacting, like dancing a tango or waltz, depends on the coordinated intermeshing of learned repertoires between the two parties. Both are forms of performance wherein certain 'moves' are expected and anticipated, and the people involved complement one another in a fluid pattern of co-responding. If one partner is unskilled, the encounter becomes much more difficult.

One of the process dimensions to have attracted considerable attention within the interpersonal communication literature is the notion of competence. Indeed, Spitzberg and Cupach (1984, p. 11) argued that 'Competence is an issue both perennial and fundamental to the study of communication.' Some theorists have conceptualised skill as being subsumed by competence. For instance, Samter (2003, p. 639) concluded that 'Social competence can thus be regarded as the manifestation of the various social skills a person possesses.' Likewise, Ridge (1993) defined competence as the ability 'to choose a strategy, then select among skills appropriate to that context and employ these skills' (p. 1), given that 'a strategy is a plan derived from a context that determines which skills to apply' (p. 8). Here, competence is regarded as the ability to choose appropriate strategies and implement these in terms of skilled performance. Spitzberg (2003, p. 97) argued, 'Competence can be viewed as an evaluative judgment of the quality of a skill.' He also concluded that *appropriateness* (the extent to which behaviour meets standards of acceptability and legitimacy) and *effectiveness* (the degree to which desired outcomes are achieved) were the two main criteria used to guide such judgements. In a comprehensive review of this area, Wilson and Sabee (2003) concluded that there are three qualities associated with competence.

1   *Knowledge.* This relates to the information that is necessary for the person to be able to communicate in a way that is perceived to be competent (e.g. what one should say in this situation, how others might feel about this, what the alternative responses are).
2   *Motivation.* This concerns the desire of the person to behave in ways that will be judged as competent.
3   *Skill.* This refers to the individual's ability to act in such a way as to promote the perception of competence.

However, it is also possible to argue that skill subsumes competence. Thus, the *Chambers English Dictionary* defines skill as 'aptitudes and competencies appropriate for a particular job'. In this way, skilled soccer players or skilled negotiators would be regarded as highly competent in many separate facets of the process in which they are engaged. Likewise, it makes sense to describe someone as 'competent but not highly skilled' at performing a particular action. Furthermore, the terms are often combined. Thus, Daly (2002, p. 153) asserted, 'Those who exhibit socially competent skills are preferred in interactions.'

If all of this is confusing, it reflects the confusion that is rife in the deliberations of some theorists who grapple with this issue. For example, the distinction proffered by Sanders (2003, p. 230) was that competence involves the acquisition of an apparently higher-order 'system of computation and reasoning' whereas skill is of a lower-order nature and concerned with having 'acquired a set of methods and techniques'. But Sanders failed to explain how one could be skilled without being competent. Moreover, his definition of competence implies that it is an abstract ability. Thus, by Sanders' distinction, someone who could provide a fluent rationale (reasoning) as to how one should be, for example, a good soccer player or negotiator, yet who in practice is disastrous at playing soccer or negotiating, would be highly competent in these contexts, yet also highly unskilled. Most theorists would regard this as an unusual state of affairs, to say the least, and would agree with Emmers-Sommer, Allen, Bourhis, Sahlstein et al. (2004, p. 2) that competence incorporates 'a combination of encoding and decoding skills'. To compound the matter, Sanders (2003, p. 230) further concluded that, in relation to the concepts of competence and skill, 'it is imperative to sharply distinguish them', but then proceeded to argue that they 'are not mutually exclusive'.

Given that the terms 'skill' and 'competence' are often used interchangeably (Hajek & Giles, 2003), it is hardly surprising that Phillips (1984, p. 25), in examining definitional issues, concluded that, 'Defining "competence" is like trying to climb a greased pole. Every time you think you have it, it slips.' Likewise, Jablin and Sias (2001), in their review of the area, concluded that there are almost as many definitions of the concept as there are researchers who investigated it.

The view taken in this chapter is that, in essence, the terms 'skilled' and 'competent', when applied to the interpersonal domain, both indicate that the individual is equipped with the range of skills required to perform effectively, and can execute apposite combinations of these as required. Skills per se are processes of which behaviours are the surface manifestations, in turn determined and driven by a whole array of cognitive, affective, and perceptual activities.

GOAL-DIRECTED

Social interaction is now widely recognised as goal-directed activity (Berger, 2002). A defining feature of skilled performance is therefore intentionality. As expressed by Dindia and Timmerman (2003, p. 686), 'Communication skill refers to an individual's ability to achieve communicative goals.' Skilled behaviours are selected by the individual to achieve a desired outcome, and as such are purposeful as opposed to chance or unintentional. The importance of goals has long been recognised. McDougall (1912), for example, claimed that a key characteristic of human behaviour is its goal-oriented nature. A distinction needs to be made between goals and plans. Once goals have been formulated, plans must be devised to attain them. The plan is the route map to the goal. However, as Berger, Knowlton and Abrahams (1996) pointed out, while a plan implies that there is a goal, a goal does not always imply that there is a plan. An unskilled person may have ambitious goals, but without carefully related action plans nothing is likely to be achieved. Carver and Scheier (1998) illustrated how, in turn, the execution of plans depends on a range of resources, such as money, access to relevant others, interpersonal skills, and cognitive ability.

Four main theories for explaining and predicting goal-directed intentions and behaviours have been proposed (Bagozzi & Kimmel, 1995).

1   The *theory of reasoned action* purports that behaviour is determined directly by one's intentions to carry it out, and these are influenced by one's attitudes (positive or negative) toward the behaviour and by perceived social pressure to perform it.
2   The *theory of planned behaviour* extends this by adding the notion of perceived behavoural control as an important predictor of intention and action. Perceived behavoural control refers both to the presence of facilitating situational conditions and to feelings of self-efficacy (personal confidence in one's ability to execute the behaviour successfully).
3   The *theory of self-regulation* emphasises the centrality of motivational commitment, or desire, to act (this aspect will be further discussed in Chapter 2).
4   Finally the *theory of trying* interprets goal-directed behaviour within three domains – trying and succeeding, trying but failing, and the process of striving per se. This theory emphasises the importance of personal attitudes to success and failure as predictors of intentions and actions, as well as attitudes to the process involved en route to the goal. For example, one may decide not to try to

lose weight because of a personal belief that one would fail anyway, or because the process of dieting and exercising is not viewed as desirable. The frequency and recency of past behaviour is also seen as important. Thus, one is likely to be less hesitant about asking a member of the opposite sex for a date if one has had lots of dates (frequency), the last of which was two days ago (recency), than if one has only ever dated three people and the last date was 10 years ago.

Although the processes of goal setting, goal implementation, and goal abandonment are affected by a range of variables (Oettingen, Bulgarella, Henderson & Gollwitzer, 2004), in essence the decision to pursue particular goals seems to be determined by two overarching factors:

1   desirability (the attractiveness of goal attainment)
2   feasibility (the strength of belief that the goal can be achieved).

Another distinction has been made between learning goals and performance goals. Those who see themselves as pursuing learning goals (e.g. to learn how to be a better salesperson) view setbacks as opportunities for learning and future development. On the other hand, those who are guided by performance goals (to sell 'x' number of products today) are more negatively affected by failure. Learning goals therefore lead to better achievements than performance goals (Oettingen et al., 2004).

In their comprehensive analysis of the nature, role, and functions of goals as regulators of human action, Locke and Latham (1990) demonstrated how goals both give incentive for action and act as guides to provide direction for behaviour. They reviewed studies to illustrate the following principles:

1   People working toward a specific goal outperform those working with no explicit goal.
2   Performance level increases with goal difficulty (providing the person is committed to the goal).
3   Giving people specific goals produces better results than vague goals (such as 'do your best').

A distinction needs to be made between long-term and short-term goals. In order to achieve a long-term goal, a number of related short-term ones must be devised and executed. Our moment-by-moment behaviour is guided by the latter, since if these are not successfully implemented the long-term goal will not be achieved. Sloboda (1986) used the term 'goal stacks' to refer to a hierarchy of goals through which one progresses until the top of the stack is reached. In this way, skilled behaviour is hierarchically organised with larger goal-related tasks comprising smaller component subunits (Spitzberg & Cupach, 2002). For example, a long-term goal may be to appoint an appropriate person for a job vacancy. In order to do so, there is a range of subgoals which must be achieved – advertising the position, drawing up a short-list of candidates, interviewing each one, and so on. These subgoals can be further subdivided. At the interview stage, the chief goal is to assess the suitability of the candidate, and this, in turn, involves subgoals such as welcoming the candidate, making introductions, and asking relevant questions. In this way, the short-term, behavioural goals provide a route to the achievement of the long-term, strategic goal.

Another aspect of skilled action is that goals are usually subconscious during performance. The skilled soccer player is not consciously aware of objectives when running with the ball, but these nevertheless govern behaviour. When shooting on goal, the player does not consciously think, 'I must lift back my left foot, move my right foot forward, hold out my arms to give me balance', and so on. The essence of skill is subconscious processing of such behaviour-guiding self-statements. Thus, the socially skilled individual does not consciously have to think, 'I want to show interest so I must smile, nod my head, engage in eye contact, look attentive and make appropriate responses.' In his comprehensive analysis of skill acquisition, Greene (2003, p. 55) concluded: 'Although people are initially cognizant of task-directed activities, with extensive practice those behaviors tend to be lost from conscious awareness. Thus, experts may have difficulty reporting just how they do what they do.'

Those involved in the process of successful learning of new skills progress through the following four sequential stages:

1   *Unconscious incompetence*. At this stage, we are blissfully unaware of the fact that we are acting in an unskilled way.
2   *Conscious incompetence*. Here we know how we should be performing but also know that we are not able to produce the level of performance required.
3   *Conscious competence*. At the early stage of skill acquisition, we are aware of behaving in a skilled manner as we act.
4   *Unconscious competence*. Once a skill has been fully assimilated, we successfully execute it without having to think about it.

Langer, Blank and Chanowitz (1978) termed behaviour that is pursued at a conscious level as *mindful* and behaviour carried out automatically as *mindless*. Burgoon and Langer (1995), in analysing these constructs, illustrated how mindful activity is guided by goals that indicate flexible thinking and careful choice making. In this way, skilled behaviour is mindful. On the other hand, a lack of skill is indicative of mindless behaviour, since this involves limited information processing, a lack of awareness of situational factors, and rigid behaviour patterns.

However, part of skill is the ability to act and react quickly at a subconscious level. In discussing the role of the unconscious, Brody (1987) made the distinction between being aware and being aware of being aware. He reviewed studies to illustrate how stimuli perceived at a subconscious level can influence behaviour even though the person is not consciously 'aware' of the stimuli (this issue is further explored in Chapter 2). At the stage of skill learning, such conscious thoughts may be present, but these become more subconscious with practice and increased competence. An example given by Mandler and Nakamura (1987, p. 301) follows:

The pianist will acquire skills in playing chords and trills and in reading music that are at first consciously represented, but then become unconscious. However, the analytic (conscious) mode is used when the accomplished artist practices a particular piece for a concert, when conscious access becomes necessary to achieve . . . changes in the automatic skills.

Boden (1972) identified the features of behaviour carried out to achieve a conscious goal as being actively attended to, under direct control, guided by precise foresight, and open to introspection in that the component features are both discriminable and describable. The individual is aware of particular responses and of the reasons why they are being employed, has planned to carry them out, and is able to explain and justify the behaviours in terms of the goals being pursued. For example, someone who has arranged a romantic date may plan a sequence of steps in order to achieve a particular goal, and be aware of the goals while executing the dating behaviour.

Thus, if person A is skilled and wishes to persuade person B to do something, A may do so by some combination of the following techniques: smiling, complimenting B, promising something in return, emphasising the limited opportunity to take advantage of a wonderful offer, using logical arguments to show the advantages of the recommended action, highlighting the dangers of doing otherwise, or appealing to the moral/altruistic side of B (Hargie, Dickson & Tourish, 2004). In this case, these behaviours are directed toward the goal of successful influence over B's behaviour (see Chapter 11 for more information on persuasion).

INTERRELATED BEHAVIOUR

Social skills are defined in terms of identifiable units of behaviour, and actual performance is in many ways the acid test of effectiveness. In recognising the centrality of behaviour, Millar, Crute and Hargie (1992, p. 26) pointed out:

> Judgements about skill are directly related to behavioural performance. We do not judge soccer players on their ability to discuss the game or analyse their own performance, but rather we regard them as skilful or not based upon what they do on the field of play. Similarly, we make judgements about social skill based upon the behaviour of the individual during social encounters.

Therefore, a key aspect of skilled performance is the ability to implement a smooth, integrated, behavioural repertoire. In a sense, all that is ever really known about others during social interaction is how they actually behave. All kinds of judgements (boring, humorous, warm, shy, and so on) are inferred about people from such behaviours. As mentioned earlier, skilled behaviour is hierarchical in nature, small elements such as changing gear or asking questions combining to form larger skill areas such as driving or interviewing, respectively. This viewpoint has guided training in social skills, whereby the emphasis is upon encouraging the trainee to acquire separately smaller units of behaviour before integrating them to form the larger response elements – a technique that has long been employed in the learning of motor skills (this issue of skills training is further discussed in Chapter 19).

Socially skilled behaviours are interrelated in that they are synchronised and employed in order to achieve a common goal. As this book illustrates, there is a wide range of differing behavioural routines, each of which can usefully be studied separately. However, to be skilled, the individual must combine appropriate elements of these as required, so as to respond appropriately in a particular interaction. As noted by Stivers (2004, p. 260), 'Social interaction requires that many different practices and systems of practices be brought together.' This is similar to the tennis player who, to improve performance, focuses on separate aspects of the game (serve, volley, lob, backhand, etc.) during training, but, to be skilled, must combine these during actual matches. In this sense, while our understanding is informed by a microanalysis of particular elements, for a fuller appreciation of skilled performance the complete picture must also be taken into consideration. One example of this is that an analysis of aspects of the channels of verbal and non-verbal behaviour combined has been found to be more effective in accurately detecting whether or not someone is being deceptive than the scrutiny of either channel on its own (Vrij, Akehurst, Soukara & Bull, 2004). Skilled performance has been likened to an orchestra (McRae, 1998). All of the instruments (behaviours) must be synchronised, and if any one is out of synch the entire performance is adversely affected. In this respect, Bellack (1983) highlighted how performance needs to be viewed as a whole when making judgements about skill, pointing out that in social presentation:

> The elements combine to form a gestalt. The contribution of any one element varies across respondents, observers, behaviours and situations. . . . Intermediate levels of many responses may play little role in forming the gestalt, while extremes may have dramatic impact. Similarly, non-context elements (e.g. posture, inflection) may be of secondary importance when consistent with verbal content, but they may dramatically alter the meaning of a response when they are discordant. (p. 34)

Skill therefore involves a coordinated meshing of behaviour, and 'is said to have been acquired when the behavior is highly integrated' (Proctor & Dutta, 1995, p. 18). The car driver needs simultaneously to operate the clutch, accelerator, gear lever, brakes, steering wheel, and light switches. Similarly, someone wishing to provide reward to another concurrently uses head nods, eye contact, smiles, attentive facial expressions, and statements such as 'That's very interesting.' These latter behaviours are all inter-related in that they are indicative of the skill of rewardingness (Dickson, Saunders & Stringer, 1993). Conversely, if someone does not look at us, yawns, uses no head nods, and yet says, 'That's very interesting', these behaviours are contradictory rather than complementary, and the person would not be using the skill of rewardingness effectively. An individual who adopted such a pattern of mixed response over a prolonged period would be judged to be low in interpersonal skills. People who always act in a socially incompetent fashion are deemed to be unskilled regardless of the depth of theoretical knowledge they may possess about interpersonal behaviour. In skill, it is performance that counts. Noel Coward, recognising his own performance deficit, once said that he could not sing although he knew how to.

An important criterion for judging skill is *accuracy*. Highly skilled individuals make fewer performance errors than those less skilled (Matthews et al., 2000). Just as a highly skilled golfer misses fewer putts than one less skilled, so, too, a skilled orator makes fewer speech dysfluencies than a less skilled public speaker. Matthews et al. divided errors into:

1   *Errors of omission.* Here an action that should have been executed is omitted. For example, a driver forgets to put the gear in neutral before switching on the

engine, or a salesperson fails to get the client's commitment to buy before attempting to close a sale.

2   *Errors of commission.* In this instance, the person carries out a behaviour that detracts from performance. For example, a learner driver releases the clutch too quickly and the car engine stalls, or an individual discloses too much deeply negative personal information on a first date and the other person terminates the encounter.

This behavioural aspect of the skills definition has been misunderstood by some theorists. For example, Sanders (2003) presented a critique of the skills approach from his background as a 'language and social interaction' scholar. In a misinterpretation of the skills perspective, Sanders made the rather absurd deduction that 'all speakers of a language are equally able to produce grammatical sentences, and thus must be equally skilled' (p. 235). Unfortunately, he does not explain how precisely he reached this conclusion, as it is the exact opposite of what is being proposed in the skills perspective. It is completely illogical to make the leap from individuals being able to produce grammatical sentences to being equally skilled, and no skills analyst would make such an error. While behaviour (both verbal and non-verbal – although the latter domain is almost entirely ignored by Sanders) is recognised as being important, it is how this behaviour is contextually employed that determines the extent to which it is deemed to be skilful.

SITUATIONALLY APPROPRIATE

The importance of contextual awareness for the effective operation of motor skill has long been recognised. In his analysis of motor skill, Welford (1976, p. 2) pointed out that 'skills represent particular ways of using capacities in relation to environmental demands, with human beings and external situation together forming a functional "system" '. Likewise, Ellis and Whittington (1981, p. 12) asserted that a core feature of social skill is 'the capacity to respond flexibly to circumstances'. For behaviour to be socially skilled, it must therefore be contextually appropriate, since behaviours that are apposite when displayed in one situation may be unacceptable if applied in another. Singing risque songs, telling blue jokes, and using crude language may be appropriate at an all-male drinking session following a rugby game. The same behaviour would, however, be frowned upon if displayed in mixed company during a formal meal in an exclusive restaurant. It is therefore essential to be able to decide which behaviours are appropriate in what situations. Simply to possess the behaviours in not enough. A tennis player who has a very powerful serve will not be deemed skilful if the ball is always sent directly into the crowd. Similarly, being a fluent speaker is of little value if the speaker always monopolises the conversation, talks about boring or rude matters, or does not listen to others when they speak. Skills must therefore be targeted to given people in specific settings.

The skills definition given in this text was criticised by Sanders (2003, p. 234) as being too 'broadly drawn and open-ended'. Sanders argued, 'It is common and meaningful to talk about skilled negotiators, skilled teachers, skilled therapists, and so forth, but not skilled interactants.' But what he failed to recognise is that this is actually in line with the skills perspective. In his criticism, Sanders completely overlooked the import of the 'situationally appropriate' component of the skills definition as presented in this chapter. The behaviour of skilled teachers will, of course, differ from that of Sanders' apparently generic 'skilled interactants', as the situational aspect is clearly defined in the former and is vague (to say the least) in the latter. Sanders, therefore, beats the 'broad and abstract' (p. 223) straw man of skill. Using the definition employed in this chapter, we would need to know in what context Sanders' hypothetical 'skilled interactant' was operating in order to make judgements about effectiveness. In other words, skill is adjudged in the light of specific contextual behaviour. Furthermore, as the chapters in this book demonstrate, we know a considerable amount about the specifics of skilled performance.

Situational factors play a central role in shaping behaviour. Magnusson (1981) argued that such factors are important for three reasons: first, we learn about the world and form conceptions of it in terms of situations experienced; second, all behaviour occurs within a given situation and so can be fully understood only in the light of contextual variables; and third, a greater knowledge of situations increases our understanding of the behaviour of individuals. There is firm evidence that certain behaviours are situationally determined. For example, Hargie, Morrow and Woodman (2000) carried out a study of effective communication skills in community pharmacy, in which they videotaped 350 pharmacist–patient consultations. They found that skills commonly employed when dealing with over-the-counter items were not utilised by the pharmacist when handling prescription-related consultations. For instance, the skill of suggesting/advising, which was defined as the offer of personal/professional opinion as to a particular course of action while simultaneously allowing the final decision to lie with the patient, fell into this category. When dealing with prescription items, suggestions or advice were not given, probably because these patients had already been advised by their doctor and the pharmacist did not wish to interfere.

Individuals skilled in one context may not be skilled in another. For example, an excellent midfielder in soccer may be a terrible goalkeeper. Likewise, experienced teachers have been shown to have difficulties in becoming skilled school counsellors (Hargie, 1988). In essence, the more similarity there is between the demand characteristics of situations, the higher the probability that skills will transfer. Thus, a professional tennis player is usually good at other racquet sports. In the same way, a successful car salesperson is likely to be effective in other related selling contexts.

One similarity between motor and social skill is that they are both sequential in nature. Thus, the skill of driving involves a pre-set sequence of behaviours that must be carried out in the correct order. In social interaction, there are also stages that tend to be followed sequentially. Checking into a hotel usually involves interacting in a set way with the receptionist, being shown to one's room and giving a tip to the porter who delivers one's cases. Likewise, going to the doctor, the dentist, or church involves sequences of behaviour that are expected and which are more or less formalised, depending upon the setting. In the case of the doctor's surgery, the sequence would be:

1   Patient enters the surgery.
2   Doctor makes a greeting.
3   Patient responds and sits down.
4   Doctor seeks information about the patient's health.

5   Patient responds and gives information.
6   Doctor makes a diagnosis.
7   Doctor prescribes and explains treatment.
8   Doctor makes closing comments.
9   Patient responds, stands up, and leaves the surgery.

This sequence is expected by the patient, who would be most unhappy if the doctor moved straight from (1) to (7) without going through the intervening steps.

It can be disconcerting and embarrassing if one is in a situation where the sequence is not as expected or has not been learned (for example, attending a church service of a different religious denomination). In such situations, however, we usually cope and, unlike the sequence of behaviours in, for example, driving a car, these behaviours are expected rather than essential. It is only in certain rituals or ceremonies that a pre-set sequence is essential (for example, weddings in church) and responses are demanded in a fixed temporal order.

Interpersonal skills are more fluid and individualised than most motor skills. Different people employ varying combinations of behaviours, often with equal success, in social contexts. This process, whereby the same goal can be achieved through the implementation of differing strategies, is referred to as *equifinality* (Shah & Kruglanski, 2000). These strategies, in turn, have alternative yet equally effective behavioural approaches. While there are common stages in social episodes (e.g. opening, discussion, closing), the behaviours used within each stage vary from one person to another. However, 'knowing' the social situation is clearly an important aspect of social skill, in order to relate behaviours successfully to the context in which they are employed. Further aspects of the situational context will be explored in Chapter 2.

LEARNING

The fifth aspect of the definition is that skills comprise behaviours that can be learned. Some theorists purport that not all skilled behaviour is learned. For example, Sanders (2003, p. 228) argued, 'There are species of behavior for which persons can produce desired results "naturally" because the skills are acquired in the course of bodily or mental development.' As an example, he cites 'speaking and understanding one's native language' (p. 228). However, most skills analysts would find the view that language just occurs 'naturally' (whatever that means) to be a rather unusual perspective. Does it mean, for example, that children reared in isolation acquire their 'native' language 'naturally'? Of course, the answer is no, they do not. While most humans are hard-wired to learn language (an exception being those suffering from cognitive impairments), all social behaviour (including non-verbal as well as verbal) still has to be learned. We know that if children are reared in isolation they do not develop 'normal' interactive repertoires and certainly will not acquire their 'native' language. In addition, it has been shown that the interactive skills of parents are key components in the development of social competence in children (Hart, Newell & Olsen, 2003). Thus, mothers who encourage their children to talk, and make elaborations on the child's responses, produce enhanced language development in the child (Thorpe, Rutter & Greenwood, 2003). Indeed, there is evidence that the degree of deprivation of appropriate learning experiences from other people differentially affects the social behaviour of individuals (Messer, 1995; Newton, 2002). In this way, children from socially deprived home backgrounds are more likely to develop less appropriate social behaviours, whereas children from culturally richer home environments tend to be more socially adept.

Bandura's (1971) social learning theory posited that all repertoires of behaviour, with the exception of elementary reflexes (eye blinks, coughing, etc.), are learned. This social learning process involves the modelling and imitation of significant others, such as parents, peers, media stars, siblings, and teachers. The individual observes how others behave and then follows a similar behavioural routine. By this process, from an early age, children may walk, talk, and act like their same-sex parent. At a later stage, however, they may begin to copy and adopt the behaviour of people whom they see as being more significant in their lives by, for example, following the dress and accents of peers regardless of those of parents. A second major element in social learning theory is the reinforcement of behaviour. As a general rule, people tend to employ more frequently responses that are positively reinforced or rewarded, and to display less often those that are punished or ignored (see Chapter 5).

This is not to say that there are not innate differences in individual potential, since some people may be more talented than others in specific areas. While most behaviours are learned, it is also true that people have different aptitudes for certain types of performance. Thus, although it is necessary to learn how to play musical instruments or how to paint, some may have a better 'ear' for music or 'eye' for art and so will excel in these fields. Likewise, certain individuals have a 'flair' for social interchange and find interpersonal skills easier to learn and perfect. However, as discussed earlier, practice is also essential for improvement. Comparisons of highly skilled people with those less skilled, across a wide variety of contexts, show that the former engage in significantly more practice (Ericsson, 1996b). As summarised by Cupach and Canary (1997, p. 290), 'Skills are developed through practice; the more we use a skill, the more we sharpen it.' This was aptly expressed by Aristotle: 'If you want to learn to play the flute, play the flute.' But while practice is a necessary factor in skill development it is not on its own sufficient, since feedback on performance is also vital (see Chapter 2). In his analysis of expert performance, Ericsson (1996a, p. 34) concluded: 'The mere duration of practice will not be a perfect predictor of attained performance. Effective learning requires attention and monitoring of goals, processes, and performance.' Practice alone does not make perfect. It is practice, the results of which are known, understood and acted upon, that improves skill.

COGNITIVE CONTROL

The final element of social skill is the degree of cognitive control that the individual has over behaviour. Thus, a socially inadequate person may have learned the basic behavioural elements of interpersonal skill but may not have developed the appropriate thought processes necessary to control their utilisation. If skill is to have its desired effect, timing is a crucial consideration. Behaviour is said to be skilled only if it is employed at the opportune moment. For example, smiling and saying 'How funny' when someone is relating details of a personal bereavement would certainly not be a socially skilled response. Indeed, saying the right thing at the wrong time is a characteristic of some social inadequates. Learning *when* to employ socially skilled behaviours is every bit as important as learning *what* these behaviours are, *where* to use them, and *how* to evaluate them. In his discussion of the notion of interpersonal competence, Parks (1994) highlighted the importance of *hierarchical control theory*, which conceives of personal action as a process controlled by nine linked and hierarchical levels. From lower to higher, these levels are as follows.

1. Intensity control

This is the level just inside the skin involving sensory receptors, muscle movements, and spinal responses. Damage at this basic level has serious consequences for communication. For example, impairments to vision, hearing or to the vocal chords can dramatically impede interpersonal ability.

2. Sensation control

Here, the sensory nuclei collected at level 1 are collated and organised into meaningful packages. The ability to portray a certain facial expression would be dependent upon activity at this level.

3. Configuration control

The basic packages developed at level 2 are in turn further organised into larger configurations, which then control movements of the limbs, perception of visual forms, and speech patterns. The ability to decode verbal and non-verbal cues occurs at this level.

4. Transition control

This level further directs the more basic configurations into fine-grained responses, such as changing the tone of voice, pronouncing a word, or using head nods at appropriate moments. Transition control also allows us to recognise the meaning of such behaviour in others.

5. Sequence control

At this level, we control the sequence, flow, intensity, and content of our communications. The ability to synchronise and relate our responses appropriately to those with whom we are interacting, and to the situational context, is handled at this level. Thus, judgements of the extent to which someone is socially skilled can begin to be made at the sequence control level.

6. Relationship control

Here the individual judges and makes decisions about larger sets of relationships (cause–effect, chronological, etc.), so that appropriate strategies can be implemented to attain higher-order goals. For example, the ability to encode and decode deceptive messages is controlled at this level. Likewise, longer-term tactics for wooing a partner, negotiating a successful business deal, or securing promotion at work all involve relational control.

7. Programme control

At this level, programmes are developed to predict, direct, and interpret communication in a variety of contexts. Skill acquisition involves a process of *knowledge compilation* (Matthews et al., 2000). Two types of knowledge are important here (Spitzberg & Cupach, 2002):

- Knowing *what* is important in social encounters. This type of *content* or *declarative knowledge* includes an awareness of the rules of social encounters, the behaviour associated with the roles that people play, and so on. In the early stages of skill learning, this knowledge predominates.
- Knowing *how* to perform in a skilled fashion. When the individual becomes skilled, declarative knowledge is 'compiled' into *procedural knowledge*. Here, the person has developed a large repertoire of procedures directly related to the implementation of interpersonal skills.

There has been increasing interest in the role of 'mental representations' in social behaviour (Smith & Queller, 2004). Highly skilled people have a huge store of such representations relating to a wide range of situations (Richman, Gobet, Staszewski & Simon, 1996). These representations, or conceptual schemas, allow existing circumstances to be compared with previous knowledge and experience, and so facilitate the process of decision making. For the development of skill, 'knowledge must be acquired in such a way that it is highly connected and articulated, so that inference and reasoning are enabled as is access to procedural action. The resulting organization of knowledge provides a schema for thinking and cognitive activity' (Glaser, 1996, pp. 305–306). A schema is a cognitive structure that is developed after repeated exposure to the same situation. It provides the person with a store of knowledge and information about how to behave in a particular context (Hogg & Vaughan, 2002). Schemas contain learned 'scripts' that are readily available for enactment as required. By adulthood, we have developed thousands of schemas to deal with a wide variety of people across a range of situations, such as checking-in at an airport, shopping at the supermarket, or giving directions to a stranger on the street.

It would seem that our implementation of schemas is guided by inner speech. In examining this field, Johnson (1993) identified three main characteristics of inner speech. Firstly, it is egocentric and used only for our own benefit, in that the producer and intended receiver of the speech are one and the same person (oneself). Secondly, it is silent and is not the equivalent of talking or mumbling to oneself out loud. Thirdly, it is compressed, containing a high degree of semantic embeddedness, so that single words have high levels of meaning. Johnson used the analogy of a shopping list to explain the operation of inner speech. When going to the supermarket, we just write *bread*, *biscuits*, *soap*, etc., on a list. In the supermarket, when we look at the word *bread* we know that we want a small, sliced, wholemeal loaf made by Bakegoods, and we select this automatically. In a similar fashion, as we enter a restaurant, inner speech reminds us of 'restaurant', and this in turn releases the schema and script for this situation, thereby enabling us to activate 'restaurant mode'. Other actions within the restaurant will also be guided by inner speech (e.g. 'ordering', 'compliment-ing', 'paying', or 'complaining'). All of this usually takes place at a subconscious level, which, as discussed earlier, is a key feature of skilled performance. Thus, as explained by cognitive accessibility theory, schemas enable individuals to use cogni-tive shortcuts when processing information and making decisions about how to respond (Shen, 2004).

New situations can be difficult to navigate, since we have not developed rele-vant schemas to enable us to operate smoothly and effectively therein. In any profession, learning the relevant schemas and scripts is an important part of profes-sional development. In their analysis of skill acquisition, Proctor and Dutta (1995) demonstrated how as skill is acquired cognitive demands are reduced (the person no longer has to think so much about how to handle the situation), and this in turn frees up cognitive resources for other activities. An experienced teacher has a number of classroom-specific schemas, such as 'class getting bored' and 'noise level too high', each with accompanying action plans – 'introduce a new activity' or 'call for order'. These schemas are used both to evaluate situations and to enable appropriate and immediate responses to be made. Experienced teachers build up a large store of such schemas, and so are able to cope more successfully than novices. The same is true in other professions. Veteran doctors, nurses, social workers, and salespeople develop a range of work-specific schemas to enable them to respond quickly and confidently in the professional context. This ability to respond rapidly and appropri-ately is, in turn, a feature of skilled performance. In fact, speed of response is a notable aspect of skilled interaction. Thus, in free-flowing interpersonal encounters, less than 200 milliseconds typically elapses between the responses of speakers. As summarised by Greene (2003, p. 53), 'Perhaps most readily apparent of the behavioral changes that occur as a person becomes more skilled at a given activity is an increase in speed of task execution.' One reason for this is that skilled indi-viduals develop a cognitive capacity to analyse and evaluate available information and make decisions about how best to respond. They will also have formulated a number of contingency plans that can be implemented instantly should the initial response fail. This flexibility to change plans, so as to adapt to the needs of the situation, is another feature of skill.

8. Principle control

Programmes must be related directly to our guiding principles or goals, and these, in turn, control their implementation. In this sense, we have to create programmes that are compatible with our goals. However, as Parks (1994) pointed out, 'unsuccessful behavior often occurs because individuals lack the necessary programming to actualize their principles' (p. 603). This is particularly true when one is confronted by unexpected events, for which programmes have not been fully developed.

9. System concept control

At the very top of this hierarchy is our system of idealised self-concepts. These drive and control our principles, which in turn determine programmes, and so on. Someone whose idealised self-concept included being a 'trustworthy person' would then develop principles such as 'always tell the truth' and 'fulfil one's obligations'. Further down the hierarchy, at the programme-control level, schemas would be formulated to enable these principles to be operationalised across various contexts.

SOCIAL SKILLS AND MOTOR SKILLS

From the above analysis, it is obvious that there are similarities and differences between social and motor skills. The parallels between the two sets of skill are not perfect. However, the analogy between motor and social performance has stimulated considerable debate, and there certainly are considerable areas of overlap. The main similarities are that both sets of skill:

- are goal-directed and intentional
- involve high levels of cognitive control
- encompass behaviour that is synchronised and situation-specific
- are learned and improved through practice and feedback.

Sloboda (1986) used the acronym *FRASK* to describe the five central elements of skilled performance: *f*luent, *r*apid, *a*utomatic, *s*imultaneous, and *k*nowledgeable.

Fluency, in the form of a smooth, almost effortless display, is a feature of skill. Compare, for example, the international ice skater with the person making a first attempt to skate on the rink. Likewise, experienced TV interviewers make what is a very difficult task look easy. Fluency subsumes two factors. Firstly, there is the overlapping of sequential events in that the preparations for action B are begun while action A is still being performed. Thus, a car driver holds the gear lever while the clutch is being depressed, while an interviewer prepares to leave a pause when coming to the end of a question. Secondly, a set of actions are 'chunked' and performed as a single unit. For instance, skilled typists need to see the whole of a word before beginning to type it, and only then is a full set of sequenced finger movements put into operation as a single performance unit. In a similar way, the greeting ritual – smiling, making eye contact, uttering salutations, and shaking hands or kissing – is performed as one 'unit'.

Rapidity is a feature of all skilled action. An ability to respond rapidly means that skilled individuals appear to have more time to perform their actions and as a result their behaviour seems less rushed. The skilled person can 'sum up' situations and respond swiftly, so that performance becomes smoother and more fluid. In one study of chess players, Chase and Simon (1973) showed novices and grandmasters chessboards on which were placed pieces from the middle of an actual game. After viewing the board for 5 seconds, they were asked to reconstruct the game on a blank board. On average, novices correctly replaced 4 out of 20, whereas masters replaced 18 out of 20, pieces. Interestingly, in a second part of this study when the subjects were shown a board on which the pieces were placed in a way that could not have resulted from an actual chess game, masters performed no better than novices. Thus, rapidity was related to actual chess *playing*. Socially skilled individuals develop a similar ability in relation to specific contexts – for example, interviewers will know how to deal with a vast array of interviewee responses. Again, this is context-related, so that an experienced detective may be highly skilled during an interrogative interview but less skilled in a counselling interview.

Automaticity refers to the fact that skilled actions are performed 'without think-ing'. We do not think about how to walk or how to talk – we just do it. Yet, in infancy, both skills took considerable time and effort to acquire, and in cases of brain injury in adulthood both may have to be relearned. The other feature of automaticity is that a skill once acquired is in a sense mandatory, in that a stimulus triggers our response automatically. When a lecture ends, the students immediately get up from their seats and walk to the exit. Likewise as we pass someone we know, we look, smile, make an eyebrow 'flash' (raised eyebrows), and utter a salutation (e.g. 'Hello, how are you?'), get a reciprocal gaze, smile, eyebrow flash, and a response (e.g. 'Fine, thanks. And your-self?'), give a reply (e.g. 'Good'), as both parties walk on without having given much thought to the encounter.

Simultaneity, or what has been termed multiple-task performance (Greene, 2003), is the fourth dimension of skill. The components of skilled activity are exe-cuted conjointly, as in depressing the clutch with a foot, changing gear with one hand, and steering the car with the other while looking ahead. Furthermore, because of the high degree of automaticity, it is often possible to carry out an unrelated activity simultaneously. Thus, experienced drivers carry out all sorts of weird and wonderful concurrent activities, not least of which include operating the in-car entertainment system, eating, drinking, shaving, reading, or applying make-up. Equally, the driver can engage in the social skill of carrying on a deep philosophical discussion with passengers while travelling at speed.

Knowledge, as discussed earlier, is important. Skill involves not just having knowledge but actually applying it at the appropriate juncture. Knowing that the green traffic light turning to amber means get ready to stop is not sufficient unless acted upon, and indeed for some drivers seems to be taken as a signal to speed up and race through the lights! Similarly, a doctor may know that a patient question is a request for further information, but choose to ignore it so as to shorten the consultation as part of a strategy of getting through a busy morning schedule.

Thus, the FRASK process applies to both social and motor skill. However, the analogy between these two sets of skill is rejected by some theorists. For example, Plum (1981) argued that the meaning of 'good' tennis playing can be easily measured by widely agreed criteria, such as accuracy and points scored, whereas the meaning of social acts cannot be so judged. Sanders (2003) later used this same analogy, contending that there were two differences here, namely that:

1   The specifics of performance outcome that can be enhanced by skill are less apparent in social interaction than in tennis.

2   There is no standardised basis for score keeping in interpersonal encounters.

However, both of these can be countered. To take the commonly used analogy between playing tennis and negotiating, the skilled negotiator, like the tennis player, can be judged upon specified outcomes (percentage of pay increase, price of goods, and so on). Secondly, behaviour analysts can evaluate negotiators along a range of behavioural criteria, such as number of questions asked, behaviours labelled, counter-proposals employed, and so on (see Rackham, 2003). This is not to say that there are not differences between the sets of skills, as will be discussed later. Plum and Sanders further argued that good motor skill equals success, yet good social skill is purely subjective; for example, what is judged as an act of empathy by one person could be viewed as an insensitive intrusion by someone else. Again, similar disputes exist regarding motor skill operators. At soccer games, the author has often debated vigorously with fellow spectators whether a forward was attempting to shoot or pass, whether a goal was the result of a great striker or a terrible goalkeeper, and whether the midfielder was capable of playing at national level or incapable even of playing for the club side. Equally, it is agreed that often the most skilful sides do not win the trophies – if they are lacking in team spirit, determination, and work-rate, or have not had 'the luck'.

Both Plum (1981) and Yardley (1979) have iterated that social skills are unique in that only the people involved in interpersonal interaction understand the real meaning of that interaction. This is certainly true in that, phenomenologically, no one else can experience exactly what another person is experiencing. However, the same is also true of motor skill operators. Television commentators frequently ask sportsmen after a competition, 'What were you trying to do at this point?' or 'What was going through your mind here?' as they watch a video replay of the action. This is to gain some further insight into the event, and how it was perceived by the participants. While such personal evaluations are important, so, too, are the evaluations of others. When people are not selected at job interviews, do not succeed in dating, or fail in teaching practice, they are usually regarded as lacking in skill, just as is the youth who fails to get picked for a sports team or the car driver who fails the driving test.

Another argument put forward by Yardley (1979) is that social skills are not goal-directed in the same way as motor skills. She opined that few individuals could verbalise their superordinate goals during social interaction and that, furthermore, social interaction is often valued in its own right rather than as a means to an end. Again, however, these arguments can be disputed. It seems very probable that nego-tiators, if asked, could state their superordinate goals during negotiations, while a doctor would be able to do likewise when making a diagnosis. Furthermore, although social interaction is often valued per se, it is likely that individuals could give reasons for engaging in such interactions (to share ideas, pass the time, avoid loneli-ness, and so on). In addition, motor skill operators often engage in seemingly aimless activities, for which they would probably find difficulty in providing superordinate goals (as when two people on the beach kick or throw a ball back and forth to one another).

What is the case is that there are gradations of skill difficulty. Thus, opening a door is a relatively simple motor action to which we do not give much thought, while using a head nod during conversation is similarly a socially skilled behaviour to which we do not devote much conscious attention. On the other hand, piloting a jumbo jet or defending a suspected murderer in court involves more complex skills, and requires much more planning and monitoring.

However, while there are numerous similarities between social and motor skills, there are also four key differences.

1   Social interaction, by definition, involves other people, whereas many motor skills, such as operating a machine, do not. The goals of the others involved in interaction are of vital import. Not only do we pursue our own goals, but we also try to interpret the goals of the other person. If these concur, social interaction will be facilitated, but if they conflict, interaction can become more difficult. Parallels can more readily be drawn with social skills when motor skill operation involves the participation of others. Thus, as mentioned earlier, an analogy is often made between a game such as tennis and a social encounter such as negotiating. Both players make moves, try to antici-pate the actions of their opponent, win 'points', and achieve a successful outcome. At the same time, of course, while the 'games' analogy is useful, there are differences between the two contexts that must be borne in mind. For example, in tennis there are strict pre-set routines that must be followed, determined by hard-and-fast rules, coupled with a rigid scoring system. None of this applies during negotiations, where the rules and routines are usually more fluid.

2   While the emotional state of the person can influence motor skill performance, the affective domain plays a more central role in interpersonal contexts. We often care about the feelings of other people, but rarely worry about the feel-ings of machines. The way we feel about others directly affects how we per-ceive their behaviour and the way in which we respond to them. The concept of 'face' is important here. Skilled individuals are concerned with maintaining the esteem of both self and others. 'Face' in this sense refers to the social identities we present to others – it is the conception of who we are and of the identities we want others to accept of us. Maintaining or saving face is an underlying motive in the social milieu. Metts and Grohskopf (2003) identified two types of facework that are important in skilled performance: (a) *preventive facework* involves taking steps to avoid loss of face before it happens; (b) *corrective facework* is concerned with attempts to restore face after it has been lost.

3   The perceptual process is more complex during interpersonal encounters. There are three forms of perception in social interaction: first, we perceive our own responses (we hear what we say and how we say it, and may be aware of our non-verbal behaviour); second, we perceive the responses of others; third, there is the field of *metaperception*, wherein we attempt to perceive how the other person is perceiving us and to make judgements about how others think we are perceiving them.

4   Personal factors relating to those involved in social interaction have an import-ant bearing upon the responses of participants. This would include the age,

gender, and appearance of those involved. For example, two members of the opposite sex usually engage in more eye contact than two males.

These differences between social and motor skill will be further discussed in Chapter 2, where an operational model of skilled performance is presented.

OVERVIEW

This chapter has examined the core elements of skilled performance as identified in the study of perceptual-motor skill, and related them directly to the analysis of social skill. While certain differences exist between the two, there are also a number of features of skilled performance that are central to each, namely, the intentionality, learning, control, and synchronisation of behaviour. The realisation that such similarities exist has facilitated a systematic and coherent evaluation of social skill. As summarised by Bull (2002, p. 22), 'The proposal that communication can be regarded as a form of skill represents one of the main contributions of the social psychological approach to communication. Indeed, it has been so influential that the term "communication skill" has passed into the wider culture.'

This has resulted in concerted efforts to determine the nature and types of communication skill in professional contexts, and guided training initiatives to encourage professionals to develop and refine their own repertoire of socially skilled behaviours. However, both of these facets are dependent upon a sound theoretical foundation. This chapter has provided a background to such theory. This will be extended in Chapter 2, where an operational model of interpersonal skill in practice is delineated. As the present chapter has shown, although there are differences between motor and social skills, there are ample similarities to allow useful parallels to be drawn between the two, and to employ methods and techniques to identify and analyse the former in the examination of the latter. In this way, interpersonal communication can be conceptualised as a form of skilled performance.

REFERENCES

Adler, R., Rosenfeld, L. & Proctor, R. (2001). *Interplay: the process of interpersonal communication*, 8th edn. Orlando, FL: Harcourt.

Argyle, M. & Kendon, A. (1967). The experimental analysis of social performance. In L. Berkowitz (Ed.), *Advances in experimental social psychology*, vol. 3. New York: Academic Press.

Bagozzi, R. & Kimmel, S. (1995). A comparison of leading theories for the prediction of goal-directed behaviours. *British Journal of Social Psychology*, **34**, 437–461.

Bandura, A. (1971). *Social learning theory*. Morristown, NJ: General Learning Press.

Becker, R., Heimberg, R. & Bellack, A. (1987). *Social skills training for treatment of depression*. New York: Pergamon Press.

Bellack, A. (1983). Recurrent problems in the behavioural assessment of social skill. *Behaviour Research and Therapy*, **21**, 29–41.

Berger, C. (2002). Goals and knowledge structures in social interaction. In M. Knapp &

J. Daly (Eds), *Handbook of interpersonal communication*, 3rd edn. Thousand Oaks, CA: Sage.

Berger, C., Knowlton, S. & Abrahams, M. (1996). The hierarchy principle in strategic communication. *Communication Theory, 6*, 111–142.

Boden, M. (1972). *Purposive explanation in psychology*. Cambridge, MA: Harvard University Press.

Book, W. (1908). *The psychology of skill*. University of Montana, Studies in Psychology, vol. 1 (republished 1925). New York: Gregg.

Brody, N. (1987). Introduction: some thoughts on the unconscious. *Personality and Social Psychology Bulletin, 13*, 293–298.

Bryan, W. & Harter, N. (1897). Physiology and psychology of the telegraphic language. *Psychological Review, 4*, 27–53.

Bryan, W. & Harter, N. (1899). Studies on the telegraphic language. The acquisition of a hierarchy of habits. *Psychological Review, 6*, 345–375.

Bull, P. (2002). *Communication under the microscope: the theory and practice of micro-analysis*. London: Routledge.

Burgoon, J. K. & Langer, E. J. (1995). Language, fallacies, and mindlessness–mindfulness in social interaction. In B. R. Burleson (Ed.), *Communication Yearbook: Vol. 18*. Thousand Oaks, CA: Sage.

Cartledge, G. & Milburn, J. (1980). *Teaching social skills to children*. New York: Pergamon Press.

Carver, C. & Scheier, M. (1998). *On the self-regulation of behavior*. Cambridge: Cambridge University Press.

Chase, W. & Simon, H. (1973). The mind's eye in chess. In W. Chase (Ed.), *Visual information processing*. New York: Academic Press.

Clampitt, P. (2001). *Communicating for managerial effectiveness*, 2nd edn. Thousand Oaks, CA: Sage.

Combs, M. & Slaby, D. (1977). Social skills training with children. In B. Lahey & A. Kazdin (Eds), *Advances in clinical child psychology*. New York: Plenum.

Cratty, B. (1964). *Movement behavior and motor learning*. Philadelphia: Lea and Febiger.

Crossman, E. (1960). *Automation and skill*. DSIR Problems of Progress in Industry, No. 9. London: HMSO.

Cupach, W. & Canary, D. (1997). *Competence in interpersonal conflict*. New York: McGraw-Hill.

Curran, J. (1979). Social skills: methodological issues and future directions. In A. Bellack & M. Hersen (Eds), *Research and practice in social skills training*. New York: Plenum.

Daly, J. (2002). Personality and interpersonal communication. In M. Knapp & J. Daly (Eds), *Handbook of interpersonal communication*, 3rd edn. Thousand Oaks, CA: Sage.

Dickson, D., Saunders, C. & Stringer, M. (1993). *Rewarding people: the skill of responding positively*. London: Routledge.

Dindia, K. & Timmerman, L. (2003). Accomplishing romantic relationships. In J. Greene & B. Burleson (Eds), *Handbook of communication and social interaction skills*. Mahwah, NJ: Lawrence Erlbaum.

Ellis, R. (1980). Simulated social skill training for interpersonal professions. In

W. Singleton, P. Spurgeon & R. Stammers (Eds), *The analysis of social skill*. New York: Plenum.

Ellis, R. & Whittington, D. (1981). *A guide to social skill training*. London: Croom Helm.

Emmers-Sommer, T., Allen, M., Bourhis, J., Sahlstein, E., Laskowski, K., Falato, W., Ackerman, J., Erian, M., Barringer, D., Weiner, J., Corey, J., Kreiger, J., Moramba, G. & Cashman, L. (2004). A meta-analysis of the relationship between social skills and sexual offenders. *Communication Reports, 17*, 1–10.

Ericsson, K. (1996a). The acquisition of expert performance: an introduction to some of the issues. In K. Ericsson (Ed.), *The road to excellence: the acquisition of expert performance in the arts and sciences, sports, and games*. Mahwah, NJ: Lawrence Erlbaum.

Ericsson, K. (Ed.) (1996b). *The road to excellence: the acquisition of expert performance in the arts and sciences, sports, and games*. Mahwah, NJ: Lawrence Erlbaum.

Fitts, P. & Posner, M. (1967). *Human performance*. Belmont, CA: Brooks-Cole.

Furnham, A. (1983). Research in social skills training: a critique. In R. Ellis & D. Whittington (Eds), *New directions in social skill training*. Beckenham: Croom Helm.

Glaser, R. (1996). Changing the agency for learning: acquiring expert performance. In K. Ericsson (Ed.), *The road to excellence: the acquisition of expert performance in the arts and sciences, sports, and games*. Mahwah, NJ: Lawrence Erlbaum.

Greene, J. (2003). Models of adult communication skill acquisition: practice and the course of performance improvement. In J. Greene & B. Burleson (Eds), *Handbook of communication and social interaction skills*. Mahwah, NJ: Lawrence Erlbaum.

Hajek, C. & Giles, H. (2003). New directions in intercultural communication competence: the process model. In J. Greene & B. Burleson (Eds), *Handbook of communication and social interaction skills*. Mahwah, NJ: Lawrence Erlbaum.

Hare, A. & Blumberg, H. (Eds) (1988). *Dramaturgical analysis of social interaction*. New York: Praeger.

Hargaden, H. & Sills, C. (2002). *Transactional analysis: a relational perspective*. London: Brunner-Routledge.

Hargie, O. (1988). From teaching to counselling: an evaluation of the role of micro-counselling in the training of school counsellors. *Counselling Psychology Quarterly, 1*, 75–83.

Hargie, O. & Dickson, D. (2004). *Skilled interpersonal communication: research, theory and practice*. London: Routledge.

Hargie, O., Morrow, N. & Woodman, C. (2000). Pharmacists' evaluation of key communication skills in practice. *Patient Education and Counseling, 39*, 61–70.

Hargie, O., Dickson, D. & Tourish, D. (2004). *Communication skills for effective management*. Basingstoke: Macmillan.

Hart, C., Newell, L. & Olsen, S. (2003). Parenting skills and social-communicative competence in childhood. In J. Greene & B. Burleson (Eds), *Handbook of communication and social interaction skills*. Mahwah, NJ: Lawrence Erlbaum.

Hogg, M. & Vaughan, G. (2002). *Social psychology*, 3rd edn. Harlow: Prentice-Hall.

Holding, D. (1989). Skills research. In D. Holding (Ed.), *Human skills*, 2nd edn. Chichester: Wiley.

Irion, A. (1966). A brief history of research on the acquisition of skill. In E. A. Bilodeau (Ed.), *Acquisition of skill*. New York: Academic Press.

Jablin, F. & Sias, P. (2001). Communication competence. In F. Jablin & L. Putnam (Eds), *The new handbook of organizational communication: advances in theory, research and methods*. Thousand Oaks, CA: Sage.

Johnson, J. (1993). Functions and processes of inner speech in listening. In A. Wolvin & C. Coakley (Eds), *Perspectives on listening*. Norwood, NJ: Ablex.

Kelly, A., Fincham, F. & Beach, S. (2003). Communication skills in couples: a review and discussion of emerging perspectives. In J. Greene & B. Burleson (Eds), *Handbook of communication and social interaction skills*. Mahwah, NJ: Lawrence Erlbaum.

Kelly, J. (1982). *Social skills training: a practical guide for interventions*. New York: Springer.

Kerr, P. (1982). *Psychomotor learning*. New York: CBS College Publishing.

Knapp, B. (1963). *Skill in sport*. London: Routledge & Kegan Paul.

Langer, E., Blank, A. & Chanowitz, B. (1978). The mindlessness of ostensibly thoughtful action. *Journal of Personality and Social Psychology, 36*, 635–642.

Locke, E. & Latham, G. (1990). *A theory of goal setting and task performance*. Englewood Cliffs, NJ: Prentice-Hall.

Magill, R. (1989). *Motor learning: concepts and applications*, 3rd edn. Dubuque, IA: W. C. Brown.

Magnusson, D. (Ed.) (1981). *Towards a psychology of situations*. Hillsdale, NJ: Lawrence Erlbaum.

Mandler, G. & Nakamura, Y. (1987). Aspects of consciousness. *Personality and Social Psychology Bulletin, 13*, 299–313.

Marteniuk, R. (1976). *Information processing in motor skills*. New York: Holt, Rinehart & Winston.

Matthews, G., Davies, D., Westerman, S. & Stammers, R. (2000). *Human performance: cognition, stress and individual differences*. Hove: Psychology Press.

McDougall, W. (1912). *Psychology: the study of behaviour*. London: Williams and Norgate.

McRae, B. (1998). *Negotiating and influencing skills*. Thousand Oaks, CA: Sage.

Messer, D. (1995). *The development of communication: from social interaction to language*. Chichester: Wiley.

Metts, S. & Grohskopf, E. (2003). Impression management: goals, strategies and skills. In J. Greene & B. Burleson (Eds), *Handbook of communication and social interaction skills*. Mahwah, NJ: Lawrence Erlbaum.

Michelson, L., Sugai, D., Wood, R. & Kazdin, A. (1983). *Social skills assessment and training with children*. New York: Plenum.

Millar, R., Crute, V. & Hargie, O. (1992). *Professional interviewing*. London: Routledge.

Newton, M. (2002). *Savage girls and wild boys: a history of feral children*. London: Faber.

Oettingen, G., Bulgarella, C., Henderson, M. & Gollwitzer, P. (2004). The self-regulation of goal pursuit. In R. Wright, J. Greenberg & S. Brehm (Eds), *Motivational analyses of social behavior*. Mahwah, NJ: Lawrence Erlbaum.

Parks, M. R. (1994). Communication competence and interpersonal control. In M. Knapp & G. Miller (Eds), *Handbook of interpersonal communication*, 2nd edn. Thousand Oaks, CA: Sage.

Phillips, E. (1978). *The social skills basis of psychopathology.* New York: Grune and Stratton.

Phillips, E. (1980). Social skills instruction as adjunctive/alternative to psychotherapy. In W. Singleton, P. Spurgeon & R. Stammers (Eds), *The analysis of social skills.* New York: Plenum.

Phillips, G. (1984). A competent view of 'competence'. *Communication Education, 33,* 25–36.

Plum, A. (1981). Communication as skill: a critique and alternative proposal. *Journal of Humanistic Psychology, 21,* 3–19.

Proctor, R. W. & Dutta, A. (1995). *Skill acquisition and human performance.* Thousand Oaks, CA: Sage.

Rackham, N. (2003). The behavior of successful negotiators. In R. Lewicki, D. Saunders, J. Minton & B. Barry (Eds), *Negotiation: readings, exercise and cases,* 4th edn. New York: McGraw-Hill.

Richman, H., Gobet, F., Staszewski, J. & Simon, H. (1996). Perceptual and memory processes in the acquisition of expert performance: the EPAM model. In K. Ericsson (Ed.), *The road to excellence: the acquisition of expert performance in the arts and sciences, sports, and games.* Mahwah, NJ: Lawrence Erlbaum.

Ridge, A. (1993). A perspective of listening skills. In A. Wolvin & C. Coakley (Eds), *Perspectives on listening.* Norwood, NJ: Ablex.

Rinn, R. & Markle, A. (1979). Modification of skill deficits in children. In A. Bellack & M. Hersen (Eds), *Research and practice in social skills training.* New York: Plenum.

Robb, M. (1972). *The dynamics of motor skill acquisition.* Englewood Cliffs, NJ: Prentice-Hall.

Samter, W. (2003). Friendship interaction skills across the life span. In J. Greene & B. Burleson (Eds), *Handbook of communication and social interaction skills.* Mahwah, NJ: Lawrence Erlbaum.

Sanders, R. (2003). Applying the skills concept to discourse and conversation: the remediation of performance defects in talk-in-interaction. In J. Greene & B. Burleson (Eds), *Handbook of communication and social interaction skills.* Mahwah, NJ: Lawrence Erlbaum.

Segrin, C. & Givertz, M. (2003). Methods of social skills training and development. In J. Greene & B. Burleson (Eds), *Handbook of communication and social interaction skills.* Mahwah, NJ: Lawrence Erlbaum.

Shah, J. & Kruglanski, A. (2000). Aspects of goal networks: implications for self-regulation. In M. Boekaerts, P. Pintrich & M. Zeidner (Eds), *Handbook of self-regulation.* San Diego, CA: Academic Press.

Shen, F. (2004). Chronic accessibility and individual cognitions: examining the effects of message frames in political advertisements. *Journal of Communication, 54,* 123–137.

Sletta, O. (1992). Social skills as exchange resources. *Scandinavian Journal of Educational Research, 36,* 183–190.

Sloboda, J. (1986). What is skill? In A. Gellatly (Ed.), *The skilful mind: an introduction to cognitive psychology.* Milton Keynes: Open University Press.

Smith, E. & Queller, S. (2004). Mental representations. In M. Brewer & M. Hewstone (Eds), *Social cognition.* Malden, MA: Blackwell.

Spence, S. (1980). *Social skills training with children and adolescents*. Windsor: NFER.

Spitzberg, B. (2003). Methods of interpersonal skill assessment. In J. Greene & B. Burleson (Eds), *Handbook of communication and social interaction skills*. Mahwah, NJ: Lawrence Erlbaum.

Spitzberg, B. & Cupach, W. (1984). *Interpersonal communication competence*. Beverly Hills, CA: Sage.

Spitzberg, B. & Cupach, W. (2002). Interpersonal skills. In M. Knapp & J. Daly (Eds), *Handbook of interpersonal communication*, 3rd edn. Thousand Oaks, CA: Sage.

Spitzberg, B. & Dillard, J. (2002). Social skills and communication. In M. Allen, R. Preiss, B. Gayle & N. Burrell (Eds), *Interpersonal communication research: advances through meta-analysis*. Mahwah, NJ: Lawrence Erlbaum.

Stivers, T. (2004). 'No no no' and other types of multiple sayings in social interaction. *Human Communication Research, 30*, 260–293.

Summers, J. (1989). Motor programs. In D. Holding (Ed.), *Human skills*, 2nd edn. Chichester: Wiley.

Thorpe, K., Rutter, M. & Greenwood, K. (2003). Twins as a natural experiment to study the causes of mild language delay. II. Family interaction risk factors. *Journal of Child Psychology and Psychiatry, 44*, 342–355.

Vrij, A., Akehurst, L., Soukara, S. & Bull, R. (2004). Detecting deceit via analyses of verbal and nonverbal behavior in children and adults. *Human Communication Research, 30*, 8–41.

Welford, A. (1958). *Ageing and Human Skill*. London: Oxford University Press (reprinted 1973 by Greenwood Press, Westport, CT).

Welford, A. (1968). *Fundamentals of skill*. London: Methuen.

Welford, A. (1976). *Skilled performance: perceptual and motor skills*. Glenview, IL: Scott, Foresman.

Welford, A. (1980). The concept of skill and its application to performance. In W. Singleton, P. Spurgeon & R. Stammers (Eds), *The analysis of social skill*. New York: Plenum.

Whiting, H. (1975). *Concepts in skill learning*. London: Lepus Books.

Wilkinson, J. & Canter, S. (1982). *Social skills training manual*. Chichester: Wiley.

Wilson, S. & Sabee, C. (2003). Explicating communicative competence as a theoretical term. In J. Greene & B. Burleson (Eds), *Handbook of communication and social interaction skills*. Mahwah, NJ: Lawrence Erlbaum.

Woodworth, R. S. (1899). The accuracy of voluntary movement. *Psychological Review Monograph Supplement* 3, No. 3.

Yardley, K. (1979). Social skills training: a critique. *British Journal of Medical Psychology, 52*, 55–62.

Chapter 2

Skill in practice: An operational model of communicative performance

Owen Hargie

T HIS CHAPTER FURTHER EXPLORES the analogy between motor skill and social skill, as discussed in Chapter 1. In particular, it examines the central processes involved in the implementation of skilled behaviour, and evaluates the extent to which a motor skill model of performance can be operationalised in the study of interpersonal communication. A model of interaction, based upon the skills paradigm, is presented. This model is designed to account for those features of performance that are peculiar to social encounters.

MOTOR SKILL MODEL

Several models of motor skill, all having central areas in common, have been put forward by different theorists. An early example of this type of model was the one presented by Welford (1965), in the shape of a block diagram representing the operation of perceptual motor skills, in which the need for the coordination of a number of processes in the performance of skilled behaviour is highlighted. As shown in Figure 2.1, this represents the individual as receiving information about the outside world via the sense organs (eyes, ears, nose, hands, etc.). A range of such perceptions is received, and this incoming information is held in the short-term memory store until sufficient data have been obtained to enable a decision to be made about an appropriate response. As explained by action assembly theory (Greene, 2000), responses are gradually assembled by the individual, taking into account information

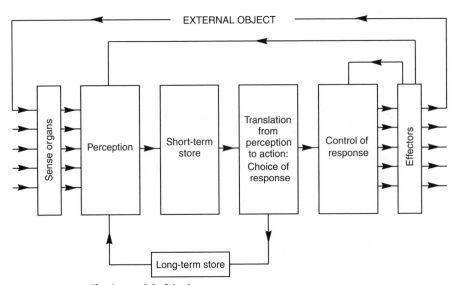

Figure 2.1 Welford's model of the human sensory-motor system

stored in long-term memory, in terms of previous responses, outcomes associated with these responses, and impinging situational factors (see Chapter 9 for further discussion on the role of memory in skilled performance). After all of this data has been sifted, a response is made by the effector system (hands, feet, voice, and so on). In turn, the outcome of this response is monitored by the sense organs and perceived by the individual, thereby providing feedback that can be used to adjust future responses.

To take a practical example, let us consider a golfer on the green about to make a putt. Here, the golfer observes (perception) the position of the ball in relation to the hole, the lie of the land between ball and hole, and the prevailing weather conditions. All of this information is held in short-term memory store and compared with data from the long-term memory store regarding previous experience of similar putts in the past. As a result, decisions are made about which putter to use and exactly how the ball should be struck (translation from perception to action: choice of response). The putt is then carefully prepared for as the golfer positions hands, body, and feet (control of response). The putt is then executed (effectors), and the outcome monitored (sense organs) to guide future decisions.

Argyle (1972) applied this model to the analysis of social skill (Figure 2.2). His model was a slightly modified version of Welford's, in which the flow diagram was simplified by: removing the memory store blocks; combining sense organs and perception, control of responses, and effectors; and adding the elements of motivation and goal. An example of how this model can be applied to the analysis of motor performance is as follows. Someone is sitting in a room in which the temperature has become too warm (motivation), and therefore wants to cool down (goal). This can be achieved by devising a range of alternative plans of action (translation), such as opening a window, removing some clothing, or adjusting the heating system. Eventually, one of these plans is carried out: a window is opened (motor response), and the situation is

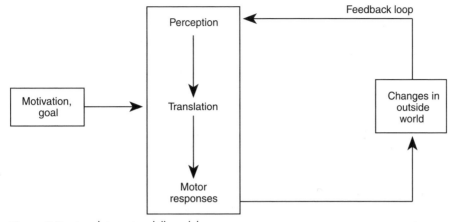

Figure 2.2 Argyle's motor skill model

monitored. Cool air then enters the room, making the temperature more pleasant (changes in outside world). This change in temperature is available as feedback that can be perceived by the individual, to enable goal achievement to be evaluated.

A simple example of the application of this motor skill model to a social context would be a woman meeting a man whom she finds very attractive (motivation), and wanting to find out his name (goal). To do so, various plans of action are translated (e.g. ask directly, give own name and pause, ask someone to effect an introduction). One of these is then carried out, such as the direct request: 'What's your name?' (response). This will result in some response from the other person: 'Norris' (changes in the outside world). His response is available as feedback, which she hears while also observing his non-verbal reactions to her (perception). She can then move on to the next goal (e.g. follow-up response, or terminate discussion).

At first sight, then, it would appear that this motor skill model can be applied directly to the analysis of social skill. However, there are several differences between these two sets of skills, which are not really catered for in the basic motor skill model. In fact, many of these differences were recognised by Argyle (1967) in the first edition of *The Psychology of Interpersonal Behaviour* when he attempted to extend the basic model to take account of the responses of the other person in the social situation, and of the different types of feedback that accrue in interpersonal encounters. However, this extension did not really succeed and was dropped by Argyle in later editions.

Subsequently, few attempts were made to expand the basic model to account for the interactive nature of social encounters. Pendleton and Furnham (1980), in critically examining the relationship between motor and social skill, did put forward an expanded model, albeit applied directly to doctor–patient interchanges. Furnham (1983) later pointed out that, although there were problems with this interactive model, it was a 'step in the right direction'. In the earlier editions of the present book, a model was presented which built upon the Pendleton and Furnham extension, in an attempt to cater for many of the special features of social skill. This model was subsequently revised and adapted by Millar, Crute and Hargie (1992); Dickson, Hargie and Morrow (1997); Hargie and Tourish (1999); and Hargie and Dickson (2004). These revised models all attempted to account for the differences between social and motor performance as discussed in Chapter 1.

However, it is difficult to devise an operational model of skilled performance that provides an in-depth representation of all the facets of interaction. Such a model would be complicated and cumbersome. As a result, a relatively straightforward, yet robust, extension has been formulated. This model, as illustrated in Figure 2.3, takes into account the goals of both interactors, the influence of the person–situation context, and the fact that feedback comes from our own as well as the other person's responses. In addition, the term 'translation' has been replaced by 'mediating factors', to allow for the influence of emotions, as well as cognitions, on performance. The interrelationship between mediation and goals, perception, and responses is also acknowledged. Thus, as a result of mediating processes, we may abandon present goals as unattainable and formulate new ones; how we perceive others is influenced (usually subconsciously) by our existing cognitive structure and emotional state (as depicted by the dashed arrow in Figure 2.3); and our responses help to shape our thoughts and feelings (as in the adage, how do I know what I think until I hear what I say?). This model can best be explained by providing an analysis of each of the separate components.

GOALS AND MOTIVATION

As discussed in Chapter 1, a key feature of skilled performance is its goal-directed, intentional nature. The starting point in this model of social interaction is therefore

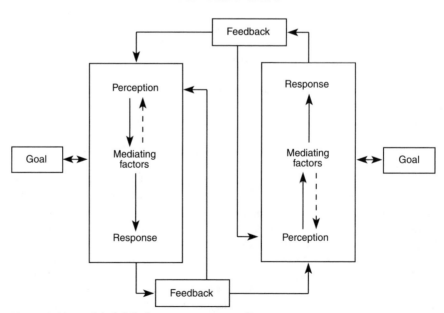

Figure 2.3 Model of skilled communicative performance

the goal being pursued, and the related motivation to achieve it. The link between needs, motivation, and goal is also recognised. As pointed out by Slater (1997, p. 137), 'The presence of various goals or motivations changes the nature of affect and cognitions generated, and of subsequent behaviors.' In essence, goals shape behaviour, while motivation determines the degree of commitment to pursue a particular goal. Carlson (1990, p. 404) described motivation as 'a driving force that moves us to a particular action.... Motivation can affect the *nature* of an organism's behavior, the *strength* of its behavior, and the *persistence* of its behavior.' The motivation that an individual has to pursue a particular goal is, in turn, influenced by needs. There are many needs that must be met in order to enable the individual to live life to the fullest. Different psychologists have posited various categorisations, but the best known hierarchy of human needs remains the one put forward by Maslow (1954), as shown in Figure 2.4.

At the bottom of this hierarchy, and therefore most important, are those physiological needs essential for the survival of the individual, including the need for water, food, heat, and so on. Once these have been met, the next most important needs are those connected with the safety and security of the individual, including protection from physical harm and freedom from fear. These are met in society by various methods, such as the establishment of police forces, putting security chains on doors, or purchasing insurance policies. At the next level are belonging and love needs, such as the desire for a mate, wanting to be accepted by others, and striving to avoid loneliness or rejection. Getting married, having a family, or joining a club, society, or some form of group, are all means whereby these needs are satisfied. Esteem needs are met in a number of ways: for instance, occupational status,

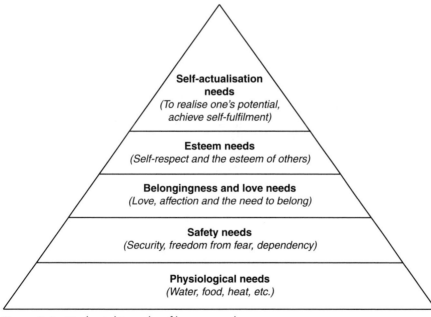

Figure 2.4 Maslow's hierarchy of human needs

achievement in sports, or success in some other sphere. At a higher level is the need for self-actualisation, by fulfilling one's true potential. People seek new challenges, feeling the need to be 'stretched' and to develop themselves fully. Thus, someone may give up secure salaried employment in order to study at college or set up in business.

Maslow argued that only when basic needs have been achieved does the individual seek higher needs. The person who is suffering from hunger will usually seek food at all costs, even risking personal safety, and is unlikely to worry about being held in high esteem. At a higher level, someone deeply in love may publicly beg a partner not to leave, thereby foregoing self-esteem. However, it should be recognised that this hierarchy does not hold in all cases. Needs can also be influenced directly by individual goals. One example of this is political prisoners starving themselves to death in an attempt to achieve particular political objectives. But for the most part this hierarchy of needs holds true, and the behaviour of an individual can be related to existing level of need. Similarly, people can be manipulated either by promises that their needs will be met, or threats that they will not be met. Politicians promise to meet safety needs by reducing the crime rate and improving law and order, computer-dating firms offer to meet love needs by providing a partner, while company management may threaten various needs by warning workers that if they go on strike the company could close and they would lose their jobs.

Skilled performers take account of the needs of those with whom they interact. For example, effective salespeople have been shown to ascertain client needs early in the sales encounter and then tailor their responses to address these needs (Hargie, Dickson & Tourish, 2004). One of the generic needs during social encounters is the quest for uncertainty reduction. We want to know what is expected of us, what the rules of the interaction are, what others think of us, what relationship we will have with them, and so on. In other words, we have a need for high predictability and are happier in familiar situations with low levels of uncertainty about what to expect and how to behave (Clampitt & Williams, 2004). In interpersonal encounters, skilled individuals take cognisance of the desire for others to have uncertainty reduced. For this reason, skilled professionals take time at the outset of consultations with clients to clarify goals and agree objectives (Hargie & Dickson, 2004).

Motivation is therefore important in determining the goals that we seek in social interaction. Indeed, traditionally, motivation has been defined as 'the process by which behavior is *activated* and *directed* toward some definable goal' (Buck, 1988, p. 5). Our behaviour, in turn, is judged on the basis of the goals that are being pursued. As the model outlined in Figure 2.3 illustrates, both parties to an interaction have goals. This is important, since those who can accurately interpret the behaviour of other people in terms of goals tend to be more successful in achieving their own goals (Berger, 2000). Our goals are determined in three main ways (Oettingen & Gollwitzer, 2004), in that they can be:

1   *Assigned.* Goals may be decided for us by others (e.g. parents, teachers, managers), who tell us what goals we should (and should not) pursue.
2   *Self-set.* Here, goals are freely chosen by the individual.
3   *Participative.* In this case, goals are openly agreed in interaction with others.

Goal conflict may occur where goals being pursued by both sides do not concur, or where there is internal inconsistency in goals. Informing a good friend of an annoying habit, while maintaining the same level of friendship, would be one example of the latter. Encounters such as this obviously require skill and tact. Yet we know little about how to ensure success in such situations. We have goals and those with whom we interact also have goals, and these may not concur. However, for relationships to develop, ways must be found of successfully negotiating mutual goal achievement. Despite a great deal of interest in the subject of goal-directed action, relatively little work has been carried out to investigate the process whereby communicators negotiate intentions.

What is clear is that goals, needs, and our motivation to satisfy these, all play a vital role in skilled performance. Once appropriate goals have been decided upon, they have an important bearing on our perceptions, behaviour, and the intervening mediating factors.

MEDIATING FACTORS

The term 'mediating factors' refers to those internal states, activities, or processes within the individual that mediate between the feedback perceived, the goal being pursued, and the responses that are made. What has been termed the 'mediated mind' (Lucariello, Hudson, Fivush & Bauer, 2004) is therefore an important feature of inter-personal communication. Mediating factors influence the way in which people and events are perceived, and determine the capacity of the individual to assimilate, process, and respond to the social information received during interpersonal encounters. It is at this stage that the person makes decisions about appropriate courses of action for goal achievement. This is part of the process of *feedforward*, whereby the individual estimates the likely outcome of particular responses in any given context. There are two core mediating factors, cognition and emotion.

Cognition

As discussed in Chapter 1, cognition plays a very important role in skilled communication, in terms of control of responses. This is because 'it is in the mind that intentions are formulated, potential courses of action considered, and efferent commands generated' (Greene, 1988, p. 37). Cognition has been defined as 'all the processes by which the sensory input is transformed, reduced, elaborated, stored, recovered and used' (Neisser, 1967, p. 4). This definition emphasises the following aspects:

- Cognition involves *transforming*, or decoding and making use of the sensory information received.
- To do so, it is often necessary to *reduce* the amount of information attended to, in order to avoid overloading the system.
- Conversely, at times, we have to *elaborate* upon minimal information by making interpretations, judgements, or evaluations (e.g. 'He is not speaking to me because I have upset him').
- Information is *stored* either in short-term or long-term memory. While there is debate about the exact nature and operation of memory, there is considerable

evidence to support the existence of these two systems (Bentley, 1993). Short-term memory has a limited capacity for storage, allowing for the retention of information over a brief interval of time (no more than a few minutes), while long-term memory has an enormous capacity for storage of data that can be retained over many years. Thus, information stored in short-term memory is quickly lost unless it is transferred to the long-term memory store. For instance, we can usually still remember the name of our first teacher at primary school, yet a few minutes after being introduced to someone for the first time we may have forgotten the name. The process of context-dependent coding is important. Remembering occurs by recalling the context of the original event. When we meet someone we recognise but cannot place, we try to think where or when we met that person before – in other words, we try to put the individual in a particular context. A similar process occurs in social situations, whereby we evaluate people and situations in terms of our experience of previous similar encounters. Short-term memory is important in skilled performance in terms of listening and retaining information about the responses of others so as to respond appropriately (see Chapter 9).

- Information that is stored is *recovered* or retrieved to facilitate the process of decision making and problem solving. As expressed by Meyer (2000, p. 183), 'Prior to addressing a communication goal, speakers retrieve from long-term memory knowledge about how that goal has been addressed in the past.'

While some thoughts are purposeful and goal-oriented, other cognitive activity may be disordered, less controlled, and more automatic, or involuntary, in nature. The extent to which these erratic thoughts determine the main direction of mental activity varies from one person to another, but is highest in certain pathological states, such as schizophrenia, where a large number of unrelated thoughts may 'flood through' the mind. Socially skilled individuals have greater control over cognitive processes and use these to facilitate social interaction. Snyder (1987) demonstrated how those high in social skill have a capacity for monitoring and regulating their own behaviour in relation to the responses of others – a system he termed *self-monitoring*. This process of regulation necessitates an awareness of the ability level of the person with whom one is interacting and of the 'way they think', since, as Wessler (1984, p. 112) pointed out, 'In order to interact successfully and repeatedly with the same persons, one must have the capacity to form cognitive conceptions of the others' cognitive conceptions.' Such metacognition is very important in forming judgements about the reasons for behaviour. However, as with many of the processes in skilled performance, there is an optimum level of metacognition, since, if overdone 'all of this thinking about thinking could become so cumbersome that it actually interferes with communication' (Lundsteen, 1993, p. 107). In other words, it is possible to 'think oneself out of' actions.

However, highly skilled individuals have the ability to 'size up' people and situations rapidly, and respond in an appropriate fashion. Such ability is dependent upon the capacity to process cognitively the information received during social interaction.

Emotion

The importance of mood and emotional state in the communication process and the part they play in shaping our relationships with others has been clearly demonstrated (Planalp, 2003). The effective control of emotion is a central aspect of socially skilled performance. For this reason, measures of the emotional domain figure prominently in interpersonal skill inventories (Bubas, 2003). Skilled individuals are adept both at encoding their own emotions, and at accurately decoding and responding appropriately to the emotional state of others (Burleson, 2003). Being responsive to the emotional needs of others is a key aspect of effective relational communication (Clark, Fitness & Brissette, 2004). Indeed, one of the characteristics of dysfunctions of personality, such as psychopathy, is emotional malfunction (Mitchell & Blair, 2000). The central role played by the affective domain in interpersonal encounters was aptly summarised by Metts and Bowers (1994) as follows:

> Emotion is a fundamental, potent, and ubiquitous aspect of social life. Affective arousal forms a subtext underlying all interaction, giving it direction, intensity, and velocity as well as shaping communicative choices. Emotion is also one of the most consequential outcomes of interaction, framing the interpretation of messages, one's view of self and others, and one's understanding of the relationship that gave rise to the feeling. (p. 508)

Differing theoretical perspectives exist concerning the nature and cause of emotion (Anderson & Guerrero, 1998; Manstead, Frijda & Fischer, 2004). An early viewpoint put forward by James (1884) was that emotions were simply a category of physiological phenomena resulting from the perception of an external stimulus. Thus, James argued, you see a bear, and the muscles tense and glands secrete hormones to facilitate escape – as a result, fear is experienced. However, this view was undermined by later research which demonstrated that patients who had glands and muscles removed from the nervous system by surgery nevertheless reported the feeling of affect. Later theorists emphasised the link between cognition and emotion, and highlighted two main elements involved in the subjective experience of the latter: first, the perception of physiological arousal; and, second, the cognitive evaluation of that arousal to arrive at an emotional 'label' for the experience (Berscheid, 1983).

However, differences persist about the exact nature of the relationship between cognition and emotion (Härtel, Kibby & Pizer, 2004). Centralist theorists purport that a direct causal relationship exists between cognitive and affective processes, the latter being caused by the former. Within this model, irrational beliefs would be seen as causing fear or anxiety, which, in turn, could be controlled by helping the individual to develop a more rational belief system. This perspective is regarded by others as being an oversimplification of what is viewed as a more complex relationship between cognition and affect. It is argued that emotional states can also cause changes in cognition, so that an individual who is very angry may not be able to 'think straight', while it is also possible to be 'out of your mind' with worry. In this sense, there does seem to be a reciprocal relationship, in that the way people think can influence how they feel and vice versa. As summarised by Parrott (2004, p. 12), 'Emotions usually occur because events have been interpreted in a certain way, and, once emotions occur, people often think in a somewhat altered manner.'

Cognition has been conceptualised as comprising two main dimensions: analytic cognition, which is rational, sequential, and reason-oriented; and, syncretic cognition, which is more holistic and affective in nature. Chaudhuri and Buck (1995), for example, found that differing types of advertisement evoked different forms of cognitive response in recipients. Thus, advertisements that employed product information strategies strongly encouraged analytic cognition and discouraged syncretic (or affective) cognition, whereas those using mood-arousal strategies had the converse effect. There may be individual differences in cognitive structure, in that with some people analytic thought drives central processing, while others are more affective in the way they think. It is also likely that when we interact with certain people, and in specific settings, affective cognition predominates (e.g. at a family gathering), whereas in other contexts analytic cognition is more likely to govern our thought processes (e.g. negotiating the price of a car with a salesperson in a garage showroom). More research is required to investigate the exact determinants of these two forms of cognition.

Emotion itself has been shown to have three main components: first, the direct conscious experience or feeling of emotion; second, the physiological processes that accompany emotions; and third, the observable behavioural actions used to express and convey them. Izard (1977, p. 10), in noting these three processes, pointed out that 'virtually all of the neurophysiological systems and subsystems of the body are involved in greater or lesser degree in emotional states. Such changes inevitably affect the perceptions, thoughts and actions of the person.' As a result, the individual who is in love may be 'blind' to the faults of another and fail to perceive negative cues, while someone who is very depressed is inclined to pick up negative cues and miss the positive ones. Similarly, a happy person is more confident, ambitious, and helpful, smiles more, and joins in social interaction, while a sad person is more cautious, makes more negative assessments of self and goal-attainment likelihood, has a flatter tone of voice, and generally avoids interaction with others (Burleson & Planalp, 2000).

Emotional states are, therefore, very important in terms of both our perception of the outside world and how we respond to it. The importance of the affective domain is evidenced by the vast array of words and terms used to describe the variety of emotional states that are experienced. Bush (1972) accumulated a total of 2186 emotional adjectives in English, while Averill (1975) identified a total of 558 discrete emotional labels, and Clore, Ortony and Foss (1987) found 255 terms referring to core emotions. The fact that we have a very large number of terms to describe emotional states is one indication of the importance of this domain. However, Power and Dalgleish (1997), in a major review of the field, concluded that these can be distilled to five basic emotions – sadness, happiness, anger, fear and disgust. They further argued that from each of these basic emotions a range of related complex emotions is derived. Thus, 'happiness' is the foundation for, *inter alia*, 'joy', 'nostalgia', and 'love'. There are also behaviours associated with the expression of these emotions, so, for example, love involves kissing, hugging, and extensive mutual gaze.

Another distinction has been made between 'secondary' emotions, which are seen as thought-imbued and unique to humans, and 'primary' emotions, which are also experienced by other animals. For example, all animals experience fear, anger, happiness, sadness, and surprise, but it is argued that feelings such as disillusionment, cynicism, respect, pride, and optimism are specific to humans. There is some evidence that messages using secondary emotional labels have greater social impact, and are more persuasive, than those employing primary emotions (Vaes, Paladino & Leyens, 2002).

While emotion and cognition are the two main aspects focused upon in this chapter, there are other related mediating factors that influence how we process information. This was highlighted by Miller, Cody and McLaughlin (1994, p. 187), who noted that 'individuals also enter into situations with preexisting experiences, beliefs and knowledge, resources, emotional tendencies, and so forth, all of which may not only affect what situation we enter but how we color and construe the current situation and make subsequent behavioral choices'. In this sense, 'communication phenomena are surface manifestations of complex configurations of deeply felt beliefs, values and attitudes' (Brown & Starkey, 1994, p. 808). Thus, our values, attitudes, and beliefs affect our perceptions, actions, cognitions, and emotions. Our political, moral, and religious beliefs and values therefore influence our actions and reactions to others. These also affect our attitudes toward other people, which, in turn, affect our thoughts, feelings, and behaviour during social encounters.

Our attitudes are affected not only by our beliefs and values, but also by previous experiences of the person with whom we are interacting, and by our experiences of similar people. All of these factors come into play at the decision-making stage during interpersonal encounters. For the most part, this mediating process of translating perceptions into actions takes place at a subconscious level, thereby enabling faster, smoother responses to be made. As highlighted in Chapter 1, a feature of skilled performance is the ability to operate at this subconscious level, while monitoring the situation to ensure a successful outcome.

RESPONSES

Once a goal and related action plan have been formulated, the next step in the sequence of skilled performance is to implement this plan in terms of social responses. It is the function of the response system (voice, hands, face, etc.) to carry out the plan in terms of overt behaviours, and it is at this stage that skill becomes manifest. Social behaviour can be categorised as shown in Figure 2.5.

Thus, an initial distinction is made between linguistic and non-linguistic behaviour. Linguistic behaviour refers to all aspects of speech, including the actual verbal content (the words used), and the paralinguistic message associated with it. Paralanguage refers to the way in which something is said (pitch, tone, speed, volume of voice, accent, pauses, speech dysfluencies, etc.). Non-linguistic behaviour involves all of our bodily communication and is concerned with the study of what we do rather than what we say. While there are many approaches to the analysis of non-verbal behaviour (Manusov, 2005), this domain encompasses the following three main categories.

1   *Tacesics* is the study of bodily contact – in other words, with what parts of the body we touch one another, how often, with what intensity, in which contexts, and to what effect.
2   *Proxemics* is the analysis of the spatial features of social presentation – that is, the social distances we adopt in different settings, how we mark and protect

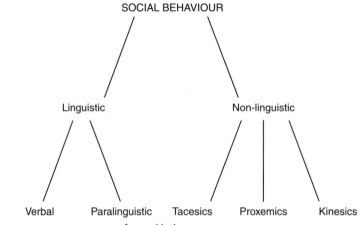

Figure 2.5 Main categories of social behaviour

       personal territory, the angles at which we orient toward one another, and the standing or seating positions we take up.

3   *Kinesics* is the systematic study of body motion – the meanings associated with movements of the hands, head, and legs, the postures we adopt, and our gaze and facial expressions.

These aspects of social behaviour are discussed fully throughout the remaining chapters of this book.

    One important element of individual behaviour is the concept of style, defined by Norton (1983) as 'the relatively enduring pattern of human interaction associated with the individual' (p. 19), involving 'an accumulation of "microbehaviors" . . . that add up to a "macrojudgment" about a person's style of communicating' (p. 38). Norton identified the following nine main communicative styles, each of which can be interpreted as a continuum:

1   *Dominant/submissive*. Dominant people like to control social interactions, give orders, and be the centre of attention; they use behaviours such as loud volume of voice, interruptions, prolonged eye contact, and fewer pauses to achieve dominance. At the opposite end of this continuum, submissive people prefer to keep quiet, stay out of the limelight, and take orders.

2   *Dramatic/reserved*. Exaggeration, storytelling, and non-verbal communication are techniques used by dramatic individuals who tend to overstate their messages. At the other end of the continuum is the reserved type of person, who is quieter, modest, and prone to understatement.

3   *Contentious/affiliative*. The contentious person is argumentative, provocative, or contrary, as opposed to the agreeable, peace-loving, affiliative individual.

4   *Animated/inexpressive*. An animated style involves making use of hands, arms, eyes, facial expressions, posture, and overall body movement to gain attention or convey enthusiasm. The converse here is the dull, slow-moving, inexpressive person.

5   *Relaxed/frenetic.* This continuum ranges from people who do not get over-excited, always seem in control, and are never flustered, to those who are tense, quickly lose self-control, get excited easily, and behave frenetically.

6   *Attentive/inattentive.* Attentive individuals listen carefully to others and display overt signs of listening such as eye contact, appropriate facial expression, and posture. Inattentive individuals, on the other hand, are poor listeners who do not make any attempt to express interest in what others are saying.

7   *Impression-leaving/insignificant.* The impression-leaving style is characterised by flamboyant individuals who display a visible or memorable style of communicating and leave an impression on those whom they meet. They are people who, for example, wear loud clothes, have unusual hairstyles, or exhibit a controversial interactive manner. The opposite of this is the insignificant individual who 'fades into the fabric' of buildings, is non-controversial, and dresses conservatively.

8   *Open/closed.* Open people talk about themselves freely, and are approachable, unreserved, candid, and conversational. At the opposite end of this continuum are very closed individuals who disclose no personal information, are guarded, secretive, and loath to express opinions, and 'keep themselves to themselves' (see Chapter 8 for further discussion on self-disclosure).

9   *Friendly/hostile.* This style continuum ranges from the friendly person who smiles frequently, and is happy, very rewarding, and generally non-competitive, to the hostile person who is overtly aggressive, highly competitive, and very unrewarding.

Most people can be evaluated overall in terms of these continua, although style of communication can also be affected by situations. A dominant teacher in the classroom may be submissive during staff meetings, while a normally friendly individual may become hostile when engaging in team sports. Nevertheless, there are elements of style that endure across situations, and these have a bearing on a number of facets of the individual. For example, someone who tends to be dominant, frenetic, inattentive, or hostile will probably not make a good counsellor. Similarly, a very dominant person is unlikely to marry someone equally dominant.

As discussed in Chapter 1, behaviour is the acid test of skill. If someone always fails miserably at actual negotiation we would not call that person a skilled negotiator. For this reason, much of this text is devoted to an analysis of a wide array of responses in terms of skills, styles, and strategies. However, in order to respond appropriately, it is also necessary to be aware of available feedback during communication.

FEEDBACK

It is now well documented that a key feature in skill acquisition is the receipt of accurate and timely feedback on performance (Greene, 2003). Feedback enables us to monitor our progress toward goal achievement (Locke & Latham, 1990). As noted by Tourish and Hargie (2004, p. 188), 'The more channels of accurate and helpful feedback we have access to, the better we are likely to perform.' 'Feedback' is a term derived from cybernetics (the study of automatic communication and control in systems), which is the method of controlling a system by reinserting into it the results of its past performance. This concept of feedback as a control process operates on the basis that the output of a system is 'fed back' into it as additional input, which, in turn, serves to regulate further output (Annett, 1969). In this way, a thermostat on a central heating unit acts as a servomechanism, automatically feeding back details of the temperature into the system, which then regulates heating output. One important difference between this mechanistic view and its application to the interpersonal domain is that people actively interpret feedback. Thus, a message intended as positive feedback by the sender may be construed as negative by the receiver. Likewise, feedback from others may be either not picked up at all, or perceived and rejected.

Nevertheless, once a response has been carried out, feedback is available to determine its effects and enable subsequent responses to be shaped in the light of this information. To perform any task efficiently, it is necessary to receive such feedback so that corrective action can be taken as required. Thus, sighted individuals would find it very difficult to write a letter, make a cup of coffee, or even walk along a straight line in the absence of visual feedback. As Sloboda (1986, pp. 32–33) put it: 'Feedback of one sort or another is essential to all skill acquisition. One cannot improve unless one has ways of judging how good present performance is, and in which direction change must occur.'

Within the sphere of social interaction, we receive feedback from the reactions of other people, as messages are received and transmitted in a continuous return loop. The importance of such feedback was illustrated in a study of advice giving during supportive encounters, which concluded: 'before giving advice, it is important to determine whether advice is even wanted. The support seeker's receptiveness to advice has a significant influence on whether the advice is liked, assists with coping, or is adopted' (MacGeorge, Feng, Butler & Budarz, 2004, p. 68). As well as getting feedback from the other person, we also receive self-feedback, which provides information about our own performance (see Figure 2.3). For example, if we ask a question which we immediately perceive to be poorly worded, we may rephrase the question before the listener has had an opportunity to respond. High self-monitors more readily access such information and by so doing control the images of self they project to others. Our self-perceptions over time help us to shape our attitudes, values, beliefs, and personality. We develop self-schemata regarding the type of person we think we are, and our self-concept in turn influences the way in which encounters with others are perceived and interpreted.

Fitts and Posner (1973) identified three main functions of feedback:

1   To provide *motivation* to continue with a task – if feedback suggests the possibility of a successful outcome. In this way, feedback enables performance to be evaluated. For example, a salesperson who believes the customer is showing interest is likely to be more motivated to try to clinch the sale.

2   To provide *knowledge* about the results of behaviour. Whether the sale is successful or not will help to shape the salesperson's future sales attempts – to replicate the same approach or make appropriate changes.

3   To act as a form of *reinforcement* from the listener, encouraging the speaker to continue with the same type of messages. Thus, during an interaction, feedback in the form of comments, such as 'I fully agree' or 'Great idea', and non-verbal behaviours, including smiles and head nods, are overt positive reinforcers (see Chapter 5).

What is referred to as *backchannel behaviour* has been shown to be a key form of feedback. This allows the listener to feed back information (agreement, disagreement, interest, involvement, etc.) to the speaker on an ongoing yet unobtrusive basis, in the form of vocalisations ('m-hm', 'uh-huh'), head nods, posture, eye movements, and facial expressions. The skilled speaker engages in *track-checking behaviour* by monitoring these backchannel cues to assess whether the message is being understood and accepted, and is having the intended impact. This enables adjustments to be made to the delivery as necessary. Research findings indicate cross-cultural differences in type and degree of backchannel behaviour, and also show that judgements of communication skill are higher where interactors display similar levels of backchannel cues (Kikuchi, 1994).

In interpersonal communication, we are bombarded by a constant stream of sensory stimulation, in the form of noises, sights, smells, tastes, and tactile sensations. While bodily olfaction has a very important communicative function that can affect the relationships we develop with others (Serby & Chobor, 1992), in Western society, bodily odours are often camouflaged by the application of various types of artificial scent. During social encounters, we therefore receive most perceptual information through the eyes and ears, and, to a lesser extent, tactile senses. Indeed, we receive such a barrage of sensory input that it is necessary to filter out some of the available stimuli, to deal more effectively with the remainder. In their analysis of skilled performance, Matthews, Davies, Westerman and Stammers (2000, p. 67) noted how, 'For more than a century, there has been explicit recognition that human cognitive performance involves a process of attentional selectivity.' This is because 'the capacity of human information processing is limited. We cannot process all stimuli that reach our sensory system' (Fiedler & Bless, 2001, pp. 125–126). Thus, we employ a selective perception filter to limit the amount of information that is consciously perceived, while storing the remainder at a subconscious level. For example, in a lecture context, students are bombarded by stimuli in terms of the voice of the lecturer, the noises made by other students, the pressure of their feet on the floor and backsides on the seat, the hum of a data projector, the feel of a pen, and so on. If the lecturer is very stimulating, other stimuli are filtered out, but if the lecturer is boring, one's aching backside may become a prime focus of attention.

Unfortunately, vital information from others may be filtered out during social interaction and less important cues consciously perceived. One reason for this is that we are not objective animals, since our 'Beliefs tell us what to listen to, how to filter incoming information' (Thompson, 1993, p. 158). Thus, from all the social stimuli available to us, we may focus upon less relevant stimuli and miss important verbal or non-verbal signals. The difference between feedback and perception is that while there is usually a great deal of feedback available, it is not all consciously perceived. Skilled individuals make appropriate use of the feedback available during interactions by perceiving the central messages and filtering out peripheral ones.

PERCEPTION

Perceptual acumen is a key feature of skilled performance. Indeed, Guirdham (2002, p. 160) argued that 'Accurate and differentiated social perception is the basis of all skilled interpersonal interaction.' Socially skilled individuals continually monitor their environment and use the available information to assess the most apposite responses. As noted by Sekuler and Blake (2002, p. 1), in general terms, 'Perception puts us in contact with the world we live in; it shapes our knowledge of that world.' Hinton (1993, p. ix) stated that, within the social domain, 'Interpersonal perception is all about how we decide what other people are like and the meanings we give to their actions.' The centrality of person perception was emphasised by Cook (1979), who illustrated how the way people perceive one another directly determines their behaviour during interaction.

One of the most common observations made of human nature is that 'people are all different'. They differ in terms of physical characteristics such as height and weight. They differ in sex, socio-economic status, cultural inheritance, educational attainments, peer group influences, and personality traits. People also differ in the way they perceive the world around them, so that they 'read' the same situation in differing ways. This is because 'social perception is not a neutral registration of objective reality, but an active construction that is influenced by concurrent processes of thought, memory, feeling, and motivation' (Martin, Frack & Strapel, 2004, p. 54). Thus, reality for each individual is constructed from the way in which incoming information is interpreted (Myers, 2002). To appreciate this more fully, we need to understand some of the factors that influence the perceptual process.

Perceptual ability is influenced by the familiarity of incoming stimuli. Bentley (1993) illustrated how knowledge is a set of associated concepts, such that new information is learned by building connections to the existing cognitive network. Consequently, if incoming material is difficult to understand, it will be harder to assimilate and conceptualise. Within social interaction, such elements as a common understandable language, recognisable dialect, and phrasing influence perceptual capacity. Thus, our speed of perception would drop if someone used technical terms with which we were unfamiliar or spoke too fast. Likewise, if the non-verbal signals do not register as understandable, or are distracting, our perceptual reception is hampered. In either situation, we may selectively filter out the unfamiliar or unacceptable and thus receive a distorted or inaccurate message. Another factor here is that we are not always consciously aware of having perceived stimuli. It has been shown that messages received at the subliminal (subconscious) level influence the way in which we judge others (Monahan, 1998; Banaji, Lemm & Carpenter, 2004).

There are two main theories of perception, namely, intuitive and inference. Intuitive theories regard perception as being innate, purporting that people instinctively recognise and interpret the behaviour and feelings of others. There is some evidence to support the existence of such an innate capacity. It has been found, for example, that monkeys reared in isolation are able to recognise and respond to the emotions displayed by other monkeys. Furthermore, people blind from birth are able to display facial expressions of emotions (albeit of a more restricted range than sighted people), and a number of such expressions seem to be common across different cultures. However, although there may be elements of emotion that are perceived intuitively, it is unlikely that many of the perceptual judgements people make are innate (for example, warm, intelligent, sophisticated). Such detailed evaluations are culture-specific and dependent upon learning. Moreover, if perception were innate and instinctive, we should be accurate in our perceptions. Yet this is patently not the case.

There is a great deal of evidence that we are often inaccurate in our perceptions and can be deceived in terms of what we appear to see (Jones, 1990). For example, a series of bulbs lit in quick succession seems like the flowing movement of light. Another example of how perception can be distorted is shown in the 'impossible object' in Figure 2.6. This object is meaningful if we look at either end of it, but when viewed in its entirety it is, in fact, an optical illusion. Likewise, in person perception, one can be deceived by appearances – for example, family and friends are often shocked when someone commits suicide without seeming to be at all unhappy.

Perceptions are also influenced by context, so that the symbol **1** will be seen as a number in the first sequence and as a letter in the second sequence below. In the same way, our perceptions of people are influenced by the social context.

1–2–3

G–H–1

Likewise, what we see often depends on how we look at things. Thus, in Jastrow's famous ambiguous illusion (Figure 2.7), we can see either a rabbit or a duck. In like vein, our perception of others depends upon the way in which we 'look' at them. The primacy and recency effects also play an important role in perception. The primacy effect refers to the way in which information perceived early in an encounter can influence how later information is interpreted. In this way, initial impressions of people we meet for the first time influence how we respond to them, despite the fact that such impressions can be misleading. Important decisions, such as whether or not to give someone a job, are influenced by the first impressions of the candidate gleaned by the interviewer (Hargie et al., 2004). The recency effect refers to the way in which the final information received can affect our judgements. For example, in a sequence of employment interviews, the final candidate is more readily remembered than those interviewed in the middle of the sequence.

It is also possible to improve perceptual ability, thereby supporting the view that learning processes are involved. Thus, while intuition plays a role in our perceptions of others, it cannot account for the entire process. The second theory of perception purports that judgements of others are based on inferences made as the result of past

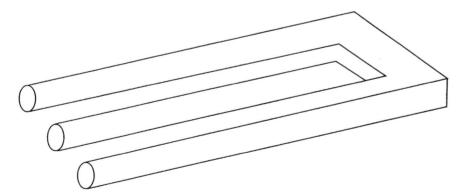

Figure 2.6 Impossible object

Figure 2.7 Jastrow's duck-rabbit

experiences. Through this process, we develop categories with which to describe others, and hold certain beliefs about which categories 'hang together'. In this way, if we were told that someone is compassionate, we might expect other related qualities to be displayed (e.g. sympathetic, kind, generous).

The process of labelling is used during person perception to enable people to be categorised and dealt with more readily. Labels are related to aspects such as age, physical appearance, sex, race, and mode of dress, as well as non-verbal and verbal behaviour. Labelling arises from the need to classify and categorise others, and to simplify incoming information, which would otherwise become unmanageable. One of the most ubiquitous types of label is that of the social stereotype (Operario & Fiske, 2004). Once a person is identified as belonging to a particular group, the charac-teristics of that group tend to be attributed irrespective of actual individual character-istics. As Fiedler (1993, p. 349) pointed out, 'perceptions and judgements of people not only reflect the objectively available stimulus information but also to a considerable extent the judge's own inferences or stereotypical expectations.'

Expectations can directly influence both the behaviour of the individual and the outcomes of interaction. This interpersonal expectancy effect, which has been shown to be operative in a range of professional contexts, including health, business, educa-tion, social research, and the courtroom (Blanck, 1993), can be either positive or nega-tive. For instance, if we are given positive information about someone, we form positive expectations and respond accordingly. In this way, a self-fulfilling prophecy can occur, in that we actually encourage the anticipated response. The effects of expectations upon behaviour can also be negative. For example, if we believe that people from a particular racial background are aggressive, when we meet someone of that race we are more likely to behave in a way that anticipates aggression, thereby provoking a more aggressive response and so confirming our original beliefs.

Thus, both intuition and inference play a part in person perception. The innate perception of certain basic emotions in others is important for the survival of the individual, but in a complex society, learned inferences enable us to recognise and interpret a range of social messages, and respond to these more appropriately. It is at the latter level that perception plays a key role in skilled performance. The more socially skilled individual possesses greater perceptual ability than someone less socially adept. To be effective in social interaction, it is necessary to be sensitive to relevant social feedback, in terms of the verbal and non-verbal behaviour being displayed both by oneself and by others. If such perceptions are inaccurate, then decisions about future responses will be based upon invalid information, and the resulting responses are likely to be less appropriate.

Perception is the final central process involved in the model of skilled performance (Figure 2.3). However, in order to comprehend fully such performance, we must take account of two other aspects, namely, personal and situational factors, which impinge upon and influence how skill is operationalised.

THE PERSON–SITUATION CONTEXT

As discussed in Chapter 1, skilled behaviour is appropriate to the situation in which it is carried out. Communication is embedded within a context and interactive messages can be fully understood only by taking cognisance of the situation (S) in which they occur. At the same time, the person (P) side of the equation is also important. Burleson (2003, p. 577) summarised it as follows:

> enduring features of the person interact with contextual factors in generating both a situated interpretation of a specific event and a situated motivational-emotional response to that event . . . [which] . . . lead, in turn, to the formation of interaction goals . . . and these ultimately generate the articulated message.

It is therefore necessary to study skilled performance within the parameters of what Hargie and Dickson (2004) termed the person–situation context. This is important since 'skill is achieved when learners can systematically adapt their performance to changing personal and contextual conditions' (Zimmerman, 2000, p. 30).

The person–situation debate has produced three perspectives. Personologists purport that behaviour is mainly a feature of inner personality traits, situationalists argue that it is primarily a function of the setting in which people find themselves, and interactionists hold that behaviour is a product of $P \times S$. In reviewing research into this debate, Argyle (1994, p. 102) concluded: 'The overall results are very clear: persons and situations are both important, but $P \times S$ interaction is more important than either.' Thus, for example, in the employment interview, what is known as the 'person–environment fit' plays a key role (Whetzel & McDaniel, 1999), in that selection interviewers attempt to assess whether or not a candidate would fit into the existing organisational environment.

Person factors

As noted by Kelley, Holmes, Kerr, Reis, Rusbult and Van Lange (2003, p. 9), 'Person factors are a necessary component of the study of social interaction because they determine the individual's perception of and response to the objective properties of the situation.' The following are the key factors pertaining to the person.

Personality

The concept of personality and the role it plays in determining behaviour has long occupied the minds of social scientists (Butt, 2004). While recognising that there are many differing perspectives on personality, and hence varying definitions, Pervin and John (2001, p. 4) defined it as 'those characteristics of the person that account for consistent patterns of feeling, thinking and behaving'. One common unit of analysis in the study of personality has been that of traits. It is argued by trait theorists that whether we are cooperative or competitive, extraverted or introverted, dominant or submissive, dependent or independent, and so on, influences both how we interpret and how we respond to situations. Although many inventories have been developed to measure a plethora of such characteristics, there is considerable debate regarding the exact number of traits, or factors, which can reliably be charted. Most agree on the validity of what have been termed the 'big five' traits of extraversion, neuroticism (or anxiety), tough-mindedness, conscientiousness, and open-mindedness.

Traits can be viewed as representing naturally occurring goal tensions within individuals. For example, extraversion–introversion represents the tension between wanting to meet and socialise with others, on the one hand, and the desire to have peace and quiet and be alone, on the other hand. It would seem that while traits are not universally reliable in predicting behaviour, they are most useful in predicting individual responses across similar situations (Miller et al., 1994). However, there is no clear agreement about the exact determinants of personality. Although a combination of hereditary and prenatal factors is contributory, experiences in infancy and early childhood seem to play a vital shaping role. Furthermore, while personality is relatively stable, it can and does change as a result of experiences throughout the lifespan. There is also some evidence that differences in personality may differentially affect skill acquisition, though research in this field is at a very early stage (see Greene, 2003). In addition, skills need to be adapted to meet the specific requirements of different types of people (see, for example, the discussion of variations in persuasion techniques in Chapter 11).

We need to interact with others for a period of time before making judgements about their personality. Yet, even before we actually talk to others, we make inferences about them based upon 'how they look'. Such judgements can markedly affect the goals we pursue, our motivation to open an interaction, the way in which we perceive the actions of others, and how we respond to them. Therefore, it is necessary to take account of those aspects of the individual that are immediately visible, namely, gender, age, and appearance.

Gender

During social interaction, we tend to respond differently to, and have differing expectations of, others depending upon whether they are male or female. All cultures recognise male/female as a fundamental divide and accord different sets of character-istics and behavioural expectations according to which side of the divide an indi-vidual is on (Eckes, 1994). The first question asked after the birth of a baby is usually whether it is a girl or a boy. Sexual differences are then perpetuated by the ways in which infants are dressed and responded to by adults. Not surprisingly, therefore, by the age of 2 years, children can readily distinguish males from females on the basis of purely cultural cues such as hairstyle and clothing (Romaine, 1999). Gender stereotypes proliferate in child rearing, with children being reminded of gender role expectations in phrases such as 'big boys don't cry' or 'that's not very lady-like'. Such practices inevitably contribute to later differences in behaviour and expectations thereof. However, the extent to which gender-specific patterns of behaviour are innate or learned remains unclear. For example, 'social constructionist' theorists view gender as being constructed through everyday discourse and relational communication (Frosh, Phoenix & Pattman, 2003). However, this perspective, which purports that masculinity and femininity exist only in relation to one another, is rejected by evolutionary theorists. The latter argue that gender variations in behaviour can be understood from an evolutionary perspective, as these arise from biological differences (Archer, 2004). Each side cites evidence to substantiate its claims. It seems likely, however, that both nature and nurture play a part in shaping gender response patterns, although the precise manner in which this occurs remains a matter of considerable debate.

Differences have been reported in studies of non-verbal behaviour, some of the trends being that women tend to require less interpersonal space, touch and are touched more, gesture less, look and are looked at more, and smile more frequently, than males (Hargie & Dickson, 2004). In addition, social skills inventories have revealed consistent gender differences on various dimensions, females scoring higher on measures of emotional expressivity and sensitivity (Riggio, 1999). Likewise, gen-der variations have been reported in several aspects of language (Mulac, Bradac & Gibbons, 2001). The male-preferred style involves being more directive, self-opinionated, and explicit, whereas females tend to be more indirect, use a greater number of 'hedges' and expressed uncertainties ('kind of', 'it could be'), speak for longer periods, and refer more to emotions. However, Jones (1999) highlighted the fact that there are many inconsistencies in the findings of studies into gender differences, concluding that gender is something that we 'do' rather than something that we 'are'. In other words, some females choose to behave in what is regarded within their particular culture as a feminine style. This is probably because males or females who deviate markedly from their expected sex role behaviour are likely to encounter prob-lems during social interaction. In this sense, the study of gender needs to take account of not only biological features but also psychological make-up. As a personality factor, gender can be divided into the following four categories:

	High femininity	*Low femininity*
High masculinity	Androgynous	Masculine
Low masculinity	Feminine	Indeterminate

In this way, for instance, a *feminine* female is likely, in various situations, to behave differently from a *masculine* female. Research bearing such psychological gender characteristics in mind is likely to be more fruitful in charting actual behavioural variants of performance.

Age

There has been increasing research into the field of social gerontology. One reason for this is that 'social aging – how we behave, as social actors, towards others, and even how we align ourselves with or come to understand the signs of difference or change as we age – are phenomena achieved primarily through communication experiences' (Nussbaum & Coupland, 2004, p. xi). Likewise, communication processes are directly affected by maturational phenomena at each stage of our lives (Yingling, 2004). It is also clear that our own age, and the age of those with whom we interact, shape our behaviour and expectations (Williams & Harwood, 2004). Skilled individuals therefore take the age of the target (and of course their own age) into consideration when framing their responses. For example, different forms of reward are appropriate for 3-year-olds, 12-year-olds, and 25-year-olds; statements such as 'You're a clever little person', 'You have really grown up', and 'I find your ideas intellectually very challenging' are apposite for one age group, but not for the others.

Reaction time, speech discrimination, and the capacity for information processing tend to decrease with age (Giordano, 2000). However, there are wide differences across individuals, with some more adversely affected than others. Furthermore, older people have accumulated a larger vocabulary, coupled with a wealth of experience of handling a wide variety of types of people across varying situations. Thus, there can be advantages and disadvantages in terms of the effects of age upon skilled performance. There has been considerable research into patterns of intergenerational communication. Hummert, Garstka, Ryan, and Bonnensen (2004) identified three positive stereotypes and four main negative stereotypes of the older adult as follows:

Positive stereotypes

1 *John Wayne conservative* (patriotic, proud, mellow)
2 *perfect grandparent* (kind, supportive, wise)
3 *golden ager* (lively, well-travelled, healthy).

Negative stereotypes

1 *despondent* (depressed, lonely, neglected, etc.)
2 *severely impaired* (feeble, incompetent, senile)
3 *shrew/curmudgeon* (complaining, selfish, ill-tempered)
4 *recluse* (quiet, timid, naive).

The possession of negative stereotypes of the elderly, especially that of being impaired, can lead younger adults to adopt an overaccommodating speech style that has been variously described as 'secondary baby talk', 'elderspeak', 'infantilising speech' and 'patronising talk'. This pattern includes the presence of simplification strategies (e.g. slower delivery, low grammatical difficulty), clarification strategies (e.g. increased volume, deliberate articulation), and diminutives (e.g. 'dear', 'love'). Such patterns, as well as being demeaning, may actually have negative effects on the self-identity of the elderly persons to whom they are directed and on their psychological and physical health (Barker, Giles & Harwood, 2004). The corollary, of course, is that older adults may underaccommodate when interacting with younger individuals, by ignoring their conversational needs (e.g. by not listening, or talking about events outside the younger person's experience). An important aspect of skilled performance is pitching responses at the apposite level, bearing in mind the ability (rather than chronological age) of the other person.

Appearance

The physical appearance of others, in terms of body size, shape, and attractiveness, also affects our behaviour and expectations. People are judged upon their appearance from a very early age, so that nursery school children have been shown to exhibit an aversion to chubby individuals and a greater liking for physically attractive peers (Stewart, Powell & Chetwynd, 1979). Attractiveness is a very important feature in social encounters. A range of research studies has shown that being rated as attractive has positive benefits (Wilson & Nias, 1999). These include being seen as more popular, intelligent, friendly, and interesting to talk to; receiving higher grades in school; dating more frequently; securing employment more readily; earning more; and being less likely to be found guilty in court. While they are also seen as more vain, materialistic, and likely to have extramarital affairs, it remains the case that 'on the whole, we seem to equate beauty with goodness' (Saks & Krupat, 1988, p. 256). Ratings of physical attractiveness are fairly consistent across variations in age, gender, socio-economic status, and geographical location. Aronson (2004) argued that cross-cultural agreement about ratings of attractiveness has been influenced by popular culture. Many children are raised on a diet of Disney cartoon characters, Ken and Barbie dolls, Scream-Dream pop stars, and TV soaps. There are clear features of attractiveness therein; for example, Disney's Cinderella and Snow White have small faces, clear complexions, thin figures, and large eyes.

It is not surprising therefore that research has shown cross-cultural agreement that attractive facial features in young women include large eyes relative to size of face, high cheek bones, and thin jaw, as well as short distance between nose and mouth and between mouth and chin (Perret et al., 1994). The male physique rated as attractive by females includes being tall and slim, with medium-thin lower trunk and medium-wide upper trunk, small buttocks, thin legs, and a flat stomach (Argyle, 1988). However, research and theory into the study of attraction have also emphasised how initial judgements of attractiveness can be tempered by psychological, sociological, contextual, and relational influences (Duck, 1995). Thus, attractiveness involves more than physical features and is not just 'skin deep'. For instance, a physically unattractive professional may be successful and popular with clients by developing an empathic interactive style coupled with a competent professional approach.

Although one of the prime functions of clothes is to protect the wearer from cold or injury, dress also serves a number of social functions (Hargie & Dickson, 2004). The importance of social signals conveyed by apparel is evidenced by the amount of money spent on fashion wear in Western society. This is because, in many situations, it is very important to 'look the part'. Socially skilled people devote time and effort to the selection of appropriate apparel for interpersonal encounters in order to project a suitable image. Thus, we 'dress up' for important occasions such as selection interviews or first dates. In addition, we also carefully select other embellishments, including 'body furniture' (rings, bangles, necklaces, brooches, earrings, watches, and hair ribbons or bands), spectacles, and make-up, to enhance our overall personal image. Since so much attention is devoted to the choice of dress, it is hardly surprising that we make judgements about others based upon this feature. In terms of impression management, it is patently advisable to dress with care.

The situation

As explained in Chapter 1, skilled performance is shaped by situational factors. There is ample evidence that social situations have a powerful impact on behaviour (Manstead, 1997). This impact can be understood by examining the core features of social situations, as initially identified by Argyle, Furnham, and Graham (1981). These are explained below, with reference to professional interaction.

Goal structure

As noted earlier in this chapter and in Chapter 1, goals represent a central aspect of skill. The goals we seek are influenced by the situation in which we are interacting, while, conversely, the goals we pursue are central determinants of situation selection (Kelley et al., 2003). Thus, in the surgery, the doctor will have goals directly related to dealing with patients. However, if the doctor has the social goal of finding a mate, social situations in which available members of the opposite sex are likely to be encountered will be sought. In this way, goals and situations are intertwined. Thus, knowledge of the goal structure for any situation is an important aspect of skilled performance.

Roles

In any given situation, people play, and are expected to play, different roles, which carry with them sets of expectations about behaviour, attitudes, feelings, and values. Thus, a doctor is expected to behave in a thorough, caring fashion, to be concerned about patients' health, and to treat their problems in confidence. The roles of those involved affect both the goals and behaviour of participants. For example, a teacher will behave differently, and have different goals, when teaching pupils in the classroom, attending a staff meeting at lunchtime, or having an interview with the principal about possible promotion.

Rules

Social interaction has been likened to a game, involving rules that must be followed if a successful outcome is to be achieved (see Chapter 1). Professionals must be aware not only of the rules of the situations they encounter, but also how to deal with clients who break them (for example, pupils misbehaving in the classroom).

Repertoire of elements

Different types of behaviour are more or less appropriate in different situations; therefore it is important for professionals to develop a range of behavioural repertoires. Thus, in one situation, fact finding may be crucial and the skill of questioning central, while in another context it may be necessary to explain carefully certain facts to a client. These behavioural repertoires are usually sequential in nature (see Chapter 1).

Concepts

A certain amount of conceptual information is necessary for effective participation in any given situation. In order to play the game of poker, one must be aware of the specific meaning of concepts such as 'flush' and 'run'. Similarly, a patient visiting the dentist may need to be aware of the particular relevance of concepts such as 'crown' or 'bridge'. One common error is to assume that others are familiar with concepts when in fact they are not. Most professionals have developed a jargon of specific terminology for various concepts, and must ensure that it is avoided, or fully explained, when dealing with clients.

Language and speech

There are linguistic variations associated with social situations, with some requiring a higher degree of language formality. Giving a lecture, being interviewed for a managerial position, or chairing a board meeting all involve a more formal, deliberate, elaborated use of language than having a chat with a friend over coffee. Equally, changes in tone, pitch, and volume of voice change across situations: there are vocal patterns associated with, *inter alia*, evangelical clergymen addressing religious gatherings, barristers summing up in court, and sports commentators describing ball games. Professionals need to develop and refine their language and speech to suit a particular context.

Physical environment

The nature of the environment influences behaviour. Humans, like all animals, feel more secure on 'home territory' than in unfamiliar environs. Thus, a social worker will tend to find clients more comfortable in their own homes than in the office, whereas the social worker will be more relaxed in the latter situation. People usually feel more at ease, and therefore talk more freely, in 'warm' environments (soft seats, concealed lights, carpets, curtains, and pot plants). The physical lay-out of furniture is also important in either encouraging or discouraging interaction.

Culture

Few aspects of the communication process have attracted as much attention in recent years as the study of culture (O'Dell, de Abreu & O'Toole, 2004). Culture can be defined as 'the sets of behaviors, beliefs, values, and linguistic patterns that are relatively enduring over time and generation within a group' (Spitzberg, 2003, p. 96). It is passed from one generation to another and, while not static, is a stable system within which people negotiate identity and relationships (Ayoko, Härtel, Fisher & Fujimoto, 2004). Furthermore, any group that is significantly different from the rest of society forms a subculture, and the actions of individuals are more readily understood in the light of subcultural influences.

Culture has been shown to have a definite influence on how interpersonal skills are enacted (Campbell & Falkowski, 2003). This is because, 'Based on the beliefs and values of our culture, we learn not only what are appropriate interaction scripts within our culture, but also the meanings that should be assigned to these inter-actions' (Pecchioni, Ota & Sparks, 2004, p. 168). The importance of *cultural expertise* as a feature of skilled performance was highlighted by Ivey, D'Andrea, Ivey and Simek-Morgan (2002). Cultural expertise refers to the ability to adapt one's responses appropriately across differing cultural settings. An example is contained in the old adage, 'When in Rome, do as the Romans do.' It necessitates the development of a knowledge and understanding of the cultural and subcultural norms, beliefs, values, and responses of those with whom we are interacting. Being a skilled person includes the possession of a high level of such cultural expertise.

While culture is a multifaceted concept (Chryssochoou, 2004), a common broad distinction is made between *collectivist* and *individualistic* cultures. Eastern cultures (e.g. Japan, China, Korea) tend to be collectivist and *high context*, in that much of the communicative meaning is implicit and attached to relationships and situations rather than to what is said. The style of communication is more indirect and self-concealing, with the result that verbal messages can be ambiguous. These cultures foster an *interdependent self* with high value placed upon external features such as roles, status, relationships, 'fitting in', being accorded one's proper place, being aware of what others are thinking and feeling, not hurting others' feelings, and minimising imposition when presenting requests. Time is conceived as being subservient to duties, relationships, and responsibilities.

Western cultures (e.g. the USA, the UK, Canada, Germany, Norway) are *low context*, with an emphasis upon open, direct communication with explicit meaning, so that verbal messages tend to be clearer, more complete, specific, and pointed. There is a discomfort with ambiguity, and anxiety when meaning depends upon something other than the words uttered. These cultures encourage the development of an *independent self* that is bounded, unitary, stable, and detached from social context, with a consequent focus upon internal abilities, thoughts and feelings, expressing oneself and one's uniqueness, and being 'up front'. Goals tend to be more personal and instrumental, and time is seen as paramount – being viewed as akin to a commodity, which can be 'spent', 'saved', 'invested', or 'wasted'.

Collectivist cultures therefore inculcate a 'we' identity as opposed to the 'I' identity in individualist cultures. This directly affects interpersonal skills. For example, cultural differences have been found in style of request, between direct forms ('Close that window'), indirect forms ('It's getting cold') and those in between ('Would it be OK to have the window closed?'). Kim and Wilson (1994) found that US undergraduates considered the direct style as the most skilful way of making a request whereas Korean undergraduates rated it as the least effective strategy. Furthermore, the US sample saw clarity as a key dimension of successful requests, while Koreans viewed clarity as counterproductive to effectiveness.

However, it has also been found that there are individual as well as cultural differences in individualism and collectivism (Iyengar & Brockner, 2001; Reykowski, 2001). As noted by Ivey (1994, p. 12), 'individuals differ as much as or more than do cultures. You will want to attune your responses to the unique human being before you.' Furthermore, at different times, in varying situations, and with different people, we may adopt either a more individualistic or a more collectivist style of communicating. Skilled individuals therefore consider both the nature of the specific individual and prevailing cultural norms when deciding how to respond.

OVERVIEW

The model described in this chapter has been designed to account for the central facets of interpersonal interaction. It will be apparent from this review that interaction between people is a complex process. Any interpersonal encounter involves a myriad of variables, some or all of which may be operative at any given time. Although each of these has been discussed in isolation, it should be realised that in reality these occur simultaneously. As we are encoding and sending messages, we are also decoding and receiving messages. Skilled communication is, in this sense, transactional. People in social encounters are therefore interdependent, and as information is perceived it is immediately dealt with and responded to so quickly that we are not usually aware that these processes are occurring. This transactional element of socially skilled performance needs to be emphasised, as it has been misunderstood by some theorists, who have then proceeded to misrepresent the skills paradigm. For example, Sanders (2003) criticised the skills approach on the specious basis that by focusing solely upon the behaviour of the individual it fails to recognise that interaction is a two-way process. Sanders patently failed to appreciate or understand that his description of how 'the quality of individual's performance . . . depends not only on their own capabilities, motives, and goals, but also on the capabilities, motives and goals . . . of the other(s) with whom they interact' (p. 224) is in fact a summary of key aspects of the skills perspective as described in this chapter.

Given the number of factors that influence the behaviour of individuals during social interaction, it is extremely difficult to make judgements or interpretations about the exact reasons why certain behaviours are, or are not, displayed. A key advantage of the model as presented in this chapter is that it provides a systematic structure for analysing skilled human behaviour. It has taken account of the central processes involved in interpersonal communication, namely, the goals people pursue and their motivation to attain them, the cognitive and affective processes which influence the processing of information, the feedback available during social encounters, the perception of this feedback, impinging personal and contextual factors, and the responses that people make.

While some of the features of the model of skilled performance (Figure 2.3) are the same as those contained in the motor skills model (Figure 2.2), there are also differences. In particular, the reciprocal nature of social interaction, the role of emotions, the nature of person perception, and the influence of the person–situation context have more impact during social than motor skill performance. However, it can be argued that the analogy between motor and social skills, as explicated in this chapter and in Chapter 1, has provided a valuable theoretical framework for interpreting interpersonal interaction.

As Hartley (1999) has exemplified, the model also illustrates how communication breakdown can occur at any of the interrelated stages. For example, an individual's *goals* may be unrealistic or inappropriate, or communicators may have competing, irreconcilable goals. At the *mediation* level, the person may suffer from disordered thought processes, have underdeveloped schemas, or lack emotional empathy. Problems can also occur because inappropriate *responses* are made, or because the person has poor *perceptual* acumen and cannot make use of available *feedback* from others. Breakdown may be a factor of the person–situation axis; for instance, it may occur because of cultural insensitivity or inappropriate personality characteristics (e.g. someone who is highly neurotic is unlikely to be a good counsellor). The model has also been shown to provide a valuable template for research investigation in the fields of health care (Skipper, 1992), negotiation (Hughes, 1994), and counselling (Irving, 1995), and among the clergy (Lount, 1997). Its applicability to communication between employees in the workplace has also been demonstrated (Hayes, 2002). Indeed, the conclusion reached by Bull (2002, p. 19), in his analysis of communication theories, was that 'the social skills model continues to be highly influential'.

The main focus in this chapter has been upon the application of the main interactive processes involved in dyadic (two-person) interaction. When more than two people are involved, although the same processes apply, interaction becomes even more complex and certainly much more difficult to represent diagrammatically. Despite the increased complexity (in terms of differing goals, motivation, and so on), knowledge of these central processes will facilitate attempts to understand and interpret the skilled performance of the individual in both group and dyadic interaction.

REFERENCES

Anderson, P. & Guerrero, L. (Eds) (1998). *The handbook of communication and emotion*. San Diego, CA: Academic Press.

Annett, J. (1969). *Feedback and human behaviour*. Harmondsworth: Penguin.

Archer, J. (2004). The trouble with 'doing boy'. *The Psychologist*, *17*, 132–136.

Argyle, M. (1967). *The psychology of interpersonal behaviour*. Harmondsworth: Penguin.

Argyle, M. (1972). *The psychology of interpersonal behaviour*, 2nd edn. Harmondsworth: Penguin.

Argyle, M. (1988). *Bodily communication*, 2nd edn. London: Methuen.

Argyle, M. (1994). *The psychology of interpersonal behaviour*, 5th edn. Harmondsworth: Penguin.

Argyle, M., Furnham, A. & Graham, J. (1981). *Social situations*. Cambridge: Cambridge University Press.

Aronson, E. (2004). *The social animal*, 9th edn. New York: Worth.

Averill, J. (1975). A semantic atlas of emotional concepts. *JSAS Catalogue of Selected Documents in Psychology*, *5*, 330.

Ayoko, O., Härtel, C., Fisher, G. & Fujimoto, Y. (2004). Communication competence in cross-cultural business interactions. In D. Tourish & O. Hargie (Eds), *Key issues in organizational communication*. London: Routledge.

Banaji, M., Lemm, K. & Carpenter, S. (2004). The social unconscious. In M. Brewer & M. Hewstone (Eds), *Social cognition*. Malden, MA: Blackwell.

Barker, V., Giles, H. & Harwood, J. (2004). Inter- and intragroup perspectives on inter-generational communication. In J. Nussbaum & J. Coupland (Eds), *Handbook of communication and aging research*, 2nd edn. Mahwah, NJ: Lawrence Erlbaum.

Bentley, S. (1993). Listening and memory. In A. Wolvin & C. Coakley (Eds), *Perspectives on listening*. Norwood, NJ: Ablex.

Berger, C. (2000). Goal detection and efficiency: neglected aspects of message production. *Communication Theory*, *10*, 135–138.

Berscheid, E. (1983). Emotion. In H. Kelley, E. Berscheid, A. Christensen et al. (Eds), *Close relationships*. New York: W. H. Freeman.

Blanck, P. (Ed.) (1993). *Interpersonal expectations: theory, research and applications*. Cambridge: Cambridge University Press.

Brown, A. & Starkey, K. (1994). The effect of organizational culture on communication and information. *Journal of Management Studies*, *31*, 807–828.

Bubas, G. (2003). The structure and agency of communion dimension in interpersonal communicative interaction. In A. Schorr, W. Campbell & M. Schenk (Eds), *Communication research and media science in Europe*. Berlin: Mouton de Gruyter.

Buck, R. (1988). *Human motivation and emotion*, 2nd edn. New York: Wiley.

Bull, P. (2002). *Communication under the microscope: the theory and practice of microanalysis*. London: Routledge.

Burleson, B. (2003). Emotional support skills. In J. Greene & B. Burleson (Eds), *Handbook of communication and social interaction skills*. Mahwah, NJ: Lawrence Erlbaum.

Burleson, B. & Planalp, S. (2000). Producing emotional messages. *Communication Theory*, *10*, 221–250.

Bush, L. E. (1972). Empirical selection of adjectives denoting feelings. *JSAS Catalogue of Selected Documents in Psychology*, *2*, 67.

Butt, T. (2004). *Understanding people*. Houndmills: Palgrave Macmillan.

Campbell, W. & Falkowski, A. (2003). A comparative study of communication skill: theory and practice. In A. Schorr, W. Campbell & M. Schenk (Eds), *Communication research and media science in Europe*. Berlin: Mouton de Gruyter.

Carlson, N. (1990). *Psychology*, 3rd edn. Boston, MA: Allyn and Bacon.

Chaudhuri, A. & Buck, R. (1995). Affect, reason and persuasion advertising strategies that predict affective and analytic-cognitive responses. *Human Communication Research*, *21*, 422–441.

Chryssochoou, X. (2004). *Cultural diversity: its social psychology*. Oxford: Blackwell.

Clampitt, P. & Williams, M. (2004). Communication about organizational uncertainty. In D. Tourish & O. Hargie (Eds), *Key issues in organizational communication*. London: Routledge.

Clark, M., Fitness, J. & Brissette, I. (2004). Understanding people's perceptions of relationships is crucial to understanding their emotional lives. In M. Brewer & M. Hewstone (Eds), *Emotion and motivation*. Oxford: Blackwell.

Clore, G., Ortony, A. & Foss, M. (1987). The psychological foundations of the affective lexicon. *Journal of Personality and Social Psychology*, *53*, 751–766.

Cook, M. (1977). The social skill model and interpersonal attraction. In S. Duck (Ed.), *Theory and practice in interpersonal attraction*. London: Academic Press.

Cook, M. (1979). *Perceiving others*. London: Methuen.

Dickson, D. (1999). Barriers to communication. In A. Long (Ed.), *Interaction for practice in community nursing*. Basingstoke: Macmillan.

Dickson, D., Hargie, O. & Morrow, N. (1997). *Communication skills training for health professionals*, 2nd edn. London: Chapman and Hall.

Duck, S. (1995). Repelling the study of attraction. *The Psychologist*, *8*, 60–63.

Eckes, T. (1994). Features of men, features of women: assessing stereotypic beliefs about gender subtypes. *British Journal of Social Psychology*, *33*, 107–23.

Fiedler, K. (1993). Constructive processes in person cognition. *British Journal of Social Psychology*, *32*, 349–364.

Fiedler, K. & Bless, H. (2001). Social cognition. In M. Hewstone & W. Stroebe (Eds), *Introduction to social psychology*. Malden: MA: Blackwell.

Fitts, P. & Posner, M. (1973). *Human performance*. London: Prentice-Hall.

Frosh, S., Phoenix, A. & Pattman, R. (2003). The trouble with boys. *The Psychologist*, *16*, 84–87.

Furnham, A. (1983). Research in social skills training: a critique. In R. Ellis & D. Whittington (Eds), *New directions in social skill training*. Croom Helm: Beckenham.

Giordano, J. (2000). Effective communication and counseling with older adults. *International Journal of Aging and Human Development*, *51*, 315–324.

Greene, J. (1988). Cognitive processes: methods for probing the black box. In C. Tardy (Ed.), *A handbook for the study of human communication*. Norwood, NJ: Ablex.

Greene, J. (2000). Evanescent mentation: an ameliorative conceptual foundation for research and theory on message production. *Communication Theory*, *10*, 139–155.

Greene, J. (2003). Models of adult communication skill acquisition: practice and the course of performance improvement. In J. Greene & B. Burleson (Eds), *Handbook of communication and social interaction skills*. Mahwah, NJ: Lawrence Erlbaum.

Guirdham, M. (2002). *Interactive behaviour at work*, 3rd edn. Harlow: Pearson Education.

Hargie, O. & Tourish, D. (1999). The psychology of interpersonal skill. In A. Memon & R. Bull (Eds), *Handbook of the psychology of interviewing*. Chichester: Wiley.

Hargie, O. & Dickson, D. (2004). *Skilled interpersonal communication: research, theory and practice*. London: Routledge.

Hargie, O., Dickson, D. & Tourish, D. (2004). *Communication skills for effective management*. Basingstoke: Macmillan.

Härtel, C., Kibby, L. & Pizer, M. (2004). Intelligent emotions management. In D. Tourish & O. Hargie (Eds), *Key issues in organizational communication*. London: Routledge.

Hartley, P. (1999). *Interpersonal communication*, 2nd edn. London: Routledge.

Hayes, J. (2002). *Interpersonal skills at work*, 2nd edn. London: Routledge.

Hinton, P. R. (1993). *The psychology of interpersonal perception*. London: Routledge.

Hughes, K. (1994). An investigation into nonverbal behaviours associated with deception/concealment during a negotiation process. University of Ulster, Jordanstown, D.Phil. thesis.

Hummert, M., Garstka, T., Ryan, E. & Bonnensen, J. (2004). The role of age stereotypes in interpersonal communication. In J. Nussbaum & J. Coupland (Eds), *Handbook of communication and aging research*, 2nd edn. Mahwah, NJ: Lawrence Erlbaum.

Irving, P. (1995). A reconceptualisation of Rogerian core conditions of facilitative communication: implications for training. University of Ulster, Jordanstown, D.Phil. thesis.

Ivey, A. (1994). *Intentional interviewing and counseling: facilitating client development in a multicultural society*, 3rd edn. Pacific Grove, CA: Brooks/Cole.

Ivey, A., D'Andrea, M., Ivey M. & Simek-Morgan, L. (2002). *Theories of counseling and psychotherapy: a multicultural perspective*, 5th edn. Boston, MA: Allyn and Bacon.

Iyengar, S. & Brockner, J. (2001). Cultural differences in self and the impact of personal and social influences. In W. Wosinska, R. Cialdini, D. Barrett & J. Reykowski (Eds), *The practice of social influence in multiple cultures*. Mahwah, NJ: Lawrence Erlbaum.

Izard, C. E. (1977). *Human emotions*. New York: Plenum.

James, W. (1884). What is emotion? *Mind*, *4*, 188–204.

Jones, C. (1999). Shifting sands: women, men and communication. *Journal of Communication*, *49*, 148–155.

Jones, E. E. (1990). *Interpersonal perception*. New York: W. H. Freeman.

Kelley, H., Holmes, J., Kerr, N., Reis, H., Rusbult, C. & Van Lange, P. (2003). *An atlas of interpersonal situations*. Cambridge: Cambridge University Press.

Kikuchi, T. (1994). Effects of backchannel convergence on a speaker's speech rate and track-checking behavior. Paper presented at the Annual Conference of the International Communication Association, Sydney, Australia, 11–15 July 1994.

Kim, M. & Wilson, S. (1994). A cross-cultural comparison of implicit theories of requesting. *Communication Monographs*, *61*, 210–235.

Locke, E. & Latham, G. (1990). *A theory of goal setting and task performance*. Englewood Cliffs, NJ: Prentice-Hall.

Lount, M. (1997). Interpersonal communication processes in the pastoral ministry of Catholic clergy. University of Ulster, Jordanstown, D.Phil. thesis.

Lucariello, J., Hudson, J., Fivush, R. & Bauer, P. (Eds) (2004). *The development of the mediated mind: sociocultural context and cognitive development*. Mahwah, NJ: Lawrence Erlbaum.

Lundsteen, S. W. (1993). Metacognitive listening. In A. Wolvin & C. Coakley (Eds), *Perspectives on listening*. Norwood, NJ: Ablex.

MacGeorge, E., Feng, B., Butler, G. & Budarz, S. (2004). Understanding advice in supportive interactions: beyond the facework and message evaluation paradigm. *Human Communication Research, 30*, 42–70.

Manstead, A. (1997). Situations, belongingness, attitudes, and culture: four lessons learned from social psychology. In C. McGarty & S. Haslam (Eds), *The message of social psychology: perspectives on mind in society*. Cambridge, MA: Blackwell.

Manstead, A., Frijda, N. & Fischer, A. (Eds) (2004). *Feelings and emotions: the Amsterdam Symposium*. Cambridge: Cambridge University Press.

Manusov, V. (Ed.) (2005). *The sourcebook of nonverbal measures: going beyond words*. Mahway, NJ: Lawrence Erlbaum.

Martin, L., Frack, F. & Strapel, D. (2004). How the mind moves: knowledge accessibility and the fine-tuning of the cognitive system. In M. Brewer & M. Hewstone (Eds), *Social cognition*. Malden, MA: Blackwell.

Maslow, A. (1954). *Motivation and personality*. New York: Harper and Row.

Matthews, G., Davies, D., Westerman, S. & Stammers, R. (2000). *Human performance: cognition, stress and individual differences*. Hove: Psychology Press.

McFall, A. (1982). A review and reformulation of the concept of social skills. *Behavioural Assessment, 4*, 1–33.

Metts, S. & Bowers, J. (1994). Emotion in interpersonal communication. In M. Knapp & G. Miller (Eds), *Handbook of interpersonal communication*, 2nd edn. Thousand Oaks, CA: Sage.

Meyer, J. (2000). Cognitive models of message production: unanswered questions, *Communication Theory, 10*, 176–187.

Millar, R., Crute, V. & Hargie, O. (1992). *Professional interviewing*. London: Routledge.

Miller, L., Cody, M. & McLaughlin, M. (1994). Situations and goals as fundamental constructs in interpersonal communication research. In M. Knapp & G. Miller (Eds), *Handbook of interpersonal communication*, 2nd edn. Thousand Oaks, CA: Sage.

Mitchell, D. & Blair, J. (2000). State of the art: psychopathy. *The Psychologist, 13*, 356–360.

Monahan, J. (1998). I don't know if I like you: the influence of nonconscious affect on person perception. *Human Communication Research, 24*, 480–500.

Mulac, A., Bradac, J., & Gibbons, P. (2001). Empirical support for the gender-as-culture hypothesis: an intercultural analysis of male/female language differences. *Human Communication Research, 27*, 121–152.

Myers, D. (2002). *Social psychology*, 7th edn. New York: McGraw-Hill.

Neisser, U. (1967). *Cognitive psychology*. New York: Appleton-Century-Croft.

Norton, R. (1983). *Communicator style: theory, application and measures*. Beverly Hills, CA: Sage.

Nussbaum, J. & Coupland, J. (2004). Preface. In J. Nussbaum & J. Coupland (Eds), *Handbook of communication and aging research*, 2nd edn. Mahwah, NJ: Lawrence Erlbaum.

O'Dell, L., de Abreu, G. & O'Toole, S. (2004). The turn to culture. *The Psychologist, 17*, 138–141.

Oettingen, G. & Gollwitzer, P. (2004). Goal setting and goal striving. In M. Brewer & M. Hewstone (Eds), *Emotion and motivation*. Oxford: Blackwell.

Operario, D. & Fiske, S. (2004). Stereotypes: content, structures, processes, and context. In M. Brewer & M. Hewstone (Eds), *Social cognition*. Malden, MA: Blackwell.

Parrott, W. (2004). The nature of emotion. In M. Brewer & M. Hewstone (Eds), *Emotion and motivation*. Oxford: Blackwell.

Pecchioni, L., Ota, H. & Sparks, L. (2004). Cultural issues in communication and aging. In J. Nussbaum & J. Coupland (Eds), *Handbook of communication and aging research*, 2nd edn. Mahwah, NJ: Lawrence Erlbaum.

Pendleton, D. & Furnham, A. (1980). A paradigm for applied social psychological research. In W. Singleton, P. Spurgeon & R. Stammers (Eds), *The analysis of social skill*. New York: Plenum.

Perret, D. I., May, K. A. & Yoshikawa, S. (1994). Facial shape and judgements of facial attractiveness, *Nature*, *368*, 239–242.

Pervin, L. & John, O. (2001). *Personality: theory and research*, 8th edn. Chichester: Wiley.

Planalp, S. (2003). The unacknowledged role of emotion in theories of close relationships: how do theories feel? *Communication Theory*, *13*, 78–99.

Power, M. & Dalgleish, T. (1997). *Cognition and emotions: from order to disorder*. Hove: Psychology Press.

Reykowski, J. (2001). Principles of social influence across cultures. In W. Wosinska, R. Cialdini, D. Barrett & J. Reykowski (Eds), *The practice of social influence in multiple cultures*. Mahwah, NJ: Lawrence Erlbaum.

Riggio, H. (1999). Personality and social skill differences between adults with and without siblings. *Journal of Psychology*, *133*, 514–522.

Romaine, S. (1999). *Communicating gender*. Mahwah, NJ: Lawrence Erlbaum.

Saks, M. J. & Krupat, E. (1988). *Social psychology and its applications*. New York: Harper and Row.

Sanders, R. (2003). Applying the skills concept to discourse and conversation: the remediation of performance defects in talk-in-interaction. In J. Greene & B. Burleson (Eds), *Handbook of communication and social interaction skills*. Mahwah, NJ: Lawrence Erlbaum.

Sekuler, R. & Blake, R. (2002). *Perception*, 4th edn. Boston, MA: McGraw-Hill.

Serby, M. & Chobor, K. (Eds) (1992). *Science of olfaction*. New York: Springer-Verlag.

Singelis, T. M. & Brown, W. J. (1995). Culture, self and collectivist communication: linking culture to individual behavior. *Human Communication Research*, *21*, 354–389.

Skipper, M. (1992). Communication processes and their effectiveness in the management and treatment of dysphagia. University of Ulster, Jordanstown, D.Phil. thesis.

Slater, M. (1997). Persuasion processes across perceiver goals and message genres. *Communication Theory*, *7*, 125–148.

Sloboda, J. (1986). What is skill? In A. Gellatly (Ed.), *The skilful mind: an introduction to cognitive psychology*. Milton Keynes: Open University Press.

Snyder, M. (1987). *Public appearances, private realities: the psychology of self-monitoring*. New York: Freeman.

Spitzberg, B. (2003). Methods of interpersonal skill assessment. In J. Greene & B. Burleson (Eds), *Handbook of communication and social interaction skills*. Mahwah, NJ: Lawrence Erlbaum.

Stewart, R., Powell, G. & Chetwynd, S. (1979). *Person perception and stereotyping*. Farnborough: Saxon House.

Thompson, B. (1993). Listening disabilities: the plight of many. In A. Wolvin & C. Coakley (Eds), *Perspectives on listening*, Norwood, NJ: Ablex.

Tourish, D. & Hargie, O. (2004). Motivating critical upward communication: a key challenge for management decision making. In D. Tourish & O. Hargie (Eds), *Key issues in organizational communication*. London: Routledge.

Vaes, J., Paladino, M. & Leyens, J. (2002). The lost-mail: prosocial reactions induced by uniquely human emotions. *British Journal of Social Psychology*, *41*, 521–534.

Welford, A. (1965). Performance, biological mechanisms and age: a theoretical sketch. In A. Welford & J. Birren (Eds), *Behavior, aging and the nervous system*. Springfield, IL: C. C. Thomas.

Wessler, R. (1984). Cognitive-social psychological theories and social skills: a review. In P. Trower (Ed.), *Radical approaches to social skills training*. Beckenham: Croom Helm.

Whetzel, D. & McDaniel, M. (1999). The employment interview. In A. Memon & R. Bull (Eds), *Handbook of the psychology of interviewing*. Chichester: Wiley.

Williams, A. & Harwood, J. (2004). Intergenerational communication: intergroup, accommodation, and family perspectives. In J. Nussbaum & J. Coupland (Eds), *Handbook of communication and aging research*, 2nd edn. Mahwah, NJ: Lawrence Erlbaum.

Wilson, G. & Nias, D. (1999). Beauty can't be beat. In L. Guerrero & J. DeVito (Eds), *The nonverbal communication reader: classic and contemporary readings*. Prospect Heights, IL: Waveland Press.

Yingling, J. (2004). *A lifetime of communication: transformations through relational dialogues*. Mahwah, NJ: Lawrence Erlbaum.

Zimmerman, B. (2000). Attaining self-regulation: a social cognitive perspective. In M. Boekaerts, P. Pintrich & M. Zeidner (Eds), *Handbook of self-regulation*. San Diego, CA: Academic Press.

Part II

Core communication skills

Chapter 3

Non-verbal behaviour as communication: Approaches, issues and research

Randall A. Gordon, Daniel Druckman,
Richard M. Rozelle and James C. Baxter

IN THIS CHAPTER, WE survey a large cross-disciplinary literature on non-verbal communication. After placing the study of non-verbal behaviour in historical perspective, we highlight the major approaches that have guided scientific explorations. Non-verbal communication can be understood best in relation to the settings in which it occurs. Settings are defined in terms of both the varying roles taken by actors within societies and the diverse cultures in which expressions and gestures are learned. Based on an example of research conducted in a laboratory simulation of international politics, we develop implications for the themes and techniques that can be used to guide analyses of behaviour as it occurs *in situ*.

NON-VERBAL BEHAVIOUR IN PERSPECTIVE

In recent years, it has become increasingly recognised that investigators in a field of enquiry – any field – bring personal perspectives and figurative comparisons to bear on their work. Such perspectives have been called paradigms, metaphors, or fundamental analogies, and their influence has been thought to be pervasive. Indeed, both philosophers and working scientists acknowledge the value and necessity of such processes in the realm of creative thought (e.g. Koestler, 1964; Glashow, 1980; Leary, 1990).

Examples of this phenomenon abound. For instance, in psychology,

Gentner and Grudin (1985) undertook a review of a sample of theoretical contributions to the field published in *Psychological Review* between the years 1894 and 1975. From the 68 theoretical papers they reviewed, they were able to identify 265 distinct mental metaphors. They defined a mental metaphor as 'a nonliteral comparison in which either the mind as a whole or some particular aspect of the mind (ideas, processes, etc.) is likened to or explained in terms of a nonliteral domain' (p. 182). These metaphors were all introduced by their contributors as ways of understanding the field. They were often based on explicit comparisons, such as James' 'stream of consciousness', but also were frequently based on subtly implied, extended comparisons only identifiable from broad sections of text. Gentner and Grudin identified four categories of analogy which characterised the period – spatial, animate-being, neural, and systems metaphors – and found clear trends in metaphor preference and rates of usage over time.

Such an examination of the field of psychology is illuminating and provocative. Recognising that the use of different metaphors places different aspects of the field in relief and interrelation, and introduces different explanatory and predictive emphasis, one can identify remarkable shifts in the ways in which psychologists have thought about their subject matter. For example, the recent emphasis on systems metaphors suggests a focus on lawfully constrained interaction among elements where organisation, precision, and mutuality of influence are stressed. Predictions are complex but specific; analysis is multifaceted and hierarchical. Fundamentally, such metaphors are thought to be constitutive of the subject matter we study (Gibbs, 1994; Soyland, 1994).

A number of contemporary cognitive scientists extended the analysis of metaphor and other linguistic forms (tropes), showing that they abound in everyday usage (even beyond scientific and creative discourse) and clearly reflect the presence of poetic aspects of mind (e.g. Lakoff, 1993; Ortony, 1993; Gibbs, 1994). Linguistic forms such as metaphor, metonymy, irony, and related expressions point to our fundamental ability to conceptualise situations figuratively (e.g. non-literally) and transpose meaning across domains. Indeed, such complex processes are assumed to occur essentially automatically and unconsciously (Gibbs, 1994). Although such analyses have focused on linguistic expression, both oral and written, the role played by non-verbal aspects of language does not seem to have been examined explicitly.

Lastly, the role that our species' evolution has played in the encoding and decoding of non-verbal behaviour has received increased attention in recent years (Zebrowitz, 2003). This has occurred, in part, as a function of the discipline-wide influence of evolutionary perspectives on the investigation of human behaviour. The observation that the scientific study of non-verbal communication began with Darwin's (1872) book on the expression of emotions primarily in the face alludes to the importance of understanding the role that adaptation plays in our non-verbal communication.

NON-VERBAL BEHAVIOUR AS COMMUNICATION

A comparable examination of contributions to the field of non-verbal behaviour may be meaningful. To this end, it is interesting to note that attention has been directed at the meaningfulness of gesture and non-verbal behaviour since earliest recorded

Western history (cf. Aristotle's *Poetics* and *Rhetoric*). According to Kendon (1981), classical and medieval works on rhetoric frequently focused on the actual conduct of the orator as he delivered his speech. They occasionally defined many forms of particular gestures and provided instructions for their use in creating planned effects in the audience.

At least as early as 1601, gesture as a medium of communication coordinate with vocal and written language was recognised by Francis Bacon (1884, 1947). He suggested that 'as the tongue speaketh to the ear, so the hand speaketh to the eye' (quoted in Kendon, 1981, p. 155). Subsequent analyses, inspired by Bacon's proposal, were undertaken to examine chirologia (manual language) as both a rhetorical and natural language form (Bulwer, 1644/1974). During the eighteenth and nineteenth centuries, scholars argued that emotional expression and gesture, the so-called 'natural languages', surely provided the foundation for the more refined and artificial verbal symbolic communication (e.g. Lavater, 1789; Taylor, 1878). Spiegel and Machotka (1974) have identified a collateral history in dance, mime, and dramatic staging beginning in the late eighteenth century. Body movement as communication has been an analogy of broad and continuing interest.

In examining the focus on non-verbal behaviour as communication, a number of somewhat different analogies can be identified. Darwin (1872) focused on facial behaviour as a neuromuscular expression of emotion and vestiges of the past, and as informative of an inner affective state. A number of investigators have extended this approach and elaborated the *affective expression* metaphor (e.g. Woodworth & Schlosberg, 1954; Tomkins, 1962, 1963; Izard, 1971; Ekman, 1992a). In delineating bodily movement, gesture, vocalisation, and particularly facial movement as expressive of affect, an emphasis is placed on the rapid, automatic, serviceable, universal aspects of behaviour. Indeed, consciousness, intention, and guile are ordinarily not central to such an analysis, although experiential overlays and culturally modified forms of expression are of interest. In examining how readily people recognise affective displays in others (Ekman & Oster, 1979; Triandis, 1994; Matsumoto, 1996) or how rules of expression are acquired (Cole, 1984), an emphasis is placed on the plastic nature of neuromuscular form.

In an ever-increasing manner, tests of hypotheses derived, at least in part, from evolutionary psychology can be found in the research literature on non-verbal behaviour and communication. In a field of enquiry where few general descriptions fail to cite Darwin's (1872) book on the expression of emotions as a starting point for the scientific investigation of non-verbal behaviour, the current increased influence of evolutionary psychology and its search for evidence of adaptation has reinforced interest and work in this area. In 2003, two issues of the *Journal of Nonverbal Behavior* were devoted to research guided by this perspective. As pointed out by Zebrowitz (2003), the studies in the issues 'take an evolutionary approach well beyond the domain of emotional expressions' (p. 133). The impact of evolutionary psychology can be seen across a number of research domains (e.g. social, developmental, cognitive-neuroscience) and is discussed as a primary influence in many contemporary models of non-verbal communication. However, this approach is problematic when it neglects the impact of more immediate situational factors.

The perceptually based (cf. Gibson, 1979) ecological approach of Zebrowitz (Zebrowitz & Collins, 1997; Zebrowitz, 2003) incorporates a focus on proximal elements and mechanisms alongside an assessment of behaviour tied to the survival of our species. In an additional commentary on evolutionary psychology and its impact on non-verbal research, Montepare (2003) echoes the need to include proximal (or situational) along with distal (or historical) influences when one studies non-verbal communication.

A related metaphor comparing non-verbal actions, especially accidents and parapraxes, to a *riddle* or *obscure text*, has been employed by psychodynamic investigators. Indeed, Freud (1905/1938, 1924) argued that such actions are usually meaningful and can often be recognised as such by a person. At the same time, Freud acknowledged that people frequently deny the significance of gestural-parapraxic actions, leaving the analyst in a quandry with respect to the validity of interpretation. Freud offered a number of interpretive strategies, including articulation with the person's life context and delayed verification as approaches to this problem. The influence of this psychodynamic perspective continues to be seen in subsequent examples of psychotherapeutic techniques that incorporate a specific focus on non-verbal behaviour (e.g., Rogers' (1961) focus on examining congruence between non-verbal and verbal expression, Perls' (1969) use of non-verbal expression as an interpretive tool in gestalt psychology). Recent data have revealed that the ability to note verbal–non-verbal inconsistency appears to be already well developed by the time we reach 4–5 years of age (Eskritt & Lee, 2003).

In dealing with the problem of denial, Freud seems to have foreshadowed the more recent concerns about the questions of consciousness and intention in determining expressive actions. In any event, Freud's approach to the investigation of non-verbal behaviour as communication appears to have taken the analogies of the riddle or perhaps the obscure text which can be made meaningful by the application of accepted interpretive (for example, hermeneutic) principles. Many psychoanalytic investigators have utilised the broad interpretive analysis of behavioural text (Deutsch, 1959; Feldman, 1959; Schafer, 1980). Feldman's examination of the significance of such speech mannerisms as 'by the way', 'incidentally', 'honest', 'before I forget', 'believe me', 'curiously enough', and many others provides an illustration of the fruitfulness of regarding speech and gesture as complex, subtle, multilevel communication.

Certainly, the reliance on an affective expression as opposed to an obscure text analogy places the process of communication in different perspectives. In the first instance, the automatic, universal, perhaps unintended and other features identified above are taken as relevant issues, while the articulation with context, uniqueness, obfuscation and necessity of prolonged scholarly examination by trained and skilful interpreters are equally clearly emphasised by the behaviour as riddle analogy.

A third approach to the behaviour as communication analogy has been provided by the careful explication of non-verbal behaviour as *code* metaphor. Developed most extensively in Birdwhistell's (1970) analogy with structural linguistics and Weiner et al.'s (1972) comparison with communication engineering, the central concern rests with the detailed, molecular examination of the structure of the code itself, modes (that is, channels) of transmission, and accuracy-utility of communication. Conventional appreciation is essential to accuracy and efficiency, as auction applications, stock and commodities trading, athletic coaching, and social-political etiquette and protocol applications may attest (Scheflen & Scheflen, 1972). Levels of communication (for instance, messages and metamessages), channel comparisons, sending and receiving strategies, and accessibility of the intention–code–channel–code–interpretation sequence as an orderly, linear process are all designed to emphasise the systematic, objective, and mechanistic features of the metaphor (Druckman et al., 1982). Indeed, the utilisation of non-verbal behaviour as metamessage is very informative, if not essential, in distinguishing ironic from literal meaning. This is perhaps especially the case for channels that allow for relatively fine-grained differentiation of non-verbal behaviour (e.g. facial expression, paralinguistic cues).

However, the boundaries of the particular variations in the 'behaviour as communication' analogies which have been identified are fuzzy, and the explicit categories of the metaphors as employed by particular investigators are difficult to articulate fully. Yet the three variations of the communication analogy seem valid as the history and current investigation in non-verbal behaviour as communication is examined. In this spirit, a fourth general communication metaphor can also be identified – non-verbal behaviour as *dramatic presentation*.

While this analogy clearly descends from mime, dance, and dramatic stage direction (Spiegel & Machotka, 1974; Poyatos, 1983), the approach has been most skilfully developed by Goffman (1959, 1969), Baumeister (1982), and DePaulo (1992) as both expressive form (that is, identity and situation presentation) and rhetorical form (that is, persuasion, impression management, and tactical positioning). The particularly fruitful features of this analogy appear to be the crafted, holistic, completely situated, forward-flowing nature of expression, with emphasis on recognisable skill, authenticity, and purpose. Strategy, guile, and deception are important aspects of this analogy, and subtlety and complexity abound (Scheibe, 1979; Schlenker, 1980; DePaulo, Wetzel, Sternglanz & Wilson, 2003).

NON-VERBAL BEHAVIOUR AS STYLE

Although the 'non-verbal behaviour as communication' analogies hold historical precedence in the area, two additional analogies can be identified: non-verbal behaviour as *personal idiom* (Allport, 1961) and non-verbal behaviour as *skill* (Argyle, 1967; Argyle & Kendon, 1967; Hargie, Saunders & Dickson, 1981; Hargie & Dickson, 2004).

Allport introduced the important distinction between the instrumental aspects of action and the expressive aspects, the latter being personalised and stylistic ways of accomplishing the tasks of life. Comparisons with one's signature, voice, or thumb print are offered. This perspective emphasises holism, consistency, and configural uniqueness, while de-emphasising complexity, skill, and authenticity. Demonstrations of the application of the analogy have been offered (certainly among the ranks of the stage impressionists, if not scientific workers), but the richness and fruitfulness of the metaphor have not yet been fully exploited.

Perhaps the most inviting metaphor of non-verbal behaviour has been the emphasis on skilled performance. The fruitfulness of the analogy of acquired skills as a way of thinking about non-verbal behaviour has been recognised for some time (Bartlett, 1958; Polanyi, 1958). However, its extension to non-verbal behaviour has been rather recent (Argyle, 1967; Knapp, 1972, 1984; Snyder, 1974; Friedman, 1979; Rosenthal, 1979; DePaulo et al., 1985; Burgoon & Bacue, 2003; Hargie & Dickson, 2004). The analogy has directed attention to the expressive or sending (encoding) and interpretive or receiving (decoding) aspects of non-verbal exchange, and has begun to highlight aspects of face-to-face interaction not investigated hitherto.

The skilled performance analogy

Since the introduction of the skilled performance metaphor is somewhat recent in the area of non-verbal behaviour analysis, it might prove useful to attempt to explicate some of the categories of such an analogy. As Bartlett (1958) pointed out, in the general case and in every known form of skill, there are acknowledged experts in whom much of the expertness, though perhaps never all of it, has been acquired by well-informed practice. The skill is based upon evidence picked up directly or indirectly from the environment, and it is used for the attempted achievement of whatever issue may be required at the time of the performance. Examples of such performance would include the sports player, the operator engaged at the workbench, the surgeon conducting an operation, the telegrapher deciphering a message, or the pilot controlling an aeroplane (see Chapter 1).

Initial examination of the comparison suggests a number of important features of skilled performance (for more detailed analysis of these, see Chapters 1 and 2) that are relevant to the investigation of non-verbal behaviour. First, skilled performances usually imply complex, highly coordinated motor acts, which may be present in unrefined form at the outset of training, but in many cases are not, and which only emerge gradually with training and development. Thus, final performances may be quite different from untutored performances. Moreover, the recognisability of individuality in the crafting of skilful expression seems clearly implied. A second feature of such performance is that it is based on perceptually differentiating environmental properties or conditions often unrecognised by the untutored. A quality of 'informed seeing' or 'connoisseurship' develops that serves to guide and structure refined action.

A third feature of skilled performances is their dependence on practice, usually distributed over extended periods of time (see Druckman & Bjork, 1991). The importance of combinations of both practice and rest as aids in acquiring desired performance levels and the occurrence of marked irregularities in progress during the attainment of desired levels is recognisable, as are the influences of age and many physical condition factors (Bilodeau, 1966). A fourth important feature of skilled performances is their persistence and resistance to decay, interference, and effects of disuse. While comparisons are difficult, the general belief is that skilled actions remain viable after verbal information has been lost to recovery. A fifth area of importance is the general assumption that individuals vary in the extent to which they display refined performances. A sixth characteristic of skilled actions is that they are ineffable, acquired best by modelling and described only imprecisely by linguistic means. Finally, the expression of skilled performances usually entails the incorporation of internalised standards of the quality of expression. Performers can recognise inadequacies or refinements in their performance, which serve to guide both practice and performance styles.

The development of the skilled performance metaphor in the investigation of non-verbal behaviour as expression seems to have suggested several areas of development and possible advance in the field. Training strategies, individual differences, the role of practice, the importance of performance feedback, and internalised criteria of achievement represent a few areas of investigation of non-verbal behaviour implied by this analogy. A number of contemporary research programmes that examine the issue of training and expertise (Frank & Ekman, 1997; Ekman, O'Sullivan & Frank, 1999; Vrij, 2000; Vrij, Evans, Akehurst & Mann, 2004) can be seen as guided, in part, by the skilled performance metaphor. In addition, current research that has revealed relationships between non-verbal decoding and interpersonal social skills among adults (Carton, Kessler & Pape, 1999) and encoding skills and social competence among adolescents (Feldman, Tomasian & Coats, 1999) points to the importance of continued investigations of these aspects of individual performance.

THE SCIENTIFIC STUDY OF NON-VERBAL BEHAVIOUR

Literature dealing with non-verbal behaviour as communication has increased dramatically in volume and complexity, particularly during the last several decades. Wolfgang and Bhardway (1984) listed 170 book-length volumes published during the previous 100 years that contained non-verbal communication materials, the vast majority of which had appeared within the last 15 years. Today's electronic databases attest to the health and continued development of the field. A search of the area, covering the time period of 1988–1995, yielded over 300 books and chapters on the subject of non-verbal behaviour as communication. A comparable search of the PsycINFO database from 1997 to the present suggests an increased empirical focus on this area of communication. The results of the search listed over 700 entries that had the descriptor term 'non-verbal behaviour' or 'non-verbal communication'. Over 500 of these entries were journal articles, the vast majority of which were empirically based.

The topic is usually presented with two different emphases: (1) a theoretical-research orientation and (2) an application-demonstration orientation. Because of its relation to the subtle and interpretative aspects of communication, there is a tendency on the part of popular lay texts to emphasise application without a balanced presentation of the theory and research which examines the validity and reliability aspects necessary for proper understanding of non-verbal behaviour as one form of communication. Indeed, an interesting piece in this vein appeared on the Internet recently, providing an extended discourse on the psychological meaning of the hand-shake. While fascinating, and probably face valid, no recognisable empirical data accompanied the analysis.

The challenge of the present chapter is to discuss non-verbal behaviour as a communication skill, while maintaining the scientific integrity needed to evaluate critically the degree to which application is appropriate for any particular reader. It is hoped that the reader will assume a critical, scientific perspective in treating non-verbal behaviour as a meaningful yet complex topic for research and application.

Behavioural dimensions

Knapp (1972) suggested seven dimensions which describe the major categories of non-verbal behaviour research as related to communication, and these are useful for placing this chapter in perspective. The first category is kinesics, commonly referred to as 'body language', and includes movements of the hand, arm, head, foot, and leg, postural shifts, gestures, eye movements, and facial expressions. A second category is paralanguage and is defined as content-free vocalisations and patterns associated with speech such as voice pitch, volume, frequency, stuttering, filled pauses (for example, 'ah'), silent pauses, interruptions, and measures of speech rate and number of words spoken in a given unit of time. A third category involves physical contact in the form of touching. Another category is proxemics, which involves interpersonal spacing and norms of territoriality. A fifth category concerns the physical characteristics of people such as skin colour, body shape, body odour, and attractiveness. Related to physical characteristics is the category of artefacts or adornments such as perfume, clothes, jewellery, and wigs. Environmental factors make up the last category and deal with the influences of the physical setting in which the behaviour occurs: a classroom, an office, a hallway, or a street corner. Knapp's seven dimensions help depict the breadth of non-verbal communication. It is interesting to note that the physical characteristic, adornment, and environmental factor categories do not involve an assessment of overt non-verbal expressions, but rather information about the actor that is communicated non-verbally.

There are numerous examples in the literature that detail these categories, either individually or in combinations (e.g. Ekman & Friesen, 1969; Argyle & Cook, 1976; Duncan & Fiske, 1977; Harper et al., 1978; LaFrance & Mayo, 1978), and the reader is referred to these for detailed discussion. This chapter will present these categories in various combinations as they pertain to non-verbal behaviour as a communication skill. It is important to stress that non-verbal behaviour is dependent upon all of these factors for meaningful communication to take place. Some of these categories are covered in the theoretical and empirical presentation; others are not, but are nevertheless important and should always be considered as part of the 'universe' comprising non-verbal communication.

Setting and role influences on non-verbal behaviour

One of the major problems in focusing on the interpretation of non-verbal behaviour is to treat it as a separate, independent, and absolute form of communication. This view of the topic is much too simplistic. The meaning of non-verbal behaviour must be considered in the context in which it occurs. Several types of contextual factors will be used to guide this discussion of non-verbal communication and the behaviours associated with it.

One involves the environmental setting of the behaviour. Both the physical and social aspects of the environment must be described in sufficient detail to assess possible contributing factors to non-verbal behaviour as meaningful communication. For example, the furniture arrangement in an office can be a major factor influencing the non-verbal behaviours exhibited therein. Body movements differ depending upon whether the person is sitting behind a desk or openly in a chair. The proximity and angle of seating arrangements have been shown to serve different functions during interaction and to affect such behaviour as eye contact, gazing, and head rotation (Argyle & Dean, 1965; Manning, 1965).

Non-verbal behaviour may have very different meanings when exhibited on the street rather than, say, in a classroom. Background noise level in a work setting may produce exaggerated non-verbal communication patterns that would have very different meaning in a more quiet setting such as a library. The influence of ecological factors on behaviour has become an increasingly important focus in the study of human behaviour (McArthur & Baron, 1983; Willems, 1985). Most research in non-verbal communication dealing with physical-environmental factors focused on inter-personal spacing, proxemics, and cultural differences in interaction patterns (Hall, 1966; Baxter, 1970; Collett, 1971).

The social climate of the environment is also an important factor in the consideration of non-verbal behaviour (Jones et al., 1985). Research has demonstrated that different behaviours are produced in stressful versus unstressful situations (Rozelle & Baxter, 1975). The formality of a setting will determine the degree to which many non-verbal behaviours are suppressed or performed. Competitive versus cooperative interaction settings will also produce different types, levels, and frequencies of non-verbal behaviours. These are just several examples of factors affecting the communicative meaning of non-verbal behaviour. The reader is encouraged systematically to survey factors that may be of importance in more personally familiar settings.

Non-verbal behaviour as communication: process and outcome factors of the interaction episode

Many communication models as applied to non-verbal behaviour have concentrated on the interpersonal level and have not elaborated to the same degree the role and situational levels of communication. An important distinction in viewing non-verbal behaviour as communication is that between the *encoder* and the *decoder*. The encoder is analogous to an actor or impression manager, producing and 'sending' the behaviours to be interpreted. The decoder is analogous to an observer 'receiving' the presented behaviours and interpreting them in some fashion. Within the context of the encoder–decoder distinction, a major concern is that of intention and whether intended and unintended messages obey the same rules and principles of communication (Dittmann, 1978).

Ekman and Friesen (1969) provided two general classifications for behavioural messages. The first is the 'informative act' that results in certain interpretations on the part of a receiver without any active or conscious intent on the part of the sender. Thus, an individual's non-verbal behaviour is unintentionally 'giving off' signals that may be either correctly or incorrectly interpreted by a decoder (Goffman, 1959). The important point is that an impression is being formed without the encoder's knowledge or intention. A second classification is termed the 'communicative act' or, in Goffman's terms, expressions that are 'given'. In this case, the encoder is intentionally attempting to send a specific message to a receiver. Goffman suggested that, as impression managers, we are able to stop 'giving' messages, but cannot stop 'giving off' information. A difficulty lies in distinguishing varying degrees of conscious intent as opposed to 'accidental' or non-specifically motivated behaviour. Extreme examples of communicative behaviours intended to convey such emotions as anger, approval, or disagreement are usually described in the literature (e.g. Jones & Pittman, 1982). Similarly, informative acts such as fidgeting and gaze aversion are presented as examples of informative behaviour indicating unintended guilt, anxiety, or discomfort.

As will be discussed later in this chapter, role and situational considerations can lead to gross misinterpretations of what is considered 'informative' or 'communicative' behaviour on the part of both encoder and decoder in an interaction. Most interactions among people involve less extreme emotion and a complexity of intentions. Many social interactions also involve changing roles between encoder and decoder as the participants take turns in speaking and listening.

A useful model dealing with the issues of social influence in non-verbal communication was presented by MacKay (1972). The distinction is made between two types of non-verbal signals exhibited by the encoder: (1) goal-directed and (2) non-goal-directed. The receiver or decoder then interprets either of these signals as being (3) goal-directed or (4) non-goal-directed. Thus, the signal and the interpretation may be similar: (1) goal-directed signal being interpreted as goal-directed; (2) non-goal-directed signal being interpreted as non-goal-directed; or dissimilar: (3) goal-directed signal being interpreted as non-goal-directed; (4) non-goal-directed signal being interpreted as goal-directed. When considering goal-directed signalling, MacKay's model assumes that the encoder is behaviourally attempting to communicate a specific internal state or presence and that the intended communication has a desired effect on the encoder. If, in the encoder's judgement, the intended effect has not been achieved, the goal-directed, non-verbal behaviour is modified to achieve the desired effect. Therefore, the encoder actively evaluates the reaction of the decoder and proceeds accordingly.

Requiring communicative behaviour to be explicitly goal-directed, with an immediate adjustment on the part of the encoder depending upon the decoder's response, limits the number of behaviours that can be considered communicative. In typical conversations, many non-verbal behaviours become automatic responses and are performed at low levels of awareness or involve no awareness at all. What was once a specifically defined, goal-directed behaviour becomes habitual and is no longer a product of conscious intention. The degree to which non-verbal behaviours involve varying levels of awareness then becomes difficult to determine.

Another consideration for the understanding of non-verbal communication is whether or not the encoder and decoder share a common, socially defined signal system. Weiner et al. (1972) argued that this is a crucial requirement for communication to occur, regardless of the degree to which any behaviour is intentional. This represents a limited perspective on what is considered communication. One of the more pervasive problems in the use of non-verbal behaviour in the encoding and decoding process is when a common system is *not* shared and misinterpretation of behaviour results. Certain encoded behaviours may have unintended effects, especially when contextual factors, such as cultural, role, and spatial factors, are inappropriately considered during an interaction. The misinterpretation of behaviour that results can lead to profound consequences and must be considered a type of communication per se.

APPROACHES TO NON-VERBAL BEHAVIOUR AS COMMUNICATION
Ekman and Friesen

Perhaps the most useful model of non-verbal communication that encompasses these issues (but does not resolve them) is one originally presented by Ekman and Friesen (1969). They began by distinguishing between three characteristics of non-verbal behaviour: (1) usage, (2) origin, and (3) coding.

Usage refers to the circumstances that exist at the time of the non-verbal act. It includes consideration of the external condition that affects the act, such as the physical setting, role relationship, and emotional tone of the interaction. For example, the encoder and decoder may be communicating in an office, a home, a car, or a street. The role relationship may involve that of interviewer–interviewee, therapist–client, supervisor–employee, husband–wife, or teacher–student. The emotional tone may be formal or informal, stressful or relaxed, friendly or hostile, warm or cold, and competitive or cooperative. Usage also involves the relationship between verbal and non-verbal behaviour. For instance, non-verbal acts may serve to accent, duplicate, support, or substitute for – or they may be unrelated to – verbal behaviours.

Usage is the characteristic Ekman and Friesen chose to employ in dealing with awareness and intentionality on the part of the encoder, as discussed previously. In addition, usage involves external feedback, which is defined as the receiver's verbal or non-verbal reactions to the encoder's non-verbal behaviours as interpreted by the encoder. This does not involve the receiver's actual interpretations of the sender's behaviour, but is only information to the sender that his or her non-verbal behaviours have been received and evaluated. Finally, usage also refers to the type of information conveyed in terms of being informative, communicative, or interactive. Informative and communicative acts have been discussed. Interactive acts are those that detectably influence or modify the behaviour of the other participants in an interaction. Thus, these three information types involve the degree to which non-verbal messages are understood, provide information, and influence the behaviour of other people.

The second characteristic of non-verbal behaviour discussed by Ekman and Friesen is its origin. Some non-verbal behaviours are rooted in the nervous system, such as reflex actions; other non-verbal behaviours are commonly learned and used in dealing with the environment: for example, human beings use their feet for transportation in one form or another. A third source of non-verbal behaviour refers to culture, family, or any other instrumental or socially distinguishable form of behaviour. Thus, we adopt idiosyncratic behaviours when driving a car; we eat in a certain manner and groom ourselves in various ways. Social customs dictate non-verbal patterns of greeting one another, expressing approval or disapproval, and apportioning appropriate distances from one another depending upon the type of interaction involved.

The third characteristic of non-verbal behaviour is coding, that is, the meaning attached to a non-verbal act. The primary distinction is between *extrinsic* and *intrinsic* codes. Extrinsically coded acts signify something else and may be either arbitrarily or iconically coded. Arbitrarily coded acts bear no visual resemblance to what they represent. A thumbs-up sign to signal that everything is OK would be an arbitrarily coded act since it conveys no meaning 'by itself'. An iconically coded act tends to resemble what it signifies, as in the example of a throat-cutting movement with a finger. Intrinsically coded movements are what they signify. Playfully hitting a person, say on the upper arm, is an intrinsically coded act in that it is actually a form of aggression.

Employing usage, origin, and coding as a basis for defining non-verbal behaviour, Ekman and Friesen went on to distinguish among the following five categories of behavioural acts.

Emblems

These are non-verbal acts that have direct verbal translation and can substitute for words, the meaning of which is well understood by a particular group, class, or culture. Emblems originate through learning, most of which is culture-specific, and may be shown in any area of the body. Examples include waving the hands in a greeting or frowning to indicate disapproval. Ekman et al. (1984) found substantial regional, national, and intranational variation in these displays, leading them to suggest compiling an international dictionary of emblems. Differences have also been found in the way cultures interpret emblems: cultures studied include the Catalans in Spain (Payrato, 1993), Dutch interpretations of Chinese and Kurdish gestures (Poortinga et al., 1993), and Hebrew speakers in Israel (Safadi & Valentine, 1988). The culture-specific nature of emblems can come into sharp focus when unintentional communication occurs as a function of an encoder and decoder having learned different meanings for identical emblematic displays.

Illustrators

These are movements that are tied directly to speech and serve to illustrate what is verbalised. Illustrators are socially learned, usually through imitation by a child of a person he or she wishes to resemble. An example of an illustrator is holding the hands a certain distance apart to indicate the length of an object.

Regulators

These non-verbal acts serve to regulate conversation flow between people. Regulators are often culture-specific and may be subtle indicators to direct verbal interaction such as head nods, body position shifts, and eye contact. Because of their subtle nature, regulators are often involved in miscommunication and inappropriate responses among people of different cultures or ethnic backgrounds. This will be examined later in greater detail when the authors' police–citizen research is described.

Adaptors

These are object or self-manipulations. The specific behaviours are first learned as efforts to satisfy bodily needs, usually during childhood. In adult expression, only a fragment of the original adaptive behaviour is exhibited. Adaptors are behavioural habits and are triggered by some feature of the setting that relates to the original need. There are three types of adaptors: (1) self-adaptors such as scratching the head or clasping the hands; (2) alter-adaptors, which may include protective hand movements and arm-folding intended to protect oneself from attack or to represent intimacy, withdrawal, or flight; and (3) object adaptors, which are originally learned to perform instrumental tasks and may include tapping a pencil on the table or smoking behaviours.

Affect displays

These consist primarily of facial expressions of emotions. There is evidence that people from different cultures agree on their judgements of expressions for the primary emotions (happiness, sadness, anger, surprise, fear, disgust, and interest) but disagree on their ratings of the intensity of these expressions (Ekman, 1992a, 1992b, 1993, 1994). However, these expressions are usually modified and often hidden by cultural display rules learned as 'appropriate' behaviour. Thus, affect displays may be masked in social settings in order to show socially acceptable behaviour. Recent findings related to this issue have led to the development of an interactionist perspective that integrates findings supportive of both cultural specificity and universality. A recent study by Elfenbein and Ambady (2003) documents the degree to which (cultural) familiarity increases decoding accuracy, and meta-analytic assessments of this question have revealed in-group advantages in decoding accuracy (Elfenbein & Ambady, 2002a, 2002b). However, evidence for such an in-group advantage has been questioned due to methodological restrictions in studies documenting the impact of culture (see Matsumoto, 2002). It may be that the events that elicit emotions vary from culture to culture, but the particular facial muscle movements triggered when a given emotion is elicited may be relatively universal.

The non-verbal characteristic-category system of Ekman and Friesen has provided a useful means of analysing and organising non-verbal behaviours used in communication, and it is readily applicable in describing processes of information and expression-exchange in normal, social interactions. Extended use of the system has focused on a number of significant topic areas, among which could be cited many investigations into the relationships between genuine and recalled emotion and facial expression (Ekman et al., 1990; Ekman, 1992a, 1993), and the utility of the system in distinguishing honest and authentic expressions from the deceptive and dissembling (Hyman, 1989; Ekman et al., 1991; Ekman & O'Sullivan, 1991; Ekman, 1992a). Perhaps one of the most promising findings to emerge from this literature is the recognition of a particular smile, 'the Duchenne smile', which seems to be a reliable indicator of genuine enjoyment and happiness. Moreover, this facial profile seems to be quite resistant to staging and dissimulation (Ekman, 1993). Results from current investigations of the Duchenne smile suggest that there may exist a universal cross-cultural response to these displays that might have evolved due to the important communicative role of such smiles (Williams, Senior, David, Loughland & Gordon, 2001).

Dittmann

Another way of organising non-verbal acts in terms of their communicative nature is by focusing on the 'communication specificity' and channel capability of message transmission. These concepts have been presented by Dittmann (1972, 1978) as part of a larger model of the communication of emotions and are an important aspect of using non-verbal behaviour as a communication skill. Dittmann focused primarily on four major channels of communication: (1) language, (2) facial expression, (3) vocalisations, and (4) body movements. These four channels can be discussed in terms of their 'capacity', defined as the amount of information each may transmit at any given moment. Channel capacity can be described along two dimensions: (1) communication specificity (communicative-expressive) and (2) information value (discrete-continuous).

The closer a channel is to the communicative end of the continuum, the more discrete its information value will be in terms of containing distinguishable units with identifiable meanings (for instance, words). The more discrete a communication is, the greater the communication specificity it will usually have. These channels have the greatest capacity for conveying the largest number of messages with a wide variety of emotional meaning.

Channels at the other end of the capacity dimension are described as being relatively more expressive and continuous. For example, foot movements or changes in posture are more continuous behaviours than are spoken words, and are more expressive than specifically communicative in their emotional content. These channels have a lower capacity for conveying information regarding how a person is feeling. Facial expressions and vocalisations (paralanguage) may vary in their capacity to convey emotional expression depending on their delivery, the role the person is playing, the setting of the behaviour, and whether the decoders are family, friends, or strangers.

Dittmann also discussed the degree to which a message varies in intentional control on the part of the encoder, and awareness on the part of the decoder. Intentional control refers to the degree to which an encoder is in control of allowing his or her emotions to be expressed. Level of awareness refers to a decoder's either being aware of, repressing, or not noticing a message being sent by an encoder.

The most useful contribution by Dittmann to the non-verbal communication area is his analysis of channels of communication. A major challenge in non-verbal behaviour research is to examine the degree to which single versus multiple channels of transmission provide more meaningful communication in human interaction.

Mehrabian

An influential approach that uses multiple non-verbal categories and attempts to organise them in terms of three dimensions is that of Mehrabian (1972). These dimensions, described as social orientations, are *positiveness, potency*, and *responsiveness*.

Positiveness involves the evaluation of other persons or objects that relate to approach–avoidance tendencies, usually described in terms of liking. Non-verbal behaviours associated with positiveness represent 'immediacy' cues such as eye contact, forward-lean, touching, distance, and orientation.

Potency represents status or social control and is demonstrated through 'relaxation' cues of posture such as hand and neck relaxation, sideways lean, reclining angle, and arm–leg position asymmetry. Responsiveness is expressed through 'activity' cues that relate to orienting behaviour and involve the relative importance of the interaction participants. Such non-verbal behaviour as vocal activity, speech rate, speech volume, and facial activity are indices of responsiveness. Mehrabian's system of non-verbal expression is thus organised into (1) dimensions, (2) associated cues, and (3) specific non-verbal indicators of the cues.

Mehrabian's system places non-verbal behaviour in socially meaningful contexts and is especially useful for non-verbal behaviour as a communication skill. The dimensions of non-verbal behaviour can be applied equally to encoding or decoding roles and are supported by numerous experimental results. For example, data collected by Mehrabian and others indicate that the positiveness dimension, with its immediacy cues, is concerned with deceptive or truthful communication. McCroskey's research on non-verbal immediacy in the classroom has also revealed positive effects on both evaluations of teachers (McCroskey et al., 1995; Rocca & McCroskey, 1999) and student learning outcomes (McCroskey et al., 1996). The potency dimension, as expressed by relaxation cues, is useful in understanding situations where social or professional status is salient, such as military rank, corporate power, teacher–student relations, and therapist–client interaction.

The responsiveness dimension, as expressed by activity cues, relates to persuasion, either as intended (encoding) or perceived (decoding). Thus, Mehrabian organised a complex set of non-verbal behaviours into manageable proportions, which are readily testable and applicable to social situations experienced daily, particularly by professionals whose judgement and influence are important to those with whom they communicate.

Patterson

A more recent attempt to organise non-verbal behaviour into basic functions or purposes of communication is presented by Patterson (1983, 1988, 2001). He argues that, as social communication, non-verbal behaviour is meaningful only when considered in terms of an exchange of expressions between participants in an interaction. It is this relational nature of behaviours that must be considered and requires sensitivity to the behavioural context each person constructs for the other (Patterson, 1983), or for third parties viewing participants in a primary relationship (Patterson, 1988). The basic functions of non-verbal behaviour are related to the management (both interpretation and presentation) of those acts primarily involved in social interaction.

Seven basic functions are suggested: (1) providing information, (2) regulating interaction, (3) expressing intimacy, (4) expressing social control, (5) presentation function, (6) affect management, and (7) facilitating service or task goals. Non-verbal behaviour is best considered as 'coordinated exchanges' and configurations of multichannel combinations as related to the seven functions. Thus, presenting non-verbal behaviour in terms of separate channels (for instance, facial expressions, arm movements, paralanguage, and so on) does not properly emphasise the inter-dependent and coordinated relationship among channels that are meaningfully involved in the functions. This configural approach is important for application to the development of communication skills. The use of emblems provides a good example of a non-verbal display that often employs multiple channels to produce a direct verbal equivalent. For example, the emblem for the verbalisation 'I don't know' involves a coordinated facial expression, shoulder movement, arm movement, and hand movement.

The information-provision function is considered to be most basic and is seen primarily from an impression formation or decoder perspective. When observing an encoder's (actor's) behaviour patterns, the decoder may infer aspects of the encoder's acquired dispositions and temporary states, or the meaning of a verbal interaction. Facial cues are emphasised (Ekman & Friesen, 1975) usually to infer emotional expressions. However, other channels of non-verbal behaviour, such as the postural, paralinguistic, and visual, are also important in formulating the impression.

The function of regulating interaction deals with the development, mainten-ance, and termination of a communicative exchange. These non-verbal behaviours are usually 'automatic' or operate at low levels of awareness. Two types of behaviour are involved in regulating interactions: the first are structural aspects that remain rela-tively stable over the course of an interaction and include posture, body orientation, and interpersonal distance; the second is dynamic and affects momentary changes in conversational exchange, such as facial expression, gaze, tone and pitch of voice, and change in voice volume (Argyle & Kendon, 1967; Duncan, 1972). Both the information and regulating functions are 'molecular' in form and represent communicative aspects of more isolated and specific non-verbal behaviours.

The last five functional categories represent broader purposes of communica-tion and are molar descriptions of more extended interactions. These are of greater importance in understanding and predicting the nature of non-verbal acts during an interaction. Intimacy refers to liking, attraction or, generally, the degree of 'union' or 'openness toward another person'. Extended mutual gazing into another's eyes, closer interpersonal spacing, and mutual touching are examples of communicating intimacy.

Social control functions to persuade others and establish status differences related to the roles of the interaction participants. Examples of non-verbal behaviours involved in social control are gaze patterns and touch to clarify status differences, and eye contact, direct body orientation, and vocal intonation to attempt to persuade someone to accept another's point of view. Much of the authors' research relates to this function and will be discussed later in the chapter.

The presentational function of non-verbal behaviours is managed by an indi-vidual or a couple to create or enhance an image, and is typically aimed not so much at the other partner as it is at others outside the direct relationship. Some authors have identified these processes as 'tie-signs' (Goffman, 1971) or 'withness cues' (Scheflen & Scheflen, 1972). Holding hands, standing close, and sharing a common focus of attention are frequent examples. Such behaviours occur more often in the presence of others. The affect-management function focuses on the expression of strong affect by demonstrative processes such as embracing, kissing, and other forms of touching associated with strong positive affect; or embarrassment, shame, or social anxiety, as in instances of decreased contact, averted gaze, and turning away from the partner.

The service-task function involves non-verbal behaviours that are relatively impersonal in nature. Role and situational factors are particularly important here since many of the same non-verbal behaviours involved in intimacy are also present in service-task functions. A good example is close interpersonal spacing and touching behaviour on the part of a physician toward a patient or between hairdresser and customer. The distinguishing feature of service-task behaviours is that they function to service the needs of individuals.

Patterson (1995) has attempted to expand his functional conception of social process maintenance by conceptualising a dynamic, multistaged, parallel-processing model of non-verbal communication. The model encompasses four classes of factors, each containing multiple processes: (1) determinants (biology, culture, gender, personality); (2) social environment (partner, setting); (3) cognitive-affective mediators (interpersonal expectancies, affect, goals, dispositions, cognitive resources, attentional focus, cognitive effort, action schemas); and (4) person perception and behavioural processes (impression formation, actor behaviour). In the broadest sense, the model attempts to describe the complex demands entailed in simultaneously initiating and monitoring interactive behaviour. It is generally recognised that if non-verbal behaviour is discussed separately by channel, it is primarily for organisational clarity; any one channel should not be considered at the exclusion of others in either managing or interpreting social behaviour. This, of course, results in a more complex task in using non-verbal behaviour as a communication skill, yet it places the topic in a more appropriate perspective vis-à-vis communication in general.

Patterson's functional approach to non-verbal behaviour is similar to Mehrabian's in its application to social-communicative processes. Both stress the importance of the multichannel use of configurative aspects of non-verbal communication. However, Patterson provides a broader framework in which to view non-verbal behaviour in role- and setting-specific conditions, by emphasising the degree of overlap in multichannel expression among the functions and the importance of interpreting these expressions in light of the psychological, social, and environmental context.

In more recent descriptions of Patterson's (1998, 2001) parallel-process model of non-verbal communication, the model is increasingly focused on the roles that goals and automatic processing play in our dealing with the tasks of simultaneously decoding our social environment and managing impressions of ourselves. Patterson observes that many relatively automatic judgements (e.g. the tendency to react in a positive and nurturing manner with baby-faced adults) may have been biologically based. However, he also suggests that due to the experience of processing social information, automatic judgements can occur as a function of forming associations between specific non-verbal cues or behaviours and learned preferred tendencies of the individual. In his commentary on the influence of evolutionary psychology on current non-verbal research, Patterson (2003) states that the evolutionary focus on the adaptive value of specific forms of expressive behaviour is consistent with the functional perspective, and that 'Evolutionary processes play a critical role in providing the foundation for this functional system of nonverbal communication' (p. 207). However, in a manner similar to that of Zebrowitz (2003), his major criticism of the evolutionary perspective is that it does not capture the parallel sending and receiving processes that represent an adequately complex interactive model of non-verbal communication.

The complexity of the task of communicative and self-presentational uses of non-verbal behaviour has been reviewed by DePaulo (1992). She examined the difficulties of communicating intended messages and emotional states through non-verbal channels. Two factors received particular emphasis. Non-verbal behaviour is more accessible to others in an interaction than it is to the actor. This makes self- (or relationship) presentational refinements and monitoring difficult for the actor, and access direct and figural for others, although such refinements have been shown to be affected by self-monitoring tendencies and strategic self-presentational goals (Levine & Feldman, 1997). Second, it is never possible to 'not act' by non-verbal channels. While one can fall silent verbally, one can never become silent non-verbally. These two features of non-verbal behaviour vis-à-vis speech highlight the significant and problematic nature of non-verbal behaviour as communication.

NON-VERBAL COMMUNICATION IN CONTEXT

This chapter has stressed that non-verbal behaviour, as a communication skill, is most usefully understood when discussed in role- and setting-defined contexts. With the possible exception of facial expressions subject to display rules, non-verbal communication cannot be discussed adequately by presenting principles that have universal application. Perhaps a useful way of presenting research results as applied to communication skills is to provide a sampling of findings in selected contexts. At present, research on non-verbal communication is incomplete and asks more questions than it provides answers, yet it is hoped that the reader will better appreciate scientific attempts to study this communication skill meaningfully.

In his review, Knapp (1984) discussed the relevance of non-verbal behaviour to communication in general and suggested several assumptions from which the research can be viewed. Among these are that human communication consists primarily of combinations of channel signals such as spatial, facial, and vocal signals operating together. Another assumption is that communication is composed of 'multilevel signals' and deals with broader interpretations of interactions such as general labelling (for example, a social or professional encounter) and inferences about longer-term relationships among the interactants. His last assumption is most crucial for the present discussion, since it points out the critical importance of context for generating meanings from human communication encounters.

Setting and role applications

A major limitation of much non-verbal behaviour research is that it is conducted in a laboratory setting devoid of many of the contextually relevant environmental and social features present in real-life interactions (Druckman et al., 1982; Davis, 1984; Knapp, 1984). This is a serious problem in attempts to generalise techniques of impression management and processes of impression formation to specific role-defined settings (such as the psychotherapeutic or counselling session), health professional–patient interactions, the employment interview, and police–citizen encounters. Professionals in these areas have a special interest in non-verbal behaviour. Accurate and effective communication is crucial to accomplishing the purposes of the interaction. One series of studies conducted over a number of years is illustrative of setting- and role-defined research and reveals the importance of the interplay among the categories of kinesics, paralanguage, proxemics, physical characteristics, adornments, and environmental factors mentioned earlier as describing major categories of non-verbal behaviour.

The specific role-defined setting was that of a standing, face-to-face, police–citizen interaction. In the initial study (Rozelle & Baxter, 1975), police officers were asked to indicate the 'characteristics and features they look for when interacting with a citizen while in the role of a 'police officer'. They were also asked to indicate cues they used in forming these impressions of the citizen. These cues or information items were classified as either behavioural (that is, the other person's verbal and non-verbal behaviour) or situational (that is, aspects of the environment, such as number of other people present, whether inside a room or on the street, and lighting conditions).

The officers were asked to compare a 'dangerous' and a 'non-dangerous' situation. Under conditions of danger, the officers indicated a broadened perceptual scan and were more likely to utilise behavioural (mainly non-verbal) and situation-environmental cues (for instance, area of town, size of room, activities on the street) in forming an impression of the citizen. Under the non-dangerous conditions, the officers concentrated almost exclusively on specific facial and vocal cues, eye contact, arm and hand movements, and dress and behavioural sequences such as body orientation and postural positions. Under these less stressful conditions, police officers indicated an impression formed that described the citizen primarily in terms of dispositional characteristics (i.e. guilty, suspicious, deceptive, honest, law-abiding).

Dispositional causes of observed behaviour are contrasted with situational causes such as attributing one's behaviour to momentary discomfort or confusion, crowding, response to another's actions, or other events in the immediate environment. Thus, in the more typical police–citizen interaction, which is non-stressful for the police officer (for instance, obtaining information from a witness to an accident or crime), the officer focused predominantly on the citizen's non-verbal behaviours and dispositional attributions, rather than situational attributions, to explain the citizen's behaviour (for example, guilty or innocent).

Actor and observer bias in explaining non-verbal behaviour

An important feature of impression-management (encoding) and formation (decoding) processes deals with differences arising out of the perspectives of the participants in the interaction (Jones & Nisbett, 1972; Ross & Nisbett, 1991). In most role-defined interactions, the person in the encoding role is considered to be the actor, whereas the decoder is the observer. It has been proposed that unless otherwise trained or sensitised (Watson, 1982), observers overemphasise dispositional qualities in inferring the causes of the actor's behaviour, while ignoring the more immediate situational factors related to the observed behaviour. Actors, on the other hand, usually overemphasise situational factors at the expense of dispositional ones in explaining their own behaviour, especially when it is self-serving to do so. It should be mentioned, however, that a number of factors, including cross-cultural differences (Choi & Nisbett, 1998; Krull, Loy, Lin, Wang, Chen & Zhao, 1999; Masuda & Kitayama, 2004) and differences in the way that individuals process information (D'Agostino & Fincher-Kiefer, 1992), have been found to moderate these general attributional tendencies.

Rozelle and Baxter (1975) concluded that police officers see themselves as observers, evaluating and judging the behaviours of the citizen with whom they are interacting. As a result, the officer makes predominantly dispositional interpretations, ignoring situational causes of the observed behaviour. It is of particular importance to note that in this type of face-to-face interaction, the officer is probably one of the more distinguishable features of the situation, and the officer's behaviour is an important situational determinant of the citizen's behaviour. Thus, the officer under-estimates or ignores personal behaviour as a contributing, situational determinant of the citizen's behaviour. This can lead to misinterpretations of behaviour, particularly when judgements must be made on the basis of a relatively brief, initial encounter. It should also be noted that the citizen may be misinterpreting his or her own behaviour in terms of reacting to the situation, including the officer's behaviour; thus, non-verbal cues are not 'managed' properly to avoid expressing or concealing appropriate behaviour for desired evaluation on the part of the officer. Other types of role-defined interactions resemble this condition in various degrees.

Interpersonal distance, roles and problems of interpretation

A more dramatic example of how this observer bias can lead to clear, yet inaccurate, interpretations of behaviour was obtained when the category of proxemics was included in the police–citizen interaction. Based on his observations of North American behaviour in a variety of settings, Hall (1959, 1966) proposed four categories of interpersonal distance that describe different types of communications in face-to-face interactions:

1   intimate distances in which interactants stand 6–18 inches from each other, types of interactions expressing intimacy being 'love-making and wrestling, comforting and protecting'
2   personal distances of 1.5–4 feet, which usually reflect close, personal relationships
3   social or consultative distances of 4–7 feet, which are typical of business and professional client interactions
4   public distances of 12–20 feet involving public speaking in which recognition of others spoken to is not required.

Hall (1966) stipulated that these distances are appropriate only for North American and possibly northern European cultures, and that other cultures have different definitions of interpersonal spacing.

A study by Baxter and Rozelle (1975) focused on a simulated police–citizen interview between white male undergraduates at a North American university and an interviewer playing the role of a police officer questioning the student-citizen about various items in his wallet. The interview consisted of four 2-minute phases in which the distance between the officer and citizen was systematically varied according to Hall's first three distance classes.

For both the experimental and control groups, the role-played officer stood 4 feet away from the student during the first 2-minute phase. At the beginning of the second 2-minute phase, the officer casually moved within 2 feet (personal distance) of the subject for both groups. For the experimental group only, the intimate or 'severe crowding' condition (due to the inappropriate distances for the roles being played) occurred during the third 2-minute phase: the officer moved to an 8-inch nose-to-nose distance from the subject, and then returned to the 2-foot distance during the fourth 2-minute phase. The 2-foot distance was maintained throughout the second, third, and fourth phases for the control group. The police interviewer was instructed to maintain eye contact during all phases of the interaction. The student was positioned next to a wall which prevented him from moving back or escaping during the crowding condition.

The non-verbal behaviours exhibited by the subjects during the crowding condition were consistent with typical reactions of people experiencing inappropriate, intimate, interpersonal spacing. As the subject was increasingly crowded during the interview, his speech time and frequency became disrupted and disorganised, an uneven, staccato pattern developing. Eye movements and gaze aversion increased, while few other facial reactions were displayed. Small, discrete head movements occurred, and head rotation/elevation movements increased. Subjects adopted positions to place their arms and hands between themselves and the interviewer, and there was a noticeable increase in hands-at-crotch positioning. Brief rotating head movements increased, while foot movements decreased.

These non-verbal behaviours were produced by a situational manipulation (that is, crowding) but were strikingly similar to those emphasised by Rozelle and Baxter's real police officers as they described behaviours indicating dispositional characteristics of guilt, suspicion, and deception. Officers in the earlier study specified facial and vocal cues, arm and hand behaviour, and posture and body orientation; they related non-verbal behaviours as being particularly reliable indices of these dispositions. At that time, the training course (at the police academy) required of all officers included instructions to stand close to the citizen and maintain maximal eye contact during such an interview. Thus, reliance on non-verbal behaviour has, in this role-specific setting, a high probability of miscommunicating intention, motivations, and other dispositions from actor to observer. The observer, by not properly including his or her own behaviour as a significant part of the situation influencing the actor's non-verbal behaviour, inaccurately forms an impression of the actor in a highly reliable and confident manner.

Cultural influences

The important role played by cultural differences in non-verbal behaviour is suggested from several directions. Early studies by Watson (1970) and by Watson and Graves (1966) have shown differences in gazing behaviour, space behaviour, body orientation, and touching behaviour among members of different cultures. More recent studies by Ekman and his colleagues distinguished the universal from the culturally specific sources for expressions of emotion (e.g. Ekman & O'Sullivan, 1988). While the underlying physiology for the primary emotions may be universal, the actual expression elicited is subject to cultural (Elfenbein & Ambady, 2002b, 2003) and situation-determined display rules, as we discussed above. Display rules serve to control an expression or to modify certain expressions that would be socially inappropriate or would reveal deception.

Klopf et al. (1991) showed that the Japanese subjects in their study perceived themselves to be less immediate – as indicated by less touching, more distance, less forward lean, less eye contact, and orientation away from the other – than their Finnish and American subjects. These variations may reflect cultural differences in rules dealing with intimacy (Argyle, 1986). Anecdotal reports also suggest distinct patterns of expression for Japanese negotiators – in the face (immobile, impassive); the eyes (gaze away from others); the mouth (closed); the hands (richly expressive gestures); and synchronous movements in pace, stride, and body angle with other members of a group (March, 1988). Understanding preferred non-verbal expressions may be a basis for communicating across cultures, as Faure (1993) illustrated in the context of French–Chinese negotiations. They may also reveal the way that members of different societies manage impressions (Crittenden & Bae, 1994).

Subcultural differences in interpersonal spacing preferences have been examined in several observational studies (Willis, 1966; Baxter, 1970; Thompson & Baxter, 1973). In general, African-Americans tend to prefer interacting at greater distances and at more oblique orientations than Anglo-Americans, who in turn prefer greater distances and more indirection than Mexican-Americans. Indeed, the Thompson and Baxter study demonstrates that African-Anglo- and Mexican-Americans, when interacting in intercultural groups in natural contexts, appear to 'work toward' inconsistent spacing arrangements through predictable footwork and orientation adjustments. A subsequent study by Garratt et al. (1981) trained Anglo-American police officers to engage in empirically determined 'African-American nonverbal behaviour and interpersonal positioning' during an interview with African-American citizens. These interviews were contrasted with 'standard' interviews conducted by the same officers with different African-American citizens. Post-interview ratings by these citizens showed a clear preference for the 'trained' policeman, along with higher ratings in the areas of personal, social, and professional competence. A similar study with comparable results had been carried out previously by Collett (1971) with trained British interviewers interacting with Arab students.

Differences were also found between African-American and white American subjects in gazing behaviour. The African-American subjects directed their gaze away when listening and toward the other when speaking (LaFrance & Mayo, 1978). Similar patterns of gaze behaviour were found in other societies (Winkel & Vrij, 1990; Vrij & Winkel, 1991). Preliminary evidence obtained by the authors of this chapter suggests that the differences in gaze may reflect differences between subcultural groups in felt stress. A comparison of decoding accuracy between African-American, African, Afro-Caribbean, and European-Americans demonstrated that decoding accuracy for the non-verbal expression of emotion through posture and tone of voice was significantly related to degree of acculturation (Bailey, Nowicki & Cole, 1998). Consistent with the likelihood that facial expressions would be more universally understood, acculturation was unrelated to the accurate interpretation of emotion from face in this study. However, more recent investigations that have compared Japanese nationals and Japanese-Americans have revealed cultural differences in 'non-verbal accents' in the facial expression of emotion (Marsh, Elfenbein & Ambady, 2003).

A few studies have investigated cultural factors in deceptive enactments. Comparing Chinese experimental truth tellers to liars, Yi Chao (1987), Cody et al. (1989), and O'Hair et al. (1989) found that only speech errors and vocal stress distinguished between the groups. Other paralinguistic variables were related more strongly to question difficulty. Like the Americans in the studies reviewed by DePaulo et al. (1985), the Chinese liars (compared to the truth tellers) experienced more difficulty in communicating detailed answers to the questions that required effort. Both the liars and truth tellers were brief in communicating negative feelings, smiling frequently and suppressing body and hand movements. With regard to Jordanian subjects, Bond et al. (1990) found that only filled pauses distinguished between the liars and truth tellers: the Jordanians expressed more filled pauses when lying than when telling the truth. Compared to a comparable sample of Americans, the Jordanian subjects (liars and truth tellers) displayed more eye contact, more movements per minute, and more filled pauses. However, the American and Jordanian subjects both used similar, inaccurate non-verbal cues (avoiding eye contact and frequent pauses) in judging deception by others. An examination of beliefs about deception cues among Jordanians by Al-Simadi (2000) revealed some similarities with data from the USA and Western Europe (expectations of increased gaze aversion and paralinguistic cues) and some notable differences (expectations of increased blinking and facial colour). For a review of other cross-cultural studies, see Druckman and Hyman (1991).

While suggestive, these studies are not sufficient probes into the cultural dimensions influencing non-verbal behaviour. None of them describes the way people from different cultures feel when they violate a social taboo, for example, or attempt to deceive or exploit an interviewer. While the studies are informative, they do not illuminate the psychological states aroused within cultures that give rise to the kind of 'leakage' which may be used to examine complex intentional structures in different cultural groups. Based on their review of deception research, Hyman and Druckman (1991) concluded that 'detection of deception would be improved if one could anticipate the sorts of settings that constitute social transgression or a guilt-producing state for particular individuals (or cultures)' (p. 188).

Some research implications

Building on the idea of cultural display rules, investigations designed to discover the situations which produce guilt for members of different cultural groups would be helpful. Situations that produce guilt are likely to vary with an individual's cultural background and experience. When identified, these situations could then be used as settings for enacting scripts that involve either deception or truth telling by subjects from those cultures. The enactments should reveal the non-verbal behaviours that distinguish deceivers and truth tellers within the cultural groups. These behaviours would be culturally specific 'leaked' cues.

Following this approach, such studies could be implemented in stages. First, interviews would be conducted to learn about a culture's 'folk psychology' of deception (see Hyman & Druckman, 1991). Respondents would be asked about the kinds of lies and lying situations that are permissible and those that are taboo within their culture. Second, experimental deception vignettes would be presented for respondents' reactions in terms of feelings of guilt, shame, and stress. The vignettes could be designed to vary in terms of such dimensions as whether the person represents a group or her/himself, the presence of an audience during the interview, and the extent to which he or she prepared for the questions being asked. Analyses would then suggest the dimensions that influence feelings of guilt or shame for each cultural group. Preliminary findings on subcultural groups, obtained by the authors of this chapter, showed differences in stress for members of different cultural groups and less guilt felt by respondents in all cultural groups when they were in the role of group representative rather than non-representative. (See also Mikolic et al., 1994, for evidence on the disinhibiting effects of being in groups.) Third, the information gathered from the interviews could provide the bases for more structured experimental studies designed to discover those non-verbal behaviours that distinguish between liars and truth tellers (the leakage cues) for each of several cultural groups. These cues could then be used for diagnostic purposes as well as for the development of training modules along the lines of work completed by Collett (1971), Garratt et al. (1981), Druckman et al. (1982), Costanzo (1992), and Fiedler and Walka (1993).

Non-verbal behaviour in professional settings: a sample of research findings

Although the police–citizen encounter was brief, and involved rather extreme situational proxemic variations with only a moderate amount of verbal exchange, it has elements similar to many professional interactions. For example, the actor–observer distinction could be applied to the employment interview. In such an interaction, the interviewer could be considered the 'observer' or decoder evaluating the verbal and non-verbal acts of the interviewee, who is the 'actor' or encoder.

In the authors' experience with the professional interview setting, the interviewer often makes an important, job-related decision regarding the interviewee based on dispositional attributions occurring as a result of behaviour observed during a 30-minute interview. Although the employment interview may be a typical experience for the interviewer during the working day, it is usually an infrequent and stressful one for the interviewee. This could increase the observer-dispositional bias, actor-situational bias effect. The interviewer, in the role of observer, proceeds 'as usual', while the interviewee reacts in a sensitive manner to every verbal and non-verbal behaviour of the interviewer. Unaware that the very role of the interviewer is an important, immediate situational cause of the interviewee's behaviours, the interviewer uses these same behaviours to attribute long-term dispositional qualities to the interviewee-actor and may make a job-related decision on the basis of the impression formed. Thus, from a non-verbal communication perspective, the impression formed is, to varying degrees, inadvertently encoded by the interviewee-actor, and possibly misinterpreted in the decoding process by the interviewer (the employment interview is discussed in detail in Chapter 16).

This miscommunication process may be particularly important during the initial stages of an interaction, since expectancies may be created that bias the remaining interaction patterns. Research indicates that first impressions are important in creating expectancies and evaluative judgements (and sometimes diagnoses) of people in interviewing, counselling, teaching, therapeutic, and other professionally role-related interactions. Zajonc (1980) stated that evaluative judgements are often made in a fraction of a second on the basis of non-verbal cues in an initial encounter. Others have shown that a well-organised, judgemental impression may be made in as little as 4 minutes.

A meta-analytic study by Ambady and Rosenthal (1992) summarized the research on 'thin slices' (defined as a 5-minute exposure or less) of expressive behaviour as a predictor for deception detection. They found a significant effect size, $r = 0.31$, across 16 studies. Neither length of exposure nor channel exposure (non-verbal vs verbal and non-verbal) significantly moderated the effect size. Babad et al. (2003) found that even very brief (10-second) exposure to teacher non-verbal behaviour while the latter was interacting with the class is predictive of students' teaching evaluations.

Those in professional roles, such as interviewing, counselling, and teaching, should constantly remind themselves of the influence they have on clients' non-verbal behaviour, and not to rely on 'favourite' non-verbal behaviours as flawless indicators of dispositional characteristics. Knowledge of the potential effects of verbal and non-verbal behaviour can be useful in impression-management techniques to create more effective communication in face-to-face interactions. For example, in a simulated employment interview setting, Washburn and Hakel (1973) demonstrated that when applicants were given a high level of non-verbal 'enthusiasm' by the interviewer (for instance, gazing, gesturing, and smiling), the applicants were judged more favourably than those given a low level of interviewer enthusiasm. Another study showed that when candidates received non-verbal approval during an employment interview, they were judged by objective observers to be more relaxed, more at ease, and more comfortable than candidates who received non-verbal disapproval from the interviewer (Keenan, 1976).

Impression-management strategies may also be utilised by the interviewee. For example, the American Psychological Association gives specific suggestions, based on research, to postgraduate school applicants on how to communicate favourable qualities non-verbally during an interview (Fretz & Stang, 1982). Research studies generally show that non-verbal behaviours, such as high levels of gaze, combinations of paralinguistic cues, frequent head movement, frequent smiling, posture, voice loudness, and personal appearance, affect impressions formed and evaluative judgements made by employment interviewers (Young & Beier, 1977; Hollandsworth et al., 1979; Forbes & Jackson, 1980). Non-verbal immediacy has also been shown to be related to positive subordinate perceptions of supervisors (Richmond & McCroskey, 2000). Caution should be advised before applying these specific behaviours, since qualifying factors have been reported. For example, one study reported that if an applicant avoids gazing at the interviewer, an applicant of high status will be evaluated more negatively than one of low status (Tessler & Sushelsky, 1978). Evidently, gaze aversion was expected, on the part of the interviewer, from a low-status applicant, but not from a higher-status one. Status differences and associated non-verbal behaviours have also been recognised in the military setting, where physical appearance, such as uniform markings, clearly identifies the ranks of the interactants (Hall, 1966).

This brief sampling of empirical results provides impressive evidence for the importance of non-verbal behaviour in managing and forming impressions in role-defined settings. However, these results also reveal that non-verbal behaviour in the form of kinesics interacts with other non-verbal categories such as proxemics, para-language, physical characteristics, and environmental factors. Although this creates a rather complex formula for applications, all of Knapp's seven dimensions are important to consider in developing communication skills in the various contexts of role-defined interactions that one experiences.

AN EXAMPLE OF RESEARCH AND APPLICATION: INTERNATIONAL POLITICS

In this section, a programme of research will be briefly presented that illustrates an attempt to identify systematically certain non-verbal behaviours associated with specific intentions of the communicator (encoder), and then to apply these findings to develop better skills in interpreting (decoding) observed behaviour of others (Druckman et al., 1982). The context selected for this research is international politics. This is an area that encompasses a broad range of situational, cultural, personal, and social factors and thus attempts to deal with the complexity of non-verbal expression and interpretation. It is also an area that contains elements similar to a variety of everyday experiences encountered by a broad range of people in professional and social interactions.

Laboratory research

The initial research project involved a role-playing study in which upper-level university students were instructed to play the role of a foreign ambassador being interviewed at a press conference. A set of pertinent issues was derived from United Nations transcripts and presented to the subjects in detail. After studying the issues, subjects were randomly assigned to one of three intention conditions which directed them to express their country's position on the issues in either an honest, deceptive, or evasive fashion. Examples of honest, deceptive, and evasive arguments and discussion points were presented to the subjects to help prepare them for the interview.

A formal, 15-minute, videotaped interview was conducted between the 'ambassador' and a trained actor playing the role of a press interviewer. An informal, 7-minute, post-interview discussion was also videotaped in which the subject was asked to be 'him/herself' and discuss his or her activities at the university. It is important to note that the subject ambassadors were not aware that the purpose of the study was to assess non-verbal behaviour exhibited by them during the interview. Thus, the study dealt with 'informative' rather than consciously controlled 'communication' acts as described by Ekman and Friesen (1969) and discussed by Dittmann (1978). Moreover, the interviewer was unaware of whether the subject was in the honest, deceptive, or evasive intention condition. Ten subjects served in each of the conditions. The videotaped interviews were coded by an elaborate process involving 200 student volunteers carefully trained reliably to observe specific channels of non-verbal behaviour patterns produced by subjects in the honest, deceptive, and evasive conditions.

Research findings

Among the detailed results presented by Druckman et al. (1982), several general findings are appropriate for this discussion. One set of analyses revealed that honest, deceptive, and evasive subjects could be classified accurately solely on the basis of their non-verbal behaviours. Using 10 non-verbal behaviours (for instance, head-shaking, gaze time at interviewer, leg movements, and so on), 96.6% of the subjects were classified correctly as being honest, deceptive, or evasive. In another segment of the interview, three non-verbal behaviours (for instance, leg movements, gaze time at interviewer, and object fidgeting) were accurate in 77% of the cases in detecting honest, deceptive, or evasive intentions of the subject.

These computer-generated results were in striking contrast to another set of judgements produced by three corporate executives selected on the basis of their experience and expertise in 'dealing effectively with people'. These executives viewed the tapes and then guessed whether the subject had been in the honest, deceptive, or evasive condition. Results indicated that the experts correctly classified the subject-ambassadors in only 43%, 30%, and 27% of the cases, respectively. Thus, even 'experts' would appear to benefit from further training and skill development in interpreting non-verbal behaviours – and actually may be in special need of such training (DePaulo et al., 1985).

The vast majority of decoding studies have involved the use of undergraduate students to assess deception. The accuracy rate across these studies tends to hover close to chance: 45% and 60% (Kraut, 1980; DePaulo et al., 1985; Vrij, 2000). Vrij (2000) points out that a more specific evaluation that distinguishes between skill at detecting honesty and skill at detecting lies reveals that we tend to be particularly poor at detecting lies (a truth bias). Some data suggest that accuracy in detecting deception may be higher among specific groups of experts such as members of the Secret Service (Ekman & O'Sullivan, 1991; Ekman, O'Sullivan & Frank, 1999) and police officers (Mann, Vrij & Bull, 2004), but this is only likely to be the case when these professional groups have learned or are trained to pay attention to the more reliable non-verbal cues and ignore non-diagnostic non-verbal behaviour.

Current research summarised by Vrij and Mann (2004) has demonstrated the utility of combining the evaluation of non-verbal behaviour with the application of various speech content analysis techniques that assess the credibility of verbal content. The accuracy rate in these studies was 77–89% (Vrij, Edward, Roberts & Bull, 2000; Vrij, Akerhurst, Soukara & Bull, 2004). Lastly, a recent study that compared decoding accuracy between individuals and small (six-person) groups revealed a significant advantage among participants in the group conditions (Frank, Paolantonio, Feeley & Servoss, 2004). However, this advantage was found only for judgements of deceptive, not honest, communication.

Another set of analyses revealed significant shifts in non-verbal behaviour patterns when the subject changed from the ambassador role to being 'him/herself' during the informal post-interview period. Generally, subjects showed more suppressed, constrained behaviour when playing the role of ambassador: for example, significantly fewer facial displays, less head nodding, fewer body swivels, and less frequent statements occurred during the interview than in the post-interview period. It would appear that the same person displays different patterns and levels of non-verbal behaviour depending upon the role that is being communicated. Moreover, different patterns of behaviour occurred in the three 5-minute segments of the formal interview. Thus, even when a person is playing the same role, different behaviours emerge during the course of an interaction. These may be due to factors of adaptation, stress, familiarity, relaxation, or fatigue.

Yet another set of analyses using subjects' responses to a set of post-interview questions indicated that certain patterns of non-verbal behaviours were related to feelings the subject had during the interview (for example, stress, relaxation, confidence, apprehension), and that these patterns were related to the intention condition assigned to the subject. Evasive and honest subjects displayed behaviours indicating involvement, while evasive and deceptive subjects displayed non-verbal indication of stress and tension. Subjects in all three conditions displayed behaviour patterns related to expressed feelings of confidence and effectiveness.

Training the decoder

Even though the results of this study were complex, they were organised into a training programme designed to improve the observer's ability to distinguish among honest, deceptive, and evasive intentions of subjects playing this role. Four training programmes were presented to different groups of decoders and represented four types of instruction, ranging from general (a global lecture and an audio-only presentation) to specific information (a technical briefing and inference training) regarding non-verbal indicators of intention. Results showed that accuracy of judgement in distinguishing between honest, deceptive, and evasive presentations improved as the specificity and applied organisation of the instructional materials increased. The strategy used for inference training was shown to be especially effective (Druckman et al., 1982).

Strategies for interpreting non-verbal behaviour: an application of experimental results

The studies reviewed above support the assumption that gestures, facial expressions, and other non-verbal behaviours convey meaning. However, while adding value to interpretation in general, an understanding of the non-verbal aspects of behaviour may not transfer directly to specific settings. Meaning must be established within the context of interest: for example, the non-verbal behaviour observed during the course of a speech, interview, or informal conversation.

Building on the earlier laboratory work, a plan has been developed for deriving plausible inferences about intentions and psychological or physical states of political leaders (see also Druckman & Hyman, 1991). The plan is a structure for interpretation: it is a valuable tool for the professional policy analyst, and it is a useful *frame-*

work for the interested observer of significant events. In the following sections, themes and techniques for analysis are discussed, and the special features of one particular context, that of international politics, are emphasised.

Themes for analysis

Moving pictures shown on video or film are panoramas of quickly changing actions, sounds, and expressions. Just where to focus one's attention is a basic analytic problem. Several leads are suggested by frameworks constructed to guide the research cited above. Providing a structure for analysis, the frameworks emphasise two general themes, namely, focusing on combinations of non-verbal behaviours and taking contextual features into account.

While coded separately, the non-verbal behaviours can be combined for analysis of total displays. Patterns of behaviours then provide a basis for inferences about feelings or intentions. The patterns may take several forms: one consists of linear combinations of constituent behaviours, as when gaze time, leg movements, and object fidgeting are used in equations to identify probable intentions; a second form is correlated indicators or clusters, such as the pattern of trunk swivels, rocking movements, head-shaking, and head nodding shown by subjects attempting to withhold information about their 'nation's' policy; another form is behaviours that occur within the same time period as was observed for deceivers in the study presented above – for example, a rocking/nodding/shaking cluster was observed during interviews with deceptive 'ambassadors'.

Patterned movements are an important part of the total situation. By anchoring the movements to feelings and intentions, one can get an idea of their meaning. But there are other sources of explanation for what is observed. These sources may be referred to as context. Included as context are the semi-fixed objects in the setting (for instance, furniture), the other people with whom the subject interacts, and the nature of the discourse that transpires. The proposition that context greatly influences social interaction/behaviour comes alive in Rapoport's (1982) treatment of the meaning of the built environment. The constraining influences of other people on exhibited expressions are made apparent in Duncan's (1983) detailed analyses of conversational turn taking. Relationships between verbal statements and non-verbal behaviour are the central concern in the analyses of stylised enactments provided by Druckman et al. (1982). Each of these works is a state-of-the-art analysis. Together, they are the background for developing systems that address the questions of *what* to look for and *how* to use the observations/codes for interpretation. Highlighted here is a structure for interpreting material on the tapes.

It is obvious that the particular intention–interpretation relationships of interest vary with particular circumstances. Several issues are particularly salient within the area of international politics. Of interest might be questions such as: What is the state of health of the leader (or spokesman)? To what degree are statements honestly expressive of true beliefs (or actual policy)? How committed is the person to the position expressed? How fully consolidated and secure is the person's political position?

Knowing where to focus attention is a first step in assessment. A particular theme is emphasised in each of the political issues mentioned above. Signs of failing health are suggested by incongruities or inconsistencies in verbal and non-verbal behaviours, as well as between different non-verbal channels. Deception is suggested by excessive body activity, as well as deviations from baseline data. Strong commitment to policy is revealed in increased intensity of behaviours expressed in a variety of channels. The careful recording of proxemic activity or spatial relationships provides clues to political status. Biographical profiles summarise co-varying clusters of facial expressions and body movements. Each of these themes serves to direct an analyst's attention to *relationships* (for health indicators and profiles), to *particular non-verbal channels* (for deception and status indicators), or to *amount* (as in the case of commitment).

Knowing specifically what to look at is the second step in assessment. Results of a number of experiments suggest particular behaviours. These provide multiple signs whose meaning is revealed in conjunction with the themes noted above. Illustrative indicators and references in each category are the following.

Health indicators

1 *pain:* furrowed brow and raised eyelids; change in vocal tone and higher pitch (Ekman & Friesen, 1975); lowered brow, raised upper lip (Kappesser & Williams, 2002); facial expression (Williams, 2002)
2 *depression:* hand-to-body motions, increased self-references, and extended periods of silence (Aronson & Weintraub, 1972); lowered facial muscle activity over the brow and cheek region (Gehricke & Shapiro, 2000)
3 *irritability:* more forced smiling (McClintock & Hunt, 1975); fewer positive head nods (Mehrabian, 1971)
4 *tension:* increased spontaneous movement (Mehrabian & Ksionzky, 1972); faster eye blinking, self-adaptive gesture (for body tension) (McClintock & Hunt, 1975)
5 *stress:* flustered speech as indicated by repetitions, corrections, use of 'ah' or 'you know', rhythm disturbances (Kasl & Mahl, 1965, Baxter & Rozelle, 1975; Fuller, Horii & Conner, 1992); abrupt changes in behaviour (Hermann, 1979); increased eye movements and gaze aversion in an otherwise immobile facial display, increased head rotation/elevation, increased placement of hands in front of the body (Baxter & Rozelle, 1975)
6 *general state:* verbal/non-verbal inconsistencies where different messages are sent in the two channels (Mehrabian, 1972).

Deception indicators

1 *direct deception:* speech errors as deviations from baseline data (Mehrabian, 1971); tone of voice (DePaulo et al., 1980); fidgeting with objects, less time spent looking at the other than during a baseline period, patterns of rocking, head shaking, and nodding movements varying together (coordinated body movements) (Druckman et al., 1982); reduction in hand movements among skilled deceivers and those high in public self-consciousness (Vrij, Akehurst & Morris, 1997); increased pauses (Anolli & Ciceri, 1997)

2   *indirect deception (evasion):* more leg movements during periods of silence (when subject feels less assertive), frequent gazes elsewhere especially during periods of stress, frequent head shaking during early periods in the interaction, increasing trend of self-fidgeting throughout the interaction (McClintock and Hunt, 1975; Druckman et al., 1982).

The search for a coherent set of reliable non-verbal cues to deception has comprised a large segment of the empirical investigation of non-verbal behaviour. However, findings from decoding accuracy studies suggest that either such a set of reliable cues simply does not exist or, alternatively, that the majority of individuals have little knowledge of how to use such a set of cues for diagnostic purposes. The most recent review of findings appears in a meta-analytic assessment conducted by DePaulo, Lindsay, Malone & Muhlenbruck et al. (2003), based on 120 independent samples. Although the review reveals consistencies with some of the indicators listed above (e.g. liars tend to talk less, provide fewer details, and tend to be perceived as more tense as a function of perceived vocal tension and fidgeting), the majority of deception cues were found to be unrelated, or only weakly related to deceit. Consistent with many individual studies, response latency was also found to be greater, but only when the lies were spontaneous (unplanned). However, specific cues to deception (e.g. increased vocal frequency or pitch) and overall assessment of non-verbal tension were found to be more pronounced when encoders were highly motivated to succeed, when lies were identity relevant, and when they were about transgressions. These findings are consistent with the recent work of Frank and Ekman (2004), Vrij (2000), and others that has documented the extent to which motivated lies ('true lies') tend to produce non-verbal cues related to the expression of negative facial affect. Motivated liars have been found to be more easily detected by experts, and high-stakes lies produce more consistent non-verbal displays.

To summarise, as documented in much of the previous research on the non-verbal encoding of deception, the review by DePaulo et al. (2003) emphasises the salience and relative utility of a number of paralinguistic cues. However, a cue's diagnosticity is moderated by a number of factors, including the liar's level of motivation, the spontaneity of the deception, whether or not the deception involved identity-relevant content, and whether or not the lie was about a transgression. In addition, given the universality of the reciprocity norm, it would seem to follow that lies about transgressions (breaching a social contract) might be especially difficult to conceal.

Commitment to policies

1   *commitment:* increased use of 'allness' terms (Hermann, 1977); increased redundancy, more trunk swivels, more time spent looking at (versus looking away from) the other (Druckman et al., 1982)
2   *persuasiveness (impact on others):* increased intensity in voice, increased object (other)-focused movements (Freedman, 1972); more facial activity and gesturing, increased head nodding, fewer self-manipulations, reduced reclining angles (Mehrabian, 1972; Washburn & Hakel, 1973)
3   *credibility (impact on others):* sustained gazing at short distances (Exline &

Eldridge, 1967; Hemsley & Doob, 1975); relaxed vocalisations (Addington, 1971); immediacy behaviours (Thweatt & McCroskey, 1998).

Political status

1   *relative status:* non-reciprocated touching, eye contact at closer distances for higher status members, more frequent use of words suggesting distance from people and objects (Frank, 1977); hand and neck relaxation, sideways lean, reclining posture, arm–leg position asymmetry (Mehrabian, 1972)

2   *changes in status:* increased physical distance from colleagues (Dorsey & Meisels, 1969); increased signs of psychological withdrawal from situations (outward-directed gestures, changed postures) for reduced status (Mehrabian, 1968); more frequent appearances at state functions for enhanced status.

Techniques for analysis

Whereas patterns of non-verbal behaviour are the basis for interpretation, it is the separate behaviours which are the constituents of the displays. A first step is to code specific, well-defined movements and expressions. Advances in technique make possible the efficient coding of a large variety of behaviours. Particularly relevant is a subset of non-verbal behaviours chosen on the basis of high reliability, as determined by independent coders, and importance, in terms of distinguishing among intentions and emotional states. Included in this list are the following: gaze time at interviewer or other person, leg movements, object fidgeting, speech errors, speaking frequency, rocking movements, head nodding, illustrator gestures, and foot movements. These are some of the movements or vocalisations coded directly from videotapes of laboratory subjects (experiments cited above) and world leaders.

Efficiency is gained by training coders to be channel specialists. Small groups are trained to focus their attention on one channel – vocalisations, eyes, face, body, legs, or spatial arrangements. Frequencies are recorded for some measures (for instance, leg movements); for others, the coder records time (for example, gaze at interviewer, speaking time). Further specialisation is obtained by assigning the different groups to specific segments of the tapes. Such a division of labour speeds the process, increases reliability, and preserves the coders for other tasks. A set of 25 non-verbal behaviours shown by subjects in 30, 20-minute tapes was coded in about 3 weeks, each individual coder contributing only 2 hours of effort.

The procedures define a coding scheme or notation system for processing video material. Computer-assisted analysis would facilitate the transforming of non-verbal measures into profiles of selected world leaders. Here, one becomes more interested in characteristic postures or movements than in particular psychological or physical states. The emphasis is on idiosyncratic styles of leaders, conditioned as they are by situational factors. Using the non-verbal notation system, these behaviours can be represented as animated displays. Recent developments in computer graphics and virtual reality technologies expand the range of programming options (Badler et al., 1991). They also contribute tools for the creative exploration of movement and expression control, such as manipulating the display to depict styles in varying situations (Badler et al., 1993).

The list of behaviours is one basis for structuring the analysis. Another basis is a more general category system that encompasses a range of situations, purposes, and verbal statements, as well as types of displayed non-verbal behaviours. Sufficient footage in each category makes possible the tasks of charting trends, making comparisons, and developing profiles. It also contributes to inventory management: systematic categorising and indexing of materials aids in the task of retrieving relevant types from archival collections. Multiple measurements provide alternative indicators that may be useful when all channels are not available to the observer (such as leg and foot movements for a speaker who stands behind a podium and eye movements for an actor seen from a distance). They also provide complementary indicators, bolstering one's confidence in the inferences made. For the time-sensitive analyst, a manageable subset of non-verbal behaviours can be identified for 'on the spot' commentary.

Systematic comparisons

Non-verbal indicators can be used to build profiles of individual foreign leaders. It is evident that such an approach emphasises Allport's (1961) concept of morphogenic analysis and stresses the analogy of expressive behaviour as personal idiom. This strategy of systematic comparison is designed to increase an analyst's understanding of his 'subject'. This is done by tracking the displays exhibited by selected individuals across situations and in conjunction with verbal statements.

Comparisons would be made in several ways: (1) examine deviations from baseline data established for each person (for instance, speech errors); (2) compare non-verbal displays for the same person in different situations (for example, within or outside home country; formal or informal settings); and (3) compare displays for different types of verbal statements (for example, defence of position, policy commitment). These analyses highlight consistencies and inconsistencies at several levels – between situations, between verbal and non-verbal channels, and within different non-verbal channels. They also alert the analyst to changes in non-verbal activity: being aware of changes from a baseline period would give one a better understanding of relatively unique expressive behaviour. Further analysis consists of comparing different persons in similar situations or dealing with similar subject matter.

The value of these comparisons is that they contribute to the development of a system of movement representation similar to the notation and animation systems described by Badler and Smoliar (1979). Extracted from the data are sets of coordinated movements which may change over time and situations. The coordinated movements can be represented in animated graphic displays. Illuminated by such displays are 'postural' differences within actors across time and between actors. When associated with events and context, the observations turn on the issue of how the feelings and intentions which are evoked by different situations are represented in body movement. When compared to displays by actors in other cultural settings, the observations are relevant to the question: What is the contribution of culture to observed non-verbal displays? (See our discussion above on cultural influences.)

Several analytic strategies enable an investigator to get to know his subject or group. Each strategy formalises the idea of 'following a subject around'. Extended coverage provides an opportunity to assemble baseline data for comparisons. It also permits execution of within-subject analytic designs for systematic comparison of displays observed in different situations and occasions, as well as when addressing different topics. These strategies enable an analyst to discriminate more precisely the meaning of various non-verbal displays.

Extensive video footage makes possible quite sophisticated analyses of leaders' behaviours. Relationships are highlighted from comparisons of responses to questions intended to arouse varying levels of stress. Profiles are constructed from the combinations of expressions and movements seen over time. Predictive accuracy of the form, 'Is this person telling the truth?' is estimated from behaviours coded in situations where a subject's intentions are known; namely, does the subset of behaviours discriminate between honest, evasive, and deceptive statements? Contributing to an enhanced analytic capability, these results reduce dependence on notation systems developed in settings removed from the critical situations of interest. They would also contribute information relevant to time-sensitive requests.

Time-sensitive requests

Demand for current assessments often places analysts on the spot, as they are frequently asked to provide interpretations without the benefit of penetrating analysis, extensive video footage, *or* hindsight. Indeed, these are the conditions often present for both technical specialist and layman. Scheibe (1979) noted that the informed observer (whom he calls the 'sagacious observer') relies on good memory for past characteristic patterns and astute observation of departure from the 'typical'. Current findings on the extent to which decoders can make rapid judgements of verbal and non-verbal cues reveal that such judgements can be made in a reliable and relatively accurate manner after training (Vrij, Evans, Akehurst & Mann, 2004). Under these conditions, notation systems are especially useful. They provide the analyst with a structure for focusing attention on relevant details. Determined largely on the basis of what is known, the relevant details are part of a larger coding system whose validity is previously established. Serving to increase the analyst's confidence in personal judgements, the codes (relevant details) highlight where to focus attention and what to look at. Examples include the following.

Abrupt changes

Readily detectable from limited data, abrupt changes may take the form of incongruities between different non-verbal channels (face and body) or increased intensity of behaviours expressed in a number of channels. The former may be construed as signs of failing health; the latter often indicates a strong commitment to policies.

Leaks

Regarded as signs of deception, leaks take the form of excessive activity in one channel (body) combined with reduced activity in another (face) (Ekman & Friesen, 1974). Based on a 'hydraulic model' analogy, the concept of leakage describes the consequences of attempts by a subject to control facial expressions during deception – to wit, the poker face.

A study designed by the authors was intended as a test of the leakage hypothesis. Subjects in one condition were asked to control their facial expression during a deceptive communication; those in another condition were asked to control their body movements. Both conditions were compared to an earlier session in which subjects were not instructed to control expressions or movements during deception. More body movements in the 'control-face' condition and more facial expressions in the 'control-body' condition than in the earlier session would support the leakage hypothesis. Although the results did not support this hypothesis, they did reveal less overall animation for deceivers in both conditions, supporting the findings by DePaulo et al. (1985) showing behavioural inhibition for motivated liars (see Druckman & Hyman, 1991, for further details).

The extent to which the deception is encoded under 'high-stakes' circumstances, as alluded to in the DePaulo et al. (2003) meta-analysis, is an additional factor related to leakage and decoding accuracy. When motivation is high (when deception success will lead to reward and failure to deceive will lead to negative consequences), research has revealed that consistency in the facial expression of emotion can betray the deception (Frank & Ekman, 1997).

Micromomentary expressions (MMEs)

Regarded as universal expressions, MMEs are the muscle activities that underlie primary emotions (happiness, sadness, surprise, anger, fear, disgust, and interest) and information-processing stages (informative seeking, pre-articulation processing, and response selection). With the aid of special instrumentation, workers have been able to identify quite precisely the muscle clusters associated with particular emotions (Ekman et al., 1980) or processing stages (Druckman et al., 1983; Karis et al., 1984). Additional research in this area has shown that MMEs may be useful in decoding body cues as well as the face (McLeod & Rosenthal, 1983).

Illustrated above are the kinds of observations that can be used for inferences from limited data: for example, behaviours that change quickly (MMEs) or obviously (incongruities), and those that occur within the time frame of a statement (leaks). However, useful as these indicators are, they are only a part of the story: missing are the cultural and contextual influences that shape what is observed. These influences are discovered through careful analysis of leaders' behaviour in the settings of interest.

Stereotypes of non-verbal deception

The empirical investigation of beliefs, expectations, and general stereotypes regarding non-verbal behaviour perceived as indicative of deception has resulted in a relatively consistent set of findings across a number of studies and reviews (Gordon et al., 1987; Vrij, 2000). In one of the earliest investigations of this issue, Zuckerman, Koestner, and Driver (1981) found that a wide variety of cues were thought to be associated with deception (e.g., gaze aversion, smiling, adaptors, body and head movements, response latency, speech errors, and hesitations). However, as mentioned in an earlier section, cross-cultural differences in such beliefs have been demonstrated (Al-Simadi, 2000). Other studies have shown that beliefs of 'experts' (police officers) are similar to those of laypersons (Akehurst et al., 1996; Vrij & Semin, 1996). Findings from an investigation by Anderson et al. (1999) also suggest that 'experts' and laypersons alike may rely on a generalised stereotype of deceptive non-verbal behaviour. This same study did show that decoders who indicated they relied on the relevant paralinguistic deception cues were indeed more accurate at detecting lies.

An examination of the stereotype content listed above, in conjunction with the findings from the encoding and decoding accuracy research, suggests that outcomes of chance level performance may be a function of decoders' stereotypes; they usually incorporate both accurate (e.g. increased response latency) and inaccurate (e.g. increased gaze aversion) components. Decoders may be relying on both diagnostic and non-diagnostic information, leading to no better than chance levels of decoding accuracy. Adding to the complexity of the deception detection task is the evidence that motivated or high-status encoders may be more likely to attempt to control leaks consciously in the channels that are more easily manipulated. It may also be that more variability is found for the encoding of behaviours in more controllable channels. Indeed, Vrij et al. (2001) found considerably more variability for the 'more easily controlled' gaze aversions than for the 'less-easily controlled' paralinguistic utterances. Deceivers showed more diverted gazes ($M = 6.4$) than truth tellers ($M = 4.3$). However, the difference was not statistically significant due to the large standard deviations (9.4 and 6.2 respectively). Confidence in this interpretation, referred to as the 'leakage-variability' hypothesis, awaits the results of further research.

OVERVIEW

Considering the large number of full-length books and papers published on non-verbal behaviour, the present chapter has provided only an up-to-date sampling of the literature on this important form of communication. Beginning with an organisational overview and historical perspective, the discussion covered general issues and theoretical and methodological frameworks, and provided some specific examples of research findings and applications. As the chapter has demonstrated, the wealth of information generated by scientific enquiry reveals the significant impact of non-verbal behaviour on communication; yet, this body of knowledge is incomplete and often complex.

The authors have argued that non-verbal behaviour, as a communication skill, is meaningful only if the context of behaviour is taken into account. Incomplete or narrow perspectives regarding others' or one's own behaviour may lead to misinterpretation of actions observed or performed. On the other hand, careful and reliable applications of non-verbal behaviour can enrich and enlighten one's understanding and control of communication in a variety of situation, role, and cultural settings.

The influence of the Darwinian focus on the issue of universality for both non-verbal encoding and decoding continues to play itself out in the research on the impact of culture-specific display rules and non-verbal 'accents' on perceptions of emotion in the face. Findings from a number of relatively diverse, contemporary non-verbal research programmes, each guided in part by evolutionary theory, illustrate the popularity of the application of such investigations to the understanding of non-verbal communication and behaviour. However, it is always important to acknowledge the manner in which factors related to our species' evolutionary heritage interact with a multitude of interpersonal motives and aspects of the situation to produce non-verbal behaviour (Patterson, 2001). Both distal and proximal factors need representation for a comprehensive assessment of non-verbal communication and behaviour (Zebrowitz, 2003).

The key theoretical issue turns on the relative power of universal versus contextual explanations for the sources of non-verbal behaviour The main practical issue is whether the diagnostic value of non-verbal behaviour is improved more by knowledge of species-wide or universal expressions or of cultural-specific (or contextually influenced) behavioural displays. Progress on these issues will depend both on more complex and dynamic theoretical frameworks and on empirical research that is sensitive to the interplay among these possible sources for behaviour. This issue is pervasive in social science. It is raised with regard to many other aspects of social behaviour and interpersonal or intergroup interactions. (See, for example, Pickering, 2001, for an insightful treatment of the issue in research on stereotyping.)

In addition to further experimental work and replication of results, one direction for future research may be to study, in greater detail, the accomplishments and strategies of performers and interpreters of non-verbal behaviour. For example, when considering non-verbal behaviour as skilled performance, aspects of style, expertise, and expression are stressed. The ways in which such crafted performances are accomplished and their effects assessed should aid in the training and development processes as well as in directing future experimental research. However, regardless of the specific approach, non-verbal behaviour must be examined rigorously by a variety of laboratory and field perspectives, such as those discussed in this chapter. Understanding is furthered and applications become possible when attempts are made to synthesise results obtained from the use of a variety of methods and frameworks. The achievements so far hold promise for significant progress in basic and applied research on this important form of communication.

REFERENCES

Addington, D. W. (1971). The effect of vocal variation on ratings of source credibility. *Speech Monographs*, **35**, 242–247.

Akehurst, L., Kohnken, G., Vrij, A. & Bull, R. (1996). Lay persons' and police officers' beliefs regarding deceptive behaviour. *Applied Cognitive Psychology*, **10**, 461–471.

Allport, G. (1961). *Pattern and growth in personality*. New York: Holt, Rinehart & Winston.

Al-Simadi, A. A. (2000). Jordanian students' beliefs about nonverbal behaviors associated with deception in Jordan. *Social Behavior and Personality*, **28**, 437–442.

Ambady, N. & Rosenthal, R. (1992). Thin slices of expressive behavior as predictors of interpersonal consequences: a meta-analysis. *Psychological Bulletin*, **111**, 256–274.

Anderson, D. E., DePaulo, B. M., Ansfield, M. E., Tickle, J. J. & Green, E. (1999). Beliefs about cues to deception: mindless stereotypes or untapped wisdom? *Journal of Nonverbal Behavior*, **23**, 67–89.

Anolli, L. & Ciceri, R. (1997). The voice of deception: vocal strategies of naïve and able liars. *Journal of Nonverbal Behavior*, **21**, 259–284.

Argyle, M. (1967). *The psychology of interpersonal behaviour*. London: Penguin.

Argyle, M. (1986). Rules for social relationships in four cultures. *Australian Journal of Psychology*, **38**, 309–318.

Argyle, M. & Dean, J. (1965). Eye-contact, distance and affiliation. *Sociometry*, **28**, 289–304.

Argyle, M. & Kendon, A. (1967). The experimental analysis of social performance. In L. Berkowitz (Ed.), *Advances in experimental social psychology*. New York: Academic Press.

Argyle, M. & Cook, M. (1976). *Gaze and mutual gaze*. New York: Cambridge University Press.

Aristotle (1927). *Poetics*. London: W. Heinemann.

Aristotle (1991). *The art of rhetoric*. London: Penguin.

Aronson, H. & Weintraub, W. (1972). Personal adaptation as reflected in verbal behaviour. In A. W. Siegman & H. Pope (Eds), *Studies in dyadic communication*. New York: Pergamon.

Babad, E., Avni-Babad, D. & Rosenthal, R. (2003). Teachers' brief nonverbal behaviors in defined instructional situations can predict students' evaluations. *Journal of Educational Psychology*, **95**, 553–562.

Bacon, F. (1884). *The essays*. Boston, MA: Lee and Shepard.

Bacon, F. (1947). *The new Atlantis*. New York: Russell F. Moore.

Badler, N. I. & Smoliar, W. W. (1979). Digital representation of human movement. *Computing Surveys*, **11**, 19–38.

Badler, N. I., Barsky, B. A. & Zeltzer, D. (1991). *Making the move: mechanics, control, and animation of articulated figure*. San Mateo, CA: Morgan Kaufman.

Badler, N. I., Phillips, C. B. & Webber, B. L. (1993). *Simulating humans: computer graphics animation and control*. New York: Oxford University Press.

Bailey, W., Nowicki, S. Jr & Cole, S. P. (1998). The ability to decode nonverbal information in African American, African and Afro-Caribbean, and European American adults. *Journal of Black Psychology*, **24**, 418–431.

Bartlett, F. (1958). *Thinking: an experimental and social study*. New York: Basic Books.

Baumeister, R. (1982). A self-presentational view of social phenomena. *Psychological Bulletin*, **91**, 3–26.

Baxter, J. C. (1970). Interpersonal spacing in natural settings. *Sociometry*, **33**, 444–456.

Baxter, J. C. & Rozelle, R. M. (1975). Non-verbal expression as a function of crowding during a simulated police–citizen encounter. *Journal of Personality and Social Psychology*, **32**, 40–54.

Bilodeau, E. (Ed.) (1966). *Acquisition of skill*. New York: Academic Press.

Birdwhistell, R. (1970). *Kinesics and context*. Philadelphia: University of Pennsylvania Press.

Bond, C., Omar, A., Mahmoud, A. & Bonser, R. (1990). Lie detection across cultures. *Journal of Nonverbal Behavior*, **14**, 189–204.

Bulwer, J. (1644/1974). *Chirologia*. Carbondale, IL: Southern Illinois University Press.

Burgoon, J. K. & Bacue, A. E. (2003). Nonverbal communication skills. In J. O. Greene & B. R. Burleson (Eds), *Handbook of communication and social interaction skills* (pp. 179–219). Mahwah, NJ: Lawrence Erlbaum.

Carton, J. S., Kessler, E. A. & Pape, C. L. (1999). Nonverbal decoding skills and relationship well-being in adults. *Journal of Nonverbal Behavior*, **23**, 91–100.

Choi, I. & Nisbett, R. E. (1998). Situational salience and cultural differences in the correspondence bias and actor–observer bias. *Personality and Social Psychology Bulletin*, **24**, 949–960.

Cody, M., Lee, W. & Chao, E. (1989). Telling lies: correlates of deception among Chinese. In J. Forgas & J. Innes (Eds), *Recent advances in social psychology: an international perspective*. New York: McGraw-Hill.

Cole, P. (1984). Display rules and the socialisation of affect displays. In G. Ziven (Ed.), *The development of expressive behaviour: biology–environment interactions*. New York: Academic Press.

Collett, P. (1971). Training Englishmen in the nonverbal behaviour of Arabs. *International Journal of Psychology*, **6**, 209–215.

Costanzo, M. (1992). Training students to decode verbal and nonverbal cues: effects on confidence and performance. *Journal of Educational Psychology*, **84**, 308–313.

Crittenden, K. S. & Bae, H. (1994). Self effacement and social responsibility: attribution as impression management in Asian cultures. *American Behavioral Psychology*, **37**, 653–671.

D'Agostino, P. R. & Fincher-Kiefer, R. (1992). Need for cognition and the correspondence bias. *Social Cognition*, **10**, 151–163.

Darwin, C. (1872). *The expression of emotion in man and animals*. London: John Murray.

Davis, M. (1984). Nonverbal behaviour and psychotherapy: process research. In H. Wolfgang (Ed.), *Nonverbal behaviour: perspectives, applications, intercultural insights* (pp. 203–229). New York: C. J. Hogrefe.

DePaulo, B. (1992). Nonverbal behavior as self-presentation. *Psychological Bulletin*, **111**, 203–243.

DePaulo, B. M., Zuckerman, M. & Rosenthal, R. (1980). Detecting deception: modality effects. In L. Wheeler (Ed.), *Review of personality and social psychology* (vol. 1). Beverly Hills, CA: Sage.

DePaulo, B. M., Stone, J. I. & Lassiter, G. D. (1985). Deceiving and detecting deceit. In B. R Schlenker (Ed.), *The self in social life*. New York: McGraw-Hill.

DePaulo, B. M., Wetzel, C., Sternglanz, R. & Wilson, M. J. (2003). Verbal and nonverbal dynamics of privacy, secrecy, and deceit. *Journal of Social Issues*, **59**, 391–410.

DePaulo, B. M., Lindsay, J. L., Malone, B. E., Muhlenbruck, L., Charlton, K. & Cooper, H. (2003). Cues to deception. *Psychological Bulletin*, **129**, 74–118.

Deutsch, F. (1959). Correlations of verbal and nonverbal communication in interviews elicited by associative anamnesis. *Psychosomatic Medicine*, *21*, 123–130.

Dittmann, A. T. (1972). *Interpersonal messages of emotion*. New York: Springer.

Dittmann, A. T. (1978). The role of body movement in communication. In A. W. Siegman & S. Feldstein (Eds), *Nonverbal behaviour and communication*. Hillsdale, NJ: Lawrence Erlbaum.

Dorsey, M. A. & Meisels, M. (1969). Personal space and self-protection. *Journal of Personality and Social Psychology*, *11*, 93–97.

Druckman, D. & Bjork, R A. (Eds) (1991). *In the mind's eye: enhancing human performance*. Washington, DC: National Academy Press.

Druckman, D. & Hyman, R. (1991). Hiding and detecting deception. In D. Druckman & R. A. Bjork (Eds), *In the mind's eye: enhancing human performance* (Ch. 9). Washington, DC: National Academy Press.

Druckman, D., Rozelle, R. & Baxter, J. (1982). *Nonverbal communication: survey, theory, and research*. Beverly Hills, CA: Sage.

Druckman, D., Karis, D. & Donchin, E. (1983). Information-processing in bargaining: reactions to an opponent's shift in concession strategy. In R. Tietz (Ed.), *Aspiration levels in bargaining and economic decision-making*. Berlin: Springer-Verlag.

Duncan, S. D. (1972). Some signals and rules for taking speaking turns in conversation. *Journal of Personality and Social Psychology*, *23*, 283–292.

Duncan, S. D. (1983). Speaking turns: studies in structure and individual differences. In J. M. Wiemann & R. P. Harrison (Eds), *Nonverbal interaction*. Beverly Hills, CA: Sage.

Duncan, S. D. & Fiske, D. W. (1977). *Face to face interaction: research, methods, and theory*. Hillsdale, NJ: Lawrence Erlbaum.

Ekman, P. (1992a). Facial expression of emotions: new findings, new questions. *Psychological Science*, *3*, 34–38.

Ekman, P. (1992b). Are there basic emotions? *Psychological Review*, *99*, 550–553.

Ekman, P. (1993). Facial expression and emotion. *American Psychologist*, *48*, 384–392.

Ekman, P. (1994). Strong evidence for universals in facial expressions: a reply to Russell's mistaken critique. *Psychological Bulletin*, *115*, 268–287.

Ekman, P. & Friesen, W. V. (1969). The repertoire of nonverbal behavior: categories, origins, usage, and coding. *Semiotica*, *1*, 49–98.

Ekman, P. & Friesen, W. V. (1974). Detecting deception from the body or face. *Journal of Personality and Social Psychology*, *39*, 228–298.

Ekman, P. & Friesen, W. V. (1975). *Unmasking the face: a guide to recognizing emotions from facial clues*. Englewood Cliffs, NJ: Prentice-Hall.

Ekman, P. & Oster, H. (1979). Facial expression of emotion. In M. Rosenzweig (Ed.), *Annual review of psychology* (pp. 527–554). Stanford, CA: Annual Reviews, Inc.

Ekman, P. & O'Sullivan, M. (1988). The role of context on interpreting facial expressions: comment on Russell & Fahr (1987). *Journal of Experimental Psychology: General*, *117*, 86–88.

Ekman, P. & O'Sullivan, M. (1991). Who can catch a liar? *American Psychology*, *46*, 913–920.

Ekman, P., Friesen, W. V. & Ancoli, S. (1980). Facial signs of emotional experience. *Journal of Personality and Social Psychology*, **39**, 1125–1134.

Ekman, P., Friesen, W. V. & Bear, J. (1984). The international language of gestures. *Psychology Today*, **May**, 64–69.

Ekman, P., Davidson, R. & Friesen, W. (1990). The Duchenne smile: emotional expression and brain physiology. *Journal of Personality and Social Psychology*, **58**, 342–353.

Ekman, P., O'Sullivan, M. & Frank, M. G. (1999). A few can catch a liar. *Psychological Science*, **10**, 263–266.

Ekman, P., O'Sullivan, M., Friesen, W. & Scherer, K. (1991). Face, voice, and body in detecting deception. *Journal of Nonverbal Behaviour*, **15**, 125–135.

Elfenbein, H. A. & Ambady, N. (2002a). Is there an in-group advantage in emotion recognition? *Psychological Bulletin*, **128**, 243–249.

Elfenbein, H. A. & Ambady, N. (2002b). On the universality and cultural specificity of emotion recognition: a meta-analysis. *Psychological Bulletin*, **128**, 203–235.

Elfenbein, H. A. & Ambady, N. (2003). When familiarity breeds accuracy: cultural exposure and facial emotion recognition. *Journal of Personality and Social Psychology*, **85**, 276–290.

Eskritt, M. & Lee, K. (2003). Do actions speak louder than words? Preschool children's use of the verbal-nonverbal consistency principle during inconsistent communications. *Journal of Nonverbal Behavior*, **27**, 25–41.

Exline, R. V. & Eldridge, C. (1967). Effects of two patterns of a speaker's visual behavior upon the perception of the authenticity of his verbal message. Paper presented at the meeting of the Eastern Psychological Association, Boston, MA.

Faure, G. O. (1993). Negotiation concepts across cultures: implementing non-verbal tools. *Negotiation Journal*, **9**, 355–359.

Feldman, R. S., Tomasian, J. C. & Coats, E. J. (1999). Nonverbal deception abilities and adolescents' social competence: adolescents with higher social skills are better liars. *Journal of Nonverbal Behavior*, **23**, 237–249.

Feldman, S. (1959). *Mannerisms of speech and gestures in everyday life*. New York: International Universities Press.

Fiedler, K. & Walka, I. (1993). Training lie detectors to use nonverbal cues instead of global heuristics. *Human Communication Research*, **20**, 199–223.

Forbes, R. J. & Jackson, P. R. (1980). Nonverbal behaviour and the outcome of selection interviews. *Journal of Occupational Psychology*, **53**, 65–72.

Frank, M. G. & Ekman, P. (1997). The ability to detect deceit generalizes across different types of high-stake lies. *Journal of Personality and Social Psychology*, **72**, 1429–1439.

Frank, M. G. & Ekman, P. (2004). Appearing truthful generalizes across different deception situations. *Journal of Personality and Social Psychology*, **86**, 486–495.

Frank, M. G., Paolantonio, N., Feeley, T. H. & Servoss, T. J. (2004). Individual and small group accuracy in judging truthful and deceptive communication. *Group Decision and Negotiation*, **13**, 45–59.

Frank, R. S. (1977). Nonverbal and paralinguistic analysis of political behaviour: the first McGovern–Humphrey California primary debate. In M. G. Hermann (Ed.), *A psychological examination of political leaders*. New York: Wiley.

Freedman, R. (1972). The analysis of movement behaviour during the clinical interview. In A. W. Siegman & B. Pope (Eds), *Studies in dyadic communication*. New York: Pergamon Press.

Fretz, B. R. & Stang, D. J. (1982). *Preparing for graduate study in psychology: not for seniors only!* Washington, DC: American Psychological Association.

Freud, S. (1905/1938). Psychopathology of everyday life. In A. A. Brill (Ed.), *The basic writings of Sigmund Freud*. New York: Random House.

Freud, S. (1924). *A general introduction to psychoanalysis*. Garden City, NJ: Doubleday.

Friedman, H. (1979). The concept of skill in non-verbal communication: implications for understanding social interaction. In R Rosenthal (Ed.), *Skill in nonverbal communication: individual differences*. Cambridge, MA: Oelgeschlager, Gunn & Hain.

Fuller, B. F., Horii, Y. & Conner, D. A. (1992). Validity and reliability of nonverbal voice measures as indicators of stressor-provoked anxiety. *Research in Nursing and Health*, *15*, 379–389.

Garratt, G., Baxter, J. C. & Rozelle, R. (1981). Training university police in black-American nonverbal behaviours: an application to police–community relations. *Journal of Social Psychology*, *113*, 217–229.

Gehricke, J. & Shapiro, D. (2000). Reduced facial expression and social context in major depression: discrepancies between facial muscle activity and self-reported emotion. *Psychiatry Research*, *21*, 157–167.

Gentner, O. & Grudin, J. (1985). The evolution of mental metaphors in psychology: a 90-year perspective. *American Psychologist*, *40*, 181–192.

Gibbs, R. (1994). *The poetics of mind*. New York: Cambridge University Press.

Gibson, J. J. (1979). *The ecological approach to visual perception*. Boston, MA: Houghton Mifflin.

Glashow, S. (1980). Toward a unified theory: threads in a tapestry. *Science*, *210*, 1319–1323.

Goffman, E. (1959). *The presentation of self in everyday life*. Garden City, NJ: Doubleday Anchor Books.

Goffman, E. (1969). *Strategic interaction*. Philadelphia: University of Pennsylvania Press.

Goffman, E. (1971). *Relations in public*. New York: Basic Books.

Gordon, R. A., Baxter, J., Rozelle, R. & Druckman, D. (1987). Expectations of honest, evasive, and deceptive nonverbal behavior. *Journal of Social Psychology*, *127*, 231–233.

Hall, E. T. (1959). *The silent language*. New York: Doubleday.

Hall, E. T. (1966). *The hidden dimension*. New York: Doubleday.

Hargie, O. & Dickson, O. (2004). *Skilled interpersonal communication: research, theory and practice*. London: Routledge.

Hargie, O., Saunders, C. & Dickson, O. (1981). *Social skills in interpersonal communication*. London: Croom Helm.

Harper, R. G., Weins, A. N. & Matarazzo, J. O. (1978). *Non-verbal communication: the state of the art*. New York: Wiley.

Hemsley, G. O. & Doob, A. N. (1975). Effect of looking behavior on perceptions of a communicator's credibility. Paper presented at the meeting of the American Psychological Association, Chicago, IL.

Hermann, M. G. (1977). Verbal behaviour of negotiators in periods of high and low stress. In M. G. Hermann (Ed.), *A psychological examination of political leaders*. New York: Free Press.

Hermann, M. G. (1979). Indicators of stress in policymakers during foreign policy crises. *Political Psychology, 1*, 27–46.

Hollandsworth, J. G. Jr, Kazelskis, R., Stevens, J. et al. (1979). Relative contributions of verbal, articulative, and nonverbal communication to employment decisions in the job interview setting. *Personnel Psychology, 32*, 359–367.

Hyman, R. (1989). The psychology of deception. In M. Rosenzweig & L. Porter (Eds), *Annual Review of Psychology, 40*, 133–154.

Hyman, R. & Druckman, O. (1991). A broader concept of deception. In D. Druckman & R. A. Bjork (Eds), *In the mind's eye: enhancing human performance* (Ch. 10). Washington, DC: National Academy Press.

Izard, C. (1971). *The face of emotion*. New York: Appleton-Century-Crofts.

Jones, A. P., Rozelle, R. M. & Svyantek, D. J. (1985). Organizational climate: an environmental affordances approach. An unpublished manuscript from the University of Houston, Houston, TX.

Jones, E. E. & Nisbett, R. E. (1972). The actor and the observer: divergent perceptions of the causes of behaviour. In E. E. Jones, O. E. Kanouse, H. H. Kelly et al. (Eds), *Attribution: perceiving the causes of behaviour*. Morristown, NJ: General Learning Press.

Jones, E. E. & Pittman, T. S. (1982). Toward a general theory of strategic self-presentation. In J. Suls (Ed.), *Psychological perspectives on the self* (vol. 1, pp. 231–262). Hillsdale, NJ: Lawrence Erlbaum.

Kappesser, J. & Williams, A. C. (2002). Pain and negative emotions in the face: judgements by health care professionals. *Pain, 99*, 197–206.

Karis, D., Druckman, D., Lissak, R. et al. (1984). A psychophysiological analysis of bargaining: ERPs and facial expressions. In R. Karrer, J. Cohen & P. Tueting (Eds), *Brain and information: event-related potentials*. Vol. 425, Annals of the New York Academy of Sciences, New York.

Kasl, S. V. & Mahl, G. F. (1965). The relationships of disturbances and hesitations in spontaneous speech to anxiety. *Journal of Personality and Social Psychology, 1*, 425–433.

Keenan, A. (1976). Effects of nonverbal behaviour of interviewers on candidates' performance. *Journal of Occupational Psychology, 49*, 171–176.

Kendon, A. (1981). The study of gesture: some observations on its history. In J. N. Deely & M. D. Lenhart (Eds), *Semiotics*. New York: Plenum.

Klopf, D. W., Thompson, C. A., Ishii, S. & Sallinen-Kuparinen, A. (1991). Nonverbal immediacy differences among Japanese, Finnish, and American university students. *Perceptual and Motor Skills, 73*, 209–210.

Knapp, M. L. (1972). *Nonverbal communication in human interaction*. New York: Holt, Rinehart & Winston.

Knapp, M. L. (1984). The study of nonverbal behaviour vis-à-vis human communication theory. In A. Wolfgang (Ed.), *Nonverbal behaviour: perspective, application, intercultural insights*. New York: C. J. Hogrefe.

Koestler, A. (1964). *The act of creation*. London: Hutchinson.

Kraut, R. E. (1980). Humans as lie detectors: some second thoughts. *Journal of Communication, 30*, 209–216.

Krull, D. S., Loy, M. H., Lin, J., Wang, C., Chen, S. & Zhao, X. (1999). The fundamental fundamental attribution error: correspondence bias in individualist and collectivist cultures. *Personality and Social Psychology Bulletin, 25*, 1208–1219.

LaFrance, M. & Mayo, C. (1978). *Moving bodies: nonverbal communication in social relationships*. Monterey, CA: Brooks Cole.

Lakoff, G. (1993). The contemporary theory of metaphor. In A. Ortony (Ed.), *Metaphor and thought*, 2nd edn. New York: Cambridge University Press.

Lavater, J. (1789). *Essays on physiognomy* (vol. 1). London: John Murray.

Leary, D. E. (1990). *Metaphors in the history of psychology*. New York: Cambridge University Press.

Levine, S. P. & Feldman, R. S. (1997). Self-presentational goals, self-monitoring, and nonverbal behavior. *Basic and Applied Social Psychology, 19*, 505–518.

MacKay, D. M. (1972). Formal analysis of communicative processes. In R. A. Hinde (Ed.), *Non-verbal communication*. Cambridge, MA: Cambridge University Press.

Mann, S., Vrij, A. & Bull, R. (2004). Detecting true lies: police officers' ability to detect suspects' lies. *Journal of Applied Psychology, 89*, 137–149.

Manning, P. (Ed.) (1965). *Office design: a study of environment*. Liverpool: Rockliff.

March, R. M. (1988). *The Japanese negotiator: subtlety and strategy beyond western logic*. Tokyo: Kodansha International.

Marsh, A. A., Elfenbein, H. A. & Ambady, N. (2003). Nonverbal 'accents': cultural differences in facial expressions of emotion. *Psychological Science, 14*, 373–376.

Masuda, T. & Kitayama, S. (2004). Perceiver induced constraint and attitude attribution in Japan and the US: a case for the cultural dependence of the correspondence bias. *Journal of Experimental Social Psychology, 40*, 409–416.

Matsumoto, D. (1996). *Culture and psychology*. Pacific Grove, CA: Brooks Cole.

Matsumoto, D. (2002). Methodological requirements to test a possible in-group advantage in judging emotions across cultures: comment on Elfennbein and Ambady (2002) and evidence. *Psychological Bulletin, 128*, 236–242.

McArthur, L. Z. & Baron, R. M. (1983). Toward an ecological theory of social perception. *Psychological Review, 90*, 215–238.

McClintock, C. C. & Hunt, R. G. (1975). Nonverbal indicators of affect and deception. *Journal of Applied Social Psychology, 1*, 54–67.

McCroskey, J. C., Richmond, V. P., Sallinen, A. & Fayer, J. M. (1995). A cross-cultural and multi-behavioral analysis of the relationship between nonverbal immediacy and teacher evaluation. *Communication Education, 44*, 281–291.

McCroskey, J. C., Sallinen, A., Fayer, J. M. & Richmond, V. P. (1996). Nonverbal immediacy and cognitive learning: a cross-cultural investigation. *Communication Education, 45*, 200–211.

McLeod, P. L. & Rosenthal, R. (1983). Micromomentary movement and the decoding of face and body cues. *Journal of Nonverbal Behavior, 8*, 83–90.

Mehrabian, A. (1968). Relationship of attitude to seated posture, orientation and distance. *Journal of Personality and Social Psychology, 10*, 26–30.

Mehrabian, A. (1971). Nonverbal betrayal of feeling. *Journal of Experimental Research in Personality, 5*, 64–73.

Mehrabian, A. (1972). *Nonverbal communication*. Chicago: Aldine.

Mehrabian, A. & Ksionzky, S. (1972). Categories of social behaviour. *Comparative Group Studies, 3*, 425–436.

Mikolic, J. M., Parker, J. C. & Pruitt, D. G. (1994). Escalation in response to persistent annoyance: groups vs. individuals and gender effects. Unpublished manuscript from the State University of New York, Buffalo, NY.

Montepare, J. M. (2003). Evolution and nonverbal behavior: adaptive social perceptions. *Journal of Nonverbal Behavior, 27,* 61–64.

O'Hair, D., Cody, M. J., Wang, X. & Yi Chan, E. (1989). Vocal stress and deception detection among Chinese. Paper presented at the annual meeting of the Western Speech Communication Association, Spokane, WA.

Ortony, A. (1993). *Metaphor and thought,* 2nd edn. New York: Cambridge University Press.

Patterson, M. L. (1983). *Nonverbal behaviour: a functional perspective.* New York: Springer.

Patterson, M. L. (1988). Functions of nonverbal behavior in close relationships. In S. Duck (Ed.), *Handbook of personal relationships: theory, research and interventions.* New York: Wiley.

Patterson, M. L. (1995). A parallel process model of nonverbal communication. *Journal of Nonverbal Behavior, 19,* 3–29.

Patterson, M. L. (1998). Parallel processes in nonverbal communication. In M. T. Palmer & G. A. Barnett (Eds), *Progress in Communication Sciences* (vol. 14, pp. 1–18). Stamford, CT: Ablex.

Patterson, M. L. (2001). Toward a comprehensive model of non-verbal communication. In W. P. Robinson & H. Giles (Eds), *The new handbook of language and social psychology.* Chichester: Wiley.

Patterson, M. L. (2003). Evolution and nonverbal behavior: functions and mediating processes. *Journal of Nonverbal Behavior, 27,* 201–207.

Payrato, L. (1993). A pragmatic view on autonomous gestures: a first repertoire of Catalan emblems. *Journal of Pragmatics, 20,* 193–216.

Perls, F. S. (1969). *Gestalt therapy verbatim.* Lafayette, CA: Real People Press.

Pickering, M. (2001). *Stereotyping: The politics of representation.* New York: Palgrave.

Polanyi, M. (1958). *Personal knowledge.* London: Routledge & Kegan Paul.

Poortinga, Y. H., Schoots, N. H. & Van de Koppel, J. M. (1993). The understanding of Chinese and Kurdish emblematic gestures by Dutch subjects. *International Journal of Psychology, 28,* 31–44.

Poyatos, F. (1983). *New perspectives in nonverbal communication.* New York: Pergamon.

Rapoport, A. (1982). *The meaning of the built environment: a nonverbal communication approach.* Beverly Hills, CA: Sage.

Richmond, V. P. & McCroskey, J. C. (2000). The impact of supervisor and subordinate immediacy on relational and organizational outcomes. *Communication Monographs, 67,* 85–95.

Rocca, K. A. & McCroskey, J. C. (1999). The interrelationship of student ratings of instructors' immediacy, verbal aggressiveness, homophily, and interpersonal attraction. *Communication Education, 48,* 308–316.

Rogers, C. R. (1961). *On becoming a person: A therapist's view of psychotherapy.* Boston, MA: Houghton Mifflin.

Rosenthal, R. (Ed.) (1979). *Skill in nonverbal communication: individual differences.* Cambridge, MA: Oelgeschlager, Gunn & Hain.

Ross, L. & Nisbett, R. (1991). *The person and the situation.* New York: McGraw-Hill.

Rozelle, R. M. & Baxter, J. C. (1975). Impression formation and danger recognition in experienced police officers. *Journal of Social Psychology*, *96*, 53–63.

Safadi, M. & Valentine, C. A. (1988). Emblematic gestures among Hebrew speakers in Israel. *International Journal of Intercultural Relations*, *12*, 327–361.

Schafer, R. (1980). Narration in psychoanalytic dialogue. *Critical Inquiry*, *7*, 29–53.

Scheflen, A. E. & Scheflen, A. (1972). *Body language and social order*. Englewood Cliffs, NJ: Prentice-Hall.

Scheibe, K. (1979). *Mirrors, masks, lies, and secrets*. New York: Praeger.

Schlenker, B. (1980). *Impression management*. Monterey, CA: Brooks Cole.

Snyder, M. (1974). Self-monitoring of expressive behaviour. *Journal of Personality and Social Psychology*, *30*, 526–537.

Soyland, A. (1994). *Psychology as metaphor*. Thousand Oaks, CA: Sage.

Spiegel, J. & Machotka, P. (1974). *Messages of the body*. New York: Free Press.

Taylor, E. G. (1878). *Research into the early history of mankind*. London: John Murray.

Tessler, R. & Sushelsky, L. (1978). Effects of eye contact and social status on the perception of a job applicant in an employment interviewing situation. *Journal of Vocational Behaviour*, *13*, 338–347.

Thompson, D. & Baxter, J. (1973). Interpersonal spacing of two person cross cultural interactions. *Man-Environment Systems*, *3*, 115–117.

Thweatt, K. S. & McCroskey, J. C. (1998). The impact of teacher immediacy and misbehaviors on teacher credibility. *Communication Education*, *47*, 348–358.

Tomkins, S. (1962). *Affect, imagery, and consciousness: the positive affects* (vol. 1). New York: Springer.

Tomkins, S. (1963). *Affect, imagery and consciousness: the negative affects* (vol. 2). New York: Springer.

Triandis, H. C. (1994). *Culture and social behavior*. New York: McGraw-Hill.

Vrij, A. (2000). *Detecting lies and deceit: the psychology of lying and the implications for professional practice*. Chichester: Wiley.

Vrij, A. & Winkel, F. W. (1991). Cultural patterns in Dutch and Surinam nonverbal behavior: an analysis of simulated police/citizen encounters. *Journal of Nonverbal Behavior*, *15*, 169–184.

Vrij, A. & Semin, G. R. (1996). Lie experts' beliefs about nonverbal indicators of deception. *Journal of Nonverbal Behavior*, *20*, 65–80.

Vrij, A. & Mann, S. (2004). Detecting deception: the benefit of looking at a combination of behavioral, auditory, and speech content related cues in a systematic manner. *Group Decision and Negotiation*, *13*, 61–79.

Vrij, A., Akehurst, L. & Morris, P. (1997). Individual differences in hand movements during deception. *Journal of Nonverbal Behavior*, *21*, 87 102.

Vrij, A., Edward, K. & Bull, R. (2001). Stereotypical verbal and nonverbal responses while deceiving others. *Personality and Social Psychology Bulletin*, *27*, 899–909.

Vrij, A., Edward, K., Roberts, K. P. & Bull, R. (2000). Detecting deceit via the analysis of verbal and nonverbal behavior. *Journal of Nonverbal Behavior*, *24*, 239–263.

Vrij, A., Akehurst, L., Soukara, S. & Bull, R. (2004). Detecting deceit via analyses of verbal and nonverbal behavior in children and adults. *Human Communication Research*, *30*, 8–41.

Vrij, A., Evans, H., Akehurst, L. & Mann, S. (2004). Rapid judgements in assessing verbal and nonverbal cues: their potential for deception researchers and lie detection. *Applied Cognitive Psychology, 18*, 283–296.

Washburn, P. V. & Hakel, M. D. (1973). Visual cues and verbal content as influences on impressions formed after simulated employment interviews. *Journal of Applied Psychology, 58*, 137–141.

Watson, D. (1982). The actor and the observer: how are their perceptions of causality divergent? *Psychological Bulletin, 92*, 682–700.

Watson, O. M. (1970). *Proxemic behavior: a cross-cultural study.* The Hague: Mouton.

Watson, O. M. & Graves, T. D. (1966). Quantitative research in proxemic behavior. *American Anthropologist, 68*, 971–985.

Weiner, M., Devoe, S., Runbinow, S. & Geller, J. (1972). Nonverbal behaviour and nonverbal communication. *Psychological Review, 79*, 185–214.

Willems, E. P. (1985). Behavioral ecology as a perspective for research in psychology research. In C. W. Deckner (Ed.), *Methodological perspectives in behavioral research.* Baltimore, MD: University Park Press.

Williams, A. C. de C. (2002). Facial expression of pain: an evolutionary account. *Behavioral and Brain Sciences, 25*, 439–488.

Williams, L. M., Senior, C., David, A. S., Loughland, C. M. & Gordon, E. (2001). In search of the 'Duchenne smile': evidence from eye movements. *Journal of Psychophysiology, 15*, 122–127.

Willis, F. N. (1966). Initial speaking distance as a function of speakers' relationship. *Psychonomic Science, 5*, 221–222.

Winkel, F. W. & Vrij, A. (1990). Interaction and impression formation in a cross-cultural dyad: frequency and meaning of culturally-determined gaze behavior in a police interview setting. *Social Behavior, 5*, 335–350.

Wolfgang, A. & Bhardway, A. (1984). 100 years of nonverbal study. In A. Wolfgang (Ed.), *Non-verbal behaviour: perspectives, applications, intercultural insights.* New York: C. J. Hogrefe.

Woodworth, R. & Schlosberg, H. (1954). *Experimental psychology.* New York: Holt, Rinehart & Winston.

Yi Chao, E. (1987). Correlates and deceit: a cross-cultural examination. Unpublished Ph.D. thesis from the University of Southern California.

Young, D. M. & Beier, E. G. (1977). The role of applicant nonverbal communication in the employment interview. *Journal of Employment Counseling, 14*, 154–165.

Zajonc, R. B. (1980). Feeling and thinking: preferences need no inferences. *American Psychologist, 35*, 151–175.

Zebrowitz, L. A. (2003). Commentary: overgeneralization effects in perceiving non-verbal behavior. *Journal of Nonverbal Behavior, 27*, 133–136.

Zebrowitz, L. A. & Collins, M. A. (1997). Accurate social perception at zero acquaintance: the affordances of a Gibsonian approach. *Personality and Social Psychology Bulletin, 1*, 204–233.

Zuckerman, M., Koestner, R. & Driver, R. (1981). Beliefs about cues associated with deception. *Journal of Nonverbal Behavior, 6*, 105–114.

Chapter 4

Questioning

David Dickson and Owen Hargie

QUESTION ASKING AND ANSWERING is one of the most prevalent and readily identifiable features of talk. Accordingly, Fritzley and Lee (2003, p. 1297) described questioning as a 'major form of speech act in interpersonal communication', while Stenstroem (1988, p. 304), in similar vein, reflected, 'It is difficult to imagine a conversation without questions and responses.' Being prosaic, however, should not be mistaken for being trivial. While at a surface level questioning seems to be a straightforward feature of communication, deeper analysis, at functional, structural, and textual levels, reveals questioning to be a complex and multifaceted phenomenon, as we shall illustrate in this chapter. Questions are principal moving parts in the engine of social interaction. Hence, the skilful use of questions is a potent device for initiating, sustaining, and directing conversation. For Hawkins and Power (1999, p. 235), 'To ask a question is to apply one of the most powerful tools in communication.' Questions are prominently positioned in what transpires during many interpersonal encounters. They can take several forms, be one of a number of possible types, and serve a range of intended purposes (Dickson, 1987). While we typically think of questions as being posed verbally, there are also non-verbal options. For example, someone can be brought into play with a quizzical look. When using American Sign Language, Crystal (1997) explained how the act of asking a question can be signalled facially by, for instance, raising eyebrows and tilting the head slightly back. Questions, then, may be non-verbal signals urging another to respond, although in this chapter we will concentrate on those that take a verbal form.

As far as question type is concerned, there is no one commonly agreed typology according to which instances can be neatly categorised.

Some questions are blatantly interrogative (*'Where did you leave the key?'*), some declarative (*'You appreciate what this will mean?'*), while others take an imperative form (*'Tell me more?'*). Furthermore, questions can be classed, *inter alia*, as open, wh-questions, closed, tag, leading, or multiple. More will be said of these later. As far as purpose served in posing a question is concerned, getting information most readily springs to mind. Heritage (2002, p. 1427), for instance, highlighted this usage when he wrote, 'In its most elemental form, a "question" is a form of social action, designed to seek information and accomplished in a turn at talk by means of interrogative syntax.' But interrogative intent can also be signalled in other ways. *Prosodic questions* are 'declarative sentences containing question cues that may be intonational, or these utterances are marked as questions by means of a variety of contextual cues' (Woodbury 1984, p. 203). Furthermore, people ask questions to which they already have the detail requested (as when a prosecuting attorney asks the accused in court during cross-examination, *'Where did you go after leaving 26 Hope Street, that evening?'*). Some may even ask questions to which they know the respondent realises they already possess the answer (e.g. a teacher asks a pupil in class, *'What's the capital of Nigeria?'*). *Expressive questions* are framed, on the other hand, not to get information but, in an oblique way, to give it (e.g. a mother asks her wayward son, following another feeble excuse, *'Do you expect me to believe that?'*). Adler, Rosenfeld, and Proctor (2001) termed these *counterfeit questions* in that they are 'really disguised attempts to send a message, not receive one'.

So what, then, is a question? In broadest terms, a definition is offered by Stewart and Cash (2000, p. 79): 'A question is *any statement or nonverbal act that invites an answer.*' In this way, these authors tacitly acknowledged the conversational rule that, in being asked a question (and with the notable exception of those that are *rhetorical*), one is obligated to respond in some way, even if only to admit one's inability to provide the detail requested. Put another way, and from a conversation-analysis perspective, questions and answers comprise *adjacency pairs* (Schegloff, 1972) (see also Chapter 5). Various interactive sequences implemented through talk are structured in this 'paired' fashion, made up of two turns that are closely linked or 'go together'. As such, a question is a *first pair part*, with the corresponding answer a *second pair part*. Importantly, the relevance of turns that are second pair parts is conditional upon the preceding first pair part. This is not to say, of course, that a question, as a first pair part, only legitimises some specific response. Rather, conversation analysts recognise a relevance gradation encompassing response alternatives. A 'preferred' response is one that is most closely aligned to the substance of the question; a 'dispreferred' alternative is one that less closely complements what was asked. (For example, the reply, *'My sister's going to Africa'*, in reply to the question, *'Why is there so much poverty in Africa?'*, would be dispreferred; *'It's a legacy of colonial exploitation'* is the preferred option.) Preference here is not a psychological entity. It is not about what will please most, but is rather a feature of the structural arrangement of the conversational elements (Koshik, 2002). To align more fully the first reply in the above example, an explanation along the lines of the person's sister going to Africa to do voluntary work and help the poor would probably have to be offered. Even then, more elaborate repair work may be necessary to prevent the conversation from stalling. In this sense, dispreferred alternatives are often more structurally complex than their preferred counterparts.

QUESTIONS IN PROFESSIONAL SETTINGS

In addition to featuring prominently in casual conversation, questions play a significant role in institutional discourse, being 'an important factor in the work of many professionals' (Waterman, Blades & Spencer, 2001, p. 477). Investigations into the use of questions in contrasting professional contexts have been carried out over some considerable period of time. The earliest of these reflect an enduring interest in how teachers put questions to use. From ancient times, exceptional teachers such as Jesus and Socrates used questions to engage their listeners and promote understanding of their messages. As shown by Ralph (1999), the reason for this interest is that 'Educational researchers and practitioners virtually all agree that teachers' effective use of questioning promotes student learning' (p. 286). However, not all teachers use questioning skilfully. An early study conducted by Corey (1940) found that, on average, the teacher asked a question once every 72 seconds. Some 30 years later, Resnick (1972), working with teachers of 5–7-year-old pupils in south-east London, reported that 36% of all teacher remarks were questions. Furthermore, this figure increased to 59% when only extended interactions were analysed.

It is clear, from a review of similar studies by Dillon (1982), that most of the questions in class are posed by teachers rather than pupils. While the former ask about two questions per minute, the latter, as a group, only manage around two questions per hour, giving an average of one question per pupil per month. This statistic, however, is quite at odds with teachers' perceptions of classroom interaction. They used three times as many questions as they estimated and reckoned that pupils asked six times more questions than they actually did. It is not that children are generally loath to question, however. Tizard, Hughes, Carmichael, and Pinkerton (1983) reported, from an observational study, that 4-year-old girls at home ask about 24 questions on an average per hour, but only 1.4 in school. Furthermore, children quickly learn how to manipulate questions to functional advantage. Thus, Lehtovaara (2002) illustrated how, at age 4 years, the 'Why?' question accounted for 46% of all questions asked by a child. These were employed to organise a still unfamiliar world and served the purposes of obtaining information, maintaining conversation, and checking rights to do certain things. By age 7 years, the proportion of questions of the 'Why?' variety fell to 22%. By this stage, the child was using the 'Why?' question in an adult fashion, demonstrating a knowledge of conversational conventions and structures which was missing from the 4-year-old's usage. The functions that this question served at age 7 were to check rules or to make accusations.

In the classroom, fear of a negative reaction from classmates may be a factor in reluctance to ask questions (Dillon, 1988). Other inhibitors include a reluctance to interrupt the teacher's flow, a deficit in pupils' questioning skills, and difficulty in recognising their own knowledge deficit (Graesser & Person, 1994). Age of pupil is a further consideration here. Daly, Kreiser, and Roghaar (1994) found a significant negative correlation between the number of questions asked and age, in pupils aged 13–16 years. White males from higher-income groups who felt accepted by the teacher and enjoyed higher self-esteem also seemed less inhibited in asking questions. However, just encouraging pupils to ask more questions is not enough, as there is no relationship between volume of pupil questions and their comprehension of material (Rosenshine, Meister & Chapman, 1996). Rather, positive benefits accrue when pupils actively ask questions at the higher levels of Bloom's taxonomy (Graesser & Person, 1994). Bloom (1956) identified six cognitive levels as follows:

Level 1 – knowledge: recalling previously learned material
Level 2 – comprehension: demonstrating an understanding of the facts by organising, comparing, interpreting, giving descriptions, or stating main ideas
Level 3 – application: applying acquired knowledge to solve problems
Level 4 – analysis: making inferences, identifying causes, and finding evidence to support judgements
Level 5 – synthesis: combining elements in different patterns to formulate new solutions
Level 6 – evaluation: giving opinions and making judgements about the validity or quality of ideas.

Daly and Vangelisti (2003, p. 886), in reviewing the literature in this field, likewise underlined the importance of teachers encouraging pupils to ask questions at the higher levels of this taxonomy:

> Because of the low rate with which learners ask questions and the importance of questioning, scholars have spent a good deal of time trying to encourage learners to ask more and better questions. The results are impressive: They demonstrate that improvements in comprehension, learning, and memory of technical materials can be achieved by training students to ask good questions.

This issue of the cognitive demands made by teachers in requesting information will be returned to later in the chapter in relation to recall/process questions.

Imbalance between professional and service receiver in the deployment of questions is not confined to the classroom, as we shall see, turning to doctor–patient interaction. Thus, West (1983) revealed that of 773 questions featured in the 21 doctor–patient consultations sampled, only 68 (9%) were initiated by patients. Indeed, in a study cited by Sanchez (2001), doctors incredibly managed to ask, on average, one question per 4.6 seconds during consultations lasting little more than 2 minutes each. Patients may even be interrupted in order for a question to be asked. In one investigation, patients got little more than 18 seconds into a description of their symptoms before the physician butted in (Epstein, Campbell, Cohen-Cole, McWhinney & Smilkstein, 1993). Summing up this state of affairs, Street (2001, p. 543) noted: 'Research consistently shows that physicians tend to talk more, ask more questions, give more directives, make more recommendations, and interrupt more than do patients.'

While in some instances patients may ask fewer questions simply because they do not know what to enquire about (Cegala & Broz, 2003), their reticence is widely acknowledge to have relational roots, reflecting an imbalance in power and control (Thompson, 1998). As observed by Sacks (1995, p. 55), 'As long as one is in the position of doing the questions, then in part one has control of the conversation.' Female patients may be (or may have been) particularly disadvantaged in this respect. While there is some evidence, presented by Cline and McKenzie (1998), that women ask more questions generally and in consultations with doctors, these latter questions are more likely than those of male patients to be ignored or responded to in a minimal way by the medical practitioner. Gender differences apart, when the patients studied did ask questions, nearly half of these were marked by speech disturbances, according to West (1983), indicating discomfort at requesting information from the doctor. Directing questions is, therefore, one way of marking a status differential, reflecting dominance, and exercising conversational control. This is a tactic not lost on medical students, who, according to Wynn (1996), quickly learned how to handle patient-initiated questions – by adopting the strategy of asking unrelated doctor-initiated ones. In so doing, they held sway. Consistent with this analysis, when patients did ask a question, they often prefaced it with a phrase such as 'I was wondering' (Skelton & Hobbs, 1999). Doctors never used this expression with patients, although they did when telephoning colleagues. Adding such pre-remarks is one way, mentioned by Tracy (2002), of making a question more 'polite' and less potentially face threatening to the person addressed. Incidentally, patients who are more active participants in the interaction have been found to express higher levels of satisfaction and commitment to what was decided (Young & Klingle, 1996). More particularly, opportunity to ask questions was one of the key elements rated most highly by patients when receiving bad news from health workers (Hind, 1997).

In the field of pharmacy, Morrow, Hargie, Donnelly, and Woodman (1993) carried out an observational study of community pharmacist–patient consultations. Patients in that context asked on average 2.5 questions per consultation compared to an average of 4.1 for pharmacists, a much higher ratio, as we have seen, than in doctor–patient consultations. Interestingly, some patient questions were requests for clarification of information previously given by the doctor. It could be that they felt more at ease asking questions of the pharmacist than admitting a lack of understanding to the doctor. Alternatively, they may have had time to reflect on the consultation and think of questions they would have liked to have asked at that time. Morrow et al. (1993) argued that the public may also see pharmacies as readily and easily accessible, and hence pharmacists become 'approachable' professionals. Furthermore, since most clients pay for the services they receive from pharmacists at the point of delivery, they may feel more empowered to ask questions of them.

It is, therefore, in general terms, the person of higher status and in control who asks the questions. As such, questions tend to be posed by teachers in classrooms, doctors in surgeries, nurses on the ward, lawyers in court, detectives in interrogation rooms, and so on. The counsellor–client relationship is typically construed differently. Here, indeed, there is evidence that HIV-prevention counsellors may actually manage the conversation in such a way as to solicit client questions in order to create a pretext for giving information and offering advice (Kinnell, 2002).

Some counselling theorists have long cautioned against the excessive use of questioning on the part of counsellors. Egan (1998, p. 101) complained that 'Helpers often ask too many questions. When in doubt about what to say or do, novice or inept helpers tend to ask questions.' Indeed, it was once thought by Rogers (1951) that questioning clients was to be avoided lest it established the counsellor as controller of the interaction. The concern of such theorists has to do with the undesirability of directing clients rather than creating space for them to 'tell their story' as they see fit. Additionally, being subjected to a particular line of questioning may place one in a certain light: others can attribute unfavourable qualities, not from answers given but from the questions asked. According to Fiedler (1993, p. 362), 'The way in which a person is questioned may have a substantial effect on his or her credibility, regardless of what s/he actually says.' For example, witnesses being interviewed or candidates at selection interviews may be treated with varying levels of respect: more or less attention may be paid to a need for face work. As well as directly affecting the respondent's self-esteem and confidence, such treatment is likely to affect how that person is perceived and evaluated by a third party.

Questions have been shown to be an important skill for a wide range of other professionals, including, to name but a few, negotiators (Rackham, 2003), psychologists (Fritzley & Lee, 2003), salespersons (Shoemaker & Johlke, 2002), organisational consultants (Dillon, 2003), journalists (Clayman & Heritage, 2002), lawyers (Kebbell, Hatton & Johnson, 2004), and police officers (Davies, Westcott & Horan, 2000).

FUNCTIONS OF QUESTIONS

As mentioned already, and at its most basic, 'the essential function of a question is to elicit a verbal response from those to whom the question is addressed' (Hawkins & Power, 1999, p. 236). More specifically, questions serve a range of functions depending upon the context of the interaction, as outlined, for instance, by Dillon (1997), Stewart and Cash (2000), Koshik (2002), and Hargie and Dickson (2004). These include, most obviously, obtaining information, although giving information is a further possibility. Maintaining control of the encounter, as we have seen with doctors talking to patients, may be at the heart of a questioning sequence, while teachers can ask questions to arouse interest and curiosity concerning a topic of study. Assessing the extent of the respondent's knowledge and encouraging critical thought and evaluation might be additional objectives for other teacher questions. Quite often conversation with a stranger gets under way with the aid of a question where it serves to express initial interest in the respondent. Follow-on questions can indicate, furthermore, that that person's attitudes, feelings, and opinions matter, at least to the one taking the trouble to ask. Depending upon the type of question framed, respondents can be encouraged to become more fully involved in the interchange. To this end, counsellors, when they do use this technique, are often advised to make their questions open. As explained by Hill and O'Brien (1999, p. 109), 'When helpers use open questions, they do not want a specific answer from clients but instead want to encourage clients to explore whatever comes to mind.'

An additional reason for questioning, in professional circles, has to do with managing the interactive process: more particularly with controlling its pace. Rackham (2003) found that skilled negotiators demonstrated very significant differences from average negotiators on their amount of questioning. Questions were put to use controlling the focus and flow of the interaction. Placing an obligation upon the other party to answer questions denies them space for detailed perusal. At the same time, the skilled negotiator creates space for personal reflection on the current state of affairs. Finally, in such conflict situations, questions can act as an alternative to an overt statement of disagreement.

Moreover, it should be appreciated that the type of question asked influences the extent to which each of these various functions can be fulfilled.

TYPES OF QUESTION

Questions can be analysed on three main linguistic levels: *form* (literal level), *content* (semantic level), and *intent* (pragmatic level) (Ulijn & Verweij, 2000). Beyond this broad distinction, different systems for classifying questions have been formulated (e.g. Quirk, Greenbaum, Leech & Svartvik, 1985; Bull & Mayer, 1993; Bowling, 1997; Gnisci & Bonaiuto, 2003). Among the most common subtypes to be specified are questions that are open, closed, wh-questions, leading, tag, process, multiple, and probing. These will feature prominently in the remainder of the chapter.

Closed/open questions

Varying the syntax of a question can have significant effects on the answer to emerge. It can reduce response choices available from a range of possibilities, limit the length of the response, lead the respondent in such a way as to make a certain reply more likely, and impose a particular set of underlying presuppositions for embedding the response (Matoesian, 1993). The most commonly cited differentiation, identifying closed and open questions, has to do essentially with the first two of these effects. Accordingly, open questions tend to be unrestricting, leaving the respondent free to choose any one of a number of possible ways in which to answer, and at length. Closed alternatives, in contrast, can typically be adequately dealt with in one or two words with that reply even being one of a limited range of options presented in the question itself.

Closed questions

These often request basic, limited, factual information, having a correct answer. They characteristically can be answered with a short response selected from a limited number of possible options. Three subtypes exist, the most frequently cited being the *yes–no question*, so called because it can be adequately responded to with a 'yes' or 'no', although this does not mean that it invariably will be, of course. In addition to affirming or negating what is asked, equivocation is a third alternative. This is the option often favoured by politicians when answering either 'yes' or 'no' has equally undesirable consequences (Bull, 2002). Incidentally, 87% of these so-called 'avoidance-avoidance' questions (i.e. ones where both preferred responses are problematic) used when politicians were interviewed in the 1992 British general election were of the yes–no type (Bull, Elliott, Palmer & Walker, 1996). Other conditions, at least among those speaking Finnish, under which respondents depart from a minimal answer to yes–no questions, are discussed by Hakulinen (2001).

This form of closed question plays a special role in courtroom discourse, where it has been found to account for over 66% of questions framed (Woodbury, 1984). It seems to be favoured by lawyers due to the levels of close control it enables them to exert over the process of evidence disclosure. Effectively, these yes–no questions enable lawyers themselves to present the evidence, the witness simply serving to affirm or deny what they say.

In community pharmacies, Morrow et al. (1993) found that almost all pharmacist questions were closed in nature with 69% being of the yes–no variety. They argued that pharmacists were thereby following the clinical algorithm approach of eliminative questioning for diagnosis. While this approach, if carried out expertly, should result in the correct clinical conclusion, it is not without drawbacks in that important information may be missed.

The *selection question* is a second variety of closed question. Here the respondent is presented with two or more alternative responses from which to choose. For this reason, it is sometimes also labelled a *disjunctive, either/or, alternative,* or *forced-choice question* (e.g. '*Do you want to travel by car or by train?*'). Here the options are given in the question itself from which an acceptable response can be selected. Sometimes the choice is more open-ended: the list is unspecified in the question per se. This is the case with the *identification question*, the third subtype of closed question. In this case, the respondent may be asked to identify, for instance, person ('*Who were you with last night?*'), place ('*Where were you born?*'), time ('*When does the meeting start?*'), or event ('*At which conference did we meet?*').

Closed questions have a number of applications, especially in fact-finding encounters where limited pieces of mainly objective information are required. These are of particular value and are often used in a variety of research and assessment-type interviews. Arroll, Khin, and Kerse (2003), for example, found that GPs could detect most cases of depression in patients by asking just two yes–no screening questions. In the research interview, responses to closed questions are usually more concise and therefore easier to record and code than those to open questions; this, in turn, facilitates comparisons between the responses of different subjects. They can also be less demanding to answer. Fritzley and Lee (2003) surveyed 377 studies into child development that used questions as a data-gathering technique with 2–6-year-olds. They found that 43.3% of all questions asked were yes–no. Interestingly, in their own subsequent investigation, they reported a consistent bias in 2-year-olds toward replying 'yes' in response to questions about objects they were both familiar and unfamiliar with, even when they did not understand the question. With those aged 4–5 years, this had changed to a 'no' bias, but only in response to incomprehensible questions. (This issue will be returned to later in the chapter when leading questions are discussed.) With adults, a heightened threat to face due to the limitations and restrictions imposed is a further consideration with this type of question (Tracy, 2002). But by the same token, and when compared with their more open counterparts, closed questions make it easier for an interviewer to control the talk, keep the respondent on a narrow path of conversational relevancy, and often require less skill on the part of the interviewer.

Open questions

In the extreme, this type of question simply extends an invitation to address a presented topic. Open questions can be answered in a number of ways, the response being left up to the respondent. They are sometimes called *wh-questions* since they frequently start with words such as 'why' and 'what'. Those beginning with 'how' also carry this classification, despite the spelling, although spelling may not be the only feature that sets them apart. In trying to get to the bottom of causes for actions, McClure, Hilton, Cowan, Ishida, and Wilson (2001) found that 'how' questions were used more frequently to unearth the precipitating preconditions, whereas 'why' questions led to explanations in terms of goals targeted.

Open questions are broad in nature, and require more than one or two words for an adequate reply. In general, they have the effect of 'encouraging clients to talk longer and more deeply about their concerns' (Hill & O'Brien, 1999, p. 113). For this reason, they tend to be the type preferred when counselling. Egan (2002, p. 121) advised that helpers, 'as a general rule, ask open-ended questions. . . . Counselors who ask closed questions find themselves asking more and more questions. One closed question begets another.' At the same time, however, some open questions impose more restriction and constraints than others. Indeed, Gnisci and Bonaiuto (2003) distinguished between broad and narrow wh-questions. The latter comprise those seeking limited specific information ('*What date is it?*', '*When did the flight touch down?*'). (We have regarded these as closed identification-type questions in this chapter.) Broad wh-questions request more general information ('*What are your views on globalisation?*').

Several advantages are attributed to open questions (Hargie & Dickson, 2004). They facilitate the in-depth expression of opinions, attitudes, thoughts, and feelings while leaving the questioner free to listen and observe. In so doing, they afford the respondent greater control over the interaction and what is to be discussed. Interviewed in this way, the respondent may reveal unanticipated, yet highly relevant, information that the questioner had not directly asked for. Furthermore, where a respondent has a body of specialised knowledge to convey, the use of open questions can be the easiest way to aid the process. On the other hand, when time is limited, or with talkative clients, they may be time-consuming and elicit irrelevant data.

Open versus closed questions

Inevitably talk of open *and* closed questions quickly gives way to talk of open *versus* closed questions. In one of the earliest investigations, Dohrenwend (1965) reported that, in research interviews, when the subject matter under discussion was objective, responses to open questions contained a higher proportion of self-revelation than did responses to closed questions. When the subject matter was subjective, however, open questions produced a lower proportion of disclosure about self. Additionally, responses to open questions were approximately three times longer than those to closed ones, but, again, subjective open questions were significantly shorter than responses to objective open questions. Length of response to closed questions was not influenced by content in this way. Similar findings have been reported by Lamb et al. (1999). They found that, in forensic interviews, open-ended questions produced responses that were three to four times longer, in terms of number of words used, than closed-ended questions, and also produced three times as many new details in the answers. Additionally, Waterman et al. (2001) showed how children were less accurate in reporting events they had experienced when answering closed rather than open questions and consequently recommended that 'interviewers should use open questions as much as possible' (p. 477).

Likewise, Kebbell et al. (2004) have shown that in the courtroom context witnesses with intellectual difficulties (and young children) produce more accurate information in relation to open, free-recall questions (e.g. '*What happened?*'). When these questions are used, those with intellectual difficulties produce accounts with accuracy rates equivalent to the general population. However, as questions become more closed (e.g. from '*describe her*' to '*describe her clothing*' to '*describe her skirt*' to '*was her skirt black?*') their responses become more inaccurate. Kebbell and colleagues explain this phenomenon in terms of level of cognitive and social demand. Free-recall questions allow those with intellectual difficulties the 'space' to recall what they can from memory. However, as questions become more closed, the task changes to one of trying to satisfy the demands of the questioner, and this, in turn, raises levels of uncertainty and stress. Feeling under pressure, the respondent with intellectual difficulties then has an increased tendency to confabulate in order to comply with perceived expectations.

Generalised discussion of the relative efficacy of open and closed questions, however, ignores a spectrum of variables relating to both individual differences among respondents and associated features of these questions themselves. Among the former can be cited gender, educational background, and cognitive ability. Thus, Moreno and Mayer (1999) found that male and female college students reacted differently to certain types of open-ended questions. After receiving instruction about the formation of light-ning, eight times as many females as males stated that they could not answer the ques-tion, '*What could you do to decrease the intensity of lightning?*', since nature could not be altered. In relation to intellectual ability, Schatzman and Strauss (1956) found that interviewers used more open questions with respondents who had spent at least one year at college than with those who had not gone beyond grammar school. Another factor here is that the respondent's perceptions of the questioner can affect how they respond. For example, children are more likely to admit they do not know the answer to a question if they feel that the interviewer is knowledgeable about the subject (Water-man, Blades & Spencer, 2004). The sheer length of the question itself may also be a con-taminating factor in any rigorous comparison. There is evidence of a positive corre-lation between length of question and length of response (Wilson, 1990). This could be due to longer questions containing more elements to be addressed by the respondent.

We have already talked about pre-remarks to questions (e.g. '*I've just arrived, where's the best place to go for Italian food?*'). Allwinn (1991) demonstrated how closed questions could be framed in this way to indicate that a detailed response was required, despite the fact that a minimal answer could be given. Moreover, the context and rules of the interaction may mean that although a question has been phrased in a closed fashion, it is clear that an open reply is expected.

Rather than placing open and close questions in all-out, head-to-head competi-tion, a more fruitful pursuit is to acknowledge their relative strengths and weaknesses. Dillon (1997) proposed a complementary arrangement in survey interviews whereby open questions are used with a range of respondents in order to produce an exhaustive list of response alternatives for later inclusion in closed-question format. He came to this recommendation upon discovering, for example, that when asked the open ques-tion of what they preferred in a job, only half as many respondents mentioned a 'feeling of accomplishment' as selected it when it was presented as one of the alterna-tives in closed format. On the other hand, good pay was the most frequently volun-teered answer to the open question, but the least frequently selected alternative in the closed variant.

Loftus (1982) also found sequencing open and closed variants to work effectively in questioning eyewitnesses to incidents. Open questions produced more accurate information, but less overall detail, than specific closed questions. She consequently recommended starting with open questions to ensure accuracy of information, followed by specific closed questions to obtain a fuller picture. This approach has been widely confirmed in studies of forensic interviewing (see Memon & Bull, 1999).

The process of beginning an interaction with a very open question, and gradually reducing the level of openness, is referred to as a *funnel sequence* (Kahn & Cannell, 1957). This is particularly apt under circumstances where respondents have the requested information readily accessible, are well motivated to offer it up, and can express themselves easily. The sequencing is favoured, for example, in counselling interviews (Hargie & Dickson, 2004), in focus groups (Morgan, 1977), and in health settings as part of the assessment interview process with patients (Cohen-Cole & Bird, 1991; Newell, 1994). It can motivate participants by providing them with more latitude at the outset to talk about issues high on their agenda, and in ways that come naturally to them (Hayes, 2002).

An *inverted funnel* (or *pyramid*) *sequence*, on the other hand, begins with narrow, closed questions and gradually introduces more open forms. A further possibility is the *tunnel sequence*, or 'string of beads' (Stewart & Cash, 2000). Here, all of the questions employed are at the same level and are usually closed. This structuring is often characteristic of screening interviews where the task is to match the respondent with some pre-set criteria. It sometimes also features as an opening gambit in interviews to map out, as it were, the conversational territory in advance of returning to some (or all) of the topics for deeper perusal.

Questions are also linked, on occasion, in a more erratic fashion. An *erratic sequence* of open and closed questions can lead to confusion and perhaps reduce the level of interviewee participation. It may be used intentionally, though, in forensic settings to catch suspects off guard and, as such, is recommended to lawyers by Kestler (1982).

Leading questions

If the closed/open dimension of questioning has to do with the degree of constraint or restriction imposed on responses, then influencing response choice from options, and the introduction of potential bias in information gathering, is the concern here. All questions have embedded sets of assumptions and presuppositions. At one level, in asking a question, there is a basic implication that the other person, for whatever reason, would not volunteer the information (Ulijn & Verweij, 2000). At another level, if I ask, '*Are you my sister?*', the presuppositions are that (a) you are female, (b) I have a sister, and (c) you are in a position to give me this information. Likewise, it would be assumed that: (a) I truly do not know (or at least am uncertain about) our familial relationship, (b) I genuinely seek this information, (c) I believe that you will answer, and (d) I want to listen to your response.

Questions can be framed in ways that seduce respondents into offering answers at odds with real perceptions, experiences, or happenings. This can be done subtly and not always with intent. Based upon empirical work completed, Conrad and

Schober (2000, p. 20) concluded, 'Surprisingly often, respondents can interpret seemingly straightforward questions differently than the survey designers intended.' Leading questions are assumption-laden in potentially problematic ways. By their wording, they entice respondents toward an expected or desired response: they 'put words in their mouths'. The anticipated answer is implied or assumed within the question (e.g. *'Aren't you my sister?'*) and may or may not be immediately obvious to the respondent, depending upon the phrasing. For this reason, they have also been labelled *misleading questions* or *suggestive questions* (Gee, Gregory & Pipe, 1999).

Some individuals are high in *interrogative suggestibility*, which 'refers to the tendency of people to yield to leading questions and submit to interrogative pressure' (Gudjonnson 1999, p. 338). Two separate phenomena come into play here. The first is *yield*, which is the extent to which the individual acquiesces in the expectations inherent in the initial leading question. The second is *shift*, which is the extent to which the respondent is induced to alter an initial answer by pressure or negative feedback from the questioner. Research indicates that individuals most susceptible to interrogative suggestibility include those who have a low IQ, poor memory, low self-esteem, higher levels of trust (less suspicious), low assertiveness, and high anxiety (Gudjonnson, 2003). There is also some evidence that there may be differences in suggestibility across countries (e.g. Pollard et al., 2004).

This process of leading has been given other names, including 'conductiveness' (Quirk et al. 1985; Heritage, 2002). As explained by Quirk et al. (1985, p. 808), questions that are conductive 'indicate that the speaker is predisposed to the kind of answer he has wanted or expected'. Koshik (2002) drew parallels between this and the concept of 'preference', already mentioned from a conversation analysis perspective, relating to adjacency pairs. Asking, *'Don't you just love the autumn?'* (rather than the more neutral form, *'How do you feel about the autumn?'*), sets up an affirmative response as the preferred second pair part. Consequently, and as observed by Sacks (1987, p. 57),

> if a question is built in such a way as to exhibit a preference as between 'yes' or 'no', or 'yes-' or 'no-like' responses, then the answerers will tend to pick that choice, or a choice of the sort will be preferred by answerers, or should be preferred by answerers.

In the context of journalists interviewing politicians, Clayman and Heritage (2002, p. 762) introduced the broader concept 'assertiveness' to refer to a similar process. It has to do with:

> the degree to which the journalist manages to suggest or imply or push for a particular response in the course of asking a question. Of course, no question is neutral in an absolute sense, but questions do vary in the degree to which they manage to express an opinion on the subject being inquired about, thereby portraying one type of answer as expected or preferred.

Four main types of leading question can be distinguished. While varying in how they work, they share this ability to direct the respondent toward an anticipated or favoured answer.

Conversational leads

As the name suggests, these crop up repeatedly in everyday conversations (which does not mean that the other three do not) (e.g. *'Have you ever seen a more beautiful morning?'*). Other examples include what Koshik (2002) termed *'reverse polarity questions'* (e.g. *'Wasn't the storm terrifying?'*). She noted the peculiar fact that while these questions are grammatically negative (i.e. *'Wasn't . . .'*) they predict a positive response. Her thesis is that they function by conveying an *epistemic stance* or position of the speaker on the topic. Indeed, on occasion, they were found to be used by teachers, not as proper questions at all in that they did not anticipate a response, but rather to convey information indirectly on the standard of students' work in conversations with them.

Simple leads

A *tag question* (e.g. *'You do smoke, don't you?'*) can act as a type of simple lead serving to favour a particular response. Not that all tag questions, though, operate in the same fashion, nor is the function invariably to elicit details. As well as satisfying the information needs of the speaker, they can also meet those of the addressee by expressing politeness, inviting conversational participation, or varying the intensity of the speech act (Holmes, 1995). Harres (1998) discovered that, at least among a small sample of Australian general practitioners in medical consultations with patients, tag questions were used to show concern and understanding and maintain control in addition to summarising and confirming medical details. However, in the legal context, they are often used deliberately by lawyers during cross-examination to confuse and lead witnesses.

Furthermore, Kebbell et al. (2004) identified two common types of simple leads, namely, *negative questions* that include the word 'not' (e.g. *'Did you not think that you should have told someone?'*) and *double-negative questions* that include the use of the word 'not' twice (e.g. *'Did Mary not go on to say that she would not have time to call?'*). Such questions, though, can have positive as well as negative outcomes. Simple leads building upon assumptions that are clearly incorrect have been known for some time to facilitate interviewee participation in order to correct these misconceptions. Beezer (1956) conducted interviews with refugees from the then East Germany in which he found that simple leading questions that were clearly incorrect yielded more information from respondents than did questions that were not leading. Thus, when respondents were asked, *'I understand you don't have to pay very much for food in the East Zone because it is rationed?'*, most replied by trying to correct the interviewer's mistaken impressions about general living conditions. However, most authors of texts on interviewing eschew this form of question as bad practice on account of its inherent potential for bias.

Implication leads

These work by presenting the choice of either going along with the lead or implicitly accepting a negative implication embedded in the question (e.g. *'Can I take it that, like all other civilised people, you oppose capital punishment?'*). They are also called *complex leading questions* and have been noted by Walton (1999) to be a common tactic when everyday argument takes place. As with the selection of dispreferred responses (i.e. *'No, I don't oppose capital punishment'*), some sort of elaboration is typically required: a justification, let us say, needs to be appended.

There are some well-documented instances where leading questions have been used in an attempt to lure politicians into entrapment. William Hague, the then leader of the UK Conservative Party, was asked in a radio interview the dual-negative implication lead, *'You're a grown-up. Do you really expect to win the next election?'* His boyish appearance (made much of by cartoonists and the press) and modest stature made an affirmative answer less tempting than would normally be the case when a politician is asked about winning elections.

Subtle leads

Bias can be introduced into questioning in less obvious and sometimes unanticipated ways through the manner in which the question is framed or the form of wording. *Directional questioning* is an alternative nomenclature. An early example, reported by Harris (1973), revealed that when subjects were asked, *'How tall was the basketball player?'*, they guessed about 79 inches but guessed 69 inches when asked, *'How short was the basketball player?'* Similarly, *'How long was the movie?'* resulted in an average estimate of 130 minutes. This dropped to 100 minutes when the parallel question, *'How short was the movie?'*, was substituted. Along similar lines, Loftus (1975) asked either, *'Do you get headaches frequently, and if so, how often?'* or *'Do you get headaches occasionally, and if so, how often?'* The reported averages were respectively 2.2 and 0.7 headaches per week.

The range of response choices in selection-type closed questions can also distort estimates given. In asking about levels of annoyance over TV advertisements, Gaskell, Wright, and O'Muircheartaigh (1993) showed that respondents given high frequencies as alternatives for responding (i.e. every day, most days, once a week, once a month, less often, never) reported significantly higher occurrences than those given low alternatives (i.e. once a week or more often, once a month, about every few months, once a year, less often, never). An explanation is that the values anchoring a scale are assumed to reflect the norm, and so respondents not wishing to be seen as 'abnormal' select an option near the midpoint (Schwarz & Hippler, 1991). Furthermore, frequencies or magnitudes represented by the given response scale can influence subjective meanings attached to the phenomenon being addressed in the question. This is especially so when the reference period applies uniquely to that particular question. When, on the other hand, it is repeatedly used with a spectrum of different questions, the effect is eliminated (Igou, Bless & Schwarz, 2002). Thus, in one study, two groups of subjects were asked to report how often they felt 'really annoyed' (Wright et al., 1997). One group was given a set of low response frequencies (i.e. from 'less than once a year' to 'more than every 3 months') while the other selected from 'less than twice a week' to 'several times a day'. When subsequently asked to define 'annoyed', those in the low-response-frequency group regarded it as referring to a state of more extreme disturbance than those in the high-frequency condition.

Other seminal work in this area has demonstrated that perceptions and recollections can also be shaped by questions asked. In a classic study on false recognition, Loftus and Zanni (1975) compared the effects of questions containing an indefinite article with the same questions containing the definite article. On being asked about a short film of a car accident, viewers asked a question containing the definite article (e.g. *'Did you see* the *broken headlight?'*) produced fewer uncertain or *'I don't know'* responses, and more false recognition of events that never happened, than did viewers asked questions which contained an indefinite article (e.g. *'Did you see* a *broken headlight?'*).

The related concept of *recovered memory* has caused much controversy. It has been argued that what is often unearthed in such in-depth interviews is more *implanted* than *recovered*, having been created through the suggestive influence of biased questioning (Pezdek & Banks, 1996). In particular, questions can encourage *imagination inflation*, 'the phenomenon that imagining an event increases subjective confidence that the event actually happened' (Loftus, 2001, p. 584).

How questions are contextualised can cause distortion of information gathered. Hirt, Lynn, Payne, Krackow, and McCrea (1999) showed that low-expectancy conditions (e.g. saying, *'If you don't remember, it's all right'*) when compared to high-expectancy conditions (*'Tell me when you get an earlier memory'*) produced earlier life memories from respondents of 3.45 years and 2.28 years respectively. Moreover, about a quarter of those led to believe that most people can recall their second birthday reported memories of a false event (i.e. getting lost in a shopping mall) when given details of this fictitious happening together with three actual events (as supplied by parents or siblings).

We have already seen how vulnerable children are to biased responding, even when answering straightforward yes–no-type, closed questions that have no obvious basis for this. Waterman et al. (2001) found that, when asked nonsensical yes–no questions (*'Is a fork happier than a knife?'*), 75% of 5–8-year-olds answered one way or the other. Subsequent exploration revealed that many who answered *'no'* were simply indicating that they did not agree with the assumption inherent in the question, but did not say so. Children, it seems, are under pressure to acquiesce in the predetermined response options (Peterson, Dowden & Tobin, 1999), especially when assuming that adults will ask reasonable questions (Siegal, 1997).

Children, principally younger children (Gee et al., 1999) and those with learning difficulties (Milne, 1999), are particularly susceptible to the effects of leading questions. Extreme caution is therefore required of those who interview these groups. However, young respondents can be protected, to some extent, by being given clear instructions about how to deal with questions (Ghetti & Goodman, 2001) and being allowed to reject a question when unsure of the answer (Endres, Poggenpohl & Erben, 1999).

Recall/process questions

This division refers to the cognitive demands placed upon the respondent in producing an answer. Recall questions are also known as *lower-order cognitive* and, as the name suggests, involve the simple recall of information. Process questions require the respondent to use some *higher mental process* in order to come up with the requested detail. Questions belonging to these categories have attracted most attention within education, particularly in classroom interaction studies.

Teachers, for a number of reasons, use questions that require pupils to do little more than reproduce what they have already been told. These are included to gauge where to begin a lesson, assess the extent of pupil knowledge about the lesson just past, and maximise pupil participation in class. Process questions, on the other hand, require the respondent to go beyond the simple recall of information by analysing, synthesising, or evaluating information in order to arrive at opinions, justifications, judgements, predictions, interpretations, or generalisations.

Research reviews of questioning in the classroom have consistently found that teachers ask more recall than process questions (Gall, 1970; Hargie, 1983; Dillon, 1997). In their review of the area, Daly and Vangelisti (2003, p. 885) concluded: 'Most of these questions are not higher-order ones – they typically are cast at low cognitive levels . . . and of the sort that generate only short answers.' Furthermore, Rousseau and Redfield (1980, p. 52), having reviewed some 20 studies, showed that 'gains in achievement . . . are greatest when higher cognitive questions are used during instruction.' This was confirmed more recently by Daly and Vangelisti, who found that, for teachers, 'Asking more penetrative questions . . . is associated with higher achievement on tests . . . perhaps because posing such questions engenders engagement on the part of learners' (p. 886).

Probing questions

Often probing or *secondary questions*, as Stewart and Cash (2000) termed them, are required as follow-ups to the initial or primary question in order to elicit the scope of information required. Inexperienced interviewers, in particular, often find that they have gathered a great deal of largely superficial data through a reluctance to explore areas in depth, according to Millar et al. (1992). But this aspect of interviewing can prove difficult to master (Hawkins & Power, 1999) and requires, on many occasions, a great deal of sensitivity (Egan, 2002). Millar and Gallagher (2000) illustrated how some interviewees may resent interviewers who probe too deeply, especially about sensitive topics.

In the contrasting setting of the political interview, not renowned for journalistic niceties, Clayman and Heritage (2002) described how *question cascading* was used to winkle specific detail out of the American presidents, Eisenhower and Reagan. This involved asking similar versions of the same question, each one being more narrowly focused than the previous. Interestingly, in group settings, there is evidence that probing may come easier to females than to males (Hawkins & Power, 1999).

In addition to benefits accruing to the inquisitor, being exposed to probing may lead to the respondent's being perceived differently by third parties. The *probing effect* is a tendency, by both the questioner and observers, to rate these people as being more honest than those not subjected to this form of enquiry. This finding has been well corroborated across a range of conditions and contexts (Levine & McCornack, 2001).

The ability to probe effectively, therefore, is at the core of effective questioning. Probes are of different types serving purposes reflected in their titles. Variants discussed by the likes of Turney, Ellis, Hatton, Owens, Towler, and Wright (1983), Hayes (2002), and Hargie and Dickson (2004) include *clarification* or *informational probes* (*'Could you go over again what happened when you opened the door?'*). *Justification probes*, also referred to as *accountability questions* (Clayman & Heritage, 2002), seek reasons for, or causes of, behaviour or happenings (*'Why did you take the purse?'*). *Relevance probes* give respondents an opportunity to reconsider the appropriateness of a response, and/or make its relevance to the topic raised in the primary question more obvious (*'How does that fit in with what we have been talking about?'*). *Exemplification probes* request specific instances of something touched upon in only vague terms. *Extension probes* are used to coax an expansion of an initial response (*'And then what happened?'*). *Accuracy probes* check the correctness of what has just been said. In *restatement probes*, the original question is repeated or rephrased, perhaps at a simpler level, to encourage a response when the initial questioning attempt has failed. This form of probe is also a way of *prompting*. *Echo probes* 'echo' a telling word or words used by the respondent in the preceding response. *Consensus probes* are a way of checking the degree to which others concur with what has just been said, either by asking the person to whom the primary question was addressed or others present in a group situation. Finally, probes can take a *non-verbal* form (e.g. raising the eyebrows and making direct eye contact).

Rhetorical questions

Adler et al. (2001), as mentioned, referred to 'counterfeit' questions that were not genuine requests for information. Although rhetorical questions were not specified in their listing, these share this same defining feature. Rhetorical questions, when posed for effect, are intended either to be answered by the speaker, not the listener, or, indeed, not to be answered (at least explicitly) at all. They may be largely expressive of the speaker's epistemic state.

Rhetorical questions have a long tradition in public speaking, stretching back at least to Aristotle. In his book *The Art of Rhetoric* (*c*330 BC), their effect, as part of the conclusion of a speech, was considered to weaken an opposing argument. However, despite their popularity as a persuasion tactic, Roskos-Ewoldsen (2003) pointed to the relative lack of research into substantiation of their effect. Still, for Turk (1985, p. 75), 'Asking questions is the best way to promote thought', and rhetorical questions have been shown to affect the type of thinking engaged in by listeners (Whaley & Wagner, 2000). While they are useful devices in providing variation and generating interest, the empirical work that has been conducted paints a more complex picture of their efficacy in actually changing attitudes and mindsets. Based upon a review of the material, Roskos-Ewoldsen (2003) concluded, tentatively, that rhetorical questions can influence persuasion (but that effects are conditional upon the counter-attitudinal nature of the message, the location of the question in the message, and the potency of the argument), influence the recipient to assess more critically the content of the message when motivation is low to engage with it cognitively, damage the speaker's credibility and likeability, and enhance the recipient's memory for message content. There is still a great deal to learn, though, about just how rhetorical questions work in persuasive discourse.

Multiple questions

These questions, also referred to as *multipart questions* (Kebbell et al., 2004), are two or more questions (which may be of the same or different type) phrased as one. (While a multiple question may contain a number of questions, quite often it comprises an open question followed by a closed one to narrow the focus (*'How is your wife? Still making fabulous Italian dishes?'*). As a rule, they tend to be frowned upon in the more prescriptive literature on interviewing technique. For Newell (1994), they are the source of problems to do with both interview process and content. As far as the latter is concerned, they are liable to wrong-foot respondents as they attempt to disentangle the various elements, and compose an ordered response. From a process point of view, the interviewer–interviewee relationship can suffer. Dickson, Hargie, and Morrow (1997) noted that patients have difficulty in formulating a reply when asked multiple questions. These questions pressurise and confuse, causing a decrease in the accuracy of information received. Switching from medicine to teaching, Wright and Nuthall (1970) found, in an early classroom study, that teachers asking one question at a time was positively related to pupil achievement, whereas asking a plurality was negatively related to this outcome variable. Likewise, in the courtroom, multipart questions have been shown to confuse witnesses, especially those with intellectual disabilities (Kebbell et al., 2004). Despite this, this type of question is often employed in various settings. Again, however, this is an aspect of questioning that remains under-researched.

Responding to questions

In a sense, all questions are an intrusion into another person's life. As a result, 'questions can cause problems for those who have to answer them, especially if the topic is very difficult, or too personal, etc.' (Ulijn & Verweij, 2000, p. 220). However, it is also the case that questions do not necessarily have to be answered. Indeed, Robert McNamara, the former US defense secretary, advised: 'Never answer the question that is asked of you, but the question you wished was asked of you. I think that's a pretty good rule' (Gibbons, 2003). However, there is an imperative, as we have seen, at least to attempt a response. Answering seems optional but yet cannot be opted out of with alacrity. It often requires a great deal of hard work and not a little skill. Politicians are notorious for failing to answer questions. Indeed, research by Bull and Mayer (1993) revealed that the UK politicians Margaret Thatcher and Neil Kinnock replied to only 37% and 39%, respectively, of the questions that they faced in political interviews. Thirty different ways of avoiding an answer were identified which could be categorised into 11 superordinate groupings, including, for instance, attacking the questioner. As already seen in relation to closed questions, equivocation is an option in 'avoid-avoid' situations: 'equivocation' was defined by Bavelas et al. (1990, p. 28) as 'nonstraightforward communication; it appears ambiguous, contradictory, tangential, obscure, or even evasive.' Wilson (1990) also discussed several techniques used by politicians to evade direct answers to questions. These included questioning the question, attacking the interviewer, or stating that the question had already been answered. The latter strategy will be returned to shortly, but in a different institutional context.

Still within the realms of the political interview, Gnisci and Bonaiuto (2003) located four types of answer that may be forthcoming: *minimal answers, elaborations, implicit answers or answers by implication*, and *non-replies*. The first includes, for example, a 'yes' or 'no' in response to a yes–no closed question. Elaborations encompass the embellishment of these with additional syntactic or semantic detail. With implicit answers or answers by implication, the reply options offered up within the question are not explicitly addressed but rather implicitly acknowledged in what is said. Non-replies fail to provide an adequate answer (e.g. explaining why an answer cannot be given).

Dillon (1997) also brought forward a categorisation of possible replies to questions, some of which coincide with those already mentioned. His 11 main types include: (l) silence, (2) overt refusal to answer, (3) unconnected response (the respondent may change the topic completely), (4) humour, (5) lying, (6) stalling, (7) evading, (8) selective ambiguity (here the respondent pretends to recognise the 'real' question, and answers that), (9) withholding and concealing, (10) distortion (respondents in many instances give the answers that they feel are socially desirable, often without consciously realising they are so doing), (11) direct honest response. Five strategies were considered by Campbell, Follender, and Shane (1998), for dealing specifically with hostile questions aimed at spokespersons for public environmental bodies in meetings with communities. Pointing out, for example, that the issue has already been addressed was found to be the most preferred approach, while an alternative agency-based option (i.e. the issue is the responsibility of another agency) was the least preferred.

OVERVIEW

Posing and responding to questions forms a conspicuous part of what we do when we talk. We may even be evaluated accordingly. Voltaire wrote: 'Judge a man not by his answers but by his questions.' Questioning also has a significant role to play in institutional talk, as in professional/service–recipient interaction in such places as classrooms, medical surgeries, community pharmacies, or counsellors' clinics. From a functional perspective, the intention is often to obtain information, although questions are also asked in situations where the speaker already has the detail supposedly requested. Sometimes asking questions seems to be more to do with giving information. Issues of relational and conversational control are also pertinent. The majority of questioning tends to be left to those in the more dominant position in the relationship.

Some of the major forms of question include open/closed, leading, multiple, recall/process, and rhetorical. Probing is an aspect entered into when primary questions fail to gain the level of detail sought. The implicit rules governing conversation stipulate that questions need to be, if not answered, at least responded to, preferably in ways that can masquerade as answers. Interesting research in this regard has emanated recently from work on interviewing politicians. However, much of how, when, and with what effect we make use of this conversational tool remains under-researched.

REFERENCES

Adler, R., Rosenfeld, L. & Proctor, R. (2001). *Interplay: the process of interpersonal communicating*, 8th edn. Fort Worth, TX: Harcourt.

Allwinn, S. (1991). Seeking information: contextual influences on question formulation. *Journal of Language and Social Interaction*, *10*, 169–184.

Arroll, B., Khin, N. & Kerse, N. (2003). Screening for depression in primary care with two verbally asked questions: cross sectional study. *British Medical Journal*, *327*, 1144–1146.

Bavelas, J. B., Black, A., Chovil, N. & Mullett, J. (1990). *Equivocal communication*. Newbury Park, CA: Sage.

Beezer, R. (1956). *Research on methods of interviewing foreign informants*. George Washington University, Hum RRO Technical Reports, No. 30.

Bloom, B. (1956). *Taxonomy of educational objectives*. New York: McKay.

Bowling, A. (1997). *Research Methods in Health*. Buckingham: Open University Press.

Bull, P. (2002). *Communication under the microscope: the theory and practice of microanalysis*. London: Routledge.

Bull, P. E. & Mayer, K. (1993). How not to answer questions in political interviews. *Political Psychology*, *14*, 651–666.

Bull, P. E., Elliott, J., Palmer, D. & Walker, L. (1996). Why politicians are three-faced: the face model of political interviews. *British Journal of Social Psychology*, *35*, 267–284.

Campbell, K. S., Follender, S. I. & Shane, G (1998). Preferred strategies for responding to hostile questions in environmental public meetings. *Management Communication Quarterly*, *11*, 401–421.

Cegala, D. J. & Broz, S. L. (2003). Provider and patient communication skills training. In T. L. Thompson, A. M. Dorsey, K. I. Miller & R. Parrott (Eds), *Handbook of health communication*. Mahwah, NJ: Lawrence Erlbaum.

Clayman, S. & Heritage, J. (2002). *The news interview: journalists and public figures on the air*. Cambridge: Cambridge University Press.

Cline, R. J. & McKenzie, N. J. (1998). The many cultures of health care: differences, dominance, and distance in physician–patient communication. In L. D. Jackson & B. K. Duffy (Eds), *Health communication research: a guide to developments and directions*. West Port, CT: Greenwood Press.

Cohen-Cole, S. A. & Bird, J. (1991). Function 1: gathering data to understand the patient. In S.A. Cohen-Cole (Ed.), *The medical interview: the three-function approach*. St Louis, MO: Mosby Year Book.

Conrad, F. G. & Schober, M. F. (2000). Clarifying question meaning in a household telephone survey. *Public Opinion Quarterly*, *64*, 1–28.

Corey, S. (1940). The teachers out-talk the pupils. *School Review*, *48*, 745–752.

Crystal, D. (1997). *The Cambridge Encyclopedia of Language*, 2nd edn New York: Cambridge University Press.

Daly, J. & Vangelisti, A. (2003). Skillfully instructing learners: how communicators effectively convey messages. In J. Greene & B. Burleson (Eds), *Handbook of communication and social interaction skills*, Mahwah, NJ: Lawrence Erlbaum.

Daly, J., Kreiser, P. & Roghaar, L. (1994). Question-asking comfort: explorations of the demography of communication in the eighth grade classroom. *Communication Education*, *43*, 27–41.

Davies, G., Westcott, H. & Horan, N. (2000). The impact of questioning style on the content of investigative interviews with suspected child sexual abuse victims. *Psychology, Crime and Law*, *6*, 81–97.

Dickson, D. (1987). Questions and questioning: a select review of research in Ireland. *Questioning Exchange, 1,* 30–32.

Dickson, D., Hargie, & Morrow, N. (1997). *Communication skills for health professionals,* 2nd edn. London: Chapman & Hall.

Dillon, J. (1982). The multidisciplinary study of questioning. *Journal of Educational Psychology, 74,* 147–165.

Dillon, J. (1988). The remedial status of student questioning. *Journal of Curriculum Studies, 20,* 197–210.

Dillon, J. (1997). Questioning. In O. Hargie (Ed.), *The Handbook of Communication Skills.* London: Routledge.

Dillon, J. (2003). The use of questions in organizational consulting. *Journal of Applied Behavioral Science, 39,* 438–452.

Dohrenwend, B. (1965). Some effects of open and closed questions on respondents' answers. *Human Organization, 24,* 175–184.

Egan, G. (1998). *The skilled helper: a problem-management and opportunity development approach,* 6th edn. Belmont, CA: Brooks/Cole.

Egan, G. (2002). *The skilled helper,* 7th edn. Belmont, CA: Brooks/Cole.

Endres, J., Poggenpohl, C. & Erben, C. (1999). Repetitions, warnings and video: cognitive and motivational components in preschool children's susceptibility. *Journal of Legal and Criminological Psychology, 4,* 129–149.

Epstein, L. H., Campbell, T. L., Cohen-Cole, S. A., McWhinney, I. P. & Smilkstein, G. (1993). Perspectives on doctor–patient communication. *Journal of Family Practice, 37,* 377–388.

Fiedler, F. E. (1993). The leadership situation and the black box in contingency theories. In M. Chemers & R. Ayman (Eds), *Leadership, theory and research: perspectives and directions.* New York: Academic Press.

Fritzley, V. H. & Lee, K. (2003). Do young children say Yes to Yes-No questions? A meta-developmental study of the affirmative bias. *Child Development, 74,* 1297–1313.

Gall, M. (1970). The use of questions in teaching. *Review of Educational Research, 40,* 709–721.

Gaskell, G., Wright, D. & O'Muircheartaigh, C. (1993). Reliability of surveys. *The Psychologist, 11,* 500–503.

Gee, S., Gregory, M. & Pipe, M. (1999). What colour is your pet dinosaur? The impact of pre-question training and question type on children's answers. *Journal of Legal and Criminological Psychology, 4,* 111–128.

Ghetti, S. & Goodman, G. (2001). Resisting distortion. *The Psychologist, 14,* 592–595.

Gibbons, F. (2003). Warning to Bush from contrite cold war veteran. *The Guardian,* 23 May, p. 11.

Gnisci, A. & Bonaiuto, M. (2003). Grilling politicians: politicians' answers to questions in television interviews and courtroom examinations. *Journal of Language and Social Psychology, 22,* 385–413.

Graesser, A. & Person, N. (1994). Question asking during tutoring. *American Educational Research Journal, 31,* 104–137.

Gudjonnson, G. (1999). Police interviewing and disputed confessions. In A. Memon & R. Bull (Eds), *Handbook of the psychology of interviewing.* Chichester: Wiley.

Gudjonnson, G. (2003). *The psychology of interrogation and confessions: a handbook.* Chichester: Wiley.

Hakulinen, A. (2001). Minimal and non-minimal answers to yes-no questions. *Pragmatics*, *11*, 1–15.

Hargie, O. (1983). The importance of teacher questions in the classroom. In M. Stubbs & H. Hiller (Eds), *Readings on language, schools and classrooms*. London: Methuen.

Hargie, O. & Dickson, D. (2004). *Skilled interpersonal communication: research, theory and practice*. London: Routledge.

Harres, A. (1998). 'But basically you're feeling well, are you?': tag questions in medical consultations. *Health Communication*, *10*, 111–123.

Harris, J. (1973). Answering questions containing marked and unmarked adjectives and adverbs. *Journal of Experimental Psychology*, *97*, 399–401.

Hawkins, K. & Power, C. (1999). Gender differences in questions asked during small decision-making group discussions. *Small Group Research*, *30*, 235–256.

Hayes, J. (2002). *Interpersonal skills at work*, 2nd edn. Hove: Routledge.

Heritage, J. (2002). The limits of questioning: negatives and hostile question content. *Journal of Pragmatics*, *34*, 1427–1446.

Hill, C. & O'Brien, K. (1999). *Helping skills: facilitating exploration, insight and actions*. Washington, DC: American Psychological Association.

Hind, C. (1997). *Communication skills in medicine*. London: BMJ Publishing Group.

Hirt, E., Lynn, S., Payne, D., Krackow, E. & McCrea, S. (1999). Expectations and memory: Inferring the past from what must have been. In I. Kirsch (Ed.), *How expectations shape experience*. Washington, DC: American Psychological Association.

Holmes, J. (1995). *Women, men and politeness*. London: Longman.

Igou, E. R., Bless, H. & Schwarz, N. (2002). Making sense of standardized survey questions: the influence of reference periods and their interpretation. *Communication Monographs*, *69*, 179–187.

Kahn, R. & Cannell, C. (1957). *The dynamics of interviewing*. New York: Wiley.

Kebbell, M., Hatton, C. & Johnson, S. (2004). Witnesses with intellectual disabilities in court: what questions are asked and what influence do they have? *Legal and Criminological Psychology*, *9*, 23–35.

Kestler, J. (1982). *Questioning techniques and tactics*. Colorado Springs, CO: McGraw-Hill.

Kinnell, A. (2002). Soliciting client questions in HIV prevention and test counseling. *Research on Language and Social Interaction*, *35*, 367–393.

Koshik, I. (2002). A conversation analytic study of yes/no questions which convey reversed polarity assertions. *Journal of Pragmatics*, *34*, 1851–1877.

Lamb, M., Sternberg, K., Orbach, Y., Hershkowitz, I. & Esplin, P. (1999). Forensic interviews of children. In A. Memon & R. Bull (Eds), *Handbook of the psychology of interviewing*. Chichester: Wiley.

Lehtovaara, K. (2002). 'Why' questions of a child at age 4 and 7 years in adult and child interaction. *Virittäjä*, *1*, 35–57.

Levine, T. & McCornack, S. (2001). Behavioral adaptation, confidence, and heuristic-based explanations of the probing effect. *Human Communication Research*, *27*, 471–502.

Loftus, E. (1975). Leading questions and the eyewitness report. *Cognitive Psychology*, *7*, 560–572.

Loftus, E. (1982). Interrogating eyewitnesses – good questions and bad. In R. Hogarth (Ed.), *Question framing and response consistency*. San Francisco, CA: Jossey-Bass.

Loftus, E. (2001). Imagining the past. *The Psychologist*, *14*, 584–587.

Loftus, E. & Zanni, G. (1975). Eyewitness testimony: the influence of the wording of a question. *Bulletin of the Psychonomic Society*, *5*, 86–88.

Matoesian, G. M. (1993). *Reproducing rape: domination through talk in the courtroom*. Chicago: University of Chicago Press.

McClure, J., Hilton, D. J., Cowan, J., Ishida, L. & Wilson, M. (2001). When people explain difficult actions, is the causal question How or Why? *Journal of Language and Social Psychology*, *20*, 339–357.

Memon, A. & Bull, R. (Eds). *Handbook of the psychology of interviewing*. Chichester: Wiley.

Millar, R. & Gallagher, M. (2000). The interview approach. In O. Hargie & D. Tourish (Eds), *Handbook of communication audits for organisations*. London: Routledge.

Millar, R., Crute, V. & Hargie, O. (1992). *Professional interviewing*. London: Routledge.

Milne, R. (1999). Interviewing children with learning disabilities. In A. Memon & R. Bull (Eds), *Handbook of the psychology of interviewing*. Chichester: Wiley.

Moreno, R. & Mayer, R. (1999). Gender differences in responding to open-ended problem-solving questions. *Learning and Individual Differences*, *11*, 355–364.

Morgan, D. (1977). *Focus groups as qualitative research*, 2nd edn. London: Sage.

Morrow, N., Hargie, O., Donnelly, H. & Woodman, C. (1993). Why do you ask? A study of questioning behaviour in community pharmacist–client consultations. *International Journal of Pharmacy Practice*, *2*, 90–94.

Newell, R. (1994). *Interviewing skills for nurses and other health care professionals*. London: Routledge.

Peterson, C., Dowden, C. & Tobin, J. (1999). Interviewing preschoolers: comparisons of yes/no and wh- questions. *Law and Human Behavior*, *23*, 539–555.

Pezdek, K. & Banks, W. (Eds) (1996). *The recovered memory/false memory*. San Diego, CA: Academic Press.

Pollard, R., Trowbridge, B., Slade, P., Streissguth, A., Laktonen, A. & Townes, B. (2004). Interrogative suggestibility in a US context: some preliminary data on normal subjects. *Personality and Individual Differences*, *37*, 1101–1108.

Quirk, R., Greenbaum, S., Leech, G. & Svartvik, J. (1985). *A comprehensive grammar of the English language*. New York: Longman.

Rackham, N. (2003). The behavior of successful negotiating. In R. Lewicki, D. Saunders, J. Minton, & B. Barry (Eds), *Negotiation: readings, exercises, and cases*, 4th edn. New York: McGraw-Hill.

Ralph, E. (1999). Oral-questioning skills of novice teachers: . . . any questions? *Journal of Instructional Psychology*, *26*, 286–298.

Resnick, L. (1972). Teacher behaviour in an informal British infant school. *School Review*, *81*, 63–83.

Rogers, C. R. (1951). *Client-centered therapy*. Boston, MA: Houghton Mifflin.

Rosenshine, B., Meister, C. & Chapman, S. (1996). Teaching students to generate questions: a review of the intervention studies. *Review of Educational Research*, *66*, 181–221.

Roskos-Ewoldsen, D. R. (2003). What is the role of rhetorical questions in persuasion?

In J. Bryant, D. Roskos-Ewoldsen & J. Cantor (Eds), *Communication and emotion: essays in honour of Dolf Zillman*. Mahwah, NJ: Lawrence Erlbaum.

Rousseau, E. & Redfield, D. (1980). Teacher questioning. *Evaluation in Education*, *4*, 51–52.

Sacks, H. (1987). On the preferences for agreement and continuity in sequences in conversation. In G. Button & J. Lee (Eds), *Talk and social organization*. Clevedon: Multilingual Matters.

Sacks, H. (1995). *Lectures on conversation*. Oxford: Basil Blackwell.

Sanchez, M. (2001). Effects of assertive communication between doctors and patients in public health outpatient surgeries in the city of Seville. *Social Behavior and Personality*, *29*, 63–70.

Schatzman, L. & Strauss, A. (1956). Social class and modes of communications. *American Journal of Sociology*, *60*, 329–338.

Schegloff, E. (1972). Notes on a conversational practice: formulating place. In D. Sudnow (Ed.), *Studies on social interaction*. New York: Free Press.

Schwarz, N. & Hippler, H. (1991). Response alternatives: the impact of their choice and presentation order. In P. Biemer, R. Groves, L. Lyberg, N. Mathiowetz & S. Sudman (Eds), *Measurement errors in surveys*. New York: Wiley.

Shoemaker, M. & Johlke, M. (2002). An examination of the antecedents of a crucial selling skill: asking questions. *Journal of Managerial Issues*, *14*, 118–131.

Siegal, M. (1997). *Knowing children: experiments in conversation and cognition*. Hove: Psychology Press.

Skelton, J. & Hobbs, F. (1999). Concordancing: use of language-based research in medical communication. *Lancet*, *353*, 108–111.

Stenstroem, A. (1988). Questions in conversation. In M. Meyer (Ed.), *Questions and questioning*. New York: de Gruyter.

Stewart, C. & Cash, W. (2000). *Interviewing: principles and practice*, 9th edn. Boston, MA: McGraw-Hill.

Street, R. (2001). Active patients as powerful communicators. In W. P. Robinson & H. Giles (Eds), *The handbook of language and social psychology*. Chichester: Wiley.

Thompson, T. L. (1998). The patient/health professional relationship. In L. D. Jackson & B. K. Duffy (Eds), *Health communication research: a guide to developments and directions*. Westport, CT: Greenwood Press.

Tizard, B., Hughes, M., Carmichael, H. & Pinkerton, G. (1983). Children's questions and adult answers. *Journal of Child Psychology and Psychiatry*, *24*, 269–281.

Tracy, S. J. (2002). When questioning turns to face threat: an interactional sensitivity in 911 call-taking. *Western Journal of Communication*, *66*, 129–157.

Turk, C. (1985). *Effective speaking*. London: E. & F. N. Spon.

Turney, C., Ellis, K. J., Hatton, N., Owens, L. C., Towler, J. & Wright, R. (1983). *Sydney micro skills redeveloped: series 1 handbook*. Sydney: Sydney University Press.

Ulijn, J. & Verweij, M. (2000). Questioning behaviour in monocultural and intercultural technical business negotiations: the Dutch-Spanish connection. *Discourse Studies*, *2*, 217–248.

Walton, D. (1999). The fallacy of many questions: on the notions of complexity, loadedness and unfair entrapment in interrogative theory. *Argumentation*, *13*, 379–383.

Waterman, A., Blades, M. & Spencer, C. (2001). Is a jumper angrier than a tree? *The Psychologist*, *14*, 474–477.

Waterman, A., Blades, M. & Spencer, C. (2004). Indicating when you do not know the answer: the effect of question format and interviewer knowledge on children's 'don't know' responses. *British Journal of Developmental Psychology*, *22*, 335–348.

West, C. (1983). Ask me no questions … an analysis of queries and replies in physician–patient dialogues. In S. Fisher & A. Todd (Eds), *The social organization of doctor–patient communication*. Washington, DC: Center for Applied Linguistics.

Whaley, B. & Wagner, L. (2000). Rebuttal analogy in persuasive messages: communicator likability and cognitive responses. *Journal of Language and Social Psychology*, *19*, 66–84.

Wilson, J. (1990). *Politically speaking: the pragmatic analysis of political language.* Oxford: Basil Blackwell.

Woodbury, H. (1984). The strategic use of questions in court. *Semiotica*, *48*, 197–228.

Wright, C. & Nuthall, G. (1970). Relationships between teacher behaviors and pupil achievement in three experimental elementary science lessons. *American Educational Research Journal*, *7*, 477–493.

Wright, D., Gaskell, G. & O'Muircheartaigh, C. (1997). How response alternatives affect different kinds of behavioural frequency questions. *British Journal of Social Psychology*, *36*, 443–456.

Wynn, R. (1996). Medical students, doctors – is there a difference? *Text*, *16*, 423–448.

Young, M. & Klingle, R. S. (1996). Silent partners in medical care: a cross-cultural study of patient participation. *Health Communication*, *8*, 29–53.

Chapter 5

Reinforcement

Len Cairns

T HE TERM 'REINFORCEMENT', AS a concept within fields such as human social communication (both non-verbal and verbal), learning theory, educational psychology, and applied behaviour therapy, has a lengthy history and very deep research base. Particularly prominent in the twentieth century in the psychological and educational literature, the concept has had less prominence in recent years, particularly in this postmodern era of thinking. Nevertheless, the significance of reinforcement as a theoretical and practical aspect of human communication, and as a key feature of skilled performance, remains today.

This chapter will examine the concept of reinforcement and its place within a social skills model of communication. The relevance of an understanding of how reinforcement plays a number of significant roles in learning to communicate effectively, and in the skilled use of communication in most of the modern forms we use, will be outlined and supported by international research findings from across the decades.

CLARIFYING THE CONCEPT

Simply put, reinforcement is a concept which has arisen as the centrepiece of what is called *operant psychology theory*, which is most associated with the writing and philosophy of the American academic, B. F. Skinner (1904–1990). Burrhus Frederic Skinner was an idealistic and inventive scholar of the twentieth century who may have changed the way we think about behaviour and life, but never quite succeeded in his professed aim to change the world in which people live (Bjork, 1993). His work was both revered and reviled by different sectors of the academic and scholarly community throughout his life and beyond into this century (for a critique, see Kohn, 1993). Fred Skinner (as he preferred to be addressed) was, and remains, a controversial theorist. For many, he was the father of modern behaviourism and its major theorist of the twentieth century.

In operant psychology (as the Skinner-led field became known), the term 'reinforcement' is usually defined in terms such as the following: the effect of a stimulus, when matched with an emitted response (*an operant action*), increases the likelihood of that action/response being repeated.

In his classic short work *About Behaviorism*, Skinner (1974) was a little more specific and also offered two examples:

> When a bit of behavior has the kind of consequence called reinforcing, it is more likely to occur again. A positive reinforcer strengthens any behavior that produces it: a glass of water is positively reinforcing when we are thirsty, and if we then draw and drink a glass of water, we are more likely to do so again on similar occasions. A negative reinforcer strengthens any behavior that reduces or terminates it: when we take off a shoe that is pinching, the reduction in pressure is negatively reinforcing, and we are more likely to do so again when a shoe pinches. (p. 51)

There are different understandings of many of the terms surrounding the operant view of the world which of necessity need to be clearly differentiated in a serious academic discussion from common-sense or common usage meanings attached to some of these words. In addition, there are those who find the whole notion of Skinnerian operant psychology an unfortunate aberration of the twentieth century.

Frequently, in normal social discourse in English, people use the terms 'reinforce', 'reinforcement', and 'punishment', as well as 'negative reinforcement', yet most of these common usages are not in line with the theory and preciseness of the operant psychology where they originated. To clarify, Table 5.1 is a useful and simple way to show the different specific meanings of the base terms in operant psychological theory.

In this table, it becomes clear that the relationship between what are called 'contingencies' and the relevant 'stimulus' is the key to understanding the concepts, particularly the difference between *punishment* and *negative reinforcement* (which are frequently erroneously used as synonyms in common parlance). The term 'contingency' in this model refers to the direct linkage or consequential relationship – what Lee (1988), in her detailed discussion of contingencies, refers to as the 'if-then relationship'; for example, 'if you talk, you hear your own voice' (p. 61). Alfie Kohn (1993), the strident critic of operant psychology, refers to this in the following terms: 'But

Table 5.1 Operant model of reinforcement contingencies and stimuli

	Positively valued stimulus	*Negatively valued stimulus*
Contingent application	Positive reinforcement	Punishment
Contingent removal	Response cost	Negative reinforcement

Skinnerian theory basically codifies and bestows solemn scientific names on something familiar to all of us: "Do this and you'll get that" will lead an organism to do "this" again' (p. 5).

Kohn's criticisms have been widely reported, but his central thesis starts with the simple, yet deceptive, argument that reinforcement is just another 'scientific' term for reward. We will return to this and other criticisms of the reinforcement concept and its applications later in the chapter.

In operant theory, the application of a positively valued stimulus (be it food, a pat on the back, or verbal praise) that is contingent (clearly linked to the emitted behaviour) will be positively reinforcing and lead to a more likely repeat of that behaviour. So, in social interaction and discourse, parents use smiles, praise, and encouragement in language and social behaviour development. Schoolteachers also make liberal use of the skill of reinforcement in social and token forms (the latter covering the gold stars and written praise comments on school work as well). This aspect has a long history in teacher education, particularly in such approaches as 'teaching skills', and was a centrepiece of microteaching over 30 years ago as a major approach to the education of teachers (Turney et al., 1973).

Similarly, the application of a negatively valued stimulus contingent upon a behaviour (such as the infliction of direct pain) will constitute punishment. The removal of a positively valued stimulus (e.g. money in a fine for speeding) is called response cost, and the removal of a negatively valued stimulus (a thorn in a sock) is negative reinforcement.

The application of this model within many fields, but significantly in education and behaviour therapy, has led to reinforcement being one of the most researched topics in modern psychology and educational research. In addition, the concept and its implications have been built into social communication skills models (e.g. Hargie, 1986, 1997) and social learning models (e.g. Bandura, 1971, 1986) for over 50 years.

While there is confusion among many non-operant theorists and researchers and particularly among the 'general public' about what the terms 'reinforcement' and 'negative reinforcement' imply in research and communication models, there is a general acceptance of the notion that a behaviour that is 'reinforced' is one that is likely to recur. People are both familiar and comfortable with the usage in relation to various child-rearing advices and pet training, so that these terms are frequently used in phone-in radio, for example, in these ways.

In most models of social communication, there are elements of both *feedback* and *response*. Some of the writing and discussion of these elements can, at times, overlap and in fact lead to confusion, depending on the way the two terms are defined and utilised within the discussions. *Feedback* figures in most models as a 'loop' or an aspect of the model where message initiators receive (or are *fed-back*) information about the messages they have sent to others (see Chapter 2). *Response* usually refers to the actions or behaviours which have resulted from a communication or inter-personal interaction initiation. It is important for this chapter to review and clarify the differences between the two key terms, *feedback* and *reinforcement*.

REINFORCEMENT AND FEEDBACK

A key issue for many readers will be the difference and application of the two terms, *reinforcement* and *feedback*. This is a significant point for any discussion of social communication models. Just as there is confusion in the popular use of the two terms *negative reinforcement* and *punishment*, there is also confusion in the use of the two terms *reinforcement* and *feedback*. This confusion is not assisted when some writers actually use the two terms either interchangeably or as synonyms in ways that indicate they are one and the same concept. There is no doubt either that for some authors in the field there are elements of both *feedback* and *response* in the way the term *reinforcement* is being used in this chapter. What this indicates clearly is that there are inherent problems in the specialised usage of such terms and general slippage when they move into everyday language and usage.

In this chapter, we are arguing that there are clear differences between these two terms. As mentioned above, the key difference between them hinges on the idea of contingency or a definite causal link between an emitted behaviour and a stimulus.

Reinforcement involves a stimulus (food, praise, tokens) that, when linked to an emitted response, will most likely lead to that response being repeated. Reinforcement implies some changes and learning in a behavioural sense.

Feedback is simply a matter of the observation of an action, or some reflection or noting that the action occurred ('I was so frightened, my heart began to beat faster and faster'). Feedback implies an information loop which may or may not have links in the learning sense or in effecting any possible repetition of the behaviour. This view of the term 'feedback' is closely aligned to the study of cybernetics (see Chapter 2). Feedback in communication can be a reflection of what was said or acknowledgement that the communication was received.

While *feedback*, particularly in the cybernetic sense, has an important role in communication models and functions, particularly in the sense of understanding automaticity, it may or may not serve some of the communication skill learning necessary for human communication development that *reinforcement* certainly does. Some may see *feedback* as a more benign term than *reinforcement*, and this is due mainly to what is, for them, a distasteful element of possible manipulative bribery or reward and/or punishment inherent in the operant model term and supposedly absent from *feedback* (see Kohn, 1993; Schunk, 2004, for different views on this aspect). Nevertheless, this chapter argues strongly that *reinforcement* is a core human communication skill which is present and utilised frequently by all communicators. An understanding of the concept and its applicability and research and practice applications will be helpful to all who study human communication.

A common model of basic language face-to-face communication, particularly relevant in classroom teacher–pupil interactions, for example, has been referred to as the I-R-F, or the I-R-E model. In this model, 'I' stands for initiation, 'R' for response and 'F' for feedback, or, in the E version, for evaluation (see Mehan, 1978, for a very early version of the latter). It is suggested that this pattern of communication is a common one in many exchanges between people and is very often the dominant pattern in most classrooms, with 'I' being a teacher-posed question, 'R' a pupil response, and 'F' or 'E' a teacher's positive comment to the pupil.

A closer examination of the F/E component and what it might entail leads to the need for some differentiation as to when the feedback is more than just feedback and actually constitutes reinforcement in purpose and result. The model may be, in many instances (particularly in the classroom setting where it has been studied so much), more an IRR model, with the second 'R' being reinforcement. For this discussion, it is essential to consider when a feedback/evaluation comment becomes, or is, *reinforcement*. Reference to the three essential elements below (validity, valence, and contingency) will assist understanding here.

For example, a teacher may *initiate* a question, gain a pupil *response*, and *reinforce* that response with social reinforcement (positively regarded comments) relevant to *that* pupil and *that* response (therefore, contingent). It is suggested here that there should be three key aspects of such utterances in verbal interaction, which would mark the statements as reinforcement or 'beyond feedback'. These characteristics are as follows:

1   *Personal validity.* This term refers to the way an utterance must have some personal real meaning for the receiver to be able to perceive it as reinforcing. The message should be clear, in language that is understood, have personal links and signage (perhaps using the receiver's name), and be meaningful to the receiver.

2   *Personal valence.* This term refers to the power within the message and the way a receiver sees it to be of some value and impact. Valence is different from validity, as the former refers to the power and affect as well as effect of the message received whereas validity refers basically to the clarity of the meaning being received by the listener.

3   *Contingency.* This term refers to the consequential linkage between the initiation and the feedback. If the message is contingently related to the response and carries some valence, it is reinforcing. A mutuality of understanding between the communicators that any such message is contingent is also a factor in this aspect.

A further point of relevance to the discussion of *reinforcement* that should be noted is the different types of possible reinforcers which may crop up in social interaction (some of these variations will be mentioned later in cited research on the topic).

As long ago as 1973, MacMillan proposed a possible hierarchy of reinforcers ranging from what he called 'primary rewards', which related to basic human needs such as food and water at the lowest level, through token and social praise, and toward a highest level of 'self-mastery' as a form of self-reinforcement. Such a hierarchy echoes very clearly the famous Maslow (1954) hierarchy of human needs, which even today figures in many basic education and business texts as an explanatory model of what tends to drive people. Of course, different people react to different potential reinforcers, and while the satisfaction of simple basic needs, such as hunger and thirst, has quite powerful effects in the reinforcement sense in training animals, people and the communication processes between them are far more complex. Aspects such as the impact of what is termed 'social reinforcement', which includes praise and approval (or even monetary rewards), have to be learned, as usually such reinforcers have little actual value in themselves, but rather, represent, or are proxies for, other personally valued aspects in life. In addition, many non-verbal reinforcers such as smiles, nods, thumbs up, and other gestures are learned and associated with particular positive elements and are often culturally bound.

The subtlety of many reinforcers in different social situations can be quite acute and even subgroup specific to the extent that it may be difficult for other out-group communicators to detect the reinforcing nature of the communication (gangs and cliques often develop in-group communications and signs to exploit this reality for exclusivity effect). In these situations, it may even be possible for the in-group reinforcers to be the opposite of what is perceived as 'normal' in the rest of society as a statement of exclusivity and differentiation. Adolescent language often uses opposite terms so that, supposedly, adults cannot penetrate their world (witness the way some cultures use as terms of endearment or 'mateship' the insult or even what is offensive language in 'normal' conversation).

A large part of social reinforcement involves social learning to imbue the comments and actions with some acceptable mutual value, which then sets the communications up as reinforcers when applied contingently. Sometimes these words or comments take on especially idiosyncratic meanings that are reinforcing only in very narrow contexts for a few individuals. Even most money is actually relatively worthless in itself; it is what it represents and what the culture, community, or nation members mutually accept it to represent as an exchange medium that makes it socially rewarding and thus a positive reinforcer. When nations are at war or in chaos, the currency often suddenly does revert to meaningless paper and coins, and has no social value. It then ceases to be a reinforcer.

REINFORCEMENT IN INTERPERSONAL COMMUNICATION

So far in this chapter, we have defined *reinforcement*, described its theoretical roots, and differentiated it from *feedback*. We now turn to the direct application of the concept in a social skills model of interpersonal communication and how research on reinforcement has, over the years, contributed to the understanding and use of the idea within a wide range of fields of study and action.

Reinforcement in non-verbal communication

Reinforcement in non-verbal communication situations has been examined from a wide range of perspectives and with some interesting results and implications (Feldman, 1992). The range of areas where non-verbal reinforcers and applications have been examined includes health (doctor–patient and nurse–patient interaction and waiting room behaviour), business, teaching, the law, and so on (Feldman, 1992, has detailed discussions on each of these aspects).

Many of us in our day-to-day communications with loved ones or those with whom we have quite close and long-standing communication utilise non-verbal reinforcers. We become quite adept at reading and transmitting facial expressions and other gestures and even body language to provide reinforcement and react to that of others. Parents usually work hard to establish certain frowns and glares as communication elements, and often develop idiosyncratic positive expressions as personal reinforcers with their children. Today, with the all pervasive use of television and its often ubiquitous partner, advertising, we have seen the development of a wide range of virtually created expressions and signs that, if successful, enter the general language as new reinforcers and 'in' expressions.

Over 30 years ago, Scheflen (1972) wrote about body language and social order, the subtitle of his book being 'communication as behavioral control', and he gave detailed illustrations of the ways people communicate and use what he called *reciprocals* in face-to-face communication, whereby body postures and gestures communicated affiliation, flirtation, and repulsion aspects. Suffice it to state at this stage that the *reciprocals* of Scheflen and the concept of reinforcement are not too far apart in meaning.

Non-verbal behaviour remains a major area of study, and aspects of this field are discussed in detail in Chapter 3, and referred to frequently in other chapters of this volume. The world of research and application of body language or non-verbal aspects of interpersonal communication is still a current issue, and numerous business, training, and other applications of research and theory are popular in the field (Feldman, 1992; Carlopio et al., 2001; Robbins et al., 2003). Most of these latter applications take early research and development and apply the findings to business behaviour or management training (e.g. Robbins et al., 2003). They are intended to familiarise managers and businessmen and -women with the ideas and possibilities of good communication and of uses and abuses of components of non-verbal (and verbal) communication in business dealings and employee management in workplaces. Some suggest effective reinforcers and other responses and how these may assist staff development or facilitate communication across teams (Hargie et al., 2004) and even cultures (Schneider & Barsoux, 2003).

Interestingly, Jones and Le Baron (2002) have argued for a convergence between verbal and non-verbal communication theory and writing. They posited that since these two aspects actually occur together, they should be studied together. In addition, they were quite critical of the division between quantitative and qualitative research paradigms and urged better use of both traditions in researching human communication. In recent years, the emergence of what is now known as 'mixed methods' (Tashakkori & Teddlie, 1998, 2003; Cresswell, 2003; Johnson & Onwuegbuzie, 2004), where both traditions/paradigms *are* more integrated, reflects such thinking.

Reinforcement in the area of non-verbal communication is usually studied within interpersonal contact and communication and has quite a long history (Argyle, 1967; Argyle & Cook, 1967; Cook, 1977, for example, were early pioneers). Most of the research and evidence on the impact of non-verbal communication aspects of relevance to the concept and use of reinforcement links clearly to how people utilise facial expressions, gestures, and postures contingently to increase or decrease the communication pattern or flow between themselves and others (Hargie & Dickson, 2004). For example, the open palms extended on either side of the body and raised shoulders with a quizzical look on the face has become an almost universal expression for 'I don't know' or 'I don't understand' and can be seen being used across many cultures. Similarly, a clenched fist shaken in front of the face with a heavy frown is also a clearly negative response to a communication attempt. The dismissive wave of the hand to a hawker or beggar is also well set as an international negative. Many of these expressions are becoming more internationally shared than in previous generations due to the massive international communications revolution of the late twentieth century. At the same time, some gestures and expressions remain relatively culture bound.

As mentioned earlier, the advertising industry deliberately and sometimes quite unsubtly manipulates the non-verbal aspects of communication to enhance sales and customer satisfaction. Fast-food chains train their 'crews' in steps which involve specific smiles, greetings, and pleasantries as positive reinforcers with the aim of generating good feelings in their customers and possible repeat business.

Non-verbal communication is now studied as a language in its own right by many researchers and writers, and the field abounds in references to elements which can be clearly seen to be linked to the ideas of employing reinforcers to facilitate and support increases in communication. In summary, reinforcement is employed non-verbally in communication in ways that are subtle and frequent in our daily lives and more manipulated in advertising and other elements of popular culture than we are prone to notice or admit.

Reinforcement in verbal communication

Of course, the majority of human social communication is verbal, with a wide range of spoken languages across the world. In each language, there is a large lexicon of words and terms that are imbued with praise and reward connotations. These are clearly meant to be used as responses to other speakers and hence figure strongly as social reinforcement in their application within communication.

Thus, whether we agree or not with the behaviourist's analysis in which the concept of reinforcement is theorised and researched, it is still patently apparent that our languages have many instances of terminology that assume words of praise and encouragement, and that these have some positive and linked effect to repetition of the behaviours to which they are responding. We use these words and terms deliberately to gain desired effects. Equally, we have a broad range of negative comments, some of which are used as severe criticism contingent on a behaviour and are meant to punish others.

As mentioned earlier, much of the research work on the place and effect of reinforcement in human communication took place in the mid- to late twentieth century. A good deal of research was also situated within the education field in two spheres: teacher education and special education. More recent work has centred on aspects such as behaviour therapy and modification of atypical behaviours in children and those with personality or communication disorders.

Some interesting recent research has highlighted the culture specificity of some aspects of reinforcement applicability. Weirzbicka (2004) presented research to show that the terms 'good boy' and 'good girl', as 'widely used in Anglo parental speech directed to children to praise them for their action', have 'no equivalents in other European languages'. In her interpretation of this assertion, she argued that the terms and their purported effects are culture specific and rooted in the English and American puritan past. Of course, many previous studies in the education sector have high-lighted the considerations, as specified above in the three criteria for reinforcement, that validity and valence are related to the individualisation of reinforcement as well as the specific contingency. General praise is not always reinforcing under these considerations, and terms such as 'good boy/girl' are general and may interplay with different attributional ideas and motivation in the hearer. Brophy (1981) has discussed in some depth the issue of whether praise is the same as reinforcement in the educational literature, and concluded that much of the praise teachers use in the classroom is actually non-contingent and therefore is not reinforcing.

Parental use of reinforcement in the development of conversation and social skill has always been a strong feature in most cultures, and current 'good-parenting' volumes attest to the use of selective praise and encouragement linked to child behaviour as evidence of best practice (Christopherson & Mortweet, 2003). Again, specific praise related to the individual child and the actions/behaviours being responded to results in better take-up and repetition of the behaviours.

Current theory of language teaching heavily emphasises the need for young students beginning school and in their early literacy and oracy years to be 'scaffolded' (that is supported and encouraged by a more skilled language user, be it parent, caregiver, or teacher) within the theoretically conceived 'zone of proximal development' (a Vygotskian concept which means that area of potential learning space just beyond current competence). Such terminology and its implications for a social construction emphasis on all language development has been pervasive in most language-teaching texts and research in the past two decades (Green & Campbell, 2003; Anstey & Bull, 2004). The implications of these theories do not necessarily support reinforcement ideology, and in some instances their advocates would take some offence at any such links, but the examples often cited include parental and teacher praise and encouragement in language that is clearly interpretable as contingent reinforcement-type feedback, rather than some neutral conversational interaction.

In business, the use and understanding of the impact of verbal reinforcers in communication and management, as well as human resource management, has a well-established background. Even a brief perusal, for example, of websites advertising workplace and management courses in such areas as 'interpersonal communication skills in the workplace' will demonstrate the centrality of elements of reinforcement theory and application in handling effective communication practices across such diverse areas from 'difficult staff at work' to 'effective productive employees'. Any reliable search engine on the World Wide Web will give results on each of the aforementioned terms as search words that will open up a myriad of websites.

As stated above, the applicability of the concept of reinforcement in understanding how we, as human communicators in social interaction, behave and develop is important within the overall communication field (Place, 1998). Most analyses of the skills we utilise to develop conversation and language will frequently bring the communication theory and research reader to the topic of reinforcement. Whether the current literature tends to offer alternative terms, such as praise and encouragement or response, is not the issue, as the underlying theory and conceptualisation remain cogent. The specificity of the concept and its roots in operant psychology are not currently mainstream in the literature, but strong elements of research and application of the ideas and principles are still evident with applicable results.

REINFORCEMENT IN THE NEW COMMUNICATION MEDIA

In the second half of the twentieth century and into this millennium, the 'new media' have become essential and central to communication patterns in most modern and postmodern nations. The new media are heavily visual (even the cellular telephone is moving into a medium for more visual content), although multimedia elements are becoming more prevalent as time goes by. Included in this general category for the purposes of this discussion are email, Web pages, interactive Internet chat rooms, blogs, and the ubiquitous text message, photo, and other image services of the modern cellular telephone networks. Many of these media are used more by the younger generations and have a linguistic edge which is starting to emerge as almost a new dialect, or even a new language with standardised English short cuts and symbolic elements at times reminiscent of rebus symbols in early twentieth-century reading instruction in schools.

Research into aspects of how these media are changing communication patterns and interactivity is emerging, and there will be much more to come in the near future. What is interesting for the purposes of this chapter is that the skill and use of *reinforcement* are easily identified when these modern-use media are investigated. Most of the symbols which are so heavily used in cellular telephone messaging, for example, include various ways of praising or rewarding, or positively reinforcing comments and messages. These symbols include emoticons, such as smiling faces and hearts, which may be attached to messages. Similar symbols in various keystroke combinations also are found in many emails, particularly between close friends who share the dialect.

Interestingly, the basis for some of the thinking about the modern media and its place in social communication theory includes recent work on what has become known as the 'computers are social actors paradigm' (CASA) (Bracken & Lombard, 2004; Bracken et al., 2004). Bracken and her colleagues have argued that computer users interact with the computers as social entities, and that reinforcement from a computer appears to have the same or similar effects as that from people in social communication (this might remind many film aficionados of the famous computer, HAL, in the film *2001: A Space Odyssey*).

It is important in this set of considerations, however, to differentiate the use of some of the media from among the remainder, in terms of the extent of interaction with a device that is a mediator of communication between two people, as compared to the situation where the computer or device is programmed in a way that appears to be non-mediating and has some apparent stand-alone qualities. Arguments for thinking computers, chaos theory, memetics, and the emergence of nanotechnology and devices with inbuilt elements of 'fuzzy logic' are starting to make the science fiction computer with a mind of its own a closer possibility than previous generations would have imagined.

Direct synchronous communication in which both parties are device connected in real time is one clear case of mediation, and the communication device is just a filter or medium between normal face-to-face encounters with all the attendant issues that may generate. There has been a long history of this type of communication through the development and use of the telephone, and many of the modern devices have merely extended this into a range of social and time and distance dimensions as a development of that paradigm. The advent of telephone etiquette, and specific language patterns of greeting, answering and conversation punctuation, enhancers, and inhibitors, has been the subject of considerable work over many decades. Asynchronous communication (where the parties are operating in different time spheres or zones but still communicating) is something which used to be only in the domain of letter writing but now also happens through email and various discussion forums and other interactive patterns.

Different from both of these situations is the computer as a programmed teaching or interactive device. Here the communication may have a range of interactive elements that allow different responses and 'conversations' or interactions to happen, depending on an algorithm or sequence which has been built into a program within the device. Some of the modern versions of such communication packages at their crudest level are the telephone-answering systems in which the caller punches in a number for a specific submenu service. The rigidity of this simplest 'voice-mail jail' version has become a modern social curse, and it is the subject of many a complaint (Hargie et al., 2004). More sophisticated aspects would include interactive games and institutional educational teaching programs. The latter may often have built-in tests and progress checks with planned reinforcement schedules and social reinforcement comments in voice or text. Early research in this area seems to indicate that computer text criticism, for example, is quite powerful in its effects on motivation and recall (Bracken et al., 2004). This field is ripe for additional detailed research and development.

At this stage of the chapter, it is important to consider that these modern media and their implications for communication theory and research are where the leading edge will be for the first half of this millennium. Whether reinforcement, as a conceptual framework, has a large place in this development and in the study of how and why and in what ways people interact with machines, and how the human communications are or are not mediated by devices, will be a fascinating aspect to watch. There is no doubt that early work in programmed instruction and computer-mediated instruction, for example, suffered from a too heavy dose of behaviourist-dominated approaches emphasising small sequenced parts as the basic learning paradigm, and that this has led to a vigorous search for alternative theories and approaches.

THE CONCEPT OF COMMUNICATION REINFORCEMENT

This chapter now moves to suggest that, in order to understand clearly the way *reinforcement* figures in human social communication, the concept of *communication reinforcement* may be a useful way to discuss and analyse the application of operant theory and models of communication. For the purposes of this chapter, *communication reinforcement* refers to the consequences of a communication from one person to others which increases the likelihood of further communication happening. The consequences of the emitted communication may be positive reinforcement in the form of social reinforcers, such as praise and other positive responses, and may be verbal or non-verbal, as with nods, facial expressions, or other gestures of approval or support.

Manipulation of communication reinforcement in research and therapy

Early research into the place and application of reinforcement theory in human communication emphasised the way positive reinforcement could be used in a deliberate sense to alter language behaviours and usage. Such research began in areas such as using reinforcement in increasing conversation skills and frequency, as, for example, in 'delinquent girls' (Minkin et al., 1976) or socially isolated elderly men in an institutional setting (Kleitsch, 1983). In addition, work employing negative reinforcement was conducted in the 1960s with a therapy group to stimulate conversation (a loud noise went off only when someone spoke) (Heckel et al., 1962). Likewise, there has always been considerable discussion of the linked (contingent) use of praise and reward by parents in assisting their children to develop language and social skills.

In the second half of the last century, particularly in the 1970s, there was a plethora of classroom-based research into the use of reinforcement in a range of forms and its effects on student classroom misbehaviour (O'Leary & O'Leary, 1977), language acquisition (Becker et al., 1981), and the shaping of various social behaviours (Kazdin, 1989). One well-known developmental programme in this genre, which has been and still remains a strongly advocated approach to early language development, is the Direct Instruction stable of materials and curriculum approaches. Commercially distributed under the DISTAR© label, this material is based on operant psychological principles and has been in existence for close to 30 years (Becker et al., 1981). The materials were developed in the USA and have been the subject of a number of specific reviews and projects, in which their applicability in developing language skills in children was well researched, showing often outstandingly successful results (Rhine et al., 1981). Basically, such materials emphasise a set curriculum sequence of behaviours that are presented with repetition and lots of positive contingent reinforcement to small groups of school-age children, and introduce small, carefully arranged elements at a time.

Another programme, aimed at language development in disabled children, that has similar reinforcement patterns as its basis is the TALK Language Development Program (Drash & Tudor, 1990). As originally described, this programme used positive reinforcement in a behaviourally oriented approach to teach language-disabled children to talk. In more recent years, these two authors have continued to work with language development in both disabled and non-disabled children, and have developed a model for the understanding and treatment of autistic children (Drash & Tudor, 2004). While their model has attracted considerable interest, it has not gone without criticism from other autism researchers (Carr & LeBlanc, 2004).

At the same time, the field of reinforcement application and behaviour modification has maintained a strong base in dealing with children with special educational and behavioural needs, as well as work in aberrant adult and child communication disorders. Speech-delayed, aphasic, and autistic children have been assisted by these techniques, based on the operant theories of language and reinforcement connections (see the Treehouse website (*www.treehouse.org.uk*) in the UK, where autistic children are taught by applied behaviour analysis (ABA) techniques featuring reinforcement).

In various places and writing across the broad field of operant psychology and its many variants, terms such as 'applied behaviour analysis', 'behaviour therapy', and other variations distinguish the many approaches to utilising reinforcement concepts and practices to affect human behaviour and communication patterns. While these may have differing elements and emphases, they all have the concept of reinforcement as central and the application of it as the major means to change or adapt behaviour and language. Within this field, a recent development is functional communication training (FCT), and a number of studies have utilised this set of techniques, which use reinforcement to improve communication in children and some adults who demonstrate severe dysfunctional behaviour (Hagopian et al., 1998; Durand, 2002).

The basic approach of FCT involves an initial functional analysis of the behaviour that is seen as at issue (be it a misbehaviour or a lack of communication). The reinforcers that apparently currently support that behaviour are also noted in this stage. The next step is to organise for the child a new or different behaviour (it may be a simple oral statement or use of some communication cards if the child cannot yet verbalise). The significant interactors with the child (or adult) concerned then actively reinforce the new behaviour/communication each time the child exhibits it. The latter behaviour/communication is termed a replacement behaviour for the previously unacceptable behaviour. In FCT, the replacement behaviour is reinforced while the unacceptable behaviour is ignored. The FCT approach has a good deal of support and research basis in the literature on treatment of severe behavioural and communication disorders (Durand & Carr, 1991, 1992; Fisher, Kuhn & Thompson, 1998).

Applications of communication reinforcement in various fields

In addition to the above specific application of reinforcement and the operant model of psychology to learning and language aspects, there have been a number of related and derivative developments which have emerged over the past two decades, and which are currently bringing some new light to the applicability of reinforcement ideas and their relationship to human communication and behaviour. Two aspects which have developed in this vein are cognitive behaviour therapy and, more recently, relational frame theory.

Cognitive behaviour therapy is an approach with direct roots in Skinnerian thinking and operant psychology. This approach blends both cognitive therapy, which was pioneered by the psychologists Beck and Ellis in the 1960s, with behavioural therapy (or behaviour-modification techniques) for maladaptive behaviours in individuals. The use of language and reinforcement is involved in such aspects of treatment of behavioural problems as the use of 'self-talk' and reinforcement of appropriate thinking about the behaviours (Greenberger & Padesky, 1995). Cognitive behaviour therapy does not, like other therapies, seek to delve into the unconscious mind, as in more psychodynamic models, and tries to treat the faulty individual schemas and behaviours with specific reinforcement approaches common in behaviour-modification approaches.

Cognitive behaviour therapy seeks to treat people with communication and social behaviour disorders and maladaptive behaviour, and, as such, is an attempt to bring the reinforcement concept into a modern approach whereby better human communication and behaviour can be assisted in such contexts. There is a good deal of research and writing on this therapy concept and its applicability to language and behavioural disorders (Goisman, 1997).

The second major recent development that has been developed from the Skinnerian operant basis, in what is termed a post-Skinnerian approach, is relational frame theory (Barnes-Holmes, Barnes-Holmes & Cullinan, 2000; Hayes, Barnes-Holmes & Roche, 2001). This is a recent and potentially powerful approach that argues for a new and different perspective on the way human language is discussed from a behaviourist point of view. As Owen (2002) states:

> Relational frame theory also suggests an entirely new theoretical approach to the *nature of language*. Specifically, it suggests that *language behavior is relational framing behavior* (see S. C. Hayes, 1994; S. C. Hayes et al., 2001, p. 144). That is, to talk about something is to frame that thing relationally in a particular way, and thereby to make a particular kind of 'sense' out of it. The value of this 'sense' can then be checked out against one's experiences.

Relational frame theory maintains that there is a place for contingencies of reinforcement in the traditional operant sense, but the basic book and theory exposition is set up as a critique of Skinner's original book, *Verbal Behavior*, and as such attempts to take the field beyond the Skinnerian views. The field of relational frame theory is emerging as one that has inspired a good deal of recent research and controversy as well. Two different reviewers of the basic book, edited by Hayes, Barnes-Holmes, and Roche (2001), have taken the group to task for a number of reasons, including that the text is difficult to read and complex (Salzinger, 2003), that the theory promises much but is less convincing to those who hold Skinnerian views (Palmer, 2004), and that there is some doubt as to the merit of seeing relational frame theory as a basic new theory. As Palmer states in the abstract of his lengthy review of the work,

> The authors dismiss Skinner's interpretation of verbal behavior as unproductive and conceptually flawed and suggest a new definition and a new paradigm for the investigation of verbal phenomena. I found the empirical phenomena important but the conceptual discussion incomplete. A new principle of behavior is promised, but critical features of this principle are not offered. In the absence of an explicit principle, the theory itself is difficult to evaluate. (p. 189)

The emergence of relational frame theory as a new paradigm with some promise is not doubted so much by writers such as Salzinger of the American Psychological Association, who concedes that the work is thought provoking and worthy of additional notice, research, and follow-up. Relational frame theory may offer a more useful approach to the place of reinforcement in human communication as a post-Skinnerian conceptualisation in this era of postmodernity, where many such behaviourist themes and approaches are anathema.

OVERVIEW

This chapter has presented the concept of reinforcement as a social skill that is essential in human communication. It has traversed the issues surrounding both the theory and the philosophical basis of the concept, which emanates from operant psychology, and the issue of distinguishing reinforcement from feedback, but with an acceptance of their linked nature in common parlance. The chapter has also offered some evidence that while the concept and understanding of reinforcement within the current communications literature in the twenty-first century is not seen as a mainstream approach in an era of postmodernity, there are still many advocates and researchers who are utilising this conceptualisation in communication, particularly in the area of treatment of language and behavioural disorders in children and adults. In addition, the emergence of approaches such as functional communication training and relational frame theory in the past few years has rejuvenated, to some extent, the place of reinforcement in the study and understanding of human communication.

REFERENCES

Anstey, M. & Bull, G. (2004). *The literacy labyrinth*, 2nd edn. Frenchs Forest: Pearson Prentice-Hall Australia.

Argyle, M. (1967). *The psychology of interpersonal behaviour*. Harmondsworth: Penguin.

Argyle, M. & Cook, M. (1967). *Gaze and mutual gaze in social interaction*. London: Cambridge University Press.

Bandura, A. (1971). *Social learning theory*. New York: General Learning Press.

Bandura, A. (1986). *Social foundations of thought and action: a social cognitive theory*. Englewood Cliffs, NJ: Prentice-Hall.

Barnes-Holmes, D., Barnes-Holmes, Y. & Cullinan, V. (2000). Relational frame theory and Skinner's verbal behavior, a possible synthesis. *Behavior Analysts, 23*, 69–84.

Becker, W. C., Englemann, S., Carnine, D. W. & Rhine, W. R. (1981). Direct instruction model. In W. R. Rhine (Ed.), *Making schools more effective: new directions from follow through*. New York: Academic Press.

Bjork, D. W. (1993). *B. F. Skinner: a life*. New York: Basic Books.

Bracken, C. C. & Lombard, M. (2004). Social presence and children: praise, intrinsic motivation, and learning with computers. *Journal of Communication (UK), 54*, 22–37.

Bracken, C. C., Jeffres, L. W. & Neuendorf, K. A. (2004). Criticism or praise? The impact of verbal versus text-only computer feedback on social presence, intrinsic motivation, and recall. *CyberPsychology and Behavior, 7*, 349–357.

Brophy, J. E. (1981). Teacher praise: a functional analysis. *Review of Educational Research, 51*, 5–32.

Carlopio, J., Andrewartha, G., Armstrong, H., Whetton, D. & Cameron, K. (2001). *Developing management skills*, 2nd edn. Frenchs Forest: Pearson Education Australia.

Carr, J. E. & LeBlanc, L. (2004). A comment on Drash and Tudor's (2004) operant theory of autism. *Analysis of Verbal Behavior*, *20* 25–29.

Christopherson, E. R. & Mortweet, S. L. (2003). *Parenting that works: building skills that last a lifetime*. Washington, DC: American Psychological Association.

Cook, M. (1977). The social skill model of interpersonal attraction. In S. Duck (Ed.), *Theory and practice in interpersonal attraction*. London: Academic Press.

Cresswell, J. W. (2003). *Research design: qualitative, quantitative and mixed approaches*. Thousand Oaks, CA: Sage.

Drash, P. W. & Tudor, R. M. (1990). Language and cognitive development: a systematic behavioral program and technology for increasing the language and cognitive skills of developmentally disabled and at-risk preschool children. In M. Hersen, R. M. Eisler & P. M. Miller (Eds), *Progress in behavior modification*, vol. 26. Newbury Park, CA: Sage.

Drash, P. W. & Tudor, R. M. (2004). An analysis of autism as a contingency-shaped disorder. *Analysis of Verbal Behavior*, *20*, 5–23.

Durand, V. M. (2002). *Severe behavior problems: a functional communication training approach*. New York: Guilford Press.

Durand, V. M. & Carr, E. G. (1991). Functional communication training to reduce challenging behavior: maintenance and application in new settings. *Journal of Applied Behavior Analysis*, *24*, 251–264.

Durand, V. M. & Carr, E. G. (1992). An analysis of maintenance following functional communication training. *Journal of Applied Behavior Analysis*, *25*, 777–794.

Feldman, R. S. (Ed.) (1992). *Applications of nonverbal behavioral theories and research*. Hillsdale, NJ: Lawrence Erlbaum.

Fisher, W. W., Kuhn, D. E. & Thompson, R. H. (1998). Establishing discriminative control of responding using functional and alternative reinforcers during functional communication training. *Journal of Applied Behavior Analysis*, *26*, 543–560.

Goisman, R. M. (1997). Cognitive-behavioral therapy today. *Harvard Mental Health Letter*, *13*, 4–7.

Green, D. & Campbell, R. (Eds) (2003). *Literacies and learners*, 2nd edn. Frenchs Forest: Prentice-Hall Australia.

Greenberger, D. & Padesky, C. (1995). *Mind over mood: a cognitive therapy treatment manual for clients*. New York: Guilford Press.

Hagopian, L. P., Fisher, W. W., Sullivan, M. T., Acquisto, J. & LeBlanc, L. A. (1998). Effectiveness of functional communication training with and without extinction and punishment: a summary of 21 inpatient cases. *Journal of Applied Behavior Analysis*, *31*, 211–236.

Hargie, O. D. W. (Ed.) (1986). *A handbook of communication skills*. London: Croom Helm.

Hargie, O. D. W. (Ed.) (1997). *The handbook of communication skills*, 2nd edn. London: Routledge.

Hargie, O. & Dickson, D. (2004). *Skilled interpersonal communication: research, theory and practice*, 4th edn. London: Routledge.

Hargie, O., Dickson, D. & Tourish, D. (2004). *Communication skills for effective management*. Houndmills: Palgrave Macmillan.

Hayes, S. C, Barnes-Holmes, D. & Roche, B. (Eds) (2001). *Relational frame theory: a post-Skinnerian account of human language and cognition*. New York: Kluwer Academic.

Heckel, R. B., Wiggins, S. L. & Salzberg, H. C. (1962). Conditioning against silences in group therapy. *Journal of Clinical Psychology*, **18**, 216–231.

Johnson, R. B. & Onwuegbuzie, A. J. (2004). Mixed methods research: a research paradigm whose time has come. *Educational Researcher*, **33**, 14–26.

Jones, S. E. & Le Baron, C. D. (2002). Research on the relationship between verbal and nonverbal communication: emerging integrations. *Journal of Communication*, **52**, 499–521.

Kazdin, A. E. (1989). *Behavior modification in applied settings*, 4th edn. Pacific Grove, CA: Brooks/Cole.

Kleitsch, E. C., Whitman, T. L. & Santos, J. (1983). Increasing verbal interaction among elderly socially isolated mentally retarded adults: a group language training procedure. *Journal of Applied Behavior Analysis*, **16**, 217–233.

Kohn, A. (1993). *Punished by rewards*. Boston, MA: Houghton Mifflin.

Lee, V. (1988). *Beyond behaviorism*. Hillsdale, NJ: Lawrence Erlbaum.

Macmillan, D. L. (1973). *Behavior modification in education*. New York: Macmillan.

Maslow, A. H. (1954) *Motivation and personality*. New York: Harper & Row.

Mehan, H. (1978). Structuring school structure. *Harvard Educational Review*, **48**, 32–64, republished in Hodge, B. (Ed.) (1983). *Readings in language and communication for teachers*. Melbourne: Longman-Cheshire.

Minkin, N., Braukmann. C. J., Minjin, B. L., Timbers, G. D., Fixsen, B. J., Phillips, E. L. & Wolf, M. M. (1976). The social validation and training of coversational skills. *Journal of Applied Behavior Analysis*, **9**, 127–139.

O'Leary, K. D. & O'Leary, S. G. (1977). *Classroom management*, 2nd edn. New York: Pergamon.

Owen, J. L. (2002). A retrospective on behavioral approaches to human language – and some promising new developments. *American Communication Journal*, **5**, 1–19.

Palmer, D. C. (2004). Data in search of a principle: a review of relational frame theory: a post-Skinnerian account of human language and cognition. *Journal of the Experimental Analysis of Behavior*, **81**, 189–204.

Place, U. T. (1998). Evidence for the role of operant reinforcement in the acquisition and maintenance of linguistic competence. *www.shef.ac.uk/~phil/connex/issu04/place2.html* (accessed 21.10.04).

Rhine, W. R., Elardo, R. & Spencer, L. M. (1981). Improving educational environments: the follow through approach. In W. R. Rhine (Ed.), *Making schools more effective: new directions from follow through*. New York: Academic Press.

Robbins, S. P., Bergman, R., Stagg, I. & Coulter, M. (2003). *Management*, 3rd edn. Frenchs Forest: Pearson Education Australia.

Salzinger, K. (2003). On the verbal behavior of relational frame theory: a post-Skinnerian account of human language and cognition. *Analysis of Verbal Behavior*, **19**, 7–9.

Scheflen, A. E. (1972). *Body language and social order: communication as behavioral control*. Englewood Cliffs, NJ: Prentice-Hall.

Schneider, S. C. & Barsoux, J.-L. (2003). *Managing across cultures*, 2nd edn. Harlow: Pearson Education.

Schunk, D. H. (2004). Continuing the controversy about reward and intrinsic motivation. *Contemporary Psychology: APA Review of Books*, **49**, 532–534.

Skinner, B. F. (1974). *About behaviorism*. New York: Vintage Books.

Tashakkori, A. & Teddlie, C. (1998). *Mixed methodology: combining qualitative and quantitative approaches*. Applied Social Research Methods Series, vol. 46. Thousand Oaks, CA: Sage.

Tashakkori, A. & Teddlie, C. (Eds) (2003). *Handbook of mixed methods in social and behavioral research*. Thousand Oaks, CA: Sage.

Turney, C., Clift, J. C., Dunkin. M. J. & Traill, R. D. (1973). *Microteaching: research, theory and practice*. Sydney: Sydney University Press.

Turney, C., Cairns, L. G., Williams, G., Hatton, N. & Owens, L. C. (1973). *Sydney micro skills. Series 1 handbook*. Sydney: Sydney University Press.

Wierzbicka, A. (2004). The English expressions *good boy* and *good girl* and cultural models of child rearing. *Culture and Psychology, 10*, 251–278.

Chapter 6

Reflecting

David Dickson

REFLECTING, AS A FEATURE of skilled interpersonal communication, is closely associated with active listening: with responding to the other in such a way as to convey interest, understanding, and engagement. The topic of listening, though, is taken up in another chapter of this book, so little more, as such, will be said about it here. Rather, the focus in this chapter is more specifically on both functional and structural aspects of the process called reflecting. Its various functions are outlined and contrasting theoretical perspectives brought to bear. A review of research into reflecting is also presented and conclusions drawn as to the interpersonal effects of this way of relating.

Before setting off in this direction, though, time spent reminding ourselves of some of the key features of interpersonal communication may be worthwhile. One of the commonly agreed characteristics of this transactional process is its multidimensionality. Messages exchanged between interactors are seldom unitary or discrete (Burgoon, 1994; Wood, 2004). In a seminal work by Watzlawick, Beavin, and Jackson (1967), attention was drawn to two separate, but nevertheless interrelated levels at which people engage. One has to do with substantive content, and the other with relational matters which help determine how participants define their association in terms of, for instance, extent of affiliation, balance of power, and degree of intimacy and trust.

Content is probably the more immediately recognisable dimension of interpersonal communication, dealing as it does with the subject matter of talk – the topic of conversation. Through relational communication, on the other hand, interactors work at establishing where they stand with each other vis-à-vis, for instance, closeness and liking. Dominance and control are also important aspects of relational communication that have to be managed, and some sort of implicit or explicit working agreement reached. While the issue of who should control the conversation may be a topic for discussion (content), such matters are more often handled in indirect and subtle ways. It is typically in *how* interactors talk about what they talk about that relational work is carried on. Dominance and control may be manifested in a plethora of verbal and non-verbal actions such as initiating topic changes, interrupting, maintaining eye contact, and speaking loudly.

INTERACTIONAL STYLE AND DIRECTNESS

An important consideration in the exercise of control is that of interpersonal style, a construct discussed extensively by Norton (1983) and more recently by Lumsden and Lumsden (2003). Style can be thought of as *how* what is done is done, with the characteristic manner in which someone handles an interactive episode. Cameron (2000) emphasised its expressive function in creating a particular 'aesthetic' presence for the other. Conversational style includes the degree of formality, elaboration, or directness adopted (Adler & Rodman, 2000). We will dwell upon the latter characteristic, directness, which has been commented upon in various domains of professional practice, including teaching (Brown & Atkins, 1988), social work (Seden, 1999), medicine (Roter & McNeilis, 2003), and counselling and psychotherapy (Corey, 1997). Referring specifically to interviewing, Stewart and Cash (2000, pp. 22–23) explained:

> In a directive approach, the interviewer establishes the purpose of the interview and attempts to control the pacing, climate, formality and drift of the interview. . . . In a nondirective approach the interviewer may allow the interviewee to control the purpose, subject matter, tenor, climate, formality and pacing.

Directness therefore involves the degree of explicit influence and control exercised or at least attempted (DeVito, 2004) and, correspondingly, the extent to which the conversational partner is constrained in responding.

Interviewers who follow a direct approach typically employ what Benjamin (1987) called 'leads': those with a less direct style make greater use of 'responses'. Although both terms are difficult to define unambiguously, responding has to do with reacting to the thoughts and feelings of interviewees, with exploring their worlds and keeping them at the centre of things. On the other hand, the interviewer who leads tends to replace the interviewee on centre stage and become the dominant feature in the interaction. Benjamin (1987, p. 206) put it as follows:

> When I respond, I speak in terms of what the interviewee has expressed. I react to the ideas and feelings he has communicated to me with something of my own. When I lead, I take over. I express ideas and feelings to which I expect the interviewee to react. . . . When leading, I make use of my own life space; when responding, I tend more to utilize the life space of the interviewee. Interviewer responses keep the interviewee at the centre of things; leads make the interviewer central.

Reflections are accordingly a type of response. They involve the interviewer striving to capture the significant message in the respondent's previous contribution and re-presenting this understanding. This has been described as mirroring back to the interviewee what the interviewee has just said, as grasped by the interviewer. Reflections can be contrasted with questions, for example, which often serve to lead in this sense.

REFLECTING: CONCEPTUAL PERSPECTIVES

Reflecting, as a topic of scholarly enquiry, is bedevilled by conceptual confusion, terminological inconsistency, and definitional imprecision, some of which has been alluded to by Hill and O'Brien (1999). An attempt is made here to disentangle the central themes. At a broad level, reflecting is operationally concerned with person A in some way grasping the significance of person B's preceding contribution and, in the form of a statement that re-presents this key message, making person B aware of A's understanding. Rogers (1951), who is commonly credited with coining the term although he later came to disparage it, regarded reflecting as a method of communicating an understanding of the other and the concerns expressed, from the other's point of view, and of 'being with' that person. Wilkins (2003) also highlighted a role in checking accuracy of understanding. Attempts to introduce greater precision and, in particular, to specify how these effects can be achieved by the interviewer have, however, led to some of the semantic difficulties mentioned above. (Causes of these incongruities, traceable to Rogers' evolving ideas and those of his colleagues, are discussed in the following section.) These inconsistencies and indeed contradictions can be illustrated by considering several definitions of the term. For French (1994, p. 188), reflecting 'is the act of merely repeating a word, pair of words or sentence exactly as it was said', a view shared by Burnard (1999, p. 85), for whom it is a technique that 'involves simply echoing back to the client the last few words spoken by him or her'. Contrast these definitions with the analysis given by Geldard and Geldard (2003, p. 76), who, in referring to a specific example provided, stressed that 'the reflection by the helper didn't repeat word for word what the person said, but expressed things differently. Thus, the helper used their own words rather than the other person's. This is essential . . .'. According to the first two definitions, reflecting comprises mere repetition of the exact words used by the client in the preceding exchange, while, in the last definition, this is precisely what reflecting is not.

Some have regarded reflecting as a unitary phenomenon (Benjamin, 1987), while others have conceived of it as a rubric subsuming a varying number of related processes. These include *reflection of content* (Manthei, 1997), *reflecting experience* (Brammer & MacLeod, 2003), *reflecting meaning* (Ivey et al., 2002; Freshwater, 2003), *content responses* and *affect responses* (Danish & Hauer, 1973), and *restatement* (Hill & O'Brien, 1999). Perhaps the most commonly cited distinction, though, is between *reflection of feeling* and *paraphrasing* (Hargie & Dickson, 2004). In some cases, ostensibly different labels have essentially the same behavioural referent (for instance, paraphrasing, reflection of content, and content responses), while in others the same label is used to denote processes differing in important respects.

To appreciate fully the issues involved and locate the sources of these confusions and inconsistencies, it is necessary to extend our discussion of communication and what it entails.

A common distinction is that between verbal and non-verbal communication. Laver and Hutcheson (1972) further differentiated between vocal and non-vocal aspects of the process. The latter relates to those methods that do not depend upon the vocal apparatus and includes, for example, facial expressions, posture, gestures, and other body movements. These have more recently become popularised as *body language* (Bull, 2002). Vocal communication incorporates all of the components of speech; not only the actual words used (verbal communication) but features of their delivery (the vocal element of non-verbal communication). The latter has been divided, although with little consistency (Robinson, 2003), into *prosody* (e.g. speed, rhythm), *paralanguage* (e.g. timbre, voice quality), and *extra-linguistics* (e.g. accent). For ease of reference, though, and because their tight specification is not central to the thrust of this chapter, the more global term *non-verbal* will be used, for the most part, to label all three, together with body language (for a review of non-verbal communication, see Chapter 3). In the face-to-face situation, therefore, people make themselves known by three potential methods: first, and most obviously, by words used; second, via the non-verbal facets of speech; and third, by means of various other bodily movements and states.

Another common distinction in this area, with respect to that which is communicated (rather than *how* it is communicated), is between the *cognitive* and the *affective*. The former has to do with the domain of the logical and rational, with facts and ideas that are mostly predicated on external reality, although they can be subjective. On the other hand, affect relates to emotional concerns, to feeling states and expressions of mood. As explained by Cormier and Cormier (1998, p. 101):

> The portion of the message that expresses information or describes a situation or event is called the *content*, or the cognitive part, of the message. The cognitive part of a message includes references to a situation or event, people, objects, or ideas. Another portion of the message may reveal how the client feels about the content; expression of feeling or an emotional tone is called the *affective* part of the message . . .

In actual practice, of course, both types of communication coalesce. In addition, both can be conveyed verbally and non-verbally (via body language, prosody, paralanguage, and extra-linguistics), although it is generally more common for cognitive information to be conveyed verbally and emotional expression non-verbally (Richmond & McCroskey, 2000). More particularly, the affective component of a message can take the following three basic forms:

1   *Explicitly stated.* Here the feeling aspect is explicitly stated in the verbal content. For example, 'I was terrified.'
2   *Implicitly mentioned.* In this case, feelings are not directly stated, but rather the affective information is implicitly contained in what is said. For example, 'I tried to scream but nothing came out.' Here the emotional message is grasped by 'reading between the lines'.
3   *Inferred.* The affective component can also be deduced from the manner in

which the verbal content is delivered – from the non-verbal accompaniments, both vocal and non-vocal. Research has shown that when the verbal and non-verbal elements of an emotional or attitudinal message conflict as, for example, when someone says glumly, 'I am overjoyed', the non-verbal often holds sway in our decoding (Knapp & Hall, 2002). In the case of inferred feelings, the verbal content of the message (i.e. *what* is said) does not play a direct part.

To summarise, communications may contain cognitive/factual material, affective/feeling information, or, indeed, as is more commonly the case, elements of both. Such content can be conveyed verbally (both explicitly and implicitly) or non-verbally (in vocal or non-vocal forms).

The cognitive-affective dimension would appear to be highly salient in this issue of reflecting, and is one factor at the centre of much of the inconsistency and confusion. A second concerns the extent of homomorphic correspondence between the reflection and the original message. In other words, does the interviewer merely repeat verbatim what was said, or is the interviewee's message reformulated in the interviewer's own words, while retaining its semantic integrity? (This dimension has more to do with the verbal than non-verbal modes of delivery. It is possible, however, for the interviewer, when repeating, to echo, more or less accurately, the original paralinguistic accompaniment. Similarly, the interviewer can mirror a non-verbal gesture. While such non-linguistic features have been regarded as an essential part of empathic communication, this has not usually been in the context of mere verbal repetition and so will not be discussed further at this point.) Since the question of repetition-reformulation has been alluded to and since it is less convoluted than the cognition-affect issue, it will be dealt with first.

Returning to the term 'reflecting', we should recall that one line of thought suggests that reflections are essentially repetitions (e.g. Burnard, 1999). Similarly, Nicholson and Bayne (1984, p. 36) wrote that, when using this technique, 'The interviewer repeats a word or phrase which the client has used ...'. They contrasted reflections with paraphrases in this respect. For others, as will be shown shortly, the cognitive-affective dimension is of greater relevance in conceptualising paraphrases. Simple repetitions have alternatively been referred to as verbatim playbacks (Gilmore, 1973), as reflections of content (Porter, 1950), but perhaps more frequently as restatements (Cormier & Hackney, 1999). In its most extreme form, according to Benjamin (1987), the restatement is an exact duplication of the original statement, including the pronoun used, although more frequently this is changed; indeed, the restatement may repeat in a more selective fashion.

Those who talk about restatements as repetitions tend to set them apart from reflections on the basis of not only form but also function. For some, restatements are of limited utility and, at best, have more to do with indicating attempts at rudimentary hearing than with understanding. Adler, Rosenfeld, and Proctor (2001) cautioned that consistent use runs the risk of making the interviewer seem foolish or even hard of hearing. Indeed, depending upon circumstances, restatements may even convey incredulity, disapproval, or sarcasm. Brammer, Shostrom, and Abrego (1989, p. 110) commented, 'Perhaps the most glaring reflection error of the novice counselor is to express the reflection in words already used by the client.' However, and more positively for Rennie (1998, p. 37), 'repeating exactly what the client has said at times is useful because it signals to the client that what was just said is significant, worthy of attention, important. By the same token, it stimulates dwelling within what was said.' Reflecting, though, is commonly regarded as going beyond this level to convey listening, and promote deep understanding (Brammer & MacLeod, 2003).

Reflections, therefore, are typically located at the reformulation end of the repetition-reformulation continuum and have been described as 'statements, in the interviewer's own words, that encapsulate and re-present the essence of the interviewee's previous message' (Hargie & Dickson, 2004, p. 148). Comparable definitions in this respect have been provided by, among others, Nelson-Jones (1990) and Geldard and Geldard (2003).

Turning to matters of content, reflections are typically held to contain the essential core of the interviewee's previous communication Thus, they may include both cognitive and affective material. It will be recalled that some who have conceived of reflections in this general way have typically made further distinctions between reflective statements that are restricted to feeling issues and those concerned with what is frequently called 'content' (e.g. Cormier & Cormier, 1998; Hayes, 2002), although it is generally accepted that the difference is more one of relative emphasis than mutual exclusion.

Reflection of feeling is the preferred term for the affective dimension of communication, while those reflective utterances that focus upon factual content, by contrast, are typically referred to as *paraphrases*. Reflecting feeling has been defined by Hargie and Dickson (2004, p. 159) as 'the process of feeding back to Person B, in Person A's own words, the essence of B's previous communication, the emphasis being on feelings expressed rather than cognitive content'. Paraphrasing is defined similarly, although here the emphasis is placed on 'facts and ideas rather than emotions' (Hayes, 2002, p. 66). In spite of this criterion, definitions of paraphrasing can be found which include both affect and cognition. For instance, Lumsden and Lumsden (2003, p. 91) instructed those paraphrasing to, 'In your own words, restate what you think the other person is saying and feeling.' Similarly, Brammer and MacLeod (2003, p. 74) pointed out, 'Usually the paraphrase has heavy cognitive content, although it includes feelings if these are an important part of the helpee's message.'

In some of these cases, as previously mentioned, the repetition-reformulation dimension, rather than the cognitive-affective, would appear to be the major consideration, with paraphrases being contrasted with simple echoic repetitions. In other cases, it would seem that a somewhat different and more subtle distinction is being exploited, although one which emerges only vaguely due to frequent lack of detail and clarity in the definitions provided. It would appear to involve primarily neither cognitive-affective content of interviewee message nor the extent of repetition-reformulation by the interviewer, but rather the mode of expression of the information divulged by the interviewee. Paraphrasing could accordingly be said to focus exclusively upon the verbal statement and, since feelings can be related in this manner, encompass both cognition and affect. Here it is very much the literal meaning of 'paraphrase' that is operationalised, and this appears to be the line followed by authors such as Lumsden and Lumsden (2003) and Wood (2004). Accordingly, although in the context of students' written work rather than face-to-face interaction, plagiarising rather than paraphrasing material was defined by Roig (1999) as involving the appropriation of a sequence of five or more consecutive words from the source.

With this literal meaning in mind, researchers such as Haase and DiMattia (1976) employed paraphrases to promote affective self-referenced statements among subjects. Paraphrases regarded in this manner are contrasted with reflections, as defined by Benjamin (1987, p. 215), for example, in the following way: 'Reflection consists of bringing to the surface and expressing in words those feelings and attitudes that lie behind the interviewee's words.' Likewise, Northouse and Northouse (1998, p. 175) explained that, rather than focusing on '*what* the client has said (the content), the focus in reflecting is on *how* something has been expressed, or the feeling dimension'. Nelson-Jones (2004, p. 129) described reflecting feeling as 'responding to clients' music and not just to their words'. While paraphrases are restricted to what is actually said, reflections concentrate upon less obvious information frequently revealed in more subtle ways.

This confusion can, in large part, be traced back to the word 'content', which features in many definitions of paraphrasing and sets it apart from reflection of feeling. Ivey and Authier (1978, p. 83), for instance, proposed that paraphrasing 'could be considered an attempt at feedback to the client of the content of what he has just said, but in a restated form'. However, 'content' has been used in slightly different ways, which have largely gone unnoticed, to refer to somewhat different aspects of the other's message, namely, mode of communication (i.e. verbal) and type of information conveyed in this manner (i.e. cognitive/factual). Note that the term is not used in a more global manner to describe *all* of the information communicated. The issue, stated as unambiguously as possible, would seem to be this: is 'content' taken to mean the verbal facet or the non-affective component of the message? It is, of course, possible for the verbal to be affective. Since the word 'content' is commonly used in the literature as the antonym of 'feeling', one would suspect the latter.

Following this line of argument, paraphrases, defined as involving content, emphasise the non-affective or factual (e.g. above definition by Hayes, 2002), while reflections of feeling deal with feelings expressed both verbally and non-verbally. This is the stance taken by authors such as Cormier and Cormier (1998, p. 101):

> The portion of the message that expressed information or describes a situation or event is called the *content*, or the cognitive part, of the message.... Another portion of the message may reveal how the client feels about the content; expression of feeling or an emotional tone is called the *affective* part of the message.

The fact that 'content' concerns factual components and that reflections of feeling can draw upon affect, verbally stated, is underlined:

> Generally, the affect part of the verbal message is distinguished by the client's use of an affective or feeling word, such as *happy, angry* or *sad*. However, clients may also express their feelings in less obvious ways, particularly through various non-verbal behaviors. (p. 101)

By contrast, others would appear to equate content solely with the verbal mode of communication. It is therefore permissible when paraphrasing to include both aspects of fact and feeling, as has already been mentioned. Unfortunately, the position is even less straightforward. Some authors seemingly straddle this particular divide. Ivey and Authier (1978, p. 539), for example, wrote that:

> responding to the feeling being expressed rather than attending solely to the content and decision issues is what is important in [reflection of feeling]. What the client is saying is the content portion of the message. One must also listen to how the client gives a message. It is this feeling portion of the communication to which you are to pay attention.

Here 'content' obviously refers to the verbal message, while non-verbal components are emphasised in relation to the communication of feeling states. Reflections of feeling utilise the latter, while paraphrases tap content. Thus, it could be assumed (and in accordance with the views of those already mentioned: e.g. Lumsden & Lumsden, 2003; Wood, 2004) that mode of expression is the defining characteristic and that paraphrases may mirror back facts and feelings *verbally* expressed. But in actual fact, Ivey and Authier (1978) stressed that paraphrases address the non-affective and, by so doing, invoke the cognitive-affective dimension as being of prime importance.

In concluding this section, it may be useful to re-present the three dimensions that seem to be conceptually central to structural aspects of reflecting, as much of the inconsistency and ambiguity existing in the literature stems from a lack of appreciation of, or confusion among, them. First, the cognitive-affective issue is concerned with the communicated message and the extent to which the reflective statement focuses upon facts, feelings, or indeed both. Second, the repetition-reformulation continuum addresses the extent to which the reflection recasts rather than merely parrots the original interviewee statement. The mode of communication of this message is the basis of the third dimension. (In actual practice, this dimension is not entirely independent of the second; that is, opportunities for repetition decrease in conjunction with decreases in explicit verbal presentation.) Was the information carried verbally or by other and often less conspicuous means? Allied to this is the implication that non-verbal messages are often more ambiguous than those verbally stated. (This, of course, is not invariably so.) The importance of the latter dimension should not be overlooked, however, especially in situations where the interviewee is striving to come to grips with a personal difficulty. Under these circumstances, a reflection which encapsulates an aspect of the problem of which the interviewee was but vaguely aware can be extremely beneficial (Egan, 2001). Mearns and Thorne (2000) explored the therapeutic significance of dealing with material on the edge of the client's awareness.

The difficulty of producing a consensual definition of reflecting should be obvious from the foregoing. Nevertheless, the following claims, although tentatively made, would appear warrantable. Reflections are statements that capture and re-present the essence of the interviewee's previous message. They can incorporate cognitive and affective components and are expressed in the interviewer's own words. Reflections which concentrate more single-mindedly upon affective issues, whether or not these were *explicitly* shared by the interviewee in the original communication, have more frequently been labelled reflections of feeling. On the other hand, those that address the non-affective content of the utterance have been called, for the most part, reflections of content or paraphrases.

REFLECTING: THEORETICAL PERSPECTIVES

The process of reflecting can be interpreted from at least three fundamentally different disciplinary positions. These are humanistic psychology, behaviourist psychology, and linguistics (more specifically, pragmatics). In keeping with the former, it is, in part, the communication of those attitudes and conditions promoting psychological growth and maturity. To the behaviourist, it is a means of influencing and modifying what people do and how they respond to their social environment. Finally, in keeping with pragmatics, reflecting can be thought of as part of the elaborate business of managing talk in the course of interaction.

The humanistic approach

The name Carl Rogers is habitually invoked in discussions of the most influential twentieth-century figures in shaping the humanistic movement in psychology. In the helping context, he is also acknowledged as the founder of the person-centred counselling movement, although Mearns and Thorne (2000) noted how uncomfortably this approach actually sits alongside other recognized humanistic therapies. A detailed consideration of Rogers' theoretical position lies far beyond the scope of this chapter. (For fuller details of Rogerian and neo-Rogerian thinking, see, for instance, Rogers, 1951, 1961, 1980; Mearns & Thorne, 2000; Thorne, 2002; McMillan, 2004.) At a rudimentary level, however, an outline of his theory of human functioning will be sketched, based upon several interlocking, key concepts. These include *the organism, actualising tendency, phenomenological field, self, positive regard*, and *incongruence*.

The *organism*, psychologically speaking, is at the centre of all experience and is a totally organised system comprising physical, cognitive, affective, and behavioural facets. It is energised by a single and immensely powerful motivating force, the *actualising tendency*. This concept lies at the heart of person-centred thought (Sanders, 2000) and refers to a positive influence toward growth and development. Wilkins (2003, p. 33) offered a broad definition along the lines of 'the tendency of life forms to develop more complex organization and to fulfil their potential'. Rogers (1951) underscored the inherent dynamism of this force in stating, 'The organism has one basic tendency and striving – to actualize, maintain, and enhance the experiencing organism' (p. 487).

Were the actualising tendency permitted to operate unimpaired, the outcome would be a person in the process of becoming *self-actualised*. Such individuals show an openness to experience, self-trust, the adoption of an internal locus of evaluation, and a willingness to continue the self-actualising process (Irving, 1995). They are not dependent upon others as a source of evaluation but are confidently self-reliant in this respect. Few, unfortunately, live self-actualising lives. The personally experienced world of the individual is called the *phenomenological field* and consists of everything that is, at least potentially, available to awareness. Part of this totality relates to the self; the child develops a particular *self-concept*. This can be thought of as a view of self together with an evaluation of it. Significant others, such as parents, have a key role to play in this process due to the individual's need for *positive regard*. This need to gain the love, respect, and esteem of others important to the person is deep felt.

Such positive regard, however, is generally not provided unconditionally. Instead, certain *conditions of worth* are attached – the child knows that behaviour of a certain type must be displayed in order to win approval. Therefore, it becomes imperative for the child to behave not only in keeping with the actualising tendency but to ensure that conditions of worth are not violated. Such dual standards invariably lead to conflicts and attempted compromises. Within the individual is held in tension, as it were, a self-concept at odds with the organismic self (Hough, 2002). The outcome is incongruence; the self-concept becomes divorced from the actual experiences of the organism (Tengland, 2001). As observed by Butt (2004, p. 50), 'Rogers' theory proposes a split between the natural and the social: an organismic process that is good and true, and a social world that impedes and hinders.' Incongruence is associated with feelings of threat and anxiety and, consequently, the falsification or indeed denial of experiences leading to the distortion of the self-concept. This is the antithesis of becoming self-actualised.

For Rogers, the source of personal problems is, to a great extent, the conditional nature of positive regard. The individual already subjected to incongruence can be encouraged to further growth and psychological maturity within the context of a particular relationship where conditions of worth are removed from positive regard. This other should manifest *congruence* and provide *unconditional* positive regard. Since no attempt is made to impose values or be judgemental, threat is reduced, thus enabling the individual to explore feelings previously denied or distorted, and to assimilate them into the self-concept. As explained by Mearns and Thorne (2000, p. 77),

> [Person-centred therapy] takes away from the encounter the notion of a leader or director who will guide the client towards health or the resolution of difficulties. Instead, person-centred therapy proposes for the therapist the role of listener and authentic companion who positively 'prizes' all dimensions of her client.

Reflecting, as a way of listening (Cormier & Cormier, 1998) and a method of responding that imposes no external evaluative comment on client disclosures, thereby satisfies these requirements.

Reflecting is, however, more commonly associated with another characteristic of the effective relationship – accurate *empathic understanding*. In his earlier writings, Rogers (1951) proposed that the empathic counsellor assumes,

> in so far as he is able, the internal frame of reference of the client, to perceive the world as the client sees it, to perceive the client himself as he is seen by himself, to lay aside all perceptions from the external frame of reference while doing so and to communicate something of this empathic understanding to the client. (p. 29)

It was considered that accurate reflecting is the most effective means of communicating this understanding to the client although, as will be outlined, subsequent views on this issue changed somewhat.

Developments have taken place in person-centred thinking over the years (see, for instance, Gelso & Carter, 1985; Mearns & Thorne, 2000; Wyatt, 2001). Three distinct phases in the ongoing evolutionary process labelled, chronologically, *non-directive, reflective,* and *experiential,* can be identified, each characterised by a particular outlook on counsellor function and style. The non-directive counsellor strove to create a permissive, non-judgemental climate by unintrusively displaying acceptance. Clarification of client contributions in order to promote increased insight gradually was also provided. With the advent of the reflective era, greater stress was placed upon effecting a more integrated self-concept and putting the client more completely in touch with his phenomenological world. As far as technique is concerned, reflecting was employed extensively during both of these phases, but particularly in the latter. However, it would seem that subtle differences in use are detectable, which go some way to shedding light on the reasons for the various nuances of definition disentangled in the previous section. Thus, a gradual switch in emphasis took place from reflecting, largely at a fairly superficial level, the factual content of the client's verbalised message (and frequently doing so by simply repeating what was said) to dealing with the affective dimension through mirroring back, in fresh words, feelings expressed. Reflection of feeling became the most widely used technique.

Subsequently, Rogers (1975) utilised the concept of experiencing to account for what takes place during counselling and to provide an updated statement on the nature of empathy. Empathy became conceived as a process of 'being sensitive, moment to moment, to the changing felt meanings which flow in this other person, to the fear, or rage . . . whatever, that he/she is experiencing' (p. 4). It requires a moving closer to the client by gaining a greater awareness of his or her presently experienced inner world of perceptions, thoughts and feelings and the personal meanings attached to these. It is this process and the corresponding commitment of the counsellor to operate within the frame of reference of the client that is important, rather than the particular technique used. In marked contrast to earlier thinking, the supremacy of reflecting feeling as a means of interaction with the client is removed. Indeed, in rejecting the confusion of earlier definitions of empathy with the wooden application of technique, Rogers (1987, p. 39) wrote, 'I even wince at the term reflection of feeling.'

Reflecting is still a legitimate activity, nevertheless, but its effectiveness is dependent upon relating directly to clients' current experiencing and encouraging them to focus more intensely upon and become more fully aware of it. Reflecting should also assist in the process of converting implicit (or unverbalised) meaning into a communicable form without misrepresentation. Rogers came to see checking on accuracy of understanding as the important task being achieved. According to Wilkins (2003), he consequently preferred the labels 'checking perceptions' and 'testing understanding' to 'reflecting feeling'. Regardless of label, the therapeutic effect of responding in this way is to promote the individual's experiencing and consequently produce change toward greater congruence. Since such responses must be directed at the felt meanings experienced by the client, there is no longer the stipulation that reflections must deal with only affective issues. Memories, experiences, thoughts, fantasies, sensations, and such like have equal legitimacy and should be responded to as well (Merry, 2000). Content in this sense becomes less important. The reflective statement may be cognitive, affective, or perhaps more usefully both. Brammer (1993) introduced the variant *reflecting experience* to describe this technique. A further development is a greater move away from the explicitly stated and obvious in the client's utterance to inchoate and vaguely expressed concerns. In offering deeper levels of empathic understanding, the reflection should move beyond the familiar to point tentatively toward experiences only faintly hinted at and less clearly grasped by the client (Egan, 2001; Tolan, 2003). Although possibilities of inaccuracy are increased, such reflections have the potential to move the client forward in experiencing to greater degrees of realisation. Here again can be identified a further source of the conceptual confusion discussed previously.

Empathy has been cast as a multidimensional construct with cognitive, affective, and behavioural aspects (Irving 1995; Irving & Dickson, 2004). According to the latter, and for empathy to make a difference, it must be actually manifested in some way. As a piece of interpersonal behaviour, reflecting is accordingly one (but only one) of a number of possible ways of making someone aware of the fact that they are being empathically understood. Indeed, the point has been put that the specific behavioural expression is largely immaterial, provided that it succeeds in communicating a strong sense to the client of being engaged with in this way (Thorne, 1992; Wilkins, 2003). (It should also be mentioned that some, from a person-centred perspective, express increasing unease at the technique-ridden connotations of any behavioural terms such as 'reflecting', 'paraphrasing', and so forth.) Nevertheless, when used appropriately, reflecting is one possible method consistently mentioned when the communicative dimension of the construct of empathy is discussed (Authier, 1986; Cormier & Cormier, 1998; Hill & O'Brien, 1999; Irving & Dickson, 2004; Nelson-Jones, 2004). Furthermore, analyses of Rogers in videotaped counselling sessions have confirmed that, in fact, he made extensive use of reflective skills (O'Farrell, Hill & Patton, 1986; Lietaer, 2004).

Changes in person-centred thinking have taken place since first formulated by Carl Rogers. Much of the definitional confusion to do with the term 'reflecting' derives from this evolution. Nevertheless, from the point of view of this branch of humanistic psychology, reflecting can be thought of as facilitative communication with the potential to convey unconditional positive regard and empathic understanding thereby pointing the way to possibilities of personal growth and maturity through enhanced self-actualisation.

The behaviourist approach

Reflecting has also been interpreted and investigated in keeping with behaviourist principles. Beginning with Watson (1913), behaviourists have traditionally regarded psychological enquiry as an extension of the natural sciences. Behaviourism, though, is far from a monolithic system of thought (O'Donohue & Kitchener, 1996) but includes, among others, *methodological* and (more prominently) *radical* variants. Philosophical underpinnings of the perspective are explored by Hocutt (1996) and will not be pursued here. Behaviourists have historically restricted psychology enquiry to behaviour, environmental happenings associated with it, and the relationship between these two types of 'in the world' happening. The individual's environment is of paramount importance in shaping what individuals do and what they become. The goal of psychology is to describe, explain, predict, and control behaviour by identifying the regularities existing between it and features of the environment in which it occurs.

The early theorists, including Pavlov and Watson, placed emphasis upon identifiable environmental stimuli serving to elicit particular responses from the organism according to predictable patterns. While some of these stimulus–response connections may be basic reflexes, others are learned. In either case, the individual was regarded as essentially passive, with responses triggered by stimuli in the form of environmental events.

Extending earlier thinking by Thorndike (1911), as enshrined in the *Law of Effect*, Skinner (1938) drew attention to the fact that the environmental consequences for an organism of those actions that are carried out have a considerable bearing upon what is done subsequently. This simple but immensely powerful idea formed the basis of his work on *operant conditioning*. Skinner stressed the *operant* rather than the *respondent* nature of behaviour. Instead of merely reacting to happenings as 'triggers', the organism was seen as emitting behaviour that operated on the environment to effect consequences which, in some cases, led to an increased likelihood of that class of behaviour being performed under comparable sets of circumstances. Such consequences are termed *reinforcers* or *reinforcing stimuli*, and operant conditioning is the process whereby they act to increase the frequency of occurrence of designated behaviour by being made contingent upon it (see Chapter 5 for a review of the area of reinforcement). As explained by Catania (2000, p. 23):

> Operant behavior is behavior that is sensitive to its consequences. When operant behavior becomes more likely because of the consequences it has had, we speak of reinforcement. Some consequences produce increases in the likelihood of operant behavior, and others do not.

Reflecting can be conceived of and researched in terms of operant conditioning procedures (Dickson, Saunders & Stringer, 1993). Reflective statements by person B, acting as reinforcing stimuli on the preceding contribution by person A, will make it more likely that person A will persist with this line of talk. The process can be thought of as one of systematic selection: 'Those responses that are selected increase in relative frequency, while most of the remainder decline' (Leslie, 2002, p. 52).

Reinforcement can take a positive or a negative form. *Positive reinforcement* is formally defined by Maag (1999, p. 71) as referring 'to any stimulus, when presented after the occurrence of a behavior, that increases the future occurrence of the behavior'. He goes on to describe it as 'the most powerful and effective method for increasing or maintaining appropriate behavior' (p. 278). With *negative reinforcement*, by contrast, an act is associated with the avoidance, termination, or reduction of an aversive stimulus that would have either occurred or continued at some existing level had the response not taken place. Behaviour resulting in the noxious stimulus being reduced, eliminated, or avoided will become more prevalent, the *sine qua non* of reinforcement in action. Examples of negative reinforcement in everyday life are common. We have a headache, take FeelFine analgesic, and the pain disappears, making it more likely that we will take FeelFine the next time a headache strikes.

Positive reinforcing stimuli can take a variety of different forms. *Primary reinforcers* include such things as food, drink, sex, etc., the reinforcing potential of which does not rely upon a process of prior learning. *Secondary, token,* or *conditioned* reinforcers, on the other hand, come to be valued through prior association with primary reinforcers, money being an obvious example in contemporary society.

Skinner (1953) also noted a group of conditioned reinforcers typically paired with several other reinforcing stimuli in a broad range of circumstances. These were labelled *generalised* reinforcers. The giving of one's attention to another is an example:

> The attention of people is reinforcing because it is a necessary condition for other reinforcements from them. In general, only people who are attending to us reinforce our behavior. The attention of someone who is particularly likely to supply reinforcement – a parent, a teacher, or a loved one – is an especially good generalized reinforcer. (Skinner, 1953, p.78)

The implication is that various verbal and non-verbal behaviours associated with attention giving, for instance, have the ability to shape how others act in interpersonal situations through selectively acting as *social reinforcers*. Lieberman (2000, p. 208) defined social reinforcers, in broad terms, as 'stimuli whose reinforcing properties derive uniquely from the behavior of other members of the same species'. Social behaviour, by definition, presupposes the involvement of other people. In the main, the types of reinforcers that govern and shape it are also contributed by those with whom we mix and intermingle and are a powerful, though often subtle, influence on our actions. Buss (1983) suggested that they be thought of as either *process* or *content*. The former are an inherent part of interpersonal contact and include, in order of increasing potency, the mere presence of others, attention from them, and their conversational responsiveness. Too much or too little of these activities can be aversive: it is only at some notional level of intermediacy that they become reinforcing.

To switch to the second element of Buss's categorisation, the content of interaction can also have reinforcing ramifications. Here, Buss mentions acts such as showing deference, praising, extending sympathy, and expressing affection. Unlike their process counterparts, these are held to operate along unipolar dimensions. In other words, there is a direct linear correlation between amount and reinforcing effect.

For some, reflecting acts as a social reinforcer because it connotes attention, interest, and acceptance, thereby serving to increase selectively verbal output of the type reflected. In an early experiment, Powell (1968) examined the effects of reinforcing subjects' self-referenced statements (statements about themselves) by means of reflections. The results showed that when, in an interview-type situation, the interviewer responded by using this technique the frequency of such statements increased significantly. In effect, subjects talked more about themselves. Other research, which is reviewed in a later section of this chapter, has produced largely comparable findings.

Some researchers, while remaining within an operant conditioning framework, see reflections working in a slightly different way. When a certain action succeeds only in eliciting reinforcement in the presence of particular accompanying stimuli, that piece of behaviour is said to be under *stimulus control* (Lieberman, 2000), and those stimuli have become *discriminating stimuli* in respect of it. They signal the availability of a reinforcer for behaving in that way. When the overall context acts in this way, *contextual control* is in operation (Sarafino, 1996). Reflections may, therefore, function more as discriminative than reinforcing stimuli. Discriminative stimuli are part of the environmental context within which the organism responds. They signal that reinforcing stimuli are available and, as such, are present at the time of respond-ing rather than afterward (and differ from reinforcing stimuli in this respect). They cue the occasion for reinforcement but do not themselves reinforce. By reflecting feeling, for example, the interviewer may actually be signalling to the interviewee that subsequent reinforcement is available for further affective responses. In the sequential stream of verbal interchange, the task of locating sources of influence is, however, fraught with difficulty. The listener's utterance can be thought of both as a response to the speaker's previous comment and as a stimulus for the next (Leslie & O'Reilly, 1999).

To summarise, reflecting is a method of influencing verbal behaviour by affecting the frequency of occurrence of particular types of response This can be accounted for in terms of the behaviourist principles of operant conditioning and behaviour analysis. As such, reflective statements act as reinforcing (and perhaps discriminative) stimuli and, by implication, promote the class of response represented in the other's preceding line of talk.

The linguistic approach

A reflective statement, whatever else it may be, is part of talk and, as such, is subject to the sphere of influence of linguistics, particularly pragmatics, and amenable to techniques of conversational analysis (CA). Pragmatics explores the factors behind our choice of language, from among a range of possibilities in any given situation, and the effects of those choices on others (Crystal, 1997). It therefore concentrates on language put to use by people as they live their lives (Mey, 1993). CA has its roots in sociology (Gee, 1999) and, as pointed out by Pridham (2001, p. 230), 'argues that conversation has its own dynamic structure and rules, and looks at the methods used by speakers to structure conversation efficiently'. People normally succeed in under-standing one another in ordinary conversations and manage their intercourse in a well-ordered fashion. But this can never be taken for granted, and the identification of the embedded rules and principles that underpin conversational coherence is of con-siderable interest to scholars of language (Jacobs, 2002). Conversationalists constantly work at making talk run smoothly. They anticipate possible confusions and mis-understandings and take avoidance action. When problems do arise, they are identi-fied and repair strategies implemented. Stokes and Hewitt (1976) referred to these management procedures that keep conversation on track as *aligning actions*, and, as specific examples, Nofsinger (1991) discussed *continuers* and *formulations*. From this background, reflections could be regarded as forming part of the complex and often subtle operation of organising and orchestrating conversation.

The process of formulating talk can be thought of as providing comment upon what has been said or what is taking place in the interaction. It has been outlined as follows:

A member may treat some part of the conversation as an occasion to describe that conversation, to explain it, or characterize it, or explicate, or translate, or summarize, or furnish the gist of it, or take note of its accordance with rules, or remark on its departure from rules. That is to say, a member may use some part of the conversation as an occasion to formulate the conversation. (Garfinkel & Sacks, 1970, p. 350)

For McLaughlin (1984), formulations serve to promote, transform, delete, or indeed terminate talk. They have also been found to be used by adults in pointing out and correcting mistakes made by children acquiring language (Chouinard & Clark, 2003), and by native speakers in conversations with adult second-language learners (Philp, 2003).

Reformulations may relate to something the person providing the formulation has contributed (A-issues or events), something the other participant has mentioned (B-issues or events), or, although less frequently, to both (AB-issues or events). A further distinction is that between formulations of *gist* and *upshot* (Heritage & Watson, 1979). The former involves extracting and highlighting the central events and issues featured in the immediately preceding utterance. Formulations of upshot go beyond this to frequently draw conclusions based upon assumptions that may or may not meet with the agreement of the other partner. It would seem that from this standpoint reflections could be regarded as essentially B-event or issue formulations of gist. (It should be also noted, though, that, in analysing Carl Rogers' verbal contributions in a counselling session, Lietaer (2004), in a study already cited, developed separate categories for reflections and reformulation.) It has been noted that formulations of this type are often tentative proposals and require a decision from the other interactor as to their acceptability. Likewise, in the helping context, counsellors have been urged to reflect feelings in a tentative way that always leaves open the opportunity of denial or correction by the client (Cormier & Cormier, 1998; Tolan, 2003). If the other is unwilling to agree to a particular representation of his or her position, one or more modifications are likely to be presented and worked through until agreement is forthcoming. The frequent association between a formulation of this type and confirmation by the other led Heritage and Watson (1979) to characterise them as *adjacency pairs*.

Adjacency pairs are a further feature of conversation that gives it structure and predictability. These are conversation sequences that are 'two turns long, having two parts said by different speakers in adjacent turns at talk' (Jacobs, 2002, p. 225). Furthermore, there is a rule-driven expectation that, in initiating this type of sequence, one positions the other in the role of respondent and places restrictions around what can be offered as an acceptable next speech turn. For example, questions beget answers; requests invoke refusals/acceptances; greetings initiate greetings, and so on. If reflection-confirmation/elaboration works in this way as an adjacency pair, then an obligation is placed upon the other either to explicitly confirm/deny the reformulation or to continue to elaborate the original pronouncement.

According to the two theoretical interpretations previously considered, reflections promote more intense experiencing or reinforce continued discussion of a particular topic. In line with this effect, Nofsinger (1991) also discussed *continuers* as conversational alignment devices that mark a listener's intention to forego making a substantive contribution to the conversation at that precise point. Following early work by Duncan and Fiske (1977) and Sacks, Schegloff, and Jefferson (1978), the mechanisms involved in *conversational turn taking* have been extensively researched. *Back-channel communication* refers to listener contributions that sustain the listener role. They seem to signal that the listener is attentive, interested, even comprehending, but does not seek the floor at that point. A further possibility is that reflections operate essentially in this way. Indeed, their role in the interviewing/counselling literature is often presented as such. If so, reflections can have an additional alignment role as continuers or *minimal responses*, promoting the continuity of the conversational status quo in respect of topic and speaker/listener arrangement. Rhys and Black (2004) showed how Carl Rogers' use of 'mm hmm' was operating in this way in at least some of the instances when used by him in counselling.

But formulations would also seem on occasion to be a way of engineering a change of topic or even the termination of conversation. It has been reported that conversational lapses are often immediately preceded by an utterance of this sort (McLaughlin & Cody, 1982). Likewise, from their detailed analysis of doctor–patient communication, Stiles and Putnam (1992) discovered that reflective statements by doctors often seemed to cut patients off conversationally, rather than encourage deeper exploration. Likewise, Beach and Dixon (2001) identified a characteristic three-step sequence in their in-depth analysis of a medical history interview between a physician's assistant and a female patient. Here a reformulation by the medic led directly to a confirmatory response by the patient followed by a shift of topic initiated in the medic's subsequent conversational turn. For the authors, 'Such actions essentially detoxify topic shift, therefore minimizing the likelihood that movement forward in the interview can be framed as [the interviewer's] heavy-handed pursuit of a medical "agenda" removed from [the patient's] concerns' (p. 29).

How can reflection act both to stimulate deeper exploration of a topic and to preface a hiatus in the conversation or mark the occasion for a change of topic? One possible explanation has to do with the broader communicative frame within which the reflective statement is delivered. In the situated interactive context of eliciting facts leading to a valid medical diagnosis, for example, patients may understand formulations as operating essentially to check the accuracy of a sequence of limited pieces of information under characteristic time pressures. At a more obviously micro-analytic level, the prosodic accompaniment of the verbal content of the reflection may also be crucially important. Variations in pitch can make a statement either interrogative or declarative (Knapp & Hall, 2002). Based upon the linguistic analysis of naturally occurring interactions, Schegloff and Sacks (1973) reported that words spoken with a downward intonation served to terminate topic discussion. Weiner and Goodenough (1977) conceived of reflections as repetition passes (that is, speech acts which serve to forego the opportunity of making a substantive contribution to the continued exploration of the topic), which can be used to bring about a conversational change. However, it was emphasised that in order for reflections to function in this fashion, they must be delivered with a downward rather than a sustained or rising vocal intonation. The corollary of this, it could be argued, is that when reflections are used to facilitate further interviewee exploration, they need to be delivered with a sustained or rising intonation pattern. The depth of the intertwining of verbal and non-verbal modes of communication is increasingly being recognised (e.g. Jones & LeBaron, 2002). Additional features of contemporaneous non-verbal behaviour are also likely to be influential in determining the conversational effects of reflective statements.

Three radically different views of reflecting have been outlined in this section.

According to the person-centred humanist, reflections are a means of accepting the other without condition, of empathising with the other, and helping that person become more fully self-actualising. To the behaviourist, reflections act as social reinforcers to influence the verbal performance of the other by increasing the amount of preordained talk. Lastly, reflections have been depicted as techniques which are used in the organisation and management of conversation not only to maintain or change it but also, under certain circumstances, to bring it to an end.

REFLECTING: FUNCTIONAL PERSPECTIVES

Functional aspects of reflecting have already been mentioned in this chapter to some extent. The present section, however, will cut across perspectives to concentrate more single-mindedly on the various potential effects claimed for the proper use of this technique (e.g. Cormier & Cormier, 1998; Brammer & MacDonald, 1999; Hill & O'Brien, 1999; Martin, 1999; Hayes, 2002). Many are applicable to reflections generally while others are more specific to paraphrasing or reflecting feeling.

One of the more basic functions of reflecting is to show respect for conversational partners by indicating that they are being fully attended to and that active listening is taking place. Reflecting is widely discussed within the context of listening actively (e.g. Levitt, 2001; Hayes, 2002). Active listening on the part of the therapist, in turn, was reported by Myers (2000) to have had a profound effect on the experiences of therapy by clients. As one client disclosed, 'When a person is not listening I notice that he or she will draw on their interpretation and dismiss my position' (p. 156). Listening demonstrates to speakers that they are sufficiently valued and accepted for another to be interested in them and prepared to become involved. Reflecting has, therefore, the potential to form the basis upon which to build a positive, facilitative relationship typified by openness, trust, respect, and empathy (for a detailed review of listening, see Chapter 9).

Reflections are also frequently used in order to clarify. An accurate paraphrase, by condensing and crystallising what has been said, can often help interviewees to see more clearly the exigencies of their situation (Lindon & Lindon, 2000). Mirroring back the core message contained in the interviewee's previous statement enables issues that are vague and confused to be thought through more clearly and objectively. Since problems and concerns, especially of a personal nature, are things experienced, for the most part at a 'gut' level rather than being intellectualised or even verbalised, it often proves difficult to find the words and indeed thoughts to express them unambiguously. By encapsulating and unobtrusively presenting the most salient features of what has just been said, the exigencies of the helped person's predicament can be made more accessible to them.

In addition to acting as a means of enabling the interviewee to appreciate more clearly experienced concerns, reflecting assists the interviewer to check accuracy of understanding and obtain a clearer realisation of the actualities of circumstances (Wilkins, 2003). By reflecting, the interviewer not only conveys a desire to get to know, but also, when it is accurate, demonstrates to the interviewee the level of understanding accomplished, despite the fact that the original message may have been inchoate and vague. Supported in this way, the interviewee is often motivated to continue to explore particular themes more deeply, concentrating upon facts, feelings, or both depending upon the content of the reflective statement (Hill & O'Brien, 1999).

Commenting more particularly upon reflecting feeling states, Cormier and Cormier (1998) pointed out that, as a result, interviewees are influenced to devote greater attention to phenomena of this type. They can be assisted to become more completely aware of their feelings by being encouraged to explore and express them in this way. This can be difficult to accomplish and requires tact but is very worthwhile. Egan (2001) noted that while some feelings are quite laudable and easily accepted, many others prompt defensive reactions and, consequently, are either consciously or subconsciously repressed and denied. As a result, people become estranged from these affective facets of their being. Through the reflection of feeling, such individuals can be put more fully in touch with these realities. By using this technique, the interviewer acknowledges the interviewee's right to feel this way and indicates that it is permissible for those feelings to be expressed and discussed (Hargie & Dickson, 2004).

Another function of reflection of feeling, which is mentioned by Brammer (1993), is to help people to 'own' their feelings – to appreciate that ultimately they are the source, and can take responsibility for their affective states. Various ploys commonly used in order to disown feelings include speaking in the second person (e.g. '*You* get depressed being on your own all the time') or third person (e.g. '*One* gets pretty annoyed'), rather than in the first person (e.g. '*I* get depressed being on my own all the time' and '*I* get pretty annoyed'). Lindon and Lindon (2000, p. 136) talked about helping the other to 'find "I" ' through reflecting. Since reflective statements make explicit others' affective experiences, and label them as clearly theirs, they help those people to acknowledge and come to terms with their emotion. Recipients are also encouraged to examine and identify underlying reasons and motives for behaviour, of which they previously may not have been completely aware. Furthermore, they are brought to realise that feelings can have important causal influences upon their actions.

Finally, the possibility of reflective statements being employed in order to regulate conversation by perhaps serving to engineer the termination of discussion should not be overlooked. Martin (1999), for instance, referred to reflections being used to regulate the pace of the transaction. The various propositions outlined in this section differ substantially in terms of their epistemological basis. While most are, for the most part, theoretically derived or experientially grounded, others have emerged from systematic empirical enquiry. The final section of this chapter selectively reviews some of the research that has been conducted into reflecting.

REFLECTING: EMPIRICAL PERSPECTIVES

The lack of consistency in the operational definition of reflections and related terms has already been discussed at length. The work of categorising individual investigations and trying to abstract broad and consistent relationships among variables is consequently making that much more difficult. Further disparities in the research conducted relate to the theoretical basis of the enquiry, research design and procedures, number and type of subjects, and dependent variables chosen for investigation. That apart, research interest in this area seems to have dwindled over the years, with little meaningful work being identified since the preparation of the version of this chapter in the previous edition of the book.

Reflections

Some studies have compared the outcomes of an indirect, reflective style with a range of alternatives, including an intrusive style (Ellison & Firestone, 1974), an evaluative style (Silver, 1970), and both interrogative and predictive approaches (Turkat & Alpher, 1984). Most of this research has an interviewing or counselling orientation. In some cases, the attitudes of both interviewees and external judges to interviewers manifesting contrasting styles have been sought. Silver (1970), for example, found that low-status interviewees felt much more comfortable with interviewers who displayed a reflective rather than a judgemental approach. Ellison and Firestone (1974) reported that subjects observing a reflective interviewer, rather than an intrusive one, who controlled the direction and pace of the interview in a particularly assertive manner, indicated a greater willingness to reveal highly intimate details. The former interviewer was also perceived as passive, easygoing, and non-assertive.

An interrogative approach in which further information was requested and a predictive style which required the interviewer accurately to predict interviewees' reactions in situations yet to be discussed were the alternatives to reflecting examined by Turkat and Alpher (1984). Although impressions were based upon written transcripts, rather than actual interviews, those interviewers who used reflections were regarded as understanding their clients. Empathic understanding together with positive regard were related to the reflective style of interviewing in a study by Zimmer and Anderson (1968), which drew upon the opinions of external judges who viewed a videotaped counselling session. From the painstaking analysis of therapy sessions undertaken by Clare Hill and her colleagues (Hill et al., 1988; Hill, 1989), not only was reflecting discovered to be one of the most common of the identified techniques utilised by therapists, but clients reported that they found it one of the most helpful. They regarded it as providing support and seldom reacted negatively to its use. Such reflections assisted clients in becoming more deeply attuned to their emotional and personal experiences, leading to more profound levels of exploration and greater insights into their circumstances and difficulties. One of the most marked outcomes was an association with significantly reduced levels of anxiety. (It should be noted that 'reflecting' in these studies was actually labelled 'paraphrasing'. Since the latter encompassed a range of different types of reflective statement, it will be included here.)

Other researchers, rather than focusing upon attitudes, have investigated the effects of reflecting upon the actual behaviour of the interviewee. Some form of interviewee self-disclosure has commonly been measured. In a study already introduced, Powell (1968) investigated the effects of reflections on subjects' positive and negative self-referent statements. 'Approval-supportive' and 'open disclosure' were the comparative experimental conditions. The former included interviewer statements supporting subjects' self-references, and the latter referred to the provision of personal detail by the interviewer. Reflections were found to produce a significant increase in the number of negative, but not positive, self-references. Kennedy, Timmons, and Noblin (1971), while failing to make the distinction between positive and negative instances, similarly reported an increase in interviewee self-statements attributable to this source.

Not all research, however, has attested to the efficacy of the technique of reflecting. According to Hill and Gormally (1977), this procedure was largely ineffective in increasing the use of affective self-referents by experimental subjects. However, not only was a non-contingent procedure of application employed in this study, but the rate of administration was low, thus militating against potential reinforcing influences.

When the effects of reflecting were looked at, not only in terms of the amount of subjects' self-disclosure but on the quality provided as well, intimate detail was associated with this style of interviewing (Vondracek, 1969; Beharry, 1976). A similar result was reported by Mills (1983) in relation to rates, rather than quality, of self-disclosure. Feigenbaum (1977) produced an interesting finding concerning sex differences of subjects. While females disclosed more, and at more intimate levels, in response to reflections, male subjects scored significantly higher on both counts in response to interviewer self-disclosure.

In an investigation of marital therapists working with couples undergoing therapy, Cline et al. (1984) discovered that therapist reflectiveness correlated positively with subsequent changes in positive social interaction for middle-class husbands but with negative changes for both lower-class husbands and wives. It was also positively related to changes in expression of personal feeling for middle-class husbands and wives. When assessed 3 months after the termination of therapy, a positive relationship emerged between therapist reflections and outcome measures of marital satisfaction, but for lower-class husbands only.

There seems to be little doubt now that there is a strong individual difference factor influencing reactions and outcomes to reflective versus directive styles of engagement. In addition to demographic variables, such as gender and class differences already mentioned, personality characteristics have also been researched. Some evidence, reviewed by Hill (1992), suggests that locus of control, cognitive complexity, and reactance of clients may be important. Locus of control refers to a belief in personally significant events deriving from either internal or external sources, while reactance is a predisposition to perceive and respond to events as restrictions on personal autonomy and freedom. Cognitive complexity relates to the conceptual differentiation and sophistication with which individuals make sense of their circumstances. Hill (1992) came to the conclusion that those high on internality of control and cognitive complexity and low on reactance were more suited to less directive interventions such as reflecting. The potential effects of cultural difference in the counselling relationship have received growing recognition (Ivey & Ivey, 1999). Here is a further variable that may well determine reactions to communication of this type.

In sum, findings would suggest that attitudes toward interviewers who use a reflective style are largely positive. At a more behavioural level, this technique would also seem capable of producing increases in both the amount and intimacy of information which interviewees reveal about themselves, although it would not appear to be significantly more effective than alternative procedures such as interviewer self-disclosures or probes. In the actual therapeutic context, there is some evidence linking reflecting with positive outcome measures for certain clients. However, the mediating effects of individual differences in demographic and personality factors should not be overlooked.

Reflections of feeling

Studies featuring this skill can be divided into two major categories and one minor. The former encompass: first, experiments, largely laboratory-based, designed to identify effects of reflecting feeling on subjects' verbal behaviour; and, second, studies that have attempted to relate the use of the technique to judgements, by either interviewees or observers, of interviewers in terms of such attributes as empathy, warmth, and respect. In many instances both types of dependent variable have featured in the same investigation. The minor category includes descriptive studies that have charted the use of reflective statements by counsellors such as Carl Rogers. In an analysis of the counselling session captured on film and entitled *Carl Rogers Counsels an Individual on Anger and Hurt*, Lietaer (2004) found that almost 53% of Rogers' contributions took the form of reflections of expressed feeling by the client. A further 5.5% were reflections of underlying feelings.

With respect to the effects of reflecting feeling on judgement of personal/relational qualities, a significant relationship was found with ratings of empathic understanding in research conducted by Uhlemann, Lea, and Stone (1976). These ratings were provided by external judges and were based upon both written responses and audio recordings of actual interviews. Likewise, Ehrlich, D'Augelli, and Danish (1979) found that interviewers who reflected feelings that had not yet been named by interviewees were regarded by the latter as being more expert and trustworthy. A similar procedure, labelled 'sensing unstated feelings' by Nagata, Nay, and Seidman (1983), emerged as a significant predictor of counsellor effectiveness when assessed by surrogate clients after a counselling-type interview.

However, not all findings have been positive. Highlen and Baccus (1977) failed to reveal any significant differences in clients' perceptions of counselling climate, counsellor comfort, or personal satisfaction between clients allocated to a reflection of feeling and to a probe treatment. Similarly, Gallagher and Hargie (1992) found no significant relationships between ratings of counsellors' reflections, on the one hand, and, on the other, separate assessments by counsellors, clients, and judges of empathy, genuineness, and acceptance displayed toward clients. As acknowledged, the small sample size may have been a factor in the outcome of this investigation.

With interviewee verbal behaviour as the dependent variable, the effects of reflections of feeling on interviewees' affective self-reference statements were explored by Merbaum (1963), Barnabei et al. (1974), Highlen and Baccus (1977), and Highlen and Nicholas (1978), among others. With the exception of Barnabei, Cormier and Nye (1974), this interviewing skill was found to promote substantial increases in affective self-talk by subjects. Highlen and Nicholas (1978), however, combined reflections of feeling with interviewer self-referenced affect statements in such a way that it is impossible to attribute the outcome solely to the influence of the former. One possible explanation for the failure by Barnabei et al. (1974) to produce a positive finding could reside in the fact that reflections of feeling were administered in a random or non-contingent manner. It has already been mentioned that paraphrases used in this indiscriminate way were equally ineffective in producing increases in self-referenced statements.

Paraphrases

Research studies on the skill of reflecting in general, and paraphrasing in particular, are limited. For the most part, these have been experimental in design, conducted in laboratory settings, and have sought to establish the effects of paraphrasing upon various measures of interviewees' verbal behaviour. In some cases, though, paraphrases are defined in such a way as to include affective material (e.g. Hoffnung, 1969), while, in others, affective content is not explicitly excluded (e.g. Kennedy & Zimmer, 1968; Haase & DiMattia, 1976). These definitional inconsistencies have also been noted by Hill and O'Brien (1999) in reviewing research in the area and should be kept in mind when interpreting the following findings.

Kennedy and Zimmer (1968) reported an increase in subjects' self-referenced statements attributable to paraphrasing, while similar findings featuring self-referenced affective statements were noted by both Hoffnung (1969) and Haase and DiMattia (1976). According to Citkowitz (1975), on the other hand, this skill had only limited effect in this respect, although there was a tendency for the association to be more pronounced when initial levels of self-referenced affect statements were relatively high. The subjects in this experiment were chronic schizophrenic in-patients, and the data were collected during clinical interviews.

The distinction between the affective and the factual has been more explicitly acknowledged by others who have researched paraphrasing. Waskow (1962), for instance, investigated the outcome of selective interviewer responding on the factual and affective aspects of subjects' communication in a psychotherapy-like interview. It emerged that a significantly higher percentage of factual responses was given by those subjects who had their contributions paraphrased. Auerswald (1974), and Hill and Gormally (1977) produced more disappointing findings. In both cases, however, paraphrasing took place on an essentially random basis. Affective responses by subjects were also selected as the dependent variable.

The few studies considering the effects of this technique on attitudes toward the interviewer, rather than behavioural changes on the part of the interviewee, have reported largely favourable outcomes. A positive relationship was detailed by Dickson (1981) between the proportion of paraphrases to questions asked by employment advisory personnel and ratings of interviewer competency provided by independent, experienced judges. A comparable outcome emerged when client perceptions of interviewer effectiveness were examined by Nagata et al. (1983).

It would therefore seem that when paraphrases are used contingently and focus upon factual aspects of communication, recipients' verbal performance can be modified accordingly. In addition, paraphrasing seems to promote favourable judgements of the interviewer by both interviewees and external judges. Counselling trainees have also indicated that this is one of the skills they found most useful in conducting interviews (Spooner, 1976).

OVERVIEW

This chapter has been concerned at conceptual, theoretical, practical, and empirical levels with reflecting as an interactive technique. After identifying and attempting to disentangle a number of conceptual confusions, three contrasting theoretical perspectives on the process deriving from humanistic psychology, behavioural psychology, and linguistics were presented. The various functional claims for the skill, based upon theoretical and experiential, as well as empirical, considerations, were discussed. From the research available (although there seems to be little recent work in this field), it would seem that reflections, whether of fact, feeling, or both, are perceived positively by both interviewees and external observers. Many from a humanistic perspective (e.g. Myers, 2000; Wilkins, 2003) are at pains, though, to ensure that qualities such as empathy and positive regard are not defined solely in terms of what they refer to as techniques such as reflecting. There is also evidence that reflections can promote interviewee self-disclosure, but that a range of psychological and demographic characteristics of the interviewee may mediate their effects.

Further research should concentrate upon more naturalistic settings than the psychology laboratory. The possible effects of such interviewer and interviewee variables as sex, status, socio-economic class, and cultural/ethnic background deserve further enquiry, as do situational factors, including the nature of the encounter. Meriting further attention is the impact of the location of the reflection in the sequence of exchanges and the effects which paralinguistic and non-verbal accompaniments may have on the other interactor.

REFERENCES

Adler, R. & Rodman, G. (2000). *Understanding human communication*, 7th edn. Fort Worth, TX: Harcourt.

Adler, R., Rosenfeld, L. & Proctor, R. (2001). *Interplay: the process of interpersonal communicating*, 8th edn. Fort Worth, TX: Harcourt.

Auerswald, M. (1974). Differential reinforcing power of restatement and interpretation on client production of affect. *Journal of Counseling Psychology*, *21*, 9–14.

Authier, J. (1986). Showing warmth and empathy. In O. Hargie (Ed.), *Handbook of communication skills*. London: Croom Helm.

Barnabei, F., Cormier, W. & Nye, L. (1974). Determining the effects of three counseling verbal responses on client verbal behavior. *Journal of Counseling Psychology*, *21*, 355–359.

Beach, W. A. & Dixon, C. N. (2001). Revealing moments: formulating understanding of adverse experiences in a health appraisal interview. *Social Science and Medicine*, *52*, 25–44.

Beharry, E. (1976). The effect of interviewing style upon self-disclosure in a dyadic interaction. *Dissertation Abstracts International*, *36*, 4677B.

Benjamin, A. (1987). *The helping interview: with case illustrations*. Boston, MA: Houghton Mifflin.

Brammer, L. (1993). *The helping relationship: process and skills*. Englewood Cliffs, NJ: Prentice-Hall.

Brammer, L. & MacDonald, G. (1999). *The helping relationship*, 7th edn. Boston, MA: Allyn and Bacon.

Brammer, L. & MacLeod, G. (2003). *The helping relationship: processes and skills*. Boston, MA: Pearson.

Brammer, L., Shostrom, E. & Abrego, P. (1989). *Therapeutic psychology: fundamentals of counseling and psychotherapy*. Englewood Cliffs, NJ: Prentice-Hall.

Brown, G. & Atkins, M. (1988). *Effective teaching in higher education*. London: Routledge.

Bull, P. (2002). *Communication under the microscope: the theory and practice of microanalysis*. London: Routledge.

Burgoon, J. (1994). Nonverbal signals. In M. Knapp & G. Miller (Eds), *Handbook of interpersonal communication*. Thousand Oaks, CA: Sage.

Burnard, P. (1999). *Practical counseling and helping*. London: Routledge.

Buss, A. (1983). Social rewards and personality. *Journal of Personality and Social Psychology*, **44**, 533–563.

Butt, T. (2004). *Understanding people*. Basingstoke: Palgrave Macmillan.

Cameron, D. (2000). *Good to talk? Living and working in a communication culture*. London: Sage.

Catania, C. (2000). Ten points every behavior analyst needs to remember about reinforcement. In J. C. Leslie & D. Blackman (Eds), *Experimental and applied analysis of human behavior*. Reno, NV: Context Press.

Chouinard, M. & Clark, E. (2003). Adult reformulations of child errors as negative evidence. *Journal of Child Language*, **30**, 637–669.

Citkowitz, R. (1975). The effects of three interview techniques – paraphrasing, modelling, and cues – in facilitating self-referent affect statements in chronic schizophrenics. *Dissertation Abstracts International*, **36**, 2462B.

Cline, V., Merjia, J., Coles, J. et al. (1984). The relationship between therapist behaviors and outcome for middle and lower class couples in marital therapy. *Journal of Clinical Psychology*, **40**, 691–704.

Corey, G. (1997). *Theory and practice of counseling and psychotherapy*. Pacific Grove, CA: Brooks/Cole.

Cormier, S. & Cormier, B. (1998). *Interviewing strategies for helpers: fundamental skills and cognitive behavioral interventions*, 4th edn. Pacific Grove, CA: Brooks/Cole.

Cormier, S. & Hackney, H. (1999). *Counseling strategies and interventions*, 5th edn. Boston: Allyn & Bacon.

Crystal, D. (1997). *The Cambridge encyclopedia of language*, 2nd edn. New York: Cambridge University Press.

Danish, S. & Hauer, A. (1973). *Helping skills: a basic training program*. New York: Behavioral Publications.

DeVito, J. (2004). *The interpersonal communication book*, 10th edn. Boston, MA: Pearson.

Dickson, D. (1981). Microcounseling: an evaluative study of a programme. Unpublished Ph.D. thesis, Ulster Polytechnic.

Dickson, D., Saunders, C. & Stringer, M. (1993). *Rewarding people*. London: Routledge.

Duncan, S. & Fiske, D. (1977). *Face-to-face interaction: research, methods and theory*. Hillsdale, NJ: Lawrence Erlbaum.

Egan, G. (2001). *The skilled helper: a problem-management and opportunity development approach*, 7th edn. Belmont, CA: Brooks/Cole.

Ehrlich, R., D'Augelli, A. & Danish, S. (1979). Comparative effectiveness of six counselor verbal responses. *Journal of Counseling Psychology*, **26**, 390–398.

Ellison, C. & Firestone, I. (1974). Development of interpersonal trust as a function of self-esteem, target status, and target style. *Journal of Personality and Social Psychology*, **29**, 655–663.

Feigenbaum, W. (1977). Reciprocity in self-disclosure within the psychological interview. *Psychological Reports*, **40**, 15–26.

French, P. (1994). *Social skills for nursing practice*. London: Chapman and Hall.

Freshwater, D. (2003). *Counseling skills for nurses, midwives and health visitors*. Maidenhead: Open University Press.

Gallagher, M. & Hargie, O. (1992). The relationship between counselor interpersonal skills and core conditions of client-centred counseling. *Counseling Psychology Quarterly*, **5**, 3–16.

Garfinkel, H. & Sacks, H. (1970). On formal structures of practical actions. In J. McKinney & E. Tirayakian (Eds), *Theoretical Sociology*. New York: Appleton-Century-Crofts.

Gee, J. P. (1999). *An introduction to discourse analysis*. London: Routledge.

Geldard, K. & Geldard, D. (2003). *Counseling skills in everyday life*. Basingstoke: Palgrave Macmillan.

Gelso, C. & Carter, J. (1985). The relationship in counseling and psychotherapy: components, consequences and theoretical antecedents. *The Counseling Psychologist*, **13**, 155–243.

Gilmore, S. (1973). *The counselor-in-training*. Englewood Cliffs, NJ: Prentice-Hall.

Haase, R. & DiMattia, D. (1976). Spatial environment and verbal conditioning in a quasi-counseling interview. *Journal of Counseling Psychology*, **23**, 414–421.

Hargie, O. & Dickson, D. (2004). *Skilled interpersonal communication: research, theory and practice*. London: Routledge.

Hayes, J. (2002). *Interpersonal skills at work*. Hove: Routledge.

Heritage, J. & Watson, D. (1979). Formulations as conversational objectives. In G. Psathas (Ed.), *Everyday language: studies in ethnomethodology*. New York: Irvington.

Highlen, P. & Baccus, G. (1977). Effects of reflection of feeling and probe on client self-referenced affect. *Journal of Counseling Psychology*, **24**, 140–143.

Highlen, P. & Nicholas, R. (1978). Effects of locus of control, instructions, and verbal conditioning on self-referenced affect in a counseling interview. *Journal of Counseling Psychology*, **25**, 177–183.

Hill, C. (1989). *Therapist techniques and client outcomes*. Newbury Park, CA: Sage.

Hill, C. (1992). Research on therapist techniques in brief individual therapy: implications for practitioners. *The Counseling Psychologist*, **20**, 689–711.

Hill, C. & Gormally, J. (1977). Effects of reflection, restatement, probe and non-verbal behaviors on client affect. *Journal of Counseling Psychology*, **24**, 92–97.

Hill, C. & O'Brien, K. (1999). *Helping skills: facilitating exploration, insight and actions*. Washington, DC: American Psychological Association.

Hill, C., Helms, J., Tichenor, V. et al. (1988). Effects of therapist response modes in brief psychotherapy. *Journal of Counseling Psychology*, **35**, 222–233.

Hocutt, M. (1996). Behaviorism as opposition to Cartesianism. In W. O'Donohue & R. F. Kitchener (Eds), *The philosophy of psychology*. London: Sage.

Hoffnung, R. (1969). Conditioning and transfer of affective self-references in a role-played counseling interview. *Journal of Consulting and Clinical Psychology*, *33*, 527–531.

Hough, M. (2002). *A practical approach to counseling*. Harlow: Pearson.

Irving, P. (1995). A reconceptualisation of Rogerian core conditions of facilitative communication: implications for training. Unpublished D.Phil. thesis, University of Ulster.

Irving, P. & Dickson, D. (2004). Empathy: towards a conceptual framework for heath professionals. *International Journal of Health Care Quality Assurance*, *17*, 212–220.

Ivey, A. & Authier, J. (1978). *Microcounseling, innovations in interviewing, counseling, psychotherapy, and psychoeducation*. Springfield, IL: C. C. Thomas.

Ivey, A. & Ivey, M. (1999). *Intentional interviewing and counseling: facilitating client development in a multicultural society*. Pacific Grove, CA: Brooks/Cole.

Ivey, A. E., D'Andrea, M., Ivey, M. B. & Simek-Morgan, L. (2002). *Theories of counseling and psychotherapy: a multicultural perspective*. Boston, MA: Allyn and Bacon.

Jacobs, S. (2002). Language and interpersonal communication. In M. Knapp & J. A. Daly (Eds), *Handbook of interpersonal communication*, 3rd edn. Thousand Oaks, CA: Sage.

Jones, S. E. & LeBaron, C. D. (2002). Research on the relationship between verbal and nonverbal communication: emerging integrations. *Journal of Communication*, *52*, 499–521.

Kennedy, T. & Zimmer, J. (1968). Reinforcing value of five stimulus conditions in a quasi-counseling situation. *Journal of Counseling Psychology*, *15*, 357–362.

Kennedy, T., Timmons, E. & Noblin, C. (1971). Non-verbal maintenance of conditioned verbal behavior following interpretations, reflections and social reinforcers. *Journal of Personality and Social Psychology*, *20*, 112–117.

Knapp, M. & Hall, J. (2002). *Nonverbal communication in human interaction*, 5th edn. London: Wadsworth/Thomson.

Laver, J. & Hutcheson, S. (Eds) (1972). *Communication in face-to-face interaction*. Harmondsworth: Penguin.

Leslie, J. C. (2002). *Essential behavior analysis*. London: Arnold.

Leslie, J. & O'Reilly, M. (1999). *Behavior analysis: foundations and applications to psychology*. Amsterdam: Harwood.

Levitt, D. H. (2001). Active listening and counselor self-efficacy: emphasis on one microskill in beginning counselor training. *Clinical Supervision*, *20*, 101–115.

Lieberman, D. (2000). *Learning: behavior and cognition*, 3rd edn. Belmont, CA: Wadsworth.

Lietaer, G. (2004). Carl Rogers' verbal responses in 'On anger and hurt': content analysis and clinical reflections. In R. Moodley, C. Lago & A. Talahite (Eds), *Carl Rogers counsels a black client: race and culture in person-centred counseling*. Ross-on-Wye: PCCS Books.

Lindon, J. & Lindon, L. (2000). *Mastering counseling skill*. Basingstoke: Macmillan.

Lumsden, G. & Lumsden, D. (2003). *Communicating with credibility and confidence: diverse people, diverse settings*, 2nd edn. Belmont, CA: Wadsworth.

Maag, J. (1999). *Behavior management: from theoretical implications to practical applications*. San Diego, CA: Singular Publishing Group.

Manthei, R. (1997). *Counseling: the skills of finding solutions to problems*. London: Routledge.

Martin, J. (1999). Communication and interpersonal effectiveness: skills training for older adults. *Educational Gerontology*, **25**, 269–284.

McLaughlin, M. (1984). *Conversation: how talk is organized*. Beverly Hills, CA: Sage.

McLaughlin, M. & Cody, M. (1982). Awkward silences: behavioral antecedents and consequences of the conversational lapse. *Human Communication Research*, **8**, 299–316.

McMillan, M. (2004). *The person-centred approach to therapeutic change*. London: Sage.

Mearns, D. & Thorne, B. (2000). *Person-centred therapy today: new frontiers in theory and practice*. London: Sage.

Merbaum, M. (1963). The conditioning of affective self-reference by three classes of generalized reinforcers. *Journal of Personality*, **31**, 179–191.

Merry, T. (2000). Person-centred counseling and therapy. In C. Feltham & I. Horton (Eds), *Handbook of counseling and psychotherapy*. London: Sage.

Mey, J. (1993). *Pragmatics: an introduction*. Oxford: Blackwell.

Mills, M. (1983). Adolescents' self-disclosure in individual and group theme-centred modelling, reflecting, and probing interviews. *Psychological Reports*, **53**, 691–701.

Myers, S. (2000). Empathic listening: reports on the experience of being heard. *Journal of Humanistic Psychology*, **40**, 148–173.

Nagata, D., Nay, W. & Seidman, E. (1983). Nonverbal and verbal content behaviors in the prediction of interviewer effectiveness. *Journal of Counseling Psychology*, **30**, 85–86.

Nelson-Jones, R. (1990). *Human relationship skills*. London: Cassell.

Nelson-Jones, R. (2004). *Practical counseling and helping skills: text and exercises for the life skills counseling model*. London: Sage.

Nicholson, P. & Bayne, R. (1984). *Applied psychology for social workers*. London: Macmillan.

Nofsinger, R. (1991). *Everyday conversation*. Newbury Park, CA: Sage.

Northouse, P. & Northouse, L. (1998). *Health communication: strategies for health professionals*. Stamford, CA: Appleton & Lange.

Norton, R. (1983). *Communicator style: theory, applications, and measures*. Beverly Hills, CA: Sage.

O'Donohue, W. & Kitchener, R. F. (1996). *The philosophy of psychology*. London: Sage.

O'Farrell, M., Hill, C. & Patton, S. (1986). A comparison of two cases of counseling with the same counselor. *Journal of Counseling and Development*, **6**, 32–41.

Philp, J. (2003). Constraints on 'noticing the gap': nonnative speakers' noticing of recastings in NS–NNS interaction. *Studies in Second Language Acquisition*, **25**, 99–126.

Porter, E. (1950). *An introduction to therapeutic counseling*. Boston, MA: Houghton Mifflin.

Powell, W. (1968). Differential effectiveness of interviewer interventions in an experimental interview. *Journal of Consulting and Clinical Psychology*, **32**, 210–215.

Pridham, F. (2001). *The language of conversation*. London: Routledge.

Rennie, D. L. (1998). *Person-centred counseling: an experiential approach*. London: Sage.

Rhys, C. S. & Black, S. (2004). Rogerian empathic listening: applying conversation analysis to 'the right to be desperate' session. In R. Moodley, C. Lago & A. Talahite (Eds), *Carl Rogers counsels a black client: race and culture in person-centred counseling*. Ross-on-Wye: PCCS Books.

Richmond, V. & McCroskey, J. (2000). *Nonverbal behavior in interpersonal relations*, 4th edn. Boston, MA: Allyn and Bacon.

Robinson, W. P. (2003). *Language in social worlds*. Oxford: Blackwell.

Rogers, C. (1951). *Client-centered therapy*. Boston, MA: Houghton Mifflin.

Rogers, C. (1961). *On becoming a person: a therapist's view of psychotherapy*. Boston, MA: Houghton Mifflin.

Rogers, C. (1975). Empathic: an unappreciated way of being. *The Counseling Psychologist*, *5*, 2–10.

Rogers, C. (1980). *A way of being*. Boston, MA: Houghton Mifflin.

Rogers, C. (1987). Comments on the issue of equality in psychotherapy. *Journal of Humanistic Psychology*, *27*, 38–39.

Roig, M. (1999). When college students' attempts at paraphrasing become instances of potential plagiarism. *Psychological Reports*, *84*, 973–982.

Roter, D. & McNeilis, K. S. (2003). The nature of the therapeutic relationship and the assessment of its disclosure in routine medical visits. In T. Thompson, A. M. Dorsey, K. I. Miller & R. Parrott (Eds), *Handbook of health communication*. Mahwah, NJ: Lawrence Erlbaum.

Sacks, H., Schegloff, E. & Jefferson, G. (1978). A simplest systematics for the organisation of turn-taking for conversation. In J. Schenkien (Ed.), *Studies in the organisation of conversational interaction*. New York: Academic Press.

Sanders, P. (2000). Mapping person-centred approaches to counseling and psycho-therapy. *Person-centred Practice*, *8*, 62–74.

Sarafino, E. (1996). *Principles of behavior change: understanding behavior modification techniques*. New York: Wiley.

Schegloff, E. & Sacks, H. (1973). Opening up closings. *Semiotica*, *8*, 289–327.

Seden, J. (1999). *Counseling skills in social work practice*. Buckingham: Open University Press.

Silver, R. (1970). Effects of subject status and interviewer response programme on subject self-disclosure in standardised interviews. *Proceedings of the 78th Annual Convention, APA*, *5*, 539–540.

Skinner, B. F. (1938). *The behavior of organisms*. New York: Appleton-Century-Crofts.

Skinner, B. F. (1953). *Science and behavior*. London: Collier Macmillan.

Spooner, S. (1976). An investigation of the maintenance of specific counseling skills over time. *Dissertation Abstracts International*, February, 5840A.

Stewart, C. & Cash, W. (2000). *Interviewing: principles and practice*, 9th edn. Boston, MA: McGraw-Hill.

Stiles, W. & Putnam, S. (1992). Verbal exchanges in medical interviews: concepts and measurement. *Social Science and Medicine*, *35*, 347–355.

Stokes, R. & Hewitt, J. (1976). Aligning actions. *American Sociological Review*, *41*, 838–849.

Tengland, P. A. (2001). A conceptual exploration of incongruence and mental health.

In G. Wyatt (Ed.), *Rogers' therapeutic conditions: evolution, theory and practice.* Vol. 1. *Congruence.* Ross-on-Wye: PCCS Books.

Thorndike, E. (1911). *Animal intelligence.* New York: Macmillan.

Thorne, B. (1992). *Carl Rogers.* London: Sage.

Thorne, B. (2002). Person-centred therapy. In W. Dryden (Ed.), *Handbook of individual therapy.* London: Sage.

Tolan, J. (2003). *Skills in person-centred counseling and psychotherapy.* London: Sage.

Turkat, I. & Alpher, V. (1984). Prediction versus reflection in therapist demonstrations of understanding: three analogue experiments. *British Journal of Medical Psychology, 57*, 235–240.

Uhlemann, M., Lea, G. & Stone, G. (1976). Effect of instructions and modeling on trainees low in interpersonal communication skills. *Journal of Counseling Psychology, 23*, 509–513.

Vondracek, F. (1969). The study of self-disclosure in experimental interviews. *Journal of Psychology, 72*, 55–59.

Waskow, I. (1962). Reinforcement in a therapy-like situation through selective responding to feelings or content. *Journal of Consulting Psychology, 26*, 11–19.

Watson, J. (1913). Psychology as the behaviorist views it. *Psychological Review, 20*, 158–177.

Watzlawick, P., Beavin, J. & Jackson, D. (1967). *Pragmatics of human communication.* New York: W. W. Norton.

Weiner, S. & Goodenough, D. (1977). A move toward a psychology of conversation. In R. Freedle (Ed.), *Discourse production and comprehension.* Norwood, NJ: Ablex.

Wilkins, P. (2003). *Person-centred therapy in focus.* London: Sage.

Wood, J. T. (2004). *Interpersonal communication: everyday encounters*, 4th edn. Belmont, CA: Wadsworth.

Wyatt, G. (Ed.) (2001). *Rogers' therapeutic conditions: evolution, theory and practice.* Vol. 1. *Congruence.* Ross-on-Wye: PCCS Books.

Zimmer, J. & Anderson, S. (1968). Dimensions of positive regard and empathy. *Journal of Counseling Psychology, 15*, 417–426.

Chapter 7

Explaining

George Brown

EXPLAINING AND QUESTIONING IN many ways represent the core skills of the professions. They underpin many of the skills discussed in this book; they are used in everyday conversation, and they are of importance to teachers, lecturers, doctors, other health professionals, lawyers, architects, and engineers. Despite the ubiquity of explaining, as an area of research, it is still neglected. The reason is, perhaps, that explaining is at the intersection of a wide range of subjects. Epistemology, psychology, linguistics, sociology, and anthropology all contribute to an understanding of the nature of explaining.

This chapter does not attempt to cover all of these areas, but it does not shirk the deeper issues of explaining. An understanding of the deeper issues will assist readers to relate explaining to their own professional and personal experiences. To assist them in this quest, a framework is provided for understanding explanations and the overviews of major findings in various professions. These findings include those primarily concerned with explaining to a group, such as a lecture, class, or a group of managers, and dyadic encounters, such as doctor–patient consultations. The chapter is based on the premise that explaining is a skill. While there have been some naive criticisms of the skills-based approach adopted in this book (e.g. Sanders, 2003), this approach is a powerful heuristic for practitioners, and it provides a useful theoretical framework in which to explore the subtleties of explaining.

A DEFINITION OF EXPLAINING

The etymological root of explaining is *explanare*, to make plain. This root suggests two powerful metaphors: 'to strip bare' and 'to reveal'. These metaphors hint at different purposes of explaining. The first has connotations of getting down to the essentials. The second leans toward revelation, to revealing subtleties, intricacies, and perhaps the uniqueness of an object, action, event, or occurrence. The first metaphor resonates with scientific approaches, such as the development of attribution theory, which seeks to identify the dimensions, through statistical analysis, on which people provide explanations of their behaviour (Hewstone, 1989). The second metaphor resonates with work in discourse analysis and hermeneutics (Antaki, 1994; Potter & Wetherall, 1994), which seeks to tease out the patterns and meanings of speech in a specific context such as a courtroom or classroom.

In standard Modern English, the term 'explain' has come to mean 'make known in detail' (*OED*). It is arguable whether providing more detail improves an explanation. Equally arguable is whether the standard definition covers the many personal meanings of explanations constructed and used by explainers. It was perhaps for this reason that Antaki (1988, p. 4) offered the general principle that explaining is 'Some stretch of talk hearable as being a resolution of some problematic state of affairs.' However, this broad definition does not cover written explanations, and it deliberately leaves open the question of intentions, meanings, and interpretations of utterances. Its core is that there is a problem to be explained in terms of causes, reasons, excuses, or justifications.

A working definition formulated by the author and a colleague (Brown & Atkins, 1986, p. 63) is as follows: 'Explaining is an attempt to provide understanding of a problem to others.' This definition was developed for pragmatic reasons. We wanted a definition that would be helpful to professionals engaged in explaining and which would link transactions between explainers and explainees and the connections made in their heads. The weight of our definition rests on the nature of understanding.

THE NATURE OF UNDERSTANDING

Given that explaining is an attempt to give understanding, it is necessary to explore the nature of understanding – otherwise, one may be accused of explaining the known in terms of an unknown. Put simply, *understanding involves seeing connections which were hitherto not seen.* The connections may be between ideas, between facts, or between ideas and facts.

This apparently simple definition has strong links with much of cognitive psychology. Dewey (1910) described five steps in arriving at understanding, which began with 'felt' difficulty and proceeded to the search for corroborative evidence. His approach also describes neatly the process of explaining to oneself. Thyne (1966) emphasises the importance of recognising the appropriate cues in the information presented. Norman and Bobrow (1975), following the work of Piaget (1954) and Bruner (1966), argued that the aim of cognitive processing is to form a meaningful interpretation of the world. Ausubel (1978) stressed that the most important single factor influencing learning is what the learner already knows. He highlighted the importance of anchoring ideas in the learner's cognitive structure, of the use of advanced organisers, and of the learner's meaningful learning set. Pask's (1976) conversational theory of understanding and research on how students learn (Entwistle & Ramsden, 1983; Entwistle & Entwistle, 1997; Biggs, 2003) are built on the proposition that understanding is concerned with forming connections.

Entwistle's (2003) more recent and qualitative work has revealed students' conceptions of understanding. He reports that, for many students, understanding was not merely cognitive but a feeling, including a feeling of satisfaction at creating meaning for themselves. They stressed, above all, coherence and connectiveness and a sense of wholeness, although many recognised that the 'wholeness' was provisional yet irreversible. Once you understood something you could not 'de-understand' it, although your understanding could increase. The composite of their views captures the essence of understanding.

> Understanding? It's the interconnection of lots of disparate things – the feeling that you understand how the whole thing is connected up – you can make sense of it internally. You're making lots of connections which then make sense and it's logical. It's as though one's mind has finally 'locked in' to the pattern. Concepts seem to fit together in a meaningful way, when before the connections did not seem clear, or appropriate, or complete. If you don't understand, it's just everything floating about and you can't quite get everything into place – like jigsaw pieces, you know, suddenly connect and you can see the whole picture. But there is always the feeling you can add more and more and more: that doesn't necessarily mean that you didn't understand it; just that you only understood it up to a point. There is always more to be added. But if you really understand something and what the idea is behind it, you can't not understand it afterwards – you can't 'de-understand' it! And you know you have understood something when you can construct an argument from scratch – when you can explain it so that you feel satisfied with the explanation, when you can discuss a topic with someone and explain and clarify your thoughts if the other person doesn't see what you mean. (Entwistle, 2003, p. 6)

Experts on human information processing have rarely considered understanding. But from Baddeley's (2004) model of memory, it is possible to deduce a model of understanding which is rich with implications for explaining as well as understanding. For an explanation to be understood, the explainee must first perceive there is a gap in knowledge, a puzzle or a problem to be explained. This perception activates the working memory to retrieve schemata from the long-term memory. These schemata may have been stored in any of the procedural, semantic (thoughts and facts) or episodic memories (narratives, events). Cues in the explanation being given are matched to the activated schemata. This matching may lead to assimilation of the explanation into the existing schemata or it may modify the existing schemata. In both, it produces new connections of concepts and/or facts. The degree of stability of those new connections depends in part upon the network of existing concepts and facts. The validity of the new connections, that is, of the understanding, can be tested only by reference to corroborative evidence, which may be from an external source or from other evidence and rules stored in the person's cognitive framework.

If the cues are clear and well-ordered, they can be rapidly processed. If they are confusing, they will not link with existing schemata and may be rapidly forgotten. Given the limitations of sensory and working memory, one should not explain too quickly, and one should chunk the information provided into meaningful and relatively brief sentences. Pauses should be used to separate the chunks of information. Too fast or too distracting explanations cannot be processed by the working memory. The use of analogies, metaphors, and similes will create new connections rapidly with the existing schemata of the explainee. The use of frequent summaries, guiding statements, and cognitive maps can help explainees to change their schemata, which they can then elaborate on subsequently. Personal narratives interwoven with concepts and findings can trigger the procedural, episodic, and semantic memories and so aid storing and retrieval of understanding.

This brief exposition of understanding has obvious implications for providing explanations in many professional contexts. The problem must be presented so as to be recognised as a problem, the cues given must take account of the existing cognitive structure of the explainees, the cues must be highlighted so they can readily be matched, and, if possible, there should be a check on whether understanding has occurred.

TYPES OF EXPLAINING

The literature abounds with typologies of explanations (e.g. Ennis, 1969; Smith & Meux, 1970; Kinneavy, 1971; Hyman, 1974; Turney, Ellis, and Hatton 1983; Rowan, 2003; Pavitt, 2000). In considering these typologies, I (together with a co-author) designed a robust, simple typology which would be relatively easy to use by researchers and practitioners (Brown & Atkins, 1986). The typology consists of three main types of explanation: *the interpretive, the descriptive, and the reason-giving*. They approximate to the questions, What? How? Why? However, the precise form of words matters less than the intention of the question. They may be supplemented with the questions, Who? When? Where? Together, these questions can rapidly provide a framework for many explanations.

Interpretive explanations address the question, 'What?' They interpret or clarify an issue or specify the central meaning of a term or statement. Examples are answers to the questions: What is 'added value'? What is a novel? What does impact mean in physics? What does it mean in management?

Descriptive explanations address the question, 'How?' These explanations describe processes, structures, and procedures, as in: How did the chairperson lead the meeting? How do cats differ anatomically from dogs? How should a chairperson lead a meeting? How do you measure sustainability?

Reason-giving explanations address the question, 'Why?' They involve reasons based on principles or generalisations, motives, obligations, or values. Included in reason-giving explanations are those based on causes and functions (Pavitt, 2000), although some philosophers prefer to distinguish causes and reasons. Examples of reason-giving explanations are answers to the questions: Why do camels have big feet? Why did this fuse blow? Why do heavy smokers run the risk of getting cancer? Why are some people cleverer than others? Why is there more crime in inner-city areas? Why am I reading this chapter? Why should I keep to deadlines? Why is Shakespeare a greater writer than Harold Robbins?

Of course, a particular explanation may involve all three types of explanation. Thus, in explaining how a bill becomes a law, one may want to describe the process, give reasons for the law, define certain key terms, and consider its implications for legal practice.

THE FUNCTIONS OF EXPLAINING

The primary function of giving an explanation is to give understanding to others, but in giving understanding, one can also fulfil a wide range of other functions. These include *ensuring learning, clarifying ambiguities, helping someone learn a procedure, reducing anxiety, changing attitudes and behaviour, enablement, personal autonomy*, and, last but not least, *improving one's own understanding*. These functions imply that explaining and understanding are not merely cognitive activities but also involve a gamut of motivations, emotions, and conation. Clearly, one needs to take account of the specific function of an explanation when considering the tasks and processes of explaining.

THE TASKS AND PROCESSES OF EXPLAINING

Explaining is an interaction of the explainer, the problem to be explained, and the explainees. The explainer needs to take account of the problem *and* the knowledge, attitudes, and other characteristics of the explainees and use appropriate approaches in the process of explaining. To assist in this process, Hargie and Dickson (2003) suggested a 'P5' approach:

*p*re-assessment of the explainees' knowledge
*p*lanning
*p*reparation
*p*resentation
*p*ost-mortem.

Their approach was developed from the work of French (1994), and our earlier work (Brown & Atkins, 1986). The model is pertinent to formally presented explanations, such as lectures or presentations, and to 'opportunistic explanations' prompted by a question from a client, patient, or student, although in the last, one may have little time to prepare. Some of Hargie and Dickson's suggestions have been incorporated into the approach advocated in this section. It follows the sequence of defining the problem, determining the process, and clarifying and estimating the outcomes.

The problem to be explained and the problem of explainees

First, the explainer has to identify and specify the problem that requires explanation. The problem may be posed initially by the explainer or by the explainee. The problem presented by a client may require clarification and refinement. It is well known by medical and legal practitioners that the problem presented by a patient or client is not necessarily *the* problem. One has to diagnose and communicate clearly the problem in a way that is acceptable to the client. Herein lies a difficulty of ownership. If patients do not perceive the problem as their own, the proposed solution may not be accepted and acted upon. Even if the problem is accepted, the solution proffered may not be acceptable. More subtly, the solution may be accepted but not acted upon. This observation is relevant to research using the health belief model. Changes in beliefs do not necessarily lead to changes in behaviour (Janz & Becker, 1984). In teaching and management, a similar difficulty may arise. If pupils, students, or employees do not perceive the problem presented as one worthy of solution, they may reject it and the process of acquiring the solution. Rhetoric, persuasion, principles of pedagogy, and power all have a part to play in the acceptance of a problem, and the solution and its implementation.

But it is not enough merely to identify the problem. To be a skilled explainer, one has also to take account of the explainees, and their social and cultural backgrounds, motivations, linguistic ability, and previous knowledge – and plan accordingly before embarking upon the explanation. An important point here is empathy. To be a good explainer, one needs to empathise with the explainees, see the world through their eyes, and relate one's explanation to their experiences. But empathy per se is not enough. As an explainer, one has to decide on one's goals *in relation to the explainees*, identify appropriate content, highlight and lowlight the content appropriately, and select appropriate methods and resources to achieve the goals. Once the problem and its possible solution(s) have been identified, the problem might helpfully be expressed in the form of a central question, and that question may be then subdivided into a series of implicit questions or hidden variables. Thus, the explanation of how local anaesthetics work contains the implicit questions, 'What is a local anaesthetic'?' and 'How are nerve impulses transmitted?' These implicit questions or hidden issues can then provide the structure of an explanation.

The process of explaining

The task of the explainer is to state the problem to be explained and present or elicit a series of linked statements, each of which is understood by the explainee and which together lead to a solution of the problem. These linked statements may be labelled 'keys' since they unlock understanding. Each of these keys will contain a key statement. A key statement may be a procedure, a generalisation, a principle, or even an appeal to an ideology or a set of personal values. The key may contain examples, illustrations, metaphors, and perhaps qualifications to the main principle. When the problem to be explained is complex, there might also be a summary of key statements during the explanation as well as a final summary.

The keys are the nub of explaining. But, as emphasised earlier, for an explanation to be understood, it follows that the explainer has to consider not only the problem to be explained but also the characteristics of the explainees. What is appropriate as an explanation of the structure of DNA to postgraduate biochemists is unlikely to be appropriate as an explanation to 11-year-olds. There is no such thing as the good explanation. What is 'good' for one group may not be good for another. Its quality is contingent upon the degree of understanding it generates in the explainees. For different groups of explainees, the keys of the explanation and the explanation itself will be different, although the *use* of keys and other strategies may not be.

The essence of the process of explaining is that its goal, understanding, is a function of the existing cognitive structure of the explainee as well as of the new information being provided: hence, the importance of similes, analogies, and metaphors. These devices may, as understanding grows, be seen as crude, perhaps even as false, explanations. Hooks and balls may be a very crude analogy for explaining atoms and molecules, but they may be a useful starting point for explaining molecular structure to young children. 'Rotting garden posts' may be an inadequate metaphor for describing the roots of a patient's teeth, but the metaphor might be a useful device for justifying extraction.

The process of explaining is not only concerned with identifying problems and proffering solutions. Sometimes, the task of the explainer is to explain the problem and sometimes to explain the connection between the problem and the solution. A problem such as the relationship between truth and meaning may not have any solution, or it may have several unsatisfactory solutions, but at least the problem may be understood. This point is emphasised, since much high-level teaching and counselling is concerned not with explaining *the* solutions of problems but with explaining the nature of a problem, exploring the possible solutions, and judging their relative merits.

The outcome

The outcome hoped for when explaining is that the explainee understands. The explainer has to check that the explanation is understood. This task is akin to feedback (see Chapter 2), and it is sometimes neglected by doctors, teachers, lawyers, and others. Understanding may be checked on by a variety of methods, including, of course, formal assessments (Brown, Bull & Pendlebury, 1997). The most primitive method is to ask, 'Do you understand?' The answer one usually gets is 'Yes'. The response is more a measure of superficial compliance than of understanding. Other methods are to invite the explainee to *recall* the explanation, to *ask questions* of specific points in the explanation, to *apply* the explanation to another situation or related problem, to provide other *examples* of where the explanation might hold, or to *identify* similar sorts of explanations. All of these may be used to measure the success of an explanation, providing the procedures are appropriate and valid.

A check on understanding much favoured by health professionals is a change in behaviour. As a measure of explanatory power, it is weak. The explanation may be understood, but it may not lead to action. The explanation may not be understood or imperfectly understood yet the patient changes behaviour. However, if the purpose of a particular explanation is to change behaviour, and understanding is a mere mediator, then changes in behaviour may be useful outcome measures. But one should bear in mind that such changes in behaviour are unlikely to be sustained unless they are integrated into the cognitive structure of the student, patient, or client.

Summary

To sum up, explaining is an attempt to give understanding to another. It involves identifying the problem to be explained, a process of explaining which uses key statements, and a check on understanding. However, it would be wrong to leave the nature of explaining without pointing out that explaining is only *usually* an intentional activity. One may intend to explain a particular problem, but one may explain points that one did not intend to explain and, alas, one may sometimes not explain what one intended to explain.

PERSPECTIVES ON EXPLAINING AND UNDERSTANDING

Aristotle provided a conceptually illuminating start to the study of explaining. His four causes (*aition*), the material, the formal, the efficient, and the final cause, are the basis of most explanations, although it should be noted that the ancient Greek term for 'cause' includes reasons. His notions of *ēthos* (personality and stance), *pathos* (emotional engagement), and *logos* (modelling and judging argument) laid the foundations of rhetoric (persuasive explanation and argument in speech and written texts) and later studies in this field (e.g. Atkinson, 1984; Cockcroft & Cockcroft, 1993).

Locke, the seventeenth-century empiricist, also had an important influence on the study of understanding and explaining. The following example of his advice is still relevant today:

Confound not his u*nderstanding* with explications or notions that are above it, or with the variety or number of things that are not to his present purpose. Mark what 'tis his mind aims at in the question and not words he expresses it in; and when you have informed and satisfied him in that you shall see how his thoughts will enlarge themselves, and how by fit answers he may be led on farther than perhaps you could imagine. (John Locke, *Some thoughts on education*, 1693)

Since the time of Galileo, there have been debates about measurement and judgement, appeals to experimentation and appeals to authority, qualitative and quantitative methods, and nomothetic and ideographic approaches. Galileo's famous dictum, *'Measure that which is measurable and make measurable that which is not'*, is at the heart of much scientific and pseudo-scientific research and of the fashionable debate of evidence-based approaches in medicine and education. This approach includes the development of models for explanation, prediction, and control. It has an underlying concern with quantitative measurement, with problems of measuring reliability and validity, and with, as far as possible, identical repetition of experiments. Associated with the mode of scientific explanation is often an interest in the organic, in disease-centred models, and in the search for mathematically based generalisations within a closed system of concepts.

In contrast, 'humanistic' or broadly 'phenomenological' approaches are more concerned with personal understanding than with 'scientific' proof; with qualitative methods; with intentions, meanings, and their constructions in different contexts; and with tentative generalisations based on themes. For example, a 'humanistic' researcher might look at how an individual doctor adduces the relevant hypotheses or explanatory principles; how he or she detects regularities, distinguishes differences, and arrives at decisions. Such a researcher often has an interest in the individual patient's conceptions of illness, in patient-centred models of management, and in a search for interpretations and meanings within the consultation. Not surprisingly, the differences between those who favour scientific explanations and those who favour searches for understanding and meaning spill over into conflicts about research, research funding, and approaches to teaching (Brown, Rohlin & Manogue, 2003). They permeate attitudes toward 'hard' and 'soft' human resources management (Storey, 1992).

The covering law model

At the core of explanation is the triadic principle derived from Aristotle's syllogistic method. There must be:

1   a generalisation or universal law
2   an evidential statement or observation that the situation being considered is an instance of that generalisation
3   a conclusion.

At first sight, procedural explanations do not fit the covering law model (Swift, 1961; Draper, 1988). Certainly, in giving a procedural explanation, it may not be necessary to use the covering law model. Indeed, its use could confuse the explainee, but there should be an explanation based upon the covering law model which justifies the procedure. If not, the procedure is likely to be faulty. Put in different terms, a good practice is always underpinned by a good theory, even if the practitioner is unaware of the theory.

The covering law model is used for scientific explanations based on strong scientific laws or in a weaker form for highly probabilistic explanations or for generalisations believed by an individual or group. Values, obligations, ideologies, or beliefs might form the first statement of an explanation. Kruglanski (1988) points out that at some point individuals stop generating hypotheses and attain closure on a belief. This 'frozen' belief becomes the regularity principle which they use to explain their behaviour.

Many of the errors in explanations can be identified by recasting the explanation in this form and examining the links between the three statements. The generalisation may not hold, the instance may not be an instance of the generalisation, and the conclusion not validly drawn from the principle and instance. More subtly, the instance may fit more appropriately into another generalisation. To complicate matters further, an explanation may be incorrect yet believed, or correct and not believed. Examples of both complications abound in the history of medicine and science, and in history itself.

One should be wary of overextending the first statement of the model lest the explanation become vacuous. Appeals to universals such as 'God's will' or the 'misfiring of neurons' do not pick out *the* reasons for a specific action or event.

Sometimes, one needs to use a counter-factual model (White, 1990) to identify the regulatory principle that has the most explanatory potency. To answer the question, 'Why did the car ferry, the *Herald of Free Enterprise*, sink so *quickly*?', one looks at the question, 'When does a car ferry sink *slowly*?', and looks for the regularity principle that accounts for the difference. This may identify a chain of reasons that could lead to the door of the boardroom.

The link between the first and second statements of the covering law model raises questions about the validity of the method used to obtain the evidence and issues concerning 'truth' and 'phenomenological' truth. Professions and academic disciplines vary in their truth criteria and what counts as acceptable evidence. What might be accepted as evidence in a research journal might not be accepted as evidence in a court of law. The link between the second and third statements raises the question of whether the conclusion is justified by the principle and the evidence (cf. arguments concerning weapons of mass destruction and the war in Iraq). But even if the covering law holds for an explanation, there is the question of whether the explanation provided would be better if it had been derived from a different principle and evidential statement, and the further question of whether the explainer was deliberately attempting to give a false explanation.

There are further difficulties here. Even if an explanation is valid, or believed to be valid, there remains the question of whether it is understood. Now, clearly, it is possible for a scientist or scholar to give an explanation that is not understood in his or her own time, or, as was more frequently the case, the explanation may have been understood but rejected by his or her peers. However, even in such extreme cases, one can assume that the scientists or scholars intended to give understanding to their audience. But is intention enough? On this issue there are various views.

On the one hand, explaining may be seen as a task word such as hunting or fishing; on the other hand, it may be seen as an achievement word such as killing or catching (Ryle, 2000). If explaining is regarded as an achievement word, then the outcome of the explanation takes primacy. As Thyne (1963, p. 126) observed: 'If the teacher really has explained something to his class, they will understand it, and if they do not understand it, despite his efforts, what purported to be an explanation was not an explanation after all.'

Our own view is that the intentional position is too weak and the outcome position too strong. We suggest there is usually an intention to explain, an attempt to explain, and a check on understanding. We recognise that some outcomes may not be attained or attainable, and some explanations, not intended, can deepen understanding. A person may carry away from an explanation much more than the intentions of the explainer.

EVIDENCE FROM THE FIELD

Most of the experimental evidence on explaining is based on studies of teaching and the doctor–patient consultation. The evidence provided in some professions, such as law and management, tends to be expertise-based rather than evidence-based. While it is easy to disparage such craft knowledge, 'practical' wisdom in a profession may run alongside the evidence collected by research and might be more influential than the research findings per se. Indeed, it could be argued that unless the research findings are integrated into craft knowledge they are unlikely to have much effect on practice.

The following sections focus primarily upon evidence-based approaches in the different professions. While it may be tempting to read only the sections related to one's own profession, there is much to be gained from exploring findings in other professions, matching these against one's own professional experience, and considering whether the findings provide a springboard for similar explorations in one's own profession.

EXPLAINING IN THE CLASSROOM

Estimates of the proportion of time spent on explaining by teachers vary from 10% to 30%, according to the definition of explaining adopted (Brophy & Good, 1986). Time spent on a task is but a crude measure of its efficacy. More important is the quality: the way the time is spent. As Gage, Belgard, Dell, Hiller, Rosenshine, Unruh et al. (1968, p. 3) wryly observed:

> Some people explain aptly, getting to the heart of the matter with just the right terminology, examples, and organisation of ideas. Other explainers, on the contrary, get us and themselves all mixed up, use terms beyond our level of comprehension, draw inept analogies, and even employ concepts and principles that cannot be understood without an understanding of the very thing being explained.

The remark is apposite to explanations in other professional contexts.

Studies show that the foremost reasons for liking a teacher are clear explanations of lessons, assignments, and difficulties, helpfulness with school work, and fairness (Wragg, 1984). Reviews of the literature (e.g. Wragg & Brown, 1993) also reveal that good explanations are not only clearly structured, but they are also interesting. The main characteristics of effective explaining are summarised in Table 7.1. They were identified in the literature, in discussions with teachers, and in the studies of explaining which the author and colleagues undertook at Nottingham and Exeter (e.g. Brown & Armstrong, 1989; Wragg & Brown, 2001).

Preparation and planning

The maxim, *'Know your subject, know your students'*, appears to be borne out by the evidence. Brown and Armstrong (1984) showed that competent planning and preparation are linked to clarity of explanations in the classroom. They also showed that student teachers trained in methods of preparing, analysing, and presenting explanations were significantly better than a comparable untrained group. The criteria were independent observers' ratings of the videotaped lessons and measures of pupil achievement and interest in the lesson. In a comparison of novice and expert teachers, Carter (1990) observed that novices tended to jump in without giving adequate thought to planning, whereas more expert teachers had developed and used tacit knowledge of pupils, organisational knowledge, and broader cognitive schemata.

Table 7.1 Planning strategies and performance skills in explaining

Planning strategies

- Analyse topics into main parts, or 'keys'
- Establish links between parts
- Determine rules (if any) involved
- Specify kinds of explanation required
- Adapt plan according to learner characteristics

Key skills

Clarity and fluency

- through defining new terms
- through use of explicit language
- through avoiding vagueness

Emphasis and interest

- by variations in gestures
- by use of media and material
- by use of voice and pauses
- by repetition, summarising, paraphrasing, or verbal cueing

Using examples

- clear, appropriate, and concrete in sufficient quantity
- positive and negative where applicable

Organisation

- logical and clear sequence pattern appropriate to task
- use of link words and phrases

Feedback

- opportunities for questions provided to test understanding of main ideas assessed
- expressions of attitudes and values sought

The study by Bennett and Carre (1993) shows there is a strong association between subject knowledge and teaching competence. However, knowledge of subject is a necessary but not sufficient condition of effective explaining. Some people are knowledgeable but remain poor explainers. In a recent study, Calderhead (1996) demonstrated that successful teachers have a sound knowledge base, and build pupil understanding, other pupil characteristics, and resources (time, space, its layout, and equipment) into their planning.

The studies and reviews by many authors provide suggestions on preparation and planning. In his studies of subject knowledge and teaching, Wragg (1993) offers some suggestions on preparation. Brown and Wragg (1993) provide suggestions in their text on questioning, on preparation and planning, including the use of mind mapping to generate ideas and methods, the use of key questions as organising principles, and a method of structuring different types of learning activities. Capel, Leask, and Turner (2002) provide guidelines on explanatory lessons in different school subjects.

Processes, structures, and outcomes

Presentation techniques have been the subject of most studies, and these have demonstrated that explanations which yield greater pupil or student achievement are based on clarity, fluency, emphasis, interest, the use of examples, summaries, and recall or application questions. Clarity, including the use of definitions, yields greater pupil or student achievement. Fluency, including the notions of emphasis, clear transitions, absence of vagueness, and absence of false starts and verbal tangles, have all been shown to be associated with effective presentation (Land, 1985; Cruikshank & Metcalfe, 1994; Brophy, 2002). Studies of expressiveness (Wragg, 1993; Brophy, 2002) show that purposeful variations in voice, gesture, manner, and use of teaching aids all contribute to the interest and effectiveness of an explanation. The pattern, not the frequency, of examples determines the effectiveness of an explanation. The pattern should be associated with both the type of explanation and the pupils' prior knowledge. In teaching an unfamiliar topic, the sequence *examples* → principle should be used; in restructuring pupils' ideas, the sequence *principle* → examples should be used. The principles should be educed or stated, and positive and negative examples provided (Brown & Armstrong, 1984; Rowan, 2003).

Research by Brown and Armstrong (1984) indicated that good explanatory lessons have more keys and more types of keys that vary the cognitive demands on the pupils. These lessons contained: more framing statements, which delineate the beginning and ending of subtopics; more focusing statements, which emphasise the key points; more relevant examples; more rhetorical questions; better use of audio-visual aids; and fewer unfinished summaries. The teachers of low-scoring lessons introduced so many ideas that the pupils became confused. The teachers of high-scoring lessons used simple language and examples to which the pupils could relate. In psychological terms, the teachers activated and built upon the cognitive schemata of their pupils. Opening excerpts from a high-scoring lesson and a low-scoring lesson taught by young teachers to 9-year-olds are given in Table 7.2. Often, one can predict the effectiveness of an explanation from its opening.

Wragg (1993) built upon the earlier work of Brown and Armstrong and, in so doing, identified two major styles of explaining, which might be labelled 'imaginative' and 'instructional'. Imaginative lessons draw out the responses of pupils through open questions and the encouragement of long responses. In instructional lessons, teachers give and elicit principles and examples, and provide summaries. Both styles could be used badly or well. Wragg's work broke new ground in the study of explaining by identifying a form of imaginative explanation. It also confirmed the important characteristics of effective explaining, as shown in Table 7.1.

Feedback and checking understanding

Two common forms of feedback, which provide checks on understanding, are the responses of pupils in class, and the performance of pupils in assignments and standardised assessment tests (SATs). The success of the former depends upon the mode of eliciting feedback. The question, 'Do you understand?', is likely to yield a compliant response. Techniques such as inviting questions in a friendly way, or

Table 7.2 High- and low-scoring explanations

High-scoring	*Low-scoring*
Orientation	**Orientation**
Teacher – 'Well, first of all I wonder if you could tell me what this is.' *Pupil* – 'A piece of concrete.' *Teacher* – 'Yes, it's a piece of concrete, a slab of concrete, out of my garden. Now, if I wanted to plant a tree or a shrub on here, what would you say was missing?' *Pupil* – 'Soil.' *Teacher* – 'Yes, the soil. And today I want to start by talking about some plants that can grow straight on to a rock.'	*Teacher* – 'I'm going to talk to you about ecological succession. It's not as difficult as it sounds.'
Keys	**Keys**
Which plants can grow straight on to rock? How do mosses replace lichens? What plants replace mosses? What is this process called? What other examples of ecological succession are there?	In what two ways can we group organisms? Which organisms are consumers? Which organisms are producers? What is it called when we group organisms that depend on each other together? What do we call it when one community takes over from another? How does ecological succession take place on bare rock?

asking recall or application questions, are more likely to be effective (see Chapter 4, for further discussion of the skill of questioning). However, not all teachers (or other professionals) are good at checking or estimating understanding. Bennett and Carre (1993) report that a sample of infant teachers often underestimated the understanding of their brighter pupils and overestimated the understanding of their less able pupils. Probing the deeper misconceptions can change the nature of understanding. For example, Brown and van Lehn (1980) identified 89 mistakes which young children make in subtraction. Resnick and Omanson (1987) used these data to show that these errors are based on two misconceptions and to suggest ways of removing them. Obviously, it is better to spend time on two misconceptions than upon 89 surface errors.

The use of assignments can provide the basis for correcting misunderstandings. The same cannot be said for SATs. Leaving aside the difficulty of determining the effects of teacher behaviour from the abilities, and social and cultural backgrounds of pupils, the feedback is too late to benefit the current pupils and the information is merely a 'mark' for the teacher. It does not provide information on how to improve understanding, although it may help a teacher to train pupils for SATs.

The conclusion to be drawn from this brief review of feedback and checks on understanding is that these are necessary, but we require more studies of processes of teaching that focus upon how teachers analyse and use responses from pupils to develop their own and pupils' understanding.

Summary

Studies of explaining in the classroom indicate that clarity and interest are crucial but complex variables. These variables are valued by pupils and lead to better achievement. Preparation and planning are important aspects of training, and using feedback to check understanding is an important, but relatively neglected, feature of explaining in the classroom.

EXPLAINING IN HIGHER EDUCATION

Most studies of explaining in higher education have focused upon the lecture, although explaining also occurs in small-group teaching, laboratory work, and clinical practice. Lectures may be considered to be sets of linked explanations or keys (Brown & Atkins, 1995), or as sets of small 'idea units' (Chafe, 1982), so many of the findings on lectures are relevant to explanations in other teaching contexts. Most of these studies have used students' evaluation of teaching (SET) as the criterion rather than student learning outcomes, although experimental studies in the 1960s did show that well-structured lectures do yield achievement gains (Bligh, 2000). The relationship between SETs and achievement is problematic, but the weight of opinion is that there are moderate to high associations between SET scores and achievement (Wachtel, 1998). This theme is discussed in the section below on checks on understanding and feedback to lecturers.

Views of students and lecturers

Structure, clarity of presentation, and interest are valued by students (Dunkin, 1986; Murray, 1997a; Light, 2001). The main dissatisfactions of students with lecturers appear to be inaudibility, incoherence, failure to pitch at an appropriate level, failure to emphasise main points, being difficult to take notes from, poor audio-visuals, and reading aloud from notes (Eble, 1995; Brown & Manogue, 2001). For lecturers, the most valued characteristics are clarity, interest, logical organisation, and selection of appropriate content. The most learnable techniques were use of diagrams, use of variety of materials, examples, and selection of appropriate content. Science lecturers valued logical and structural characteristics more highly than arts lecturers; science lecturers also considered more features of explaining to be learnable than did arts lecturers (Brown & Daines, 1981). Subsequent research on training in explaining confirmed the views of scientists (Brown, 1982). No recent surveys of these themes have been found in the literature.

Planning and preparation

These areas of research also remain neglected, but Bligh (2000) provides a comprehensive description of possible structures of lectures, while Light and Cox (2001) and Brown and Race (2002) offer some useful guidance in this area. Brown and Manogue (2001) also outline a method of preparation that new lecturers have found helpful.

Structures and processes

Lecturers report that their most common method of organising lectures is the classical approach of subdividing topics and then subdividing subtopics (Brown & Bakhtar, 1988).

Other methods are described by Brown and Manogue (2001). Structured moves which yield high ratings of clarity are shown in Table 7.3. Seven opening moves associated with giving the framework and setting the context were identified by Thompson (1994). Often lecturers mixed these moves in ways which confused students and obscured the links between structure, content, and context.

The key to generating interest is expressiveness supported by the use of examples, a narrative mode of explaining, and the stimulation of curiosity (Brown

Table 7.3 Effective structuring moves in explaining

1. **Signposts**: *These are statements which indicate the structure and direction of an explanation:*
(a) 'I want to deal briefly with lactation. First, I want to outline the composition of milk; second, its synthesis; third, to examine normal lactation curves.'
(b) 'Most of you have heard the old wives' tale that eating carrots helps you to see in the dark. Is it true? Let's have a look at the basic biochemical processes involved.'

2. **Frames**: *These are statements which indicate the beginning and end of the subtopic:*
(a) 'So that ends my discussion of adrenaline. Let's look now at the role of glycogen.'
Framing statements are particularly important in complex explanations which may involve topics, subtopics, and even subtopics of subtopics.

3. **Foci**: *These are statements and emphases which highlight the key points of an explanation:*
(a) 'So the main point is . . .'
(b) 'Now this is very important . . .'
(c) 'But be careful. This interaction with penicillin occurs only while the cell walls are growing.'

4. **Links**: *These are words, phrases, or statements which link one part of an explanation to another part, and the explainees' experience:*
(a) 'So you can see that reduction in blood sugar levels is detected indirectly in the adrenaline gland and directly in the pancreas. This leads to the release of two different hormones.'

& Atkins, 1995). All of these features can raise levels of arousal and attention and thereby increase the probability of learning.

Expressiveness includes enthusiasm, friendliness, humour, and dynamism of speech and gesture. It is based largely upon gesture, eye contact, body movement, facial expression, vocal inflection, and apt choice of vocabulary. It has long been regarded as an essential ingredient of explaining and lecturing. In a review of meta-analyses, d'Appolonia and Abrami (1997) report that highly expressive lecturers score about 1.2 standard deviations higher than low expressives on student ratings. Expressiveness does exert an influence on student learning (Murray, Rushton & Paunonen, 1990). However, expressiveness is only a mediating variable for sustaining attention and generating interest. As indicated, examples, similes, metaphors, the use of a narrative mode, and the use of 'teases', such as provocative questions, also have a role in generating interest as well as contributing to understanding. So, too, does the judicious use of technological aids (Brown & Race, 2002; Downing & Garmon, 2002).

Persuasive explaining may also have a part to play in higher education to motivate students and to help them to accept the challenge of difficult tasks. Some people may object to the use of persuasion, but the order and quality of presentations always have an influence upon an audience, so one should be aware of the processes and use them to good effect (see Chapter 11 for a full discussion of influencing and persuasion). Various rhetorical devices are used in persuasive explaining and lecturing, including pairs of contrasting statements, asking rhetorical questions and then pausing, the use of triple statements, pausing before important points, summarising with punchlines, and powerful metaphors and analogies. Metaphors and analogies are particularly useful when explaining unfamiliar topics or ideas (Cockcroft & Cockcroft, 1993; Atkinson, 1984). Studies of attitude change (e.g. Zimbardo, Ebbesen & Maslach, 1977; Baron & Byrne, 1997) conducted in a wide variety of contexts suggest some basic principles of persuasive explaining and how new attitudes are formed. These are summarised in Table 7.4.

Checks on understanding and feedback from students

A disadvantage of lectures is they do not provide any immediate checks on understanding; hence, some writers advocate the use of activities during lectures (Brown & Atkins, 1995; Biggs, 2003). If these are not used, then observation of non-verbal reactions of the students can provide a clue (see Chapter 3 for further information on non-verbal communication). Subsequent assignments and tests provide measures of achievement, but it is difficult to separate the various effects of student variables such as study time, availability of resources, prior knowledge, and motivation.

Feedback, in the form of SETs, can help lecturers to improve their capacity to explain, providing the right questions are asked and the lecturer wishes to change. Murray's comprehensive review of this area concludes, 'under certain conditions, student evaluation of teaching does lead to improvement of teaching' (Murray, 1997b, p. 41). Earlier studies reported by McKeachie (1994) showed that student evaluations improved teaching only when the ratings were in the middle range and when the lecturers wanted to improve their teaching. A recent study by Blackburn and Brown (2005) identified four clusters of lecturers in physiotherapy who held differing views

Table 7.4 The art of persuasive explanation

1. Know your audience and decide what kinds of arguments may be appealing and interesting.
2. People are more likely to listen to you and accept your suggestions if you are perceived as credible and trustworthy and have expertise.
3. When there are arguments in favour and against your proposal, it is usually better to present both sides (especially with an intelligent audience).
4. If you have to stress risks in what you are proposing, don't overdo the arousal of fear.
5. Say what experts or expert groups do when faced with the problem you are discussing.
6. If the problem is complex for the group, you should draw the conclusions or give them time for discussion. If it is not too complex, let the group members draw their own conclusions.
7. If the suggestions you are making are likely to be challenged by others, describe their views in advance and present your counter-arguments.
8. If you are dealing with a cherished belief, don't dismiss it as an old wives' tale. Instead, say, 'People used to think that . . . but now we know . . .'
9. If the task you are asking a group to perform is highly complex, prepare them for the possibility of failure. Never say a task is easy; rather, say it may not be easy at first.
10. If a task is threatening, admit it and describe how people might feel and what they can do to reduce their anxiety.

on the value of feedback from SETs: *strong positives* who used the ratings to make changes, *thinkers* who reflected upon student evaluations when considering change, *negatives* who rejected SETs, and *non-discriminators* who were uncertain.

Evidence from the meta-analyses of SETs indicates that students' perceptions of teaching effectiveness accounts for 45% of the variations in student learning. One of the three major factors involved includes explaining, clarity, and organisation; the other factors are facilitation, and assessment of student learning, known as 'evaluation' in the USA (d'Apollonia & Abrami, 1997). The most reliable and valid ratings were those based on simple global ratings rather than detailed specific items. These results suggest that carefully designed SETs can be useful for feedback purposes, but using only SETs is not sufficient.

Summary

Studies of explaining in higher education have been confined largely to the lecture method. Students value clear, well-structured, and, to a lesser extent, interesting explanations. Training in explaining can improve the clarity, structure, and interest of explanations. Explanations with these characteristics also yield higher measures of recall and understanding. Feedback to lecturers can improve their performance, providing that the evaluation forms are well designed and the lecturers are open to the possibility of change.

EXPLAINING IN THE HEALTH PROFESSIONS

It is sometimes forgotten that today's health professionals spend much of their time talking to managers or other health professionals or teaching students. Much of the research reported in this book, including this chapter, is relevant to these tasks. In this section, we focus upon the specific task of talking with patients, which is referred to as the medical consultation or medical interview.

Explaining in the medical consultation

Since most doctors give about 200,000 consultations in a lifetime (Pendleton, Schofield, Tate & Havelock, 2004), it is clear that explaining and questioning are important skills for doctors – and patients. However, studies of the doctor–patient consultation do not usually isolate the skill of explaining from the other skills involved in the consultation. An exception is the study by Kurtz, Silverman, Benson and Draper (2003). But it is possible to identify features of the research on doctor–patient interactions which are relevant, if not crucial, to the processes of explaining.

Views and beliefs

Patients want their doctors to be knowledgeable, trustworthy, interested in them as persons, and able to explain in terms which they understand (Pendleton & Hasler, 1983; Hall & Dornan, 1988; Levinson et al., 1993). For doctors to explain in ways which the patients understand, it is necessary to explore the explanatory framework and health beliefs of patients and take account of these in providing an explanation (Tuckett, Boulton & Olson, 1985; Robinson, 1995). Robinson (1995, p. 12) argues in her review of patients' contribution to the consultation: 'The most important predictor of a positive outcome is that the doctor offers information and advice which fits easily in to the patients pre-consultation framework.'

This suggestion is of particular importance when a doctor is working with patients from relatively unfamiliar cultures or subcultures (Johnson, Hardt & Kleinman, 1995; Ferguson & Candib, 2002). However, one should be wary of overgeneralising on the basis of cultural stereotypes.

Doctors have their own explanatory frameworks and health beliefs, which are culturally bound and influenced by the scientific and organically based culture of their medical education (Brown, Rohlin & Manogue, 2003). For example, anecdotal evidence from numerous workshops that I have given indicates that doctors prefer to work with patients who are able to explain clearly, are not aggressive, accept the doctor's advice, and are clean.

All medical schools in the UK now provide courses on communication, although the duration, quality, and location of these courses vary widely (Hargie, Dickson, Boohan & Hughes, 1998). The recent recommendations of the General Medical Council (2002) include learning outcomes such as the ability to communicate with a diverse range of people and give patients information in a way which they can understand. There is now strong evidence that communication skills, including explaining, can be taught effectively and are sustainable (Aspegren, 1999; Maguire & Pitceathly, 2002).

Structures, processes, and outcomes

The tasks of the consultation have been framed in different formats (Pendleton et al., 2004). The model based on the Calgary-Cambridge Observation Guide (Kurtz, Silverman, Benson & Draper, 2003) consists of *initiation of the session, gathering information, building a relationship, explaining and planning*, and *closing the session*. These tasks are common to the four modes of consultation identified by Roter, Stewart, Putnam, Lipkin, Stiles and Inui (1997) as *paternalisitic* (doctor-centred), *consumerist* (heavily patient-centred), *laissez-faire*, and *mutuality* (patient-centred). The last is the patient-centred or disease-illness model, which is strongly advocated by researchers. The model has been shown to yield greater patient recall, understanding, and compliance, and better health outcomes (Roter, 1989; Roter & Hall, 1992; Ley & Llewelyn, 1995; Stewart, 1995). However, evidence for the use of this model is sparse. Tuckett et al. (1985) reported that it was used in less than 10% of 1300 videotaped consultations. Few consultations contained detailed explanations in response to patients' questions. Pendleton et al. (2004) reported a similar finding based on analyses of videotapes submitted by 3000 candidates for the MRCGP examination. Among the common reasons for failure in the examination were *not* fulfilling the criteria of sharing management options, explaining diagnosis and the effects of treatment, or explaining in language appropriate to the patient. These results are not surprising given the neglect of personal understanding and holistic approaches in medical schools (Brown, Rohlin & Manogue, 2003).

Clear explanations and a friendly approach have been shown to be important determinants of patient recall and satisfaction. Clear explanations take account of a patient's beliefs, concepts, and linguistic register (Tuckett et al., 1985). The use of structuring moves such as signposting, frames, foci, and links, the use of simple visual aids, and summarising and checks on understanding have all been shown to improve clarity (Ley & Llewelyn, 1995; Maguire, 2000). Maguire (2000) and also Harrigan, Oxman and Rosenthal (1985) and Kinnersley, Stott, Peters and Harvey (1999) have shown that friendliness, warmth, and courtesy contribute to patient recall, understanding, and satisfaction. DiMatteo, Hays, and Prince (1986) in a series of laboratory experiments demonstrated that expressiveness and the decoding of patients' non-verbal cues were strongly associated with patient satisfaction.

Most studies have focused upon the doctor's skills rather than those of the patients. However, the effectiveness of a consultation depends also on the patient's ability to explain. Evidence from discourse analyses shows that there may be disjunctions in intentions, meanings, and belief systems of patients and doctors (Greenhalgh & Hurwitz, 1998; Herxheimer, McPherson, Miller, Sheppherd, Yaphe & Ziebland, 2000).

Such approaches focus upon developing a personal understanding of the patient. Other studies have demonstrated that patients, like doctors, can be trained to provide better explanations and that such training improves both doctor and patient satisfaction with the consultation (Kaplan, Greenfield & Gandek, 1996).

For many medical practitioners, the most powerful test of a consultation is the compliance of patients. Ley and Llewelyn (1995) argue that compliance is a product of satisfaction, which in its turn is a product of understanding and recall. Their review shows well-defined links between recall, understanding, and satisfaction but more tenuous links between satisfaction and compliance. Skilled information gathering and explaining also influence emotional satisfaction, physiological measures, and pain control (Stewart, 1995).

Other researchers prefer the terms 'adherence' or 'concordance'. The latter has connotations of mutually agreed understanding and treatment, which is at the heart of the patient-centred model. Whatever the label, compliance is not high. Silverman, Kurtz, and Draper (1998) reported that about half of patients do not take their medication at all or take it erratically; non-adherence in medications for acute illness is 30–40% and for recommendations on diet about 72%. Stevenson, Cox, Britten, and Dundar (2004) in their review of concordance between health professionals and patients conclude that a patient-centred model is likely to produce greater concordance (compliance) on medication, but evidence for its use is scant. On the basis of a review of improving concordance, Elwyn, Edwards, and Britten (2003) offer useful advice in this area.

However, non-compliance cannot be solely attributed to inadequate information gathering or explaining by a doctor. The better predictors include patients' attitudes, health beliefs, and intentions to comply (Butler, Rollnick & Stott, 1996). Compliance is likely to be influenced by earlier experiences of compliance and non-compliance and the perceived cost/benefits of complying/non-complying. Patients with an 'external' locus of control tend to be fatalistic and feel helpless; those with an internal locus believe events are controllable to some extent through their own actions. 'Externals' *tend* to be poorer compliers than 'internals'. 'Internals' who have a positive attitude to health are more likely to comply and attempt health-related actions (Strickland, 1978). Modifying patients' private theories and causal attributions through discussion and explanation, as well as treating their physical condition, has been shown to contribute to long-term health (Law & Britten, 1995; Marteau, 1995). A summary of processes and outcomes in health improvement is provided in Table 7.5.

Summary

Studies of the medical consultation indicate that what patients value in doctors is warmth, care, concern, and the ability to explain clearly. Patient recall and understanding is enhanced when doctors provide simple, clear, and well-structured explanations. Improved recall and understanding lead to higher patient satisfaction and higher patient compliance, and contribute to health improvement.

Table 7.5 Health improvement: processes and outcomes

Doctor	Patient	Outcome
Friendly, attentive, creates partnership with patient, encourages, is supportive, explains clearly	Tells own story clearly, is encouraged to ask questions, develops treatment with doctor, and takes responsibility for own health tasks	Increases probability of positive health outcome
Cold, distant, non-attentive, frequently interrupts patient, has quick-fire questions, gives several instructions, offers several pieces of advice	Passive, does not ask questions, unduly deferential, superficially agrees to comply	Decreases probability of positive health outcome

EXPLAINING IN OTHER HEALTH PROFESSIONS

Research on explaining in other health professions follows a similar pattern to that of the medical profession.

Dentistry

The General Dental Council (GDC) (2003) recommends that communication skills should be part of the undergraduate curriculum. A survey of the nature and type of courses offered is being undertaken (Manogue, July 2004, personal communication). Furnham (1983) produced evidence-based arguments for the training of dentists in explaining and other communication skills. Pendlebury and Brown (1997) developed courses for vocational trainees on consultation skills, including explaining. Corah (1984) and Gale, Carlsson, Erikson, and Jontell (1984) showed that inadequate explaining led to less anxiety reduction, less positive attitudes to dentistry, and lower levels of satisfaction with dental care. Jepson (1986) reported that co-participation, in which the dentist explains various options of treatment and their probable outcomes, leads to higher levels of compliance. Pendlebury (1988) was the first to propose that the meeting between dentists and patients should be described as a consultation. He outlined the tasks and skills of the consultation and argued for a model based on mutual understanding and agreed treatment. Subsequently, he showed that young dentists who had been trained in communication skills received higher ratings of patient satisfaction and more favourable reports from their senior partners than those who had not received training. This work is to be published posthumously. Overall, however, there remains much work to be done on the dentist–patient consultation.

Nursing

Various nursing initiatives (e.g. CINE, 1986; UKCC, 2001) have strongly advocated training in communication skills. Yet, studies of what nurses actually do, do not appear to be consonant with official wisdom or the wishes of patients or nurses. In her review of nurse–patient communication, Macleod-Clarke (1985) showed that nurses usually only talk to patients when performing some aspect of physical care, and avoided providing explanations on treatment or care. Maguire (1985) in his analysis of nurse–patient interactions pointed to inadequate recognition of patients' problems, insufficient provision of information, and inadequate reassurance and support. In their comprehensive review of nurse–patient communication, Chant, Jenkinson, Randle, and Russell (2002) identified the barriers to effective nurse–patient communication. These findings suggest that the organisational context, role definitions, ward culture, and workloads of nurses inhibit the use of explanations and other communications with patients. At the same time, when nurses are given the opportunity and encouragement to provide explanations to patients, the outcomes are good (Faulkner, 1998). For example, pre-operative information given to patients is related to lower levels of post-operative physiological anxiety, lower analgesic consumption, better sleep patterns, and quicker return to normal appetite. Various intensive qualitative studies, such as McCabe (2004), demonstrate the importance of patient-centred approaches, empathic explanations, continuity of care, and timely reassurances. However, it is not always clear from these studies whether explaining leads to understanding, or whether explaining is merely a signal to patients that their nurses and doctors care. But it is likely that the act of explaining does dispel anxiety, provide reassurance, and, for some patients, at least, provide a deeper understanding.

Pharmacy

Community pharmacists are often the last health professional to see patients before they embark upon self-treatment. Hence, they have an important role in reinforcing and clarifying previously presented information, explaining and justifying procedures, offering suggestions, providing reassurance, and responding to patients' questions. Hospital pharmacists work with a wide range of patients including the terminally ill, the elderly, and stroke patients. Courses on communication skills are now offered in most pharmacy degrees. A communication skills package developed by Morrow and Hargie in 1987 is still in use. Hargie, Morrow, and Woodman (2000) conducted a field study of pharmacist–patient interactions, and found that building rapport and explaining were the primary skills employed, accounting for over 50% of total skill usage. Further support for the use of this skill was produced by Stevenson et al. (2004), who reported that training (interventions), including explaining and questioning, by pharmacists led to increased satisfaction and adherence, and a decrease in the use of over-the-counter medicines and prescribed medicines.

Other health professions

Evidence and training protocols for explaining and other communication skills for other health professionals have been developed in the School of Communication, University of Ulster over the past 25 years. Among the many health professions studied have been speech therapists (Saunders & Caves, 1986), health visitors (Crute, 1986), counsellors (Gallagher, 1987), radiographers (Hargie, Dickson & Tourish, 1994), and physiotherapists (Adams, Bell, Saunders & Whittington, 1994). Although social work is not, strictly speaking, part of health care, apparently its clients too appreciate the ability of a social worker to structure explanations, to specify tasks, to provide clear directions, to listen responsively, and to express concern (Dickson & Bamford, 1995). Dickson, Hargie, and Morrow (1997) have published a most useful text on communication skills training for health professions, and Hargie and Dickson (2003) have provided a comprehensive text on skilled interpersonal communication, both of which contain reviews and guidance on explaining.

Law

A substantial part of the work of solicitors and barristers is concerned with explaining orally or in writing to lay or professional clients, colleagues or opposing lawyers, lay or expert witnesses, and members of the judiciary. Interviewing, advocacy, drafting a case, and opinion writing all involve the tasks of identifying the problem to be explained, taking account of the explainees' prior knowledge, and providing clear, persuasive explanations. All legal practice courses approved by the Law Society of England are now required to include practical exercises in *drafting, research, advocacy, interviewing, and negotiation* (DRAIN). Despite the obvious importance of explaining in law, there are no evidence-based studies of the efficacy of training.

Discourse analysts have shown that judges (Tiersma, 2001) often overestimate what patients or jurors know and consequently give poor, ill-planned explanations. The language used by lawyers, judges, and other court officials, and the procedures used to handle evidence, influence the outcomes of cases (Drew, 1992; Brown, 1996; Lacey, 1997; Lees, 1997). Witnesses and victims often feel demeaned by court procedures and resentful that they cannot give their own narrative (Whitehead, 2001).

Much of this research does not appear to have influenced policy or advice on legal skills training. Instead, the profession tends to draw heavily upon its long history of craft knowledge and expertise-based opinions (LeBrun & Johnstone, 1994). Nor has the profession, as yet, appeared to consider analyses from other high-level professions of generic skills. The exception is Nathanson (1997), who has highlighted the importance of explaining, analysing, listening, and questioning as important competences for lawyers.

The interview or consultation in law has, officially, always been regarded as primarily for the benefit of the client. The recent consultation paper of the Law Society of England on regulations for the twenty-first century again stresses that legal competence should focus on client care, an approach which is similar to the emerging view of concordance in the medical profession. It remains to be seen whether evidence will be forthcoming on the practice of this approach.

Management

All members of the professions are enmeshed in a web of professional and governmental organisations, so it is pertinent to consider how organisations manage and might improve communications, including explanations. Successful organisations use internal and external communications effectively (Blundel, 1998; Hargie, Dickson & Tourish, 2004) and explaining, particularly clear, persuasive explaining, is, arguably, an important feature of organisational effectiveness, but it is rarely singled out from other communication skills. However, there are studies of organisational communication which are relevant to explaining, and some of these may serve as salutary warnings to the professions and their managers.

Much of organisational communication is predicated on two assumptions: training is effective, and if only employees understand, they will comply. The assumption that training in explaining is effective does not appear to have been tested in management, and, as in the professions, good working conditions are probably as important as training. The second assumption is based on a misunderstanding of understanding, or, at least, a misuse of the term. The assumption that understanding will necessarily lead to change in attitudes and culture is not borne out by the evidence (Thompson & Findlay, 1999). This finding is not surprising. Organisations are interdependent hierarchies that do not necessarily share common values. Groups and individuals may see how more senior groups behave and become cynical about the official 'culture'.

Power difference, language usage, and cultural diversity have been shown to affect organisational communication (Hargie, Dickson & Tourish, 2004). The latter is of particular importance in international organisations. The studies by Hofstede (1991) and Javidian and House (1999) reveal differential effects across countries in power distance (status), uncertainty avoidance, assertiveness, commitment to individualism–collectivism, and attitudes to masculinism–femininism. For example, American managers score high on assertiveness and individualism, whereas Hong Kong and Taiwanese score higher on concerns for status and collectivism, and the latter prefer to avoid assertive strategies. All of these affect the processes and success of explanations and of understanding between members of different cultures. Of course, it is also important to recognise that within any cultural group there are individual variations which arise out of the microcontexts of family, school, and community.

High-power talking strategies, which include persuasion, decisive speaking, and clear-cut views, have been shown to be effective in many contexts, whereas low-power talking, which has the characteristics of hesitations, uncertainty, and qualifying statements, does not (Huczynski, 2004). The US presidential election in 2004 provided an example of high- and low-power talkers. However, these characteristics may be culture bound and, even within UK and US cultures, high-power talking strategies may lead to superficial compliance rather than understanding and fundamental change.

Impression management, which includes expressiveness and appearance, contributes to persuasive presentations and reputation (Rosenfeld, Giacolone & Riordan, 2001). Feldman and Klitch (1991) offer somewhat cynical advice on promoting one's self image through ingratiation, exaggeration of one's successes, intimidation of peers, *appearing to be* a team player, distancing oneself from failure, and *displaying* loyalty. These characteristics, they argue, should permeate all aspects of one's work, including presentations. Again, caution is advocated in the use of such tactics in some organisations and national cultures.

The ethos, or subculture, of an organisation influences the willingness of its members to provide information and explanations. Here the concept of open and closed climates is relevant. Characteristics of open climates are empathy, understanding, transparency, egalitarianism, respect for persons, trust, and honesty. Gibb (1961) argued that these characteristics promote collaboration and willingness to provide information, ideas, and explanations. Closed climates are non-caring, controlling, and deceitful; they generate distrust and unwillingness to share intellectual capital, unless such sharing is to the advantage of the communicator.

Tactics of obfuscation, vagueness, illogical explanations, and language which masks personal meanings can be associated with closed climates. For example, 'right-sizing' may mean, for employees, 'redundancy'; 'team-working' may mean limiting an individual's discretion; 'new working patterns' may mean reducing full-time jobs; 'core' and 'periphery' may mean reducing the organisation's commitments to its staff; and 'flexibility' might mean 'management can do what it wants'. These tactics may be unintentional, but often are not. Hargie, Dickson, and Tourish (2004) provide other examples of miscommunication and offer practical guidance on oral and written communication in organisations.

Although written explanations are not part of the brief of this chapter, it is worth pointing out that there is a hierarchy of communication modes. At the top of the hierarchy are face-to-face communications followed by videoconferencing, telephone conversations, e-mails, and memoranda. As one descends the hierarchy, clues of meaning, opportunities to clarify understanding, or checks on understanding become fewer. Different approaches to explaining are required in these modes. For these reasons alone, it is worth considering the use of communication audits (Hargie & Tourish, 2000), which explore the structures and quality of the communication processes in an organisation. As Hargie, Dickson, and Tourish (1999, p. 313) point out, independent communication audits provide an 'objective picture of what is happening compared with what senior executives think (or have been told) is happening'. The advice is pertinent to all workplaces and organisations, including yours!

OVERVIEW

This chapter has provided a conceptual framework for the exploration of explaining and has brought together studies of explaining from a variety of professions. The framework provides a basis for analysing and providing explanations. The evidence indicates that clear explanations are valued by students, patients, and clients. It leads to better learning gains in educational institutions and, in consultations, to better patient understanding, satisfaction, and improved health outcomes. Expressiveness is valued highly in teaching and in consultations. These contribute to learning gains and health outcomes respectively. Studies in law and in the management of organisations provide some further evidence and some cautionary notes on explaining. The evidence indicates that members of professions can be trained to be better explainers, but one needs also to take account of the contexts and cultures in which they work. The chapter has not reviewed all aspects of explaining – that would be a lifetime's work.

But it has provided a sufficiently robust framework to permit observations and suggestions for further research and development.

The most obvious of these is there is a gap between the findings of researchers and professional practice. Without any further research, closing this gap would improve professional practice. But, in addition, each profession could, with advantage, examine its own approaches to research and practice. In teaching, one might examine ways in which students could be encouraged to incorporate models of explaining into their own thinking. In medicine and law, studies of language and power might unravel the complexities of explaining and personal meaning. Hypotheses derived from practice wisdom should be investigated. Such studies will probably confirm much of practice wisdom – it would be odd if they did not. The studies might also identify dissonances between official policies, the value system of a profession, its practice wisdom, and actual practice. These studies could include explaining to singletons and groups, and they would have implications for training. More importantly, they might lead to a shift from descriptions of practice rooted in ideologies to descriptions of ideologies rooted in practice.

But perhaps the greatest challenge is strengthening the links between explaining in a professional context and its outcomes. This task will require an exploration of explaining, not merely as a cognitive act, but also as an affective act through which persuasion and influence lead to changes in attitudes, which, in their turn, may lead to long-term changes in cognition and behaviour. However, the approach and measurement of such outcomes is a vexing problem for all the professions. It is relatively easy to take short-term measures of understanding and satisfaction; it is more difficult to measure whether changes in cognition and attitudes have stabilised. The difficulties are partly technical, ethical, and economic. There is no satisfactory answer to this issue. One may simply have to rely upon 'weak' generalisations based on the covering law model, referred to in this chapter, and continue to explore explaining and understanding by a diverse range of methods. While the goal of explaining will always remain understanding, it may be that the goal of the professions is understanding that leads to action. It is hoped that this chapter will assist professionals in this task.

ACKNOWLEDGEMENTS

I wish to thank Madeline Atkins, who contributed to the chapter in the previous edition of this handbook; Joy Davies and Catrin Rhys for drawing my attention to some studies in law; and David Dickson and Owen Hargie for their suggestions and comments on this chapter.

REFERENCES

Adams, N., Bell, J., Saunders, C. & Whittington, D. (1994). *Communication skills in physiotherapist–patient interaction*. University of Ulster, Jordanstown.

Antaki, C. (Ed.) (1988). *Analysing everyday explanation: a case book of methods*. London: Sage.

Antaki, C. (1994). *Explaining and arguing: the social organisation of accounts.* London: Sage.

Aspegren, K. (1999). Teaching and learning communication skills in medicine: a review with quality grading of articles. *Medical Teacher, 21,* 563–572.

Atkinson, M. (1984). *Our master's voice.* London: Methuen.

Ausubel, D. (1978). *Educational psychology: a cognitive view.* New York: Holt, Rinehart & Winston.

Baddeley, A. D. (2004). *Your memory: a user's guide.* London: Carlton Books.

Baron, R. & Byrne, D. (1997). *Social psychology.* Boston, MA: Allyn and Bacon.

Bennett, N. & Carre, C. G. (1993). *Learning to teach.* London: Routledge.

Biggs, J. (2003). *Teaching for quality at university,* 2nd edn. Maidenhead: McGraw-Hill/ Open University.

Blackburn, M. & Brown, G. (2005). Views of lecturers on the use of student rating scales for the improvement of teaching. Paper presented at the AMEE Conference, Amsterdam, September.

Bligh, D. A. (2000). *What's the use of lectures?,* 5th edn. San Francisco, CA: Jossey Bass.

Blundel, R. (1998). *Effective business communication: principles and practice for the information age.* London: Prentice-Hall.

Brophy, J. (Ed.) (2002). *Advances in research on teaching.* New York: Elsevier.

Brophy, J. & Good, T. L. (1986). Teacher behaviour and student achievement. In M. Wittrock (Ed.), *Handbook of research on teaching.* New York: Macmillan.

Brown, B. (1996). *Law and the sexual politics of interpretation.* London: Athlone.

Brown, G. A. (1978). *Lecturing and explaining.* London: Methuen.

Brown, G. A. (1982). Two days on explaining and lecturing. *Studies in Higher Education, 2,* 93–104.

Brown, G. A. & Daines, J. (1981). Can explaining be learnt? Some lecturers' views. *Higher Education, 10,* 575–580.

Brown, G. A. & Armstrong, S. (1984). On explaining. In E. C. Wragg (Ed.), *Classroom teaching skills.* London: Croom Helm.

Brown, G. & Atkins, M. (1986). Explaining in professional contexts. *Research Papers in Education, 1,* 60–86.

Brown, G. & Bakhtar, M. (1988). Styles of lecturing: a study and its implications. *Research Papers in Education, 3,* 131–153.

Brown, G. A. & Armstrong, S. (1989). Explaining and explanations. In E. C. Wragg (Ed.), *Classroom teaching skills,* 2nd edn. London: Croom Helm.

Brown, G. A. & Wragg, E. C. (1993). *Questioning.* London: Routledge.

Brown, G. & Atkins, M. (1995). *Effective teaching in higher education,* rev. edn. London: Routledge.

Brown, G. & Manogue, M. (2001). Refreshing lecturing: a guide for lecturers. *The Medical Teacher, 24,* 231–244.

Brown, G., Bull, J. & Pendlebury, M. (1997). *Assessing student learning in higher education.* London: Routledge.

Brown, G., Rohlin, M. & Manogue, M. (2003). Collaborative learning, collegiality and critical thinking. In J. Sweet (Ed.), *Effective teaching and learning in medical, dental and veterinary education.* London: Kogan Page.

Brown, J. S. & van Lehn, K. (1980). Repair theory: a generative theory of bugs in procedural skills. *Cognitive Science, 4,* 379–426.

Brown, S. & Race, P. (2002). *Lecturing: a practical guide*. London: Kogan Page/Routledge.

Bruner, J. S. (1966). *Towards a theory of instruction*. Cambridge, MA: Belkapp Press.

Butler, C., Rollnick, S. & Stott, N. (1996). The practitioner, the patient and resistance to change: recent ideas on compliance. *Canadian Medical Association*, *154*, 1357–1362.

Calderhead, J. (1996). Teachers: beliefs and knowledge. In D. Berliner (Ed.), *The handbook of educational psychology*. New York: Macmillan.

Capel, S., Leask, M. & Turner, A. (2002). *Starting to teach in the secondary school: a companion for the newly qualified teacher*. London: Routledge.

Carter, K. (1990). Teachers' knowledge and learning to teach. In W. R. Houston (Ed.), *Handbook of research on teacher education*. New York: Macmillan.

Chafe, W. I. (1982). Integration and involvement in speaking, writing and oral literature. In D. Tannen (Ed.), *Spoken and written language*. Norwood, NJ: Ablex.

Chant, S., Jenkinson, T., Randle, J. & Russell, G. (2002). Communication skills: some problems in nursing education and practice. *Journal of Clinical Nursing*, *11*, 12–21.

CINE (1986). *Report on the communication in nursing education curriculum development project (Phase One)*. London: Health Education Council.

Cockcroft, R. & Cockcroft, S. M. (1993). *Persuading people: An introduction to rhetoric*, 3rd edn. London: Macmillan.

Corah, N. (1984). Reduction of patient stress and the patient-dentist relationship. *New York State Dental Journal*, *30*, 478–479.

Cruikshank, D. R. & Metcalfe, K. K. (1994). Explanation in teaching and learning. In T. Husen & T. N. Postlethwaite (Eds), *International encyclopaedia of educational research: Vol. 10*, 2nd edn, pp. 6143–6148. Oxford: Pergamon.

Crute, V. (1986). Microtraining in health visiting education. Unpublished Ph.D. thesis, University of Ulster, Jordanstown.

d'Apollonia, S. & Abrami, P. C. (1997). Navigating student ratings of instruction. *American Psychologist*, *52*, 1198–1208.

Dewey, J. (1910). *How we think*. Boston, MA: D. C. Heath.

DiMatteo, M. R., Hays, R. D. & Prince, L. M. (1986). Relationship of physicians' non-verbal communication skill to patient satisfaction, appointment non-compliance and physician workload. *Health Psychology*, *5*, 581–594.

Dickson, D. & Bamford, D. (1995). Improving the communication skills of social work students: the problem of transfer of training and what to do about it. *British Journal of Social Work*, *25*, 85–105.

Dickson, D., Hargie, O. & Morrow, N. (1997). *Communication skills for health professionals*, 2nd edn. London: Chapman & Hall.

Downing, J. & Garmon, C. (2002). A guide to implementing Powerpoint and overhead LCD projectors in communication classes. *American Journal of Communication*, *5*. (retrieved 25 March 2004 from www.acjournal.org/holdings/vol5/iss2/articles/guide/.pdf).

Draper, S. (1988). What's going on in everyday explanations? In C. Antaki (Ed.), *Analysing everyday explanation: a casebook of methods*. London: Sage.

Drew, P. (1992). Contested evidence in courtroom cross-examination: the case of trial for rape. In P. Drew & J. Heritage (Eds), *Talk at work*. Cambridge: Cambridge University Press.

Dunkin, M. J. (1986). Research on teaching in higher education. In M. Wittrock (Ed.), *Handbook of research on teaching*. New York: Macmillan.

Eble, K. (1995). *The craft of teaching*, 2nd edn. San Francisco, CA: Jossey-Bass.

Elwyn, G., Edwards, A. & Britten, N. (2003). 'Doing prescribing': how doctors can be more effective. *British Medical Journal, 327*, 864–867.

Ennis, R. H. (1969). *Logic in teaching*. New York: Prentice-Hall.

Entwistle, A. & Entwistle, N. J. (1997). Revision and experience of understanding. In N. F. Marton, D. Hounsell & N. J. Entwistle (Eds), *The experience of learning*. Edinburgh: Scottish University Press.

Entwistle, N. J. (2003). Conceptions of learning, understanding and teaching in higher education (retrieved 24 July 2004 from www.scre.ac.uk/fellow/fellow98/entwistle.html).

Entwistle, N. J. & Ramsden, P. (1983). *Understanding student learning*. London: Croom Helm.

Faulkner, A. (1998). *Effective interaction with patients*, 2nd edn. London: Churchill Livingstone.

Feldman, D. & Klitch, N. (1991). Impression management and career strategies. In K. Giacolone & P. Rosenfeld (Eds), *Applied impression management: how image making affects managerial decisions*. London: Sage.

Ferguson, W. J. & Candib, L. M. (2002). Culture, language, and the doctor–patient relationship. *Family Medicine, 34*, 353–361.

French, P. (1994). *Social skills for nursing practice*, 2nd edn. London: Chapman & Hall.

Fry, J. (1992). *General practice: the facts*. Oxford: Radcliffe Medical Press.

Furnham, A. (1983). Social skills and dentistry. *British Dental Journal, 154*, 404–408.

Gage, N. L., Belgard, M., Dell, D., Hiller, J. E. Rosenshine, B. & Unruh, W. R. (1968). *Explanations of the teacher's effectiveness in explaining*. Technical report No. 4. Stanford, CA: Stanford University Center for Research and Development in Teaching.

Gale, E., Carlsson, S., Erikson, A. & Jontell, M. (1984). Effects of dentists' behaviour on patient attitudes. *Journal of the American Dental Association, 109*, 444–446.

Gallagher, M. (1987). *The microskills approach to counsellor training*. Unpublished Ph.D. thesis, University of Ulster, Jordanstown.

General Dental Council (2003). *The first five years*, 2nd edn. London: General Dental Council.

General Medical Council (2002). *Tomorrow's doctors*, 2nd edn. London: General Medical Council.

Gibb, J. R. (1961). Defensive communication. *Journal of Communication, 11*, 41–49.

Greenhalgh, T. & Hurwitz, B. (1998). *Narrative based medicine: dialogue and discourse in clinical practice*. London: British Medical Journal.

Hall, J. & Dornan, H. C. (1988). What patients like about their medical care and how often are they asked: a meta-analysis of the satisfaction literature. *Social Sciences and Medicine, 27*, 935–939.

Hargie, C., Dickson, D. & Tourish, D. (1994). Communication skills training and the radiography profession: a paradigm for training and development. *Research in Radiography, 3*, 6–18.

Hargie, O. & Tourish, D. (Eds) (2000). *Handbook of communication audits for organizations*. London: Routledge.

Hargie, O. & Dickson, D. (2003). *Skilled interpersonal communication: research, theory and practice*, 4th edn. London: Routledge.

Hargie, O., Dickson, D. & Tourish, D. (1999). *Communication in management*. Aldershot: Gower.

Hargie, O., Morrow, N. & Woodman, C. (2000). Pharmacists' evaluation of key communication skills in practice. *Patient Education and Counseling*, *39*, 61–70.

Hargie, O., Dickson, D. & Tourish, D. (2004). *Communicating skills for effective management*. Houndmills: Palgrave/Macmillan.

Hargie, O., Dickson, D., Boohan, M. & Hughes, K. (1998). A survey of communication skills in UK schools of medicine: present practices and prospective proposals. *Medical Education*, *32*, 25–34.

Harrigan, J. A., Oxman, T. E. & Rosenthal, R. (1985). Rapport expressed through non-verbal behaviour. *Journal of Non-verbal Behavior*, *2*, 486–489.

Herxheimer, A., McPherson, A., Miller, R., Shepperd, S., Yaphe, J. & Ziebland, S. (2000). A database of patients' experiences (DIPex): new ways of sharing experiences and information. *Lancet*, *355*, 1540–1543.

Hewstone, E. (1989). *Causal attribution from cognitive processes to collective beliefs*. Oxford: Blackwell.

Hofstede, G. (1991). *Cultures and organizations: software of the mind*. London: McGraw-Hill.

Huczynski, A. A. (2004). *Influencing within organisation: getting in, rising up and moving on*, 2nd edn. London: Routledge.

Hyman, R. T. (1974). *Teaching: vantage points for study*. New York: Lippincott Press.

Janz, N. K. & Becker, M. H. (1984). The health belief model a decade later. *Health Education Quarterly*, *11*, 1–47.

Javidian, M. & House, R. J. (1999). Cultural acumen for the global managers: lessons from the project GLOBE. *Organisational Dynamics*, *29*, 289–305.

Jepson, C. (1986). Some behavioural aspects of dental compliance. *Journal of Dental Practice Administration*, *3*, 117–122.

Johnson, T. M., Hardt, E. J. & Kleinman, A. (1995). Cultural factors. In M. Lipkin, Jr, S. M. Putnam & A. Lazare (Eds), *The medical interview, clinical care, education and research*. New York: Springer-Verlag.

Kaplan, S. H., Greenfield, S. & Gandek, B. (1996). Characteristics of physicians with participatory decision-making styles. *Annals of Internal Medicine*, *124*, 497–504.

Kinneavy, J. L. (1971). *A theory of discourse*. New York: W. W. Norton.

Kinnersley, P., Stott, N., Peters, T. J. & Harvey, I. (1999). The patient-centeredness of consultations and outcomes. *British Journal of General Practice*, *13*, 41–45.

Kruglanski, A. (1988). *Basic processes in social cognition; a theory of lay epistemology*. New York: Plenum.

Kurtz, S., Silverman, J., Benson, J. & Draper, J. (2003). Marrying content and process in clinical method teaching: enhancing the Calgary–Cambridge Guides. *Academic Medicine*, *78*, 802–809.

Lacey, N. (1997). Criminology, criminal law and criminalisation. In M. Maguire, R. Morgan & R. Reiner (Eds), *The Oxford book of criminology*. Oxford: Oxford University Press.

Land, M. L. (1985). Vagueness and clarity in the classroom. In T. Husen & T. N. Postlethwaite (Eds), *International encyclopaedia of education: research studies.* Oxford: Pergamon Press.

Law, S. & Britten, N. (1995). Factors that influence the patient-centredness of a consultation. *British Journal of General Practice, 45,* 520–524.

LeBrun, M. & Johnstone, R. (1994). *The quiet revolution: improving student learning in law.* London: Law Book Company.

Lees, S. (1997). *Ruling passions: sexual violence and the law.* Buckingham: Open University Press.

Levinson, W., Stiles, W. B. & Inui, T. S. (1993). Physician frustration in communicating with patients. *Medical Care, 31,* 285–295.

Ley, P. & Llewelyn, S. (1995). Improving patients' understanding, recall and satisfaction and compliance. In A. Broome & S. Llewelyn (Eds), *Health psychology.* London: Chapman & Hall.

Light, G. & Cox, R. (2001). *Learning and teaching in higher education: the reflexive professional.* London: Sage.

Light, R. J. (2001). *Making the most of college: students speak their minds,* Boston, MA: Harvard University Press.

Locke, J. (1693). *An essay on human understanding* (retrieved 1 May 2004 from oregonstate.edu/instruct/phl302/texts/locke).

Locke, J. (1693). *Some thoughts on education.* Oxford: Oxford University Press, 1995.

Macleod-Clarke, J. (1985). The development of research in interpersonal skills in nursing. In C. Kagan (Ed.), *Interpersonal skills in nursing: research and applications.* London: Croom Helm.

Maguire, P. (1985). Deficiencies in key interpersonal skills. In C. Kagan (Ed.), *Interpersonal skills in nursing: research and applications.* London: Croom Helm.

Maguire, P. (2000). *Communication skills for doctors.* London: Arnold.

Maguire, P. & Pitceathly, C. (2002). Key communication skills and how to acquire them. *British Medical Journal, 325,* 697–700.

Marteau, T. M. (1995). Health beliefs and attributions. In A. Broome & S. Llewelyn (Eds), *Health psychology.* London: Chapman & Hall.

McCabe, C. (2004). Nurse–patient communication: an exploration of patients' experiences. *Journal of Clinical Nursing, 13,* 41–49.

McKeachie, W. J. (1994). *Teaching tips,* 9th edn. Lexington, MA: D. C. Heath.

McKeachie, W. J. (2002). *McKeachie's teaching tips: strategies, research and theories for college and university teachers.* Boston, MA: Houghton Miffin.

Murray, H. G. (1997a). Effective teaching behavior in the college classroom in higher education. In R. P. Perry & J. C. Smart (Eds), *Effective teaching in higher education: research and practice.* New York: Agathon Press.

Murray, H. G. (1997b). Does evaluation of teaching lead to improvement of teaching? *International Journal of Academic Development, 2,* 20–41.

Murray, H. G., Rushton, J. P. & Paunonen, S. V. (1990). Teacher personality traits and student instructional ratings in six types of university courses. *Journal of Educational Psychology, 82,* 250–261.

Nathanson, S. (1997). *What lawyers do: a problem solving approach to legal practice.* London: Sweet & Maxwell.

Norman, D. & Bobrow, D. (1975). Active memory processing perception and cognition.

In C. N. Cofer (Ed.), *The structure of human memory*. San Francisco, CA: W. H. Freeman.

Pask, G. (1976). Styles and strategies of learning. *British Journal of Educational Psychology*, **46**, 128–148.

Pavitt, C. (2000). Answering questions requesting scientific explanations for communication. *Communication Theory*, **10**, 379–404.

Pendlebury, M. (1988). Let's call it the 'dental' consultation. *British Dental Journal*, **165**, 276–277.

Pendlebury, M. & Brown, G. (1997). Communicating with dental patients. In R. Dennick (Ed.), *Innovations in teaching and clinical medicine*. Birmingham: Staff and Educational Development Association

Pendleton, D. & Hasler, J. (Eds) (1983). *Doctor patient communication*. London: Academic Press.

Pendleton, D. Schofield, T., Tate, P. & Havelock, P. (2004). *The new consultation: developing doctor–patient communication*. Oxford: Oxford University Press.

Piaget, J. (1954). *The construction of reality in the child*. New York: Basic Books.

Potter, J. & Wetherell, M. (1994). *Discourse and social psychology: beyond attitudes and behaviour*. London: Sage.

Resnick, L. & Omanson, S. (1987). Learning to understand arithmetic. In R. Glaser (Ed.), *Advances in instructional psychology*. Hillsdale, NJ: Lawrence Erlbaum Associates.

Robinson, A. (1995). Patients' contribution to the consultation. In A. Broome & S. Llewelyn (Eds), *Health psychology*. London: Chapman & Hall.

Rosenfeld, P., Giacolone, R. A. & Riordan, C. A. (2001). *Impression management: building and enhancing reputations at work*. London: Thomson.

Roter, D. (1989). Which aspects of communication have strong effects on outcomes? In M. Stewart & D. Roter (Eds), *Communicating with medical patients*. London: Sage.

Roter, D. L. & Hall, J. A. (1992). *Doctors talking with patients: patients talking with doctors*. Westport, CT: Auburn House.

Roter, D. L., Stewart, M., Putnam, S. M., Lipkin, M., Stiles, W. & Inui, T. S. (1997). Communication patterns of primary care physicians. *Journal of the American Medical Association*, **277**, 350–356.

Rowan, K. E. (1999). Explanatory skills. In A. L. Vangelisti, J. A. Daly & G. W. Friedrich (Eds), *Teaching communication: theory, research and methods*, 2nd edn. Mahwah, NJ: Lawrence Erlbaum.

Rowan, K. E. (2003). Informing and explaining skills: theory and research on informative communication. In J. O. Greene & B. R. Burleson (Eds), *Handbook of communication and social interaction skill*. Mahwah, NJ: Lawrence Erlbaum.

Ryle, G. (2000). *The concept of mind*. London: Penguin.

Sanders, R. (2003). Applying the skills concept to discourse and conversation: the remediation of performance defects in talk-in-interaction. In Greene, J. & Burleson, R. (Eds), *Handbook of communication and social interaction skills*. Mahwah, NJ: Lawrence Erlbaum.

Saunders, C. & Caves R. (1986). An empirical approach to the identification of communication skills with reference to speech therapy. *Journal of Further and Higher Education*, **10**, 29–44.

Silverman, J., Kurtz, S. & Draper, J. (1998). *Skills for communicating with patients*. Oxford: Radcliffe Medical Press.

Smith, B. O. & Meux, M. O. (1970). *A study of the logic of teaching*. Urbana, IL: University of Illinois Press.

Stevenson, F. A., Cox, K., Britten, N. & Dundar, Y. (2004). A systematic review of the research on communication between patients and health care professionals about medicine: the consequences for concordance. *Health Expectations, 7*, 235–245.

Stewart, M. A. (1995). Effective physician–patient communication and health outcomes: a review. *Canadian Medical Association Journal, 152*, 1423–1433.

Storey, J. (1992). *Developments in the management of human resources: an analytical review*. Oxford: Blackwell.

Strickland, B. (1978). Internal-external expectancies and health-related behaviour. *Clinical Psychology, 46*, 1192–1211.

Swift, L. F. (1961). Explanation. In R. H. Ennis & B. O. Smith (Eds), *Language and concepts in education*. Chicago: Rand McNally.

Thompson, P. & Findlay, P. (1999). Changing the people: social engineering in the contemporary workplace. In L. Ray & A. Sayer (Eds), *Culture and economy after the cultural turn*. London: Sage.

Thompson, S. (1994). Frameworks and contexts: a genre-based approach to analysing lectures. *English for Specific Purposes, 13*, 171–186.

Thyne, J. M. (1963). *The psychology of learning and techniques of teaching*. London: University of London Press.

Tiersma, P. (2001). The problem of jury instructions. Paper presented at the annual conference of the American Association for the Advancement of Science, San Francisco, CA.

Tuckett, D. A., Boulton, M. G. & Olson, C. S. (1985). *Meetings between experts: a study of medical consultations*. London: Tavistock.

Turney, C., Ellis, K. J. & Hatton, N. (1983). *Sydney microskills redeveloped*. Sydney: University of Sydney.

UKCC (2001). *Fitness for practice: the UKCC commission for nursing and midwifery education*. London: United Kingdom Central Council for Nursing, Midwifery and Health Visiting.

Wachtel, H. C. (1998). Student evaluation of teaching effectiveness. *Assessment and Evaluation in Higher Education, 23*, 191–211.

White, P. A. (1990). Ideas about causation in philosophy and psychology. *Psychological Bulletin, 108*, 3–18.

Whitehead, E. (2001). *Witness satisfaction: findings from the witness satisfaction survey*. London: Home Office.

Wragg, E. C. (Ed.) (1984). *Classroom teaching skills*. London: Croom Helm.

Wragg, E. C. (1993). *Primary teaching skills*. London: Routledge.

Wragg, E. C. & Brown, G. A. (1993). *Explaining*. London: Routledge.

Wragg, E. C. & Brown, G. A. (2001). *Explaining in the secondary school*. London: Routledge.

Zimbardo, P., Ebbesen, E. & Maslach, C. (1977). *Influencing attitudes and changing behavior*. Reading, MA: Addison-Wesley.

Chapter 8

Self-disclosure: Strategic revelation of information in personal and professional relationships

Charles H. Tardy and Kathryn Dindia

SELF-DISCLOSURE, THE PROCESS whereby people verbally reveal themselves to others, constitutes an integral part of all relationships. As stated by Rubin, 'In every sort of interpersonal relationship, from business partnerships to love affairs, the exchange of self disclosure plays an important role' (1973, p. 168). People disclose to friends and spouses, to physicians and hairdressers, to solicitors and pub governors. The importance of self-disclosure for individuals and their relationships is not always apparent. Revelation of such mundane matters as the events of the day may be a cherished ritual in a marriage (Sigman, 1991; Vangelisti & Banski, 1993), while people sometimes confide personal problems to virtual strangers (Cowen, 1982).

The pervasiveness and importance of self-disclosure accounts for the intense interest in this phenomenon shown by social scientists. Literally thousands of quantitative studies have been conducted over a period extending 40 years. The periodic publication of reviews of this literature has helped provide coherence and helped organise this body of knowledge. Both reviews of thematic issues (e.g. Dindia & Allen, 1992) and more comprehensive treatments (e.g. Derlega et al., 1993) enable readers to cope with a mounting body of knowledge.

The present review offers a strategic perspective on self-disclosure by highlighting the motivations and means by which people manage the disclosure of information in personal and work relationships. We review literature that describes the disclosure of personal information in friendships and romantic relationships as well as in relationships with supervisors, subordinates, and co-workers. We focus on three facets of disclosure in these two contexts: self-disclosure and relationship development, factors affecting self-disclosure, and risky self-disclosure.

SELF-DISCLOSURE IN PERSONAL RELATIONSHIPS

Self-disclosure is one of the defining characteristics of intimate relationships (Brehm, Miller, Perlman & Campbell, 2002): 'Two people cannot be said to be intimate with each other if they do not share some personal, relatively confidential information with one another' (p. 138). Self-disclosure serves important functions in relationship development. We can not initiate, develop, or maintain a relationship without self-disclosure. We terminate relationships, in part, by terminating self-disclosure. Self-disclosure has other important relational consequences, including eliciting liking and reciprocal self-disclosure. Requests for disclosure are common when individuals want information about their partner, including details about the partner's sexual history in order to engage in safer sex.

Self-disclosure and relationship development

Self-disclosure performs important relational functions (Derlega & Grzelak, 1979; Derlega et al., 1993). Revealing information about self can help people as they attempt to initiate and develop relationships with others. Some authors even suggest that self-disclosure may be a strategy by which people seek to obtain desirable responses from others (Schank & Abelson, 1977; Baxter, 1987; Miller & Read, 1987). On the other hand, self-disclosing some information creates problems for individuals and relationships. Telling others exactly how we feel can be cruel and destroy trust. Consequently, individuals must learn how to regulate their disclosures. Below we discuss both the role of self-disclosure in different stages of relationship development and the necessity of managing personal information by regulating self-disclosures (see Chapter 15 for a detailed discussion of relational communication).

Relationship initiation and development

Self-disclosure is used to initiate relationships. In initial interaction, people reveal their names, hometowns, hobbies, and so on. As stated by Derlega et al. (1993, pp. 1–2), 'it is hard to imagine how a relationship might get started without such self-disclosure.' Self-disclosure is typically superficial and narrow in breadth in the early stages of a relationship. Although this self-disclosure may not be intimate, it is the prelude to more intimate self-disclosure. Self-disclosure in the initial phases of a relationship functions to promote liking and to help people get to know each other. Self-disclosure provides information that helps us reduce uncertainty about the other person's attitudes, values, personality, and so on, thereby enabling the relationship to develop (Berger & Bradac, 1982). Similarly, through self-disclosure we acquire mutual knowledge, or knowledge that two people share, know they share, and use in interacting with one another (Planalp & Garvin-Doxas, 1994).

Self-disclosure is also an important component in the development of a relationship; thus,

> If you like this person, you will want to know more about him or her, and you will, in turn, be willing to share more information about yourself. You will begin to talk about attitudes, feelings, and personal experiences; in brief, you will begin to disclose more personal information. If your new friend likes you, he or she also will disclose personal information. (Derlega et al., 1993, p. 2)

Research indicates that people strategically use self-disclosure to regulate the development of a relationship. In Miell and Duck's (1986) study of strategies individuals use to develop and restrict the development of friendships, participants described how they got to know others and how they chose appropriate topics of conversation for interacting with someone they just met and a close friend. They also indicated strategies they would use to restrict and intensify a relationship's development. Superficial self-disclosure, appropriate for conversing with a stranger, was also used to restrict the development of a relationship. Similarly, intimate self-disclosure, appropriate for conversing with friends, was used to intensify a relationship.

In Tolhuizen's (1989) study of romantic relationships, seriously dating college students reported self-disclosing information about self ('I told my partner a great deal about myself – more than I had told anyone before') as a strategy to intensify dating relationships. Another strategy was to disclose things about the relationship, feelings in the relationship, and what is desired for the future of the relationship ('We sat down and discussed our relationship so far, how we felt about each other and what we wanted for the relationship'). Thus, disclosing information about yourself as well as your thoughts and feelings about the relationship is a strategy to increase the intimacy of a relationship.

Relational maintenance

Self-disclosure about the events of the day, referred to as 'catching up' or 'debriefing', is an important relationship maintenance strategy. All relationships involve periods when the partners are away from each other (e.g. while they are at work). One of the behaviours used by partners to maintain the continuity of their relationship across these periods of physical absence is catching up (Sigman, 1991; Gilbertson, Dindia & Allen, 1998). When couples are reunited at the end of the day, they often talk about what happened during the day: how their day went, who they saw, what they did, and so on. Research indicates that debriefing one another is a relationship maintenance strategy that is positively related to marital satisfaction (Vangelisti & Banski, 1993).

Self-disclosure of intimate information is also important for maintaining a relationship. Once partners feel they know each other, the exchange of objective or factual information about the self probably decreases (Fitzpatrick, 1987). As a relationship progresses, the amount of subjective or emotional information that can be exchanged between partners increases; not only how the speaker feels about himself or herself but also how the speaker feels about the partner and the relationship can be revealed. Thus, self-disclosure in relationships continues to include the disclosure of facts and feelings about the self, but it also includes feelings about the partner and the relationship.

Self-disclosure is essential for preventing problems in relationships and solving problems after they have occurred. Discussing our relationship and the rules in our relationship is important for preventing relational transgressions, and it is also important in repairing relationships after relational transgressions have occurred (Dindia & Emmers-Sommers, 2006).

In the late 1960s and early 1970s, total and complete openness was advocated, and open communication was considered the essence of a good relationship. Jourard (1971), as well as others, advocated full disclosure in relationships: 'the optimum . . . in any relationship between persons, is a relationship . . . where each partner discloses himself without reserve' (p. 46). More recently, others (Bochner, 1982; Parks, 1995) have argued that moderate levels of self-disclosure lead to satisfaction in long-term relationships. Gilbert's (1976) review of research found support for a curvilinear relationship between self-disclosure and satisfaction; moderate degrees of self-disclosure appeared to be most conducive to maintaining relationships over time.

Baxter and Wilmot (1985) have shown how most relationships involve taboo topics, topics that partners do not talk about. In developing relationships, one of the most common taboo topics is the state of the relationship itself. Other common taboo topics are other current relationships, past relationships, relationship norms, conflict-inducing topics, and negatively valenced self-disclosure. 'People are often keenly interested in the likely future of their partnerships and are eager to learn their partner's expectations and intentions, but they don't ask' (Brehm et al., 2002, p. 141). Instead, they create secret tests (Baxter & Wilmot, 1984) to get the desired information. For example, if I want to find out how much my partner loves me, I might watch how he/she responds to other attractive people (triangle test), or ask my partner's best friend how my partner feels about me (third-party test), and so on. Why do partners engage in secret tests when they could simply ask their partner how they feel about them? The answer is that in many relationships, such matters are too intimate to be discussed (Brehm et al., 2002). It takes a high level of trust to talk about such intimate matters. Ironically, it takes discussing such intimate matters to develop a high level of trust. However, even in the most committed relationships, there are still some things that are left unsaid and are better left unsaid.

An alternative conclusion is that openness is an effective communication strategy for some types of couples, but not others. Fitzpatrick (1987) described three types of couples, traditionals, independents, and separates, and argued that there are similarities within and differences among the types of couples in the degree to which they self-disclose and value self-disclosure in their marriage. Fitzpatrick argued that these couple types establish different norms about what is appropriate to reveal in their relationship, and that these norms determine the relationship between communication and satisfaction. Fitzpatrick found that traditionals value self-disclosure in marriage and that they self-disclose to their spouses. However, their self-disclosure is limited to positive feelings and topics about the partner and the relationship. Independent couples value self-disclosure, disclose substantially more to their spouses than other types of couples, and are willing to disclose both positive and negative feelings to one another. Separates do not value openness and self-disclosure in marriage and also do not self-disclose to their spouses. Thus, self-disclosure is important to maintain a relationship, but full disclosure is not universally prescribed.

Relational de-escalation

Self-disclosure is also used to terminate relationships (Baxter, 1985, 1987). Some relationships gradually fade away; in this case, self-disclosure gradually and incrementally decreases over time. This may happen without either party intending to end the relationship. For example, it may be the result of one partner moving away to go to college. Some relationships terminate suddenly, typically as the result of a relational transgression (such as infidelity). In this case, relationship disengagement may be accomplished through strategic communication by one or both relational partners.

Baxter (1987) argued that there are multiple stages to the dissolution of relationships and that self-disclosure is used differently in the stages. Baxter divided relationship disengagement into three stages: private decision making, decision implementation, and public presentation. During private decision making, the individual contemplates existing dissatisfactions with the partner and with the relationship, reaching the decision to end the relationship. Self-disclosure is strategically employed during this stage to acquire information about the partner's satisfaction with the relationship, to acquire information on the likelihood that the partner would be willing to repair the relationship, and to acquire information from the social network regarding their perceptions of self, partner, and the relationship. Relational disclosure, in which the discloser reveals personal feelings about the relationship, is a strategy used to induce reciprocal relational disclosure from the partner and from social network members. The likelihood of using this strategy is low but increases if alternative strategies have failed, the disengager lacks sufficient skill in enacting indirect information acquisition strategies, or the secondary goal of saving face is relatively unimportant to the disengager.

During the decision implementation stage, the disengager seeks to accomplish the dissolution of the relationship through actions directed at the partner. Withdrawal, including reduced self-disclosure, is the most common strategy, and it is used to terminate relationships indirectly (Baxter, 1985). Relational self-disclosure, in which a person directly presents the partner with direct personal feelings about the relationship ('I don't love you anymore'), is used less frequently to terminate relationships.

At the public presentation stage, the dissolution of the relationship becomes official to social network members. Here the goal of self-disclosure is to make public the dissolution of the relationship while simultaneously maintaining face with the social network. These goals require selective self-disclosure to others.

Relational dialectics/boundary management theory

One of the important principles of a strategic perspective on self-disclosure is that individuals have multiple goals in interaction and relationships. Sometimes, the goals are compatible and the pursuit of one goal facilitates the accomplishment of the other. However, sometimes goals are contradictory and the fulfilment of one goal conflicts with the fulfilment of the other (Schank & Abelson, 1977). For example, the goal of being open and honest with your partner may conflict with the goal of maintaining the relationship. Recent theories have elaborated the forces working against self-disclosure in relationships.

Early theories on personal relationships, such as Altman and Taylor's (1973) social penetration theory, argued that there is a linear relationship between self-disclosure and relationship development, self-disclosure gradually and incrementally increasing as the relationship develops. Many scholars have rejected the idea that the development of relationships always follows a unidirectional and cumulative path, with ever-increasing openness of self-disclosure (Altman, Vinsel & Brown, 1981). As argued by these authors, initial theory and research on self-disclosure were simplistic. Instead, more recent theories recognise the possibility that developing or continuing relationships might exhibit cycles of openness and closedness, or that some relationships might not progress toward increased openness at all (Altman et al., 1981). Although some relationships may generally proceed toward greater openness, they probably have cycles or phases of openness or closedness within this overall developmental pattern.

Recent scholarship views relationships as involving contradictory and opposing forces (Baxter, 1988; Montgomery, 1993; Baxter & Montgomery, 1996a & b). These theorists posit openness–closedness or expressiveness–protectiveness as a dialectical tension in relationships. Individuals continually face the contradictory impulses to be open and expressive versus protective of self and/or other. Self-disclosure is necessary to achieve intimacy and trust in a relationship, but self-disclosure opens areas of vulnerability, and to avoid hurting each other people must undertake protective measures. Thus, the contradictory dilemma between being open and closed requires decisions to reveal or conceal personal information.

Rawlins (1983) identified two conversational dilemmas resulting from the contradictory impulses to be open and expressive and to be protective of self and/or other. First, an individual confronts the contradictory dilemma of striving to be open or to protect self. Disclosing personal information to another makes one susceptible to being hurt by the other. The decision for self-disclosure will be a function of at least two things, an individual's perceived need to be open about a given issue, and the individual's trust of the partner's discretion (the latter's abilities to keep a secret and exercise restraint regarding the self's sensitivities). The decision to reveal or conceal involves assessing what will be gained or lost by either choice.

In deciding whether to disclose statements regarding the partner (e.g. 'I don't like your haircut'), an individual confronts the second contradictory dilemma of protecting partner versus striving to be open and honest. The decision for self-disclosure or to restrict disclosure of negative information will be a function of the self's perceived need to be honest about a given issue and the amount of restraint appropriate to the topic. An individual develops an awareness of topics which make the other vulnerable to hurt or anger. In particular, *self must determine whether telling the truth is worth causing the other pain and breaching the other's trust in self's protective inclinations* (Rawlins, 1983, p. 10).

Individuals can respond to the dialectical tension of openness–closedness with a number of strategic responses. Baxter (1990) found the predominant strategy reported for the openness–closedness contradiction to be segmentation, which involves a differentiation of topic domains into those for which self-disclosure is appropriate and those regarded as 'taboo topics' (i.e. topics that are 'off limits' in a relationship).

Similarly, privacy regulation is a strategic response to the dialectical nature of self-disclosure. Altman (1975) defined privacy as 'an interpersonal boundary process by which a person or group regulates interaction with others. By altering the degree of openness of the self to others, a hypothetical personal boundary is more or less receptive to social interaction with others' (p. 6). Similarly, communication boundary management theory (Petronio, 1991, 2002) argues that individuals manage their communication boundaries in balancing the need for disclosure with the need for privacy. The basic thesis of communication boundary management theory is that revealing private information is risky because one is potentially vulnerable when revealing aspects of the self. To manage disclosing private information, individuals erect a metaphoric boundary as a means of protection and to reduce the possibility of being rejected or getting hurt. Thus, privacy regulation is a strategic response to the dialectical tension of the need to reveal and conceal. By regulating privacy, we engage in a strategy designed to satisfy the oppositional forces of openness and closedness.

The dialectical perspective paints a more complex picture of the skills involved in competent self-disclosure. Competent self-disclosure is responsive to partners' needs for intimacy and privacy. Rawlins' (1983) analysis suggests that it may be just as important for an individual to develop skill at restrained remarks and selective disclosure of intimate information: 'An apt handling of the dialectic means that self limits self's own vulnerability and strives to protect other while still expressing thoughts and feelings' (Rawlins, 1983, p. 5).

Factors affecting self-disclosure

Some variables affect self-disclosure, such as gender, requests for self-disclosure, and another person's self-disclosure. In this section, we explore some of the factors facilitating and inhibiting the process of self-disclosure.

Sex differences

Who discloses more, men or women? Gender stereotypes would have us believe that women are far more disclosive than men. However, a meta-analysis of sex differences in self-disclosure indicates that while women disclose more than men, the difference is small. Dindia and Allen (1992) examined over 200 studies on sex differences in self-disclosure published between 1970 and 1989. Regardless of whether self-disclosure was observed between strangers or measured by self-report or observational measures between partners in intimate relationships, approximately 85% of men and women overlapped in their self-disclosure. The results were similar in a follow-up meta-analysis (Dindia & Malin; 2003) of 75 studies published in the 1990s; women disclosed more than men but the difference was small.

235

Reciprocal disclosures

Perhaps the most enduring generalisation from the literature on self-disclosure is that self-disclosure is reciprocal. The pioneering researcher, Sidney Jourard, noted: 'in ordinary social relationships, disclosure is a reciprocal phenomenon. Participants in dialogue disclose their thoughts, feelings, actions, etc., to the other and are disclosed to in return. I called this reciprocity the "dyadic effect": disclosure begets disclosure' (1971, p. 66).

A recent meta-analysis of over 60 studies (Dindia, 2002) found that self-disclosure is reciprocal, although the degree of matching depends on how reciprocity was measured. But in all cases, whether self-disclosure was measured by self-report or observational measures, whether self-disclosure was to strangers or intimates, self-disclosure was highly reciprocal.

Several theories explain reciprocity of self-disclosure, including trust attraction, social exchange, and modelling (Archer, 1979). The trust-attraction hypothesis assumes that disclosing intimate information to a recipient indicates that the other is liked and trusted and this then leads the recipient to disclose as a sign of liking and a willingness to trust the original discloser. The social exchange perspective suggests that receiving disclosure is a rewarding experience and that when we receive something of value we feel obligated to return something of similar value, such as a similar disclosure. The modelling hypothesis posits that one person's self-disclosure serves as a model for the other person's self-disclosure. More recent theoretical explanations attribute reciprocity to more global constraints of conversational norms, that is, rules that indicate the kinds of comments that would be appropriate given previous comments (Derlega, Metts, Petronio & Margulis, 1993).

Reciprocity of self-disclosure is assumed to be a time-bound process in which people mutually regulate their self-disclosure to one another at some agreed-on pace. But little more is known about the temporal aspects of reciprocity. The rate at which it occurs, how it ebbs and flows, and factors that accelerate or retard reciprocity of exchange have not been discussed in detail. Some people have argued that the need for immediate reciprocity declines as the relationship increases in intimacy and commitment (e.g. Altman, 1973); however, one study indicated that married couples reciprocate self-disclosure within a 10-minute conversation (Dindia, Fitzpatrick & Kenny, 1997).

Berg and Archer (1980) noted that a variety of responses to self-disclosure are appropriate and that a common reaction to receiving intimate self-disclosure is to express concern or support, rather than to reciprocate self-disclosure. In their experimental study, Berg and Archer observed that the most favourable impressions were made by listeners who expressed concern for a discloser rather than listeners who responded with self-disclosures. Thus, it may be more important to respond to self-disclosure with interest and support than immediately to reciprocate self-disclosure.

Self-disclosure and liking

Self-disclosure and liking are thought to be related in at least three ways: self-disclosure to another person causes the other person to like the discloser, liking another person causes an individual to self-disclose, and individuals like another person as a result of having disclosed to them. A meta-analysis (Collins & Miller, 1994) of the research on self-disclosure and liking confirmed that we like people who self-disclose to us, we disclose more to people we like, and we like others as a result of having disclosed to them.

The effect of self-disclosure on a recipient's liking for the discloser has been of greatest theoretical interest, and studies examining this effect make up the bulk of the studies on self-disclosure and liking (Collins & Miller, 1994). This effect is typically referred to as the 'disclosure-liking hypothesis'. Though the research indicates that self-disclosure leads to liking, there are at least two qualifications to the disclosure–liking relationship. First, disclosure that violates normative expectations will not lead to liking. Low-intimacy, descriptive self-disclosures that reflect positively on the self are normative in initial interactions. Revealing information that deviates from this norm may produce negative evaluations (Bochner, 1982). Even in developed relation-ships, norms exist specifying appropriate and inappropriate topics for discussion (Baxter & Wilmot, 1985). Research also indicates that the disclosure of negatively valanced information does not lead to liking (Gilbert & Horenstein, 1975). As Bochner stated, 'discriminating disclosers are more satisfied and more likely to remain attrac-tive to their partners than are indiscriminating disclosers' (1982, p. 120). Second, people who disclose a lot to everyone are not liked more than low disclosers. Miller (1990) observed that sorority women who generally disclosed more to others were not more popular than other members. However, women who disclosed more to a particular partner than they generally disclosed to others were liked more by that partner.

People make attributions regarding another person's disclosure, and the reasons or motivations we attribute to another person's self-disclosure are an important part of what the self-disclosure will mean to the relationship (Derlega et al., 1993). People can attribute another person's self-disclosure to the person's disposition or personality ('he disclosed to me because he is an open person') or to their relationship ('he dis-closed to me because he likes me or because we have an intimate relationship'). When we perceive another person's self-disclosure as personalistic (revealed only to the target) rather than non-personalistic (revealed to many people), research indicates that it leads to increased liking (Berg & Derlega, 1987). Collins and Miller (1994) concluded from their meta-analysis of the research on self-disclosure and liking that the relationship between disclosure and liking is stronger if the recipient believes that the disclosure was shared only with the recipient.

Requests for disclosures

For a variety of reasons, people frequently desire personal information about others. Berger and Calabrese (1975) suggested that 'when strangers meet, their primary con-cern is one of uncertainty reduction' (1975, p. 100). To reduce that uncertainty, initial interactants engage in high levels of information-seeking. There are several strategies for acquiring information about a partner in interactions, the most obvious being asking questions. However, because norms of social appropriateness restrict the use of information requests (Berger, Gardner, Parks, Schulman & Miller, 1976; Berger, 1979), initial interactants are hypothesised to use less direct strategies as well. In particular, participants in initial interaction may use self-disclosure to acquire information about each other (Berger & Bradac, 1982; Archer & Earle, 1983). Because of the norm of reciprocity, self-disclosure is a 'potentially powerful way to induce the other to disclose similar information about himself' (Berger, 1979, p. 141). This is especially true in initial interaction, where the need to reciprocate self-disclosure immediately and on a tit-for-tat basis is strong.

Douglas (1990) found that self-disclosure occurred more frequently than asking questions during a 6-minute initial conversation between strangers; across the entire conversation, 49% of the utterances were coded as self-disclosures, whereas 18% of the utterances were coded as questions. As the conversation continued, individuals' uncertainty level and question asking decreased, but their self-disclosure increased. Thus, disclosure appears to be a more appropriate strategy than asking questions for acquiring information in initial interaction.

Self-disclosure on the Internet

In the 1980s and early 1990s interpersonal communication researchers began considering how computer-mediated communication (CMC) compares to face-to-face (f2f) communication. Early views of CMC were that on-line communication is impersonal in comparison to f2f communication due to the lack of non-verbal cues. Social information-processing theory (Walther, 1992) rejected the view that the absence of non-verbal communication restricts communicators' ability to engage in interpersonal communication. Walther argued that communicators are just as motivated to reduce interpersonal uncertainty, form impressions, and develop affinity in on-line settings as off-line. When denied non-verbal communication, communicators substitute other cues to engage in impression formation and relational messages, such as content, style, and timing of verbal messages. The rate of information exchange is slower on-line but, given enough time, relationships conducted through CMC can be just as personal as f2f communication. Research supports the proposition that CMC can be just as personal as f2f communication (Walther 1992; Walther & Parks, 2002).

More recently, a third view has emerged in which on-line relationships, because of the characteristics of CMC, are often hyperpersonal (more personal and involve higher levels of self-disclosure and attraction than f2f) (Walther, 1996, Walther & Parks, 2002). Some have argued that Internet users come to know one another more quickly and intimately than in f2f relationships. They argue that the features of CMC may make it easier to self-disclose on-line versus f2f. Individuals in CMC often are anonymous, and the psychological comfort that comes from such anonymity may lead them to reveal more information about themselves (Wallace, 1999). Walther (1996) argued that CMC is hyperpersonal because of sender, receiver, message, and channel effects. Receivers initially engage in stereotypically positive and idealised attributions of on-line partners. Senders exploit CMC's absence of non-verbal communication for the purpose of selective self-presentation, presenting a positive and idealised image of self. The channel facilitates goal-enhancing messages by allowing sources greater control over message construction. The process of feedback creates self-fulfilling prophesies among senders and receivers.

Cooper and Sportolari (1997) refer to this as the 'boom and bust' phenomenon:

When people reveal more about themselves earlier than they would in F2F interactions, relationships get intense very quickly. Such an accelerated process of revelation may increase the chance that the relationship will feel exhilarating at first, and become quickly eroticized, but then not be able to be sustained because the underlying trust and true knowledge of the other are not there to support it. (p. 12)

Cooper and Sportolari highlight media accounts of people who are certain they have found their 'soulmate' and leave an established relationship, travelling across the country, to meet people who do not turn out to be what they seemed.

Others have noted that Internet romantic relationships progress through an inverted developmental sequence (Merkle & Richardson, 2000). In real life, we meet people, then get to know them; on-line, we get to know people and then choose to meet them (Rheingold, 1993). Some, say this makes for an unstable relationship (Levine, 2000). However, the opposite is plausible. CMC may be characterised by a higher degree of personal investment of time and self-disclosure than is typical in f2f relationships. This greater investment may result in a stronger relationship (Merkle & Richardson, 2000).

Overall, there is little evidence that on-line communication is more personal than f2f communication (Walther & Parks, 2002). Nor is there empirical evidence to support the boom and bust phenomenon. Nonetheless, some have cautioned that when developing relationships on-line one should move from virtual to f2f in a short period of time before unrealistic expectations have time to build up (Levine, 2000).

Another dimension along which the nature of self-disclosure in CMC versus f2f communication may differ is that of sex differences in self-disclosure. The issue of gender differences in self-disclosure in CMC has yet to be empirically examined; however, some have speculated that such differences would be less evident (Merkle & Richardson, 2000). That is, in CMC, the anonymity of the Internet may permit users to step outside constricting gender roles of communication, and may allow men and women to self-disclose equally. However, it should be remembered that technology and the uses of technology (for instance, the relatively recent use of Web cameras) change so quickly that any generalisations regarding self-disclosure on the Internet are problematic.

Revealing risky information

Self-disclosure always involves a certain amount of risk, but the risk becomes acute when disclosing highly intimate and negative information about self. Sometimes, not engaging in self-disclosure can result in serious consequences, such as not talking about safer sex. Sometimes, engaging in self-disclosure can result in serious consequences, such as disclosing stigmatised information about self.

Self-disclosure and safer sex

Though attaining information about past relationships, other present relationships, sexual habits, and sexual experiences is necessary for making informed choices for sexual intimacy (Cline, Freeman & Johnson, 1990), these topics are taboo in developing relationships (Baxter & Wilmot, 1985). Several studies have been conducted of college students and the extent to which they attempt to talk with their partners about AIDS prevention, either to know the partner or to obtain the partner's sexual history (Chervin & Martinez, 1987; Bowen & Michal-Johnson, 1989; Cline, Johnson & Freeman, 1992). The results of these studies indicate that only a minority of students talk about AIDS prevention (e.g. condom use, sexual history, monogamy) with a sex partner. From condom use (Edgar, Freimuth, Hammond, McDonald & Fink, 1992) to AIDS prevention (Cline & Johnson, 1992; Cline et al., 1992), researchers have found that talking about safe sex is relatively rare. For example, Buysse and Ickes (1999) observed 120 dating couples; half were paired with their partner and the other half were paired with a stranger. Half the pairs were asked to discuss safe sex practices, and the other half were asked to discuss joint leisure time activities. Buysse and Ickes found that dating couples had a more difficult time discussing safe sex practices than did their non-acquainted counterparts. Furthermore, dating couples had a more difficult time discussing safe sex practices than they did discussing joint leisure activities. In other words, it seems that sexual self-disclosure is a difficult proposition for dating couples. This is catastrophic, given that sexual communication has been linked to lower HIV risk behaviour (Wingood & DiClemente, 1998; Quina, Harlow, Morokoff, Burkholder & Deiter, 2000).

Even less is known about how people go about talking about AIDS prevention. Edgar et al. (1992) examined the type of information-seeking strategies individuals use to reduce uncertainty about a potential partner prior to the first sexual encounter. The most frequently reported interaction strategy was asking questions; 39% of the sample reported asking the partner directly about the partner's sexual history and health, etc. The second most common interaction strategy was unsolicited self-disclosure (17%); the other person volunteered the information. Eight per cent of the participants reported that they introduced the topic into a conversation in hopes that the information would come out while they were talking. Five per cent of the sample reported reciprocal self-disclosure: 'I disclosed this information to him or her in hopes that she or he would reciprocate and disclose the same information to me.' This study indicates that although more direct methods of information seeking (questions) may be used when soliciting information about something as important as AIDS prevention, less direct methods, such as requests for self-disclosure, unsolicited self-disclosure, bringing up the topic with the hopes that the other person will self-disclose, and reciprocal self-disclosure, also function to provide information and reduce uncertainty about a potential sexual partner. Edgar et al. (1992) concluded that mere willingness to bring up condom use is more important than the particular strategy employed. It is extremely important that people engage in sexual self-disclosure for the simple reason that their health may depend on it.

Revelation of stigmatising information

The term 'stigma' refers to a stable characteristic or attribute of an individual that is perceived as damaging to the individual's reputation (Goffman, 1963). Stigmas include, but are not limited to, physical disability, membership in some stigmatised group, character defects that are manifested by some discrediting event in the person's past or present, and disease. The literature on stigma disclosure includes research on disclosure of homosexuality, positive HIV status, AIDS, sexual abuse, drug addiction, alcoholism, mental illness, epilepsy, and other stigmatised conditions. Individuals are stigmatised because they presently possess or display these characteristics (e.g. being HIV positive or having AIDS), because they formerly manifested these characteristics (e.g. former drug addiction, former mental illness), or because they are associated with someone who is stigmatised (e.g. the lover, relative, or caregiver of a person with AIDS; the parent of a gay son or lesbian daughter).

Research on stigma disclosure indicates that individuals are highly selective in choosing their targets for stigma disclosure (Wells & Kline, 1987; Siegel & Krauss, 1991; Marks, Bundek, Richardson, Ruiz, Maldonado & Mason, 1992; Murphy & Irwin, 1992; Herman, 1993; Dindia, 1998). Disclosure of stigmatised conditions is a reasoned action that follows from the perceived social, psychological, and material consequences of informing others (Marks et al., 1992).

Disclosure of stigmatised conditions is based on decision-making rules; individuals make decisions regarding disclosure of stigma. Petronio, Reeder, Hecht & Mon't Ros-Mendoza (1996) studied the decision-making rules used in children's and adolescents' disclosures of sexual abuse. They found three rules to grant access: *tacit permission* (i.e. disclose in response to an inquiry or in response to another person's self-disclosure), *selecting the circumstances* (i.e. choose a situation that makes you feel comfortable and reduce fears of disclosure), and *incremental disclosure* (i.e. disclose in an incremental fashion, testing the reaction to each self-disclosure before deciding whether to increase self-disclosure). Individuals denied access to disclosure of sexual abuse based on *target characteristics* (i.e. do not disclose if recipient is untrustworthy, unresponsive, or lacks understanding) and *anticipated negative reactions* (i.e. do not disclose if you anticipate negative reactions from the target, including gossip and loss of control of the information). Dindia (1998) found that *relationship characteristics* is a decision-making rule for disclosure of homosexuality (i.e. do not disclose if the relationship is not close). The US military policy, *don't ask, don't tell*, is a decision-making rule used for revealing/concealing homosexuality in the military (Herek, Jobe & Carney, 1996). More interestingly, Dindia, (1998) found that this rule was used outside the military (i.e. 'my parents know but they don't ask and I don't tell').

Individuals use specific verbal strategies when revealing their stigma to others. *Selective disclosure and concealment* can take the following forms: avoidance of selected 'normals', redirection of conversations, withdrawal, the use of disidentifiers (misleading physical or verbal symbols that prevent others from discovering their stigma), and the avoidance of stigma symbols (e.g. symbols of gay pride) (Herman, 1993). Petronio et al. (1996) have shown how children and adolescents select the circumstances (when and where) for disclosure of abuse.

In *staging information*, also referred to as 'testing the waters', the boundaries of self-disclosure are progressively relaxed (or tightened) depending on the listener's reactions (positive or negative) to disclosure (Petronio, 1991). Specifically, the discloser reveals a minimal amount of information and tests the reaction of the target before self-disclosing in more depth or detail. A number of researchers have found that staging information is a key strategy used to manage stigma disclosure (MacFarlane & Krebs, 1986; Limandri, 1989; Petronio et al., 1996; Dindia, 1998).

Another strategy for revealing stigma is *indirect disclosure*. In studying disclosure of homosexuality, Dindia (1998) found that participants reported dropping hints about themselves, wearing 'freedom rings' (a symbol of gay pride), and T-shirts and caps that symbolise gay identity in a more or less explicit manner.

Limandri (1989) found that some participants engaged in *concealment or non-disclosure* of HIV antibodies, AIDS, and abuse, in which they kept their secret to themselves and would do anything possible to deny their stigma to others, including lying. Powell-Cope and Brown (1992) found that many caregivers of persons with AIDS lived with secrecy. Specific strategies used to 'pass' included making excuses, lying, witholding information, changing jobs or places of residence, and avoiding certain social situations and family gatherings.

Several studies have found that a few people engage in *open and complete disclosure* (Limandri, 1989; Powell-Cope & Brown, 1992; Dindia, 1998); they do not hide their stigma from anyone. Additional strategies include *invitational disclosure*, in which a discloser provides sufficient cues that 'something is wrong' to invite the respondent to request self-disclosure (Limandri, 1989). Limandri (1989) and Dindia (1998) also report *reciprocal self-disclosure* and *responses to inquiry* as common types of stigma disclosure.

SELF-DISCLOSURE IN WORK RELATIONSHIPS

Although considerable efforts have been expended in assessing the role of self-disclosure in personal relationships, social scientists have only begun to examine systematically the revelation of personal information in task or work relationships. Although this situation has improved slightly since the publication of our chapter in the second edition of this volume, the relative deficiency of programmatic research on this topic is unfortunate because work consumes a significant portion of most people's daily lives, and talking about personal experiences at work is perhaps the most common activity among people in disparate occupations and professions. Moreover, a close examination of relevant organisational research indicates that self-disclosure serves many important functions in the employment context (see Steele, 1975, for a practical discussion of these issues). Consequently, in this section, we describe the role of self-disclosure in the development and maintenance of relationships in the work environment, identify factors affecting the revelation of personal information at work, and discuss the dilemmas faced by individuals contemplating the revelation of risky information in the context of work relationships.

Disclosure and the development of work relationships

Self-disclosure plays a pivotal role in the development and maintenance of work relationships, just as it does in personal relationships. Subsequently, we discuss the strategic use of self-disclosure in the employment interview, the ritualised interaction in which people begin their relationship with co-workers and employers, and organisational socialisation, the process by which individuals acquire the values, knowledge, and behaviours necessary for successfully performing job functions.

Employment interviews

Although performing numerous functions, the initial job interview primarily serves to provide the employer with information allowing the discrimination of applicants and provides the interviewee with information concerning potential employment (see Chapter 16 for a full review of the employment interview). Although both the interviewer and interviewee roles require the selective revelation of information, disclosures by the interviewee are much more likely to be personal than are disclosures revealed by and about the employer. The standard script for employment interviews includes a section where questions are asked about the applicant's personal, educational, and work history (Tullar, 1989). Additionally, some interview research (e.g. Janz, 1989) suggests that interviewers should rely less on speculative questions, such as, 'what would you do *if* . . . ?' (p. 160) and more on questions requiring recollection of specific behaviours, such as, 'what did you do *When* . . . ?' (p. 160). Interviews based on these questions have been shown to improve the selection process and result in hiring people who perform better on the job (Jablin & Krone, 1994). Additionally, a review of research on interviewing (Jablin & Miller, 1990) concluded that interviewees infrequently seek information about or opinions of interviewers. Thus, personal revelations by interviewees are an integral part and may reasonably be said to be the primary focus of employment interviews.

What kind of disclosures do interviewees reveal? Given the importance of making a positive impression, it might be expected that the interviewee will reveal largely attributes and experiences that portray the speaker favourably. As one guide suggests, interviewees 'try to demonstrate the characteristics of the interviewers' ideal employee through answers and references to their education and experience' (Stewart & Cash, 1988, pp. 157). Research predictably indicates that interviewers rate more highly interviewees who present favourable information (Rowe, 1989), elaborate answers, and talk fluently (Jablin, 1987). Gilmore and Ferris (1989) stated:

> Most job seekers try to present their positive qualities in an interview, with self-enhancing statements intending to create a good impression. Statements that suggest positive qualities or traits, if credible, should positively influence the interviewer. This somewhat obvious ingratiation technique is employed frequently by applicants seeking to bolster their image in an interview. (p. 200)

Moreover, interviewers ask more questions designed to elicit positive information than ones to get negative information (Sackett, 1982; Binning, Goldstein, Garcia, Harding & Scattaregia, 1988). Thus, the interview may be thought of as 'a search for confirmation of a positive hypothesis' (Rowe, 1989, p. 87).

The preference for positive disclosure should not result in a standardisation of interviews such that everyone professes honesty, dependability, helpfulness, and so on. Rather, interviewees would be best advised to reveal experiences indicating personal traits consistent with job characteristics (Jackson, Peacock & Smith, 1980). For example, a person interviewing for a job as a counsellor might describe incidents of helping others, while a candidate for a job writing advertising copy might disclose experiences that reveal independence and creativity.

Disclosures are, however, so commonly self-flattering that interviewers may discount as exaggeration some of the information revealed (Giacalone & Rosenfeld, 1986). One study suggested that 25% of interviewees falsified information (Kennan, 1980), while Barlund's polygraph study of 400 job applicants concluded that 20% of interviewees falsified or concealed information that might jeopardise their employment (cited in Ekman, 1992). Trinkaus's (1986) survey reported that most respondents would not disclose information that would potentially adversely and unfairly affect their employer's evaluation. Thus, self-revelations may be viewed sceptically by interviewers. One professional publication even offered suggestions for detecting deception in employment interviews (Waltman & Golen, 1993). Interviewees can deflect such scepticism by providing supporting evidence, such as curricula vitae, letters of references, and portfolios, when appropriate. Interviewers might also take steps to improve the accuracy or honesty of disclosures made by interviewees. For example, explaining why information is being requested could increase the interviewee's willingness to reveal job-relevant information (Fletcher, 1992).

Ordinarily, people who reveal too much positive information may be perceived as bragging (Miller, Cooke, Tsang & Morgan, 1992) or overly aggressive (Dipboye & Wiley, 1977). However, interviewers expect a positive bias in information revealed, and the general tendency of interviewees is to reveal only favourable information. Consequently, the thresholds will probably be very high for making these negative assessments and attributions. Moreover, aggressiveness may even be seen as a desirable trait in some occupations. Because the failure to reveal relevant qualifications or attributes may put the interviewee in a relatively unfavourable position relative to other interviewees, and negative attributions are unlikely to be made because of overly positive disclosures, people should reveal information in the employment interview that otherwise might appear self-serving.

Because of the bias toward positive information in the interview, negative information about the interviewee significantly and adversely affects interviewer perceptions and selection decisions (Rowe, 1989). These circumstances make it difficult for people to reveal past failures, shortcomings, or problems. For example, several studies suggest that voluntary disclosures about a disability may jeopardise an individual's prospects of being hired (Tagalakis, Amsel & Fichten, 1988; Herold, 1995) and reduce opportunities for advancement (Dalgin & Gilbride, 2003). One study indicated that 80% of a sample of individuals with learning disabilities did not discuss their condition with their employer while seeking their current job (Price, Gerber & Mulligan, 2003). For individuals with disabling illnesses or conditions, such as rheumatoid arthritis, the issue of concealment or disclosure is a recurring one (Allen & Carlson, 2003). However, a person who does not disclose this information in the employment interview may be subsequently perceived as devious or untruthful for withholding the information. These alternatives clearly present a dilemma. One strategy for managing this no-win situation is to reveal the negative after the positive information has been disclosed (Tucker & Rowe, 1979). Herold (2000) describes other strategies that disabled people can use to enhance their credibility in job interviews.

Socialisation/inculturation

Becoming a productive employee involves acquiring the values and skills required of organisational members. This inculturation or socialisation process involves active strategies by both individuals and organisations (e.g. Griffin, Collela & Goparaju, (2000). Self-disclosure may be linked to socialisation in several ways. Many people develop an identity that includes their occupation, job, or company. People sometimes define themselves by what they do for a living or whom they work for. Statements such as 'I work for Merrill-Lynch' or 'I am a barrister with the Inns of Court' not only describe facts but can also reveal personal priorities, pride, or even at times embarrassment or shame. (For a formal discussion of the process of identification, see Cheney, 1983). Self-disclosures perform a role in the process by which people acquire these work identities. Disclosure of personal information will accompany the development of relationships between new and older or senior employees of a company. Sharing personal history will allow people to establish commonalities and mutual bonds. Without developing a network of supportive peers, a person will remain or become an isolate and will unlikely develop a corporate identity.

Van Maanen and Kunda (1989) noted that personal disclosures can affect transmission of the organisation's culture. Their field notes from an ethnographic study of an engineering company recount one example from an employee orientation session:

> Toward the end of the session, the instructor gives a short, apparently impromptu speech of a personal, almost motherly sort: 'Be careful, keep a balance, don't overdo it, don't live off vending machines for a year. I've been there; I lived underground for a year, doing code. Balance your life. Don't say, "I'll work like crazy for four years then get married." Who will marry you? Don't let the company suck you dry. After nine or ten hours, your work isn't worth much anyway' (p. 79)

That such strategic disclosure can increase not only credibility but also cohesiveness, task commitment, and productivity has been demonstrated in an experimental study of small group interaction (Elias, Johnson & Fortman, 1989).

Other people's disclosures can have positive consequences for the recipient's identification with and inculturation in the organisation. Bullis and Bach's (1989) study of the socialisation of postgraduate students indicated that socialising allowed 'students to talk about themselves, their interests, and their professors' (p. 282) and accounted for one of the largest changes in identification. Participating in these types of informal conversations increased students' identification with their new roles. Additionally, as established employees reveal stories of their work career, new employees will learn not only the procedures and policies of the organisation but something of its values as well. Thus, disclosures by long-term employees will be personally and practically helpful to new employees. Cheney's (1983) study of employees from a divisional office of a large industrial corporation revealed that employees in divisions that were relatively isolated, that is, did not have frequent contact with other offices, had relatively lower levels of organisational identification (see also Eisenberg, Monge & Miller, 1983). One recent study of untenured faculty in colleges and universities revealed that friendship and collegiality of mentors were among the strongest predictors of organisational commitment and connectedness (Schrodt, Cawyer & Sanders, 2003). The opportunity to engage in disclosure, then, may facilitate the development of useful employee attitudes.

Factors affecting disclosure at work

Self-disclosures can have functional and dysfunctional effects for organisations, and the people in them. Self-disclosures may promote effective decision making by initiating the resolution of problems, or self-disclosures may cause resentment, as when an employee learns from a co-worker that the latter earns a higher salary. By intent or default, organisational policies and practices can encourage and discourage these appropriate and inappropriate behaviours. In this, and the subsequent section on risky disclosures, we describe factors that facilitate or discourage the occurrence of different kinds of self-disclosures in the work context.

Organisational practices and policies that discourage self-disclosure

As mentioned earlier, the US military's *don't ask, don't tell* policy on homosexuality is perhaps the most widely known example of an overt attempt by an organisation to control the disclosure of personal information. Some corporations prohibit employees from revealing their salary or wages in an attempt to minimise conflicts due to perceived inequities, though these policies may be illegal (Kleiman, 2002). An employee who does not know how much money her peer is receiving, cannot complain about salary inequity. Below, we describe a few examples of organisational policies and practices that affect self-disclosure.

Organisational norms that inhibit the disclosure of felt emotions

Hochschild's (1983) pioneering work on emotional labour demonstrated that organisations can enforce expectations about how employees express their feelings. For example, one worker describing the organisational culture of Disneyworld noted that employees 'may complain of being "too tired to smile" but at the same time may feel guilty for having uttered such a confession' (Van Maanen & Kunda, 1989, p. 69). Thus, the culture of the organisation may be a control system that discourages employees from honestly revealing their emotions.

Legal constraints on the request for information

In many countries, legislation now prohibits employers from giving preference in hiring, compensating, or promoting individuals based on their sex, race, age, marital status, or disabilities, unless these characteristics are fundamental to the performance of the job. Information that can be used for illegal discrimination cannot be lawfully requested. For example, an employer may not ask job applicants who would babysit their children if they were offered the job (Stewart & Cash, 2003). However, interviewers may skirt the legal requirements by indirect tactics to acquire desired information. For example, interviewers may give interviewees the opportunity to discuss the cause of their disabilities by making general enquiries, such as 'tell me about yourself' or 'what were the significant events of your life?' (Hequet, 1993).

In both the inappropriate, illegal explicit request and the veiled request for self-disclosure, a person confronts the dilemma of being unhappily cooperative or combatively closed. Stewart and Cash (2003) describe how to make tactful denials in employment interviews, to use these as opportunities to provide supportive information, and playfully to remind interviewers that these questions are inappropriate. Bavelas, Black, Chovil, and Mullett (1990) showed how people use equivocal messages, that is, messages open to multiple interpretation, to extricate themselves in such situations. Thus, responses other than denial of the request or open disclosure provide people an alternative to the dilemma faced when receiving requests for inappropriate or undesired disclosures.

Prohibitions against disclosure

As numerous reports and court cases attest, self-disclosures from co-workers can be considered not only inappropriate but also illegal in the USA if they contribute to a hostile or threatening work environment (for a discussion of the legal issues, see Paetzold & O'Leary-Kelly, 1993). Although offensive compliments are one of the least offensive, threatening, and recognised forms of sexual harassment (Konrad & Gutek, 1986; Padgitt & Padgitt, 1986; Powell, 1986), they occur frequently and constitute a significant problem for many people. Studies also indicate that women are more likely than men to see these behaviours as problematic (e.g. Powell, 1986). Additionally, Pryor and Day's (1988) experimental study noted that attributions of sexual harassment and negative intentions to a sexual compliment are greater when spoken by a superior than a peer. Witteman (1993) suggested that persistent sexual disclosures that are non-reciprocated and non-negotiated constitute a 'severe' form of sexual harassment. In order to discourage sexual harassment, organisations have exerted considerable efforts over the last decade to increase employee awareness of this problem and to prevent it from happening.

Organisational ideologies that limit disclosure

In a recent study of a research and development corporation, Meares, Oetzel, Torres, Derkacs, and Ginossar (2004) observed that members of minority groups are less likely than others to raise concerns of mistreatment with supervisors. This has been confirmed in studies of majority–minority interaction within organisations in Northern Ireland (Hargie & Dickson, 2004). These findings are consistent with muted group theory, which contends that the communication practices of majority groups make it difficult for members of minority groups to express themselves in ways that are seen as legitimate. These authors recommend that companies proactively seek the input of minority members to prevent these problems and to make effective use of their employees. Hence, organisations may institute policies and practices to circumvent more endemic, societal pressures.

Factors facilitating disclosure in work relationships

Reciprocal disclosures

As discussed in the section on personal relationships, research consistently demonstrates that self-disclosure is reciprocal in social relationships. A similar phenomenon occurs in formal, task relationships. In work as well as social contexts, relationships in which mutual disclosure occurs evidence desirable characteristics or outcomes. For example, a study by Waldron (1991) indicated that respondents who had better relationships with their supervisors reported more frequent personal contacts (e.g. 'Ask about their personal life'; 'Share my future career plans with them') and direct negotiation of the relationship (e.g. 'Make it known when I am unhappy about something at work'; 'Speak up when I feel I have been treated unjustly') than workers who perceived their relationship with their supervisor to be lower in quality. Jablin (1987) suggested that new employees may disclose information to supervisors to elicit reciprocal disclosures that reveal the supervisor's expectations concerning the employee's work habits and values. Another study of new employees and transferees indicated that people who developed relationships characterised by mutual disclosure of ideas and feelings had clearer expectations and fewer uncertainties about their role in the organisation (Kramer, 1994).

Mutual disclosure can also have adverse consequences for the individual and the organisation. Bridge and Baxter (1992) noted that people who develop personal friendships with their work colleagues experience common problems or tensions. Likewise, the organisation can experience problems from mutually disclosive relationships, such as cohesive work groups that develop norms and goals that are contrary to those of the employers or the organisation.

Revealing risky information

Revealing some information engenders risk. Employees should, and sometimes no doubt do, consider the possibility of adverse consequences for the discloser. Because of these important potentials, we describe below several distinct types of self-disclosures that present dilemmas for employees.

Bad news and negative job appraisals

Organisational researchers have long noted the problem of 'upward distortion', whereby negative information is withheld and only positive information is communicated up the organisational structure (for a discussion of the general bias against revealing negative information, see Tesser & Rosen, 1975; Tourish & Hargie, 2004). Research consistently indicates that information will be distorted if it is unfavourable to the discloser (Dansereau & Markham, 1987). For example, the accountant does not want to tell the supervisor that inflation was not considered when estimating next year's expenses, and the sales representative would not want the manager to know about the customer who took business to another company because of the representative's failure to return telephone calls. Although troubling for the individual, such information is crucial for the effective functioning of organisations. Weick (1990) described one dramatic example in which job stress and organisational command structures contributed to pilots' and air traffic controllers' unwillingness to reveal their confusion or uncertainty, resulting in airliners crashing and killing hundreds of people. Although few failures to disclose have such dramatic and costly consequences, the incident illustrates how important employee disclosures can be.

Morrison and Milliken (2000) conceptualise this problem as one of 'organizational silence' and suggest that organisational or systemic factors account for people's unwillingness to disclose opinions. More specifically, they suggest that managers' beliefs about the harms of dissent, self-interest of employees, and relative value of their own opinions create a climate that discourages input. Moreover, Morrison and Milliken (2000) specify organisational, environmental, and individual characteristics that foster these beliefs.

Few empirical investigations assess the factors that facilitate these revelations, although Steele (1975) recommended organisational development strategies for facilitating openness. Research consistently suggests that trust plays a decisive role in the disclosure of negative information. Fulk and Mani (1986) reported that employees are more likely to distort or withhold information from supervisors perceived to distort and withhold information. This conclusion supports the earlier findings of Mellinger (1956) that people are less likely to distort information communicated to people they trust. Consequently, supervisors who provide accurate information to subordinates should be more likely to receive negative disclosures than supervisors who provide distorted information. Likewise, Roberts and O'Reilly's (1974) frequently cited study indicated that perception of trust in a supervisor is negatively correlated with reports of withholding and distorting information. In general terms, then, trust plays an influential role in decisions affecting disclosure in the work environment just as it does outside work (e.g. Larzelere & Huston, 1980). A survey of recent graduates of a college business programme and employees of an accounting firm indicated that willingness to voice dissatisfaction was related to satisfaction with the organisation and perceived efficacy of complaining (Withey & Cooper, 1989). A similar conclusion was reached by Dutton, Ashford, Lawrence, and Miner-Rubino (2002), whose survey of female managers suggested that the only factor that predicted their willingness to voice gender equity issues was perceived cultural exclusivity, that is, how open or exclusive their superiors were thought to be. Such affective constructs as trust, satisfaction, and sense of belonging appear to facilitate the disclosure of negatively valenced information to superiors.

Seeking support for personal problems

To gain assistance, emotional support, or practical aid from others, people must reveal their problems (see review in Derlega et al., 1993). Organisations can either encourage or discourage such revelations. In the last 20 years, many organisations have instituted procedures and programmes to foster employee disclosure of personal problems. People who seek this help must disclose events, incidents, and issues from their lives that warrant change (see Sonnenstuhl, Staudenmeier & Trice, 1988, for a discussion of differences among self-referrals and other referrals). Employee assistance programmes (EAPs) are seen by organisations as the preferred alternative for minimising the workplace effects of employee problems ranging from drug abuse to childcare (e.g. Rosen, 1987; Soloman, 1992). Over the last two decades, many organisations have instituted EAPs to help employees with personal problems that interfere with job performance. For example, one report estimates there are more than 10,000 EAPs in the USA and that more than 75% of Fortune 500 companies sponsor EAPs (Luthans & Walersee, 1990). Although reports of the success of these programmes abound, the empirical evidence is limited (Luthans & Walersee, 1990).

One review of the literature on this subject suggested that four steps are necessary to encourage self-referrals: eliminate stigma, ensure anonymity, train employees, and encourage employee self-analysis (Myers, 1984). The few quantitative studies of employee decisions to utilise EAPs indicate that employee confidence in the EAP is the most important attitudinal factor affecting propensity to use this service (Harris & Fennell, 1988; Milne, Blum & Roman, 1994). Corporations are discouraged from giving these divisions names that accentuate negative connotations, such as 'drug rehabilitation programme'. This advice is particularly appropriate because only a small percentage of the problems dealt with by EAPs are drug and alcohol related (e.g. Success Story, 1991). Numerous authors note the importance of confidentiality (e.g. Feldman, 1991). However, the required secrecy that prevents peers from learning of the problems experienced by their co-workers also reduces the opportunity for peer support (e.g. Koch, 1990).

Stigmatising personal information

Examples of stigmatising information that are particularly salient in the work context include previously being fired from a job, disability, and ill health, such as HIV infection or AIDS (Koch, 1990). The vast majority of individuals with learning disabilities in one study reported that they never discuss their condition with supervisors or co-workers for fear of losing credibility, status, and opportunities (Price, Gerber & Mulligan 2003), while in another study almost 70% reported not disclosing their condition to supervisors, with about 50% reporting that their condition was not relevant and 50% reporting fear of negative consequences (Madaus, Foley, McGuire & Ruban, 2002). Several authors suggest that persons with disabilities can lessen the uncertainties and tensions of their interactional partners by acknowledging their disability (e.g. Evans, 1976; Thompson, 1982). However, such disclosures may prove effective only if the disabled person reassures the other 'that a disabled person is not hypersensitive about the disability' (Coleman & DePaulo, 1991, p. 82).

Another type of information that is risky for employees to reveal, both to employers and to peers, is preference for alternative lifestyles or non-heterosexual identities. Revealing a lesbian or homosexual identity may allow a person to 'be' herself or himself, remove the individual's fear of being 'outed', and/or relieve the person of feelings of shame, self-doubt, or hypocrisy. However, revealing an alternative lifestyle or sexual orientation has potential negative consequences; personal rejection, loss of job, and disrupted relationships also can occur. Sexual orientation is not a protected status in the USA, and is therefore not protected information as would be gender, age, race, and religious affiliation (Badgett, 1996).

Schneider (1986) reported a study of factors that predict the revelation of lesbian identity to co-workers. She found that women working with adults, working in female-dominated settings, and making low incomes more frequently reported disclosing their sexual identity. Loss of prior job because of sexual identity discrimination militated against disclosure. These factors apparently affect the risk of negative consequences resulting from disclosure. The process by which lesbians weigh these factors is described by Hitchcock and Wilson (1992).

Incidents of sexual harassment

A recent estimate suggested that 59% of working women in the USA may have been sexually harassed (Illies, Hauserman & Schwochau, 2003). Women who have been harassed have to decide whether to discuss their experience with others. As Wood (1993) noted, even recounting the incidence of sexual harassment invokes 'a range of fierce emotions . . . from shame and feeling wrong or stupid, to feeling violated, to guilt about allowing it to occur, to entrapment with no viable alternatives, to anger at being impotent to stop harassment' (p. 22). Consequently, sexual harassment necessarily involves subsequent considerations and enactments of self-disclosure.

Perhaps the most frequent recommendation is for the victim of sexual harassment to tell someone about the problem. Passively responding to the event legitimises and perpetuates the offence (Claire, 1993). Offensiveness of the harassment and perceived efficacy of reporting harassment influence victims' responses (Brooks & Perot, 1991). Options available to the victim include confronting the perpetrator, telling friends, and formal reporting to appropriate supervisory personnel.

Some organisations recommend writing a letter to the offender describing how the statements made the victim feel. Bingham and Burleson (1989) concluded that attempting to change the harasser's behaviour while maintaining a cordial relationship with that person is required for the production of messages that others see as competent and effective. They point out that telling an offender:

> We've got a great working relationship now, and I'd like us to work well together in the future. So I think it's important for us to talk this out. You're a smart and clear-thinking guy, and I consider you to be my friend as well as my boss. That's why I have to think you must be under a lot of unusual stress lately to have said something like this. I know what it's like to be under pressure. Too much stress can really make you crazy. You probably just need a break. (p. 193)

251

is perceived by observers to be a much better response than:

> You are the most rude and disgusting man that I have ever met. You're nothing but a dirty old man. Where do you get off thinking you could force me to have an affair with you? You make me sick. I'm going to make sure you get kicked out on your ass for this – just you wait and see. (p. 192)

Whether this strategy is effective or not, the victim of sexual harassment has the additional option of revealing the incident to friends, co-workers, and management. Sharing reactions with others serves to document the occurrence of the offence, an important step if subsequent legal or other formal remedies are pursued. Additionally, disclosure to others enables a person to receive support from trusted friends, although undesired 'blame the victim' reactions may also be experienced.

All of these suggestions recognise the importance of actively rather than passively responding to the sexual harassment. However, research on the viability of disclosive and non-disclosive responses yields no clear recommendations (see also Bingham, 1991, and Clair, McGoun & Spirek, 1993, for a comparison of alternative typologies of responses to sexual harassment). For example, from experience as a mediator, Gadlin (1991) suggested that mediation is an effective alternative for resolving allegations of sexual harassment and recommended that disputants enlist the help of a supporter throughout the process. Phillips and Jarboe (1993) advocated that women experiencing even severe forms of harassment should cope by subterfuge and manipulation rather than by revealing their true reactions, a conclusion strongly opposed by Kreps (1993). In a study of university faculty and staff, Bingham and Scherer (1993) noted that talking to the harasser in a non-confrontational style about the problem resulted in more favourable outcomes than did talking with friends. Yount's (1991) ethnographic study of female coal miners suggested that women's revelations of distress after incidents of sexual harassment resulted in perceptions of weakness and exacerbated their problems. Livingston's (1982) analysis of US Merit System Protection Board data indicated that assertive reactions were perceived by the victim to be no more successful than non-assertive reactions to sexual harassment. A study of the perceived effectiveness of responses to sexual harassment in the US military indicated that women had the most success with active, formal strategies, such as giving bad reports, transferring, and threatening (Firestone & Harris, 2003). No doubt many factors determine the response and its success to incidents of sexual harassment (Tempstra & Baker, 1989; Jones & Remland, 1992), and, clearly, more research is needed before specific recommendations can be confidently made.

SELF-DISCLOSURE BEYOND PERSONAL AND WORK RELATIONSHIPS

Although this chapter focuses on personal and work relationships, we should recognise that the use of self-disclosure by human beings, and the research on self-disclosure by social scientists, extends to additional contexts and aspects of self-disclosure. Because of the intense interest by many people in the idea that self-disclosure may affect health and well-being, this topic is introduced below. We conclude by noting that self-disclosure is proliferating in the public sphere.

Disclosure and health

Sidney Jourard (1959), an early and important advocate of self-disclosure research as well as practice, was perhaps the first social scientist to argue that disclosure of one's innermost thoughts and feelings would enhance psychological well-being. However, the connection between disclosure and health was not studied systematically before James Pennebaker's pioneering research almost 20 years later. The development of these ideas and the subsequent research are adequately summarised elsewhere (Pennebaker, 1989; Pennebaker, 1997; Pennebaker, Mehl & Niederhoffer, 2003). Consequently, we will only sketch these ideas and supporting studies, emphasising their implication for the topic of this chapter.

Pennebaker contends that the act of verbally encoding, by writing or speaking, one's most traumatic life experiences alters the way those events are stored in memories, resulting in improved physical and mental health (Pennebaker, 1997). In many experimental studies, Pennebaker and others have demonstrated that individuals who write or speak anonymously about their traumas, compared to individuals in control groups who describe mundane daily activities, show improved subjective well-being, declines in the use of health-care resources, and enhanced physiological markers of health (Pennebaker, 1997). These findings have been replicated not only in studies of college students, but also of university employees, unemployed workers, Holocaust victims, and others (Pennebaker, 1997), although Pennebaker's predictions are not always supported (e.g. Kloss & Lisman, 2002). The potential importance of this phenomenon has been recognised by scholars in a variety of fields. Consequently, there have been attempts to assess the utility of Pennebaker's theory to address problems ranging from asthma and arthritis (Smyth, Stone, Hurewitz & Kaell, 1999) and sleeping disorders (Harvey & Farrell, 2003) to athletic performance (Scott, Robare, Raines, Knowinski, Chanin & Tolley, 2003).

The exact processes by which these disclosures affect health are not clear. Pennebaker suggests that the use of explanatory language either facilitates or is primarily responsible for these effects (Pennebaker, 1993). Other researchers have noted, however, that these findings may also occur when individuals talk not only about traumas but also about positive, meaningful events (King, 2001), suggesting that disclosure facilitates self-regulatory processes.

From the earliest formulations of this theory, Pennebaker has argued that the effects of disclosure are more likely to occur when made in private, as by writing in a journal, because these disclosures are different than ones made to other individuals (Pennebaker, 1997, 2002). Self-disclosures to friends, acquaintances, and even doctors will be adapted or altered in some important ways because of self-presentational concerns. Consequently, this literature does not suggest that indiscriminate self-disclosure results in improved health. In fact, indiscriminate disclosure might lead to arguments and hurt feelings, which can impede immune system functioning or accelerate the deleterious consequences of stress. However, it is also possible that some relationships might encourage or permit open disclosure of important life events, and result in positive health outcomes. In fact, some self-report studies, even one by Pennebaker (Pennebaker & O'Heeron, 1984), support the conclusion that naturally occurring self-disclosures of important concerns can positively affect mental health (Bolton, Glenn, Orsillo, Roemer & Litz, 2003). Thus, this research conclusively demonstrates that certain types of verbalisations about important life events produce positive health benefits. Exactly why and how these occur is unknown and of considerable interest to researchers, a great number of whom are currently trying to determine not only the extent, but also the limitation of the connections between health and self-disclosure.

Public disclosures

Self-disclosures are made not only to our friends and cohorts, but also in public to complete strangers. Ranging from the sensational to the profound, there are three places where public disclosure can be observed: entertainment media, the World Wide Web, and public forums.

Every day, newspapers, magazines, and television transmit to readers and viewers worldwide the self-disclosures of the famous, the infamous, and the previously unknown. On scores of television 'talk show' programmes, entertainers, politicians, and other celebrities are prompted to share their lives and experiences, discuss their sexual identity, and recount how they dealt with substance abuse, martial infidelity, personal tragedies, etc. This form of entertainment is not limited to English-speaking media (e.g. Acosta-Alzuru, 2003). Part of the current appeal of 'realilty' television shows is that they allow viewers by the millions to observe self-disclosures that otherwise would be private. Clearly, these cultural performances suggest that not only do some people have unfulfilled needs to disclose, but also that the disclosures of unacquainted others are apparently appealing to many, indeed millions. This form of self-disclosure warrants the attention of social scientists, but has been examined infrequently (e.g. Priest & Dominick, 1994).

The advent of the World Wide Web provided individuals with another medium in which to present themselves to others. On personal 'home pages', individuals routinely describe their interests, affiliations, and accomplishments and sometimes reveal their beliefs, aspirations, and so on (for a review of communication issues related to home pages, see Doing, 2002). Web logs, or blogs, which first appeared in the mid-1990s, are websites consisting of dated entries in reverse chronological order so that the reader sees the most recent post first. A blog is like an online journal where people express their thoughts, feelings, and experiences on any number of topics. On blogs, individuals may leave reports of their daily ruminations, activities, observations, etc., either anonymously or openly. These digital disclosures can contain the same content as those made in initial conversations, and can perform somewhat the same functions, that is, establish and maintain relationships (e.g. Adamic & Adar, 2003), and are subject to some of the same processes of self-presentation (Miller & Arnold, 2001). However, the public availability and transmission clearly suggest that these revelations must be performing additional purposes as well. These disclosures also warrant the additional serious attention of social scientists.

One additional public forum for self-disclosure that has received considerable attention is South Africa's Truth and Reconciliation Commission hearings and report. As a compromise between political factions that wanted to prosecute or pardon individuals who committed criminal acts in the perpetuation of apartheid, the government offered amnesty to individuals who would confess their crimes (see Gobodo-Madikizela, 2002, and Rey & Owens, 1998, for a more detailed description of these events). In order to document incidents of human rights violations, testimony was taken, some in public forums, around the country, so that victims as well as perpetrators could describe their personal experiences during this period of political repression and rebellion. The goal of these investigations was to promote healing by providing a forum for reporting and recognising these crimes. The families of people killed would finally learn of the events and responsible individuals, thus enabling them to achieve a sense of closure for their loss. The perpetrators of crimes, and their supporters, would be allowed to show their remorse and be forgiven, and in some, but not all, cases receive amnesty (Gobodo-Madikizela, 2002).

Countries around the world have used similar procedures 15 times since 1970 (Hayner, 1994, as cited in Allan, 2000). However, the efficacy of these public disclosures in South Africa has been contested. Some studies conclude that the testimony enabled healing (Rey & Owens, 1998; Skinner, 2000), and one of the Truth and Reconciliation Commission members argues that the process made forgiveness possible (Gobodo-Madikizela, 2002). Others assessments are less positive (Allan, 2000; Statman, 2000). Clearly, research on the effectiveness of these forums to achieve the goals of personal healing and social unification is needed so that procedures may be formulated for effectively implementing such policies. And unfortunately, there are too many other regions of the world that will some day, hopefully, face comparable problems of reconciliation.

OVERVIEW

Self-disclosure is a basic and pervasive social phenomenon. How we come to know others, get others to like us, learn our jobs, get along with spouses, select employees, and get others to help us all depend, in part, on the selective revelation of personal information. Prescriptions of more, or less, self-disclosure oversimplify the complex and dialectical nature of human relationships. Individuals must weigh the potential rewards (personal, relational, and professional) against the potential risks in making decisions regarding self-disclosure. In short, managing personal and professional relationships requires strategic self-disclosure. Understanding how self-disclosure functions in personal and work relationships can only help people use it effectively.

REFERENCES

Acosta-Alzuru, C. (2003). Change your life! Confession and conversation in Telemundo's Cambia Tu Vida. *Mass Communication and Society*, *6*, 137–159.

Adamic, L. A. & Adar, E. (2003). Friends and neighbors on the web. *Social Networks*, *25*, 211–230.

Albrecht, T. L. & Hall, B. (1991). Facilitating talk about new ideas: the role of personal relationships in organizational innovation. *Communication Monographs*, *58*, 273–288.

Allan, A. (2000). Truth and reconciliation: a psycholegal perspective. *Ethnicity and Health*, *5*, 191–204.

Allen, S. & Carlson, G. (2003). To conceal or disclose a disabling condition? A dilemma of employment transition. *Journal of Vocational Rehabilitation*, *19*, 19–30.

Altman, I. (1973). Reciprocity of interpersonal exchange. *Journal for the Theory of Social Behavior*, *3*, 249–261.

Altman, I. (1975). *The environment and social behavior: privacy, personal space, territory, and crowding*. Belmont, CA: Wadsworth.

Altman, I. & Taylor, D. A. (1973). *Social penetration: the development of interpersonal relationships*. New York: Holt, Rinehart, and Winston.

Altman, I., Vinsel, A. & Brown, B. H. (1981). Dialectic conceptions in social psychology: an application to social penetration and privacy regulation. In L. Berkowitz (Ed.), *Advances in experimental social psychology*, vol. 14 (pp. 107–160). New York: Academic Press.

Archer, R. L. (1979). Anatomical and psychological sex differences. In G. J. Chelune & Associates (Eds), *Self-disclosure: origins, patterns, and implications of openness in interpersonal relationships* (pp. 80–109). San Francisco, CA: Jossey-Bass.

Archer, R. L. & Earle, W. B. (1983). The interpersonal orientations of disclosure. In P. B. Paulus (Ed.), *Basic group processes* (pp. 289–314). New York: Springer-Verlag.

Badgett, M. V. L. (1996). Employment and sexual orientation: disclosure and discrimination in the workplace. In A. L. Ellis & E. D. B. Riggle (Eds), *Sexual identity on the job: issues and services* (pp. 29–52). New York: Harrington Park Press.

Bavelas, J. B., Black, A., Chovil, N. & Mullett, J. (1990). *Equivocal communication*. Newbury Park, CA: Sage.

Baxter, L. A. (1985). Accomplishing relational disengagement. In S. Duck & D. Perlman (Eds), *Understanding personal relationships: an interdisciplinary approach* (pp. 243–265). Thousand Oaks, CA: Sage.

Baxter, L. A. (1987). Self-disclosure and relationship disengagement. In V. J. Derlega & J. H. Berg (Eds), *Self-disclosure: theory, research, and therapy* (pp. 155–174). New York: Plenum.

Baxter, L. A. (1988). A dialectical perspective on communication strategies in relationship development. In S. W. Duck (Ed.), *A handbook of personal relationships* (pp. 257–273). Chichester: Wiley.

Baxter, L. A. (1990). Dialectical contradictions in relationship development. *Journal of Social and Personal Relationships*, *7*, 69–88.

Baxter, L. A. & Wilmot, W. W. (1984). 'Secret tests': social strategies for acquiring information about the state of the relationship. *Human Communication Research*, *11*, 171–201.

Baxter, L. A. & Wilmot, W. W. (1985). Taboo topics in close relationships. *Journal of Social and Personal Relationships*, *2*, 253–269.

Baxter, L. A. & Montgomery, B. M. (1996a). *Relating: dialogues and dialectics*. New York: Guilford Press.

Baxter, L. A. & Montgomery, B. M. (1996b). Rethinking communication in personal relationships from a dialectical perspective. In S. Duck (Ed.), *Handbook of personal relationships*, 2nd edn, Chichester: Wiley.

Berg, J. H. & Archer, R. L. (1980). Disclosure or concern: a second look at liking for the norm-breaker. *Journal of Personality*. *48*, 245–257.

Berg, J. H. & Derlega, V. J. (1987). Themes in the study of self-disclosure. In V. J. Derlega & J. H. Berg (Eds), *Self-disclosure: theory, research and therapy* (pp. 1–80). New York: Plenum.

Berger, C. R. (1979). Beyond initial interaction: uncertainty, understanding, and the development of interpersonal relationships. In H. Giles & R. St. Clair (Eds), *Language and social psychology* (pp. 122–144). Oxford: Basil Blackwell.

Berger, C. R. & Calabrese, R. J. (1975). Some explorations in initial interaction and beyond: toward a developmental theory of interpersonal communication. *Human Communication Research*, *1*, 99–112.

Berger, C. R. & Bradac, J. J. (1982). *Language and social knowledge: uncertainty in interpersonal relationships*. London: Edward Arnold.

Berger, C. R. & Douglas, W. (1992). Thought and talk: 'Excuse me, but have I been talking to myself?' In F. E. X. Dance (Ed.), *Human communication theory* (pp. 42–60). New York: Harper and Row.

Berger, C. R., Gardner, R. R., Parks, M. R., Schulman, L. & Miller, G. R. (1976). Interpersonal epistemology and interpersonal communication. In G. R. Miller (Ed.), *Explorations in interpersonal communication* (pp. 149–171). Beverly Hills, CA: Sage.

Bingham, S. G. (1991). Communication strategies for managing sexual harassment in organizations. *Journal of Applied Communication Research*, *19*, 88–115.

Bingham, S. G. & Burleson, B. R. (1989). Multiple effects of messages with multiple goals: some perceived outcomes of responses to sexual harassment. *Human Communication Research*, *16*, 184–216.

Bingham, S. G. & Scherer, L. L. (1993). Factors associated with responses to sexual harassment and satisfaction with outcome. *Sex Roles*, *29*, 239–269.

Binning, J. F., Goldstein, M. A., Garcia, M. F., Harding, J. L. & Scattaregia, J. H. (1988). Effects of preinterview impressions on questioning strategies in same- and opposite-sex employment interviews. *Journal of Applied Psychology*, *73*, 30–37.

Bochner, A. P. (1982). On the efficacy of openness in closed relationships. In M. Burgoon (Ed.), *Communication yearbook 5* (pp. 109–142). New Brunswick, NJ: Transaction Books.

Bolton, E. F., Glenn, D. M., Orsillo, S., Roemer, L. & Litz, B. T. (2003). The relationship between self-disclosure and symptoms of posttraumatic stress disorder in peacekeepers deployed to Somalia. *Journal of Traumatic Stress*, *16*, 203–210.

Bowen, S. P. & Michal-Johnson, P. (1989). The crisis of communicating in relationships: confronting the threat of AIDS. *AIDS and Public Policy*, *4*, 10–19.

Brehm, S. S., Miller, R. S., Perlman, D. & Campbell, S. M. (2002). *Intimate relationships*, 4th edn. New York: McGraw-Hill.

Bridge, K. & Baxter, L. A. (1992). Blended relationships. *Western Journal of Speech Communication*, *56*, 200–225.

Brooks, L. & Perot, A. R. (1991). Reporting sexual harassment: exploring a predictive model. *Psychology of Women Quarterly*, *15*, 31–47.

Bullis, C. & Bach, B. W. (1989). Socialization turning points: an examination of change in organizational identification. *Western Journal of Speech Communication*, *53*, 273–293.

Buysse, A. & Ickes, W. (1999). Communication patterns in laboratory discussions of safer sex between dating versus nondating partners. *Journal of Sex Research*, *36*, 121–134.

Cheney, G. (1983). On the various and changing meanings of organizational membership. *Communication Monographs*, *50*, 352–362.

Chervin, D. D. & Martinez, A. M. (1987). *Survey on the health of Stanford students*. Stanford, CA: Colwell Student Health Center.

Clair, R. P. (1993). The use of framing devices to sequester organizational narratives. *Communication Monographs*, *60*, 113–136.

Clair, R. P., McGoun, M. J. & Spirek, M. M. (1993). Sexual harassment responses of working women: an assessment of current communication-oriented typologies and perceived effectiveness of the response. In G. L. Kreps (Ed.), *Sexual harassment: communication implications* (pp. 209–233). Creskill, NJ: Hampton Press,

Cline, R. J. W. & Johnson, S. J. (1992). Mosquitoes, doorknobs, and sneezing: relationships between homophobia and AIDS mythology among college students. *Health Communication*, *4*, 273–289.

Cline, R. J. W., Freeman, K. E. & Johnson, S. J. (1990). Talk among sexual partners about AIDS: factors differentiating those who talk from those who do not. *Communication Research*, *17*, 792–808.

Cline, R. J. W., Johnson, S. J. & Freeman, K. E. (1992). Talk among sexual partners about AIDS: interpersonal communication for risk reduction or risk enhancement? *Health Communication*, *4*, 39–56.

Coleman, L. M. & DePaulo, B. M. (1991). Uncovering the human spirit: moving beyond disability and 'missed' communications. In N. Coupland, H. Giles & J. M. Weimann (Eds), *'Miscommunication' and problematic talk* (pp. 61–84). Newbury Park, CA: Sage.

Collins, N. L. & Miller, L. C. (1994). The disclosure-liking link: from meta-analysis toward a dynamic reconceptualization. *Psychological Bulletin*, *116*, 457–475.

Cooper, A. & Sportolari, L. (1997). Romance in cyberspace: understanding online attraction. *Journal of Sex Education and Therapy*, *22*, 7–14.

Cowen, E. L. (1982). Help is where you find it. *American Psychologist*, *37*, 385–395.

Dalgin, R. B. & Gilbride, D. (2003). Perspectives of people with psychiatric disabilities on employment disclosure. *Psychiatric Rehabilitation Journal*, *26*, 306–310.

Dansereau, F. & Markham, S. E. (1987). Superior–subordinate communication: multiple levels of analysis. In F. M. Jablin, L. L. Putnam, K. H. Roberts & L. W. Porter (Eds), *Handbook of organizational communication: an interdisciplinary perspective* (pp. 343–388). Newbury Park, CA: Sage.

Derlega, V. & Grzelak, J. (1979). Appropriateness of self-disclosure. In G. J. Chelune (Ed.), *Self-disclosure: origins, patterns, and implications of openness in interpersonal relationships* (pp. 151–176). San Francisco, CA: Jossey-Bass.

Derlega, V. J., Metts, S., Petronio, S. & Margulis, S. T. (1993). *Self-disclosure*. Newbury Park, CA: Sage.

Dindia, K. (1998). 'Going into and coming out of the closet': the dialectics of stigma disclosure. In B. M. Montgomery & L. A. Baxter (Eds), *Dialectical approaches to studying personal relationships* (pp. 83–108). Mahwah, NJ: Lawrence Erlbaum.

Dindia, K. (2002). Self-disclosure research: knowledge through meta-analysis. In M. Allen, R. W. Preiss, B. M. Gayle & N. Burrell (Eds), *Interpersonal communication: advances through meta-analysis* (pp. 169–186). Mahwah, NJ: Lawrence Erlbaum.

Dindia, K. & Allen, M. (1992). Sex-differences in self-disclosure: a meta-analysis. *Psychological Bulletin, 112*, 106–124.

Dindia, K. & Malin, M. (2003). Sex differences in self-disclosure: a meta-analysis of studies published between 1990 and 1999. Paper presented at the National Communication Association convention, Miami, FL, November 2003.

Dindia, K. & Emmers-Sommer, T. M. (2006). What partners do to maintain their close relationships. In P. Noller & J. Feeney (Eds), *Close relationships*. New York: Psychology Press.

Dindia, K., Fitzpatrick, M. A. & Kenny, D. A. (1997). Self-disclosure in spouse and stranger dyads: a social relations analysis. *Human Communication Research, 23*, 388–412.

Dipboye, R. L. & Wiley, J. W. (1977). Reactions of college recruiters to interviewee sex and self-presentation style. *Journal of Vocational Behavior, 10*, 1–12.

Doing, N. (2002). Personal home pages on the web: a review of research. *Journal of Computer-Mediated Communication, 7* (retrieved 30 October 2004 from www.ascusc.org/jcmc/vol7/issue3/doering.html).

Douglas, W. (1990). Uncertainty, information-seeking, and liking during initial interaction. *Western Journal of Speech Communication, 54*, 66–81.

Dutton, J. E., Ashford, S. J., Lawrence, K. A. & Miner-Rubino, K. (2002). Red light, green light: making sense of the organizational context for issue selling. *Organization Science, 13*, 355–369.

Edgar, T., Freimuth, V. S., Hammond, S. L., McDonald, D. A. & Fink, E. L. (1992). Strategic sexual communication: condom use resistance and response. *Health Communication, 4*, 83–104.

Eisenberg, E. M., Monge, P. R. & Miller, K. I. (1983). Involvement in communication networks as a predictor of organizational commitment. *Human Communication Research, 10*, 179–201.

Ekman, P. (1992). *Telling lies: clues to deceit in the marketplace, politics, and marriage.* New York: Norton.

Elias, F. G., Johnson, M. E. & Fortman, J. B. (1989). Task-focused self-disclosure: effects on group cohesiveness, commitment to task, and productivity. *Small Group Behavior, 20*, 87–96.

Evans, J. H. (1976). Changing attitudes toward disabled persons: an experimental study. *Rehabilitation Counseling Bulletin, 19*, 572–579.

Feldman, S. (1991). Trust me. *Personnel, 68*, 7.

Firestone, J. M. & Harris, R. J. (2003). Perceptions of effectiveness of responses to sexual harassment in the US military, 1988 and 1995. *Gender, Work, and Organization, 10*, 42–64.

Fitzpatrick, M. F. (1987). Marriage and verbal intimacy. In V. J. Derlega & J. H. Berg, (Eds), *Self-disclosure: theory, research and therapy* (pp. 131–154). New York: Plenum.

Fletcher, C. (1992). Ethical issues in the selection interview. *Journal of Business Ethics, 11*, 361–367.

Fulk, J. & Mani, S. (1986). Distortion of communication in hierarchical relationships. *Communication Yearbook, 9* (pp. 483–510). Beverly Hills, CA: Sage.

Gadlin, H. (1991). Careful maneuvers: mediating sexual harassment. *Negotiation Journal, 7*, 139–153.

Giacalone, R. A. & Rosenfeld, P. (1986). Self-presentation and self-promotion in an organizational setting. *Journal of Social Psychology, 126*, 321–326.

Gilbert, S. J. (1976). Self-disclosure, intimacy, and communication in families. *Family Coordinator, 25*, 221–229.

Gilbert, S. J. & Horenstein, D. (1975). The communication of self-disclosure: level versus valence. *Human Communication Research, 1*, 316–322.

Gilbertson, J., Dindia, K. & Allen, M. (1998). Relational continuity constructional units and the maintenance of relationships. *Journal of Social and Personal Relationships, 15*, 774–790.

Gilmore, D. C. & Ferris, G. R. (1989). The politics of the employment interview. In R. W. Eder & G. R. Ferris (Eds), *The employment interview: theory, research, and practice* (pp. 233–245). Newbury Park, CA: Sage.

Gobodo-Madikizela, P. (2002). Remorse, forgiveness, and rehumanization: stories from South Africa. *Journal of Humanistic Psychology, 42*, 7–32.

Goffman, E. (1963). *Stigma: notes on the management of spoiled identity*. Englewood Cliffs, NJ: Prentice-Hall.

Griffin, A. E. C., Collela, A. & Goparaju, S. (2000). Newcomer and organizational socialization tactics: an interactionist perspective. *Human Resources Management Review, 10*, 453–474.

Hargie, O. & Dickson, D. (Eds) (2004). *Researching the troubles: social science perspectives on the Northern Ireland conflict*. Edinburgh: Mainstream.

Harris, M. M. & Fennell, M. L. (1988). Perceptions of an employee assistance program and employees' willingness to participate. *Journal of Applied Behavioral Sciences, 24*, 423–438.

Harvey, A. G. & Farrell, C. (2003). The efficacy of a Pennebaker-like writing intervention for poor sleepers. *Behavioral Sleep Medicine, 1*, 115–124.

Hequet, M. (1993). The intricacies of interviewing. *Training, 30*, 31–36.

Herek, G. M., Jobe, J. B. & Carnery, R. M. (Eds) (1996). *Out in force: sexual orientation and the military*. Chicago: University of Chicago Press.

Herman, N. J. (1993). Return to sender: reintegrative stigma-management strategies of ex-psychiatric patients. *Journal of Contemporary Ethnography, 22*, 295–330.

Herold, K. (1995). The effects of interviewee's self-disclosure and disability on selected perceptions and attitudes of interviewers. Unpublished doctoral dissertation, University of Southern Mississippi, Hattiesburg, MS.

Herold, K. (2000). Communication strategies in employment interviews for applicants with disabilities. In D. O. Braithwaite & T. L. Thompson (Eds), *Handbook of communication and people with disabilities: research and application* (pp. 159–175). Mahwah, NJ: Lawrence Erlbaum.

Hitchcock, J. M. & Wilson, H. S. (1992). Personal risking. *Nursing Research, 41*, 178–183.

Hochschild, A. R. (1983). *The managed heart: commercialization of human feeling*. Berkeley, CA: University of California Press.

Illies, R., Hauserman, N. & Schwochau, S. (2003). Reported incidence rates of work-related sexual harassment in the United States: using meta-analysis to explain reported rate disparities. *Personnel Psychology, 56*, 606–631.

Jablin, F. M. (1987). Organizational, entry, assimilation, and exit. In F. M. Jablin, L. L. Putnam, K. H. Roberts & L. W. Porter (Eds), *Handbook of organizational communication: an interdisciplinary perspective* (pp. 389–419). Newbury Park, CA: Sage.

Jablin, F. M. & Miller, V. D. (1990). Interviewer and applicant questioning behavior in employment interviews. *Management Communication Quarterly, 4*, 51–86.

Jablin, F. M. & Krone, K. J. (1994). Task/work relationships: a life-span perspective. In M. L. Knapp & G. R. Miller (Eds), *Handbook of Interpersonal Communication*, 2nd edn (pp. 621–675). Newbury Park, CA: Sage.

Jackson, N., Peacock, A. & Smith, J. P. (1980). Impressions of personality in the employment interview. *Journal of Personality and Social Psychology, 39*, 294–307.

Janz, T. (1989). The patterned behavior description interview: the best prophet of the future is the past. In R. W. Eder & G. R. Ferris (Eds), *The employment interview: theory, research, and practice* (pp. 158–168). Newbury Park, CA: Sage.

Jones, T. S. & Remland, M. S. (1992). Sources of variability in perceptions of and responses to sexual harassment. *Sex Roles, 27*, 121–142.

Jourard, S. M. (1971). *The transparent self*, rev. edn. New York: Van Nostrand Reinhold.

Jourard, S. M. (1959). Healthy personality and self-disclosure. *Journal of Mental Hygiene, 43*, 499–507.

Kennan, A. (1980). Recruitment on campus. *Personnel Management, March*, 43–46.

King, L. A. (2001). The health benefits of writing about life goals. *Personality and Social Psychology Bulletin, 27*, 798–807.

Kleiman, C. (2002). Salary policies sometimes a revelation. *Chicago Tribune*, 3 December (retrieved 31 October 2004 from Newspaper Source database).

Klos, D. & Lisman, S. A. (2002). An exposure-based examination of the effects of written emotional disclosure. *British Journal of Health Psychology, 7*, 31–46.

Koch, J. J. (1990). Employee assistance: Wells Fargo and IBM's HIV policies help protect employees' rights. *Personnel Journal, 69*, 40–48.

Konrad, A. M. & Gutek, B. M. (1986). Impact of work experience on attitudes toward sexual harassment. *Administrative Science Quarterly, 31*, 422–438.

Kramer, M. W. (1994). Uncertainty reduction during job transitions: an exploratory study of communication experiences of newcomers and transferees. *Management Communication Quarterly, 7*, 384–412.

Kreps, G. L. (1993). Providing a sociocultural evolutionary approach to preventing sexual harassment: metacommunication and cultural adaptation. In G. L. Kreps (Ed.), *Sexual harassment: communication implications* (pp. 310–318). Creskill, NJ: Hampton Press.

Larzelere, R. E. & Huston, T. L. (1980). The dyadic trust scale: toward understanding interpersonal trust in close relationships. *Journal of Marriage and the Family, 42*, 595–606.

Levine, D. (2000). Virtual attraction: what rocks your boat. *CyberPsychology and Behavior, 3*, 565–573.

Limandri, B. (1989). Disclosure of stigmatizing conditions: the discloser's perspective. *Archives of Psychiatric Nursing, 3*, 69–78.

Livingston, J. A. (1982). Responses to sexual harassment on the job: legal, organizational and individual actions. *Journal of Social Issues*, *38*, 5–22.

Luthans, F. & Walersee, R. (1990). What do we really know about EAPs? *Human Resource Management*, *28*, 385–401.

MacFarlane, I. & Krebs, S. (1986). Techniques for interviewing and evidence gathering. In K. MacFarlane & J. Waterman (Eds), *Sexual abuse of young children* (pp. 67–100). New York: Guilford Press.

Madaus, J. W., Foley, T. E., McGuire, J. M. & Ruban, L. M. (2002). Employment self-disclosure of postsecondary graduates with learning disabilities: rates and rationales. *Journal of Learning Disabilities*, *35*, 364–369.

Marks, G., Bundek, N., Richardson, J., Ruiz, M., Maldonado, N. & Mason, J. (1992). Self-disclosure of HIV infection: preliminary results from a sample of Hispanic men. *Health Psychology*, *11*, 300–306.

Meares, M. M., Oetzel, J. G., Torres, A., Derkacs, D. & Ginossar, T. (2004). Employee mistreatment and muted voices in the culturally diverse workplace. *Journal of Applied Communication Research*, *32*, 4–27.

Mellinger, G. D. (1956). Interpersonal trust as a factor in communication. *Journal of Abnormal Social Psychology*, *52*, 304–309.

Merkle, E. R. & Richardson, R. A. (2000). Digital dating and virtual relating: conceptualizing computer mediated romantic relationships. *Family Relations*, *49*, 187–192.

Miell, D. E. & Duck, S. (1986). Strategies in developing friendships. In V. J. Derlega & B. A. Winstead (Eds), *Friends and social interaction* (pp. 129–143). New York: Springer-Verlag.

Miller, H. & Arnold, J. (2001). Breaking away from grounded identity? Women academics on the web. *CyberPsychology and Behavior*, *41*, 95–108.

Miller, L. C. (1990). Intimacy and liking: mutual influence and the role of unique relationships. *Journal of Personality and Social Psychology*, *59*, 50–60.

Miller, L. C. & Read, S. J. (1987). Why am I telling you this? Self-disclosure in a goal-based model of personality. In V. J. Derlega & J. H. Berg (Eds), *Self-disclosure: theory, research, and therapy* (pp. 35–58). New York: Plenum.

Miller, L. C., Cooke, L. L., Tsang, J. & Morgan, F. (1992). Should I brag? Nature and impact of positive and boastful disclosures for women and men. *Human Communication Research*, *18*, 364–399.

Milne, S. H., Blum, T. C. & Roman, P. M. (1994). Factors influencing employees' propensity to use an employee assistance program. *Personnel Psychology*, *47*, 123–145.

Montgomery, B. M. (1993). Relationship maintenance versus relationship change: a dialectical dilemma. *Journal of Social and Personal Relationships*, *10*, 205–224.

Morrison, E. W. & Milliken, F. J. (2000). Organizational silence: a barrier to change and development in a pluralistic world. *Academy of Management Review*, *25*, 706–725.

Murphy, S. & Irwin, J. (1992). 'Living with the dirty secret': problems of disclosure for methadone maintenance clients. *Journal of Psychoactive Drugs*, *24*, 257–264.

Myers, D. W. (1984). *Establishing and building employee assistance programs*. Westport, CT: Quorum Books.

Padgitt, S. C. & Padgitt, J. S. (1986). Cognitive structure of sexual harassment: implications of university policy. *Journal of Student Personnel*, *27*, 34–39.

Paetzold, R. L. & O'Leary-Kelly, A. M. (1993). Organizational communication and the legal dimensions of hostile work environment sexual harassment. In G. L. Kreps (Ed.), *Sexual harassment: communication implications* (pp. 63–80). Creskill, NJ: Hampton Press.

Parks, M. (1995). Ideology in interpersonal communication: beyond the couches, talk shows, and bunkers. In B. R. Burleson (Ed.), *Communication yearbook 18* (pp. 480–497). London: Sage.

Pennebaker, J. W. (1989). Confession, inhibition, and disease. In L. Berkowitz (Ed.), *Advances in experimental social psychology* (vol. 22, pp. 211–244). New York: Academic Press.

Pennebaker, J. W. (1993). Putting stress into words: health, linguistic, and therapeutic implications. *Behavioral Research and Therapy*, *31*, 539–548.

Pennebaker, J. W. (1997). *Opening up: the healing power of expressing emotions*. New York: Guilford.

Pennebaker, J. W. (2002). Solitary disclosure allows people to determine their own dose. *British Medical Journal*, *324*, 544.

Pennebaker, J. W. & O'Heeron, R. C. (1984). Confiding in others and illness rate among spouses of suicide and accidental death victims. *Journal of Abnormal Psychology*, *93*, 473–476.

Pennebaker, J. W., Mehl, M. R. & Niederhoffer, K. G. (2003). Psychological aspects of natural language use: our words, our selves. *Annual Review of Psychology*, *54*, 547–577.

Petronio, S. (1991). Communication boundary management: a theoretical model of managing disclosure of private information between marital couples. *Communication Theory*, *1*, 311–335.

Petronio, S. (2002). *Boundaries of privacy: dialectics of disclosure*. Albany, NY: State University of New York Press.

Petronio, S., Reeder, H. M., Hecht, M. L. & Mon't Ros-Mendoza, T. (1996). Disclosure of sexual abuse by children and adolescents. *Journal of Applied Communication Research*, *24*, 181–189.

Phillips, G. M. & Jarboe, S. (1993). Sycophancy and servitude: harassment and rebellion. In G. L. Kreps (Ed.), *Sexual harassment: communication implications* (pp. 281–309). Creskill, NJ: Hampton Press.

Planalp, S. & Garvin-Doxas, K. (1994). Using mutual knowledge in conversation: friends as experts in each other. In S. Duck (Ed.), *Understanding relationship processes IV: the dynamics of relationship* (pp. 1–26). New York: Guilford.

Powell, G. N. (1986). Effects of sex role identity and sex on definition of sexual harassment. *Sex Roles*, *14*, 9–19.

Powell-Cope, G. M. & Brown, M. A. (1992). Going public as an AIDS family caregiver. *Social Science Medicine*, *34*, 571–580.

Price, L., Gerber, P. J. & Mulligan, R. (2003). The Americans with disabilities act and adults with learning disabilities as employees. *Remedial and Special Education*, *24*, 350–358.

Priest, P. J. & Dominick, J. R. (1994). Pulp pulpits: self-disclosure on 'Donahue'. *Journal of Communication*, *44*, 74–97.

Pryor, J. B. & Day, J. D. (1988). Interpretations of sexual harassment: an attributional analysis. *Sex Roles*, *18*, 405–417.

Quina, K., Harlow, L. L., Morokoff, P. J., Burkholder, G. & Deiter, P. J. (2000). Sexual communication in relationships: when words speak louder than actions. *Sex Roles, 42*, 523–549.

Rawlins, W. (1983). Openness as problematic in ongoing friendships: two conversational dilemmas. *Communication Monographs, 50*, 1–13.

Rey, C. & Owens, I. (1998). Perception of psychosocial healing and the Truth and Reconciliation Commission in South Africa. *Peace and Conflict: Journal of Peace Psychology, 4*, 257–270.

Rheingold, H. (1993). *The virtual community: homesteading on the electronic frontier.* Reading, MA: Addison-Wesley.

Roberts, K. R. & O'Reilly, D. A. (1974). Failures in upward communication in organizations: three possible culprits. *Academy of Management Journal, 17*, 205–215.

Rosen, T. H. (1987). Identification of substance abusers in the workplace. *Public Personnel Management, 16*, 197–207.

Rowe, P. M. (1989). Unfavorable information and interview decisions. In R. W. Eder & G. R. Ferris (Eds), *The employment interview: theory, research, and practice* (pp. 77–89). Newbury Park, CA: Sage.

Rubin, Z. (1973). *Liking and loving.* New York: Holt, Rinehart and Winston.

Sackett, P. R. (1982). The interviewer as hypothesis tester: the effects of impressions of an applicant on interviewer questioning strategy. *Personnel Psychology, 35*, 789–804.

Schank, R. C. & Abelson, R. P. (1977). *Scripts, plans, goals, and understanding.* Hillsdale, NJ: Lawrence Erlbaum.

Schneider, B. E. (1986). Coming out at work: bridging the private/public gap. *Work and Occupations, 13*, 463–487.

Schrodt, P., Cawyer, C. S. & Sanders, R. (2003). An examination of academic mentoring behaviors and new faculty members' satisfaction with socialization and tenure and promotion processes. *Communication Education, 52*, 17–29.

Scott, V. B., Robare, R. D., Raines, D. B., Knowinski, S. J., Chanin, J. A. & Tolley, R. S. (2003). Emotive writing moderates the relationship between mood awareness and athletic performance in collegiate tennis players. *North American Journal of Psychology, 5*, 311–325.

Siegel, K. & Krauss, B. J. (1991). Living with HIV infection: adaptive tasks of seropositive gay men. *Journal of Health and Social Behavior, 32*, 17–32.

Sigman, S. J. (1991). Handling the discontinuous aspects of continuing social relationships: toward research on the persistence of social forms. *Communication Theory, 1*, 106–127.

Skinner, D. (2000). An evaluation of a set of TRC public hearings in Worcester: a small rural community in South Africa. *Psychology, Health, and Medicine, 5*, 97–106.

Smyth, J. M., Stone, A. A., Hurewitz, A. & Kaell, A. (1999). Effects of writing about stressful experiences on symptom reduction in patients with asthma or rheumatoid arthritis. *Journal of the American Medical Association, 281*, 1304–1309.

Soloman, C. M. (1992). Work/family ideas that break boundaries. *Personnel Journal, 71*, 112–117.

Sonnenstuhl, W. J., Staudenmeier, W. J. & Trice, H. M. (1988). Ideology and referral categories in employee assistance program research. *Journal of Applied Behavioral Science*, *24*, 383–396.

Statman, J. M. (2000). Performing the truth: the social-psychological context of TRC narratives. *South African Journal of Psychology*, *30*, 23–32.

Steele, F. (1975). *The open organization: the impact of secrecy and disclosure on people and organizations*. Reading, MA: Addison-Wesley.

Stewart, C. J. & Cash, W. B. Jr (1988). *Interviewing: principles and practices*. Dubuque, IA: W. C. Brown.

Stewart, C. J. & Cash, S. B. Jr (2003). *Interviewing: principles and practices*, 10th edn. Dubuque, IA: W. C. Brown.

Success story: getting substance abusers into an EAP (1991). *Personnel*, *68*, 24.

Tagalakis, V., Amsel, R. & Fichten, C. S. (1988). Job interviewing strategies for people with a visible disability. *Journal of Applied Social Psychology*, *18*, 520–532.

Tesser, A. & Rosen, S. (1975). The reluctance to transmit bad news. *Advances in Experimental Social Psychology*, *8*, 193–232.

Tempstra, D. E. & Baker, D. D. (1989). Identification and classification of reactions to sexual harassment. *Journal of Organizational Behavior*, *10*, 1–14.

Thompson, T. L. (1982). Disclosure as a disability-management strategy: a review and conclusions. *Communication Quarterly*, *30*, 196–202.

Tolhuizen, J. H. (1989). Communication strategies for intensifying dating relationships: identification, use and structure. *Journal of Social and Personal Relationships*, *6*, 413–434.

Tourish, D. & Hargie, O. (2004). Motivating critical upward communication: a key challenge for management decision making. In D. Tourish & O. Hargie (Eds), *Key issues in organizational communication*. London: Routledge.

Trinkaus, J. W. (1986). Disclosure of a physical disability: an informal look. *Perceptual and Motor Skills*, *62*, 157–158.

Tucker, D. H. & Rowe, P. M. (1979). Relationship between expectancy, causal attribution and final hiring decisions in the employment interview. *Journal of Applied Psychology*, *64*, 27–34.

Tullar, W. L. (1989). The employment interview as a cognitive performing script. In R. W. Eder & G. R. Ferris (Eds), *The employment interview: theory, research, and practice* (pp. 233–245). Newbury Park, CA: Sage.

Vangelisti, A. L. & Banski, M. A. (1993). Couples' debriefing conversations: the impact of gender, occupation, and demographic characteristics. *Family Relations*, *42*, 149–157.

Van Maanen, J. & Kunda, G. (1989). 'Real feelings': emotional expression and organizational culture. *Research in Organizational Behavior*, *11*, 43–104.

Waldron, B. (1991). Achieving communication goals in superior–subordinate relationships. *Communication Monographs*, *58*, 289–306.

Wallace, P. (1999). *The psychology of the Internet*. New York: Cambridge University Press.

Walther, J. B. (1992). Interpersonal effects in computer-mediated interaction: a relational perspective. *Communication Research*, *19*, 52–90.

Walther, J. B. (1996). Computer-mediated communication: impersonal, interpersonal, and hyperpersonal interaction. *Communication Research*, *23*, 342–369.

Walther, J. B. & Parks, M. R. (2002). Cues filtered out, cues filtered in. In M. L. Knapp & J. A. Daly (Eds), *The handbook of interpersonal communication* (pp. 529–563). Newbury Park, CA: Sage.

Waltman, J. L. & Golen, S. P. (1993). Detecting deception during interviews. *Internal Auditor, 50*, 61–63.

Weick, K. (1990). The vulnerable system: an analysis of the Tenerife air disaster. *Journal of Management, 16*, 571–593.

Wells, J. W. & Kline, W. B. (1987). Self-disclosure and homosexual orientation. *Journal of Social Psychology, 127*, 191–197.

Withey, M. J. & Cooper, W. H. (1989). Predicting exit, voice, loyalty, and neglect. *Administrative Science Quarterly, 34*, 521–539.

Witteman, H. (1993). The interface between sexual harassment and organizational romance. In G. L. Kreps (Ed.), *Sexual harassment: communication implications* (pp. 27–62). Creskill, NJ: Hampton Press.

Wingood, G. M. & DiClemente, R. J. (1998). Partner influences and gender-related factors associated with noncondom use among young adult African-American women. *American Journal of Community Psychology, 26*, 29–51.

Wood, J. T. (1993). Naming and interpreting sexual harassment: a conceptual framework for scholarship. In G. L. Kreps (Ed.), *Sexual harassment: communication implications* (pp. 9–26). Creskill, NJ: Hampton Press.

Yount, K. R. (1991). Ladies, flirts, and tomboys: strategies for managing sexual harassment in an underground coal mine. *Journal of Contemporary Ethnography, 19*, 396–422.

Chapter 9

The process of listening

Robert N. Bostrom

T HE ABILITY TO PERCEIVE and process information presented orally – 'listening' – has traditionally been viewed as a communication skill, such as interviewing and public speaking. However, as discussed in Chapter 1, there has been a great deal of debate about the exact meaning and delineation of the concept of 'skill'. Some skills involve considerable overt activity, whereas others consist primarily of covert mental processing. Listening seems to fall in this latter category, in that one can listen without exhibiting any external activity that would indicate that listening is taking place. Traditionally, we have distinguished between cognitive events as opposed to behaviour, although today most researchers are suspicious of such simplistic categories in almost every discipline (Dawkins, 1998). It still may be correct to say that listening is a cognitive process, but we are less sure of this designation than we once were (Hargie & Dickson, 2004).

The importance of listening would seem to be obvious. Whenever individuals are asked about the nature of their organisational activities, listening is cited as one of the most central. For example, in a recent survey of the Law School Admission Council (Luebke, Swygert, McLeod, Dalessandros & Roussos, 2003), listening activities were described as central to the practice of law and success in law school. Nor is the concern for listening confined to organisational settings. Paul Krugman, describing the stresses of modern politics, notes that neoconservatives today actually seem to have an aversion to listening to others (Krugman, 2003). Given some of this concern, it seems that knowing more about the nature of listening would be of great benefit.

Most early research in listening grew out of the cognitive tradition. This research was importantly influenced by an assumption that listening and reading were simply different aspects of a single process – the acquisition and retention of information. (It should be noted that most early research was conducted in university settings, and the universal assumption was that college students learned by reading textbooks and listening to lectures). If listening and reading produce the same outcomes, it is easy to assume that they are similar (if not exactly the same) skills. Success or failure of listening activity was therefore couched in cognitive (linguistic) terms. This assumption has been the dominant paradigm in listening and other communication research for the last 50 years. In other words, we have believed that linguistic events are central to the educational experience, and that relational and affective issues are less important.

This paradigm is firmly rooted in Western philosophical thought. The emphasis on symbols and the universal acceptance of philosophy has been the dominant paradigm in Western intellectual life ever since. The study of philosophy has been intermingled with the study of language ever since its inception. We use language according to certain well-established principles, and even though a strong case can be made that this usage is 'hard-wired', or determined by the physiological nature of the human brain (Pinker, 1994, 1997), the principles seem to be 'inherently' true – so much so that philosophers were led to contend that they indicate 'reality'. More recently, 'social' reality has been invoked as the aim of research in social interactions, especially communication. Language is primary in 'constructing' this reality. The nature of language is so intermingled with the 'proofs' of the reality hypotheses that it is impossible to approach them separately.

From the point of view of the cognitive/linguistic paradigm, communication (or symbolic behaviour) was an early evolutionary step in the development of human beings, leading to social behaviour and the beginning of civilisation. This explanation asserts that human beings somehow acquired the ability to communicate and subsequently were able to engage in social behaviour.

This paradigm, then, tells us that to improve our abilities in communication we should improve our facility with language. Words (cognitions) are either generated by internal processing or received from others, and then behaviour follows the words. A popular example of this paradigm is 'symbolic interactionism', which takes as its basic assumption that our social life is constructed of words. Some organisational communication theorists (Eisenberg & Goodall, 1993) have taken the position that a symbolic interactionist perspective is the most productive way in which to study organisations, and they draw on symbolic interactionism as a basic conceptual framework for organisational study.

Symbolic interactionism begins with the assumption that all life is a search for 'meaning', which, according to symbolic interactionists, is found in the way that each of us interacts with other persons, our institutions, and our culture. These interactions are *symbolic*, in that they take place primarily through language and symbols. This is in contrast to the well-known 'hierarchy of needs' (Maslow, 1943), which proposes that 'self-actualisation' (meaningful) needs are addressed only when the more basic needs of food and shelter are satisfied (see Chapter 2). This approach relies both on interpretation and the acceptance of principles derived from linguistic frameworks. The recipe for social change, therefore, involves a change in the symbol system, and behaviour is assumed to follow. Whether the changes are political, social, or organisational, the communicator must only 'manage meaning' to have significant effect. So if we are to increase the numbers of women and minorities in our organisational systems, we should concentrate on building symbol systems that will facilitate changes in hiring and promotional practices.

There is no doubt that changes in behaviour sometimes do follow changes in symbol systems. But at the same time, there is abundant evidence that changes in behaviour more often occur through coercion, social pressure, physiological and chemical changes, and sometimes random events. These changes, often termed 'mindless' ones, are then 'justified' by subsequent explanations by the participant. An individual who bows to social pressure in making a group decision then 'rationalises' the event by constructing evidence and logical processes. When this occurs, it is the case that language follows behaviour, rather than the other way around.

While communicative outcomes have traditionally been described as symbolic or behavioural, there are other communicative activities that may be as important, or even more important than these. The development and maintenance of relationships may be far more important than any other aspect of our daily life. Concerns with relationships are clearly facilitated through interactive activity (Knapp, Miller, and Fudge, 1994). We communicate in order to maintain and develop relationships with others, and the 'content' of the interaction may be only secondary to the process. Whether we use terms like 'affinity-seeking' or 'homophily' (Rogers, 1962), interpersonal relationships are a fundamental human characteristic, and are a significant outcome of communicative activity.

In summary, researchers in communication have placed an inordinate amount of emphasis on the linguistic, or cognitive, aspects of the communicative process. This focus on language led to ideas of 'reality' as dominant paradigms governing communicative activity. The rationale for this emphasis on language assumes that social change and behavioural alteration follow from changes in language and linguistic systems. The opposite view – that language follows behavioural change – is just as defensible but has not received as much attention. Recently, researchers in interpersonal communication have pointed out the importance of interactive behaviour, as well as the central role that relationships play in interpersonal communication (see Chapter 15). While these more recent trends would seem to lead to questioning the dominance of the language-centredness of traditional 'reality-based' research, we still see linguistic assumptions as pervasive ones. Since these assumptions have affected most thinking in communication, it is not surprising to see that this tradition has also affected examination of the process of listening.

RESEARCH IN LISTENING

Research in listening, like most communication research, has focused on symbolic rather than behavioural or relational outcomes, and, as a result, has had some of the same conceptual problems that have afflicted communication in general. Symbol-oriented definitions of information acquisition assume that since reading, writing, listening, and speaking are all communicative activities, they should share the same methods and outlook, and aim for the same end product – the processing of information. Larger differentiation of communicative outcomes has not traditionally been a part of the research in listening. Instead, we have focused on the inherent differences *in persons*, looking to research to help us understand why people differ in communicative skill.

Individuals vary widely in their ability to receive information that is presented symbolically, and the causes of this variation are poorly understood. Clearly, contexts and media affect the reception of messages. But individual differences are probably the most important source of variability in communication activities. The most logical explanation for differences in receiving ability would seem to be the possession of a generalised facility to manipulate and remember symbols. To this end, individual variations in reading, both in speed and comprehension, have been extensively studied. A 'general ability' explanation, however, is elusive. For example, reading and writing skills are not closely associated (Bracewell, Fredericksen and Fredericksen, 1982). The lack of a strong association between reading and writing skills leads us to expect that listening and speaking abilities are similarly unrelated to reading skill. But these individual differences in listening ability, if any, have attracted much less attention. This seems anomalous, since listening is probably the most common communication activity.

In a much-cited study, Paul Rankin (1929) asked persons to report how much time they spent in various types of communication. They reported that they listened 45% of the time, spoke 30%, read 16%, and wrote 9%. In a more recent study, Klemmer and Snyder (1972) studied the communicative activity of technical persons. These persons spent 68% of their day in communicative activity, and of that time 62% was 'talking face-to-face'. Klemmer and Snyder did not distinguish between speaking and listening, but it seems safe to assume that at least half of the face-to-face activity was listening. Brown (1982) estimated that corporate executives spend at least 60% of their day listening. To say that listening is an essential communication skill is to risk restating the obvious.

Early attempts at measurement

Whether or not listening is a distinct skill – that is, different from reading and writing skills – is a different question. Academic interest in listening is a relatively recent phenomenon, probably beginning with discussions by Wesley Wiksell (1946) and Ralph Nichols (1947) in the *Quarterly Journal of Speech*. Nichols' approach to studying listening was to assume that the methods used in studying reading could be used to examine listening, and Nichols' early research (Nichols, 1948) attempted to discover what, if anything, could help us predict good listening. In this pioneering study, Nichols adopted an information-based, cognitive definition of good listening. He constructed lectures with factual content in them, read them to respondents, and then measured subsequent retention in tests. 'Listening', in other words, was defined as what students do in a classroom.

Nichols examined the participants' retention and its relationship to many different factors, such as distance from the speaker, previous training in subject matter, hearing loss (!), size of family, and parental occupation. He concluded that retention was 'related to' intelligence, ability to discern organisational elements, size of vocabulary, and very little else. In other words, he found that intelligent persons retained more information than did unintelligent ones, those who understood organisational principles also retained more, and those with a large vocabulary retained more than those with a smaller vocabulary. Since Nichols' research, many investigators have used this criterion as a basis for an assessment of listening success. Studies of this type have been conducted by Beighley (1952, 1954), McClendon (1958), Thompson (1967), Hsia (1968), Klinzing (1972), Palamatier and McNinch (1972), Rossiter (1972), Buchli and Pearce (1974), and Beatty and Payne (1984).

Not long after Nichols' research was published, the 'factors' relating to listening skill were used as the theoretical justification for a commercial test of listening skill (Brown & Carlsen, 1955). But instead of using the actual findings of the Nichols study, this test made use of subscales which measured vocabulary, recognition of transitions, ability to follow directions, immediate recall, and the retention of facts from a lecture. With the exception of 'following directions', the subscales were all clearly language related. Since Brown's principal training and expertise was in reading, this bias was understandable. The Brown–Carlsen test has been used to measure listening ability as an independent variable by a few researchers (Ernest, 1968; Petrie & Carrell, 1976).

A similar 'listening' test was published by the US Educational Testing Service (ETS) (1957); it also was a language-related, cognitive test (Dickens & Williams, 1964). At first, it was considered part of the STEP (Sequential Tests of Educational Progress) test group, and then (after much revision) was incorporated into part of the communication skills assessment of the US National Teacher Examination (NTE) (ETS, 1984). Today, these tests are described as the *Praxis* examinations and the listening test is no longer one of the required elements, although it is still available.

The development of these tests and the research following from them seemed to demonstrate that persons do indeed vary in their ability to retain information from spoken messages, and that often instructional efforts to improve this ability were successful. This research considered that listening took place if information from spoken discourse was retained. A person who scored better on a test of retention was assumed to be a better listener. A person's listening ability was assumed to be a unique skill, not related to other cognitive skills.

The assumption that the ability to listen is a separate and unitary skill was sharply attacked in the middle of the 1960s by Charles Kelly. He reasoned that if listening tests did indeed measure a separate ability, the Brown–Carlsen and the STEP tests of listening would be more highly correlated with each other than with other measures of cognitive ability. He found that the tests of listening were not highly correlated with each other; in fact, they were more highly correlated with tests of intelligence. These data led Kelly, reasonably enough, to the conclusion that the ability that had previously been termed 'listening ability' was in fact only an aspect of intelligence, and that the Brown–Carlsen and the STEP tests were only different kinds of intelligence tests (Kelly, 1965, 1967). A clue to Kelly's findings was already present in Nichols' data, in that the single best predictor was cognitive ability, with a correlation of 0.54 (Nichols, 1948). While 'intelligence' is clearly not a unitary factor, defining listening as the remembering of facts from a lecture is definitely isomorphic with at least one of them. In his theory of multiple intelligences, Gardner (1983) clearly indicates that verbal processing is one of the many intelligences, and listening as defined as efficient word processing would fit well into this definition. If we take Sternberg's (1985) definition of intelligence as the ability to manipulate the environment, we probably would not see the same strong relationship exhibited by the Kelly and Nichols data.

The relationship of lecture-defined listening and intelligence is certainly not clear-cut. Cognitive ability interacts with difficulty of material and rate of presentation in predicting retention (Sticht & Glassnap, 1972). Kelly's discovery that 'listening' (as defined by the retention model) is probably not a separate and distinguishable mental ability complicates the problem. Almost everyone involved in the practical study of communication has had experience of persons who are obviously intelligent but could never be called 'good listeners'.

Attitudes and listening

One method of reconciling Kelly's findings with everyday experience is to redefine listening so that it includes something other than intelligence. Many invoked an 'attitude' about listening to explain why some persons listen better than others. This attitude could also be termed a 'willingness' to listen – a basic interest in others' ideas. Often when we say that someone is a 'good listener', we mean that they have a good attitude about the process, rather than retentive ability.

Carl Weaver was one of the first researchers to incorporate the attitudinal dimension into a formal definition of listening. He referred to research in perception showing that attitudinal predispositions affect both selection and perception of incoming stimuli. Listening, to Weaver, was 'the selection and retention of aurally received data' (1972, p. 12). Weaver went on to discuss 'selective exposure', an attitudinally and culturally determined activity. Weaver also included information seeking as an important component.

Weaver's approach, while popular, still avoided the basic question of whether or not listening 'ability' is a separate and distinct psychological characteristic. Normally attitudes, even social attitudes, are not considered to be permanent traits or abilities. Kelly had pointed out that good listeners were intelligent, and now Weaver asserted that good listeners were those who had respect and interest in others. 'Other orientation' was a popular theme in academic life in the early 1970s, and the 'humanistic psychology' movement seemed to be in tune with concern for other people expressed in the goal of being 'good listeners'. But more sceptical theorists looked at listening as simply a redescription of other, better-known psychological processes, notably selective perception and intelligence.

'Interpersonal' attitudes form the basis of much popular writing about listening today. This writing assumes that a good listener is one that is 'other oriented', in that respect, and that concern for others is the foundation for effective listening. The process of becoming a better listener is akin to the process of becoming a better spouse or work partner, in that the relational elements are deemed to be paramount. It is, of course, possible to call this respect a 'skill' of a kind, and it is also possible to encourage these attitudes in workshops and seminars. But at the same time, it is hard to see how any careful definition of listening can ignore the processes involved in human memory.

Listening and memory

When one listens, one captures, however briefly, the message in memory. One of the most interesting results of recent memory research was the discovery that memory is of various types and is used in different ways. Some researchers, noting that the information in messages is almost always words, have called this process 'semantic memory'. Squire (1986), for example, distinguished semantic memory from episodic memory. When we remember episodes, we remember what someone did, and when we remember words, we remember what they said. Semantic memory and episodic memory affect one another, even though one uses percepts and the other uses language (Chang, 1986). So 'memory' research offers a distinct alternative to primarily symbolic approaches to listening.

Semantic memory is definitely related to the probabilistic nature of information. It has been studied from the point of view of 'category sizes' (Collins & Quillian, 1972), 'relatedness', (Kintsch, 1980), and 'familiarity' (McCloskey, 1980). And though Baddely and Dale (1968), Kintsch and Busche (1969), and Squire (1986) consider semantic memory to be part of long-term storage, Schulman (1972) has demonstrated that some semantic decoding does take place in shorter temporal situations. Further evidence is furnished by Pellegrino et al. (1975), who showed that short-term memory for words is different from that for pictures.

Monsell (1984), for example, speculated that it is the job of the 'input register' to hold the words or phonemes long enough for semantic encoding processes to be brought into play. If so, persons who cannot activate the input register would either encode immediately or lose everything. If they conduct the kind of grammatical processing suggested by Heen Wold's data (1978), material presented in a grammatically coherent structure would be easily processed, while material not having structure would be more difficult.

The standard description of how items are processed into long-term storage is highly linear (Loftus & Loftus, 1976). If this linear description is accurate, then a deficiency at one point of the process would clearly result in deficiencies at later temporal stages. A good way to identify such deficiencies would be to compare persons with different aptitudes at each stage in the process and see how the end product is affected. But the most important finding, and one that affects conceptions of listening most directly, is that memory has several stages, most probably best described as short term, intermediate term, and long term. The use of this memory model led to the hypothesis that verbal decoding can be divided into several components: short-term listening, short-term listening with rehearsal, and lecture listening. When investigated, these three 'types' (aspects) of listening were initially shown to differentiate among one another (Bostrom & Waldhart, 1980); furthermore, short-term listening seemed to have little relationship to cognitive abilities, as shown in intelligence tests.

Alternative approaches to listening

If the linguistic/symbolic view is an acceptable one, and if listening is primarily a cognitive process, then the research reported above, including the memory-based models, would suffice for productive investigations into listening behaviour. The principal research tasks would be the development of reliable and valid tests of the process, and investigation into some of the varying relationships involved in the communicative process. However, many aspects of listening are not easily subsumed under a typical linguistic/symbolic framework.

To begin with, the process of communication is a much more broadly defined activity than a linguistic/symbolic process alone. Defensible distinctions can be made among typical communicative functions such as relaying, stimulating, activating, and linguistic functions (Bostrom, 1988). On a more global level, communication often aims at both instrumental and relational goals.

The discovery that short-term listening (STL) was different from other aspects of listening and that individuals differ systematically in this ability was hardly earth-shaking. But what was more interesting was that the linear model proposed by Loftus and Loftus (1976) could not be maintained for listening, because long-term retention did not depend on short-term retention (Bostrom & Bryant, 1980). Further, a curious finding appeared in a large-scale investigation of public-speaking 'performance' – good short-term listeners apparently performed better in oral presentations (Spitzberg & Hurt, 1983). Another interesting study of 'managerial effectiveness' demonstrated that STL is the best discriminator between good and poor branch managers in banks (Alexander, Penley & Jernigan, 1992). Another, even more interesting finding appeared in a long-term study of organisational success. Short-term listening was the best single predictor of upward mobility in the organisation (Sypher, Bostrom & Seibert, 1989). Bussey (1991) found that those respondents with good short-term skills asked more questions in an interview than those with poor short-term skills.

The discovery that short-term listening skill is qualitatively different from long-term listening skill was an important step in separating listening research from the more traditional, symbol-oriented frameworks, but did not go very far. More recently, Thomas and Levine (1994) raised two fundamental questions about the memory model of listening: (1) What is the relationship between the memory for symbols and the listening process? (2) How can relational factors be introduced into the model? Thomas and Levine pointed out that there is no real basis for assuming a connection between short-term listening and interactive skill. While some of the studies cited above (e.g. Sypher et al., 1989; Alexander et al., 1992) demonstrate that some kind of relationship exists, there is no compelling theoretical or observational basis for such an assumption. Further, Thomas and Levine (1994), in contending that a conversation based on short-term memory alone would be 'nearly incoherent', offered an alternative definition of listening that is primarily relational. In their study, they examined relational cues – eye gaze, head nods, short 'backchat', and long 'backchat'. Short backchat consists of utterances such as 'yes' or 'hmm' during speech, and long back-chat comprises typically restatements of the speaker's utterances. Long backchat is identical to the 'statements and questions' aspect of the NTE listening test, but the other three are traditionally defined as 'non-verbal' factors. Nods and gaze are clearly visual stimuli.

In short, while some research indicates that STL is closely implicated in inter-personal activities, apparently much more than long-term skills (or ability), just how these abilities relate to one another is not known. These and other studies led to the conclusion that perhaps short-term listening is not a cognitive skill, but an interpersonal skill (Bostrom, 1990) and should not be confused with other forms of listening. 'Lecture' listening, on the other hand, seems to be very closely related to common definitions of intelligence (Bostrom & Waldhart, 1988). In other words, listening was originally modelled on memory models, which contain a minimum of short- and long-term components. Dividing listening into those two kinds of abilities produced the serendipitous finding that short-term listening is apparently closely connected with interpersonal skills in a variety of settings.

But clearly (as Thomas and Levine pointed out), no good theoretical explanation exists for this finding. On the other hand, several other aspects of listening are much more important in communication. Prominent among these is the expression and understanding of affective messages. Typically, this has been termed 'interpretive listening'.

Interpretive listening

Interpretive listening is identical to vocalic decoding. This is usually understood to mean the processing of emotional or affective content from a message, primarily from 'tone' of voice, inflection, and other variations of voice. Most persons feel that they are skilled in vocalic listening, but generally do poorly when called on to decode affect. For example, in one study using a standardised vocalic listening task, a very large sample of college students and adults identified correct answers only 55% of the time (Bostrom, 1990). In other words, more than half of the time, people misinterpret vocalic signals. And while accessing this kind of information is universally considered to be of great importance, no one seems to have a clear idea as to how it should be improved. One factor here is that individuals vary in their 'affect orientation' (Booth-Butterfield & Booth-Butterfield 1990).

Research indicates that improvements in interpretive listening can be accomplished with training procedures, such as sensitivity training, role playing, and the like (Wolvin & Coakley, 1988). Interpreting the underlying affect implied in spoken messages may involve personal schemas (Fitch-Hauser, 1990), constructs, or 'cultural literacy' (Hirsch, 1987). These changes, however, are changes in attitude, awareness, or knowledge, not changes in basic ability. Changes in basic ability are much more difficult.

A substantive body of research clearly indicates that interpretive listening is also strongly affected by an individual's ability to decode the non-verbal cues present in the exchange (Burgoon, 1994). Often when non-verbal signals contradict the verbal ones, individuals typically accept the non-verbal as a more valid expression of the true feelings of the interactant (Leathers, 1979; Burgoon, 1994). Most investigations of non-verbal cues centre on visual displays, such as facial expression, posture, and so on. Others have investigated 'vocalic' messages, such as pitch, intonation, and inflection. Visual cues have typically been shown to be of greater influence than the vocalic ones in most situations. However, some studies show that vocalic cues are of more use in detecting deception than visual ones (Streeter et al., 1977; Littlepage & Pineault, 1981).

However, Keely-Dyreson, Burgoon, and Bailey (1991) examined decoding differences in isolation. They compared the ability of respondents to decode visual cues with their ability to decode vocal cues, and found that visual cues are more accurately perceived than vocal ones. Some gender differences were also observed. In short, the division of messages into 'verbal' and 'non-verbal' categories may be too simple. Visual and vocal cues, both of which have been categorised as non-verbal messages, would seem to differ in important ways. Comparisons of decoding abilities are rare. What the relationships might be among visual/non-verbal decoding ability, vocal/ non-verbal decoding ability, and verbal decoding ability is not known.

In summary, decoding of non-verbal messages is an important aspect of all inter-actions, and this decoding usually involves visual and aural cues. Research indicates that visual cues are decoded with much greater accuracy and that the ability to decode vocalic messages is not nearly as good as most persons suppose. Lateral asymmetry of brain function may well be an unsuspected contributor to the lack of accuracy in vocalic decoding. Vocalic decoding is quite important because in mediated communi-cations, such as the telephone, visual cues are not available. Other circumstances may preclude the inspection of facial expression and other body movements.

Schematic listening

Another way of examining the acquisition of information in spoken messages may involve the use of schemas (Fitch-Hauser, 1990). How would you interpret the following passage?

> When the Kiwis took the field, they began their infamous Maori wardance. The Sydney team was forced to wait an inordinately long time for this dance to conclude, and at that time, were not mentally ready. As a consequence, and as a result of the emotionality of the ceremony, the Kiwis won easily.

If you did not know that the event described was taking place in Australia, and involved Australian football, and that the Kiwis were distinctly the underdogs (and a host of other details), the passage would mean little to you. A good name for all the interlocking knowledge represented here would be an 'Australian football schema'.

Richard Mayer (1983) noted that schemas underlie almost all important cogni-tive activities, and sometimes have been investigated using terms like 'frames' and 'scripts'. Nonetheless, it is clear that quite often interpreting a prose passage is impos-sible without knowledge of the 'big picture' in the situation. Hirsch (1987) extended the schema concept to general educational outcomes, calling for colleges and uni-versities to teach a core of cultural knowledge that could serve as common schemas to assist in understanding one another.

Thain (1994) used aspects of schema theory in formulating his definition of 'authentic' listening. Thain reasoned that many aspects of listening skill are 'pure traits', such as memory and vocabulary, but an integrative act is vital to put the entire message into meaningful relationships. He presented an example of a situation in which decoding cannot take place without a larger understanding of the situation involved, similar to the 'Kiwi' example above.

Further evidence for the distinctiveness of schematic listening is furnished by the ETS. Consider the following test item (presented on audiotape):

MAN'S VOICE: Well, what do you think is the most effective way of dealing with this matter?

WOMAN'S VOICE: William has a great deal of respect for his parents. I suggest we set up a meeting with them.

MAN'S VOICE: I think William may feel threatened if we ask his parents to come in. I'd like to have the school staff try a bit longer before we call them.

WOMAN'S VOICE: I think that we could involve them in such a way that William would not feel threatened.

QUESTIONER: Why does the man hesitate to call William's parents?

a. William could feel threatened if his parents were called.
b. William is threatened by those who work with him at school.
c. Children usually do not respect their parents.
d. The man does not like to involve parents in school problems.

The correct answer is *a*. Notice that the information given is provided in the man's second statement. However, the *implicit* information in the dialogue is clear: the two speakers were either teachers or school counsellors, and this kind of conversation does not take place unless there is some kind of trouble. If you had absolutely no information about the 'school' schema, you would not understand that. Your ability to respond correctly to questions like that would be determined by your knowledge of the schema, and not your ability to listen (what Thain called a 'pure trait').

This item, together with other similar items, is part of the 40-item, listening portion of the NTE. Other items reflect interest in short-term listening (short statements and answers, interpretive listening (the affective content of statements or dialogues), and 'lecture' listening (responding to 'talks'). The NTE scores only 'statements and questions', 'dialogues', and 'talks' however.

Table 9.1 presents the intercorrelations of the varying measures on the NTE, including the results of an essay (writing) test, a reading test, a 'usage' test that measures grammatical choices, and a sentence-completion test of comprehension (ETS, 1984). Unfortunately, a correlation table does not present a comprehensive view

Table 9.1 Intercorrelations of various sections of the National Teacher Examination (NTE)

Test section	List A	List B	List C	Reading	Writing A	Writing B
1A. S & Q	1.00					
1B. Dlg	.56	1.00				
1C. Talks	.59	.48	1.00			
2. Reading	.72	.58	.68	1.00		
3A. Usage	.63	.49	.58	.71	1.00	
3B. SC	.56	.44	.52	.65	.68	1.00
Essay	.46	.39	.41	.52	.53	.50

S & Q: statements and questions; Dlg: dialogue; SC: sentence comprehension.

of the interrelationships in the data. To get a better idea of the relationships among these scales, factor analysis can be employed. Table 9.2 presents a simple factor analysis of the variables in Table 9.1 (it should be noted that this is certainly not a sophisticated analysis. Principal components were used, rather than an oblique solution, and the five-factor solution is clearly arbitrary. Nonetheless, it does illustrate some of the internal characteristics of these abilities).

It is clear from Table 9.2 that the ETS data do conform to the tripartite model (Bostrom, 1990) very well. The 'statements and questions' measure, the 'dialogue' task, and the 'talks' measure are clearly individual and distinct factors, as is the ETS 'essay'. What exactly 'reading' and 'usage' are is not clear, but it seems that the original statements made in this paper about communication and language are borne out in this analysis. But most importantly, it is clear that the 'dialogues' portion of the test is very distinct from the other subscales, and, as the example of the test item above shows, the 'dialogues' measure is dependent upon possession of a fairly well-articulated 'school' schema. In other words, the 'schematic' aspects of the model are distinct (i.e. different) from the other skills involved.

As we review the history of listening research, we see that traditional studies of communication have centred on linguistic competence – understandably, since it has taken place in the traditional 'learning paradigm' in the Western world. The cognitive/linguistic approach has affected our basic orientation to almost every effort in studying communicative competence. Unfortunately, sometimes, it is not efficacious. Communication often needs to focus on behaviour, on relationships, and on affect. Traditional studies in listening assessment have not examined the overall communicative process, but have focused primarily on individual differences in the processing of orally presented symbols.

BROADER ASPECTS OF THE STUDY OF LISTENING

Clearly, it is time to take another look at the research on listening as a whole. As discussed above, definitions of listening began with symbolic processing (synonymous with intelligence) and then were supplemented with other aspects, such as attitudes. Memory models were introduced, as well as an emphasis on schemas of various types.

Table 9.2 Factors generated by intercorrelations of ETS 'communication skills' assessments

	I	II	III	IV	V
Statements and questions	.27	.85	.23	.24	.17
Dialogue	.20	.24	.19	.91	.14
Talks	.26	.25	.89	.18	.15
Reading	.45	.52	.44	.27	.22
Usage	.68	.39	.26	.17	.25
Sentence comprehension	.88	.17	.19	.11	.19
Essay	.25	.17	.15	.14	.92

If we look carefully at all of the previous research in listening, we can see that the one common element in all of these different approaches has been information processing. This common thread is strong enough for us to say that the best definition of listening is the *acquisition, processing, and retention of information in the interpersonal context*. This is a much more inclusive definition, but has a number of advantages. One advantage of using this more inclusive model of listening is that visual stimuli are just as important as aural stimuli. The inclusion follows logically from integrating interpretive, relational, and behavioural aspects of communication.

Some interesting research has been conducted on the comparison of audio and video modalities, much of which has important implications for the assessment of listening. In the next section, we will examine some of these.

Audio or video?

Comparisons of audio and video modalities are recent ones, and have only been made possible because modern technology has enabled researchers to control each artificially. In interpersonal situations, audio and video occur simultaneously. The introduction of electronic communication devices – the telephone, and then radio – separated audio from video. Television, of course, restored video, but in its own way. Commercial news broadcasts provided pictures of explosions and earthquakes while an announcer described the carnage, but, typically, the audio and video, *as presented by broadcasters*, have little to do with one another. Some early research (Anderson, 1966, 1968) illustrates the way researchers thought at that time. Anderson compared the way that *adding* video could improve retention and effect. In essence, the audio contained *the message*. This way of thinking still persists, as we will see. Contrasts between audio and video are relatively new.

In other words, we see that the linguistic/symbolic bias in early research in telecommunication determined how investigations were conducted. We can also see this dominance in later research. 'Effectiveness' has been defined as simple retention of news content (Gunter, 1987; Graber, 1988). Studies of violence and other antisocial effects have been related only to 'content', a global term, which usually does not distinguish between modalities.

This is a truly odd assumption, given the universal assumption of most theorists of the pre-eminence of the video mode. The preoccupation with video by news directors is well known, at least in the USA. Michael Deaver, the media manager of the US president Ronald Reagan, was extremely cooperative in providing the candidate for video but kept absolute control of the video content. The CBS News correspondent Lesley Stahl reported that she would present a feature in which, for example, pictures of the president at the Handicapped Olympics and the opening of a home for the elderly were matched with Stahl's voice-over of budget cuts for the disabled and the elderly. But the video always showed a smiling, genial, nice guy. Stahl concluded that she had been 'had' by Deaver and the other Reagan managers, since, as she said about the viewers: 'They didn't hear you. They only saw [the] pictures' (*http://hypertextbook. com/eworld/president.shtml*).

Nonetheless, research seems to focus on 'propositional content' of news programmes. This content is not always well remembered. For example, Stauffer, Frost, and Rybolt (1983) telephoned viewers immediately after they watched network news programmes, and reported that the viewers contacted did not remember much news content. Of an average of 13.3 news items, only 2.3 were recalled (17.2%) A 'cued' group did better, but even this group never exceeded 25% recall. Better educated persons did slightly better than the average, but the overall picture is a dismal one.

Barrie Gunter (1987) conducted careful research in 'memory for news' as a function of the 'modality' of presentation. His research bears out much of Stauffer et al.'s findings. Gunter pointed out that there are significant differences between modalities (audio plus video versus audio alone, and print). Gunter's research utilised illustrative tapes (one featured riots in the streets of Seoul), and his data show us that video added to audio improves the retention of headlines significantly. Table 9.3 presents some of these data (from Gunter, 1987, p. 235).

While the film and the still pictures improved the retention of headlines, adding video to the message when it consisted of a newscaster (a talking head) was quite the opposite. In these circumstances, the audio alone was superior. In other words, talking-head presentations are a poor way to utilise video. This finding has been repeated in other research (Searle & Bostrom, 1990).

Nonetheless, we can see that print is better than audio and audio-visual presentations. When Gunter examined these differences, he also found that gender plays a role. Table 9.4 (from Gunter, 1987, p. 225) presents these differences. Males in

Table 9.3 Percentages of news headlines correctly recalled as a function of visual format and modality

| Modality | | Visual format | | | |
		Film	Stills	Newscaster	Mean
	Audio-visual	90	54	29	51
Experiment 1	Audio only	44	41	50	45
	Mean	57	48	40	48
	Audio-visual	74	60	35	56
Experiment 2	Audio only	50	46	48	48
	Mean	62	53	42	52

Table 9.4 Recall of news as a function of presentation modality

| Presentation modality | Experiment 1 | | | Experiment 2 | | |
	Males	Females	All	Males	Females	All
Audio-visual	12.1	8.0	10.1	9.9	9.9	9.9
Audio only	10.4	7.1	8.8	13.1	11.6	12.4
Print	13.3	11.6	12.5	15.7	17.0	16.4
All modalities	11.9	8.9	10.5	12.9	12.8	12.9

Gunter's studies remembered better – almost universally. In a similar study, however, Searle and Bostrom (1990) found that females remembered more data from viewing a talking-head presentation than did males. Reports of gender differences of this type probably should not be taken seriously unless gender is defined psychologically rather than physiologically.

Gunter generally explains the retention of information presented in the news as a function of the varying 'cognitive structures' that may or may not affect processing the news. His assumption is that the cognitive structure for all processing is the same. Gunter reviews memory structures, such as semantic and episodic memory. He also reviews memory processes, such as encoding, arousal, selective attention, spacing, organising, and retrieval. He applies all of these concepts (in a theoretic sense) to the manner in which television news is presented. Here is Gunter's explanation of the way news is remembered:

> Sentences that readily conjure up visual scenes in the minds of individuals can be assigned a context more easily than sentences that do not, leading to better memory performance. In other words, it may be easier to relate new sentence input whose content can also be 'pictured' to existing propositional knowledge structures in memory derived from other linguistic or picture inputs, providing an abundance of connections from permanent memory into the new information (1987, p. 257).

The pre-eminence of the linguistic/symbolic paradigm is evident in this explanation.

A 'true' comparison of the differences between sound and sight as information inputs would occur only if the audio and video presented *exactly the same material or content*. Grimes (1991) conducted such a comparison. He compared 'attentional factors' in what he called redundant, quasi-redundant, and non-redundant video–audio comparisons. In the redundant condition, the video and audio exactly corresponded. Grimes prepared a videotape of a farmer drilling a hole in a tree to tap maple sap, and added audio saying, 'farmers drill holes in trees to tap maple sap'. In the quasi-redundant condition, the video was taken at a distance so that details were hard to make out, and in the non-redundant condition, the audio was the principal method of gaining information. Grimes examined the degree to which receivers attended to the message. Messages were inserted in the stimulus tape instructing watchers to press a lever. When the lever pressing was delayed, Grimes reasoned that they were not paying attention as well as when the lever pressing was instantaneous. The reaction times in these three conditions did not vary significantly.

Then Grimes examined recognition scores of information presented in newscasts to see whether the degree of redundancy made a difference there. Video was superior only in a condition where no redundancy was present. Table 9.5 presents these scores.

Grimes' research has probably the best theoretical and methodological instances of the comparison of sound and sight, and suggests that there is little difference between the modalities.

Newhagen and Reeves (1992) provided an interesting analysis of the research on memory for television. They noted that most of these studies rely on propositional memory – an obvious problem. 'Visual' memory is tremendously difficult to measure, so Newhagen and Reeves relied on a 'recognition' technique; that is, they asked, 'Did

Table 9.5 Recognition scores

Redundancy	Visual	Audio
High	23.84	29.76
Medium	19.71	28.44
None	23.10	18.35

you see this before?' These recognitions were inhibited by negative images preceding the stories or stimuli.

Further evidence for a hypothesis of no differences comes from research in deception. Bauchner, Brandt, and Miller (1977) studied the ability of receivers to detect deception. Messages were presented by four different media: face-to-face, video, audio, and printed transcript. No significant differences could be seen – judgemental accuracy was not more effective on any channel. So in two very careful studies of communication effectiveness, media 'effects' seem to be exaggerated.

In short, the way that commercial television operates probably has *created* the assumed superiority of the 'video modality' rather than any innate superiority of one medium over another. Researchers have designed their studies to mirror what is practised, and the consequence is that the 'superiority' is demonstrated by the research.

Nonetheless, there is no question that future research in listening should expand to a search for explanations concerning the processing of information in general, not simply the oral channel. Interpersonal interactions do contain a strong visual component, and the visual component should be combined with what we know about non-verbal communication to add to our existing knowledge. But the contrasts between audio and video should be conducted only in a framework of interpretive listening, and not modelled after existing broadcasting practice.

Reading and listening

Few studies have compared reading and listening as modalities for gaining information. Such studies would seem to be one of the most obvious kinds of comparisons, especially in educational research, yet, even in research reports which purport to examine the differences between reading and listening (Horowitz & Samuels, 1987), no instances of direct comparisons are reported. Comparisons of this kind are difficult to make directly, because of the problem in elapsed time. Reading can occur at roughly four or five times the rate of an audio or video signal. Announcers speak at a rate of 100–125 words per minute. If you can process information at 500 words per minute and it is coming to you only at 150, there is a great gap here. This certainly explains why good short-term listeners who are also high sensation seekers, do much more poorly on lecture listening than low sensation seekers (Bostrom, 1990).

We do know that both reading and listening are affected by 'sensation seeking' on the part of the receiver (Donohew, Nair & Finn 1984; Bostrom, 1990). The basic similarity in these two processes would seem to indicate that productive investigations should be possible in the future.

Listening and behaviour

Examining the 'behaviour' in listening would seem to be a difficult task. Recall that Thomas and Levine (1994) examined immediate behavioural responses to listening – eye gaze, head nods, short 'backchat', and long 'backchat' – all of which are typically accepted indicators of attentional constancy. But other than attending to the speaker, what behavioural indications are there of listening? Simply acquiring and storing information does not suffice to bring about behavioural change. Smokers know that cigarettes harm their health, but continue to smoke. Drivers know that wearing seat belts is wise, but most are careless about the actual compliance. Likewise, Steinhauer (1995) reported that knowledge of the nutritional value of foods had no appreciable effect on consumers' choices of foods. If listening is only an informational process, little, if any, behavioural change will result. On the other hand, if individuals listen with an eye to changes in behaviour, we would have to conclude that earlier models of listening might not be sufficient.

'Information seeking' is a rather well-researched phenomenon in communication research. The uses and gratifications that individuals seek from television have been carefully explored (Palmgreen, 1984). If individuals seek information proactively in media consumption, why not in interpersonal interactions?

Behavioural research in listening probably would depend heavily on the use of schemas as explanatory mechanisms. Recall that both Graber (1988) and Gunter (1987) depended heavily on this mechanism as an explanatory paradigm. But both of these researchers have missed some of the essential characteristics of schematic research, especially some of the implications for behavioural modification. Thain (1994) proposed that the term 'authentic listening' be used to describe the broader aspects of the process, and Fitch-Hauser (1990) proposed an outline for looking at schemas in the listening process. The ETS's NTE provided some compelling data that schematic processes are different from the more specific skills. But behavioural change is a communicative effect that goes beyond simple retention effects, and may be a communicative outcome that is ultimately more important.

Many persons believe that dramatic programmes on television are affecting our culture in important ways. The best explanation of this phenomenon is the development of an elaborate schema system and the attachment of propositional content to this system. Mary John Smith (1982) demonstrated how this effect seems to work. In a straightforward message, she told individuals that 'high-risk' people make better fire-fighters, or in other words, that a personality test with 'riskiness' as a personality trait is a useful way to screen applicants for a fire department recruiting task. Then she asked these people to construct (a) a short message supporting the belief, (b) a short message refuting the belief, (c) both pro and con arguments, or (d) messages irrelevant to the schemata. Then she acknowledged to everyone that the message was false – no such research existed. Those who wrote arguments defending the belief stubbornly refused to change, even though they knew that the foundation for their belief was faked.

Smith attributed the phenomenon to 'plugging in' the proposition to existing schemas, but an explanation that utilises 'scripts' or 'semantic networks' would be as defensible. Clearly, the event is related to connection making of some type. Research in listening that explored such structures would be very productive.

PROBLEMS IN LISTENING RESEARCH

Clearly, two very important questions in communication research are the following: (a) 'How do people process information received from others' and (b) 'How can this processing be improved?' Common sense tells us that to claim that something has been improved, we must be able to demonstrate that individuals are different in some fashion as a result of something that they perceived. If we believe something can be improved, the most logical way to demonstrate this is to measure its level prior to the improvement procedure hypothesised and then measure it after the procedure has been applied.

Unfortunately, self-report is not a highly reliable way to discover characteristics about an individual's behaviour. Questionnaires often probe respondents about their past, specifically getting to quantitative issues. 'During the past 2 weeks, on days when you drank alcohol, how many drinks did you have?'; 'In the past 12 months, how often did you go to your dentist?'; 'When did you last work at a full-time job?' are all examples of these kinds of questions. They make an implicit demand to remember and enumerate specific autobiographical episodes. However, respondents frequently have trouble complying because of limits on their ability to recall. In these situations, respondents resort to inferences that use partial information from memory to construct a numeric answer. Feinberg and Tanur (1989) have suggested reducing the error by placing 'embedded experiments' in survey design, and this seems to be a promising method. This method randomly administers alternative questionnaires or other variations in procedure to subsets of the sample. Statistically, these subsets are partialled out as part of the error variance in the analysis of variance. Essentially, what results is an embedded, randomised block design. Feinberg and Tanur (1989) demonstrated this technique by designing two sets of questionnaires, both of which contained items about abortion. In one questionnaire, the question context contained items generally relating to women's rights, followed by questions about abortions. In a second questionnaire, the items related to medical practice and health issues, followed by questions about abortion. The questionnaires produced dramatically different results. Feinberg and Tanur explained their results by invoking schema theory.

The implications of these findings for listening research are clear – reliance on past events is probably poor practice. If responses can be designed to assess immediate responses, a greater degree of reliability can be produced.

In another examination of questionnaire behaviour, Bradburn, Rips, and Shevell (1987) discovered strong evidence of schema theory in survey reports. Their respondents tended to group recalled happenings in terms of memory reconstructions, rather than in any straight, linear form. They concluded that people use any information they have available to generate any kind of reasonable answer. This is especially true when recalling events in their own lives. In other words, respondents may remember one or two pertinent facts, and they produce an answer using some kind of inductive inference. Most of us are familiar with the 'telescoping' phenomenon that occurs in surveys – we remember material as having occurred in smaller units of time. Since people recall events in terms of autobiographical experiences, surveys can and should be designed to trigger these events in the respondent's memory. For example, if asking a respondent about behaviour concerning or reaction to the Chernobyl disaster, it would be useful to anchor the responses in terms of the respondents' own lives, by tagging the response to events more familiar, such as graduations, marriages, etc.

Results from surveys certainly throw light on individual interpretation of activities, but listening research ought to aim at specific responses in which a clear indication of behaviour is present. This is especially important if the phenomena involved deal with situations that inhibit or facilitate recall, and the accuracy of the respondent's answers is at issue.

OVERVIEW: IMPLICATIONS FOR PRACTICE

In our organisational life, listening is most often invoked as an interpersonal skill, and supervisors clearly are considered competent when they 'listen well'. Individuals prize good listening in others even when they are unwilling to engage in it themselves. This well-known characteristic opens a manipulative channel that many have exploited. Supervisors may learn to offer the appearance of listening only to build a good attitude in a subordinate. When they proclaim, 'I am a good listener', it is only an internal strategy to get others to go along. This strategy was utilised on a grand scale when a large US computer corporation adopted 'We listen better' as a theme for a series of television advertisements. The series was frankly copied from the Avis 'We try harder' slogan. In order to give the campaign credibility, the corporation decided to train its employees in listening, offering a series of seminars around the country. To everyone's surprise, the employees enjoyed the training and reported that learning about listening not only helped them in their organisational lives, but was instrumental in building better relationships at home! Training in listening, however inspired, is a worthwhile activity, and, whether administered by experts or not, can convey benefits.

The 'measurement' approach to listening research should convince us all that individuals differ in their listening ability, and that these differences can make organisational coordination very difficult. Results from almost every aspect of listening measurement show that less than half of what is transmitted is retained, even within a few minutes. Clearly, managers need to explore the information requirements of the organisation and examine the communicative tasks very closely.

The first major task is to make sure communicative interactions have a clear, specific purpose. Consider the following communicative situations, all of which occur in daily life in organisations:

- a school board listening to a teacher advocating a new reading programme
- a social worker explaining the food stamp programme to a group of welfare mothers
- a group of new employees listening to a personnel supervisor explaining how to use the company's cash register system
- a soccer coach going over a new play with the team
- a lifeguard at a municipal pool explaining the rules to a newly formed swim club

- an army officer giving instructions to a unit before a training exercise
- a student testifying before the city council concerning parking problems.

All of these situations have several common elements. Each is an example of one individual presenting an extended message to a large group. In addition, certain agreed-upon rules contribute to an element of formality in these occasions:

1 Some mutual goal or purpose is assumed, whether organisational or societal.
2 Minimal structure and role expectations divide the group into one source (speaker) and many receivers (listeners).
3 The receivers assume that the source has some expertise.
4 The receivers assume specific preparation on the part of the source.
5 The receivers do not talk as much as the source.

If all of these five requirements are met, sensible enquiries can be made concerning differences in listening skills. If not, then problems in retention of messages may be lodged in one of the five characteristics above.

What does research tell us about improving our listening effectiveness? Actually, there is a good deal to be learned from the research efforts.

1 We all vary in our ability to listen. This means that in a given situation some receivers will retain only half as much as others. This ability is uncorrelated with other cognitive skills, meaning that even if you did well in school, you may be a poor listener. Probably the only way to ascertain an individual's skill level is to use a standardised abilities test. Those who are poorer in this ability need to work harder in the process.
2 Sensation seeking contributes negatively to lecture listening. This means that if you are a high sensation seeker (e.g. you enjoy events such as auto racing or downhill skiing), you will have difficulty concentrating during a lecture. Individuals can introduce 'self-interesting' strategies during lectures to counteract these problems.
3 Schematic listening is probably more important than most researchers have previously thought. This means that individuals new to an organisation or a manufacturing system will have much more difficulty than those who have an extensive history in it. Managers need to be aware of these differences.
4 The organisation or system needs to be clear about the goal of the communicative interaction. Cognitively oriented data can be reduced to writing or stored in a computer. Interpersonal interactions are probably better suited to relational matters and affective messages.

There is, sadly, an unfortunate tendency among managers or others in authority to assume that, if a communication is not efficacious, it is the fault of the receivers. Many managers are notoriously poor transmitters, but since they enjoy organisational power, they are generally attended to. It is obviously true that individuals differ in receiving ability, but these differences are usually not ones that can be easily overcome with short courses or 'quick-fix' programmes. A broader, more functional programme in listening research might help in finding new applications.

REFERENCES

Alexander, E. R., Penley, L. E. & Jernigan, I. E. (1992). The relationship of basic decoding skills to managerial effectiveness. *Management Communication Quarterly*, **6**, 58–73.

Anderson, J. (1966). Equivalence of meaning among statements present through various media. *AV Communication Review*, **14**, 499–505.

Anderson, J. (1968). More on the equivalence of statements presented in various media. *AV Communication Review*, **16**, 25–32.

Baddely, A. & Dale, H. (1968). The effect of semantic similarity on retroactive interference in long- and short-term memory. *Journal of Verbal Learning and Verbal Behavior*, **5**, 471–420.

Bauchner, J. E., Brandt, D. R. & Miller, G. R. (1977). The truth/deception attribution: effects of varying levels of information availability. In B. D. Rubin (Ed.), *Communication Yearbook*, vol. 1. New Brunswick, NJ: Transaction Books.

Beatty, M. & Payne, S. (1984). Listening comprehension as a function of cognitive complexity. *Communication Monographs*, **51**, 85–89.

Beighley, K. (1952). The effect of four speech variables on listener comprehension. *Speech Monographs*, **19**, 249–258.

Beighley, K. (1954). An experimental study of the effect of three speech variables on listener comprehension. *Speech Monographs*, **21**, 248–253.

Booth-Butterfield, M. & Booth-Butterfield, S. (1990). Conceptualizing affect as information in communication production. *Human Communication Research*, **16**, 451–476.

Bostrom, R. N. (1980). Altered physiological states: the central nervous system and persuasive communications. In G. Miller & M. Roloff (Eds), *Persuasion: new directions in theory and research*. Beverly Hills, CA: Sage.

Bostrom, R. N. (1983). *Persuasion*. Englewood Cliffs, NJ: Prentice-Hall.

Bostrom, R. N. (1988). *Communicating in public*. Minneapolis, MN: Burgess.

Bostrom, R. N. (1990). *Listening behavior: measurement and applications*. New York: Guilford.

Bostrom, R. N. & Bryant, C. (1980). Factors in the retention of information presented orally: the role of short-term memory. *Western Speech Communication Journal*, **44**, 137–145.

Bostrom, R. N. & Waldhart, E. S. (1980). Components in listening behavior: the role of short-term memory. *Human Communication Research*, **6**, 211–227.

Bostrom, R. N. & Waldhart, E. S. (1988). Memory models and the measurement of listening. *Communication Education*, **37**, 1–18.

Bostrom, R. & Donohew, L. (1992). The case for empiricism: clarifying fundamental issues in communication theory. *Communication Monographs*, **59**, 109–128.

Bostrom, R. N. & Prather, M. E. (1992). Birth order and communicative characteristics of individuals. Paper presented at the International Communication Association Annual Meeting, Miami, FL (May).

Bracewell, R. J., Fredericksen, C. H. & Fredericksen, J. D. (1982). Cognitive processes in composing and comprehending discourse. *Education Psychologies*, **17**, 146–164.

Bradburn, N. M., Rips, L. J. & Shevell, S. K. (1987). Answering autobiographical questions: the impact of memory and inference on surveys. *Science, 236,* 157–161.

Brown, J. & Carlsen, R. (1955). Brown–Carlsen listening comprehension test. New York: Harcourt, Brace & World.

Brown, L. (1982). *Communicating facts and ideas in business.* Englewood Cliffs, NJ: Prentice-Hall.

Brown, M. H., Waldhart, E. S. & Bostrom, R. N. (1990). Differences in motivational level in listening tasks. In R. Bostrom (Ed.), *Listening behavior: measurement and applications.* New York: Guilford.

Buchli, V. & Pearce, W. (1974). Listening behavior in coorientational states. *Journal of Communication, 24,* 62–70.

Burgoon, J. (1994). Nonverbal signals. In M. Knapp & G. Miller (Eds), *Handbook of interpersonal communication,* 2nd edn. Beverly Hills, CA: Sage.

Burns, K. & Beier, E. (1973). Significance of vocal and visual channels in the decoding of emotional meaning. *Journal of Communication, 23,* 118–130.

Bussey, J. (1991). Question asking in an interview and varying listening skills. Paper delivered at the Annual Meeting of the Southern Communication Association, Tampa, Florida (April).

Chang, T. (1986). Semantic memory: facts and models. *Psychological Bulletin, 99,* 199–220.

Collins, A. & Quillian, M. (1972). Experiments on semantic memory and language comprehension. In L. Gregg (Ed.), *Cognition in learning and memory.* New York: Wiley.

Dawkins, R. (1998). *Unweaving the rainbow: science, delusion, and the appetite for wonder.* New York: Houghton Mifflin.

Dickens, M. & Williams, F. (1964). An experimental application of cloze procedure and attitude measures to listening comprehension. *Speech Monographs, 31,* 103–108.

Donohew, L., Nair, M. & Finn, S. (1984). Automaticity, arousal, and information exposure. In R. Bostrom (Ed.), *Communication Yearbook Eight.* Beverly Hills, CA: Sage.

Eisenberg, E. W. & Goodall, H. L. Jr (1993). *Organizational communication: balancing creativity and constraint.* New York: St Martin's Press.

Ernest, C. (1968). Listening comprehension as a function of type of material and rate of presentation. *Speech Monographs, 35,* 154–156.

ETS (Educational Testing Service) (1957). *Sequential tests of educational progress.* Princeton, NJ: Educational Testing Service.

ETS (Educational Testing Service) (1984). Test analysis: core battery. Unpublished statistical report, February. Princeton, NJ: Educational Testing Service.

Ewen, S. (1983). The implications of empiricism. *Journal of Communication, 33,* 219–225.

Festinger, L. (1957). *A theory of cognitive dissonance.* New York: Harper and Row.

Feinberg, S. E. & Tanur, J. M. (1989). Combining cognitive and statistical approaches to survey design. *Science, 243,* 1017–1022.

Fitch-Hauser, M. (1990). Making sense of data: constructs, schemas, and concepts. In R. Bostrom (Ed.), *Listening behavior: measurement and applications.* New York: Guilford.

Frandsen, K. (1963). Effects of threat appeals and media of transmission. *Speech Monographs*, *30*, 101–104.

Gardner, H. (1983). *Frames of mind: the theory of multiple intelligence*. New York: Basic Books.

Graber, D. A. (1988). *Processing the news*. New York: Longman.

Griffin, D. & Buehler, R. (1993). Role of construal processes in conformity and dissent. *Journal of Personality and Social Psychology*, *65*, 657–669.

Grimes, T. (1991). Mild auditory-visual dissonance in television news may exceed viewer attentional capacity. *Human Communication Research*, *18*, 268–209.

Gunter, B. (1987). *Poor reception: misunderstanding and forgetting broadcast news*. Hillsdale, NJ: Lawrence Erlbaum.

Hargie, O. & Dickson, D. (2004). *Skilled interpersonal communication: research, theory and practice*. London: Routledge.

Heen Wold, A. (1978). *Decoding oral language*. London: Academic Press.

Hirsch, R. (1987). *Cultural literacy*. New York: Houghton Mifflin.

Horowitz, R. & Samuels, S. J. (1987). *Comprehending oral and written language*. New York: Academic Press.

Hsia, H. (1968). Output, error, equivocation, and recalled information in auditory, visual, and audiovisual information processing with constant noise. *Journal of Communication*, *18*, 325–353.

Keely-Dyreson, M., Burgoon, J. & Bailey, W. (1991). The effects of stress and gender on noverbal decoding accuracy and vocalic channels. *Human Communication Research*, *17*, 584–605.

Kelly, C. (1965). An investigation of the construct validity of two commercially published listening tests. *Speech Monographs*, *32*, 139–143.

Kelly, C. (1967). Listening: a complex of activities or a unitary skill? *Speech Monographs*, *34*, 455–466.

Kintsch, W. (1980). Semantic memory: a tutorial. In R. S. Nickerson (Ed.), *Attention and performance VIII*. Hillsdale, NJ: Lawrence Erlbaum.

Kintsch, W. & Busche, H. (1969). Homophones and synonyms in short-term memory. *Journal of Experimental Psychology*, *80*, 403–407.

Klemmer, E. & Snyder, F. (1972). Measurement of time spent communicating. *Journal of Communication*, *22*, 142–158.

Klinzing, D. (1972). Listening comprehension of pre-school age children as a function of rate of presentation, sex and age. *Speech Teacher*, *21*, 86–92.

Knapp, M. (1984). *Interpersonal communication and human relationships*. Boston, MA: Allyn & Bacon.

Knapp, M. L., Miller, G. R. & Fudge, K. B. (1994). Basic concepts in interpersonal communication. In M. L. Knapp & G. R. Miller (Eds), *Handbook of interpersonal communication*, 2nd edn. Newbury Park, CA: Sage.

Krugman, P. (2003). *The great unraveling: losing our way in the twentieth century*. New York: W. W. Norton.

Leathers, D. (1979). The impact of multichannel message inconsistency on verbal and nonverbal decoding behaviors. *Communication Monographs*, *46*, 88–100.

Littlepage, G. E. & Pineault, M. A. (1981). Detection of truthful and deceptive interpersonal communications across information transmission modes. *Journal of Social Psychology*, *114*, 57–68.

Loftus, G. & Loftus, E. (1976). *Human memory: the processing of information.* New York: Wiley.

Luebke, S. W., Swygert, K. A., McLeod, L. D., Dalessandro, S. P. & Roussos, L. A. (2003). *LSAC skills analysis: Law School Task Survey.* Newtown, PA: Law School Admission Council.

Maslow, A. (1943). A theory of human motivation. *Psychological Review, 50*, 370–396.

Mayer, R. (1983). *Thinking, problem solving, and cognition.* San Francisco, CA: Freeman.

McClendon, P. (1958). An experimental study of the relationship between the notetaking practices and listening comprehension of college freshmen during expository lectures. *Speech Monographs, 25*, 222–228.

McCloskey, M. (1980). The stimulus familiarity problem in semantic memory research. *Journal of Verbal Learning and Verbal Behavior, 19*, 485–502.

Miller, R. W. (1987). *Fact and method.* Princeton, NJ: Princeton University Press.

Monsell, S. (1984). Components of working memory underlying verbal skills: a 'distributed capacities' view. In H. Bouma & D. G. Bowhuis (Eds), *Attention and performance*, vol. 10. Hillsdale, NJ: Lawrence Erlbaum.

Mosco, V. (1983). Critical research and the role of labor. *Journal of Communication, 33*, 237–248.

Motley, M. T. (1992). Mindfulness in solving communicator's dilemmas. Communication: inherently strategic and primarily automatic. *Communication Monographs, 59*, 306–314.

Myrdahl, G. (1967). *Objectivity in social research.* New York: Random House.

Newhagen, J. E. & Reeves, B. (1992). The evenings's bad news: the effects of compelling negative television news images on memory. *Journal of Communication, 42*, 25–41.

Nichols, R. (1947). Listening: questions and problems. *Quarterly Journal of Speech, 33*, 83–86.

Nichols, R. (1948). Factors in listening comprehension. *Speech Monographs, 15*, 154–163.

Palamatier, R. & McNinch, G. (1972). Source of gains in listening skill: experimental or pre-test experience. *Journal of Communication, 22*, 70–76.

Palmgreen, P. (1984). Uses and gratifications: a theoretical perspective. In R. Bostrom (Ed.), *Communication Yearbook Eight.* Beverly Hills, CA: Sage.

Pellegrino, J., Siegel, A. & Dhawan, M. (1975). Short term retention for pictures and words: evidence for dual coding systems. *Journal of Experimental Psychology, 104*, 95–101.

Petrie, C. & Carrell, S. (1976). The relationship of motivation, listening capacity, initial information, and verbal organizational ability to lecture comprehension and retention. *Communication Monographs, 43*, 184–187.

Pinker, S. (1994). *The language instinct: how the mind creates language.* New York: William Morrow.

Pinker, S. (1997). *How the mind works.* New York: W. W. Norton.

Pollock, D. & Cox, J. R. (1991). Historicizing 'reason': critical theory, practice and postmodernity. *Communication Monographs, 58*, 170–178.

Prather, M. E. (1991). Birth order and listening ability. Paper presented at the annual meeting of the Southern Speech Association, Tampa, FL (April).

Rankin, P. (1929). Listening ability. *Proceedings of the Ohio State Educational Conference*. Columbus, OH: Ohio State University Press.

Ray, E. B. & Bostrom, R. N. (1990). Listening to medical messages: the relationship of physican gender and patient gender to long- and short-term recall. In R. Bostrom, *Listening behavior: measurement and applications*. New York: Guilford.

Rogers, E. M. (1962). *Diffusion of information*. New York: Free Press.

Rossiter, C. (1972). Sex of the speaker, sex of the listener, and listening comprehension. *Journal of Communication, 22*, 64–69.

Schulman, H. (1972). Semantic confusion errors in short-term memory. *Journal of Verbal Learning and Verbal Behavior, 11*, 221–227.

Searle, B. H. & Bostrom, R. N. (1990). Encoding, media, affect and gender. In R. Bostrom, *Listening behavior: measurement and applications*. New York: Guilford.

Smith, M. J. (1982). Cognitive schema theory and the perseverance and attenuation of unwarranted empirical beliefs. *Communication Monographs, 42*, 116–126.

Spitzberg, B. & Hurt, T. (1983). *Essays on human communication*. Lexington, MA: Ginn.

Squire, L. (1986). Mechanisms of memory. *Science 232*, 1612–1619.

Stauffer, J., Frost, R. & Rybolt, W. (1983). The attention factor in recalling network news. *Journal of Communication, 33*, 29–37.

Steinhauer, J. (1995). Food labels don't change eating habits. *New York Times*, 10 May 1995, p. B1.

Sternberg, R. (1985). Human intelligence: the model is the message. *Science, 230*, 1111–1118.

Sticht, T. & Glassnap, D. (1972). Effects of speech rate, selection difficulty, association strength, and mental aptitude on learning by listening. *Journal of Communication, 22*, 174–178.

Streeter, L. A., Krauss, R. M., Geller, V., Olson, C. & Apple, W. (1977). Pitch changes during attempted deception. *Journal of Personality and Social Psychology, 35*, 345–350.

Sypher, B. D., Bostrom, R. N. & Seibert, J. H. (1989). Listening, communication abilities, and success at work. *Journal of Business Communication, 26*, 293–303.

Thain, J. W. (1994). Improving the mesaurement of language aptitude: the potential of the L1 measures. Paper presented at the Language Aptitude Improvement Symposium, Washington, DC (September).

Thomas, L. T. & Levine, T. R. (1994). Disentangling listening and verbal recall: related but separate constructs? *Human Communication Research, 21*, 103–127.

Thompson, E. (1967). Some effects of message structure on listener's comprehension. *Speech Monographs, 34*, 51–57.

Weaver, C. (1972). *Human listening: process and behavior*. Indianapolis, IN: Bobbs-Merrill.

Wiksell, W. (1946). The problem of listening. *Quarterly Journal of Speech, 32*, 505–508.

Wolvin, A. & Coakley, C. (1988). *Listening*, 3rd edn. Dubuque, IA: Brown.

Chapter 10

Humour and laughter

Hugh Foot and May McCreaddie

Humour is a source of power and healing and may be a key to survival.

(Gregg, 2002, p. 1)

W HEN THE FIRST EDITION of this handbook was published in 1986, the notion that humour and laughter might have beneficial effects on health, work, and personal life was only just starting to catch our imagination. Research was relatively sparse, and much of the subsequent upswing in professional interest in the use of or need for humour was a development based more upon an act of faith than on any substantial research evidence. Nevertheless, a stream of humour-related websites and programmes has emerged in recent years, extolling the virtues of humour and laughter and holding out the carrot of enhanced well-being and a healthy body and mind. One of the best known of these programmes was Robert Holden's Happiness Project, a series of workshops designed for health professionals and company managers, among others. This followed from his laughter clinics set up in the UK in 1991. As Mauger (2001) reports, there are now websites for those with phobias, panic attacks, and anxiety states which advise subscribers to 'laugh yourself calm'; and there is an on-line Laughter Therapy Centre, which offers guidance on how to put more laughter into your life, a sentiment shared by those in the Laughter Club Movement (Kataria, 2002). Patty Wooten (1992) developed the 'jest for the health of it' workshops for nurses with the aim of reducing burn-out or loss of caring. It is currently fashionable to appreciate the psychological benefits that humour can bring, but whether humour is an easy recipe or solution for self-help is still somewhat questionable.

Beyond doubt, humour is a very complex phenomenon involving cognitive, emotional, physiological, and social aspects (Martin, 2000, 2004). It is surprising neither that humour research has spilled over into fields of psychology such as personality, emotion, and motivation, nor that there is such a diverse range of conceptualisations of sense of humour. To many, however, the idea of humour as a communicative or social skill is still relatively novel, perhaps because we tend to think of it as a relatively stable expression of personality. Unless we are planning a career as a professional comedian, we tend not to think of humour as something that needs nurturance and cultivation.

The manner in which the exploitation of humour is occasionally catapulted into the public eye, however, can be breathtaking. In October 1995, the national press carried the story of British Airways' sudden 'discovery' that 'criticism softened by humour may be more effective than traditional forms of communication' (*The Guardian*, 12 October 1995). To implement this notion, BA had appointed a 'Corporate Jester' to stalk executive offices and tell top managers where they are going wrong while putting a smile on their faces at the same time. First-quarter profits were up by 57% according to *The Guardian*, but the Confederation of British Industry remained sceptical!

Part of the apparent ludicrousness of this venture is the implication that humour can be marshalled and deployed to order, without immediately losing any of the positive impact that it may have had. It might work once, but how can any beneficial effect possibly be sustained? There is a wide gulf in the potential effectiveness of humour which is spur of the moment, arising directly from the situation one is in, and humour that is rehearsed and carefully groomed to fit a particular occasion. Perhaps this is why there is a degree of discomfort in considering humour as a skill: a skill by its very nature is practised and studied; humour is spontaneous, fleeting, situation-specific, and so essentially frivolous and playful.

Much of the research on humour has occupied itself with explaining why we find jokes funny and why we are amused by certain episodes in real life. So the focus of attention has been primarily on the features or ingredients of the joke or episode which render it humorous. Rather less attention has been paid to the creation or production of humour, either in terms of the task facing the professional comedian in consciously constructing new jokes for a comedy show, or in terms of the ordinary individual deciding when or how to initiate humour in a social situation. Sometimes, we might argue, such a 'decision' to initiate humour is not under our conscious control; an amusing event occurs and quite spontaneously an apt comment or witticism 'pops out' which neatly captures the feeling of the moment. This is probably a naive view; with few exceptions, we are in control of what we say and we do 'initiate' humour in order to achieve some interpersonal goal.

Essentially, the distinction we are drawing here is that between the 'decoding' of humour – understanding the meaning of a joke that we have just read or heard – and the 'encoding' of humour – understanding how and when we use humour to convey a message to others. To consider humour and laughter as social skills, therefore, is to be concerned with encoding characteristics, the reasons why we initiate humour. The bulk of this chapter is devoted to the social uses to which humour and laughter are put.

Before we embark upon this analysis, some of the main humour theories are briefly summarised.

THEORIES OF HUMOUR AND LAUGHTER

There are probably well over 100 theories of humour, some quite narrowly focused and some more general in nature. However, it is recognised that no single theory of humour can ever do justice to the rich array of characterisations of humour. Researchers and theoreticians have even been somewhat reluctant to define humour and laughter. Most have chosen to emphasise some particular elements, such as incongruity or surprise, as necessary prerequisites for a stimulus to appear humorous. Most of the theories address the question of humour appreciation and the outcome of our responses to humour rather than dealing with our motivation for encoding humour.

Historical conceptions of humour and laughter and problems of definition have been outlined in more detail in Goldstein and McGhee (1972), Chapman and Foot (1976), and McGhee (1979). Broadly, humour theories fall into four main groups.

Incongruity and developmental theories of humour

These theories stress the absurd, the unexpected, and the inappropriate or out-of-context events as the basis for humour. While these incongruities are necessary, they are not sufficient prerequisites for humour alone (McGhee, 1979). After all, incongruous events or statements can lead to curiosity or anxiety rather than to humour; so the perception of humour is dependent upon how the incongruity is understood in the context in which it occurs. Suls (1972) suggested that not only does an incongruity have to be perceived for humour to be experienced, but it has to be resolved or explained. Rothbart (1976), on the other had, proposed that the incongruity itself is sufficient to evoke humour as long as it is perceived in a joking or playful context. And, of course, the same ludicrous idea can continue to evoke merriment long after the surprise has gone.

This debate has proved exceptionally fertile ground for cognitive investigations. McGhee (1979) carried the debate forward by interpreting 'resolution' as the need to exercise 'cognitive mastery', without which the incongruity cannot be accepted and used in the humour context. He has proposed a developmental-stage approach which maps out the types of incongruity understood by children across the stages of their increasing cognitive development. For example, the child first recognises incongruity when making pretend actions with an absent object, based upon an internal image of that object. Then the child learns the fun of deliberately giving incongruous labels to objects: 'girls' may be called 'boys'; 'cats' may be called 'dogs'. Later come more subtle forms of incongruity such as endowing animals with human characteristics ('the dog is talking to me') and learning that words and phrases may have multiple meaning (puns and riddles).

Forabosco (1992, p. 60) has extended the cognitive model to show that mastery involves understanding the cognitive rule and identifying both aspects of congruity and incongruity with that rule:

> There is therefore a succession (diachronicity) of incongruity–congruence configurations that terminates in a contemporaneousness (synchronicity) of

incongruity/congruence. What is more, typical of the final act in the process is an attention-shift situation in which the subject passes from the perception of congruence to the perception of incongruity and, sometimes, vice versa, with several shifts.

Seen from this perspective, both the perception of the incongruity and its resolution are essential components for the humour process.

Ruch and Hehl (1986) argued that we should not look for a general model of humour but rather just accept that there are at least two kinds of humour, one in which the solubility of the incongruity is important (e.g. congruous build-up to an unexpected and cognitively incongruent punchline) and one in which the incongruity alone is sufficient (e.g. nonsense or absurd jokes). Research suggests that preference for these major dimensions of humour correlates with personality variables such as conservatism (Ruch, 1984).

Superiority and disparagement theories of humour

These theories have a tradition going back at least three centuries to the work of the philosopher Thomas Hobbes (1588–1679), and for some they are the the key to humour (Gruner, 1997). They are based upon the notion that humour stems from the observations of others' infirmities or failures. Hobbes spoke of 'sudden glory' as the passion which induces laughter at the afflictions of other people, and it results from favourable comparison of ourselves with these others. So, at one level, for example, we find it amusing when our companion slips on a banana skin; at another level, we take delight in the downfall of our enemies. Zillmann and Cantor (1976) and Zillmann (1983) proposed a 'dispositional' view that humour appreciation varies inversely with the favourableness of the disposition toward the person or object being disparaged. In other words, the less well disposed we are toward someone, the more humorous we find jokes or stories in which that person is the butt or victim. The source of the disparagement is also important; we are highly amused when our friends humiliate our enemies but much less amused when our enemies get the upper hand over our friends. These ideas relate very much to jokes and humour involving social, national, ethnic, and religious groupings with which we personally identify.

What is interesting, as Ruch and Hehl (1986) pointed out, is that this model works well in predicting the behaviour of groups which believe they are traditionally 'superior': for example, men appreciate jokes in which women are disparaged but show less appreciation for jokes in which a woman disparages a man. However, 'inferior' group members are no more amused at jokes which disparage a man than at jokes disparaging a member of their own sex. Indeed, sometimes the inferior groups laugh more at jokes putting down a member of their own group. Clearly, some moderating variables are at work here. From their factor analytic studies, Ruch and Hehl (1986) suggest that the personality dimensions of conservatism and tough-mindedness are conjointly associated with enjoyment of disparagement humour. This does not say much for the humour of men, who are more likely to score higher on these scales than women. Tough conservatives (chauvinistic, ethnocentric, and authoritarian) appreciate disparagement jokes directed at outside groups but tender-minded liberals do not.

Authoritarians tend to be preoccupied with power relationships, the strengthening of in-group bonds, and feeling of superiority over the weak or out-group members (Adorno, Frenkel-Brunswick, Levinson & Sanford, 1950). One might, however, question their sense of humour. Perhaps those who enjoy disparagement humour are singularly lacking in appreciation of other kinds of humour. We certainly might expect this if, as Allport (1954) claimed, sense of humour and ability to laugh at oneself are a clear measure of self-insight.

Arousal theories of humour

A number of theories suggest that the most important qualities of humour operate at a physiological level. These theories assume that the initiation of humour brings about measurable arousal changes, which directly influence the experience of amusement. Berlyne (1972) has linked humour with fluctuations in arousal in two ways: first, humour is associated with the reduction of high arousal; second, it is associated with moderate increases in arousal followed by a sudden drop. This 'arousal boost-jag', as he terms it, accounts for the pleasure derived from many jokes. The build-up to the joke is moderately arousing in that it attracts attention (for example, the audience latches on to the fact that a joke is being told and becomes attentive). The joke may be additionally stimulating by virtue of having a sexual, aggressive, or anxiety-arousing theme, or it may be intellectually arousing. The punchline comes when the audience is suitably aroused and seeking a resolution to the joke; timing can be crucial here. The resolution produces a rapid dissipation of arousal frequently associated with laughter. The build-up and subsequent dissipation of arousal are rewarding and pleasurable, and produce the experience of amusement. An important aspect of Berlyne's position is his belief that there is a curvilinear relationship between arousal level and amount of pleasure experienced: that is, moderate levels of arousal are more enjoyable than either very low or very high levels.

Arousal theories of laughter also feature in explanations of certain kinds of non-humorous laughter. For example, *nervous laughter* occurs in states of tension after periods of shock and fright or acute embarrassment; more extreme *hysterical laughter* is conceived of as a psychogenic disorder (Pfeifer, 1994) and is often exhibited cyclically with weeping, possibly shouting, in an uncontrolled outburst after periods of intense stress or prolonged deprivation of some kind. Laughter through arousal can also be easily induced by tactile stimulation, normally *reflexive laughter*, rather than involving any cognitive process. Tickling is a more complicated kind of stimulus because the desired response may be achieved only when a mood of fun, compliance, or self-abandonment is already operating. If unexpected, or in the wrong company or environment, tickling can be a very aversive stimulus and elicits an aggressive response.

Psychoanalytic and evolutionary theories of humour

Freud's (1928, 1938) view of the function of humour is akin to his view of dreaming, namely, that they both serve to regulate sexual and aggressive desires. Humour is the outcome of repressed sexual and aggressive wishes, which have been pushed into the unconscious due to society's prohibition of their expression. Wit and humour are not forbidden; indeed, they may be socially valued and therefore present an acceptable outlet for such repressed feelings. The process of repression, according to Freud, involves the use of 'psychic energy', which is saved once the joke has been emitted; thus, repression is no longer necessary. The experience of humour and laughter flows directly from the saving of psychic energy whose repressive function is (momentarily) relaxed.

Freud's theory shares with arousal theory the basic view that humour serves a physical as well as a psychological function by manipulating arousal or the level of felt tension. The well-known criticism that psychoanalytic theory is rarely amenable to scientific investigation does not debase the insights and ideas that the theory has generated.

Another psychodynamic view has been expressed by Bokun (1986), who has linked humour with our over-serious construction of the world. This view stresses the need for humour as a means of offering us a more realistic vision of ourselves and the world around us, stripped of all our self-imposed fears, frustrations, and suffering. Having a sense of humour, therefore, provides us with the ability to cope with the trials and tribulations of everyday life.

Freud's ideas represent one strand of what are more widely referred to as evolutionary or biological theories of humour, in which laughter is viewed as an adaptive response with an early onset. Just as play has evolved to allow children to rehearse and develop the practical and social skills they will need as adults, so humour has evolved to allow rehearsal of more abstract cognitive skills (McGhee, 1979). Laughter is also a release from the inevitable tensions of daily life and permits the flights of imagination that lead to innovations and ways of coping (Christie, 1994). It is adaptive because it can operate as a circuit-breaker, momentarily disabling people and preventing them from continuing with misguided behaviour patterns (Chafe, 1987).

OUR SOCIAL EXPERIENCE OF HUMOUR AND LAUGHTER

As Norrick (1993, p. 1) put it, 'Everyday conversation thrives on wordplay, sarcasm, anecdotes, and jokes. Certainly these forms of humor enliven conversation, but they also help us break the ice, fill uncomfortable pauses, negotiate requests for favors and build group solidarity.'

Above all else, humour is an essentially shared experience. While, on solitary occasions, we may savour a joke or funny incident which we remember, or may laugh privately at a funny sketch on television, our appreciation of humour is expressed much more expansively in company. Among research participants, Provine and Fischer (1989) reported 30 times more emissions of laughter in social than in solitary settings. In social situations, there are few more useful social skills than humour, and there are probably no contexts, however dire, in which humour is not a potentially appropriate response. Throughout history, the more frequently remembered and oft-quoted last remarks of those waiting to be led to the gallows are their rueful witticisms about their fate, society, humankind, or life after death. There is humour in chronic sickness and adversity; humour about old age, adolescence and puberty, aggression and war, sex, love, and marriage. The most formidable and powerful feature of humour as a source of social influence is its inherent ambiguity (Kane, Suls & Tedeschi, 1977). We can use humour to communicate a message that we mean; we can use it to communicate the opposite of what we mean. Because humour is playful and can be interpreted in several different ways at the same time, we can retract our message at any time, if it suits us. According to the reaction of our audience and the impression we wish to create, we can choose, through the use of humour, whether to claim or disclaim responsibility for our message or action.

The idea that humour can be interpreted in several different ways reflects our everyday experience of it; it has also been empirically supported. In a politically somewhat dated study by Suls and Miller (1976), a male speaker's joke about 'women's libbers' was interpreted entirely from the reaction of his audience. If the audience consisted of a group of liberated women who laughed at his joke, the speaker was attributed with liberated views and as one who did not agree with the content of the joke. If the same group glared at him, he was seen as chauvinistic. Thus, the response of the audience is taken as evidence of whether the speaker is merely teasing or in deadly earnest.

Hostile reactions to sarcastic humour can, of course, be readily countered by the reply, 'Can't you take a joke?' Then, not only does the aggrieved party suffer from the affront to his or her own attitudes, knowledge, or self-image provoked by the original joke, but also has matters made worse by virtue of appearing humourless. The only satisfactory way of parrying humour of which one is the target may be to retaliate with humour, but, too often, the moment is past and the opportunity lost.

Although the mechanics of encoding humour are poorly understood, and there are wide individual differences, a variety of motives can be identified quite easily for our skilled use of humour and laughter. We shall now review what these motives are.

Humour as a search for information

Social probing

A common objective in social interaction, especially when striking up conversations with comparative strangers, is to discover what attitudes, motives, and values the other individual possesses. Standards of propriety may prohibit us from directly asking their views on certain issues and, in any case, we may not initially want to engage in a detailed conversation about politics, religion, or anything else which direct questioning may commit us to. Introducing a topic in a light-hearted way helps to probe indirectly the other person's general attitudes and values about an issue and to reveal 'touchy' subjects. We can take our cue in pursuing or changing the topic of conversation from the other person's response. Whether or not the humour is reciprocated may determine whether the discussion becomes more personal and intimate and whether the relationship moves forward.

Social acceptance

In addition to probing for information about others, we may also be interested in finding out how others respond to us. Telling jokes is a way not only of drawing attention to ourselves but of gauging others' acceptance of us and disposition toward us. It is their response to our humour that provides the social barometer by which we assess our popularity or lack of it. This constitutes a reason for encoding humour and is not to be confused with social laughter, whose primary function is to win social approval.

Humour as a means of giving information

Self-disclosure

Humour may often be used as a vehicle for conveying to others our motives and intentions, and it is especially useful when we wish to intimate feelings that we might not normally wish to reveal publicly: for example, fears about imminent hazards and anxieties about forthcoming ordeals. The use of humour can, of course, offset the embarrassment of revealing highly personal information (Bloch, 1987). Humour may also convey fairly explicit sexual interest in our companion in a light-hearted and socially acceptable way which is easily revoked or shrugged off if the message is not reciprocated. Of course, such 'humour' can become excessive and may reach the proportions of sexual harassment if carried too far.

Humour used as a tactic to disclose sexual interest was demonstrated in a study by Davis and Farina (1970). Male subjects were asked to rate the funniness of a series of sexual and aggressive jokes in front of either a rather plain female experimenter or in front of the same experimenter made up to be sexually attractive and provocative. The ratings were made privately on paper and pencil scales by half the subjects but reported orally to the experimenter by the other half. The sex jokes were rated as funniest by those subjects who made their ratings orally to the sexually attractive experimenter. Davis and Farina took this to indicate that the male subjects wanted the experimenter to know that they enjoyed sex and were sexually attracted to her. It could be argued further that self-disclosure is not an end in itself but a means of trying to elicit reciprocated feelings or interest by others, so it serves to obtain information as well as give it (see Chapter 8 for further discussion of self-disclosure).

Self-presentation

Humour is an expression of character in times of adversity or stress. A humorous perspective on one's problems allows one to distance oneself from them, to take them less seriously, and thereby to experience them as less distressing or threatening. Martin (1989) has hypothesised that humour may reduce stress by means of several different processes, including appraisal-focused, emotion-focused, and problem-focused coping. Lefcourt and Martin (1986) have demonstrated that sense of humour moderates the relation between stressful life events and mood disturbance. Individuals with a low sense of humour typically experience greater upset (mood disturbance) during high levels of stress than individuals with a high sense of humour. Sense of humour is, therefore, related to more positive self-esteem and more realistic standards for evaluation of self-worth. Putting on a brave face and being 'seen to cope' also sustains the image of ourselves which we wish to maintain to the outside world.

Denial of serious intent

Kane et al. (1977, p. 14) referred to this function of humour as 'decommitment', whereby, 'When a person faces failure, a false identity is about to be unmasked, an inappropriate behaviour is discovered or a lie uncovered, he or she may attempt to save the situation by indicating that the proposed or past action was not serious, but was instead meant as a joke.' Recourse to humour, then, is self-serving: a way of backing down without injury in the event of having our credibility or motives challenged. A serious confrontation, or one in which our actions or intentions are likely to be maligned, can be converted into jocular repartee, by which we admit we were jesting all the time.

Unmasking hypocrisy

Another information-giving function of humour is when we use ridicule or sarcasm to show that we do not believe the ostensible motivation for someone's behaviour. Political cartoons are rife with examples of satirists' attempts to highlight what they believe to be the essential motivation for the actions or pronouncements of a prestigious political figure or the absurdity of professional pretensions, privileges of class, or institutional rules. At an interpersonal level, our jest at the expense of other people may serve as a gentle hint that we do not accept the image of themselves that they are projecting; for example, the eager and overearnest trainee doctor presenting an identity as an experienced and competent expert on a medical symptom.

Humour in interpersonal control

Expression of liking and affiliation

Humour is valued as a social asset and, exercised judiciously, confers upon its encoder the animated interest and welcoming approval of others. Sharing humour fosters rapport and intimacy and promotes friendship by showing common sentiment and reducing tensions. As a basis for developing friendship and attraction, therefore, humour signals three affective ingredients of its encoder: first, as a jovial person who is rewarding and fun to be with; second, as a sensitive person who has a friendly interest and willingness to enter relationships with others; and third, as one who seeks, and probably wins, the social approval of others (or likes to be liked). Mettee, Hrelec, and Wilkens (1971) found that a job candidate giving a short lecture was rated as more likeable by an audience when he used humour.

Expression of dislike and hostility

We have already seen under the heading 'Unmasking hypocrisy' that humour can be used to inform others that we do not accept the image of themselves that they are trying to project. In a more general manner, humour is one way, possibly the only socially acceptable way, of expressing personal antagonism. We are inclined to enjoy cruel forms of humour, obtaining amusement from incompetence and deformity, and from the oddities and incongruities of others' behaviour. On the one hand, we may not be able, on occasion, to conceal our amusement at the faux pas of our friends; our suppressed aggression leads us to savour their little defeats with gentle relish. On the other hand, against those we do not like, our ridicule and amusement at their undoing may be out of proportion to their defeat; we revel in their downfall out of the feeling of superiority that it gives.

Among social equals and friends, the use of reciprocal sarcasm and derision may constitute a normal and regular feature of their interactive style. Indeed, what may appear to an outsider as a hostile slanging match may seem playful bantering to the participants. Those with power and authority may avoid being cast as figures of fun to their face but may frequently be the butt of ribald laughter and ridicule behind their backs. In group situations, an individual can be unjustly selected (scapegoated) as a target of repeated aggressive humour.

Controlling social interaction

Humour, like laughter, helps to maintain the flow of interaction in daily encounters, 'filling in pauses in our conversations and maintaining the interest and attention of our conversational partner' (Foot & Chapman, 1976, p. 188). In terms of sheer social expediency, therefore, the motive in encoding humour may be little more than to create and sustain a congenial atmosphere, as when breaking the ice at a party. Humour helps to regulate interactions and serves as a social mechanism to facilitate or inhibit the flow of conversation (LaGaipa, 1977). Hostile wit within a group, for example, may dampen the social interaction or the tempo of conversation because it threatens the cohesiveness of the group.

Humour also provides a smooth and acceptable means of changing the level or direction of a conversation. It provides spontaneous comic relief in the context of a turgid or boring conversation and draws attention away from a topic of conversation which one of the participants does not wish to pursue. It also helps to indicate to others that they are taking things too seriously and need to look at their problems from a more detached or balanced perspective. As will be illustrated later, this is a particularly useful tactic in psychotherapy when the patient is over-anxious and completely bound up with personal problems.

Ingratiation

While humour can be used to win from others approval that is genuinely sought and valued for no other motive than friendship, it can also be employed to capture the approval of others from whom favours are sought or who happen to be in powerful positions. The humour may be self- or other-enhancing, or it may be self-disparaging as a tactic to express a submissive, dependent posture (Wilson, 1979). The risk with ingratiation humour is always that its insincerity will be revealed.

Humour as a device for group control

Intragroup control

Studies of group process and of emergent leadership have frequently revealed two types of process that need to be operative if a group is to be effective in its task (Bales, 1950, 1958). One process, unsurprisingly, relates to task-relevant variables such as ensuring that the group gathers relevant information, examines appropriate views, and directs itself toward a solution. The second process is related to the maintenance of the cohesion and well-being of the group ('socio-emotional' process is Bales' term). Sometimes, these functions are channelled through one leader within the group; sometimes through two or more group members. Basically, if the group is to 'survive' intact as a group, it needs safe outlets by which to express its feelings, sustain its morale, and deal with internal conflicts. Humour has an important role to play in this process. Yalom (1985) and Bloch and Crouch (1985) have identified humour as one important factor which gives group members a sense of belonging and acceptance and fosters caring and mutual support. Within a group context humour can also be used to reinterpret or reframe distressing events to preserve or re-establish feelings of perspective and safety (Mauger, 2001).

Building on the earlier work of Middleton and Moland (1959), Martineau (1972) provided a model of the intragroup processes that humour serves, based upon how the humour is judged by the members of the group. It is, of course, within such a group context that in-group jokes can thrive, often barely understood by others outside the group. As LaGaipa (1977, p. 421) says, 'Jocular gripes require some common experiences. Teasing requires knowledge about the butt of the joke and an acceptance and accurate perception of intent. Hostile wit is often not expressed unless the group has achieved a level of cohesiveness able to tolerate it ... situational jokes are likely to reflect the dynamics underlying the social interactions at any given point in time.'

According to Martineau, when the humour is judged as esteeming the in-group, it functions to galvanise the group. When it is judged as disparaging the in-group, it may still serve positively to solidify the group (for example, the football coach using sarcasm to motivate his players against imminent defeat) or to control group members who step out of line. But disparagement may also provoke demoralisation, conflict within the group, and ultimately the disintegration of the group.

Intergroup control

Martineau's model also addresses itself to the effects of humour upon the in-group when that humour emanates from a member or members of an out-group. Zillmann and Cantor (1976) have stressed that hostile or derogatory jokes are least appreciated when they attack ourselves or group members whom we like or with whom we identify. And one reason for humorous disparagement in the first place is to bring about dissension in the out-group. An ethnic in-group, for example, will use anti-out-group humour not only to express hostility against that out-group, and in an attempt to undermine the morale of its members, but also to strengthen the morale and solidarity of its own members (Bourhis, Godfield, Giles & Tajfel, 1977).

Anti-out-group humour can, therefore, be a creative and effective way of asserting in-group pride and distinctiveness from a dominant out-group. But it cuts both ways because hostile humour directed at the in-group from an out-group may also tend to produce greater consensus and cohesion on the part of the in-group members as they close ranks to meet and challenge the implied threat to their position. Intergroup disparagement and hostile wit, therefore, serve only to increase the tension and conflict between the groups, and they are tactics used the world over in parliamentary wrangling, professional disputes, industrial strife, and international gamesmanship.

Anxiety management

Saving face

Humour offers a path to control and restraint in more tense interpersonal encounters. An individual encodes humour, for example, to defuse a tense or hostile situation prevailing between two other interactors, thus enabling the contesting parties to back off from the confrontation without loss of face. At the very least, such humour may make it difficult for the parties to continue their altercation without incurring the wrath or scorn of other bystanders. The humour serves both as a corrective to restore the normal boundaries of social etiquette, and an admonition that the argument has gone quite far enough.

Coping with embarrassment

Humour is invoked as a control to restore composure and self-presentation on occasions when they are undermined by some sudden and perhaps unexpected event – for example, being caught out in a lie. More commonly, we are embarrassed by some little accident which spoils the image we wish to convey at that particular moment: the elegantly dressed lady at a formal dinner party tripping on the carpet as she is about to be presented to her fellow guests, the spilling of a drink down someone else's clothes, or some clumsy or unscripted act by a well-known politician or television personality that becomes typical subject matter for satirical television programmes. Joking is about the only way to save the situation, treating the event as a trivial one, merely an accident that could have happened to anyone.

Safety valve for under- and over-arousal

Humour has already been suggested as a mechanism of social control inasmuch as it brings comic relief to a boring conversation or relieves the tedium of an uneventful activity such as waiting for a bus or queuing for an exhibition. On the other side of the coin, humour can help to reduce unwanted and unpleasantly high levels of anxiety and stress. Laughter, according to Berlyne's (1969) arousal theory of humour, results from the tension release that follows heightened arousal, albeit pleasant arousal, such as that created by the build-up of a joke before the punchline. It may be that the impetus for encoding humour in times of anxiety stems from anticipation of the release of tension which dissipates pleasurably through laughter. Perhaps doctors and dentists could help to alleviate their patients' anxieties before the consultation by the liberal provision of humorous literature and cartoons in their waiting rooms! Some do, of course.

But solitary amusement may not be the answer here. In stressful situations, sharing humour with a fellow sufferer may be a more potent way of dissipating unwanted anxiety. The pleasurable experience of mutually appreciating a joke may establish rapport and reduce concern over one's own plight. Laughing with people is compassionate; laughing at them is immoral (Mauger, 2001).

Humour may be experienced as a direct consequence of realising that one is safe after a threatening stimulus has been removed (Rothbart, 1973, 1976). Shurcliff (1968) varied the level of anxiety in three groups of college students. In the low-anxiety group, the students were told they would be asked to pick up a docile white rat and hold it for 5 seconds. In the moderate- and high-anxiety groups, students were asked to take a blood sample from a white rat. In the moderate-anxiety condition, a small sample only was requested and the students were told it would be an easy task. In the high-anxiety condition, the students were asked to remove 2 cc of blood from a rat that might be expected to bite through their glove. Having then discovered that the rat they were given was only a toy, the students were asked to rate how funny this trick was to them. Of the three groups, students in the high-anxiety condition found the trick most amusing. Shurcliff attributes this to their greater sense of sudden relief at realising that they were completely safe from a potentially harmful situation. He does not comment on their annoyance about the deception.

Humour as a means of changing and sustaining the status quo

Freedom from conventional thought

Writers and social commentators have waxed lyrical about the emancipating power of humour. Mindess' book *Laughter and Liberation* (1971) outlines and illustrates all the many ways in which humour frees us from the shackles of our mundane daily lives. Humour is an escape; as Mindess put it, 'In the most fundamental sense, it (humour) offers us release from our stabilising systems, escape from our self-imposed prisons. Every instance of laughter is an instance of liberation from our controls' (p. 23).

It is also a frame of mind which transcends both reality and fantasy. It frees us from moral inhibitions, from the constraints of language, from rationality, and from a sense of inferiority and feelings of inadequacy. It is a guilt-free release from frustration and aggression.

This perspective accords with Freud's (1938) view that humour and laughter occur when repressed energy, which normally keeps one's thoughts channelled in socially prescribed and rational directions, is momentarily freed from its static function of keeping something forbidden away from consciousness. A witticism starts with an aggressive tendency or intent that is repressed. The aggressive intentions are manipulated and disguised in the unconscious mind with 'playful pleasure repressed since childhood and waiting for a chance to be satisfied' (Grotjahn, 1957, p. 256). The thoughts emerge into consciousness when they are socially acceptable and the energy originally activated to keep the hostility under repression is freed. By this time, the repressed energy is no longer needed and the shock of this freedom from repression spills out in pleasure and laughter.

Joking, therefore, may be seen as a revolt against the structure of society. It may not, in practical terms, bring about much change in the world, but it is enjoyable for its own sake in making the unthinkable thinkable.

The reinforcement of stereotypes

While this freedom of thought may be characteristic of the way humour is used to perceive and experience life, it is paradoxical but also true that, in its overt expression, humour serves to sustain and reinforce narrow-minded attitudes and blinkered vision within society. Wilson (1979) put his finger on the same point when he wrote, 'Joking is a powerful conservative. Its effects reinforce existing ideology, power, status, morality and values within a society' (p. 230). So much of the content of our humour concerns human weakness and foolishness that if we were freed from ignorance, inhibitions, fear, and prejudice there would be little room left for humour: 'though jokes feed on subversive thought, on deviations from the normal and expected, they reinforce established views of the world. Though their content appears to undermine norms, mores, established power and authority, jokes are potent in preserving that status quo' (Wilson, 1979, p. 228).

In the present authors' view, the power of humour in perpetuating myths and reinforcing stereotyped and traditional attitudes is greatly under-estimated. How else, except through humour, do we derive our stereotyped views about the Irish, the English, the Scots, the Welsh, the Latin-American temperament, Protestants, Jews, and Catholics? Because the joke is a socially acceptable form, the message it conveys is extremely powerful and the recipient or target, however much offended, can scarcely denounce it without standing accused of the greatest crime of all – lacking a sense of humour. While real institutional changes have been taking place in the outside world through legal and social reform in relation to, say, homosexuality, equal pay, and equal opportunities, the old attitudes about 'poofs' and 'women's libbers' still remain enshrined in jokes which can span a generation and may still be as popular as ever, even though usually disguised or suppressed under the veil of 'political correctness'.

We are undoubtedly caught in a cleft stick. In an ironic way, as Husband (1977) pointed out in relation to racial humour in the mass media, such humour reinforces existing prejudice and yet its mere usage sustains the mythology of our national tolerance, since racial jokes are supposed to be characteristic of a tolerant society.

THE SOCIAL FUNCTIONS OF LAUGHTER

Although the foregoing section outlined different sources of motivation for encoding *humour*, it offers little guidance about the functions of *laughter* as social skill. The reasons for laughing may have nothing whatever to do with humour, and it may occur in situations where nothing humorous has actually happened. Pfeifer (1994, p. 170) expresses this rather aptly:

> One of the interesting things about laughter is that it's a 'middle range' behavior, in the sense that it falls between such physiologically determined behavior as blinking on the one hand and such culturally determined behavior as language on the other. We sometimes laugh at nothing, or else laugh at something, but for no particular reason. That's more or less at the level of what a dog does when it's barking.

Of course, laughter itself may be a response to a situation in which a cognitive failure has occurred and where the individual is at a loss to know how to respond. This is not to deny that, on many occasions, humour and laughter may function as displays of the same social purpose: we may well be laughing as we encode humour.

McGhee (1977) drew particular attention to the problem of low intercorrelation between funniness ratings and laughter (or smiling) and suggested that researchers should use both measures as dependent variables in their studies. He also suggested that they report the correlation obtained between these measures to provide a database from which hypotheses can be made concerning factors which will influence the relationship between expressive and intellectual measures of appreciation. Ruch (1990) has proposed that exhilaration is a consistent emotion elicited by humour and that this accounts for the behavioural, physiological, and experiential changes typically occurring in response to some non-humorous (e.g. tickling) as well as humorous stimuli. Ruch (1995) has also shown that correlation size may be a methodological artefact: for example, within-subject designs tend to yield higher correlations than between-subject designs.

To understand laughter, one must enquire into the situational context from which it emerges. In her book *Laughter: A Socio-Scientific Analysis*, Hertzler (1970) made the useful point about the function of laughter in society that it is an economical aid ('almost a gift') in getting things done. It is a quick, spontaneous reaction to the immediate situation which, often because it is not subject to the normal controls of deliberate speech, gives away directly the perpetrator's thoughts, feelings, or desires: 'A good laugh may contribute more than vocal or written admonitions or commands; it may be easier, cheaper, and more successful than laws and ordinances, police and supervisors, hierarchical chains of command, or other regulative and operative personnel and organisational machinery' (Hertzler, 1970, p. 86).

This is not to signify that laughter is not regulated by conscious control. There would be little point considering it as a social skill if it were entirely outside one's control. As in the case of most other habitual behaviours, we have each developed our own particular style of expressing ourselves: for some, laughter is free-flowing and virtually automatic; for others, it is a scarce commodity, reserved for a more limited range of social occasions.

Attempts to distinguish between different functions of laughter based upon the physical characteristics of laughs (for example, their intensity or amplitude) have generally failed, although small effects from measures of laughter duration have sometimes been reported. For example, LaGaipa (1977) found that hostile wit directed toward an out-group generated longer laughter than either teasing or 'jocular gripes', whereas laughter lasted longer when teasing an in-group member than when teasing an out-group member.

Within everyday language, one talks about laughs as being 'hollow', 'forced', 'mocking', 'bubbling', and so on, as if they possessed characteristic attributes which were uniquely disparate. There is also a rich vocabulary by which to denote types of laughter – giggle, titter, chortle, guffaw, cackle, roar, crow, snigger, and jeer – a fact that also gives substance to the view that there are many types of laughter which qualitatively differ from each other. No one would deny this. What humour researchers have failed to show is any systematic correlation between particular types of social situations and particular types of laughter. So when an individual displays incompetence in front of others, audience reaction is just as likely to consist of raucous guffaws as a quiet chuckle or a restrained snigger. The interpretation of what the laugh means, therefore, comes from the participants' understanding of the social situation they are in, and not from any inherent characteristics of the laugh itself.

The functions and purposes of laughter have been reviewed at length by Gruner (1978) and Hertzler (1970). Giles and Oxford (1970), Foot and Chapman (1976), and Pfeifer (1994) have summarised these functions. For the purposes of this social skills analysis, it is important to recognise that laughter is wholly a social phenomenon. As Hertzler (1970) pointed out, it is 'social in its origin, in its processual occurrence, in its functions and in its effects' (p. 28). Let us briefly outline these functions here.

Humorous laughter

Following Giles and Oxford's (1970) analysis, humorous laughter may be regarded as an overt expression of rebellion against social pressures, codes, and institutions. Continually conforming to such social constraints places an insufferable limitation on individual freedom, causing an accumulation of frustration, which, in turn, is perfectly displaced through humorous laughter. Such laughter is, of course, very responsive to social facilitation effects, and the frequency and amplitude of its emission is governed by the responsiveness of those around us (Chapman, 1973, 1974, 1975; Chapman & Chapman, 1974; Chapman & Wright, 1976).

Social laughter

Social laughter serves the primary purpose of expressing friendship and liking, of gaining social approval, and of bolstering group cohesiveness. This function of laughter for integrating ourselves within a particular group does not depend upon the individual's having experienced anything amusing, and, far from expressing rebellion against social pressures, it can be viewed as an act of social conformity, fulfilling normative group expectations. It is more intended to convey an image of good-natured 'sociability'. Possibly as much as humour, social laughter is used for controlling conversations and 'oiling the wheels' of social interaction, as through polite laughter when we laugh at what others have said, not because we find it funny but out of consideration for them.

Ignorance laughter

This type of laughter implies both the presence of humour stimuli and the presence of others. Typically, we recognise that a joke has been told but wish to conceal our ignorance or inability to comprehend it. So we laugh along with everyone else in the group in order not to be left out or not to look stupid. Ignorance laughter is also a version of imitative or feigned laughter as described by Pfeifer (1994).

Evasion laughter

In an important way, laughter, like humour, may serve as an emotional mask behind which to hide our true feelings. If a friend or acquaintance of ours is being attacked or ridiculed by others behind their back, we have a choice to defend our friend or, out of expediency, go through the motions of joining in the ridicule in order not to appear different. Laughter gives the impression of sharing in the prevailing feeling of the group. Embarrassment laughter is another example of masking our feelings or of a circuit-breaker to stall for time. We laugh because we are not quite sure what the other person's comments to us mean, or whether his or her intentions toward us are amicable or hostile.

Apologetic laughter

Related to embarrassment laughter and laughter designed to mask our feelings is apologetic or defensive laughter. This may precede an action on our part, the outcome of which we are uncertain about. We sometimes say, 'I've never done this before' or 'I can't guarantee what's going to happen' when we embark upon a novel task. Laughter may either accompany or substitute for the oral statement, and its meaning is clear. We are paving the way for possible failure or for making ourselves look foolish and thereby preparing the audience to believe that we are not taking the situation too seriously ourselves. We may also preface the telling of bad news with laughter, perhaps partly in an attempt to soften the blow and partly by way of apologising for being the one to announce it.

Anxiety laughter

Tension in social encounters stems from anxiety as well as from embarrassment, and anxiety laughter is a manifestation of tension release to a specific anxiety-provoking situation. Such laughter may be provoked directly by the feeling of relief when a period of acute tension comes to an end. To cite an extreme example, the hostages from a hijacked aircraft may, when suddenly freed, break down in laughter (often alternating with weeping) bordering on the hysterical at the sheer relief that they are safe and the crisis has passed. Rothbart (1976) has noted the close relation between laughter and fear in young children and has argued that laughter is a consequence of the child's realisation of being safe again, the moment the fear or distress is over.

Derision laughter

Derision laugher (also referred to as sinister, sarcastic, mocking, or acerbic laughter) is another category of laughter that is obviously an alternative, or an additive, to the encoding of hostile humour in situations where one wishes to express superiority to another. It is particularly prevalent among children whose laughter may be deliberately cruel or mocking, as in the face of another child's physical or mental deformity, or stupidity. Adults use derision laughter as a weapon in more subtle, psychological ways and less for deriding the physical abnormalities of their victims (for which they cannot be blamed) and more for ridiculing the odd behaviours, mannerisms, accent, attitudes, or incompetence of their victims (for which they can more readily be blamed).

Joyous laughter

One final category of laughter might be described as joyous laughter, which is a pure expression of excitement or *joie de vivre* (Foot & Chapman, 1976). This is a spontaneous reaction to pleasurable and exhilarating activities and is often an expression of mastery, like riding a horse without a saddle, climbing a difficult mountain, or experiencing a fairground roller coaster. Joyous laughter is of less interest in the present context because it is largely non-functional, other than as a signal of shared enjoyment.

APPLICATIONS OF HUMOUR

Humour and laughter have been hailed as good for the body and good for the mind. According to Keith-Spiegel (1972), the body benefits because they 'restore homeostasis, stabilise blood pressure, oxygenate the blood, massage the vital organs, stimulate circulation, facilitate digestion, relax the system and produce a feeling of well-being' (p. 5). Reviewing the evidence, Goldstein (1987) points to the inevitable conclusion that most studies on the arousal and tension-reducing properties of laughter are short-term experimental studies. Studies that examine the long-term consequences of laughter are almost non-existent (Mantell & Goldstein, 1985). Popular books on humour, however, clearly imply that it unquestionably leads to a healthy and prolonged life. Norman Cousins (1979) has documented his relief and 'cure' (through laughing at 'Candid Camera' episodes) from a painful rheumatic inflammation of the vertebrae. Yet to associate humour and laughter with longevity is hardly compatible with the clear evidence that professional comedians and comic writers do not live longer than anyone else. As Goldstein (1987) put it: 'the quality of life is surely enhanced by a sense of humour and not necessarily its duration' (p. 13). It should, however, be noted that laughter is not totally unconnected with the life-threatening states. Fry (1979) has suggested that laughter is actively related to the reduction of stress and hypertension that can lead to risk of heart attack, especially in those who smoke, are overweight, lack exercise, or have tension-related conditions. Mantell and Goldstein (1985) suggest that 'type B' personalities displace anger, anxiety, and aggression through humour, while 'type A' personalities are more at risk of heart attacks because of the seriousness and impatience (and therefore lack of humour) which they typically display.

Most recent literature, however, does not support the view that physical and psychological well-being is necessarily facilitated by a sense of humour. Individuals with high daily levels of laughter do not generally show greater positive emotion (Kuiper & Martin, 1998), nor do they display higher levels of intimacy in interpersonal relationships (Nezlek & Derks, 2001). Kuiper and Olinger (1998) and Martin (2001) have proposed models which specify the conditions under which a sense of humour may or may not benefit physical and psychological health, and on the assumption that there are negative as well as positive elements to having a sense of humour. Kirsh and Kuiper (2003) identified three higher-order patterns of humour:

1   positive, socially skilled, adept sense of humour that entails an ability to generate humour effortlessly and elicit laughter from others
2   boorish, aggressive humour, involving coarse or vulgar humour or poking fun at others
3   'belaboured' humour reflecting a strained or obsequious style, more designed to gain the approval of others and mask personal and social anxieties.

Martin et al. (2003) also developed a multidimensional approach, which identifies styles of humour as either adaptive or maladaptive, and focused on self or other. Individuals with self-focused adaptive humour styles have a humorous outlook on life and can maintain a humorous perspective even under stress. Other-related adaptive humour is essentially affiliative humour used to enhance interpersonal and social relationships. Maladaptive humour is potentially destructive and injurious to self (self-disparagement) or to others (aggressive humour). By drawing attention to the different functions served by different styles of humour, these models reveal very clearly why a sense of humour may produce mechanisms which result in detrimental as well as facilitative effects on psychological well-being (Kuiper et al. 2004). Other research by Kerkkanen et al. (2004), on Finnish police officers, suggests that a sense of humour can negatively affect a number of health indices, such as obesity, smoking, and risk of cardiovascular disease.

The general notion that a sense of humour facilitates health and psychological well-being has, therefore, received equivocal support. Research shows that it is not a unidimensional positive attribute. Whether or not facilitative effects are demonstrated depends upon how a sense of humour is measured or what elements of humour are explored. Most of us probably have the capacity to display both adaptive and mal-adaptive humour when it suits our purpose. This looser linkage between sense of humour and healthy adjustment may also explain why there is little evidence to connect lack of humour appreciation with poor mental health. Derks et al. (1975) were unable to pinpoint any particular differences in the kinds of humour appreciated by samples of neurotic, schizophrenic, and normal individuals. Ecker et al. (1973) found that patients from clinical populations may fail to see humour in jokes closely related to their own area of conflict, but not necessarily fail to appreciate other kinds of humour.

With respect to a healthy, adaptive sense of humour, there are several mechanisms by which humour may promote health. Martin (2004) identified four such mechanisms:

1   the physiological changes accompanying vigorous laughter in the muscular-skeletal, cardiovascular, endocrine, and neural systems
2   positive emotional mood states accompanying humour and laughter which may, for example, increase pain tolerance (Bruehl et al., 1993) or enhance immunity (Stone et al., 1987)
3   the moderation of adverse effects of psychological stress by enabling individuals to cope more effectively with stress (Martin et al., 1993)
4   the level of social support enhanced by more satisfying social relationships brought about by a healthy indulgence in humour.

Humour in therapy

Whether drawing on research or on their own experience, some professional helpers have begun to see humour as something to be cultivated and strategically deployed rather than ignored or used purely incidentally. Most therapists accept that humour is an index of self-knowledge, a prerequisite for personal exploration (Bloch, 1987). Mauger (2001) argues that humour can provide an emotional bonding between client and therapist that demonstrates the therapist's supportiveness and acceptance of the client, and enhances the 'therapeutic alliance' by confirming parity between them.

Let us be quite clear what kind of humour we are talking about in relation to therapy. Clearly, it is not the intrusion of jokes nor any direct attempt to make the patient or client laugh. Mindess (1971) endeavours to define it as conveying an 'inner condition, a stance, a point of view, or in the largest sense an attitude to life' (p. 214). As a therapeutic tool, it must be flexible, unconventional, and playful, the kind of humour which erupts as a spontaneous reaction to the patient's account of a tale of sorrow or state of mind. Killinger (1987) describes humour in therapy as an inter-active personal experience that occurs between client and therapist. Its potential lies in its usefulness as a tool to enable people to view their problems from a new perspective. It serves to broaden clients' self-awareness by improving their ability to take stock of themselves and others more objectively and to develop fuller affective reactions (Rosenheim, 1974). Mauger (2001) describes it as a means of 'untwisting' a client's cognitive distortions.

This broadening of perspective, from which clients begin to see the irony or absurdity of their own predicament, must nonetheless be facilitated cautiously and sensitively. Kubie (1971) has warned that humour introduced by the therapist too soon can be destructive if the therapist is assumed to be laughing at (maladaptive) rather than with (adaptive) the client. Mauger (2001), too, sees laughing with people as compassionate, and laughing at them as immoral and unethical.

Therapeutic contexts vary, of course, and the literature on therapy methodology gives examples of therapists' experience of using humour in individual contexts, in group therapy and in family therapy.

Individual therapy

Killinger (1987) believes fundamentally in the creative, but spontaneous, development of humour to capture and crystallise the essence or meaning within the immediate client–therapist interchange. Her clinical approach emphasises gentleness and therapeutic sensitivity to a client's needs. She (1987, p. 31) believes that this sensitivity can be best achieved through 'verbal picture painting or framing an image' that is designed to open the client's eyes while at the same time maintaining some 'psychic distance':

> In the process of active listening and attempting to understand what clients are thinking or saying about themselves, the therapist can focus the intervention at a significant point by creating a humorous word picture to frame the essence of the client's dynamics. The humorous interpretation hopefully serves to shift clients from a fixed view of themselves or their situation while simultaneously reinforcing the *now* by expanding on what clients are saying about themselves. By focusing the subject matter of the humor onto objects, people or situations slightly removed from the client this change of focus can be achieved without being 'too close' and raising undue anxiety in the client.

Mauger (2001) also uses humour to reinterpret or reframe distressing events in such a way as to distance the client sufficiently from the stressor while creating a feeling of perspective and safety.

Group therapy

Most long-established groups (such as therapy groups) whose members develop a sense of belonging and loyalty create what Yalom (1985) called a 'social microcosm' – shared experiencing of a broad array of emotions. Inevitably, humour becomes an intrinsic feature of the therapy group and, far from repressing it, the main concern is how it can be optimally built into a group's culture without making it too contrived.

Bloch (1987) has considered the various advantages and disadvantages of using humour in long-term group therapy. In particular, he has stressed the desirability of adopting an interactional model in which change stems mainly from the relationship between members rather than from the relationship between each client and the therapist. Thus, it is important that humour revolves around or emanates from the clients' relationships with each other rather than with the therapist. Bloch has identified 10 ways in which humour can be therapeutically useful. Three of these are classified as therapist-related uses, four as client-related, and three as group-related.

Therapist-related uses include *modelling* – good-natured expressions of attitude or behaviour which help to dislodge obstacles to a client's more spontaneous self-expression, *transparency* – self-disclosure by the therapist which shows a willingness to laugh at oneself, and *interpretation* – helping clients, through humour, to examine themselves in a different way.

Client-related uses include several techniques to help clients perceive the light-hearted nature of some experiences which arise during discussion among group members. These involve helping clients to put their experiences into a proper *sense of proportion*, to *overcome earnestness*, to *promote social skills* (by forging social relationships), and to provide opportunities for *catharsis and self-disclosure*.

Group-related uses include *cohesiveness* – the use of humour within the group to foster cordiality and friendliness, *insight into group dynamics* – helping group members to appreciate the relevance of processes such as undue dependency on the therapist and avoidance of distressing topics, and *reduction of tension* – the use of humour to handle conflict and embarrassment.

Family therapy

According to Madanes (1987), a therapist can follow one of two broad approaches in using humour to change the 'drama of a family': one is based on the use of language to redefine situations; the other relies on organising actions that change a course of events and modify sequences of interaction.

In relation to language, the art of the therapist is much the same as we have just been discussing (i.e. to facilitate the family members' reinterpretation of the meaning of their behaviour toward each other). Often humorous interventions do not appear humorous to the family members at the time; only in retrospect do they appear so. The therapist can sometimes revisit with the family events which happened earlier in the therapy and help them, through humour, to penetrate the family system, to loosen their grasp of cyclical dysfunctional patterns of family behaviour, and to reorganise the tasks which alter the interactions among family members.

In relation to action, the use of comic or slapstick routines may be helpful in situations where the behaviour of one family member irritates another. Madanes' device here is to have the behaviour deliberately practised by the perpetrator but responded to in an exaggeratedly affectionate way by the individual who is irritated (e.g. a sulky pout of the lips or angry finger-stabbing). This draws attention to the behaviour in a non-threatening way that can release amusement by both family members in the exchange. In all humour, there may be an element of defiance of authority – of rules or socially accepted norms. Defiance can be used in ways that are not only humorous but also therapeutic, as antagonism is changed into playful challenge.

Most therapists agree that if humour is to be used in therapy it must be used sensitively and caringly, in a way which indicates that the therapist values and respects clients and is concerned about their well-being. Many warn against the sudden and unguarded insertion of humour into therapy and view its introduction as a delicately judged business. This view of the psychological fragility of clients, however, has been questioned. Farrelly and Matthews (1981) and Farrelly and Lynch (1987) describe the technique of provocative therapy in which humour is explicitly used as a means of challenging clients' disorders and provoking them into a strong emotional reaction designed to make them relinquish their self-defeating behaviours. However, this is potentially a dangerous strategy if not handled very carefully.

Medical and caring contexts

In medical and nursing relationships, humour helps cement the bond and feeling of trust between patient and health-care provider (e.g. Beck, 1997; Astedt-Kurki, Tammentie & Kervinen, 2001). It also helps to establish the perception of a more egalitarian relationship, serving to offset the obvious asymmetry of a relationship in which one person (patient) is dependent upon another (carer), and effectively passes over control for their well-being. This does not mean to imply that the humour relationship actually becomes symmetrical. Haakana (2002) has shown that doctors typically laugh less than their patients during consultations and do not invite laughter as much as their patients do. When doctors do initiate humour, however, it is very likely to be reciprocated.

In one large-scale study of medical consultations, Sala and Kapat (2002) found a strong association between the use of humour and reported satisfaction with medical care by the patient. Female patients in particular used humour more than males in consultation visits with which they were satisfied. Where such visits were judged to be unsatisfactory, patients used more self-disparaging (maladaptive) humour; where visits were judged by patients to be more satisfactory, the physicians themselves were more likely to use self-deprecating humour. Perhaps the level of satisfaction was related more to patients' perception of their relative parity with their doctor during the consultation than to anything to do with their confidence in the doctor's competence or the medical outcome. Sala and Kapat also reported that patients were less likely to sue physicians for malpractice on the basis of more humorous consultation visits!

Several other results have emerged from research which has examined the use of humour in medical care and consultations. For example, there is some evidence that the use of humour helps to manage conflict, difficult caring situations, and difficult patients (Mallet & Ahern, 1996; Beck, 1997). Similarly, use of humour can help restore patients' feelings of control (Wooten, 1992) and reassert their autonomy and self-esteem, especially after a stroke (Heath & Blonder, 2003). Humour has also emerged as a means of providing hope to residents (and staff) in an 'assisted living facility' (Westburg, 2003), as a means of coping and improving the working climate (Astedt-Kurki et al., 2001), and as an antidote to burn-out, emotional exhaustion, and depersonalisation (Wooten, 1992; Talbot & Lumden, 2000).

Much of the research involving use of humour in medical and nursing contexts has been relatively small-scale, often qualitative, and even anecdotal in nature. The foregoing thumbnail sketch illustrates that the focus of this research has been largely upon the relationship between practitioner and patient rather than upon the relationship between practitioners themselves or with their organisations. Yet, what makes many stressful working situations tolerable, or even enjoyable, is not just the way humour can be deployed with clients, patients, customers, or students, with whom contact may be relatively brief and transient. Rather, for those in an organisational setting, it is the humour engendered by their working relationships with colleagues, co-practitioners, and those above and below them in authority that creates the cultural climate by which they judge their own competency, efficiency, and work satisfaction.

This organisational focus for humour emerged in a study of British social workers (Broussine, Davies & Scott, 1999), social work being considered the third most stressful job in the UK (Cooper, 1997). From open-ended descriptions of the social workers' personal work experiences, the researchers identified six main areas of tension which humour tends to target in their working lives:

1   confronting the overwhelming awfulness and sadness of clients' situations
2   dealing with a paradoxical role of being both powerful and powerless
3   tolerating an ever-increasing amount of control, bureaucracy, and loss of professional autonomy
4   balancing the need for efficiency (throughput) with the desire to care for and help disadvantaged people
5   handling the increasing formality required by and toward management
6   engaging in subversion and resistance while maintaining attachment and loyalty to the organisation.

Although these are descriptions within an organisation dealing with people at the edge of society, it is very likely that they will resonate within other work environments.

HUMOUR AND TEACHING

Humour in the classroom can clearly make lessons more enjoyable. 'Sesame Street' is an obvious example of an educational television programme designed to present teaching in an atmosphere of fun by use of 'muppets' as well as to inject humour into specific lessons to be taught. The question is, does humour actually help children to learn? Unfortunately, the evidence is equivocal; studies showing that humour does not aid memory outnumber the studies that show a positive or negative effect.

Clearly, humour may distract from the lesson in the sense that it draws the child's attention toward the joke and away from the message, but if the humour is related to and integrated directly with the items to be learned, it may assist the learning of those items (Chapman & Crompton, 1978). Davies and Apter (1980) argue that the type of humour, length of the joke, temporal position of the insertion of the humour, and the method of presentation may all contribute to the humour's effectiveness, and the type of lesson or material to be learned may also be crucial. So there are no easy answers. The case for humour as a means of aiding subsequent recall is not yet proven, but this is no reason why teachers should abandon it as a means of maintaining their pupils' attention (see also Brown & Bryant, 1983). There is very little evidence supporting the view that it could be detrimental. Some evidence suggests that it makes individuals more creative by improving their flexibility of thinking (Isen et al., 1987). Furthermore, appropriate humour is entertaining and renders the communicator more popular (Gruner, 1976).

OVERVIEW

For whatever purposes we use humour in our daily lives, it is above all else a coping mechanism: it buffers us against stress and against the criticism of others; it enables us to maintain and possibly enhance our own self-concept and preserve our self-esteem (Martin et al., 1993). The evidence we have surveyed in this chapter demonstrates just how goal-directed humour is and how it comes to be involved in a broad range of human activities and functioning. Not only does humour appear to be an effective means of reducing stress, but it also appears to be associated with a greater enjoyment of positive life experiences and a more positive orientation toward self (Martin et al., 1993). Patently, humour is a subtle and complex skill, and some are more proficient in its use than others. The origins and development of the skill are poorly understood, and little is known about why some adults and children become particularly versed and adept at using it to express themselves. As a social skill, however, humour is an ability, and everyone has the capacity to develop it. As Fry (1994, p. 112) expressed it:

> The sense of humor of each person is slightly different from everyone else's sense of humor. A sense of humor is a kind of psychological fingerprint, distinctive for each person. There are broad overlaps of humor appreciation among groups – family, community, regional, national, cultural. There is humor which has universal appeal, humor recognised as humor and enjoyed throughout the world. But each person develops a sense of humor which is slightly different from that of each other person.

There seems little danger that the intrinsic pleasure of humour will be destroyed by our serious attempts to comprehend and exploit it.

REFERENCES

Adorno, T. W., Frenkel-Brunswick, E., Levinson, D. J. & Sanford, R. N. (1950). *The authoritarian personality*. New York: Harper & Row.

Allport, G. W. (1954). *The nature of prejudice*. London: Addison-Wesley.

Astedt-Kurki, P., Tammentie, T. & Kervinen, U. (2001). Importance of humor to client–nurse relationships and clients' well-being. *International Journal of Nursing Practice*, *7*, 119–125.

Bales, R. F. (1950). *Interaction process analysis: a method for the study of small groups*. Reading, MA: Addison-Wesley.

Bales, R. F. (1958). Task roles and social roles in problem-solving groups. In E. Maccoby, T. Newcomb & E. Hartley (Eds), *Readings in social psychology*, 3rd edn. New York: Holt, Rinehart & Winston.

Beck, C. T. (1997). Humor in nursing practice: a phenomenological study. *International Journal of Nursing Studies*, *34*, 346–352.

Berlyne, D. E. (1969). Laughter, humor and play. In G. Lindzey & E. Aronson (Eds), *Handbook of social psychology*, vol. 3, 2nd edn. Reading, MA: Addison-Wesley.

Berlyne, E. E. (1972). Humor and its kin. In J. H. Goldstein & P. E. McGhee (Eds), *The psychology of humor*. New York: Academic Press.

Bloch, S. (1987). Humor in group therapy. In W. F. Fry & W. A. Salameh (Eds), *Handbook of humor and psychotherapy*. Sarasota, FL: Professional Resource Exchange.

Bloch, S. & Crouch, E. (1985). *Therapeutic factors in group psychotherapy*. Oxford: Oxford University Press.

Bokun, B. (1986). *Humour therapy*. London: Vita Books.

Bourhis, R. Y., Gadfield, N. J. Giles, H. & Tajfel, H. (1977). Context and ethnic humour in intergroup relations. In A. J. Chapman & H. C. Foot (Eds), *It's a funny thing, humour*. Oxford: Pergamon.

Broussine, M., Davies, F. & Scott, J. C. (1999). Humour at the edge: an inquiry into the use of humour in British social work. *Bristol Business School Teaching and Research Review*, *1*, 1–8.

Brown, D. & Bryant, J. (1983). Humor in the mass media. In P. McGhee & J. Goldstein (Eds), *Handbook of humor research*, Vol. 1: *Applied Studies*. New York: Springer.

Bruehl, S., Carlson, C. R. & McCubbin, J. A. (1993). Two brief interventions for acute pain. *Pain*, *54*, 29–36.

Chafe, W. (1987). Humor as a disabling mechanism. *American Behavioral Scientist*, *3*, 15–23.

Chapman, A. J. (1973). Social facilitation of laughter in children. *Journal of Experimental Social Psychology*, *9*, 528–541.

Chapman, A. J. (1974). An experimental study of social facilitated 'humorous laughter'. *Psychological Reports*, *35*, 727–734.

Chapman, A. J. (1975). Humorous laughter in children. *Journal of Personality and Social Psychology*, *31*, 42–49.

Chapman, A. J. & Chapman, W. A. (1974). Responsiveness to humor: its dependency upon a companion's humorous smiling and laughter. *Journal of Psychology*, *88*, 245–252.

Chapman, A. J. & Foot, H. C. (Eds) (1976). *Humour and laughter: theory, research and applications*. Chichester: Wiley.

Chapman, A. J. & Wright, D. S. (1976). Social enhancement of laughter: an experimental analysis of some companion variables. *Journal of Experimental Child Psychology*, *21*, 201–218.

Chapman, A. J. & Crompton, P. (1978). Humorous presentations of material and presentations of humorous material: a review of the humour and memory literature and two experimental studies. In M. M. Gruneberg, P. E. Morris & R. N. Sykes (Eds), *Practical aspects of memory*. London: Academic Press.

Christie G. (1994). Some psychoanalytic aspects of humour. *International Journal of Psychoanalysis*, *75*, 479–489.

Cooper, C. (1997). Stress at work: how your job rates? *The Sunday Times*, Stress Manager Supplement, Point 1: In the workplace, pp. 8–9, 18 May.

Cousins, N. (1979). *Anatomy of an illness as perceived by the patient*. New York: Norton.

Davies, A. P. & Apter, M. J. (1980). Humour and its effects on learning in children. In P. E. McGhee & A. J. Chapman (Eds), *Children's humour*. Chichester: Wiley.

Davis, J. M. & Farina, A. (1970). Humor appreciation as social communication. *Journal of Personality and Social Psychology*, **15**, 175–178.

Derks, P. L., Leichtman, H. M. & Carroll, P. J. (1975). Production and judgement of 'humor', by schizophrenics and college students. *Bulletin of the Psychonomic Society*, **6**, 300–302

Ecker, J., Levine, J. & Zigler, E. (1973). Impaired sex-role identification in schizophrenia expressed in the comprehension of humor stimuli. *Journal of Personality*, **83**, 67–77.

Farrelly, F. & Lynch, M. (1987). Humor in provocative therapy. In W. F. Fry & W. A. Salameh (Eds), *Handbook of humour and psychotherapy*. Sarasota, FL: Professional Resource Exchange.

Farrelly, F. & Matthews, S. (1981). Provocative therapy. In R. Corsini (Ed.), *Handbook of innovative psychotherapies*. New York: Wiley.

Foot, H. C. & Chapman, A. J. (1976). The social responsiveness of young children in humorous situations. In A. J. Chapman & H. C. Foot (Eds), *Humour and laughter: theory, research and applications*. Chichester: Wiley.

Forabosco, G. (1992). Cognitive aspects of the humor process: the concept of incongruity. *Humor: International Journal of Humor Research*, **5**, 45–68.

Freud, S. (1928). Humour. In *Collected papers*, vol. 5, pp. 215–221. London: Hogarth Press.

Freud, S. (1938 [1905]). *Wit and its relationship to the unconscious* In A.A. Brill (Ed.), *Basic writings of Sigmund Freud* (pp. 633–803). Random House, New York: Modern Library.

Fry, W. F. (1979). Humor and the cardiovascular system. In H. Mindness & J. Turek (Eds), *The study of humor: proceedings of the Second International Humor Conference*. Antioch College, Los Angeles, CA.

Fry, W. F. (1994). The biology of humor. *Humor: International Journal of Humor Research*, **7**, 111–126.

Giles, H. & Oxford, G. S. (1970). Towards a multi-dimensional theory of laughter causation and its social implications. *Bulletin of the British Psychological Society*, **23**, 97–105.

Goldstein, J. H. (1987). Therapeutic effects of laughter. In W. F. Fry & W. Salameh (Eds), *Handbook of humor and psychotherapy*. Sarasota, FL: Professional Resource Exchange.

Goldstein, J. H. & McGhee, P. E. (Eds) (1972). *The psychology of humor*. New York: Academic Press.

Gregg, J. (2002). Laughter's good medicine. Oregon State University Extension Service, Leader Guide, HE4–970, pp. 1–7.

Grotjahn, M. (1957). *Beyond laughter: humor and the subconscious*. New York: McGraw-Hill.

Gruner, C. R. (1976). Wit and humour in mass communication. In A. J. Chapman and H. C. Foot (Eds), *Humour and laughter: theory, research and application*. Chichester: Wiley.

Gruner, C. R. (1978). *Understanding laughter: the workings of wit and humour*. Chicago: Nelson-Hall.

Gruner, C. R. (1997). *The game of humor*. New Brunswick, NJ: Transaction Books.

Haakana, M. (2002). Laughter in medical interaction: from quantification to analysis and back. *Journal of Sociolinguistics, 6*, 207–235.

Heath, R. L. & Blonder, L. X. (2003). Conversational humor among stroke survivors. *Humor; International Journal of Humor Research, 16*, 91–106.

Hertzler, J. O. (1970). *Laughter: a socio-scientific analysis*. New York: Exposition.

Husband, C. (1977). The mass media and the functions of ethnic humour in a racist society. In A. J. Chapman & H. C. Foot (Eds), *It's a funny thing, humour*. Oxford: Pergamon.

Isen, A. M., Daubman, K. A. & Nowicki, G. P. (1987). Positive affect facilitates creative problem solving. *Journal of Personality and Social Psychology, 52*, 1122–1131.

Kane, T. R., Suls, J. M. & Tedeschi, J. (1977). Humour as a tool of social interaction. In A. J. Chapman & H. C. Foot (Eds), *It's a funny thing, humour*. Oxford: Pergamon.

Kataria, M. (2002). *Laugh for no reason*, 2nd edn. Mumbai, India: Madhuri International.

Keith-Spiegel, P. (1972). Early conceptions of humor: varieties and issues. In J. H. Goldstein & P. E. McGhee (Eds), *The psychology of humor*. New York: Academic Press.

Kerkkanen, P., Kuiper, N. A. & Martin, R. A. (2004). Sense of humor, physical health, and well-being at work: a three-year longitudinal study of Finnish police officers. *Humor: International Journal of Humor Research, 17*, 1–36.

Killinger, B. (1987). Humor in psychotherapy: a shift to a new perspective. In W. F. Fry & W. A. Salameh (Eds), *Handbook of humor and psychotherapy*. Sarasota, FL: Professional Resource Exchange.

Kirsh, G. & Kuiper, N. A. (2003). Positive and negative aspects of sense of humor: associations with the constructs of individualism and relatedness. *Humor: International Journal of Humor Research, 16*, 32–62.

Kubie, L. S. (1971). The destructive potential of humor in psychotherapy. *American Journal of Psychiatry, 127*, 861–886.

Kuiper, N. A. & Martin, R. A. (1998). Laughter and stress in daily life: relation to positive and negative affect. *Motivation and Emotion, 22*, 133–153.

Kuiper, N. A. & Olinger, L. J. (1998). Humor and mental health. In H. Friedman (Ed.), *Encyclopedia of mental health*, vol. 2, pp. 445–457. San Diego, CA: Academic Press.

Kuiper, N. A., Grimshaw, M., Leite, C. & Kirsh, G. (2004). Humor is not always the best medicine: specific components of sense of humor and psychological well-being. *Humor: International Journal of Humor Research, 17*, 135–168.

LaGaipa, J. J. (1977). The effects of humour on the flow of social conversation. In A. J. Chapman & H. C. Foot (Eds), *It's a funny thing, humour*. Oxford: Pergamon.

Lefcourt, H. M. & Martin, R. A. (1986). *Humor and life stress: antidote to adversity*. New York: Springer.

Madanes, C. (1987). Humor in strategic family therapy. In W. F. Fry & W. A. Salameh (Eds), *Handbook of humor and psychotherapy*. Sarasota, FL: Professional Resource Exchange.

Mallet, J. & Ahern, R. (1996). Comparative distribution and use of humour within nurse–patient communication. *International Journal of Nursing Studies, 33*, 530–550.

Mantell, M. & Goldstein, J. H. (1985). Humour and the coronary-prone behaviour pattern. Paper presented at the Fifth International Conference on Humour, Cork, Ireland.

Martin, R. A. (1989). Humor and the mastery of living: using humor to cope with the daily stresses of growing up. In P. E. M.Ghee (Ed.), *Humor and children's development: a guide to practical applications*. New York: Haworth Press.

Martin, R. A. (2000). Humor. In A. E. Kazdin (Ed.), *Encyclopaedia of psychology*, vol. 4, pp. 202–204. Washington DC: American Psychological Association.

Martin, R. A. (2001). Humor, laughter and physical health: methodological issues and research findings. *Psychological Bulletin*, *127*, 504–519.

Martin, R. A. (2004). Sense of humor and physical health: theoretical issues, recent findings and future directions. *Humor*, *17*, 1–19.

Martin, R. A., Kuiper, N. A., Olinger, L. J. & Dance, K. A. (1993). Humor, coping with stress, self-concept and psychological well-being. *Humor: International Journal of Humor Research*, *6*, 89–104.

Martin, R. A., Puhlik-Doris, P., Larsen, G., Gray, J. & Weir, K. (2003). Individual differences in uses of humor and their relation to psychological well-being: development of the Humor Styles Questionnaire. *Journal of Research in Personality*, *37*, 48–75.

Martineau, W. H. (1972). A model of the social functions of humor. In J. H. Goldstein & P. E. McGhee (Eds), *The psychology of humor*. New York: Academic Press.

Mauger, S. (2001). The use of humour in stress management. *Stress News*, *13*, 1–4.

McGhee, P. E. (1977). Children's humor: a review of current research trends. In A. J. Chapman & H. C. Foot (Eds), *It's a funny thing, humour*. Oxford: Pergamon.

McGhee, P. E. (1979). *Humor: its origin and development*. San Francisco. CA: Freeman.

Mettee, D. R., Hrelec, E. S. & Wilkens, P. C. (1971). Humor as an interpersonal asset and liability. *Journal of Social Psychology*, *85*, 51–64.

Middleton, R. & Moland, J. (1959). Humor and Negro and white subcultures: a study of jokes among university students. *American Sociological Review*, *24*, 61–69.

Mindess, H. (1971). *Laughter and liberation*. Los Angeles, CA: Nash.

Nezlek, J. & Derks, P. (2001). Use of humor as a coping mechanism, psychological adjustment and social interaction. *Humor: International Journal of Humor Research*, *14*, 395–413.

Norrick, N. R. (1993). *Conversational joking: humor in everyday life*. Bloomington, IN: Indiana University Press.

Pfeifer, K. (1994). Laughter and pleasure: *Humour: International Journal of Humor Research*, *7*, 157–172.

Provine, R. R. & Fischer, K. R. (1989). Laughing, smiling and talking: relation to sleeping and social context in humans. *Ethology*, *83*, 295–305.

Rosenheim, E. (1974). Humor in psychotherapy: an interactive experience. *American Journal of Psychotherapy*, *28*, 584–591.

Rothbart, M. K. (1973). Laughter in young children. *Psychological Bulletin*, *80*, 247–256.

Rothbart, M. K. (1976). Inconguity, problem-solving and laughter. In A. J. Chapman & H. C. Foot (Eds), *Humour and laughter: theory, research and applications*. Chichester: Wiley.

Ruch, W. (1984). Conservatism and the appreciation of humor. *Zeitschrift für Differentielle und Diagnostische Psychologie*, *5*, 221–245.

Ruch, W. (1990). The emotion of exhilaration. Unpublished habilitation thesis, University of Dusseldorf, Dusseldorf.

Ruch, W. (1995). Will the real relationship between facial expression and affective experience please stand up: the case of exhilaration. *Cognition and Emotion*, *9*, 33–58.

Ruch, W. & Hehl, F.-J. (1986). Conservation as a predictor of responses to humour. II. The location of sense of humour in a comprehensive attitude space. *Personality and Individual Differences*, *7*, 861–874.

Sala, F. & Kapat, E. (2002). Satisfaction and the use of humour by physicians and patients. *Psychology and Health*, *17*, 269–280.

Shurcliff, A. (1968). Judged humor, arousal, and the relief theory. *Journal of Personality and Social Psychology*, *8*, 360–363.

Stone, A. A., Cox, S., Valdimarsdottir, L. J. & Neale, J. M. (1987). Evidence that secretory IgA antibody is associated with daily mood. *Journal of Personality and Social Psychology*, *52*, 988–993.

Suls, J. J. (1972). A two-stage model for the appreciation of jokes and cartoons: an information-processing analysis. In J. H. Goldstein and P. E. McGhee (Eds), *The psychology of humor*. New York: Academic Press.

Suls, J. M. & Miller, R. L. (1976). Humor as an attributional index. Cited by T. R. Kane, J. Suls & J. Tedeschi, in A. J. Chapman & H. C. Foot (Eds), *It's a funny thing, humour*. Oxford: Pergamon.

Talbot, L. A. & Lumden, D. B. (2000). On the association between humor and burnout. *Humor: International Journal of Humor Research*, *13*, 419–428.

Westburg, N. G. (2003). Hope, laughter and humour in residents and staff at an assisted living facility. *Journal of Mental Health Counselling*, *25*, 16–32.

Wilson, C. P. (1979). *Jokes: form, content, use and function*. London: Academic Press.

Wooten, P. (1992). Does a humour workshop affect nurse burnout? *Journal of Nursing Jocularity*, *2*, 46–47.

Yalom, I. D. (1985). *The theory and practice of group psychotherapy*. New York: Basic Books.

Zillman, D. (1983). Disparagement humor. In P. E. McGhee & J. H. Goldstein (Eds), *Handbook of humor research*, vol. 1. *Basic issues*. New York: Springer.

Zillman, D. & Cantor, J. R. (1976). A dispositional theory of humour and mirth. In A. J. Chapman & H. C. Foot (Eds), *Humour and laughter: theory, research and applications*. Chichester: Wiley.

Chapter 11

Persuasion

Daniel J. O'Keefe

T HE SKILL THAT IS most fundamental to persuasive success is
that of adapting messages to audiences. Skilled persuaders adapt
their messages to those they seek to influence. The general idea of
adaptation, however, can usefully be unpacked into two separate (but
related) tasks. One is the task of identifying the current obstacles to
agreement or compliance, that is, the bases of the audience's resistance
to the advocated action or viewpoint. The other is the task of constructing effective messages aimed at removing or minimising such obstacles.
In what follows, each of these tasks is analysed further through the lens
of current theory and research concerning effective persuasive communication. The extensive social-scientific research literature concerning persuasion offers a number of principles and guidelines that can
be useful in illuminating the nature of, and possibilities for, adapting
persuasive messages to audiences.

As an initial observation, however, it should be remembered that
the circumstances persuaders face can be quite diverse, if only because
persuasion itself is a ubiquitous human activity. Persuasion occurs in
the marketplace (e.g. consumer advertising), the courtroom, the political
arena, family and interpersonal settings, the workplace, and so on. This
diversity of persuasion situations in turn guarantees that there can be
no simple, completely dependable directives for skilful persuasion; what
is needed in one persuasion setting may be quite different from what is
needed in another. But the task of adapting to the particular circumstance at hand is a task faced by all persuaders, and what follows is
meant to provide a general guide to skilful adaptation by discussing, in
turn, the identification of obstacles to compliance and the creation of
messages aimed at those obstacles.

IDENTIFYING OBSTACLES TO COMPLIANCE

One common obstacle to the audience's embracing the persuader's advocated action or viewpoint is the audience's current attitudes, that is, the audience's general evaluations (of the advocated action, policy, product, and so on). For instance, low participation in recycling programmes might be the result of negative attitudes about recycling; in that case, a persuader who wants to encourage recycling would obviously be well advised to try to change those negative attitudes.

However, skilful persuaders will realise that it is a mistake to assume that what lies behind a person not performing a given action is a negative attitude. To be sure, sometimes current attitudes are indeed the obstacle, and in such circumstances (as will be discussed) attitude change is needed. But sometimes the basis of the audience's resistance lies somewhere other than attitude. Thus, it is useful to distinguish two broad persuasion circumstances – one in which the audience already has the desired attitudes (but for some reason is not acting consistently with them) and the other in which the audience lacks the desired attitudes.

When the audience has the desired attitudes

When the audience already has the desired attitudes in place, the persuader's challenge is that of encouraging people to act consistently with those attitudes. This circumstance is actually not uncommon. For example, people almost certainly already have favourable attitudes toward good health; what is needed is to persuade people to make attitude-consistent behavioural choices about exercise, diet, medical care, and the like. Similarly, persons who have positive attitudes toward energy conservation and environmental protection might not act consistently with those views – might not choose appropriate thermostat settings, engage in recycling, and so on. Two broad (not mutually exclusive) approaches are available to persuaders here. One is to attempt to connect more closely the existing attitudes with the desired behaviour; the other is to focus on non-attitudinal influences on behaviour.

Connecting the existing attitude with the desired behaviour

When a persuader seeks to have persons connect their existing attitudes more closely to a behavioural choice (so as to shape that choice), three general strategies recommend themselves: enhancing the perceived relevance of the attitude to the behaviour, inducing feelings of guilt or hypocrisy, and enhancing the salience of the current attitude.

One strategy for enhancing attitude-consistent behaviour is to encourage people to see their attitudes as relevant to their behavioural choices. The general principle here is that persons are more likely to act consistently with their attitudes if they see the attitudes as relevant to the behaviour in question; hence, increasing perceived attitudinal relevance will increase the likelihood of attitude-consistent behaviour.

For example, in a study by Snyder and Kendzierski (1982), participants completed measures of their attitudes toward affirmative action, read arguments in an affirmative-action court case, and rendered individual verdicts in the case. Some participants received instructions from the judge emphasising that the case dealt with a contemporary issue (affirmative action) and thus that decisions in this case could have implications not only for the involved parties, but also for affirmative-action programmes generally (because of the precedent-setting nature of judicial decisions); these instructions underscored the relevance of participants' attitudes to their decision. Participants who did not receive these instructions displayed little consistency between their affirmative-action attitudes and their decisions, but those who received the instructions exhibited substantial attitude-behaviour consistency.

In short, emphasising the relevance of an existing attitude to a current behavioural choice can be one means of inducing attitude-consistent conduct. Indeed, one need think only of the computers, computer programs, tutoring sessions, academic camps, and similar products or services that have been purchased by parents who had been led to see that various of their current attitudes were relevant to the purchase decision ('You want your children to have an advantage at school? To get a good education? To succeed in life?'). (For related research and discussion, see Borgida & Campbell, 1982; Snyder, 1982; Shepherd, 1985; Prislin, 1987.)

A second strategy for encouraging attitude-consistent behaviour is that of inducing feelings of hypocrisy or guilt. When people have previously acted inconsistently with their attitudes, drawing their attention to the hypocrisy can lead them to act more consistently with their attitudes. Specifically, the research evidence suggests that when both the existing attitude and the previous inconsistent behaviour are made salient, persons are likely subsequently to act more consistently with their attitudes. For example, Stone, Aronson, Crain, Winslow, and Fried (1994) varied the salience of participants' positive attitudes about safe-sex practices (by having some participants write and deliver a speech about the importance of safe sex) and varied the salience of previous behaviour that was inconsistent with such attitudes (by having some participants be reminded of their past failures to engage in safe-sex practices). The combination of salient attitudes and salient inconsistency induced greater subsequent attitude-behaviour consistency (reflected in greater likelihood of buying condoms at the end of the experiment) than either one alone. Similarly, Aitken, McMahon, Wearing, and Findlayson (1994) reported that households given feedback about their water consumption, combined with a reminder of their previously expressed belief in their responsibility to conserve water, significantly reduced their subsequent consumption. Feedback alone did reduce consumption, but was not as effective as the combination of feedback and the reminder. (For similar findings, see Kantola, Syme & Campbell, 1984; Linz, Fuson & Donnerstein, 1990; Aronson, Fried & Stone, 1991; Fried & Aronson, 1995.)

Plainly, then, one means of inducing attitude-behaviour consistency may be to lead people to recognise their hypocrisy (which may involve making them feel guilty about their past inconsistency). But this strategy can easily backfire if not deployed carefully. For instance, persons made to feel hypocritical about apparent attitude-behaviour inconsistency might resolve that inconsistency not by changing their behaviour so as to align it with their attitudes, but by changing their attitudes so as to justify (be consistent with) their previous behaviour (for an example of such a backfire effect, see Fried, 1998). Similarly, several studies have found that although more explicit guilt appeals do arouse greater guilt than less-explicit appeals, those more-explicit appeals are significantly less persuasive than less-explicit appeals, perhaps because the strategy generates anger or resentment (e.g., Englis, 1990; Pinto & Priest, 1991; Coulter & Pinto, 1995; Coulter, Cotte & Moore, 1997; Cotte, Coulter & Moore, 2005; for reviews and discussion, see O'Keefe, 2000, 2002a).

A third means of encouraging attitude-consistent behaviour is simply to ensure that the relevant attitudes are sufficiently salient. In the right circumstances, persuasion can be effected through relatively straightforward prompts or reminders.

For example, Conn, Burks, Minor, and Mehr (2003) found that mail and telephone prompts led to significant increases in the exercise behaviour of older women compared to conditions without such reminders; Andersen, Franckowiak, Snyder, Bartlett, and Fontaine (1998) reported that stair use in a shopping mall was significantly increased by placing signs (mentioning the benefits of stair use) next to escalators that had adjacent stairs; Austin, Alvero, and Olson (1998) found that when a restaurant hostess prompted departing patrons by adding 'don't forget to buckle up' to her usual parting comments, seat belt use increased by over a third; Alemi et al. (1996) found that computerised reminder telephone calls to parents significantly increased the likelihood that children would be immunised on schedule; Ferrari, Barone, Jason, and Rose (1985a) reported that persons who had signed a pledge card to donate blood were significantly more likely to fulfil that pledge (more likely to report to give blood) if they received a reminder telephone call a day or two before the blood drive began. As these findings illustrate, when the relevant attitudes are already in place, effective persuasion can simply be a matter of making those attitudes salient.

Focus on non-attitudinal factors

However, even if the audience has the appropriate attitudes and is prepared to act consistently with them (e.g. even if the attitude is seen as relevant to the desired action), attitude-consistent behaviour may nevertheless not occur, because other (non-attitudinal) factors can outweigh any influence of attitude on behaviour. Two such additional factors deserve special mention: normative considerations and the person's perceived ability to perform the behaviour.

Concerning normative considerations, a number of generalised models of intentional behaviour recognise that both attitudinal (personal) and normative (social) factors can influence conduct. Thus, even when an individual has the desired attitudes, perceived normative pressures might prevent the person from engaging in the desired action.

The most extensively studied model that incorporates both attitudinal and normative influences on intentional conduct is Fishbein and Ajzen's (1975; Ajzen & Fishbein, 1980) theory of reasoned action (for reviews and discussion, see Eagly & Chaiken, 1993, pp. 168–186; Conner & Sparks, 1996; Sutton, 1998; O'Keefe, 2002b, pp. 101–113). The theory of reasoned action is based on the idea that the primary determinant of a person's (volitional) conduct is that person's behavioural intention (what the person intends to do). Behavioural intentions, in turn, are seen to be a function of two factors: the person's attitude toward the behaviour in question and the person's 'subjective norm', which represents the person's general perception of whether others who are important to the person (e.g. friends, spouse, parents, and so on) desire the performance of the behaviour. These two factors may not have equal influence on a given intention, so the theory acknowledges that these factors may have varying 'weights'. This is expressed algebraically in the following formula:

$$BI = (A_B)w_1 + (SN)w_2$$

BI represents behavioural intention, A_B represents the attitude toward the behaviour, SN represents subjective norm, and w_1 and w_2 are weighting factors. As this model makes clear, even if an individual has a positive attitude toward the recommended behaviour, perceived normative pressures can override that attitude. In such a circumstance, the appropriate persuasive target is obviously not attitude, but subjective norm.

Hence, altering the subjective norm can be a mechanism for influencing behaviour. For example, Kelly et al. (1992; St. Lawrence, Brasfield, Diaz, Jefferson, Reynolds & Leonard, 1994) identified a number of 'trendsetters', who were then recruited to communicate HIV risk-reduction information to gay men in their communities. This intervention produced substantial and sustained risk-reduction behaviour and illustrates how alterations in subjective norms can affect behaviour.

But the individual's subjective norm is not the only sort of norm that might influence a person's conduct. A person's 'descriptive norm' – the person's perception of what most people do – can also play a role. Several studies have found that behavioural intentions can be influenced by descriptive norms; the more one perceives that others engage in a behaviour, the more likely one is to intend to engage in it (e.g. Heath & Gifford, 2002; Okun, Karoly & Lutz, 2002).

Thus, one avenue to influencing intentions and behaviour can be to change perceived descriptive norms. For example, college students appear often to overestimate the frequency of drug and alcohol use on their campuses (e.g. Perkins, Meilman, Leichliter, Cashin & Presley, 1999; cf. Wechsler & Kuo, 2000). Interventions aimed at correcting such descriptive-norm misperceptions might be helpful in reducing drug and alcohol abuse (for some relevant findings, see Haines & Spear, 1996; Steffian, 1999; Miller, Monin & Prentice, 2000, pp. 106–107; Carter & Kahnweiler, 2000; Werch, Pappas, Carlson, DiClemente, Chally & Sinder, 2000; Thombs & Hamilton, 2002).

Concerning perceived behavioural control, another non-attitudinal obstacle to compliance with the persuader's advocated action can be the audience's perceived inability to perform the desired behaviour. A number of theoretical perspectives on intentional behaviour have emphasised this possibility, but for present purposes Ajzen's (1991) theory of planned behaviour provides a convenient example. The theory of planned behaviour provides an elaboration of the theory of reasoned action, by adding perceived behavioural control as a third predictor of behavioural intention. Perceived behavioural control refers to the person's perception of the ease or difficulty of performing the behaviour, that is, the person's perceived self-efficacy with respect to the behaviour. Thus, the algebraic expression of the theory of planned behaviour is

$$BI = (A_B)w_1 + (SN)w_2 + (PBC)w_3$$

where PBC refers to perceived behavioural control and w_3 is the corresponding weighting factor.

It is easy to imagine circumstances in which perceived behavioural control is the key obstacle to compliance. For example, a person might have a positive attitude toward exercising regularly ('I think exercising regularly would be a good thing') and a positive subjective norm ('Most people who are important to me think I should exercise regularly'), but negative perceived behavioural control ('I don't have the time, and the health club is too far away'), and so the person does not form the intention to exercise regularly. A large number of studies have confirmed that perceived behavioural control does indeed often have a significant influence on behavioural intentions (for reviews and discussion, see Godin & Kok, 1996; Conner & Armitage, 1998; Notani, 1998; Sutton, 1998; Albarracin, Johnson, Fishbein & Muellerleile, 2001; Armitage & Conner, 2001; Hagger, Chatzisarantis & Biddle, 2002; O'Keefe, 2002b, pp. 113–127). To take one example of the distinctive role of perceived behavioural control, in a comparison of householders who recycled and those who did not, De Young (1989) found recyclers and non-recyclers to have similar positive attitudes toward recycling, but non-recyclers perceived recycling to be much more difficult to do than did recyclers and indicated uncertainty about exactly how to perform the behaviour; that is, the barrier to behavioural performance appeared to be a matter of a perceived inability to perform the action, not a negative attitude toward the behaviour.

Given that a lack of perceived behavioural self-efficacy is sometimes the primary obstacle to gaining the audience's compliance, the question becomes one of identifying ways in which persuaders might enhance self-efficacy. Broadly speaking, persuaders have at least four different means by which they can attempt to influence a person's perceived behavioural control. The usefulness of these various mechanisms will depend on the particular behaviour of interest, but each can be helpful in the right circumstances.

First, sometimes persuaders will be able to remove some barrier to behavioural performance. In cases where the barrier is a lack of information, persuaders can simply supply the necessary information. Cardenas and Simons-Morton (1993), for instance, found that parents' self-efficacy for lowering the temperature setting of a water heater (so as to prevent tap-water scalding of infants) could be enhanced by an informational brochure describing how to perform the action. In cases where the barrier is substantive (rather than informational), persuaders may sometimes be able to remove the barrier. For example, among low-income patients whose initial medical test results indicate a need for a return hospital visit, transportation problems might represent a significant barrier to returning; Marcus et al. (1992) found that providing such patients with free bus passes or parking permits significantly increased the likelihood of a visit for follow-up procedures. Similarly, if a political party finds that its potential voters do not know the location of their polling places (informational barrier) or lack transportation to polling places on election day (substantive barrier), the party might well take steps directly to remove those impediments to performance of the desired behaviour.

Second, audiences can be given examples of other people performing the behaviour successfully. Such modelling can enhance self-efficacy (by receivers reasoning, in effect, 'if they can do it, so can I'). For example, Anderson (2000) found that viewing a video in which successful breast self-examination was modelled produced significantly greater perceived behavioural self-efficacy than various control conditions. (For some additional studies of the effects of modeling on self-efficacy, see Mahler, Kulik & Hill, 1993; Anderson, 1995; Hagen, Gutkin, Wilson & Oats, 1998; Ng, Tam, Yew & Lam, 1999.)

Third, persuaders can sometimes create opportunities for successful perform-ance of the target behaviour. Rehearsal of the behaviour – that is, practice at accomplishing the behaviour – will presumably enhance perceived self-efficacy ('I've done it before, I can do it again'). For example, Steffen, Sternberg, Teegarden, and Shepherd (1994) found that practising testicle self-examination on a life-like model significantly increased participants' reported ability to perform the examination. And a number of studies have reported that self-efficacy for condom use can be enhanced by practice at using condoms correctly, role-playing (or mental rehearsal) of conversations with sexual partners, and similar interventions (Maibach & Flora, 1993; Weeks, Levy, Zhu, Perhats, Handler & Flay, 1995; Weisse, Turbiasz & Whitney, 1995; Yzer, Fisher, Bakker, Siero & Misovich, 1998). (For examples of other research concerning the effects of successful practice on perceived behavioural control, see Luzzo, Hasper, Albert, Bibby & Martinelli, 1999; Duncan, Duncan, Beauchamp, Wells & Ary, 2000.)

Finally, self-efficacy can apparently be enhanced by receiving encouragement from others. A persuader who indicates confidence in the receiver's behavioural abilities can sometimes thereby increase the receiver's perceived self-efficacy. For example, assuring people that they can successfully prevent a friend from driving while drunk can enhance their perceived ability to do so (Anderson, 1995).

Of course, these are not mutually exclusive possibilities. Indeed, several studies have indicated that combinations of these elements (e.g. combining modelling with rehearsal) can be especially valuable as a means of influencing self-efficacy (Eden & Kinnar, 1991; Maibach & Flora, 1993). But whether deployed individually or jointly, these various mechanisms all offer good prospects for enhancing perceived behavioural control.

Summary

Persuaders often seem prone to suppose that the primary reason that the audience currently fails to embrace the advocated action or viewpoint is that the audience does not have the appropriate attitudes, that is, the appropriate general evaluations of the action or object. Thus, it might be assumed that, for instance, the reason that house-holds do not participate in recycling programmes is negative attitudes toward recycling; the reason that consumers do not purchase one's product is negative evaluations of the product; and so forth.

But as should now be apparent, the audience's resistance to the advocated action need not necessarily lie in negative attitudes. On the contrary, often the audience already has the desired attitudes. In such circumstances, skilful persuaders will want to identify carefully the locus of such non-attitudinal resistance. It might be that the attitudes are insufficiently connected to the behaviour (for instance, they are insuffi-ciently salient), or it might be that other influences on behaviour (such as norms or behavioural self-efficacy) represent the key obstacles to compliance.

When the audience lacks the desired attitudes

When the audience has a negative evaluation of the desired action or viewpoint, the persuader may face the job of changing those attitudes. Sometimes, as should be apparent, the audience's negative attitudes will not necessarily be a barrier to compliance (if, for example, normative pressures are sufficiently great). But when the primary obstacle to compliance is attitudinal, attitude change becomes the persuader's objective.

Changing people's attitude about an object (a policy, a behaviour, a product, or a political candidate) is fundamentally a matter of changing people's beliefs about the object. If consumers believe that a given cleaning product is expensive, difficult to use, and does not do a good job of cleaning, they will surely have rather negative attitudes toward the product – and changing those attitudes will require somehow changing the underlying beliefs (by altering those existing beliefs or by adding new, more positive beliefs). Thus, the question becomes: which beliefs should be addressed by one's message, that is, what particular appeals (arguments) should the message emphasise? Unfortunately, it turns out to be all too easy for persuaders to be mistaken about which beliefs need to be addressed – and hence mistaken about which appeals will be most successful.

For example, one argument against marijuana use that might naturally seem to be especially powerful is the argument that regularly using marijuana leads to the use of stronger drugs (drugs that have especially harmful consequences); health educators and anti-drug campaign planners commonly suppose that this 'marijuana is a gateway drug' argument will be an effective tool in reducing marijuana use. But Yzer, Cappella, Fishbein, Hornik, and Ahern's (2003) study of anti-marijuana campaign appeals using such arguments found them to be largely ineffective – and indeed yielded some indications that the gateway argument might sometimes produce boomerang effects (that is, changes opposite to those sought by the campaign).

Similarly, one might suppose that one reason that teenagers do not seek appropriate protection from sun exposure is that they do not understand the relationship between sun exposure and skin cancer. But an intervention aimed at underscoring that connection, although successful in increasing participants' knowledge of the risk factors for skin cancer, did not significantly change attitudes about tanning and sunbathing (Kristjansson, Helgason, Mansson-Brahme, Widlund-Ivarson & Ullen, 2003).

As another example, it seems plausible to assume that for altruistically oriented behaviours such as donating blood and agreeing to be an organ donor, altruistically oriented appeals (emphasising advantages to others, the prosocial nature of the behaviour, and so forth) will naturally have some special purchase that self-oriented appeals (focused on benefits to the individual) do not. And yet in a number of studies, altruistic appeals on these topics have been found to be less persuasive than self-oriented appeals (Fink, Rey, Johnson, Spenner, Morton & Flores, 1975; Ferrari, Barone, Jason & Rose, 1985b; Barnett, Klassen, McMinimy & Schwarz, 1987).

These findings illustrate the importance of determining, rather than assuming, which beliefs and appeals are most important for a persuasive message. And in attempting to identify the key relevant beliefs and appeals, persuaders should bear in mind an important complexity: a given attitude might have different substantive bases for different receivers, requiring corresponding adaptation of persuasive messages.

For example, in the evaluation of consumer products, persons differ in their relative general emphases on different kinds of product attributes. This difference is related to variation in 'self-monitoring', which refers to the control or regulation (monitoring) of one's self-presentation (Snyder, 1974). High self-monitors are concerned about the image they project to others and tailor their conduct to fit the particular circumstances they are in; low self-monitors are less concerned about their projected image and are less likely to adapt their behaviour to external circumstances. In evaluating consumer products, high self-monitors are relatively more interested in symbolic or image-related aspects of the product (the kind of image projected by the car; what the watch says about me as a person), whereas low self-monitors are relatively more interested in instrumental or product-quality attributes (whether the car gets good gas mileage; whether the watch is accurate).

These differences (in what high and low self-monitors value in products) are reflected in corresponding differences in the relative effectiveness of different persuasive appeals. A number of studies have found that high self-monitors react more favourably to image-oriented advertisements than to product-quality-oriented ones, with the opposite effect found for low self-monitors (e.g. Snyder & DeBono, 1985; Lennon, Davis & Fairhurst, 1988; Zuckerman, Gioioso & Tellini, 1988; DeBono & Packer, 1991). Obviously, then, a persuader will want different kinds of appeals in messages aimed at these two different sorts of audiences.

To take another example, persuading people to wear protective headgear when they engage in activities such as bicycling, horseback riding, and the like might naturally be assumed to require the same kinds of arguments across the different leisure activities. But, at least sometimes, participants in these different activities have had different bases for negative attitudes toward wearing protective headgear. Many bicyclists have been unaware of the importance of protective helmets (DiGuiseppi, Rivara & Koepsell, 1990); by contrast, many equestrians recognise the need for helmets but have negative attitudes because of beliefs about how hot, heavy, and uncomfortable helmets are (Condie, Rivara & Bergman, 1993). Naturally, then, different persuasive messages will be appropriate for these two audiences given the difference in underlying beliefs.

In short, it is easy to be mistaken about which beliefs should be targeted by persuasive appeals aimed at changing attitudes. Appeals that might seem plausible can turn out not to be especially effective (e.g. altruistic appeals for altruistic behaviours); appeals that are successful for one group of receivers might not be so successful with another (as illustrated by the differences between high and low self-monitors).

Summary

Accurate diagnosis of the bases of resistance is fundamentally important to effective persuasion. Given the great variability of persuasion circumstances, there is naturally corresponding variability in the possible sources of resistance. Still, it can be useful to notice that models such as the theory of reasoned action and the theory of planned behaviour provide what amounts to abstract templates that identify possible bases of resistance; the theory of planned behaviour, for instance, identifies attitude toward the behaviour, subjective norm, and perceived behavioural control as three general possible sources of resistance. However, in certain specialised persuasion circumstances, it is possible to sketch correspondingly more particular possible loci of resistance.

A useful example concerns persuading people to take action to protect themselves against possible threats or risks (for example, quitting smoking so as to avoid lung cancer, or adopting an exercise programme to reduce the risk of heart disease). Protection motivation theory (Rogers, 1975, 1983; Rogers & Prentice-Dunn, 1997) identifies two general elements that contribute to one's motivation to undertake such protective behaviours. The first is threat appraisal, the person's assessment of the threatening or risky event. Threat appraisal is a joint function of perceived threat severity (that is, the perceived severity of the problem) and perceived threat vulnerability (one's perception of the likelihood that one will encounter or be susceptible to the threat); as persons perceive the threat to be more severe and as they perceive themselves to be more vulnerable to the threat, they are expected to have higher protection motivation. The second general element is coping appraisal, the person's assessment of the recommended way of coping with the threat. Coping appraisal is a joint function of perceived response efficacy (the degree to which the recommended course of action is perceived to be effective in dealing with the problem) and perceived self-efficacy (one's perceived ability to adopt or perform the protective action, that is, perceived behavioural control); as the perceived efficaciousness of the response increases and as perceived ability to perform the action increases, persons are expected to have greater protection motivation. (For some reviews of research on protection motivation theory, see Floyd, Prentice-Dunn & Rogers, 2000; Milne, Sheeran & Orbell, 2000.)

This abstract characterisation of the elements underlying protection motivation offers a general template for designing persuasive messages, in the sense that it identifies four fundamental possible concerns underpinning a person's decisions about protection-motivation behaviour: perceived threat severity, perceived threat vulnerability, perceived response efficacy, and perceived self-efficacy. Correspondingly, persuasive appeals might have any of these as their focus, depending on the particular persuasion situation.

For example, consider the task of persuading an audience to take up an exercise programme to prevent heart disease. Protection motivation theory identifies four different possible issues to be addressed, and skilful persuasion will require learning which of these are most important in a given circumstance. For instance, if the audience believes that they are unlikely to have heart disease (low perceived threat vulnerability), messages aimed at convincing the audience of their ability to perform regular exercise (that is, messages aimed at perceived self-efficacy) will be of little persuasive value. (For an example of the use of protection-motivation theory to guide the development of persuasive messages, see Pechmann, Zhao, Goldberg & Reibling, 2003.)

In sum, then, effective persuasion depends upon accurate identification of the bases of the audience's current resistance to the advocated view. The nature of the resistance will vary from circumstance to circumstance, but it also possible to specify some abstract possible sources of resistance, and these can serve as useful devices for guiding identification of the relevant concerns in any given situation.

CONSTRUCTING EFFECTIVE MESSAGES

Given a diagnosis of the bases of the audience's current resistance to the persuader's advocated action or viewpoint, the persuader can turn to the task of constructing effective messages that are targeted at those obstacles. Some aspects of this task have already been implicitly discussed in the course of indicating how various specific obstacles to compliance might be overcome (e.g. the use of modelling as a means of enhancing perceived behavioural control). But the research literature on persuasion also offers a number of general recommendations concerning effective message construction; here attention is drawn to three particularly important guidelines. (For further discussion, see O'Keefe, 2002b, pp. 215–240; Perloff, 2003, pp. 176–210.)

Meeting objections

Sometimes receivers will have objections (stated or unstated) to the advocate's viewpoint. The question that arises is how a persuader should handle such objections. There are three broad alternative courses of action for a persuader: ignoring the opposing arguments (commonly termed a 'one-sided' message), attempting to refute the opposing arguments (a 'refutational two-sided' message), and mentioning the opposing arguments without undermining them (a 'non-refutational two-sided' message). A considerable body of research evidence bears on the question of the relative persuasiveness of these alternatives. The evidence suggests that refutational two-sided messages are significantly more persuasive than their one-sided counterparts; non-refutational two-sided messages, on the other hand, are significantly less persuasive than one-sided messages (for reviews and discussion, see Allen, 1998; O'Keefe, 1999). That is to say, persuaders are well advised to meet counter-arguments head-on by attempting to refute them (a refutational two-sided message) rather than ignoring them (a one-sided message) or – even worse – mentioning them without undermining them (a non-refutational two-sided message).

Being clear and specific

For various reasons, persuaders will sometimes be tempted not to be especially clear about exactly what position they are advocating. This might be motivated by concerns about possible resistance or by a belief that leaving the message's point implicit will be more persuasive than making it explicit (because with the conclusion implicit, the audience will need actively to reason its way to the desired point).

But two lines of research evidence suggest that persuasiveness is commonly enhanced by clarity and specificity. The first compares the relative persuasiveness of messages in which the conclusion is stated explicitly or is omitted from the message. For example, Struckman-Johnson and Struckman-Johnson (1996) compared two versions of safer-sex public service announcements, one with and one without an explicit recommendation to use condoms. Across a number of such studies, the predominant finding is that messages with explicit conclusions are more persuasive than those with implicit conclusions (e.g. Cope & Richardson, 1972; Feingold & Knapp, 1977; for a review, see O'Keefe, 1997).

The second line of work concerns the specificity with which the communicator's recommended action is described. The contrast is between messages that provide only a general description of the advocated action and messages that provide a more detailed, specific description. For instance, Evans, Rozelle, Lasater, Dembroski, and Allen (1970) compared messages giving relatively general, unelaborated recommendations concerning dental care and messages providing more specific, detailed recommendations. These studies have commonly found messages to be more persuasive when the message contained a more specific description of the advocated behaviour (e.g. Leventhal, Jones & Trembly, 1966; Tanner, Day & Crask, 1989; for a review, see O'Keefe, 1997).

In sum, persuaders would do well to ensure that their advocated position is made clear to the audience, including being specific about the particulars of any advocated action.

Following-up

Persuaders sometimes seem not to realise that an initially successful persuasive effort may not be sufficient to ensure sustained results. But, for two reasons, follow-up persuasive efforts may be crucial.

First, after making a decision, people often immediately experience feelings of regret. (For some readers, this may be familiar as what is sometimes called 'buyer's remorse'.) Such feelings are not entirely irrational. Any given choice inevitably involves choosing between two imperfect options (not one perfectly good option versus some completely terrible option); hence, no matter which option is chosen, there will inevitably be some desirable aspects of the unchosen alternative and some undesirable aspects of the chosen option. In the course of trying to rationalise one's choice, one might quite naturally come to think about those various elements that are inconsistent with one's choice (e.g. drawbacks of the product that was just purchased) on the way to eventually concluding that those inconsistent aspects are in fact trivial (hence, one did indeed make the correct choice). But before that process reaches its conclusion, people will quite naturally experience feelings of regret, given that their attention has been drawn to all the considerations that argued against the choice that was made. Indeed, these feelings of regret can be so great as to induce people to want to change (back out of) their initial decision. (For classic treatments of these matters, see Festinger & Walster, 1964; Walster, 1964.)

Obviously, persuaders might find it useful to engage in follow-up efforts aimed at minimising such feelings of regret. The potential value of such efforts has been nicely illustrated in a study of automobile purchases. During the period between the time the purchase decision is made and the time the vehicle is delivered, some automobile buyers back out of their initial decision (a reversal that can be induced by regret). But when two follow-up telephone calls were made to the buyer – calls that emphasised the desirable aspects of the chosen automobile and that reassured the buyer of the wisdom of the decision – the number of buyers who reversed their initial decisions was significantly reduced (Donnelly & Ivancevich, 1970).

Second, quite apart from any immediate regret-based reversals of persuasive effects, there is good reason to suppose that, in general, persuasive effects are likely to decay over time (for some general reviews and discussion, see Cook & Flay, 1978; Zanna, Fazio & Ross, 1994). Old habits can return, competing persuasive messages can be received, new obstacles and constraints can emerge – and all these can serve to diminish any previous persuasive effects.

For example, in consulting with teachers, school psychologists often seek to convince teachers to adopt some new teaching method or approach. But 'ideas that sound simple during the course of consultation may, in fact, require skills that the consultee [teacher] does not possess to an adequate degree.' Unfortunately, this may not become apparent until the teacher is 'actually attempting to implement the strategy in question' (Gutkin & Curtis, 1990, p. 584). Of course, when this obstacle arises, the teacher's enthusiasm for the new approach may well fade. Only close attention to the necessity for follow-up efforts will permit the identification and resolution of such problems.

OVERVIEW

Skilful persuasion requires adaptation to the basis of the audience's resistance to the advocated view. Discerning the current obstacles to compliance is not always easy, and fashioning effective messages aimed at those barriers can be difficult. However, as should be apparent, the research literature on persuasive effects provides a number of useful insights into the diagnosis and management of obstacles to persuasion.

REFERENCES

Aitken, C. K., McMahon, T. A., Wearing, A. J. & Finlayson, B. L. (1994). Residential water use: predicting and reducing consumption. *Journal of Applied Social Psychology*, *24*, 136–158.

Ajzen, I. (1991). The theory of planned behavior. *Organizational Behavior and Human Decision Processes*, *50*, 179–211.

Ajzen, I. & Fishbein, M. (1980). *Understanding attitudes and predicting social behavior*. Englewood Cliffs, NJ: Prentice-Hall.

Albarracin, D., Johnson, B. T., Fishbein, M. & Muellerleile, P. A. (2001). Theories of reasoned action and planned behavior as models of condom use: a meta-analysis. *Psychological Bulletin*, *127*, 142–161.

Alemi, F., Alemagno, S. A., Goldhagen, J., Ash, L., Finkelstein, B., Lavin, A., Butts, J. & Ghadiri, A. (1996). Computer reminders improve on-time immunization rates. *Medical Care*, *34*, OS45–OS51.

Allen, M. (1998). Comparing the persuasive effectiveness of one- and two-sided messages. In M. Allen & R. W. Preiss (Eds), *Persuasion: advances through meta-analysis*. Cresskill, NJ: Hampton Press.

Andersen, R. E., Franckowiak, S. C., Snyder, J., Bartlett, S. J. & Fontaine, K. R. (1998). Can inexpensive signs encourage the use of stairs? Results from a community intervention. *Annals of Internal Medicine, 129*, 363–369.

Anderson, R. B. (1995). Cognitive appraisal of performance capability in the prevention of drunken driving: a test of self-efficacy theory. *Journal of Public Relations Research, 7*, 205–229.

Anderson, R. B. (2000). Vicarious and persuasive influences on efficacy expectations and intentions to perform breast self-examination. *Public Relations Review, 26*, 97–114.

Armitage, C. J. & Conner, M. (2001). Efficacy of the theory of planned behaviour: a meta-analytic review. *British Journal of Social Psychology, 40*, 471–499.

Aronson, E., Fried, C. & Stone, J. (1991). Overcoming denial and increasing the intention to use condoms through the induction of hypocrisy. *American Journal of Public Health, 81*, 1636–1638.

Austin, J., Alvero, A. M. & Olson, R. (1998). Prompting patron safety belt use at a restaurant. *Journal of Applied Behavior Analysis, 31*, 655–657.

Barnett, M. A., Klassen, M., McMinimy, V. & Schwarz, L. (1987). The role of self- and other-oriented motivation in the organ donation decision. *Advances in Consumer Research, 14*, 335–337.

Borgida, E. & Campbell, B. (1982). Belief relevance and attitude-behavior consistency: the moderating role of personal experience. *Journal of Personality and Social Psychology, 42*, 239–247.

Cardenas, M. P. & Simons-Morton, B. G. (1993). The effect of anticipatory guidance on mothers' self-efficacy and behavioral intentions to prevent burns caused by hot tap water. *Patient Education and Counseling, 21*, 117–123.

Carter, C. A. & Kahnweiler, W. M. (2000). The efficacy of the social norms approach to substance abuse prevention applied to fraternity men. *Journal of American College Health, 49*, 66–71.

Condie, C., Rivara, F. P. & Bergman, A. B. (1993). Strategies of a successful campaign to promote the use of equestrian helmets. *Public Health Reports, 108*, 121–126.

Conn, V. S., Burks, K. J., Minor, M. A. & Mehr, D. R. (2003). Randomized trial of two interventions to increase older women's exercise. *American Journal of Health Behavior, 27*, 380–388.

Conner, M. & Sparks, P. (1996). The theory of planned behaviour and health behaviours. In M. Conner & P. Norman (Eds), *Predicting health behaviour*. Buckingham: Open University Press.

Conner, M. & Armitage, C. J. (1998). Extending the theory of planned behavior: a review and avenues for further research. *Journal of Applied Social Psychology, 28*, 1429–1464.

Cook, T. D. & Flay, B. R. (1978). The persistence of experimentally induced attitude change. In L. Berkowitz (Ed.), *Advances in experimental social psychology* (vol. 11). New York: Academic Press.

Cope, F. & Richardson, D. (1972). The effects of reassuring recommendations in a fear-arousing speech. *Speech Monographs, 39*, 148–150.

Cotte, J., Coulter, R. A. & Moore, M. (2005). Enhancing or disrupting guilt: the role of ad credibility and perceived manipulative intent. *Journal of Business Research, 58*, 361–368.

Coulter, R. H. & Pinto, M. B. (1995). Guilt appeals in advertising: What are their effects? *Journal of Applied Psychology*, *80*, 697–705.

Coulter, R. H., Cotte, J. & Moore, M. L. (1997). Guilt appeals in advertising: are you feeling guilty? In D. T. LeClair & M. Hartline (Eds), *1997 AMA winter educators' conference: marketing theory and applications*. Chicago: American Marketing Association.

DeBono, K. G. & Packer, M. (1991). The effects of advertising appeal on perceptions of product quality. *Personality and Social Psychology Bulletin*, *17*, 194–200.

De Young, R. (1989). Exploring the difference between recyclers and non-recyclers: the role of information. *Journal of Environmental Systems*, *18*, 341–351.

DiGuiseppi, C. G., Rivara, F. P. & Koepsell, T. D. (1990). Attitudes toward bicycle helmet ownership and use by school-age children. *American Journal of Diseases of Children*, *144*, 83–86.

Duncan, T. E., Duncan, S. C., Beauchamp, N., Wells, J. & Ary, D. V. (2000). Development and evaluation of an interactive CD-ROM refusal skills program to prevent youth substance use: 'refuse to use'. *Journal of Behavioral Medicine*, *23*, 59–72.

Eagly, A. H. & Chaiken, S. (1993). *The psychology of attitudes*. Fort Worth, TX: Harcourt Brace Jovanovich.

Eden, D. & Kinnar, J. (1991). Modeling Galatea: boosting self-efficacy to increase volunteering. *Journal of Applied Psychology*, *76*, 770–780.

Englis, B. G. (1990). Consumer emotional reactions to television advertising and their effects on message recall. In S. J. Agres, J. A. Edell & T. M. Dubitsky (Eds), *Emotion in advertising: theoretical and practical applications*. New York: Quorum Books.

Evans, R. I., Rozelle, R. M., Lasater, T. M., Dembroski, T. M. & Allen, B. P. (1970). Fear arousal, persuasion, and actual versus implied behavioral change: new perspective utilizing a real-life dental hygiene program. *Journal of Personality and Social Psychology*, *16*, 220–227.

Feingold, P. C. & Knapp, M. L. (1977). Anti-drug abuse commercials. *Journal of Communication*, *27*, 20–28.

Ferrari, J. R., Barone, R. C., Jason, L. A. & Rose, T. (1985a). The effects of a personal phone call prompt on blood donor commitment. *Journal of Community Psychology*, *13*, 295–298.

Ferrari, J. R., Barone, R. C., Jason, L. A. & Rose, T. (1985b). The use of incentives to increase blood donations. *Journal of Social Psychology*, *125*, 791–793.

Festinger, L. & Walster, E. (1964). Post-decision regret and decision reversal. In L. Festinger (Ed.), *Conflict, decision, and dissonance*. Stanford, CA: Stanford University Press.

Fink, E. L., Rey, L. D., Johnson, K. W., Spenner, K. I., Morton, D. R. & Flores, E. T. (1975). The effects of family occupational type, sex, and appeal style on helping behavior. *Journal of Experimental Social Psychology*, *11*, 43–52.

Fishbein, M. & Ajzen, I. (1975). *Belief, attitude, intention, and behavior*. Reading, MA: Addison-Wesley.

Floyd, D. L., Prentice-Dunn, S. & Rogers, R. W. (2000). A meta-analysis of research on protection motivation theory. *Journal of Applied Social Psychology*, *30*, 407–429.

Fried, C. B. (1998). Hypocrisy and identification with transgressions: a case of undetected dissonance. *Basic and Applied Social Psychology*, *20*, 145–154.

Fried, C. B. & Aronson, E. (1995). Hypocrisy, misattribution, and dissonance reduction. *Personality and Social Psychology Bulletin*, **21**, 925–933.

Godin, G. & Kok, G. (1996). The theory of planned behavior: a review of its applications to health-related behaviors. *American Journal of Health Promotion*, **11**, 87–98.

Gutkin, T. B. & Curtis, M. J. (1990). School-based consultation: theory, techniques, and research. In T. B. Gutkin & C. R. Reynolds (Eds), *The handbook of school psychology*, 2nd edn. New York: Wiley.

Hagen, K. M., Gutkin, T. B., Wilson, C. P. & Oats, R. G. (1998). Using vicarious experience and verbal persuasion to enhance self-efficacy in pre-service teachers: 'priming the pump' for consultation. *School Psychology Quarterly*, **13**, 169–178.

Hagger, M. S., Chatzisarantis, N. L. D. & Biddle, S. J. H. (2002). A meta-analytic review of the theories of reasoned action and planned behavior in physical activity: predictive validity and the contribution of additional variables. *Journal of Sport and Exercise Psychology*, **24**, 3–32.

Haines, M. & Spear, S. F. (1996). Changing the perception of the norm: a strategy to decrease binge drinking among college students. *Journal of American College Health*, **45**, 134–140.

Heath, Y. & Gifford, R. (2002). Extending the theory of planned behavior: predicting the use of public transportation. *Journal of Applied Social Psychology*, **32**, 2154–2189.

Kantola, S. J. Syme, G. J. & Campbell, N. A. (1982). The role of individual differences and external variables in a test of the sufficiency of Fishbein's model to explain behavioral intentions to conserve water. *Journal of Applied Social Psychology*, **12**, 70–83.

Kelly, J. A., St. Lawrence, J. S., Stevenson, L. Y., Hauth, A. C., Kalichman, S. C., Diaz, Y. E., Brasfield, T. L., Koob, J. J. & Morgan, M. G. (1992). Community AIDS/HIV risk reduction: the effects of endorsements by popular people in three cities. *American Journal of Public Health*, **82**, 1483–1489.

Kristjansson, S., Helgason, A. R., Mansson-Brahme, E., Widlund-Ivarson, B. & Ullen, H. (2003). 'You and your skin': a short-duration presentation of skin cancer prevention for teenagers. *Health Education Research*, **18**, 88–97.

Lennon, S. J., Davis, L. L. & Fairhurst, A. (1988). Evaluations of apparel advertising as a function of self-monitoring. *Perceptual and Motor Skills*, **66**, 987–996.

Leventhal, H., Jones, S. & Trembly, G. (1966). Sex differences in attitude and behavior change under conditions of fear and specific instructions. *Journal of Experimental Social Psychology*, **2**, 387–399.

Linz, D., Fuson, I. A. & Donnerstein, E. (1990). Mitigating the negative effects of sexually violent mass communications through preexposure briefings. *Communication Research*, **17**, 641–674.

Luzzo, D. A., Hasper, P., Albert, K. A., Bibby, M. A. & Martinelli, E. A., Jr (1999). Effects of self-efficacy-enhancing interventions on the math/science self-efficacy and career interests, goals, and actions of career undecided college students. *Journal of Consulting Psychology*, **46**, 233–243.

Mahler, H. I. M., Kulik, J. A. & Hill, M. R. (1993). A preliminary report on the effects of videotape preparations for coronary artery bypass surgery on anxiety and self-efficacy: a simulation and validation with college students. *Basic and Applied Social Psychology*, **14**, 437–453.

Maibach, E. & Flora, J. A. (1993). Symbolic modeling and cognitive rehearsal: using video to promote AIDS prevention self-efficacy. *Communication Research, 20,* 517–545.

Marcus, A. C., Crane, L. A., Kaplan, C. P., Reading, A. E., Savage, E., Gunning, J., Bernstein, G. & Berek, J. S. (1992). Improving adherence to screening follow-up among women with abnormal pap smears: results from a large clinic-based trial of three intervention strategies. *Medical Care, 30,* 216–230.

Miller, D. T., Monin, B. & Prentice, D. A. (2000). Pluralistic ignorance and inconsistency between private attitudes and public behaviors. In D. J. Terry & M. A. Hogg (Eds), *Attitudes, behavior, and social context: the role of norms and group membership.* Mahwah, NJ: Lawrence Erlbaum.

Milne, S., Sheeran, P. & Orbell, S. (2000). Prediction and intervention in health-related behavior: a meta-analytic review of protection motivation theory. *Journal of Applied Social Psychology, 30,* 106–143.

Ng, J. Y. Y., Tam, S. F., Yew, W. W. & Lam, W. K. (1999). Effects of video modeling on self-efficacy and exercise performance of COPD patients. *Social Behavior and Personality, 27,* 475–486.

Notani, A. S. (1998). Moderators of perceived behavioral control's predictiveness in the theory of planned behavior: a meta-analysis. *Journal of Consumer Psychology, 7,* 247–271.

O'Keefe, D. J. (1997). Standpoint explicitness and persuasive effect: a meta-analytic review of the effects of varying conclusion articulation in persuasive messages. *Argumentation and Advocacy, 34,* 1–12.

O'Keefe, D. J. (1999). How to handle opposing arguments in persuasive messages: a meta-analytic review of the effects of one-sided and two-sided messages. *Communication Yearbook, 22,* 209–249.

O'Keefe, D. J. (2000). Guilt and social influence. *Communication Yearbook, 23,* 67–101.

O'Keefe, D. J. (2002a). Guilt as a mechanism of persuasion. In J. P. Dillard & M. Pfau (Eds), *The persuasion handbook: developments in theory and practice.* Thousand Oaks, CA: Sage.

O'Keefe, D. J. (2002b). *Persuasion: theory and research.* Thousand Oaks, CA: Sage.

Okun, M. A., Karoly, P. & Lutz, R. (2002). Clarifying the contribution of subjective norm to predicting leisure-time exercise. *American Journal of Health Behavior, 26,* 296–305.

Pechmann, C., Zhao, G., Goldberg, M. E. & Reibling, E. T. (2003). What to convey in antismoking advertisements for adolescents: the use of protection motivation theory to identify effective message themes. *Journal of Marketing, 67,* 1–18.

Perkins, H. W., Meilman, P. W., Leichliter, J. S., Cashin, J. R. & Presley, C. A. (1999). Misperception of the norms for the frequency of alcohol and other drug use on college campuses. *Journal of American College Health, 47,* 253–258.

Perloff, R. M. (2003). *The dynamics of persuasion,* 2nd edn. Mahwah, NJ: Lawrence Erlbaum.

Pinto, M. B. & Priest, S. (1991). Guilt appeals in advertising: an exploratory study. *Psychological Reports, 69,* 375–385.

Prislin, R. (1987). Attitude–behaviour relationship: attitude relevance and behaviour relevance. *European Journal of Social Psychology, 17,* 483–485.

Rogers, R. W. (1975). A protection motivation theory of fear appeals and attitude change. *Journal of Psychology*, *91*, 93–114.

Rogers, R. W. (1983). Cognitive and physiological processes in fear appeals and attitude change: a revised theory of protection motivation. In J. T. Cacioppo & R. E. Petty (Eds), *Social psychophysiology: a sourcebook*. New York: Guilford.

Rogers, R. W. & Prentice-Dunn, S. (1997). Protection motivation theory. In D. Gochman (Ed.), *Handbook of health behavior research*, vol. 1. *Personal and social determinants*. New York: Plenum.

Shepherd, G. J. (1985). Linking attitudes and behavioral criteria. *Human Communication Research*, *12*, 275–284 [Erratum, 358].

Snyder, M. (1974). Self-monitoring of expressive behavior. *Journal of Personality and Social Psychology*, *30*, 526–537.

Snyder, M. (1982). When believing means doing: creating links between attitudes and behavior. In M. P. Zanna, E. T. Higgins & C. P. Herman (Eds), *Consistency in social behavior: the Ontario symposium*, vol. 2. Hillsdale, NJ: Lawrence Erlbaum.

Snyder, M. & Kendzierski, D. (1982). Acting on one's attitudes: procedures for linking attitude and behavior. *Journal of Experimental Social Psychology*, *18*, 165–183.

Snyder, M. & DeBono, K. G. (1985). Appeals to image and claims about quality: understanding the psychology of advertising. *Journal of Personality and Social Psychology*, *49*, 586–597.

Steffen, V. J., Sternberg, L., Teegarden, L. A. & Shepherd, K. (1994). Practice and persuasive frame: effects on beliefs, intention, and performance of a cancer self-examination. *Journal of Applied Social Psychology*, *24*, 897–925.

Steffian, G. (1999). Correction of normative misperceptions: an alcohol abuse prevention program. *Journal of Drug Education*, *29*, 115–138.

St. Lawrence, J. S., Brasfield, T. L., Diaz, Y. E., Jefferson, K. W., Reynolds, M. T. & Leonard, M. O. (1994). Three-year follow-up of an HIV risk-reduction intervention that used popular peers. *American Journal of Public Health*, *84*, 2027–2028.

Stone, J., Aronson, E., Crain, A. L., Winslow, M. P. & Fried, C. B. (1994). Inducing hypocrisy as a means of encouraging young adults to use condoms. *Personality and Social Psychology Bulletin*, *20*, 116–128.

Struckman-Johnson, D. & Struckman-Johnson, C. (1996). Can you say condom? It makes a difference in fear-arousing AIDS prevention public service announcements. *Journal of Applied Social Psychology*, *26*, 1068–1083.

Sutton, S. (1998). Predicting and explaining intentions and behavior: how well are we doing? *Journal of Applied Social Psychology*, *28*, 1317–1338.

Tanner, J. F. Jr, Day, E. & Crask, M. R. (1989). Protection motivation theory: an extension of fear appeals theory in communication. *Journal of Business Research*, *19*, 267–276.

Thombs, D. L. & Hamilton, M. J. (2002). Effects of a social norm feedback campaign on the drinking norms and behavior of Division I student-athletes. *Journal of Drug Education*, *32*, 227–244.

Walster, E. (1964). The temporal sequence of post-decision processes. In L. Festinger (Ed.), *Conflict, decision, and dissonance*. Stanford, CA: Stanford University Press.

Wechsler, H. & Kuo, M. (2000). College students define binge drinking and estimate its prevalence: results of a national survey. *Journal of American College Health*, *49*, 57–64.

Weeks, K., Levy, S. R., Zhu, C., Perhats, C., Handler, A. & Flay, B. R. (1995). Impact of a school-based AIDS prevention program on young adolescents' self-efficacy skills. *Health Education Research, 10*, 329–344.

Weisse, C. S., Turbiasz, A. A. & Whitney, D. J. (1995). Behavioral training and AIDS risk reduction: overcoming barriers to condom use. *AIDS Education and Prevention, 7*, 50–59.

Werch, C. E., Pappas, D. M., Carlson, J. M., DiClemente, C. C., Chally, P. S. & Sinder, J. A. (2000). Results of a social norm intervention to prevent binge drinking among first-year residential college students. *Journal of American College Health, 49*, 85–92.

Yzer, M. C., Fisher, J. D., Bakker, A. B., Siero, F. W. & Misovich, S. J. (1998). The effects of information about AIDS risk and self-efficacy on women's intentions to engage in AIDS preventive behavior. *Journal of Applied Social Psychology, 28*, 1837–1852.

Yzer, M. C., Cappella, J. N., Fishbein, M., Hornik, R. & Ahern, R. K. (2003). The effectiveness of gateway communications in anti-marijuana campaigns. *Journal of Health Communication, 8*, 129–143.

Zanna, M. P., Fazio, R. H. & Ross, M. (1994). The persistence of persuasion. In R. C. Shank & E. Langer (Eds), *Beliefs, reasoning, and decision making: psycho-logic in honor of Bob Abelson*. Hillsdale, NJ: Lawrence Erlbaum.

Zuckerman, M., Gioioso, C. & Tellini, S. (1988). Control orientation, self-monitoring, and preference for image versus quality approach to advertising. *Journal of Research in Personality, 22*, 89–100.

Part III

Specialised contexts

Chapter 12

Asserting and confronting

Richard F. Rakos

If not I for myself, who then?
And being for myself, what am I?
And if not now, when?

Hillel

THE ABOVE WORDS BY the ancient sage, though discussing knowledge and meritorious behavior in general (Goldin, 1957), also apply
to the effective use of assertive skills: the right to express one's desires,
the social responsibilities that accompany rights, and the decision to
engage in such expression. Hundreds of studies over the past 35 years
have confirmed that Hillel's wisdom remains highly relevant even when
the societal *Weltanschauung* has evolved from Judaic monotheism to
secular humanism.

Assertiveness rose to prominence in the mid-1970s as both a pop
psychology fad that promised to be a panacea for human unhappiness
and as a new clinical focus of behaviour therapy (Rakos, 1991). While
the 1990s saw the popular obsession with assertion recede and the
research interest in it wane, the concept today is widely accepted as
an appropriate way to influence others and resolve conflicts. The contemporary notion of assertiveness emerged from the cultural philosophies and social changes that the USA, and to a lesser extent other
Western industrialised nations, experienced in the late 1960s and early
1970s (Rakos, 1991). These include the *rationality* that helped to meet
the demands of an accelerating scientific and technological society,
the *social and political activism* that promoted personal empowerment, the
ethical relativism that expanded the range of socially acceptable
behaviours, and, finally, the *pragmatism* (cf. Dewey, 1957) that prioritised
outcome over ideology. Today these four attributes remain at the heart
of assertion as an *option* for coping with, and adjusting to, the rapidly
changing postmodern technological environment.

The contexts in which assertion has acquired increased importance are now quite varied compared to the clinical settings in which it originated. For instance, its value in the work environment is recognised widely (Back & Back, 1999; Hayes, 2002; Hargie, Dickson & Tourish, 2004), particularly within predominantly female professions, such as nursing (Hansten, Washburn & Kenyon, 1999) and social work (McBride, 1998), where deference by women can undermine job satisfaction. The benefits of assertion extend beyond the immediate conflict situation by empowering workers as well as managers. For example, Korsgaard, Roberson, and Rymph (1998) found that assertively skilled persons, compared to non-assertive individuals, received fairer performance appraisals and also evidenced more positive attitudes toward the appraisal and more trust in the manager.

Assertiveness also contributes to physical wellness as consumers negotiate increasingly complex contemporary health-care systems. For example, the skill helps low socio-economic status cancer patients access the most appropriate medical care (Adler, McGraw & McKinlay, 1998; Krupat et al., 1999), and permits women to respond to stress as a challenge rather than as a threat (Tomaka, et al., 1999). Assertiveness training is an integral component of interventions for problems that compromise the quality of life, such as chronic pain (Winterowd, Beck & Gruener, 2003) and depression (Klosko & Sanderson, 1999). It also can empower vulnerable individuals, such as the chronic mentally ill, who are at risk of contracting HIV infection (Weinhardt, Carey, Carey & Verdecia, 1998), women with intellectual disabilities who need to be partners in their health care (Lunsky, Straiko & Armstrong, 2003), children at risk of being abused or bullied (MacIntyre, Carr, Lawlor & Flattery, 2000), and adolescents who face decisions about substance use (Trudeau, Lillehoj, Spoth & Redmond, 2003). Furthermore, self-help books continue to be published, including *The Complete Idiot's Guide to Assertiveness* (Davidson, 1997), which surely marks assertion's full acceptance as a legitimate contemporary skill.

Though the social value of assertion is widely embraced, it does not automatically follow that use of these skills is invariably the preferred option; in many cases, in fact, it is not. The purpose of this chapter, therefore, is to summarise the current understanding of the conditions under which assertive behaviour in conflict situations is both appropriate and effective.

DEFINING ASSERTIVE BEHAVIOUR

The early definitions of assertion emphasised the individual's right to express personal desires while simultaneously respecting the rights of the other person (e.g. Alberti & Emmons, 1970; Lange & Jakubowski, 1976). They were developed by clinicians from the pioneering formulations introduced by Salter (1949) and Wolpe (1969), and specified components (be direct, use a firm but respectful tone, and maintain eye contact) derived from face or content validity. However, such conceptualisations were unable to promote systematic theoretical and empirical enquiry, due to their insensitivity to situational, individual, and cultural factors. This led Rich and Schroeder (1976) to propose a functional, contentless operant definition: '[Assertive behaviour is] the skill to seek, maintain, or enhance reinforcement in an interpersonal situation through the expression of feelings or wants when such expression risks loss of reinforcement or even punishment ... the degree of assertiveness may be measured by the effectiveness of an individual's response in producing, maintaining, or enhancing reinforcement' (p. 1082).

This definition highlights the core features of assertion (Rakos, 1991):

a) it is a *learned skill* that varies as a function of the situation, not a 'trait' that a person 'has' or 'lacks'
b) it occurs only in an *interpersonal* context
c) it is an *expressive* skill, involving verbal and non-verbal components
d) it always involves *risk* that the recipient may react negatively to and/or fail to comply with the assertion
e) it is frequently measured by *outcome*, which some consider to be the 'ultimate criterion for evaluating performance'. (McFall, 1982, p. 17)

However, assertion must be evaluated by more than a simple *outcome criterion* (Rakos, 1991). Because assertion involves risk, even technically proficient behaviour may fail to produce reinforcement in any given instance. This *technical criterion* assesses response quality. Additionally, assertion may achieve its immediate goals but significantly injure the relationship. Such a response 'works' only in a limited way; the net effect of even a 'self-enhancing' skill (Masters et al., 1987) must be determined by a *cost-benefit criterion*. Finally, behaviour must have social validity – legitimacy through social acceptability (Kazdin, 1977; Wolf, 1978). Since unskilled behaviour can still produce reinforcement, a *cultural criterion* that judges social appropriateness is usually necessary. Thus, the immediate effectiveness of the response is but one way to measure assertiveness, and, in fact, trainers emphasise technical expertise, net benefit, and cultural appropriateness far more than immediate outcome (Heimberg & Etkin, 1983). Indeed, when numerous instances of assertion are aggregated, each of the four standards defines self-enhancing yet socially responsible behaviour.

Criteria such as technical expertise and cultural appropriateness reintroduce some content into the functional definition of assertion. But a consensus has been elusive; St. Lawrence (1987), for example, identified more than 20 distinctly different definitions of assertion in use in research and training. Thus, a discussion of ways to approach the concept of assertion is essential.

CLARIFICATION OF THE ASSERTION CONCEPT

Response classes of assertion

Assertive behaviour comprises a number of partially independent response classes. Schroeder et al. (1983), after an extensive review of the literature, identified four 'positive' response classes – admitting personal short-comings (self-disclosure), giving and receiving compliments, initiating and maintaining interactions, and expressing positive feelings – and three 'negative' or 'conflict' response classes – expressing unpopular or different opinions, requesting behaviour changes by other people, and refusing unreasonable requests.

The asserter's initiative also has been used to categorise responses. Trower

(1995) identified active assertive skills (self-disclosure, asking favours, disagreeing, and expressing negative and positive feelings) and reactive assertive skills (refusing requests, responding to disagreement, and responding to negative and positive feelings). Similarly, Gambrill (1995) classified negative assertion as a response to another's initiative (refusing unwanted and tempting requests, and responding to criticism) or as an initiative response (requesting a behaviour change, disagreeing, apologising, and ending interactions). She categorised positive assertion as an initiative response (asking favours and complimenting others). However, this approach has had a limited impact because it was articulated after the majority of the assertion studies had been published.

The conflict response classes have received the bulk of the research and clinical attention, probably due to social and historical factors (such as the dominance of male values) rather than to scientific or clinical ones. While the focus here will remain on conflict assertion, it is important to recognise that assertiveness encompasses interpersonal expressiveness in both positive and negative contexts (Rakos, 1991; Gambrill, 1995).

Distinguishing assertion from aggression

Assertion typically has been conceptualised as the midpoint on the continuum between non-assertion and aggression. While research has generally supported this approach (Galassi, Galassi & Vedder, 1981), more recent data suggest that assertion may incorporate elements of aggressive and submissive behaviour (Wilson & Gallois, 1993). Furthermore, though a single continuum highlights the appropriateness of assertiveness training for aggressive as well as timid individuals, it fails to offer a clear differentiation between socially appropriate conflict assertive behaviour and inappropriate aggressive behaviour (Hargie & Dickson, 2004). This is a critical distinction since laypersons often fail to distinguish the two styles of responding: describe assertion as pushy, rude, and insensitive; and label conflict assertion as aggression (Rakos, 1991). Such confusion compromises the social validity of assertive response alternatives.

Most attempts to distinguish between assertion and aggression employ one or more of the four criteria discussed earlier. Alberti and Emmons (2001) and Lange and Jakubowski (1976) both suggested that appropriate conflict assertion, unlike aggression, respects the other person's rights and dignity through the use of non-hostile verbal content and vocal attributes. Assertion is expected to produce strong relationships and relatively few negative emotions, whereas aggression is predicted to result in a strained emotionally charged relationship. Hollandsworth (1977), however, argued that such formulations fail to establish objective criteria; he proposed instead that aggressive responses are defined by their use of coercive content (verbal disparagement, name-calling, and verbal threat of punishment). Alberti (1977) further contended that the distinction cannot rest on content alone, but must also acknowledge intentions, consequences, and context. Thus, Rakos (1979) noted that it might be appropriate to 'escalate' (Masters et al., 1987) the response by including reasonable threats (e.g. to initiate legal action, appeal to higher authority, refuse to cooperate further, withdraw resources) after repeated non-compliance with an assertion.

Pure functional definitions also are problematic because they exclude critical context such as social values, behavioural goals, and cultural expectations. For instance, Wilson and Gallois (1993) demonstrated that people commonly endorse 'the general goals of avoiding conflict and not straining the relationship' (p. 99). However, Rakos (1979) suggested that the functional definition can serve as the basis from which other functionally related behaviours with specified but general content can be identified. Assertion, which is generally viewed as a discrete behaviour and a personal right, should instead be considered as a chain of overt and covert responses encompassing rights (actually, *rights behaviours*) and their functionally related antecedent and consequent responsibilities (*obligation behaviours*). Verbalisation of the rights behaviour alone, without the attendant social obligation behaviours, is *expressive behaviour* and, by itself, aggressive. Conflict assertion, in contrast, requires the emission of specific categories of socially responsible behaviour. There are the following antecedent obligations (emitted prior to expressive behaviour):

- engaging in sufficient overt and covert behaviour to determine the rights of *all* participants
- developing a verbal and non-verbal response repertoire that is intended to influence the other person's offending behaviour but not the self-evaluation of his or her 'worth'
- considering the potential negative consequences the other person may experience as a function of expressive behaviour.

There are also the following subsequent obligations (emitted after expressive behaviour):

- providing a brief, honest, but non-apologetic explanation for the expressive behaviour
- providing clarifying or alternative interpretations of the expressive behaviour and empathic communications concerning its implications, in an attempt to minimise any hurt, anger, or unhappiness experienced by the other person as a consequence of the expressive behaviour
- protecting the other person's rights if that person is unable to do so
- seeking a mutually acceptable compromise when legitimate rights of both parties exist and are in conflict.

The antecedent obligations are necessary prerequisites to expressive behaviour in all conflict situations, and the subsequent ones are the key socially sanctioned elements that preserve relationships while contentious issues are addressed directly (Rakos, 1991; Wilson, Lizzio, Whicker, Gallois & Price, 2003). Because women are inclined to employ interpersonal sensitivity to resolve disagreements (Wilson & Gallois, 1993), they rely strongly on obligations, in contrast to men, who tend to focus on rights (Wilson et al., 2003). While the subsequent obligations can be emitted as part of an assertion to a stranger with whom no further contact is anticipated, they do not improve the social reaction in such situations (Heisler & McCormack, 1982) and are unnecessary – there is no relationship to enhance – and potentially problematic, as they extend the interaction and expand the content that is open for discussion.

Furthermore, when the legitimate rights of strangers conflict, the nature of the situation usually precludes a search for a mutually acceptable compromise.

The behaviour chain conceptualisation provides a way to distinguish assertion, which includes the emission of the appropriate obligation behaviours as well as the expressive ones, from aggressive behaviour, which involves only the expression of rights. Expressing rights alone violates the general norm of conflict minimisation and employs dominance and power to achieve an outcome (Wilson & Gallois, 1993). It is not surprising, therefore, that in conflict situations persons exhibiting the dominating, hostile, type A behaviour pattern are less likely than type Bs to include obligation components within assertive responses (Bruch, McCann & Harvey, 1991). Thus, the chain definition classifies the reply to your supervisor of 'Janice, I'm sorry, I can't work late tonight' as an expressive response and, by itself, aggressive. In a continuing relationship with a supervisor, both antecedent and subsequent responsibilities define assertive behaviour. These obligations encompass general and flexible content, so that variability due to situational, social, and cultural norms and values can be accommodated. The components themselves have little meaning apart from the chain. Nevertheless, sufficient specificity is included so that competent emission of the individual components can be reliably trained and then effectively generalised to the natural environment (Rakos & Schroeder, 1979).

THE SKILL OF CONFLICT ASSERTION

Research in clinical, school, and work contexts convincingly indicates that conflict assertive skills characterise psychologically adaptive, 'healthy' individuals and facilitate personal growth and satisfaction, particularly, but by no means exclusively, in cultural contexts dominated by secular Western norms and values (see Rakos, 1991, for an extensive review). But exactly what behaviours constitute this valuable skill? Certainly, overt response elements, such as verbalisations and eye contact, are important components. However, because the response must be sensitive to the context, covert behaviours must be integrally involved in selecting the overt responses that best meet the needs of the situation. Fortunately, the extensive research provides a good number of general guidelines for the development of a diverse behavioural repertoire that can be adapted to the specific circumstance.

Overt behavioural components of conflict assertion

The overt response elements can be categorised as follows:

- content: the verbal behaviour of the asserter, or what the person *says* to the other person(s)
- paralinguistic elements: the vocal characteristics of the verbal behaviour, or how the asserter *sounds*
- non-verbal behaviours: the body movements and facial expressions that accompany the verbal behaviour, or how the asserter *appears*
- social interaction skills: the timing, initiation, persistence, and stimulus control

skills that enhance the impact of the verbal behaviour, or how the asserter behaves in the *process* of the interaction.

Content

The verbal content of conflict assertion includes the expression of rights and the emission of obligations, as described by the chain conceptualisation presented above.

Expression of rights

The expression of rights is the core of any assertion, its *raison d'être*. The specific content will vary as a function of the response class and situation, but will always include a statement of desire, affect, or opinion (Romano & Bellack, 1980; Kolotkin et al., 1984). For example:

Refusal: 'No thank you, I am not interested.'
Behaviour change request: 'I feel that I am doing most of the housework' (statement of opinion or affect). 'I would like to sit down with you and revise our agreement' (request for new behaviour).
Expression of unpopular or different opinion: 'I don't think your job performance is up to our expectations.'

These rights statements exemplify several important topographical features of skilled responding. First, they utilise 'I-statements', in which the speaker assumes responsibility for personal feelings, rather than 'you-statements', which attribute responsibility for personal feelings to the other person (Lange & Jakubowski, 1976; Winship & Kelly, 1976). For example, 'You make me angry when you don't do your share of the housework' is a very different communication than 'I am angry because I feel I am doing more than my share of the housework'. Note also that the 'I-statement' offers a legitimate but unconfirmed perception, while the 'you-statement' presents a statement of fact that must be denied. Thus, it is not surprising that 'I-statements' are strongly related to judgements of overall assertion, while 'you-statements' are associated with aggression (Kolotkin et al., 1984). However, because 'I-statements' do not characterise ordinary conversation and may be difficult for many individuals to adopt (Gervasio, 1987), their use may be limited to specific situations, as when the recipient of an assertion is likely to be very sensitive to blame or when there is a continuing emotionally charged dispute.

Expressions of rights are also direct, specific, and respectful. A *direct* statement contains a clear, honest, and succinct message that describes the relevant feelings, desires, perceptions, or opinions. However, brevity should not violate conversational rules; compound sentences joined by 'and' or 'but' should be employed (cf. Gervasio & Crawford, 1989). Additionally, an introductory 'orienting statement' that signals the topic to be discussed is usually appropriate (e.g. 'I have some concerns about the plans we made'; Kolotkin et al., 1984). Explanations or apologies are not included in the rights statement, as they obscure the focus of concern and dilute the impact of the assertion; they may, however, be appropriately emitted later (see below). A *specific* statement delineates the central issue clearly and avoids generalisations. 'I have concerns about how we divide the housework' is much more specific than 'I have concerns about how we divide our responsibilities'. The latter statement introduces a myriad of other issues (child care, financial matters, etc.) that can only confuse the discussion, dilute the focus, increase perceived demands, and impede problem solving. A *respectful* expression adheres to norms of politeness and avoids labelling, blaming, demeaning, attacking, or making motivational assumptions about the other person.

Thus, a direct, specific, and respectful behaviour change request simply describes the offending behaviour and then politely asks for a behaviour change. The expression of an unpopular opinion is similarly constructed: 'I feel Issue 1 fails to recognise the real needs of the schools' is quite different from 'Anyone who supports Issue 1 is deceiving himself and rationalising'. The latter generalises ('anyone'), labels ('self-deceiving'), and makes motivational assumptions ('rationalising'). Refusal of unreasonable requests also incorporates these three features: 'No thank you, I'm not interested' is all that is necessary in terms of expression of rights. Conflict assertions that lack directness are likely to be seen as non-assertive, those lacking respect as aggressive, and those lacking both as passive-aggressive, while lack of specificity may characterise all three alternatives to assertion.

Several comments regarding the content of behaviour change requests and refusals are necessary. Behaviour change requests are conceptualised as containing a statement of feeling and a specific request for altered behaviour. While the specific request component is judged to be part of an assertive response by trained judges, untrained judges evaluate it as bordering on aggressiveness and of little functional value (Mullinix & Galassi, 1981). This suggests that the specific request statement may be most appropriate and useful when a desired response to the conflict statement alone is not forthcoming (escalation and persistence are discussed below). Refusals do include the stereotypical 'no', but its direct verbalisation may be socially awkward and breach conversational conventions (Gervasio, 1987; Gambrill, 1995), as when a spouse responds to the partner, 'No, I don't want to see that film. Let's choose one we both want to see.' An alternative approach is to embed the refusal within the obligation components: 'I know I will really dislike that film. Let's find one that we will both enjoy.'

A conflict assertion that expresses only a right has been termed a 'standard assertion'. Research consistently has demonstrated that such communications are judged (1) to be equally potent to, and somewhat more desirable than, conventional aggressive behaviour, and (2) to be distinctly less likeable, but more socially competent than, non-assertive behaviour (see Rakos, 1991, for an extensive review of this literature). Further, standard assertion is judged to be less likeable and more unpleasant than ordinary non-conflict conversation (Wildman & Clementz, 1986) and the expression of positive feelings (Cook & St. Lawrence, 1990). However, a few studies suggest that situational variables may moderate the social reaction: standard assertion is viewed as a more highly valued conflict resolution style than non-assertion for competitive (Levin & Gross, 1987) and socially skilled (Frisch & Froberg, 1987) persons, and for persons working in corporations (Solomon et al., 1982) and psychiatric hospitals (Dura & Beck, 1986). Overall, however, the standard assertion is likely to introduce an identifiable risk of social disapproval and may be labelled by others as aggressive behaviour.

Expression of obligations

Experienced clinicians have always recognised that the standard assertion (expressing a right) does not address the social context, cultural norms, or growth potential of a continuing relationship. Researchers began to investigate the obligations that accompany rights with Woolfolk and Dever's (1979) study showing that a short explanation and an acknowledgement of the other person's feelings enhanced the evaluation of the assertion without detracting from its potency. Additional studies soon suggested that other responses also improved the social reaction to assertion while maintaining its efficacy, including compromises and alternatives, reasons, praise, and apologies (Pitcher & Meikle, 1980; Romano & Bellack, 1980; Twentyman et al., 1981), providing support for the behaviour chain strategy proposed by Rakos (1979) to distinguish assertion from aggression.

Subsequent research confirmed that the obligations moderate the negative social reaction to conflict assertion. Assertions that include explanations, acknowledgements of feelings, compromises, and praise have been termed *empathic assertions* (Rakos, 1986), and are judged to be as potent as, but more likeable and appropriate than, standard assertions. Empathic assertions are as effective as aggressive responses but provoke less anger. They are comparable to non-assertions in terms of likeability but more efficacious. Finally, they are as pleasant as neutral non-conflict conversation (see Rakos, 1991, for a comprehensive review).

These qualities have made the empathic assertion, with its feminine-influenced approach toward conflict resolution, the generally preferred training goal, particularly when maintenance or enhancement of a continuing relationship is important (Wilson & Gallois, 1993). The specific components, which can be easily operationalised and reliably assessed (Bruch et al., 1981) as well as successfully trained (Rakos & Schroeder, 1979), include:

- a short, truthful, non-defensive explanation for the expression of rights
- a statement conveying understanding of the effects of the expression of rights on the other person
- praise or another positive comment directed toward the other person
- a short apology that is directed toward the inconvenience or disappointment that will result from the expression of rights (e.g. 'I am sorry you will have to miss the concert'), rather than an apology that refers to the necessity for the expression of rights (e.g. 'I am sorry I have to say no')
- an attempt to achieve a mutually acceptable compromise when legitimate rights conflict, recognising that such a solution may not always be possible. (The determination of legitimate rights involves covert response components to be discussed below.)

Paralinguistic and non-verbal components

The paralinguistic and non-verbal features of a verbalisation are critical components of effective communication (see Chapter 3), social skill (see Chapter 1), and assertion (Gambrill, 1995). Women in particular strive to demonstrate emotional control and a conscious non-stereotypical presentation in confrontations (Wilson & Gallois, 1993). These elements of skilled communication have been the focus of a great deal of research, which is summarised below.

Paralinguistic characteristics

The features commanding the greatest attention are voice volume, firmness and intonation, response latency, duration, and fluency. An extensive review of the numerous research studies can be found in Rakos (1991).

LATENCY The observation that non-assertive people hesitate before responding suggested that a short response latency is an important component of assertion. However, the research has failed to confirm this hypothesis, indicating instead the importance of situational variables such as sex of the participants and type of assertion. For example, latency is greater in conflict situations than in positive ones, with conflict assertions to males producing the longest latency (Pitcher & Meikle, 1980). The speed with which a person responds will be related to his or her ability to process the situational information and determine the desired and appropriate response (see covert skills, below). In practical terms, a short latency is less important for effective conflict resolution than is the avoidance of a very long latency. If the desired response is difficult to determine or not in the current behavioural repertoire, then the appropriate assertion, with modest delay, would be to request additional time to formulate a reply or to arrange a specific time for further discussion.

RESPONSE DURATION Originally, a short duration was assumed to be characteristic of assertion, since non-assertive persons tend to produce excuses, lies, apologies, and long explanations. However, because appropriate assertion involves verbalising obligations as well as rights, the duration of an assertion may be longer than other responses (Gervasio, 1987), especially when (as is the case for latency) the assertion involves conflict and is directed toward a male (e.g. Pitcher & Meikle, 1980). The assertion must be sufficiently long to communicate effectively in a given context; mere verbiage in and of itself is neither assertive nor unassertive. In fact, Heimberg et al. (1979) found a curvilinear relationship between assertiveness and duration: moderately assertive individuals exhibited much shorter duration than either highly assertive or non-assertive persons. Although excessive verbalisation increases the chances of confusion, diversion, and irrelevancy, response duration must be sufficient to meet the demands of unique circumstances.

RESPONSE FLUENCY Fluency is considered to be an important paralinguistic feature of assertion, yet it has been poorly investigated. In fact, the few studies directly to address the issue found a very weak relationship (e.g. Kolotkin et al., 1984). However, hesitant, choppy speech is associated with anxiety (Linehan & Walker, 1983), which is presumed to be detrimental to and perhaps even incompatible with effective assertion (Wolpe, 1990). Thus, common sense suggests fluency will contribute to the judgement of skill. Interestingly, speech *rate* has not attracted the attention of researchers or clinicians. It, too, makes intuitive sense: non-anxious, assertive individuals would be expected to adjust their rate of talking to reflect the particular context.

VOICE VOLUME The data on loudness, in contrast to the previous characteristics, are fairly consistent: effective conflict assertion is characterised by an appropriate, moderate volume that is louder than the speech produced in ordinary conversation (e.g. Rose & Tryon, 1979) and by non-assertive persons (e.g. Eisler et al., 1973).

INTONATION (INFLECTION) Laypersons consider intonation to be one of the most important features of effective assertion (Romano & Bellack, 1980), but, like response duration, both highly assertive and non-assertive people evidence greater inflection than moderately assertive individuals (Heimberg et al., 1979). Inflection is therefore an important attribute of assertion, but not a distinguishing characteristic. As with many of the other paralinguistic components, intermediate levels of intonation are judged to be most appropriate (Rose & Tryon, 1979).

FIRMNESS (AFFECT) High levels of firmness are strongly correlated with judgements of assertion (Bordewick & Bornstein, 1980; Kolotkin et al., 1984) and may even contribute more than actual content (Kirschner & Galassi, 1983). Assertive psychiatric patients manifest greater affect than non-assertive ones (Eisler et al., 1973), particularly in conflict situations (Eisler et al., 1975). With the exception of a study by Bourque and Ladouceur (1979), the data suggest that the absence of vocal firmness is likely to detract from the impact of a conflict assertion, and that the development of an appropriately firm 'tone' should be a high training priority.

Summary of paralinguistic qualities

Firmness, intermediate levels of volume and intonation, and moderate response latency and duration appear to characterise effective conflict assertion. Intuitively, a fluent response and a moderate speech rate make sense but lack definitive empirical support. Latency and duration have shown a particular sensitivity to situational variables: they are likely to increase in conflict interactions and when directed toward a male. In general, appropriate conflict assertion requires flexible paralinguistic abilities that are sensitive to changing environmental conditions.

Non-verbal characteristics

Motoric behaviours convey a great deal of information in an assertive interaction (McFall et al., 1982), as they do in interpersonal communication in general (see Chapter 3). Research has examined the contribution eye contact, facial expression, gestures, and 'body language' make to effective conflict assertion.

Eye contact

Western culture regards eye contact as a key aspect of interpersonal communication (Kleinke, 1986) and social skill (Trower, 1980; Caballo, 1995). Predictably, it emerges as an important component of conflict assertion. The duration of eye contact is longer in conflict situations than in positive ones (Eisler et al., 1975). However, the actual amount of eye contact is not a clear distinguishing feature of assertion: skilled and unskilled persons do not consistently differ in its duration (Bourque & Ladouceur, 1979; Heimberg et al., 1979). The topography of eye contact, rather than simple duration, may be the critical feature: it must be emitted flexibly and somewhat intermittently (as opposed to a fixed stare), especially since it is engaged in by the listener, and not by the speaker, in general social conversation between Caucasians (LaFrance & Mayo, 1976).

Facial expression

Deception and anxiety are both betrayed by a variety of facial movements and expressions (Ekman, 2001). Thus, it is not surprising that judgements of assertion, a presumably honest and non-anxious communication, are strongly influenced by overall facial expression (Romano & Bellack, 1980), as well as by specific mouth, eyebrow, and forehead cues (McFall et al., 1982). Uncontrolled fidgety mouth movements, wrinkled forehead, and animated, constantly moving eyebrows communicate unassertiveness. These cues convey more information when the speaker is male but are more influential in evaluating female asserters (McFall et al., 1982). While McFall et al. did not detect differences in the way males and females used these cues, Romano and Bellack (1980) found that 'males and females differed substantially in the number, pattern and valence of the cues used . . . female judges seemed to be sensitive to and made use of more behavioral cues' (p. 488). In particular, they noted that smiles, which in general contribute minimally to perceptions of assertiveness (Kolotkin et al., 1984), strongly detracted from women's – but not from men's – evaluations of female asserters. More recent research has confirmed that women asserters are more effective when their responses to men include smiles (cf. Carli, 2001).

Facial expression, then, is an important component of assertion, especially for women. Females may be more astute than men at discriminating these cues in others, but as asserters they emit them in more subtle ways that nevertheless strongly influence the perception of their assertion. Thus, their concern with controlling their emotional personas (Wilson & Gallois, 1993) appears fully warranted.

Gestures

Socially competent persons increase their use of gestures in conflict situations (Trower, 1980). They also use their arms and hands differently than less skilled individuals – arm movements that are smooth and steady while speaking and inconspicuous while listening are the greatest non-verbal contributors to judgements of male assertion (McFall et al., 1982). Such movements are also highly influential in the perception of female assertion, especially when rated by males: physical gestures enhance the evaluation while extraneous and restrained movements are viewed negatively (Romano & Bellack, 1980). Arm and hand gestures may be most important when the conflict interaction involves opposite sexed participants (Rose & Tryon, 1979). Thus, an appropriate repertoire of gestures is likely to enhance the effectiveness of conflict assertion.

Body language

Experts discount the importance of body language (Kolotkin et al., 1984), but laypersons consider it significant (Romano & Bellack, 1980). Head, neck, shoulder, and torso positions that are upright, exhibit minimal extraneous movement, squarely face the other person, and involve purposive movement while speaking yet remain quiet while listening are associated with assertive behaviour. Non-assertiveness is associated with excessive nodding and head tilting; stooped, hunched, or shrugging shoulders; and squirming, rotating, or rocking torsos (McFall et al., 1982). These cues are more influential in the evaluation of male asserters, but, overall, are the least important non-verbal responses (Romano & Bellack, 1980; McFall et al., 1982). Finally, while meaningful posture shifts are appropriate (Trower, 1980), actually approaching the other person while asserting is perceived by laypersons as aggressive (Rose & Tryon, 1979). These data suggest that body language contributes modestly to perceptions of assertion, and is more important for males.

Summary of non-verbal responses

Eye contact, facial expression, gestures, and, to a lesser extent, body language, all influence evaluations of conflict assertion. Facial expression for female asserters and gestures for male asserters may be especially important variables. Overall, steady but not rigid eye contact; a calm, sincere, serious facial expression; flexible use of arm and hand gestures; and a relaxed, involved body posture characterise behaviour judged to be assertive. Body movements should be fluid and purposeful when speaking but quiet and inconspicuous when listening.

Process (interactive) skills

The overt skill components are emitted within social interaction. Their impact, therefore, depends on competence in the process skills of response timing, initiation and persistence, and stimulus control.

Response timing

Socially unskilled persons fail to time their statements and gestures accurately (Fischetti et al., 1977; Peterson et al., 1981) and respond inappropriately to situational cues (Fischetti et al., 1984). Trower (1980), for example, found that skilled individuals spoke more than unskilled persons, and did so at socially proper moments. This suggests that the effectiveness of an assertion will be related to the appropriateness with which it is introduced into the conflict interaction. It is essential that individuals discriminate among the verbal, non-verbal, and situational cues that indicate when it is appropriate to respond. When these stimuli fail to provide clear guidelines, other communication skills may be required (e.g. questioning, paraphrasing, reflecting, self-disclosing, explaining, or reinforcing, as detailed in other chapters of this volume).

Initiation and persistence

The decision to emit an assertive response in a particular situation involves covert responses to be discussed shortly. On occasion, passivity or compliance may be preferred options, as when the realistic risk of assertion is excessive or the offending person's situation invites extraordinary 'understanding' (Rakos, 1991). However, when assertion is the selected option, the initial verbalisation should be the *minimal effective response* (MER), defined as 'behaviour that would ordinarily accomplish the client's goal with a minimum of effort and of apparent negative emotion (and a very small likelihood of negative consequences)' (Masters et al., 1987, p. 106). The MER operationalises the social rules of minimising conflict and relationship strain (cf. Wilson & Gallois, 1993). If the MER proves ineffective, and the decision is made to persist, *escalation* is appropriate. This may involve increasing the intensity of paralinguistic qualities (voice volume, intonation, affect, and response duration) and/or expanding the use of non-verbal behaviours such as gestures and body language. Typically, the verbal content will be modified in some manner. For example, in continuing relationships, further explanation may be provided, empathy increased, or additional potential compromises suggested. Aversive consequences may be articulated or the specific behaviour change request added if the statement of the problem alone fails to alter the behaviour in question. Consider, for example, a cosmetic salesperson in a department store who approaches you with a product you do not want and does not respect your lack of interest. Appropriate assertion might involve the following:

MER: 'No, I am not interested. Good day.'
Escalation 1: 'No, I told you: I am not interested.'
Escalation 2: 'I am *not* interested.' (Louder volume, firmer affect and intonation.)
Escalation 3: 'I told you three times I am not interested. Please respect that, or I will contact your supervisor.' (Volume, affect, intonation maintained or increased slightly from previous response, and aversive contingency specified.)

Determination of the MER is critical because an escalated response emitted as an initial assertion (a common error by novices) will likely be evaluated as inappropriate and aggressive, and may result in negative consequences for the asserter and reinforce beliefs that such behaviour is indeed risky. For instance, escalation 2 above would likely be perceived as aggressive if emitted as the initial response.

Effective persistence requires that the asserter maintain the conflict focus and resist manipulation (Rakos, 1991). In non-continuing relationships, the asserter must basically provide a repetitive response that avoids the introduction of new material. If the cosmetic salesperson persists, and begins to describe the 'free' travel bag, umbrella, and perfume that accompany a purchase, and that can be given as extra 'gifts' or used for oneself, the appropriate assertive response remains: 'No, thank you, I am not interested.' This avoids the manipulative ploy of discussing gifts or uses of products; such a shift in focus allows the interaction to continue and may soon force the asserter into explaining gift giving or cosmetic usage, neither of which is the issue. Maintaining the assertive focus in such a situation usually means simple repetition without qualification. If you say, 'I am not interested at this time,' you may be asked why not 'now', and then 'when', and if 'cost' is the problem, there is a smaller size, and if no person is available to receive the 'gift' now, it will be good to have a gift handy when that person surely comes upon the scene.

Maintaining the focus is particularly difficult when a valued continuing relationship is involved and the asserter is starting to behave less submissively. The new behaviour is not consistent with the expectations of the other person and is likely to arouse negative feelings, such as hurt, anger, rejection, depression, or vengeance. Therefore, persistence by the novice asserter in relationships is a greater challenge than for experienced asserters, who have taught their social environment to expect self-enhancing behaviour. Escalation must be highly skilful to maintain the focus while simultaneously addressing the issues that affect the long-term integrity of the relationship. The escalations must embed repetitions in diverse syntactic surface structures (Gervasio, 1987) and in layers of elaborations. For example, suppose a father whose grown daughter comes to his house for dinner every Sunday now learns that she will not be coming this week:

MER: 'Dad, I won't be coming to dinner this Sunday. I've made plans to see some friends – we're going to a party. I hope you won't be too disappointed. I'll see you again next Sunday as usual.' (This MER expresses the unpopular communication along with an explanation, attention to feelings, and a potential mutually acceptable compromise.)

Father: 'But I look forward to your visits so much. I don't get out often any more, and your company is so special. Couldn't you meet your friends after dinner?' (Father at this point is responding with an appropriate assertion of his own – a request for a behaviour change – and includes an explanation and potential compromise.)

Escalation 1: 'Dad, if I come to dinner, I'll miss a good deal of the party. I know how much you enjoy my visits, but this is an exception. It's a special party that I really want to attend. I know you'll miss me, but it's only one time.' (Repeated expression of the unpopular content, with additional explanation and empathy, all offered with a changed surface structure.)

Father: 'Then go with your friends to your party! I'll be fine. I'm sorry they are more important to you. One day you'll see how important it is that your kids care, and show that they care!'

Here we are dealing with one of the most complex of continuing relationships, that of an adult child with a parent. The daughter initiates assertive behaviour, resulting in the father experiencing an unexpected loss of reinforcement and the feelings of hurt and anger that frequently accompany disappointment. Protecting the relationship and maintaining the focus in this situation involves an increased attention to underlying feelings, repetition and possible expansion of the explanation, and a wider search for a mutually acceptable compromise. The focus will be maintained best if the asserter can manage the exceptionally difficult task of addressing these verbalisations to the *existence* of the feelings rather than to the *content* of the feelings.

Escalation 2: 'Dad, I can see how angry and disappointed you are that I will not be coming for dinner this Sunday. I know how important our dinners together are to you, but as I said, I very much want to go to this party. There will be a lot of new people there, and I've been feeling a bit isolated lately. I hope you understand my feelings. I'm thinking about how to solve this problem, and I know I'm free Wednesday evening – I can stop by for a few hours after work instead of waiting until next Sunday. How does that sound?'

This escalated response repeats the assertion, attends to the feelings the father is experiencing, expands the explanation, offers a new compromise, and changes the surface structure. It does not lose the focus by becoming defensive through a debate on the extent of 'caring' for father or the relative 'importance' of different relationships. Caring, if present, can be demonstrated through the compromise. Sometimes, however, the interaction will continue and the content of the feelings will have to be addressed more directly, resulting in an increased probability of losing the assertive focus.

Escalation 3: 'Dad, I really do understand how much you look forward to our Sunday dinners and the time we spend together. I enjoy our dinners too, but sometimes other important engagements occur on Sundays. I feel very close to you, and care about you very much. My missing dinner this week has nothing to do with how I feel about you. I wish you saw this as I do, but all I can do is try to explain my point to you. Anyway, as I said, I am free Wednesday evening. I'd like to stop by then – how does that sound to you?'

Escalation in continuing relationships will always involve expanded content (and hence response duration), but louder volume, greater firmness and inflection, or increased use of non-verbal cues will depend on the context. If the other person continues to experience negative feelings as a consequence of the assertion, and the relationship is a valued one, an assertion directed at the negative feelings may be necessary, either immediately or at a later, planned time. Persistence should be conceptualised as the behaviours required to solve the problem as best as possible. As the interaction continues, issues may shift, and further escalation may become counterproductive. A new, legitimate issue usually indicates the need for a new MER rather than endless escalation:

MER: 'Dad, I want to talk to you about our phone conversation last week. You sounded quite hurt and angry, and seemed to feel that if I cared about you I would always make the Sunday dinner. I would like to talk about that because I think I need some flexibility in my plans.' (This MER includes an orienting verbalisation and the conflict statement component of a behaviour change request.)

Persistence increases the chances for a desired outcome but cannot guarantee it. The car mechanic may not reduce unwarranted charges regardless of the extent of escalation. An ineffective assertion that specifies a future contingency ('you will hear from my attorney') will not be very satisfying. Even when a desired outcome is achieved in a continuing relationship, the possibility of arousing negative feelings introduces additional risks. Skilful use of the covert components of assertion (see below) is necessary to assess the situation accurately; avoid rationalisations that justify passivity; and decide, first, whether to assert, and second, the extent of escalation that is desirable given the importance of the conflict, the nature of the relationship, and the realistic probability of potential positive and negative outcomes.

Stimulus control skills

Antecedent and consequent stimulus control skills facilitate effective, socially acceptable assertion by altering the context in which the assertion is emitted. Antecedent stimulus control involves arranging the environment prior to asserting so that the likelihood of a favourable outcome is maximised. These skills are assertive behaviours themselves: requests to move to a private room prior to a confrontation, requests for a delay prior to making a decision (which provides time to identify and rehearse appropriate responses), or enquiries to the other person regarding convenient times to set aside for the discussion of concerns. They may also involve self-management skills that inhibit assertions judged to be inappropriate or counter-productive. Conflicts that are discussed in private, at the right time, without time pressures, and with prior deliberation are more likely to be resolved satisfactorily.

Consequent stimulus control refers to reinforcing the other person (see Chapter 5) for listening to and/or complying with the assertion. Providing contingent verbal reinforcement for desired behaviour in response to an assertion is likely to encourage similar behaviour in the future and may also minimise negative perceptions of the conflict interaction (Levin & Gross, 1984; St. Lawrence et al., 1985).

Covert behavioural components of conflict assertion

Cognitive skills are central elements in contemporary conceptualisations of social skill (see Chapter 1). They categorise and manipulate information and are essential for the self-monitoring, self-evaluation, and self-reinforcement that comprise behavioural self-regulation (Kanfer & Schefft, 1988). For example, socially skilled and unskilled persons differ in the standards they employ to evaluate their actions. Skilled persons utilise objective criteria based on situational and interpersonal cues that generate social roles, norms, and rules, as well as empirically grounded expectations generated by personal experience. Unskilled individuals, on the other hand, rely on subjective standards that focus on idiosyncratic, non-empirical beliefs, perceptions, and expectations (Trower, 1982). An illustration of this is provided by Hung et al. (1980), who found that non-assertive persons performed more assertively after exposure to a severely passive model than to a moderately or minimally submissive model, presumably because their subjective performance standards were modified.

The ability to use empirically based, objective criteria requires conceptual complexity (CC) (Schroder et al., 1967), through which individuals

- make increasingly precise discriminations among situational cues, allowing consideration of broader and more varied viewpoints
- increase the use of internally but rationally developed standards for problem solving
- integrate more information and increase tolerance for conflict.

The importance of CC for assertive performance is clear: assertive individuals demonstrate greater CC than non-assertive persons; furthermore, high-CC people, compared to low-CC ones, manifest a better knowledge of assertive content, superior delivery skills, and more effective use of adaptive cognitions. Moreover, high-CC individuals behave more assertively and include more obligations in conflicts involving continuing relationships (Bruch, 1981; Bruch et al., 1981). Such relationships demand the greatest ability to utilise multiple perspectives and internal rational standards to resolve conflict and enhance the relationship. Conflicts involving non-continuing relationships require less CC, since social norms provide fairly straightforward behavioural guidelines.

The specific cognitive abilities necessary to produce a sophisticated, rational, empirical analysis of, and response to, a conflict include knowledge, self-statements, expectancies, philosophical beliefs, problem-solving skills, social perception skills, and self-monitoring skills.

Knowledge

Both non-assertive and assertive individuals can accurately categorise and differentiate passive, assertive, and aggressive responses (Bordewick & Bornstein, 1980; Alden & Cappe, 1981). In addition, non-assertive individuals can describe or enact appropriate assertive responses (see Rakos, 1991), reflecting clinical observations that deficiencies in *response content knowledge* account for some but by no means all instances of non-assertive performance.

A second category of essential knowledge concerns the social rules, norms, and expectations that are likely to operate in particular contexts or circumstances, so that an array of appropriate response options can be generated (Wilson & Gallois, 1993). Unskilled persons, as noted above, are likely to lack accurate *social cue knowledge* (Trower, 1982).

Self-statements

A 'negative internal dialogue' interferes with competent social responding (Meichenbaum et al., 1981). Negative self-statements are exemplified by 'I will be embarrassed if I speak up,' or 'He won't like me unless I agree'. Positive versions might be 'My opinions are valuable' and 'I have the right to express myself'. In fact, assertive persons emit approximately twice as many positive as negative self-statements when confronted with social conflict, while non-assertive individuals produce approximately equal numbers of each (Rakos, 1991). Further, the 'mix' of positive and negative self-statements may be as important as the absolute frequency of each (Blankenberg & Heimberg, 1984). For example, assertive persons often use negative self-statements as cues to verbalise positive coping ones (Bruch, 1981).

Wine (1981) noted that the self-verbalisations that are labelled as 'negative' or 'dysfunctional' typically focus on the needs of others and fear of rejection, and stem from the 'feminine' emphasis on relationships (Gilligan, 1982; Wilson & Gallois, 1993). An implicit masculine bias can be avoided if such self-statements are conceptualised as conciliatory, nurturant, and communal. This would remove a biased ('positive/negative') continuum from the analysis and replace it with two orthogonal dimensions, autonomy and affiliation, each of which makes important but incomplete contributions to adjustment.

Nevertheless, it is important to recognise that effective conflict assertion clearly entails significant use of autonomous self-statements. In fact, direct training in these self-instructions, apart from any other intervention, has resulted in significant gains in assertiveness (e.g. Craighead, 1979).

Expectancies

An expectancy is a cognitive behaviour that makes a specific prediction about performance in a particular situation. *Outcome expectancies* predict the probability that specific consequences will be produced by a particular response. Assertive and non-assertive persons expect standard assertion, and to a lesser extent empathic assertion, to have greater negative long-term effects on a relationship than non-assertion (Zollo et al., 1985). However, assertive individuals expect conflict assertion to produce more positive short-term consequences and fewer negative ones than do non-assertive persons (see Rakos, 1991). Non-assertive and assertive persons do not differ in their identification of the *possible* consequences but in the *probability* that the potential outcomes will actually occur. Further, the possible outcomes are evaluated differently: assertive individuals perceive the potential positive consequences of assertion as more desirable and the potential negative ones as more unpalatable (Kuperminc & Heimberg, 1983; Blankenberg & Heimberg, 1984). Non-assertive persons may rationalise to reduce the perceived demand for engaging in a conflict interaction.

Self-efficacy expectations refer to a person's belief that he or she can emit a specific response in a particular circumstance (Bandura, 1977). Assertive individuals evidence much stronger self-efficacy in conflict situations than do non-assertive persons (Chiauzzi & Heimberg, 1986). Finally, assertive individuals demonstrate greater *situational efficacy expectancies*, which describe the confidence a person has of being able to generate any successful response to deal with a specific situation (Chiauzzi & Heimberg, 1986). Thus, assertive persons approach conflict situations with an adaptive appraisal of the context and a realistic self-confidence in their ability to emit appropriate behaviours.

Philosophical beliefs

Ellis (1962; Ellis & Grieger, 1977) has identified at least a dozen 'irrational' beliefs, of which six are directly related to assertion:

- demands for perfection in self and others in important situations
- blaming self or others for fallible behaviour
- demands for universal and unwavering approval from significant others
- defining personal rights and self-worth by external achievement in subjectively important areas
- catastrophising, or exaggerating the meaning of an undesired outcome
- viewing passivity as preferable to active intervention, in the belief that things will 'work out' eventually without 'rocking the boat'.

These irrational thoughts are generally produced only in response to subjectively important issues: the person fails to accept that events in the world occur without regard to the personal value ascribed to a particular situation. Thus, someone may very rationally tolerate incompetence in a meaningless hobby (e.g. failure to perform well in a volleyball game), yet react with extraordinary emotion to an objectively similar event of subjective import (e.g. failure to get a leading role in a community play).

Underlying all irrational thinking is a basic logical error: things, people, or events *should* be a certain way. Ellis argues that the use of 'should' elevates desires into demands and prevents rational analysis of the situation. Unmet demands lead to upset, which does not facilitate effective problem resolution. If, on the other hand, unfulfilled desires are viewed as unfortunate events that one wished were otherwise ('it would be better if . . .' rather than 'it should not have happened . . .'), the person will exhibit concern that can contribute to resolution of the problem.

Ellis' theory has been investigated in terms of assertive skills (see Rakos, 1991, for a review). Non-assertive individuals endorse more irrational ideas than do assertive individuals. In conflict situations, non-assertive persons entertain the possibility of many more negative 'overwhelming consequences' than positive ones, while assertive persons consider similar frequencies of each. As with self-statements, the 'mix' of extreme outcome expectancies may be more important than their intensity or frequency. Thus, rational alternatives to the irrational beliefs are likely to facilitate assertive responding.

The typical non-assertive person might engage in the following thought process: 'I must assert myself without any mistakes or the assertion will fail [self-perfection], the other person will think I'm weird or will be hurt or angry [universal approval], and that would be absolutely terrible [catastrophising]. It would be my fault [self-blame] and confirm that I am no good [self-denigration]. It will work out better if I let it pass and see what happens [inaction].' These belief statements might be prefaced by additional irrational ideas: 'I don't have the right to infringe or make demands on this other person [self-denigration]' and/or 'I should not even have to deal with this situation because the other person should not be acting this way [other-perfection/ other-blame].'

Rational alternatives to the irrational beliefs can be taught fairly directly. The initial step requires the identification of the specific irrational thought(s) produced in the particular context. Non-assertive people frequently are so practised in irrational thinking that they do not actually verbalise the irrational thoughts, but behave 'as if' they did. After specification of the actual or implicit thought, the individual is taught to challenge it and actively substitute a rational alternative, first in safe and structured rehearsal and later in the actual situation. The general content of the rational alternatives would include the following principles.

Acceptance of imperfection

I am human and the world is very complicated; therefore, I will make mistakes even when the situation is important to me and I very much want to behave competently. The importance of an issue to me does not increase its objective status: there is no reason I should behave competently simply because it is important that I do so, although it would be nice if I were able to respond competently. The other person is also human, lives in the same complex world, and will also make mistakes in situations that are important to me. There is no reason that others should act in a desirable fashion, just because it is important to me, although it would be nice if they were able to do so. (These thoughts avoid self- or other-blaming and accept the inevitable frailty and imperfection of the human condition.)

Acceptance of disapproval

I cannot always satisfy everyone who is important to me, even if I always place their needs ahead of my own, because the world is too complicated and its operation too capricious. It would be nice if I could, but I must recognise that there is no reason why I should do so. (These beliefs recognise that some rejection or disapproval from others is unavoidable.)

Non-catastrophising

Negative outcomes are unfortunate, inconvenient, unpleasant, perhaps even bad – but not terrible, horrible, awful, or unbearable. I will try to resolve the problem when possible and adapt to the situation when change is not feasible. I must do this even when the undesired outcome involves a personally important issue, because the world does not know or care what is important to me. Things are as they should be, and demanding that they should be different ignores the complexity of the world – although it would be nice if they indeed were different. (These cognitions clarify the nature of the world and foster a realistic understanding and acceptance of one's place in it.)

Action

Since the world is not oriented toward fulfilling my desires, active attempts to influence it will increase the probability that my wishes will be achieved. Without action on my part, it is unlikely that events in the complex world will fortuitously meet my desires. (These thoughts promote personal responsibility for change, though they do not demand that such efforts be successful.)

Self-worth

I am worthy, and have the same basic human rights as anyone else, regardless of how much or how little I or others have achieved. I have the basic right to assert myself, if I so choose, in an effort to influence the situation and maximise my rewards. (These ideas accept one's unconditional self-worth and human rights.)

The direct modification of irrational thinking has been an important component of assertiveness-training programmes since the early 1970s (Rich & Schroeder, 1976). While 'rational relabelling' or 'cognitive restructuring' alone improves conflict assertive performance, it contributes only minimally to a comprehensive training package (see Rakos, 1991). This supports Bandura's (1978) contention that though performance may be cognitively mediated, those cognitions are most efficaciously changed when the behaviours upon which they are based are first changed. Rational relabelling procedures may prove to be more important in promoting generalisation of assertive responses to novel people and situations (Scott et al., 1983) than in facilitating initial acquisition of the response.

Social perception skills

Accurate perception and empathic role-taking are two distinct cognitive skills involved in interpersonal perception (Argyle et al., 1981). These skills are now conceptualised as components of 'emotional intelligence' (Burgoon & Bacue, 2003). Accurate perception has been investigated more thoroughly and the evidence strongly suggests that non-assertive individuals are deficient in this skill. They are less sensitive to external cues (Trower, 1980), misjudge the amount of anger communicated by assertive and aggressive responses (Morrison & Bellack, 1981), and place exaggerated emphasis on the status of the other person and the extent of social norm transgression when analysing conflict situations (Rudy et al., 1982). A realistic assessment of social norms provides an important guideline for judging behaviour; for example, the reasonableness of a request influences compliance and emotional responses to the asserter (Epstein, 1980). However, non-assertive persons perceive 'reasonableness', and therefore social norms and the legitimate rights of the other person, differently from assertive individuals (Blankenberg & Heimberg, 1984; Chiauzzi & Heimberg, 1986), especially when requests are consensually evaluated to be of low or moderate legitimacy.

Conflict situations of moderate legitimacy pose a particular challenge to accurate perception: in such situations, assertive as well as non-assertive persons produce more thoughts but fewer objective ones (Chiauzzi & Heimberg, 1983) and report a decreased intention to assert and weakened self-efficacy beliefs (Chiauzzi & Heimberg, 1986). The legitimate rights of all participants are most difficult to determine in ambiguous contexts, requiring refined conceptual skills that can assess situational considerations, make appropriate reasonableness determinations, and synthesise the resulting increase in positive and negative thoughts into adaptive, accurate discriminations. Distorted judgements of circumstances may be a prime contributor to a decision to behave non-assertively.

A second important perceptual skill is the ability to understand the viewpoint of the other person, termed 'role-taking' (Meichenbaum et al., 1981) or 'metaperception' (Argyle et al., 1981). It provides the basis for determining the impact of an assertion on the recipient (an antecedent obligation), and it is the foundation upon which the asserter develops an empathic statement (a subsequent obligation) (Rakos, 1991). The superior social evaluation of the empathic assertion relative to the standard one highlights the importance of this skill in conflict resolution. A key element of this skill is the discrimination of the cues that indicate an empathic response will facilitate the interaction. For example, Fischetti et al. (1984) found that heterosocially skilled and unskilled persons differed in their ability to recognise when a vocal or gestural response from them would help a speaker continue to talk. The ability to discriminate such cues may explain why skilled and unskilled persons differ in the timing or placement of vocalisations and gestures, but not in the frequency (Fischetti et al., 1977; Peterson et al., 1981).

Interpersonal problem-solving skills

The systematic problem-solving skills necessary for social competence (Meichenbaum et al., 1981; Trower, 1982) are deficient in a variety of clinical populations (Schroeder & Rakos, 1983). The problem-solving sequence involves problem recognition and acceptance, problem definition and goal setting, generation of potential response alternatives, decision making (assessment of alternatives in terms of likely outcomes), and solution implementation and evaluation (D'Zurilla & Nezu, 2001). Chiauzzi and Heimberg (1986) found that non-assertive persons manifested deficits in problem recognition and assessment (a social perception skill) and in their ability to select an appropriate response. No inadequacies were observed in their capacity to generate response alternatives, in terms of either number or quality. However, therapist-generated alternatives produce higher outcome expectancies than client-generated ones (Arisohn et al., 1988), suggesting that unskilled individuals lack confidence in their own alternatives. Robinson and Calhoun (1984) also found a situational effect: more complex and assertive alternatives were produced in response to an angry than to a pleasant male. Finally, Deluty (1981, 1985) found that assertive, aggressive, and submissive children generated equal numbers of alternatives in conflict situations, but that the assertive children's possibilities included assertive options to a proportionately greater extent.

Problem-solving skills assume a central role in assertion when it is conceptualised as a sequence of overt and covert responses. The antecedent obligations are involved in problem definition and assessment (determining the rights of all participants and whether assertion is the preferred option). The subsequent obligation to seek a mutually acceptable compromise is largely dependent on the ability to generate alternative solutions. Because these features contribute to conceptual complexity, problem-solving skills may provide the means through which the former attribute can be operationalised and trained.

Self-monitoring skills

Responsible assertion is based on an accurate perception that the situation appropriately calls for such action; in other words, an assertion situation must be distinguished from other social ones and acquire the properties of a discriminative stimulus. This learned cue, which will prompt the early behaviours in the assertion chain (the antecedent obligations), will comprise the person's own reactions. Thus, the assertive person must learn to attend to his or her own behaviours and discriminate those reactions that indicate assertion should be considered.

The self-monitored discriminative stimuli can be behaviours, emotions, and/or cognitions (Rakos & Schroeder, 1980). Behavioural cues include coping strategies that are indirect, hostile, or avoidant (e.g. hinting at desires, using phoney excuses or excessive apologies; engaging in withdrawal, aggression, passive-aggression, or submission). Emotional cues include frustration, resentment, shame, guilt, anger, depression, and upset. Cognitive cues are present when the person engages in excessive ruminations and self-statements that blame or denigrate the self and others, rationalise the unimportance of the concern, and are generally affiliative ('negative') or irrational. When these behavioural, emotional, and cognitive reactions are produced in response to a social conflict, they are the primary signals that assertion should be considered.

THE SOCIAL VALIDITY OF CONFLICT ASSERTION

Technical proficiency, immediate outcome, overall net cost-benefit, and social validity were discussed earlier as four distinct and partially independent measurements of the assertive response. For instance, a skilled assertion that meets social and cultural norms may still fail to produce desired short-term outcomes or enhance the long-term stability of a relationship. But because the functional value of an assertion will provide the tangible benefits, the social reaction to assertion assumes critical importance.

General findings

The social validity of standard assertion (expression of the assertive right without the inclusion of obligations) was discussed earlier. Briefly, it is judged to be more socially competent, but less likeable, than non-assertive behaviour, and to be at least as potent as, and more favourably evaluated than, aggressive behaviour. Empathic assertions, which express rights and obligations, are judged more favourably than standard assertions and comparably to non-assertion. The obligations are consistent with social expectations and thereby enhance the potency of the assertion (Wilson et al., 2003).

The evaluation is less positive when the assertion requires a significant sacrifice on the part of the recipient or is in response to a relatively reasonable request (Epstein, 1980; McCampbell & Ruback, 1985). Adults judge assertion to be most appropriate when directed toward strangers rather than toward friends or intimates (Linehan & Siefert, 1983), but college students perceive it to be the preferred option for resolving conflicts with friends and relatives (Heisler & McCormack, 1982).

These studies demonstrate that empathic and standard conflict assertions are judged by observers to be socially appropriate and competent, if not always exceptionally likeable. However, the person whose reaction is most important is the real-life recipient, not an observer. Although an observer may appreciate the abstract value of an assertion, the natural social environment may react differently. Not surprisingly, the appraisal may be relative to the alternatives. Evaluations by recipients of assertion delivered by confederates in staged encounters confirm that non-assertive behaviour is judged to be more likeable than standard or empathic assertion (Gormally, 1982; Delamater & McNamara, 1991). Furthermore, *in vivo* and abstract comparisons between standard assertion and aggression suggest that the superior observer evaluation of assertion is magnified in the *in vivo* situation (Christoff & Edelstein, 1981; McCampbell & Ruback, 1985).

The social acceptance of a standard assertion can be increased by use of the empathic assertion's obligations, as noted above, and also by more extensive inter-action with the asserter that includes experience with non-conflict as well as conflict behaviours, as will occur in most continuing relationships. Thus, individuals who emit positive assertions (such as requesting or offering help, or expressing compliments or thanks), general conversational comments, and task-oriented interactions are viewed as more likeable and competent than persons exhibiting standard assertion alone (Rakos, 1991). For instance, in a naturalistic investigation, Kern and Paquette (1992) found that college students' evaluation of their roommates' likeability and social competence was significantly correlated with the roommates' level of conflict asser-tion ability. Thus, empathic elaborations and contextual experience can moderate the evaluation of assertion. Nevertheless, concerns regarding social evaluation remain highly relevant in continuing relationships, unlike transient interactions in which instrumental utility is usually the primary consideration.

Gender

Conflict assertion has been seen as a powerful tool through which pervasive societal sexism can be challenged (see Rakos, 1991; Wilson & Gallois, 1993; Gambrill, 1995, for extensive discussions) – including its failure to include assertion as a component of healthy (Broverman et al., 1970) or appropriate (Broverman et al., 1972) female behaviour. Some feminists, however, contend that the assertion construct is 'andro-centric' (Cameron, 1994) and blames women rather than challenging societal prejudice (Crawford, 1995). Further, women writers have long contended that behaving assert-ively entails significantly greater risks for females than for males (e.g. Fodor, 1980; Kahn, 1981; MacDonald, 1982; Gervasio & Crawford, 1989), even though 30-plus studies published in the 1970s and 1980s failed to confirm such a bias (see Rakos, 1991; Wilson & Gallois, 1993, for reviews).

However, this body of research on gender was conducted primarily with US college students in contexts that established arbitrary social interactions and at a time when the notion of assertiveness was trendy and the conservative social and political Zeitgeist that was to suffuse the West was still nascent. The handful of studies that appeared in the 1990s strongly indicate that conflict assertion is riskier for women than for men. This may be why the *social rules* governing conflict assertion by women – but not by men – emphasise obligation behaviours and even submission (Wilson & Gallois, 1993). Even so, women still expect empathic assertion to result in more problematic long-term consequences than do men (Zollo et al., 1985).

In the work environment, for example, women who promote themselves in a direct and confident manner decrease their social attractiveness (Rudman, 1998) and are perceived as less socially skilled than males who engage in similar behaviour (Rudman & Glick, 1999). These devaluations are in response to socially dominant behaviours (e.g. competitiveness) rather than to demonstrations of competence, such as autonomy and ambition. Women can, however, temper the unfavourable judgements by meeting expectations of communality, such as by exhibiting warmth, sensitivity, and caring (Rudman & Glick, 2001). In addition, assertive women are valued by business people who are outcome oriented (Mullinix & Galassi, 1981; Solomon et al., 1982; Sigal et al., 1985; Gallois et al., 1992; Rudman, 1998).

Women, to a much greater degree than men, must assert themselves in a rule-consistent manner and rely on obligations in their efforts to resolve conflict (Wilson et al., 2003). To accomplish this, they must (a) learn to discriminate gender-based social rules and (b) integrate self-interest with a transparently warm and communal interpersonal style. These skills are considerably more sophisticated and complex than the relatively straightforward response that characterises effective assertion by males (Carli, 2001). For Rudman and Glick (2001), this means women must be 'bilingual' – simultaneously competent and nice. The greater demands and risks women face constrain their assertion and result in significant real-world consequences such as salary and promotion disadvantages (Wade, 2001; Babcock & Laschever, 2003). For instance, women ask for less than men when negotiating starting salary, which has a significant impact on future earnings as small initial differences become compounded over the years into major discrepancies. In addition, women make fewer requests related to working conditions, and those that they do make are more likely to involve home rather than job concerns (Babcock & Laschever, 2003).

Unfortunately, women struggle to promote their own interests within a culture that even today teaches preschoolers that assertion is a component of social competence and acceptance for boys, but not for girls (Killen & Naigles, 1995; Sebanc, Pierce, Cheatham & Gunnar, 2003). As adults, men and women who have internalised a traditional view of women's role in society devalue assertion by females (Sterling & Owen, 1982; Kern et al., 1985). Women, therefore, must discriminate the context fully, including the gender biases of the recipient and the social rules that establish expectations, in order to make an informed decision about the value of assertion (Gallois, 1994). In this regard, females do appear to be making slow but steady progress in successfully juggling social demands and costs: they increased their assertiveness in the last third of the twentieth century by a significant though modest amount (0.46 standard deviations), as measured by two common behavioural self-report scales and the dominance scales of three trait instruments (Twenge, 2001).

Response classes

The studies assessing the perception of various response classes of standard assertion have produced conflicting data. Schroeder and his colleagues (Hull & Schroeder,

1979; Schroeder et al., 1983) determined that expressing unpopular opinions involved the greatest amount of assertiveness, behaviour change requests the next most, and refusals the least. Behaviour change requests were perceived to be most socially acceptable and expressing unpopular opinions the least appropriate. Lewis and Gallois (1984), on the other hand, obtained contradictory results: behaviour change requests (conflict statement only) were judged most assertive but least socially desirable, while expressing unpopular opinions was perceived most favourably. Furthermore, expressions of different opinions by friends were more positively evaluated than such behaviour by strangers or refusals by friends. Refusals by strangers were judged more positively than refusals by friends or the conflict statement component of a behaviour change request. Finally, Crawford (1988) found no differences in the reactions to the expression of negative feelings, positive self-presentation, and the setting of limits. However, these three response categories appeared to be variations of behaviour change requests rather than representatives of distinct response classes.

The conflicting data obtained by Schroeder and Lewis and Gallois may be due to cultural differences between the USA and Australia or to a variety of methodological differences, such as varying response topographies and specification of degree of familiarity of friends. Furthermore, these investigations evaluated standard assertion only. Friends, as part of their relationship, may very well accept a difference of opinion without explanation, compromise, or empathy, but are likely to expect those elaborations to accompany the refusal of a request. These data, then, are consistent with the emphasis on employing empathic assertion for resolving conflicts in continuing relationships.

Level of assertiveness

Socially competent persons judge assertive responses to be more likeable, effective, and appropriate than aggressive and non-assertive ones (e.g. Frisch & Froberg, 1987). Because non-assertive persons expect more negative outcomes from assertion, it is not surprising that many studies find that their perception of such behaviour is relatively unfavourable (see Rakos, 1991). However, when non-assertive persons have the opportunity to evaluate a spectrum of behaviour that is broader than a single standard assertive interaction, their evaluation of the asserter is similar to that of assertive persons (Alden & Cappe, 1981; Levin & Gross, 1984; Wojnilower & Gross, 1984; Delamater & McNamara, 1991; Kern & Paquette, 1992). Non-assertive persons, with their lower level of conceptual complexity, may moderate their judgement of conflict assertion only when it is portrayed concretely and in concert with other responses that have unambiguous social acceptability.

Racial and cultural values

The activism, pragmatism, rationality, and ethical relativism that legitimise assertion embody middle-class, US, Caucasian male values (Wine, 1981). Thus, the specific behaviours and attitudes fostered by this ideology will not be congruent with cultural assumptions of all societies or ethnic groups (Furnham, 1979; Rakos, 1991). In US society, for example, the issue of race must be considered directly. A system of cultural values that originated in Africa and the legacy of brutal discrimination (e.g. inter-racial discomfort, the development of distinct communication and linguistic patterns) raise questions about the social acceptability of assertion by African-Americans. In fact, the research suggests that there are important differences in the way African-Americans and whites react to conflict assertion. In general, African-Americans perceive assertive behaviour by an African-American as more aggressive than similar behaviour emitted by a white person, and value aggressive and standard assertive behaviour more, and empathic assertion less, than do whites (see Rakos, 1991, for summary).

When the race of all participants in an assertive interaction is examined, even finer distinctions emerge. Hrop and Rakos (1985) compared the reactions of African-American and white observers to standard and empathic assertion emitted in white–white, white–black, black–white, and black–black male dyads. White observers were influenced by race of asserter but not by race of recipient. They felt more intimidated by either style of assertion by an African-American than by a white. Furthermore, they judged the empathic assertion more positively than the standard assertion when the asserter was white but not when he was African-American. These data suggest that the obligation components are appropriate training goals for whites asserting to whites, but that the goals for blacks asserting to whites might place greater emphasis on strategies to foster awareness of, and then to decrease, whites' discomfort with black assertiveness. African-American judges had relatively unfavourable perceptions of both styles of assertion when performed by a white as compared to a black, judging the behaviour to be more aggressive. In addition, African-Americans were influenced by the race of both asserter and recipient. They perceived empathic assertion by whites to blacks as less positive than standard assertion in the same context, but reversed their judgement for black-to-black interactions, in which the obligations significantly enhanced the evaluation of assertion. Therefore, different training goals for assertion to African-Americans may be indicated: standard assertion for white asserters, empathic assertion for black asserters.

Generalisations about the appropriateness of assertive response styles for members of diverse cultural and ethnic groups must be made cautiously. Japanese, Malaysian, and Filipino adults (Niikura, 1999), Asian-American adults (Zane, Sue, Hu & Kwon, 1991), and Turkish adolescents (Mehmet, 2003) are less likely to engage in conflict assertion than their Western counterparts. Nevertheless, assertion that accommodates cultural norms is an accepted communication style in a wide range of societies (e.g. the Igbo in Nigeria; Onyeizugbo, 2003). Furthermore, sensitivity to cultural values that are more communitarian and tradition bound than mainstream US can form the basis of successful intervention with a wide array of ethnic groups (Wood & Mallinckrodt, 1990; Fodor, 1992). More recently, this approach has been articulated in a novel and idealistic manner: Dwairy (2004) proposed that a broad-based effort to train Palestinian-Arab citizens of Israel in conflict assertion skills could help these persons coexist more effectively and harmoniously within the indi-vidualistically oriented Israeli milieu, particularly if a companion intervention helped Israelis to understand the communitarian-authoritarian foundation of Palestinian society.

OVERVIEW

Assertion is a situation-specific social skill that has been touted in the pop psychology literature as a panacea for all social frustrations, and then chastised by many researchers as a concept that has outlived its usefulness. Despite these polarised judgements, assertiveness and its accompanying training procedures have settled into a comfortable role in an increasing number of professional settings. As the peoples of the world experience rapid changes that bring them in closer contact with each other, it is likely that increasing numbers will conclude that their society's long-term interests are served when its members personify assertiveness. This is because assertiveness is an egalitarian social philosophy that encourages responsible individual action to challenge the legitimacy of barriers (interpersonal, societal, cultural, legal, or whatever) that prevent fair and equitable sharing of power and resources. Human nature being what it is, conflict assertion skills will remain central for all who seek to redress societal inequities.

REFERENCES

Adler, S. R., McGraw, S. A. & McKinlay, J. B. (1998). Patient assertiveness in ethnically diverse older women with breast cancer: challenging stereotypes of the elderly. *Journal of Aging Studies*, **12**, 331–350.

Alberti, R. E. (1977). Comments on 'Differentiating assertion from aggression: some behavioral guidelines'. *Behavior Therapy*, **8**, 353–354.

Alberti, R. E. & Emmons, M. L. (1970). *Your perfect right: a guide to assertive behavior*. San Luis Obispo, CA: Impact.

Alberti, R. E. & Emmons, M. L. (1986). *The professional edition of 'Your perfect right': a manual for assertiveness trainers*. San Luis Obispo, CA: Impact.

Alberti, R. E. & Emmons, M. L. (2001). *Your perfect right: assertiveness and equality in your life and relationships*, 8th edn. Atascadero, CA: Impact.

Alden, L. & Cappe, R. (1981). Non-assertiveness: skill deficit or selective self-evaluation? *Behavior Therapy*, **12**, 107–115.

Argyle, M., Furnham, A. & Graham, J. (1981). *Social situations*. Cambridge: Cambridge University Press.

Arisohn, B., Bruch, M. A. & Heimberg, R. G. (1988). Influence of assessment methods on self-efficacy and outcome expectancy ratings of assertive behavior. *Journal of Counseling Psychology*, **35**, 336–341.

Babcock, L. & Laschever, S. (2003). *Women don't ask: negotiation and the gender divide*. Princeton, NJ: Princeton University Press.

Back, K. & Back, K. (1999). *Assertiveness at work: a practical guide to handling awkward situations*. London: McGraw-Hill.

Bandura, A. (1977). Self-efficacy: toward a unifying theory of behavior change. *Psychology Review*, **84**, 191–215.

Bandura, A. (1978). The self-system in reciprocal determinism. *American Psychologist*, **33**, 344–358.

Blankenberg, R. W. & Heimberg, R. G. (1984). Assertive refusal, perceived consequences, and reasonableness of request. Paper presented at the annual convention of the Association for Advancement of Behavior Therapy, Philadelphia, PA (November).

Bordewick, M. C. & Bornstein, P. H. (1980). Examination of multiple cognitive response dimensions among differentially assertive individuals. *Behavior Therapy*, *11*, 440–448.

Bourque, P. & Ladouceur, R. (1979). Self-report and behavioral measures in the assessment of assertive behavior. *Journal of Behavior Therapy and Experimental Psychiatry*, *10*, 287–292.

Broverman, I. K., Broverman, D. M., Clarkson, F. E., Rosenkrantz, P. S. & Vogal, S. R. (1970). Sex-role stereotypes and clinical judgments of mental health. *Journal of Consulting and Clinical Psychology*, *34*, 1–7.

Broverman, I. K., Vogal, S. R., Broverman, D. M., Clarkson, F. E. & Rosenkrantz, P. S. (1972). Sex-role stereotypes: a current appraisal. *Journal of Social Issues*, *28*, 59–78.

Bruch, M. A. (1981). A task analysis of assertive behavior revisited: application and extension. *Behavior Therapy*, *12*, 217–230.

Bruch, M. A., Heisler, B. D. & Conroy, C. G. (1981). Effects of conceptual complexity on assertive behavior. *Journal of Counseling Psychology*, *28*, 377–385.

Bruch, M. A., McCann, M. & Harvey, C. (1991). Type A behavior and processing of social conflict information. *Journal of Research in Personality*, *25*, 434–444.

Burgoon, J. K. & Bacue, A. E. (2003). Nonverbal communication skills. In J. O. Greene & B. R. Burleson (Eds), *Handbook of communication and social interaction skills* (pp. 179–219). Mahwah, NJ: Lawrence Erlbaum.

Caballo, V. E. (1995). A Spanish contribution to molecular factors, assessment, and training of social skills. *Revista Mexicana de Psicolgia*, *12*, 121–131.

Cameron, D. (1994). Verbal hygiene for women: linguistics misapplied? *Applied Linguistics*, *15*, 382–398.

Carli, L. L. (2001). Gender and social influence. *Journal of Social Issues*, *57*, 725–741.

Chiauzzi, E. & Heimberg, R. G. (1983). The effects of subjects' level of assertiveness, sex, and legitimacy of request on assertion-relevant cognitions: an analysis by post performance videotape reconstruction. *Cognitive Therapy and Research*, *7*, 555–564.

Chiauzzi, E. & Heimberg, R. G. (1986). Legitimacy of request and social problem-solving: a study of assertive and non-assertive subjects. *Behavior Modification*, *10*, 3–18.

Christoff, K. A. & Edelstein, B. A. (1981). Functional aspects of assertive and aggressive behavior: laboratory and in vivo observations. Paper presented at the annual meeting of the Association for Advancement of Behavior Therapy, Toronto, Canada (November).

Cook, D. J. & St. Lawrence, J. S. (1990). Variations in presentational format: effect on interpersonal evaluations of assertive and unassertive behavior. *Behavior Modification*, *14*, 21–36.

Craighead, L. W. (1979). Self-instructional training for assertive-refusal behavior. *Behavior Therapy*, *10*, 529–542.

Crawford, M. (1988). Gender, age, and the social evaluation of assertion. *Behavior Modification*, *12*, 549–564.

Crawford, M. (1995). *Talking difference: on gender and language*. London: Sage.

Davidson, J. P. (1997). *The complete idiot's guide to assertiveness*. New York: Alpha Books.

Delamater, R. J. & NcNamara, J. R. (1991). Perceptions of assertiveness by women involved in a conflict situation. *Behavior Modification, 15*, 173–193.

Deluty, R. H. (1981). Alternative-thinking ability of aggressive, assertive, and submissive children. *Cognitive Therapy and Research, 5*, 309–312.

Deluty, R. H. (1985). Cognitive mediation of aggressive, assertive, and submissive behavior in children. *International Journal of Behavior Development, 8*, 355–369.

Dewey, J. (1957). *Reconstruction in philosophy*. Boston, MA: Beacon Press.

Dura, J. R. & Beck, S. (1986). Psychiatric aides' perceptions of a patient's assertive behaviors. *Behavior Modification, 10*, 301–314.

Dwairy, M. (2004). Culturally sensitive education: adapting self-oriented assertiveness training to collective minorities. *Journal of Social Issues, 60*, 423–436.

D'Zurilla, T. J. & Nezu, A. M. (2001). Problem-solving therapies. In K. S. Dobson (Ed.), *Handbook of cognitive-behavioral therapies* (pp. 211–245). New York: Guilford.

Eisler, R. M., Miller, P. M. & Hersen, M. (1973). Components of assertive behavior. *Journal of Clinical Psychology, 29*, 295–299.

Eisler, R. M., Hersen, M., Miller, P. M. & Blanchard, E. (1975). Situational determinants of assertive behavior. *Journal of Consulting and Clinical Psychology, 43*, 330–340.

Ekman, P. (2001). *Telling lies: clues to deceit in the marketplace, politics, and marriage*, 3rd edn. New York: Norton.

Ellis, A. (1962). *Reason and emotion in psychotherapy*. New York: Lyle Stuart.

Ellis, A. & Grieger, R. (1977). *Handbook of rational-emotive therapy*. New York: Springer.

Epstein, N. (1980). The social consequences of assertion, aggression, passive aggression and submission: situational and dispositional determinants. *Behavior Therapy, 11*, 662–669.

Fischetti, M., Curran, J. P. & Wessberg, H. W. (1977). Sense of timing: a skill deficit in heterosexual-socially anxious males. *Behavior Modification, 1*, 179–194.

Fischetti, M., Peterson, J. L., Curran, J. P., Alkire, M., Perrewe, P. & Arland, S. (1984). Social cue discrimination versus motor skill: a missing distinction in social skill assessment. *Behavioral Assessment, 6*, 27–32.

Fodor, I. G. (1980). The treatment of communication problems with assertiveness training. In A. Goldstein & E. B. Foa (Eds), *Handbook of behavioral interventions: a clinical guide* (pp. 501–603). New York: Wiley.

Fodor, I. G. (Ed.) (1992). *Adolescent assertiveness and social skills training: a clinical handbook*. New York: Springer.

Frisch, M. B. & Froberg, W. (1987). Social validation of assertion strategies for handling aggressive criticism: evidence for consistency across situations. *Behavior Therapy, 18*, 181–191.

Furnham, A. (1979). Assertiveness in three cultures: multidemensionality and cultural differences. *Journal of Clinical Psychology, 35*, 522–527.

Galassi, J. P., Galassi, M. D. & Vedder, M. J. (1981). Perspectives on assertion as a social skills model. In J. Wine & M. Smye (Eds), *Social competence* (pp. 287–345). New York: Guilford Press.

Gallois, C. (1994). Group membership, social rules, and power: a social-psychological perspective on emotional communications. *Journal of Pragmatics, 22*, 301–324.

Gallois, C., Callan, V. J. & McKenzie Palmer, J. (1992). The influence of applicant communication style and interviewer characteristics on hiring decisions. *Journal of Applied Social Psychology*, *22*, 1041–1060.

Gambrill, E. (1995). Assertion skills training. In W. O'Donohue & L. Krasner (Eds), *Handbook of psychological skills training: clinical techniques and applications* (pp. 81–117). Boston, MA: Allyn and Bacon.

Gervasio, A. H. (1987). Assertiveness techniques as speech acts. *Clinical Psychology Review*, *7*, 105–119.

Gervasio, A. H. & Crawford, M. (1989). Social evaluations of assertiveness: a critique and speech act reformulation. *Psychology of Women Quarterly*, *13*, 1–25.

Gilligan, C. (1982). *In a different voice*. Cambridge, MA: Harvard University Press.

Goldin, J. (1957). *The living Talmud*. New York: Mentor.

Gormally, J. (1982). Evaluation of assertiveness: effects of gender, rater involvement and level of assertiveness. *Behavior Therapy*, *13*, 219–225.

Hansten, R. I., Washburn, M. J. & Kenyon, V. (1999). Home care nursing delegation skills: a handbook for practice. Gaithersburg, MD: Aspen.

Hargie, O. & Dickson, D. (2004). *Skilled interpersonal communication: research, theory and practice*. London: Routledge.

Hargie, O. Dickson, D. & Tourish, D. (2004). *Communication skills for effective management*. Basingstoke: Macmillan.

Hayes, J. (2002). *Interpersonal skills at work*, 2nd edn. Hove: Routledge.

Heimberg, R. G. & Etkin, D. (1983). Response quality and outcome effectiveness as factor in students' and counselors' judgements of assertiveness. *British Journal of Cognitive Psychotherapy*, *1*, 59–68.

Heimberg, R., Harrison, D. F., Goldberg, L. S., DesMarais, S. & Blue, S. (1979). The relationship of self-report and behavioral assertion in an offender population. *Journal of Behavior Therapy and Experimental Psychiatry*, *10*, 283–286.

Heisler, G. H. & McCormack, J. (1982). Situational and personality influences on the reception of provocative responses. *Behavior Therapy*, *13*, 743–750.

Hollandsworth, J. G. (1977). Differentiating assertion and aggression: some behavioral guidelines. *Behavior Therapy*, *9*, 640–646.

Hrop, S. & Rakos, R. F. (1985). The influence of race in the social evaluation of assertion in conflict situations. *Behavior Therapy*, *16*, 478–493.

Hull, D. B. & Schroeder, H. E. (1979). Some interpersonal effects of assertion, non-assertion, and aggression. *Behavior Therapy*, *10*, 20–29.

Hung, J. H., Rosenthal, T. L. & Kelley, J. E. (1980). Social comparison standards spur immediate assertion: 'So you think you're submissive?'. *Cognitive Therapy and Research*, *4*, 223–234.

Kahn, S. E. (1981). Issues in the assessment and training of assertiveness with women. In J. D. Wine & M. S. Smye (Eds), *Social competence* (pp. 346–367). New York: Guilford Press.

Kanfer, F. H. & Schefft, B. K. (1988). *Guiding the process of therapeutic change*. Champaign, IL: Research Press.

Kazdin, A. E. (1977). Assessing the clinical or applied importance of behavior change through social validation. *Behavior Modification*, *1*, 427–452.

Kern, J. M. & Paquette, R. J. (1992). Reactions to assertion in 'controlled' naturalistic relationships. *Behavior Modification*, *16*, 372–386.

Kern, J. M., Cavell, T. A. & Beck, B. (1985). Predicting differential reactions to males' versus females' assertions, empathic assertions, and non-assertions. *Behavior Therapy, 16,* 63–75.

Killen, M. & Naigles, L. R. Preschool children pay attention to their addresses: effects of gender composition on peer disputes. *Discourse Processes, 19,* 329–346.

Kirschner, S. M. & Galassi, J. P. (1983). Person, situational, and interactional influences on assertive behavior. *Journal of Counseling Psychology, 30,* 355–360.

Kleinke, C. L. (1986). Gaze and eye contact: a research review. *Psychological Bulletin, 100,* 78–100.

Klosko, S. & Sanderson, W. C. (1999). *Cognitive-behavioral treatment of depression.* Northvale, NJ: Jason Aronson.

Kolotkin, R. A., Wielkiewicz, R. M. Judd, B. & Weiser, S. (1984). Behavioral components of assertion: comparison of univariate and multivariate assessment strategies. *Behavioral Assessment, 6,* 61–78.

Korsgraad, M. A., Roberson, L. & Rymph, R. D. (1998). What motivates fairness? The role of subordinate assertive behavior on mangers' interactional fairness. *Journal of Applied Psychology, 83,* 731–744.

Krupat, E., Irish, J. T., Kasten, L. E., Freund, K. M., Burns, R. B., Moskowitz, M. A. & McKinlay, J. B. (1999). Patient assertiveness and physician decision-making among older breast cancer patients. *Social Science and Medicine, 49,* 449–457.

Kuperminc, M. & Heimberg, R. G. (1983). Consequence probability and utility as factors in the decision to behave assertively. *Behavior Therapy, 14,* 637–646.

LaFrance, M. & Mayo, C. (1976). Racial differences in gaze behavior during conversations: two systematic observational studies. *Journal of Personality and Social Psychology, 33,* 547–552.

Lange, A. J. & Jakubowski, P. (1976). *Responsible assertive behavior.* Champaign, IL: Research Press.

Levin, R. B. & Gross, A. M. (1984). Reactions to assertive versus nonassertive behavior: females in commendatory and refusal situations. *Behavior Modification, 8,* 581–592.

Levin, R. B. & Gross, A. M. (1987). Assertiveness style: effects on perceptions of assertive behavior. *Behavior Modification, 11,* 229–240.

Lewis, P. N. & Gallois, C. (1984). Disagreements, refusals, or negative feelings: perception of negatively assertive messages from friends and strangers. *Behavior Therapy, 15,* 353–368.

Linehan, M. M. & Seifert, R. F. (1983). Sex and contextual differences in the appropriateness of assertive behavior. *Psychology of Women Quarterly, 8,* 79–88.

Linehan, M. M. & Walker, R. O. (1983). The components of assertion: factor analysis of a multimethod assessment battery. *British Journal of Clinical Psychology, 22,* 277–281.

Lunsky, Y., Straiko, A. & Armstrong, S. (2003). Women be healthy: evaluation of a women's health curriculum for women with intellectual disabilities. *Journal of Applied Research in Intellectual Disabilities, 16,* 247–253.

MacDonald, M. L. (1982). Assertion training for women. In J. P. Curran & P. M. Monti (Eds), *Social skill training: a practical guide for assessment and treatment* (pp. 253–279). New York: Guilford Press.

MacIntyre, D., Carr, A., Lawlor, M. & Flattery, M. (2000). Development of the stay safe programme. *Child Abuse Review, 9,* 200–216.

Masters, J. C., Burish, T. G., Hollon, S. D. & Rimm, D. C. (1987). *Behavior therapy: techniques and empirical findings*, 3rd edn. New York: Harcourt Brace Jovanovich.

McBride, P. (1998). *The assertive social worker*. Aldershot: Arena.

McCampbell, E. & Ruback, R. B. (1985). Social consequences of apologetic, assertive, and aggressive requests. *Journal of Counseling Psychology, 32*, 68–73.

McFall, M. E., Winnett, R. L., Bordewick, M. C. & Bornstein, P. H. (1982). Nonverbal components in the communiation of assertiveness. *Behavior Modification, 6*, 121–140.

McFall, R. (1982). A review and reformulation of the concept of social skills. *Behavioral Assessment, 4*, 1–33.

Mehmet, E. (2003). Self-reported assertiveness in Swedish and Turkish adolescents: a cross-cultural comparison. *Scandinavian Journal of Psychology, 44*, 7–12.

Meichenbaum, D., Butler, L. & Gruson, L. (1981). Toward a conceptual model of social competence. In J. Wine & M. Smye (Eds), *Social competence* (pp. 36–60). New York: Guilford Press.

Morrison, R. L. & Bellack, A. E. (1981). The role of social perception in social skill. *Behavior Therapy, 12*, 69–79.

Mullinix, S. B. & Galassi, J. P. (1981). Deriving the content of social skills training with a verbal response components approach. *Behavioral Assessment, 3*, 55–66.

Niikura, R. (1999). The psychological processes underlying Japanese assertive behavior: comparison of Japanese with Americans, Malaysians and Filipinos. *International Journal of Intercultural Relations, 23*, 47–76.

Onyeizugbo, E. U. (2003). Effects of gender, age, and education on assertiveness in a Nigerian sample. *Psychology of Women Quarterly, 27*, 12–16.

Peterson, J. L., Fischetti, M., Curran, J. P. & Arland, S. (1981). Sense of timing: a skill defect in heterosocially anxious women. *Behavior Therapy, 12*, 195–201.

Pitcher, S. W. & Meikle, S. (1980). The topography of assertive behavior in positive and negative situations. *Behavior Therapy, 11*, 532–547.

Rakos, R. F. (1979). Content consideration in the distinction between assertive and aggressive behavior. *Psychological Reports, 44*, 767–773.

Rakos, R. F. (1986). Asserting and confronting. In O. Hargie (Ed.), *A handbook of communication skills* (pp. 407–440). London: Croom Helm.

Rakos, R. F. (1991). *Assertive behavior: theory, research, and training*. London: Routledge.

Rakos, R. F. & Schroeder, H. E. (1979). Development and empirical evaluation of a self-administered assertiveness training program. *Journal of Consulting and Clinical Psychology, 47*, 991–993.

Rakos, R. F. & Schroeder, H. E. (1980). *Self-administered assertiveness training*. New York: BMA Audio Cassettes.

Rich, A. & Schroeder, H. (1976). Research issues in assertiveness training. *Psychological Bulletin, 83*, 1084–1096.

Robinson, W. L. & Calhoun, K. S. (1984). Assertiveness and cognitive processing in interpersonal situations. *Journal of Behavioral Assessment, 6*, 81–96.

Romano, J. M. & Bellack, A. S. (1980). Social validation of a component model of assertive behavior. *Journal of Consulting and Clinical Psychology, 4*, 478–490.

Rose, Y. J. & Tryon, W. W. (1979). Judgements of assertive behavior as a function of speech loudness, latency, content, gestures, inflection and sex. *Behavior Modification, 3,* 112–123.

Rudman, L. A. (1998). Self-promotion as a risk factor for women: the costs and benefits of counterstereotypical impression management. *Journal of Personality and Social Psychology, 74,* 629–645.

Rudman, L. A. & Glick, P. (1999). Feminized management and backlash toward agenic women: the hidden costs to women of a kinder, gentler image of middle managers. *Journal of Personality and Social Psychology, 77,* 1004–1010.

Rudman, L. A. & Glick, P. (2001). Prescriptive gender stereotypes and backlash toward agenic women. *Journal of Social Issues, 57,* 743–762.

Rudy, T. E., Merluzzi, T. V. & Henahan, P. T. (1982). Construal of complex assertion situations: a multidimensional analysis. *Journal of Consulting and Clinical Psychology, 50,* 125–137.

Salter, A. (1949). *Conditioned reflex therapy.* New York: Farrar, Straus & Giroux.

Schroder, H., Driver, M. & Streufert, S. (1967). *Human information processing.* New York: Holt, Rinehart and Winston.

Schroeder, H. E. & Rakos, R. F. (1983). The identification and assessment of social skills. In R. Ellis & D. Whitington (Eds), *New directions in social skill training* (pp. 117–188). London: Croom Helm.

Schroeder, H. E., Rakos, R. F. & Moe, J. (1983). The social perception of assertive behavior as a function of response class and gender. *Behavior Therapy, 14,* 534–544.

Scott, R. R., Himadi, W. & Keane, T. M. (1983). A review of generalization in social skills training: suggestions for future research. In M. Hersen, R. Eisler & P. Miller (Eds), *Progress in behavior modification* (vol. 15, pp. 113–172). New York: Academic Press.

Sebanc, A. M., Pierce, S. L., Cheatham, C. L. & Gunnar, M. R. (2003). Gendered social worlds in preschool: dominance, peer acceptance and assertive social skills in boys' and girls' peer groups. *Social Development, 12,* 91–106.

Sigal, J., Braden-Maguire, J., Hayden, M. & Mosley, N. (1985). The effect of presentation style and sex of lawyer on jury decision-making behavior. *Psychology: A Quarterly Journal of Human Behavior, 22,* 13–19.

Solomon, L. J., Brehony, K. A., Rothblum, E. D. & Kelly, J. A. (1982). Corporate managers' reaction to assertive social skills exhibited by males and females. *Journal of Organizational Behavior Management, 4,* 49–63.

Sterling, B. S. & Owen, J. W. (1982). Perceptions of demanding versus reasoning male and female police officers. *Personality and Social Psychology Bulletin, 8,* 336–340.

St. Lawrence, J. S. (1987). Assessment of assertion. In M. Hersen, R. M. Eisler & P. M. Miller (Eds), *Progress in behavior modification* (vol. 21, pp. 152–190). Newbury Park, CA: Sage

St. Lawrence, J. S., Hansen, D. J., Cutts, T. F., Tisdelle, D. A. & Irish, J. D. (1985). Situational context: effects on perceptions of assertive and unassertive behavior. *Behavior Therapy, 16,* 51–62.

Tomaka, J., Palacios, R., Schneider, K. T., Colotla, M., Concha, J. B. & Herrald, M. M. (1999). Assertiveness predicts threat and challenge reactions to potential stress among women. *Journal of Personality and Social Psychology, 76,* 1008–1021.

Trower, P. (1980). Situational analysis of the components and processes of behavior of socially skilled and unskilled patients. *Journal of Consulting and Clinical Psychology*, *48*, 327–339.

Trower, P. (1982). Toward a generative model of social skills: a critique and syntheses. In J. Curran & P. Monti (Eds), *Social skills training: a practical handbook for assessment and treatment* (pp. 399–427). New York: Guilford Press.

Trower, P. (1995). Adult social skills: state of the art and future directions. In W. O'Donohue & L. Krasner (Eds), *Handbook of psychological skills training: clinical techniques and applications* (pp. 54–80). Boston, MA: Allyn and Bacon.

Trudeau, L., Lillehoj, C. Spoth, R. & Redmond, C. (2003). The role of assertiveness and decision making in early adolescent substance initiation: mediating processes. *Journal of Research on Adolescence*, *13*, 301–328.

Twenge, J. M. (2001). Changes in women's assertiveness in response to status and roles: a cross-temporal meta-analysis, 1931–1993. *Journal of Personality and Social Psychology*, *81*, 133–145.

Twentyman, C. T., Zimering, R. T. & Kovaleski, M. E. (1981). Three studies investigating the efficacy of assertion training techniques. *Behavioral Counseling Quarterly*, *1*, 302–316.

Wade, M. E. (2001). Women and salary negotiation: the costs of self-advocacy. *Psychology of Women Quarterly*, *25*, 65–76.

Weinhardt, L. S., Carey, M. P., Carey, K. B. & Verdecia, R. N. (1998). Increasing assertiveness skills to reduce HIV risk among women living with a severe and persistent mental illness. *Journal of Consulting and Clinical Psychology*, *66*, 680–684.

Wildman, B. G. & Clementz, B. (1986). Assertive, empathic assertive, and conversational behavior: perception of likeability, effectiveness, and sex role. *Behavior Modification*, *10*, 315–332.

Wilson, K. & Gallois, C. (1993). *Assertion and its social context*. Oxford: Pergamon Press.

Wilson, K. L., Lizzio, A. J., Whicker, L., Gallois, C. & Price, J. (2003). Effective assertive behavior in the workplace: responding to unfair criticism. *Journal of Applied Social Psychology*, *33*, 362–395.

Wine, J. D. (1981). From defect to competence models. In J. D. Wine & M. D. Smye (Eds), *Social competence* (pp. 3–35). New York: Guilford Press.

Winship, B. J. & Kelly, J. D. (1976). A verbal response model of assertiveness. *Journal of Counseling Psychology*, *23*, 215–220.

Winterowd, C., Beck, A. T. & Gruener, D. (2003). *Cognitive therapy with chronic pain patients*. New York: Springer.

Wojnilower, D. A. & Gross, A. M. (1984). Assertive behavior and likability in elementary school boys. *Child and Family Behavior Therapy*, *6*, 57–70.

Wolf, M. M. (1978). Social validity: the case for subjective measurement or how applied behavior analysis is finding its heart. *Journal of Applied Behavior Analysis*, *11*, 203–214.

Wolpe, J. (1969). *The practice of behavior therapy*. Oxford: Pergamon Press.

Wolpe, J. (1990). *The practice of behavior therapy*, 4th edn. Elmsford, NY: Pergamon Press.

Wood, P. S. & Mallinckrodt, B. (1990). Culturally sensitive assertiveness training for ethnic minority clients. *Professional Psychology: Research and Practice, 21,* 5–11.

Woolfolk, R. L. & Dever, S. (1979). Perceptions of assertion: an empirical analysis. *Behavior Therapy, 10,* 404–411.

Zane, N. W. S., Sue, S., Hu, L. & Kwon, J. (1991). Asian-American assertion: a social learning analysis of cultural differences. *Journal of Counseling Psychology, 38,* 63–70.

Zollo, L. J., Heimberg, R. G. & Becker, R. E. (1985). Evaluations and consequences of assertive behavior. *Journal of Behavior Therapy and Experimental Psychiatry, 16,* 295–301.

Chapter 13

Interacting in groups

Arjaan Wit

T HERE ARE SEVERAL RELATED reasons for members of a task group to communicate with one another. Imagine a number of students and faculty members who have volunteered to participate in a committee to update the current curriculum. Before they can plan any specific actions, they first have to arrive at a common understanding of their task. If they differ among themselves in their interpretation of the group task, as is often the case, the divergence in cognitions should be resolved by mutually exchanging pieces of information. The first part of this chapter discusses how communication affects the process of *cognitive tuning* to arrive at a common understanding of the group task.

A group cannot successfully complete a task unless its members reach agreement about the division of the work that has to be carried out. Group members may realise that their common and private interests coincide with respect to successful completion of the group task, but all of them may nevertheless feel tempted to act in their private interest by, for example, leaving unpleasant work to fellow group members. The second part of this chapter elaborates on the role of communication in the process of *tuning common and private interests*.

Cognitive tuning and tuning of interests are two basic processes in groups (Wilke & Meertens, 1994). In both tuning processes, communicating group members exert strong pressures on one another to consider the cognitions and interests that they have in common. Although essential for successful completion of the group task, strong normative conformity pressure to arrive at a common understanding of the task may have its drawbacks when it comes to innovative thinking. At the end of the first part of this chapter, we will discuss some preventive measures that can be taken to weaken dysfunctional normative conformity

383

pressures. In the process of tuning of interests, by contrast, normative pressures on group members to consider their common interests cannot be strong enough. As we will see at the end of the second part of this chapter, groups often take additional normative measures to counteract group members' temptation to enjoy a free ride on fellow members' cooperative efforts.

COGNITIVE TUNING

Newly formed task groups or existing groups faced with a new task can formulate solutions only after a common understanding of the task is achieved. There are three basic modalities of cognitive tuning toward a commonly shared frame of reference (Moscovici, 1985), namely, normalisation, conformity, and innovation. *Normalisation* occurs when there is no a priori shared interpretation of the group task. When the task is very ambiguous and fluid, group members mutually and gradually converge on a common frame of reference that serves from then on as a group norm. *Conformity* assumes prior normalisation since it involves the attempts of a majority of the group members to maintain their socially anchored representation of the task by putting pressure on deviating individuals to go along, or risk being rejected by the majority. When a persisting minority of deviates tries to introduce a new frame of reference an explicit cognitive conflict is created. *Innovation* occurs when this cognitive conflict is resolved through persuasion of members of the majority by the minority.

The three modalities of cognitive tuning embody increasing levels of cognitive conflict in a task group (Moscovici & Doise, 1994). The following three sections will describe some classic studies on the role of communication in group members' attempts to form, maintain, and change their common frame of reference, respectively. These studies are often cited as starting points for more recent research on cognitive-tuning processes in task groups. To illustrate some implications of the research findings, we will use the example of an educational committee.

Normalisation

Although all of the members of the committee may share the conviction that the current curriculum needs an update, their participation in the committee may initially feel like a leap in the dark to (some of) them. How will they arrive at a common frame of reference when there is not yet an a priori shared interpretation of the group task?

In a very literal sense, darkness has been employed by Sherif (1936) in a classic series of experiments on the formation of a shared representation of an ambiguous task. Sherif made use of the so-called autokinetic phenomenon, a compelling optical illusion to a person who stares at a tiny light bulb in an otherwise completely darkened room. Even though the light is in fact stationary, after the person watches it for a minute or two it appears to move, due to (unconscious) eye movements and neural processes in the eyes of the perceiver. The illusion occurs when the room is pitch-dark and when experimental participants are unfamiliar with the room's size so that they lack any physical standard against which to compare the position of the dot of light. Their task is to estimate the apparent movement of the light after each of a number of exposures.

Sherif's first series of studies investigated the formation of a personal frame of reference. Participants were run in isolation and there was no opportunity to communicate. It appeared that a participant's initial responses varied widely from one exposure to the next, but with repeated exposures, a participant's responses gradually converged on a single estimate. This single value that each participant eventually arrived at differed widely across participants, suggesting that each participant built up a stable personal frame of reference to judge subsequent task stimuli.

In Sherif's second series of studies, inexperienced participants were placed together in the pitch-dark room and were allowed to communicate with one another. It appeared that, as in the first series of studies, participants' individual estimates showed a pattern of extreme initial variability. However, as a result of mutual adjustment between group members' estimates in the process of communicating, participants' responses soon converged on a single group estimate. These group estimates differed widely across groups, suggesting that each of the groups developed its own frame of reference. The question arises as to why some groups converged on a high, while other groups converged on a low, group estimate. To address the role of the content of the communication, in some studies Sherif paid experimental confederates, acting as if they were regular fellow group members, to offer extremely high (or low) estimates. In response to these extreme estimates given by the confederates, the naive group members drastically increased (or decreased) their estimates to converge on a high (or low) group estimate. Subsequent studies (e.g. MacNeil & Sherif, 1976) observed that, once such a high (or low) group estimate had been established, it acquired a life of its own as a group norm. When the experimenter removed the confederates from the group after a number of trials and replaced them by new naive participants, the artificially high or low group norm still continued to affect the group's judgements in subsequent trials.

In the above studies, the naive, inexperienced participants felt very unsure about the correctness of their own estimates. In the absence of any communication with fellow participants in the first series of studies, the internal cognitive conflict about the correctness of their own estimates had to be resolved by the individual participant himself or herself. In the second series of studies, the possibility to communicate with fellow group members helped participants to resolve their internal cognitive conflict. Participants were so uncertain about their own initial responses, that they gave much weight to the estimates expressed by their fellow group members. As a result, they developed a common understanding of the task and a common response: a group estimate.

In a subsequent study, a much stronger cognitive conflict was experienced by the participants, not merely at an intrapersonal level (as in the above mentioned studies) but also at an interpersonal level. It appeared that participants that had first been exposed to a number of trials in isolation before they were placed in a group were less willing to adjust their own initial estimates to those of their fellow group members. Many of the participants stuck to their personal way of responding that they had developed in isolation before they entered the group. As a result, the progress of cognitive tuning toward a socially anchored norm, that is, a single group estimate, took much more time and was far less complete than when no personal way of responding had been previously established.

The strongest interpersonal cognitive conflict was felt by participants in yet another study. After having naive, inexperienced participants respond to repeated trials in separate groups so that a socially anchored local group norm had been developed within each group, Sherif took individuals from these separate groups and created new groups for another series of exposures. Unlike completely inexperienced participants or participants who had already built up a personal norm in isolation before entering a group, these participants were least easily influenced by the fellow members of their present, newly created group. They persisted in the norm that they had developed by communicating with fellow members of their previous group.

Taken together, Sherif's studies suggest that once task ambiguity has been cognitively resolved by the formation of an internalised frame of reference, group members attach less weight to new perspectives, which may then be seen as discrepant from their own frame of reference. These results imply that the communicative process of cognitive tuning toward a commonly shared frame of reference depends on group members' previous experiences. For example, if (some of the) members enter the educational committee with well-developed ideas about the task, which may differ widely from one member to another due to previous normalisation in other social settings (such as student meetings or faculty meetings), the formation of a common frame of reference will not be easily achieved. This is very likely to happen, since one usually does not recruit naive, inexperienced candidates to participate in advisory committees. When (some) members stick to their previously developed, socially anchored frame of reference, the committee should find ways to resolve the cognitive conflict between the group members.

Under these conditions of prior normalisation, the question arises as to whether a group member faced with a number of fellow group members advocating a discrepant perspective that does not seem correct will go along or stick to their previously developed, socially anchored frame of reference (Falcione & Wilson, 1988; Teboul, 1997). This group member may be displaying attitudes or behaviours that have gained them personal acceptance in other groups to which they belong. In a newly formed group, the person may be met with disapproval. What happens if such an individual is faced with a discrepant majority?

Conformity pressures from a majority

How will a group member respond upon learning that a personal frame of reference, established by previous experience, differs from the one held by the majority of the fellow members of the present group?

The classic experimental paradigm for studying this issue has been developed by Asch (1952), who asked small groups of participants to make a series of relatively simple judgements. Their task was to state publicly, and in the same fixed order, which of three comparison lines matched a fourth 'target' line in length. The correct answer was obvious. When making these simple judgements in isolation, participants made no mistakes. In the typical group experiment, only one of the group members was a naive participant, who had to respond next to last in the row after hearing the responses of the preceding group members, who (unknown to the naive participant) were all confederates of the experimenter. The group judged a series of stimulus sets, and on many of these (the 'critical' trials) the confederates had been instructed to agree on a clearly incorrect response. By having the confederates advocate a clearly incorrect response, Asch assessed an individual group member's willingness to conform to a majority when this individual could be completely certain of being right and that the majority was wrong. Being faced with a unanimous majority that offered an obviously incorrect answer created a strong intra- and interpersonal cognitive conflict for the naive participant. This participant was puzzled by the discrepancy between personal judgement and the unanimous judgement of all of the fellow group members. Should the person comply with the unanimous majority of the present group or stick to their internalised frame of reference? It appeared that only 25% of the naive participants showed no conformity at all and remained independent of the social pressure from the majority throughout the session. Only a few participants conformed on all of the critical trials to the blatantly incorrect judgement of the majority. However, 33% of all participants conformed to the clearly incorrect majority position on more than half of the critical trials.

What can be learned from these results? On the one hand, they demonstrate the impact of majority influence. One out of every three naive participants solved the cognitive conflict by adjusting their own response to the incorrect responses of the majority on many (but not all) of the critical trials. On the other hand, the same results demonstrate that conformity in a group is not easily achieved when group members are strongly convinced that they themselves are right and that the majority of their fellow group members are wrong. At least one out of every four naive participants remained completely independent of the majority pressure, whereas two-thirds of all naive participants remained independent on more than half of the critical trials. Note that such a reluctance to conform to the judgements of fellow group members was also observed in Sherif's studies, by participants who had previously developed a socially anchored frame of reference before they entered their present group.

The case of one (naive participant) against all other group members (confederates) is a special case, however. Whereas a lone individual will find it hard to resist the pressure of the majority since the one view can be dismissed as a personal idiosyncrasy, the presence of some fellow dissenters in the group may cast doubt on the majority view. In follow-up studies, Asch (1955) instructed one of the confederates to give the correct response on some of the critical trials. When the naive participant found that they were not alone in disagreeing with the clearly incorrect majority, conformity rates were much lower. In yet another variation, Asch arranged for one confederate to disagree with the majority, but also to disagree with the (correct) answer of the naive participant. It appeared that even the presence of such a fellow deviate who did not agree with the majority nor with the participant made it easier for a naive participant to express a personal viewpoint during the group discussion and to withstand pressures from the majority. Apparently, the cognitive conflict of being faced with a unanimous majority is more intense (and, as a result, elicits more conformity) than the cognitive conflict of being faced with a non-unanimous majority.

Subsequent research by Asch revealed that naive participants were less willing to go along with the majority when they were not required to state their judgements publicly but were allowed to state their judgements privately in writing. Thus, conformity to a majority position does not necessarily reflect a participant's true opinion. Indeed, in private, post-experimental interviews (away from the group), participants who had publicly agreed with their fellow group members in the group session pointed out that they did not believe that the others were correct, but that they themselves did not want to appear different. Their anxiety about appearing different was not unrealistic. In a reversal of the above described studies, Asch (1952) replaced the confederates by naive participants, so that there was a majority of naive participants facing one incorrect confederate. Under these conditions, the naive participants expressed strong confidence in the correctness of their majority position and exposed the persisting deviate to amusement and scorn.

The relationship between non-conformity and rejection by fellow group members has also been demonstrated by Schachter (1951). He showed that, throughout group discussions, communication directed toward disagreeing group members tends to increase over time in order to put pressure on these deviants to conform to the majority. At a later stage of the discussion, the amount of communication with deviants decreases, either because initial deviants yield to the majority pressure or because the majority gives up trying to influence a persisting deviant. In the latter case, the deviant is literally excommunicated.

Reviewing the above classic studies and many recent studies that used a large variety of tasks (ranging from perceptual tasks to attitude tasks), Wheeler (1991) concluded that the need to communicate in a group increases when the issue has more relevance for the group and when group members feel the need to maintain a congenial group atmosphere. Furthermore, pressures to communicate in the direction of a specific group member are stronger when the perceived likelihood that communication will change that person in the desired direction is greater. Communication with an unyielding deviate will eventually stop. Applied to the process of cognitive tuning in the educational committee, these studies suggest that its members may feel compelled to conform to the opinions of the majority of their present group, that is, the committee. Learning that a majority of the committee has reached agreement about their understanding of the task that differs from one member's own understanding may lead the individual to doubt whether personal views are valid and whether a deviant will be liked as a group member. With increasing group cohesion or when the topic of discussion has more relevance for the committee, it will be harder for a deviant to withstand the majority's conformity pressures. Resistance to majority pressure is more likely, however, when there is still another group member advocating a perspective that differs from the one held by the majority. Whereas a single dissenter's arguments can be dismissed as personal idiosyncrasies, more than one dissenter in the group may cast doubt on the validity of the majority's perspective. In the next paragraph, we will elaborate on the potential innovative impact of such a few persisting dissenters.

Innovative pressures from a minority

Members of a minority who challenge the prevailing group norm by maintaining their own discrepant views in a consistent and confident way may not only successfully withstand the conformity pressures of the majority, but may also have innovative impact on the group. Consistency in the responses of the minority in the face of majority opposition (and sometimes even ridicule) may be considered by the members of the majority as a sign of self-confidence and commitment to a coherent idea and thereby may focus their attention on the minority's line of reasoning. Herein lies the potential of minority influence. It can purposely create cognitive conflict, and doubt and uncertainty about the prevailing group norm, exploiting most group members' dislike of cognitive conflict and their need for uniformity. When the cognitive conflict cannot be resolved by mutual convergence (as participants did in Sherif's autokinetic effect studies), it may be solved either by excommunicating the deviant minority (as in Asch's and Schachter's studies) or by an attitudinal shift of members of the majority in the direction of the minority.

Effective minority influence has been demonstrated in a classic series of ingenious studies by Moscovici, Lage, and Naffrechoux (1969). Groups of six individuals were shown a series of blue slides, which varied in brightness. The participants' task was to judge the colour of the slides and to announce judgements aloud. When the group consisted of six naive participants, 99% of all participants labelled the slides as blue. By instructing two confederates in the six-person groups to advocate an unusual response, that is, labelling the blue slides as green, Moscovici and his co-workers were able to assess naive participants' willingness to go along with a discrepant minority. It was unlikely that the unusual responses by these confederates would be dismissed as blatantly incorrect, as had been the case in Asch's studies, since the colour perception task faced participants with more ambiguity about the correct response than Asch's line-matching tasks. The results showed that when the judgements of the two confederates were consistent, both over time and across themselves, the four naive participants eventually described the slide more often as green (8% of all responses given by the naive participants were green) than when the judgements of the two confederates were inconsistent, that is, sometimes labelling the slides as blue, sometimes as green (resulting in only 1% of all responses being green). Thus, it appears that a consistent minority may exert innovative influence, whereas an inconsistent minority may have virtually no impact on the group.

Although naive participants in the six-person groups were more likely to agree publicly with the unusual colour judgements when these were made by a majority (four confederates labelling the slides as green) than when these were made by a consistent minority (two confederates labelling the slides as green), their private beliefs were influenced more deeply by minority influence than by majority influence. From private interviews (away from the group) after the group sessions, it appeared that participants who had followed the minority's suggestion that the slides were green had a stronger belief that the slides were green than participants who had yielded to a majority labelling the slides as green. These results were conceptually replicated with various other tasks, such as discussion tasks (Maass & Clark, 1984). Several studies show that naive participants' private beliefs are more strongly affected by minority influence than by majority influence. When naive participants can express their opinion at the end of the discussion in private, they tend to agree more often with the minority. However, they tend to agree more often with the majority when they have to express their opinion in the presence of fellow group members.

Taken together, majority influence appears to be particularly effective in eliciting public compliance, whereas group members' private beliefs are more strongly affected by minority influence (De Vries, De Dreu, Gordijn & Schuurman, 1996). These results suggest that a small subgroup within the educational committee may create a cognitive conflict by demonstrating a consistent and confident behavioural style in expressing a discrepant perspective. This subgroup may be able to introduce a new frame of reference. Its innovative impact may not be visible right away, however. Minority influence may not immediately come to the surface during plenary meetings, but only in the absence of the majority of the committee members, for example, during private discussions between individuals after a plenary meeting (Pearce, Stevenson & Porter, 1986). In order to enhance its innovative impact, a minority should encourage group members who have been privately persuaded by the minority's arguments to support publicly the new frame of reference. To increase the size of the minority (and thereby its impact), the minority should persuade individual converts that some fellow committee members have also privately expressed their support for the minority position. The assumed presence of fellow dissenters makes it less threatening for individual converts to adhere publicly to the minority position during a follow-up, plenary committee meeting.

Informational versus normative pressures

The preceding sections have dealt with cognitive-tuning processes in groups in which there exists either a broad range of perspectives or in which a majority or minority favours one particular perspective. The three associated modalities of cognitive tuning, that is, normalisation, conformity, and innovation, respectively, can be described in terms of two basic social pressures in groups: informational pressure and normative pressure (Deutsch & Gerard, 1955; Zimbardo & Leippe, 1991).

Informational pressure is based on group members' tendency to rely upon fellow group members to acquire accurate information to form an appropriate frame of reference in an ambiguous task environment. Open communication may induce group members to converge on a common frame of reference or social norm. This process of normalisation has been observed in Sherif's groups of inexperienced participants, who were literally put in the dark and lacked any standard against which to compare the position of the dot of light. Internalisation of such a socially anchored frame of reference may result in individual group members attaching less weight to new, discrepant perspectives, but it does not immunise them, since group members rely on others to acquire not only accurate information but also approval.

When faced with a majority holding a discrepant perspective, individual group members may yield to *normative* pressures of a majority to reward conforming group members and reject persisting deviates. A comparison between Asch's and Sherif's research findings suggests, however, that conformity in the interest of being liked as a group member has less powerful ramifications than conformity that results from viewing fellow group members for the purpose of gaining accurate information. Many of Asch's participants, who were confident that their own frame of reference was correct and that the fellow group members were wrong (no informational social pressure), publicly conformed to the local majority norm because they were afraid to be seen as different. Their compliance persisted only as long as they felt normative pressure. Once outside the group, they were more likely to express their private beliefs. By contrast, a local group norm that had been established through communication between inexperienced naive participants in Sherif's studies (on the basis of their informational needs to arrive at an accurate representation of ambiguous task stimuli) acquired a life of its own and tended to persist even in the absence of fellow group members with whom the norm had previously been developed.

Not only a majority, but also a consistent minority may induce individual group members to shift their opinion. Particularly when the task environment leaves some room for different interpretations (Moscovici et al., 1969), a minority's discrepant perspective cannot easily be dismissed as blatantly incorrect. Since minorities lack the numerical advantage of majorities and their positions are often quite unpopular, minorities cannot exert normative pressure on individual members of the majority. By intentionally raising doubt about the validity of the prevailing opinion of the majority, minorities may instead set the stage for *informational* social influence. To be effective, arguments supporting the minority position must be well communicated. In addition, minorities should evoke elaborate discussions in the group. Such discussions are less likely to be initiated by members supporting the majority opinion. When the content of the minority's persuasive arguments eventually becomes clear, minorities may induce a real change in group members' private beliefs.

Following this line of reasoning, Nemeth (1992) argues that majority influence may induce a fixation in thought, because it focuses group members mainly on the normative requirement of conformity. The fear of being rejected by the majority of one's group impedes creative and divergent thinking. By contrast, given a minority's inability to exert normative pressure, minority influence relies on informational pressure. The cognitive conflict evoked by a persistent minority is likely to promote careful consideration of the reasons for the apparent discrepancy. Nemeth and Kwan (1987) demonstrated that group members not only express more, but also more divergent and original, ideas in response to a discrepant minority than group members exposed to a discrepant majority. Thus, a dissenting minority appears to stimulate creativity and openness in the exchange of information rather than adaptation and fixation.

Although normative and informational pressures can be distinguished conceptually, they are closely related. Normative pressures can inhibit informational pressures by determining what information gets exchanged in a task group. During discussions, group members may be so concerned with receiving social approval from their peers (rather than with careful evaluation of the available information) that some information never gets expressed. As a result, they tend to discuss information that they assume to share in common and fail to mention distinguishing pieces of information that are known only to single individuals within the group (Stasser & Titus, 1985), or information that might contradict an emerging group consensus. In its most extreme form, normative pressures may lead to premature concurrence-seeking in decision-making groups ('groupthink'). Failure to take relevant alternative perspectives into account may result in serious policy disasters (Janis, 1982). Given the importance of open-mindedness to alternative perspectives at various stages of task completion, task groups should find ways to row against the current of normative pressures. The next section will elaborate on some formal techniques to push group members past the bounds of restrictive thinking along the lines of the prevailing local group norm.

Overcoming dysfunctional normative pressures

How can premature concurrence-seeking and biased information exchange be avoided? *Brainstorming* may stimulate group members to generate divergent ideas (Osborn, 1957). Group members receive instructions from a group facilitator, who introduces several rules to encourage group members to express as many ideas as possible within a certain time interval. Group members should not screen their own ideas. In order to generate even more ideas, they are encouraged to piggyback on ideas expressed by their fellow group members. One person records all the expressed ideas and presents the list to the group as rapidly as possible, without discussion, clarification, or comment. Evaluation of one's own and others' ideas has to be postponed.

In a review of many studies, McGrath (1984) concluded that, in spite of the popularity of interactive brainstorming and common beliefs about its efficacy, there is little empirical evidence that groups that follow this procedure generate more ideas of superior quality than individuals working separately. On the contrary, separate individuals may produce even more and better ideas than the same individuals acting as members of an interactive brainstorming group (Diehl & Stroebe, 1987; Paulus, Larey & Ortega, 1995). One of the reasons that conventional interactive brainstorming groups fall short in producing creative ideas seems to be that group members, despite the instruction not to evaluate one another's contributions, fear negative evaluations from their fellow group members. Normative conformity pressures are often too strong for free expression of one's idiosyncratic ideas. Furthermore, it has been demonstrated that members of a conventional interactive brainstorming group tend to converge on similar amounts of idea expressions. This convergence appears to be biased in the direction of the least productive group members (Paulus & Dzindolet, 1993). Real group interaction leads to mutual matching that normalises a low performance level. How can these drawbacks be prevented?

In order to overcome these dysfunctional normative pressures, a modification of the traditional face-to-face brainstorming method has been developed. The so-called *nominal group technique* (NGT) involves a process with two formally distinct stages (Delbecq, Van de Ven & Gustafson, 1975). In the first or elicitation stage, individual group members work separately, generating alternative perspectives on the issue at hand. In order to minimise normative pressures, group members are not required to express their ideas aloud in the presence of the fellow group members, but write their ideas down (cf. Asch's research findings, suggesting that normative conformity pressures can be weakened when group members are not required to express their opinions publicly, but are allowed to state them privately in writing). The second or evaluation stage involves the collective listing and evaluation of the perspectives that have been generated during the first stage. In a series of studies by Van de Ven and Delbecq (1974) to compare NGT with conventional interactive brainstorming techniques, NGT was found to produce superior results. This suggests that interaction and communication between members of brainstorming groups may be most useful if individual group members have first generated ideas separately and thereafter get additional social stimulation of other members' ideas.

Some groups may install a 'devil's advocate' to evoke discussion about alternative perspectives. In order to promote the examination of both supporting and detracting evidence, one group member presents any information that may lead to the disqualification of the prevailing frame of reference (Herbert & Estes, 1977). Unlike the lone dissenter in Asch's studies, this dissenting group member's popularity in the group is not harmed, since this person is formally installed to play that role. Moreover, the role may be shifted regularly from one group member to another. The cognitive conflict created by having one group member disagree consistently with the majority position sets the stage for informational social influence, as in the case of minority influence. Severe cognitive stress should be avoided, however, by instructing the devil's advocate to present arguments carefully in a low-key, non-threatening manner.

Yet another technique to inhibit dysfunctional normative conformity pressures may be to arrange that members of the group meet in *separate subgroups*, which will each develop their own frame of reference (Wheeler & Janis, 1980). The presence of two subgroups in a subsequent combined meeting may elicit discussion and critical examination of the reasons for the differences between the perspectives that have been developed within each of the subgroups. If the subgroups eventually come to agreement, which may not be easily achieved (cf. Sherif's research findings, suggesting less convergence to a common group opinion in the case of prior normalisation), it is less likely that any important considerations will be overlooked or ignored. The common frame of reference on which the subgroups eventually come to agree may then be adopted with more confidence than if only a single group had worked on it.

Although normative conformity pressures can be dysfunctional and may produce erroneous group judgements (cf. Asch's research findings and Janis' studies on 'groupthink'), one should acknowledge the potential benefits of normative pressure to ensure mutual social control. Mutual control becomes increasingly important when group members are motivated to act in their own way. As long as they are merely concerned with tuning their cognitions, group members' motivation to act in their own way may be relatively weak: they may publicly conform to the local group norm, despite keeping strong private reservations about its correctness (as in Asch's studies). In later stages of task completion, however, group members may become increasingly concerned with their private positions and interests. When the division of labour becomes an issue, for instance, the costs of giving in to the group (i.e. living up to normative expectations to contribute as much as possible to promote group success) may be more tangible than the costs of conformity in the process of cognitive tuning. To save themselves costly personal contributions, some of the group members may feel tempted to leave unpleasant work to fellow members. As we will see in the next section, the tuning of interests requires very strong normative pressures to complete the group task successfully.

TUNING OF INTERESTS

Once a common cognitive frame of reference has been developed, group members have to reach agreement about the division of labour to complete the group task. The division of labour may give rise to a conflict between common and private interests. Groups have to ensure that members' common and private interests are properly tuned, because the unrestrained pursuit of private interests will cause the whole group to fail or fall apart. Communication plays a crucial role in this process of tuning of conflicting interests.

Entwining of common and private interests

Since a group member's outcomes do not depend solely upon their own performance but also on the performance of fellow group members, members of a task group are mutually interdependent. Two basic types of interdependence can be distinguished, positive and negative interdependence (Deutsch, 1949).

To the extent that one group member's successful performance directly promotes the interests of fellow group members, group members are *positively interdependent*. As far as their private interests coincide, group members will be motivated to cooperate to serve their common interest. Cooperation requires coordinated action. For example, it is in the common interest of all members of the educational committee that each of them submits proposals to change the curriculum before a certain deadline, so that all individual proposals can be assembled and sent to all the members of the committee before the next meeting. Group members' private interests coincide, since it is in nobody's private interest to be late in submitting proposals. Coordination requires clear communication (e.g. about submission deadlines) to structure the interaction process in such a way that group members optimally combine their contributions. If the group falls short in optimally combining its members' contributions, the group suffers from 'coordination losses' (Steiner, 1972). In the next section, we will elaborate on this type of productivity loss.

By contrast, group members are *negatively interdependent* to the extent that a gain by one group member entails a loss by other group members. Usually, the distribution of benefits and costs among group members increases the salience of this type of interdependence. For example, when the educational committee has to elect a chairperson, a candidate can achieve personal success only at the expense of other group members. Since only one of them can be installed, the election may create a competitive atmosphere between members of the committee. To give another example of conflicting interests, it may be in the students' best interest to increase the number of seminars and tutorials in the curriculum, whereas faculty members of the committee may advocate student self-tuition in order not to increase their own teaching load. Students can achieve success only if the faculty members give in. As long as problems arising from negative interdependence remain unsolved, the resulting competition within the group may pose a serious threat to group productivity.

The above dichotomy is an oversimplification, however, since pure positive and pure negative interdependence are rare. The *mixture of positive and negative interdependence* in almost any task group evokes a motivation to cooperate (group success can be achieved only by cooperating with fellow group members) as well as a motivation to act in a self-interested way (what is to be gained by one group member in the division of benefits and costs can often be obtained only at the expense of fellow group members). Even when the motivation to act in a self-interested way seems to prevail, as in the election of a chairperson or in the final phrasing of the committee's recommendations, opposing parties should communicate to serve their common interest. In an attempt to resolve the conflict of interests between the parties, they may start negotiating and bargaining (see Chapter 14). The present chapter focuses on such so-called mixed motive task situations, in which the motivation to cooperate prevails. But even under predominantly cooperative circumstances, group members' self-interest may lead them (un)consciously to reduce their personal contributions to the group and take advantage of fellow group members' cooperative efforts to achieve group success. Reduced individual contributions in task groups reflect the second type of productivity loss, namely, 'motivation losses' (Steiner, 1972; Kerr, 1983). Before we elaborate on group members' communicative attempts to overcome motivation losses, we will first address the issue of coordination losses.

Coordination losses

To the extent that group members are positively interdependent, they are eager to contribute to their common interest, since there is no incentive for any of them to refrain from contributing. Cooperation requires good coordination. Group interactions need to be structured in such a way that members optimally combine their efforts. Coordination losses occur when the group falls short in optimally combining its members' efforts. The behavioural requirements may not be immediately clear to all group members. Some tasks, for instance, require simultaneity in group members' efforts. A group whose members are properly tuned to focus simultaneously on one and the same part of the task performs better than a group in which individual contributions are less well tuned in time (Tschan, 1995; see also Hackman, Brousseau & Weiss, 1976; Harper & Askling, 1980). Communication is essential to make sure that everyone is aware of what has been achieved so far and to ensure that people will make further contributions that are compatible. Successful committees, compared to those that fail, stimulate task-relevant communication by focusing their members' attention on simultaneity in submitting individual proposals, evaluating these proposals, and reaching agreement upon one particular course of action and its subsequent implementation and evaluation.

The completion of a group task will always benefit from simultaneity in group members' contributions, however. In interactive brainstorming groups, for example, it would be unproductive if all participants were to express their ideas aloud at the same time. While one group member speaks, other group members have to keep silent. Group members have to wait for others to express their own ideas. This type of coordination loss, which is called 'production blocking' (Diehl & Stroebe, 1987), may hinder group members in presenting or even remembering their own ideas. One way to prevent production blocking in the generation of ideas is the NGT discussed earlier. Another way is computerised brainstorming, in which individuals are exposed to ideas from others on their computer screen as they generate their own ideas. As in the NGT, the absence of face-to-face interaction in computerised brainstorming may prove particularly fruitful in larger task groups (Valachich, Dennis & Connolly, 1994).

Unfortunately, group members rarely show much interest in planning the coordination process. Yet, controlling the process by communicating about how properly to sequence group members' contributions has strong positive effects on group productivity.

Motivation losses

Even if the processes in task groups are so well organised that virtually all losses due to faulty coordination are eliminated, group productivity might still suffer from motivation losses. Motivation losses occur because task groups are seldom character-ised by pure positive interdependence, but almost always involve a mixture of posi-tive and negative interdependence (Baron, Kerr & Miller, 1992). The conflict between common and private interests lays the ground for motivation losses, reflecting the (un)conscious tendency to decrease one's personal share in the collective burden by letting one's fellow group members do the work.

Motivation losses are more likely if group members can take advantage of cir-cumstances in which their own contribution to the group product is hardly identifiable (such as in large groups) while they still share in the collective benefits of group success. When motivation losses are more or less unconscious, the decrease of indi-vidual contributions to the group is termed 'social loafing'. When group members intentionally let others do the work, we speak of 'free riding' (Kerr, 1983). A very likely reaction in response to the (assumed) presence of free riders in the group is to reduce one's own efforts, too, rather than to take the risk of being exploited (being the 'sucker').

The scientific study on productivity losses started with studies by Ringelmann (his classic paper (1913) is reprinted in Kravitz & Martin, 1986), who had young men pull a rope, either alone or in groups of varying size. Participants working alone pulled with an average force of 63 kg, participants working in dyads pulled with a force of 118 kg (i.e. an average of 59 kg per person), participants working in triads pulled with a force of 106 kg (i.e. an average of 53 kg per person), and eight-person groups pulled with an average of 31 kg per person. Thus, the average individual performance decreased with increasing group size. To estimate the relative impact of motivation losses in the total productivity loss, Ingham, Levinger, Graves, and Peckham (1974) employed an experimental method that eliminated all coordination losses (i.e. productivity losses due to faulty coordination, such as a lack of simul-taneity of the muscular contractions of the individuals). Ingham et al. blindfolded the rope-pulling participant and contrived that the participant was ahead of any other participants on the rope, closest to the gauge to measure the performance. In actuality, there were no other people pulling on the rope. In this way, Ingham et al. assessed the performance of a naive participant that believed himself to be part of a group. It appeared that, as the apparent group size increased, the individual performance of the naive participant declined. This suggests that group members are less motivated to do their ultimate best when the size of their (imagined) group increases (see also Latané, Williams & Harkins, 1979). Subsequent research has shown that motivation losses also occur in cognitive and perceptual group tasks (Petty, Harkins & Williams, 1980; Jackson & Williams, 1985).

Normative pressures to prevent motivation losses

Communication may help to overcome motivation losses, since it sets the stage for normative social pressure on group members to contribute their fair share (or even: as much as they can). Communicating simply to get better acquainted with one's fellow group members is not sufficient, however (Dawes, McTavish & Shaklee, 1977). So, what might be relevant topics to discuss?

In the first place, communication may facilitate group members' understanding of the extent to which they are positively interdependent. When their attention becomes focused on their common interests, group members may come to understand that mutual cooperation is preferable to mutual non-cooperation. Thus, communication may help them to agree on mutual cooperation as a shared goal. However, it is rather risky to cooperate unless you can count on your fellow group members to cooperate. If others cannot be trusted, those who cooperate run the risk of being 'the sucker'. Therefore, the second important function of communication is to reduce group members' uncertainty about fellow group members' actual contributions. Shared cooperative goals and mutual trust are the two key concepts in Pruitt and Kimmel's (1977) goal-expectation theory about cooperation in mixed-motive situations. Group members who share a cooperative goal, *and* expect fellow group members to cooperate, may eventually establish a cooperative group norm (see also Kramer, 1999).

Two group norms are of particular importance, namely, the commitment norm and the norm of equity or reciprocity. The *commitment* norm prescribes that group members should actually carry out those actions which they have publicly promised to perform. Communication may present an opportunity for group members to establish mutual commitment to cooperate as a binding social contract (Orbell, Dawes & Van der Kragt, 1988).

The *equity norm* prescribes that the rewards of group performance should be in proportion to group members' individual contributions. When all group members have an equal share in the collective outcomes of group success, as often is the case in task groups that provide a common good, the equity norm prescribes that all of them should exert equal amounts of effort. The equity norm may both encourage and discourage cooperation in task groups, however. When a group member learns that fellow group members exert more effort, personal failure to work as hard as these others would violate the equity norm. Equity considerations may then induce this person to cooperate, since free riding would violate the equity norm. However, if the same group member learns that fellow group members are free riding upon their cooperative effort, the most likely response would simply be to cease cooperating himself. Few group members will endure the inequitable 'sucker' role in their task group. A cooperation-inducing strategy, based upon the equity norm, may be to start cooperating and keep cooperating just as long as fellow group members cooperate; whenever fellow group members act uncooperatively, then refrain from cooperation. Group members who employ this reciprocal 'tit-for-tat' strategy (Axelrod, 1984) communicate that they are willing to cooperate as long as fellow group members do the same.

Research findings that normative pressures to conform to group norms are stronger in cohesive groups (Wheeler, 1991) suggest that the above discussed cooperative norms are stronger when the salience of a common group membership is high. Communication in groups appears to enhance feelings of being a part of the group and creates a sense of group identity or group cohesion (Orbell et al., 1988). Communication among group members in mixed motive situations indeed tends to focus on the normative requirement of cooperation and on how angry the group will be at group members who do not take their fair share of the collective burden (Bonachich, 1976). Furthermore, the more group members feel part of their group, the less strongly they distinguish between their common and private interests (Brewer & Kramer, 1986; Tyler & Blader, 2000). Members who strongly identify with their group are also more likely to perceive fellow group members in generally favourable terms as trustworthy and cooperative (Brewer, 1981). Such favourable attributions may lay the ground for trust in the cooperative intentions of fellow group members, even in the absence of information about the extent to which they actually cooperate.

Additional measures to strengthen normative pressures

Even under these normative pressures to cooperate, a task group remains vulnerable to motivation losses of (some of) its members. If only one of the group members refrains from cooperating, this 'bad apple' may elicit non-cooperative responses from fellow group members, who may feel justified to do so on the basis of the equity/reciprocity norm. Reciprocal cooperation is not easily established in task groups with more than two members. Many studies suggest that cooperation declines as groups become larger (e.g. Fox & Guyer, 1977). Other factors inhibiting the evolution of cooperation in large task groups may be the perceived efficacy of one's own contribution, the extent to which one's own contribution is identifiable and can be evaluated, and the extent to which one feels responsible for the achievement of the common interest.

A second reason for task groups' vulnerability to motivation losses is that the beneficial effects of enhanced group identification on individuals' willingness to conform to cooperative group norms may be weakened by subordinate group boundaries (Kramer & Brewer, 1984; Wit & Kerr, 2002). For example, members of the educational committee may refrain from taking their fair share of the work to be done because they may be more concerned with their particular subgroup (students or staff) than with work that has to be done in the interest of the committee as a whole.

Therefore, communicative attempts to promote cooperation often have to be combined with additional measures. Since cooperative behaviour is the result of normative pressures to serve the common interest, cooperation can be further promoted by enhancing the salience of cooperative norms and/or increasing the severity of social sanctions for non-cooperation. Several lines of research confirm this assumption. First, enforcement of any social norm requires the ability to monitor inputs and outcomes so that norm violations can be detected. Social loafing (more or less unconsciously hiding in the crowd) and free riding (its deliberate pendant, when one expects that fellow group members will do the necessary work) are less likely to occur when identification and evaluation of one's own contribution are more likely. Group members appear to be very sensitive to the risk of being detected as an underperforming group member (Harkins & Jackson, 1985). As a result, higher levels of cooperation are achieved when group members have to make their contributions publicly than when their contributions remain unidentifiable (cf. Asch's findings, suggesting that participants are more likely to comply with the local group norms when they have to state their opinions publicly than when they are allowed to express their opinions in the absence of any social control by their fellow group members). Record keeping, for instance, allows group members to check whether each of them does their fair share of the work. It promotes social control that encourages group members to conform to cooperative norms.

Second, a group may increase social control over its members by the use of explicit promises to reward cooperators or threats to punish non-cooperators. Promises seem to yield more beneficial effects than threats, as the latter communicate that fellow group members cannot be trusted to be internally motivated to cooperate (Yamagishi, 1992; Mulder, 2004). However, even promises may arouse reactance and prove counter-effective if group members perceive the rewards as an attempt to bribe them (Wit & Wilke, 1990).

Third, when group members learn that soft interventions do not suffice to ensure satisfactory levels of cooperation and fairness in individuals' share in the collective burden, they are quite willing to hand their decisional freedom over to one of the (cooperative) group members to make decisions on behalf of all of them (Rutte & Wilke, 1984; Wit & Wilke, 1988; Van Vugt & De Cremer, 2002).

OVERVIEW

By communicating, members of a task group exert strong normative pressure on one another to consider the cognitions and interests that they have in common. However, in the process of cognitive tuning, normative pressure is a double-edged sword. On the one hand, normative pressures lead group members to converge on a common understanding of the task, necessary to achieve group success. On the other hand, normative pressures make group members so concerned with receiving social approval from their peers that innovative perspectives that might contradict the emerging group consensus never get expressed. Since premature concurrence-seeking constitutes a serious threat to group success, some formalised communication techniques (such as NGT or installing a devil's advocate) may be employed so that important alternative perspectives are less likely to be overlooked.

When group members are tuning their interests, normative pressures to consider common interests cannot be strong enough. Normative expectations that all group members will contribute their fair share may promote cooperation, but may at the same time increase the temptation for some of them to free ride upon other's cooperative efforts. Therefore, task groups often take additional measures to sanction non-cooperation.

In sum, preventing or overcoming productivity losses is a continuous concern for task groups. Even if group members realise that time and energy must be devoted to find effective solutions to these threats to their common interest, many of them may prefer not to become involved in the activities necessary to implement these solutions and leave this task to (one or some of the) cooperative fellow group members.

REFERENCES

Asch, S. E. (1952). *Social psychology*. Englewood Cliffs, NJ: Prentice-Hall.

Asch, S. E. (1955). Opinions and social pressures. *Scientific American*, **193**, 31–35.

Axelrod, R. (1984). *The evolution of cooperation*. New York: Basic Books.

Baron, R. S., Kerr, N. L. & Miller, N. (1992). *Group process, group decision, group action*. Buckingham: Open University Press.

Bonachich, P. (1976). Secrecy and solidarity. *Sociometry*, *39*, 200–208.

Brewer, M. B. (1981). Ethnocentrism and its role in interpersonal trust. In M. Brewer & B. Collins (Eds), *Scientific inquiry and the social sciences*. San Francisco, CA: Jossey-Bass.

Brewer, M. B. & Kramer, R. M. (1986). Choice behavior in social dilemmas: effects of social identity, group size, and decision framing. *Journal of Personality and Social Psychology*, *50*, 543–549.

Dawes, R. M., McTavish, J. & Shaklee, H. (1977). Behavior, communication, and assumptions about other people's behavior in a commons dilemma situation. *Journal of Personality and Social Psychology*, *35*, 1–11.

Delbecq, A. L., Van de Ven, A. H. & Gustafson, D. H. (1975). *Group techniques for program planning*. Glenview, IL: Scott, Foresman.

Deutsch, M. (1949). A theory of cooperation and competition. *Human Relations*, *2*, 129–152.

Deutsch, M. & Gerard, H. B. (1955). A study on normative and informational social influence upon individual judgement. *Journal of Abnormal and Social Psychology*, *51*, 629–636.

De Vries, N. K., De Dreu, C. K. W., Gordijn, E. & Schuurman, M. (1996). Majority and minority influence: a dual role interpretation. In W. Stroebe & M. Hewstone (Eds), *European review of social psychology* (vol. 7, pp. 145–172). Chichester: Wiley.

Diehl, M. & Stroebe, W. (1987). Productivity losses in brainstorming groups: towards the solution of a riddle. *Journal of Personality and Social Psychology*, *53*, 497–509.

Falcione, R. L. & Wilson, C. E. (1988). Socialization processes in organizations. In G. Goldhaber & G. Barnett (Eds), *Handbook of organizational communication* (pp. 151–169). Norwood, NJ: Ablex.

Fox, J. & Guyer, M. (1977). Group size and others' strategy in an N-person game. *Journal of Conflict Resolution*, *21*, 323–338.

Hackman, R. J., Brousseau, K. R. & Weiss, J. A. (1976). The interaction of task design and group performance strategies in determining group effectiveness. *Organizational Behavior and Human Performance*, *16*, 350–365.

Harkins, S. & Jackson, J. (1985). The role of evaluation in eliminating social loafing. *Personality and Social Psychology Bulletin*, *11*, 457–465.

Harper, N. L. & Askling, L. R. (1980). Group communication and quality of task solution in a media production organization. *Communication Monographs*, *47*, 77–100.

Herbert, T. T. & Estes, R. W. (1977). Improving executive decisions by formalizing dissent: the corporate devil's advocate. *Academy of Management Review*, *2*, 662–667.

Ingham, A. G., Levinger, G., Graves, J. & Peckham, V. (1974). The Ringelmann effect: studies on group size and group performance. *Journal of Experimental Social Psychology*, *10*, 371–384.

Jackson, J. M. & Williams, K. D. (1985). Social loafing on difficult tasks. *Journal of Personality and Social Psychology*, *49*, 937–942.

Janis, I. L. (1982). *Victims of group think*, 2nd edn. Boston, MA: Houghton Mifflin.

Kerr, N. L. (1983). Motivation losses in task-performing groups: a social dilemma analysis. *Journal of Personality and Social Psychology*, *45*, 819–828.

Kramer, R. M. (1999). Trust and distrust in organizations: emerging perspectives, enduring questions. *Annual Review of Psychology*, *50*, 569–598.

Kramer, R. M. & Brewer, M. B. (1984). Effects of group identity on resource use in a simulated commons dilemma. *Journal of Personality and Social Psychology*, *46*, 1044–1057.

Kravitz, D. A. & Martin, B. (1986). Ringelmann rediscovered: the original article. *Journal of Personality and Social Psychology*, *50*, 936–941.

Latané, B., Williams, K. & Harkins, S. (1979). Many hands make light the work: the causes and consequences of social loafing. *Journal of Personality and Social Psychology*, *37*, 822–832.

Maass, A. & Clark, R. D. (1984). Hidden impact of minorities: fifteen years of minority influence research. *Psychological Bulletin*, *95*, 428–450.

MacNeil, M. K. & Sherif, M. (1976). Norm change over participant generations as a function of arbitrariness of prescribed norm. *Journal of Personality and Social Psychology*, *34*, 762–773.

McGrath, J. E. (1984). *Groups: interaction and performance*. Englewood Cliffs, NJ: Prentice-Hall.

Moscovici, S. E. (1985). Social influence and conformity. In G. Lindzey & E. Aronson (Eds), *The handbook of social psychology, 3rd edn, vol. 2*. New York: Random House.

Moscovici, S. E. & Doise, W. (1994). *Conflict and consensus; a general theory of collective decisions*. London: Sage.

Moscovici, S. E. Lage, E. & Naffrechoux, M. (1969). Influence of a consistent minority on the responses of a majority in a color perception task. *Sociometry*, *32*, 365–380.

Mulder, L. B. (2004). Throwing light on the dark side of sanctions; sanctioning systems in social dilemmas re-examined. Doctoral dissertation. Leiden: Kurt Lewin Institute Dissertation Series.

Nemeth, C. J. (1992). Minority dissent as a stimulant to group performance. In S. Worchel, W. Wood & J. Simpson (Eds), *Group processes and productivity*. Newbury Park, CA: Sage.

Nemeth, C. J. & Kwan, J. L. (1987). Minority influence, divergent thinking and detection of correct solutions. *Journal of Applied Social Psychology*, *17*, 786–797.

Orbell, J., Dawes, R. M. & Van der Kragt, A. (1988). Explaining discussion induced cooperation. *Journal of Personality and Social Psychology*, *54*, 811–819.

Osborn, A. F. (1957). *Applied imagination*. New York: Scribner's.

Paulus, P. B. & Dzindolet, M. T. (1993). Social influence processes in group brainstorming. *Journal of Personality and Social Psychology*, *64*, 575–586.

Paulus, P. B., Larey, T. S. & Ortega, A. H. (1995). Performance and perceptions of brainstormers in an organizational setting. *Basic and Applied Social Psychology*, *17*, 249–265.

Pearce, J. L., Stevenson, W. B. & Porter, L. W. (1986). Coalitions in the organizational context. In R. Lewicki, B. Sheppard & M. Bazerman (Eds), *Research on negotiation in organizations* (vol. 1, pp. 97–115). Greenwich, CT: JAI Press.

Petty, R., Harkins, S. & Williams, K. (1980). The effects of diffusion of cognitive effort on attitudes: an information processing view. *Journal of Personality and Social Psychology*, *38*, 81–92.

Pruitt, D. G. & Kimmel, M. J. (1977). Twenty years of experimental gaming: critique, synthesis, and suggestions for the future. *Annual Review of Psychology*, *28*, 363–392.

Rutte, C. G. & Wilke, H. A. M. (1984). Social dilemmas and leadership. *European Journal of Social Psychology*, *14*, 105–121.

Schachter, S. (1951). Deviation, rejection and communication. *Journal of Abnormal and Social Psychology*, *46*, 190–207.

Sherif, M. (1936). *The psychology of social norms*. New York: Harper and Row.

Stasser, G. & Titus, W. (1985). Pooling of unshared information in group decision making: biased information sampling during group discussion. *Journal of Personality and Social Psychology*, *48*, 1467–1478.

Steiner, I. D. (1972). *Group process and productivity*. New York: Academic Press.

Teboul, J. B. (1997). Scripting the organization: new hire learning during organizational encounter. *Communication Research Reports*, *14*, 33–47.

Tschan, F. (1995). Communication enhances small group performance if it conforms to task requirements: the concept of ideal communication cycles. *Basic and Applied Social Psychology*, *17*, 371–393.

Tyler, T. & Blader, S. L. (2000). *Cooperation in groups: procedural justice, social identity, and behavioral engagement*. Philadelphia: Psychology Press.

Valachich, J. S., Dennis, A. R. & Connolly, T. (1994). Idea generation in computer-based groups: a new ending to an old story. *Organizational Behavior and Human Decision Processes*, *57*, 448–476.

Van de Ven, A. H. & Delbecq, A. L. (1974). The effectiveness of nominal, Delphi and interacting group decision-making processes. *Academy of Management Journal*, *17*, 605–621.

Van Vugt, M. & De Cremer, D. (2002). Leader endorsement in social dilemmas: comparing the instrumental and relational perspectives. *European Review of Social Psychology*, *13*, 155–184.

Wheeler, D. D. & Janis, I. L. (1980). *A practical guide for making decisions*. New York: Free Press.

Wheeler, L. (1991). A brief history of social comparison theory. In J. Suls & T. Wills (Eds), *Social comparison: contemporary theory and research*. Hillsdale, NJ: Lawrence Erlbaum.

Wilke, H. A. M. & Meertens, R. (1994). *Group performance*. London: Routledge.

Wit, A. P. & Kerr, N. L. (2002). 'Me vs. just us vs. us all' categorization and cooperation in nested social dilemmas. *Journal of Personality and Social Psychology*, *83*, 616–637.

Wit, A. P. & Wilke, H. A. M. (1988). Subordinates' endorsement of an allocating leader in a commons dilemma. *Journal of Economic Psychology*, *9*, 151–168.

Wit, A. P. & Wilke, H. A. M. (1990). The presentation of rewards and punishments in a simulated social dilemma. *Social Behaviour*, *5*, 231–245.

Yamagishi, T. (1992). Group size and the provision of a sanctioning system in a social dilemma. In W. Liebrand, D. Messick & H. Wilke (Eds), *Social dilemmas: theoretical issues and research findings* (pp. 267–287). Oxford: Pergamon Press.

Zimbardo, P. G. & Leippe, M. R. (1991). *The psychology of attitude change and social influence*. New York: McGraw-Hill.

Chapter 14

Negotiation and bargaining

Ian E. Morley

T HE PURPOSE OF THIS chapter is to review theories which examine psychological aspects of negotiation, in an attempt to say what, of practical value, has been learned about the skills of negotiation, and how it has been learned. There are many theoretical models that may be relevant. How they are classified is partly a matter of preference, and certainly linked to the pedagogical purposes one has in mind. However, I still find it convenient to classify models into five main types: analytic models[1], behavioural models, information-processing models, personal models, and discursive models (as in Morley, 1996). I shall consider each kind of model in turn.

My own preference is for some sort of language-action perspective in which negotiators have to handle cognitive and political problems (Morley, Webb & Stephenson, 1988; Morley, 1992, 1996). The cognitive problems arise because negotiators have to work out (individually and collectively) what is going on and why. This looks like a purely intellectual task, but the negotiators have to agree how to describe their worlds, and this introduces both informational and normative sources of influence. This is the 'language' part of the perspective. The political problems arise because negotiators have to commit themselves to lines of action that make sense of the past and provide hope for the future. This is the 'action' part of the perspective. I shall use this perspective both to criticise previous research and to provide a framework for integrating much of the literature.

ANALYTIC MODELS

Analytic models of negotiation are formal models which use simple and elegant notations to describe the process of negotiation in abstract and, therefore, very general terms. They are used to analyse the ways of thinking that may occur in negotiation and bargaining, and to explain why they may have certain effects. It is a matter of controversy to what extent such models are useful in guiding our understanding of particular cases.

There are two main kinds of abstraction. They are connected by considerations of what it means to act rationally in certain contexts. In the first case, the context is defined by an abstract statement of 'the bargaining problem' developed in contexts of interest in microeconomics. In the second case, the context is defined by models of strategic interaction in the mathematical theory of games.

The bargaining problem

The phrase '*the* bargaining problem' should give some indication of the generality of the analysis that is involved. It is intended to apply to any example of bargaining or negotiation. The abstraction works – if it works – by assuming that the way to understand the problem is to start by considering a two-person or two-party negotiation and then to generalise (or to think about generalising) such results to any multiperson or multiparty negotiations.

Such models (often called utility models) begin by describing a contractor, P, and a client, O. It is assumed that they have wants which conflict to a greater or lesser extent, and that bargaining is a process of deciding on an allocation of goods. The process is one in which they exchange bids, where each bid is a proposal to allocate some goods to P and others to O. It is assumed that P and O will each estimate the various costs and benefits each will expect if the other agreed with the proposal on the table. It is also assumed that each will estimate the costs and benefits they would each face in the event of a failure to agree. An agreement is reached when the process of bid and counter-bid converges on to a proposal both P and O find acceptable and both think is the best they could have obtained in the circumstances.

Such models have two advantages. They capture the idea that each proposal has a net worth (expected utility or expected value) for each of the bargainers, so that the process of bargaining may be described as an allocation of utility (or value) between P and O. They also suggest that competition and cooperation are not at opposite ends of a continuum.

Formally, the bargaining problem is represented on a set of orthogonal axes: the vertical axis representing the utility to P (from high to low) and the horizontal axis representing the utility to O (from high to low). The high-high quadrant contains those agreements that are positively valued by both P and O; the low-low quadrant contains those that both P and O wish to avoid; and the other two quadrants represent options P will want but O will not and that O will want but P will not. The location of agreements within and between quadrants represents the allocation of utility.

If we superimpose a new set of orthogonal axes such that the new axes divide the old quadrants into two equal segments, we will have a line that, firstly, bisects the high-high quadrant and the low-low quadrant and a line that, secondly, bisects the high-low quadrant and the low-high quadrant. Both P and O wish to gain outcomes in the high-high quadrant and avoid outcomes in the low-low quadrant so that the first line represents an axis of common interest. By contrast, the second line represents an axis of competition. The main lesson is that cooperation and competition are not at opposite ends of a continuum. Rather, there are two perpendicular axes: from low cooperation to high cooperation and from low competition to high competition. Consequently, utility models capture the very important idea that conflicting interests always occur in the context of common interests.

Some writers focus on the high-high quadrant and translate talk about utilities into talk about aspiration zones, contract zones, and settlement ranges. For example, Walton and McKersie (1965) argue that P and O each form an aspiration zone with a target and a resistance point. The target is determined by their highest estimate of what is needed, by their most optimistic estimates of what is possible, and by their most favourable estimates of their bargaining skill. The resistance point (sometimes called the minimum necessary share) is determined by their lowest estimate of what is needed, by their most pessimistic assumptions about what is possible, and by their least favourable estimates of their bargaining skill. The four points may be plotted on a single line, known as the conflict line. The distance between A's resistance point and B's resistance point is known as the settlement range. When these points are compatible, there is a contract zone or positive settlement range (because both prefer some agreement to their best alternative to a negotiated agreement). When these points are incompatible, there is a negative settlement range, and agreement will be impossible until either A or B or both change their minimum terms. Analyses of this kind have been used to gain insight into historical cases. To take one example, it has been shown that the Berlin Wall was built because it was the only option preferred to no agreement by both Soviet and Western negotiators (Snyder & Diesing, 1977).

Although there is a common statement of the bargaining problem, there are many different solutions.

- Some describe constraints that proposals must satisfy if they are to be turned into outcomes that are fair, acceptable, optimum, etc. Such constraints are known as arbitration schemes (see Nash, 1950; Braithwaite, 1955).
- Some locate the main impetus for concession making in estimates of the risks of disagreement, but give different treatments of the nature of those risks (Coddington, 1968; Lockhart, 1979; Bacharach & Lawler, 1981).
- Some view the process of bargaining as a learning process in which various expectations are revised (Coddington, 1968).

Each kind of solution points to different kinds of skill.

- The focus on arbitration schemes has prepared the way for a consideration of principled bargaining (e.g. Fisher & Ury, 1981).
- The focus on perception of risk has prepared the way for a more general consideration of negotiators' reputations for resolve (Snyder & Diesing, 1977).
- The focus on learning has prepared the way for more detailed explorations

of how negotiators define issues, interpret feedback, and revise expectations (Snyder & Diesing, 1977; Lockhart, 1979).

The theory of games

The mathematical theory of games was an ambitious theory that attempted to define rational action in contexts where the outcomes for each person depended partly on their own actions and partly on the actions of others (Morgenstern, 1949). Negotiation was seen as a game of strategy in which P and O make separate choices: either to make concessions or to maintain their current level of demand, or to choose between cooperative or competitive approaches.

The outcome of the game depends on the choices made by P and O so that what P gets depends on O's choices, and vice versa. The logic of the game may be represented in the form of a two-person, two-choice matrix with four cells: both P and O stand firm; both P and O make concessions; P stands firm but O does not; O stands firm but P does not. When some estimate of utility or value is entered into each cell for each player, it may be possible to identify some of the reasons why negotiators act as they do (Snyder & Diesing, 1977; Pruitt & Carnevale, 1993; Morley, 1996). Two of the games, known as the prisoners' dilemma game and chicken, have been related to dilemmas in the process of negotiation (see Morley, 1996).

Evaluation

It is clear that analytic models treat only some aspects of negotiation. The models are intended to be simple but powerful. Thus, bargaining is described in terms of a small number of processes, capable of mathematical treatment. Other activities are either ignored, or somehow interpreted in terms of the variables included in the model. Such drastic simplification is not without value. It helps us to realise that negotiation begins when someone sees change, or the possibility of change, in the status quo; and it helps us to realise that different people might look at the status quo in very different ways.

Once negotiation begins, it is important to realise that the process is one which engages mixed motives. The description of lines of conflict and lines of common interest given above has encouraged some writers to draw a distinction between distributive bargaining and integrative bargaining (Walton & McKersie, 1965; Raiffa, 1982). In the two-person case, distributive bargaining is competitive bargaining in which P and O struggle to get as much as they can of something that they each desire. Integrative bargaining is collaborative bargaining in which P and O actively search for new agreements from which each will gain.

Because distributive bargaining is competitive and integrative bargaining is collaborative, negotiators face certain strategic dilemmas. Typically, distributive bargaining is bargaining in which negotiators struggle to exploit asymmetries in power. However, to the extent that they misrepresent their own positions, they make it difficult to explore ways in which the requirements of the parties might be reconciled. Such dilemmas may be particularly acute when negotiations are complex (Raiffa,

1982). Raiffa's own solution is to advise negotiators to keep secret their minimum necessary terms, but otherwise to behave openly and honestly.

Nevertheless, models of this kind have very important weaknesses. The way they simplify the bargaining problem is too drastic. Consequently, they provide inadequate models of people, parties, processes, and contexts.

- They provide inadequate models of people because they take the character of the conflict for granted (Lockhart, 1979; Morley, Webb & Stephenson, 1988).
- They provide inadequate models of parties because they treat parties just like people (so that P and O stands just as well for person and other, or party and opponent). In reality, party and opponent are usually loose coalitions in which negotiation within sides is as important as negotiation between sides (Snyder & Diesing, 1977; Morley, 1992).
- They provide inadequate models of processes because they neglect the ways in which parties identify issues, develop solutions, choose between alternatives, and implement policies (Morley, Webb & Stephenson, 1988; Hosking & Morley, 1991).
- They provide inadequate models of contexts because they abstract away from the historical relationship between the sides. They neglect the fact that agreements have to be justified as rules that make sense – because they link what is happening now to what has happened in the past, and to what needs to happen in the future (Morley, 1992).

Despite such criticisms, some analytic models deserve to be taken very seriously, notably those of Walton and McKersie (1965) – who deal with industrial negotiations – and Snyder and Diesing (1977) – who deal with international negotiations. Both have recognised the importance of dilemmas in negotiation; both have recognised the intellectual demands placed on negotiators, and both have realised the importance of bargaining within and between groups. For the moment, I shall ignore Snyder and Diesing and concentrate on Walton and McKersie.

Walton and McKersie's (1965) model of social negotiations

Ostensibly, Walton and McKersie (1965) describe strategy and tactics in industrial negotiations. However, they treat industrial negotiation as a special case of 'social negotiation', meaning those 'systems of activity' involving 'complex social units' in attempts to define or redefine 'their terms of their interdependence'. They identify four *separate* systems: namely, those concerned with distributive bargaining, integrative bargaining, attitudinal structuring, and intraorganisational bargaining. The first three systems are concerned with relationships between groups and the fourth is concerned with relationships within groups. Talk about distributive bargaining and integrative bargaining is used to identify strategies and tactics designed to move opponents along the line of conflict or the line of cooperation, respectively. Attitudinal structuring is activity designed to change the basic 'bonds' between the negotiators. Intraorganisational bargaining is internal negotiation designed to achieve consensus about what to do in the external negotiations between groups.

Walton and McKersie's theory is a very welcome attempt to provide better analytic models of people, parties, processes, and contexts, but it has not been without critics, such as Morley (1984, 1992), Tracy and Peterson (1986), and, most fundamentally, Anthony (1977). Anthony has argued that almost all bargaining involving representatives of groups is distributive bargaining, but agrees that negotiators may take a more competitive or a more cooperative approach. From his perspective, 'attitudinal structuring' is not a separate system of activities, but a set of tactics available to those who wish to take a collaborative approach. Furthermore, intraorganisational bargaining is not a new kind of bargaining. It is to be explained in just the same ways as external negotiations that take place between organisations. I shall follow Anthony in his attempt to understand internal and external negotiation in the same general kinds of way (also see Morley, 1992).

BEHAVIOURAL MODELS OF NEGOTIATION

Behavioural models attempt to describe what negotiators do. In this sense, Walton and McKersie's theory is a behavioural model because it is an attempt to classify the activities observed in collective bargaining with distinctions from utility theory and from the theory of games. In this section, I include four kinds of research. On the one hand, there are attempts to predict the outcomes of experimental negotiations by examining the process of negotiation and its preconditions, background factors, and concurrent conditions (Rubin & Brown, 1975; Druckman, 1977; Morley & Stephenson, 1977; Pruitt, 1981; Pruitt & Carnevale, 1993; Kramer & Messick, 1995). On the other hand, there are attempts to describe 'phase sequences', 'critical transformations', or 'turning points' in negotiation by experimental methods, category schemes, or comparative analyses of individual cases (Morley & Stephenson 1977; Rackham & Carlisle, 1978a; Putnam & Jones, 1982; Druckman, 2004).

The outcomes of experimental negotiations

The various experimental tasks which have been used include: matrix games (such as prisoner's dilemma and chicken); distribution games, in which participants negotiate the division of a quantified scarce resource; games of economic exchange, in which participants take the roles of buyers and sellers; role-playing debates, in which participants learn the details of a particular dispute, and then negotiate as if they were representing a party in that dispute; and substitute debates, in which an encounter which occurs in laboratory conditions is substituted for one which might have occurred elsewhere (Morley & Stephenson, 1977). It is still the case that the vast majority of experimental research has used matrix games or tasks in which negotiation is limited to little more than the exchange of bids, although there are some signs that research is becoming more likely to recognise the complexities of real life (Kramer & Messick, 1995). For further discussion of matrix games, the interested reader is referred to the work of Snyder and Diesing (1977), Colman (1982), and Morley (1996).

The process of bid and counter-bid

The most popular experimental task simulates a situation of bilateral monopoly in which there is integrative potential because there is more than one issue. Sometimes a buyer (P) and seller (O) have to agree on the price–quantity combination at which a particular product will be traded. Sometimes there are several products, for which P and O agree a price for each, regardless of quantity. Sometimes there is a single product, but P and O agree prices for linked elements such as delivery time, discounts, and finance. Typically, the buyer and seller have complete information about their own profits but none about those of their opponent.

Two features of the profit tables are important. First, P and O are able to offer a variety of possible contracts at a given level of profit. Two contracts that are of equal (or near equal) value to P may differ considerably in their value to O, and vice versa. Second, the profit tables contain some agreements which are Pareto optimal – meaning that they maximise the joint gain or profit (MJP) available to the participants.

The most important finding from this research is that P and O often fail to find agreements which are Pareto optimal (Pruitt, 1981; Pruitt & Carnevale, 1993). This means that there is some other agreement which would give either P or O or both significant gains, at little or no cost to the other. According to Pruitt and his associates, the main predictor of MJP outcomes is that P and O each adopt a problem-solving strategy. One obvious possibility is that this will occur when P and O each exhibit high concern for their own outcomes and high concern for the other's outcomes (but see Morley, 1996). The model which specifies the factors which lead to this combination of motives is known as the dual-concern model (Carnevale & Keenan, 1992; Pruitt & Carnevale, 1993). It has been used to integrate findings which deal with negotiators' assigned goals, with their relationship to their constituents, with the possibility of future interaction, and with the effects of mood. One suggestion that seems to have a more general significance is that MJP outcomes are more likely when negotiators are motivated to engage in systematic trial and error (Pruitt, 1981; Carnevale & Isen, 1986). However, the possible reasons for this are not clear.

If prospect theory is correct (see Tversky & Kahneman, 1981), negotiators who are most concerned to maximise gains rather than minimise losses are more likely to reach MJP outcomes (Bazerman, Magliozzi & Neale, 1985). This suggests that it is often important to adopt a problem-solving or collaborative approach. Furthermore, such a conclusion is compatible with a great deal of evidence that 'powerful and persistent images of a mythical fixed pie' lead to an 'incompatibility bias' and mean that negotiators in experimental negotiations fail to extract maximum value from negotiations (Thompson, 1998). At the same time, there is evidence that negotiators will fail to reach MJP agreements if they are too anxious to reach agreements (Fry, Firestone & Williams, 1983). In these respects, the results of experiments are consistent with the analyses of real-life negotiations, meaning that it is important both to disagree and not to let the disagreement go too far (Douglas, 1962; Morley & Stephenson, 1977; Snyder & Diesing, 1977; Rackham & Carlisle, 1978a, 1978b; Morley, 1981, 1986).

More recently, there has been an emphasis on group process and on social norms – both long overdue. The emphasis on group process has been conducted mainly within the context of social decision scheme theory (for a general review, see Baron & Kerr, 2003). One of the main findings has been that majority rules and sequential agendas lead to compromise rather than integrative agreements (Thompson, Mannix & Bazerman, 1988; Mannix, Thompson & Bazerman, 1989; Bazerman, Mannix, Sondak & Thompson, 1990). Other research is summarised in Morley and Stephenson (1977), Pruitt (1981), and Bazerman et al. (2000). Consideration of the effects of social norms has led to a critique of Fisher and Ury's (1981) account of principled negotiation. Fisher and Ury urge negotiators to insist from the beginning that any agreements be based on norms of fairness. They also urge them to seek objective evidence to show that their claims are consistent with those norms. While some see principled negotiation as part of a problem-solving strategy that offers an opportunity to make mutual gains, others see it as limited to special cases. The reader will find a useful summary of the arguments in Johnson (1993) and Pruitt and Carnevale (1993).

Recent analyses have confirmed the view that most experimental studies of integrative bargaining do little more than scratch the potential for integration between the sides. In the end, I think that they fail to give participants sufficient detail of the historical contexts in which they are supposed to be operating. Because of this, they do little to illuminate why negotiators have to 'look beyond interpersonal process to the underlying substance of the problem, seeking to figure where potential value exists and how to embody it in sustainable agreements' (Lax & Sebenius, 2002, p. 6).

The analysis of real-life negotiations

With hindsight, it is possible to integrate much of this research by describing its purpose as the identification of those transitions that are necessary and sufficient if negotiation is to succeed. Two methods have been used. The first involved the use of category schemes to describe units of discourse[2] identified according to 'objective' rules[3]. Such coding schemes were used to identify transitions within negotiations. The second method identified larger units, using frameworks for case analysis, as in Druckman (2004).

The earliest research used Bales' (1950) interaction process analysis (Landsberger, 1955) and saw the key transitions as those that shifted between task problems and social-emotional problems. Next, research identified the key transitions as those that involved a shift between interparty and interpersonal aspects of the negotiation task (Douglas, 1962; Morley & Stephenson, 1977; Morley, 1981). When the interparty role was salient, the negotiators were forced to come to terms with the imperative of representing their parties. When the interpersonal role was salient, the negotiators were forced to come to terms with imperatives of maintaining personal relationships with their opponents. Later research (using a coding scheme derived from the work of Toulmin, Rieke, and Janik, 1979) was concerned with the ways in which transitions were linked to arguments in negotiation. To quote Putnam and Geist (1985): 'What emerges from presenting proposals and counterproposals are significant issues that must be discussed to uncover or create interpretations that lead to a settlement' (p. 230). Recently, Putnam (2004) has suggested four 'mechanisms' or 'shifts in levels in abstraction' that may be crucial turning points in such discussions. The first is a shift from the specific to the general; the second is a shift from part to whole; the third is a shift from the individual level to the system level; and the fourth is a shift from the literal level to the symbolic level. My own preference would be to relate what

Putnam says to descriptions of dilemmas in any decision-making process, such as those identified by Friend and Hickling (1987).

The second kind of analysis has involved the systematic comparison of individual cases to identify 'precipitants' of turning points (whether procedural, substantive, or external), 'departures' (what happens next), and longer-term 'consequences' (whether the parties move closer together or further apart) (Druckman, 2001, 2004). Druckman (2004) has reviewed some of the 'social and psychological dimensions of departure' by reviewing 'changes in individuals, interactions, and collectivities'. His paper provides some new ways of looking at old literature and makes some interesting suggestions about the forces for change (primarily external when security issues are at stake but primarily internal in other cases).

Other research is not so much concerned with transitions in the process of negotiation as with comparisons between negotiators with or without a track record of success (Rackham & Carlisle, 1978a, 1978b). The coding schemes involved are essentially a development of Bales' interaction process analysis, adapted so that the categories form more convenient contrasts, and may be applied to speech units larger than a simple sentence. The net effect is that the categories are easier to use reliably in real time. This research is interesting and important but is more behaviourist than that of Bales. Consequently, I have chosen to give it an interpretation that links it to a broader psychological context (within cognitive psychology) and to a particular model of social skill (see below).

Evaluation

Behavioural models have been applied to both experimental and real-life negotiations. Much of the experimental literature is individualistic in the sense that it ignores historical variables at the level of the small group or the larger organisation (or even the culture), and perhaps it has to do so in the search for abstractions that are simple but powerful. On the other hand, social psychologists are paying much more attention to the ways in which experimental studies may be integrated with studies of naturalistic decision making, and this is to be applauded. Attempts to describe the process of real-life negotiations are important because they make it abundantly clear that there is more to negotiation than a process of bid and counter-bid. Negotiation *is* a kind of argument even if the argument does not always conform to the canons of academic debate. Such argument is not only possible but almost inevitable given that all social actions are ambiguous, cannot be completely described, and will be described from a particular point of view (Morley & Ormerod, 1996). To understand the nature of this argument, it is important to link it to wider psychological concerns that arise within cognitive psychology and social psychology.

INFORMATION-PROCESSING MODELS

So far, negotiation has been treated *mostly* as an exercise in bargaining, dominated by strategic or tactical concerns. However, as negotiations become more complex (e.g. because of the number of participants, information overload, or uncertainty), it seems likely that questions of strategy (how can P outwit O, or vice versa?) must be subordinated to questions of structure (how to find a definition of the bargaining problem that compels assent) (Winham, 1977; Winham & Bovis, 1978; Putnam, 1985). The reason is that negotiators may find that their capacities to process information are insufficient to cope with the demands of the task. In consequence, they may find it difficult to understand the issues (the 'language' problem), and because of this they may find it difficult to find practical ways of handling them, so that they are able to justify commitments to particular lines of action (the 'action' problem).

Making sense of change

To make sense of change, negotiators must organise a collective process in which they identify issues, develop solutions, choose between alternatives, and implement policies (Hosking & Morley, 1991). There is evidence that more-skilled and less-skilled negotiators structure these processes in different ways.

Let us suppose that some change in existing circumstances has created a circumstance in which P must confront O. P and O must plan suitable responses. Furthermore, they must plan those responses in contexts which are ambiguous and cannot be completely described. This means that negotiators interpret changes in the status quo in terms of more or less well-organised systems of attitudes, values, and beliefs, and pass on those interpretations to others, in summary form (George, 1969; Holsti, 1970; Jervis, 1970, 1976; Snyder & Diesing, 1977; Marengo, 1979). Such construct systems allow negotiators to identify threats and opportunities and work out what to do about them (Hosking & Morley, 1991).

What is important is that, through the experience of negotiation, skilled negotiators have been able to build up more or less systematically organised knowledge of the negotiation task, and how to work in it. This means that they have schooled and highly specific ways of perceiving, and are able to see relatively quickly what other people may never see at all (see Hosking & Morley, 1991). Thus, the skilled negotiator is a skilled perceiver (see Chapter 2, for further discussion of the role of perception in skilled performance).

There are good reasons to believe that learning about the world requires people to use organised systems of belief to anticipate the future and to explain the past[4]. However, if they are not to see only what they expect to see, they must also be sensitive to new information. There is a dialectical contradiction between these two requirements (Neisser, 1986; Hosking & Morley, 1991), and this means that some negotiators find it extremely difficult to learn from the process of negotiation (Snyder & Diesing, 1977). Early research located the problems in the structure of the belief systems (Holsti, 1970; Jervis, 1970). Later research has implicated a wide range of cognitive, social, and contextual factors (Hosking & Morley, 1991; Kramer, 1995).

Probably, negotiators will always disagree about how to describe events, and how they contributed to the development of social settings (Snyder & Diesing, 1977; Friedman & Meredeen, 1980). They will maintain general images of their opponents which are not likely to change. However, a combination of cognitive, social, and contextual conditions combine to produce two kinds of activity, which Snyder and

Diesing have articulated in terms of a 'rational bargaining module' and an 'irrational bargaining module'.

Two features of the rational bargaining module are important in the present context. First, Snyder and Diesing found that rational bargainers had low confidence in their initial diagnoses of what had happened, and why. They used the process of bargaining to test hypotheses: to root out ideas which were plausible, but false or incomplete. Second, they initiated an active search for information to find out which aspects of others' positions were flexible, and to what extent. (Presumably, they used both verbal and non-verbal cues. See Walton & McKersie, 1965; Miron & Goldstein, 1979.)

Matching capacities to demands

This is a part of cognitive psychology that we just cannot ignore from an applied perspective. Much of the early work in cognitive psychology was intended to establish which features of our cognitive systems limit our ability to process information. One clear implication of this work is that effective performers find ways of working that allow them to match their intellectual capacities to the information-processing demands of the task (Welford, 1980). A second implication is that those who are effective performers in social domains recognise the processing problems faced by other people. Consequently, they use a variety of techniques designed to reduce ambiguity, clarify communications, and slow things down.

Methods of behaviour analysis have been used to identify some of the ways in which effective negotiators tailor their performances to help their opponents deal with the information-processing demands of the negotiation task (e.g. Rackham & Carlisle, 1978a, 1978b). Effective negotiators recognise that social actions are inherently ambiguous. Consequently, unless special care is taken, it is all too easy for people to see only what they want to see. So, effective negotiators take pains to label their actions, making frequent use of verbal forms such as, 'May I ask you a *question*?', 'If I could make a *suggestion* . . .', and so on. They are significantly more likely than average negotiators to *test understandings*, often by *summarising* what has been said.

Much of the work which has contributed to the Harvard Program on Negotiation fits within the framework of matching capacities to demands (see Fisher & Ury, 1983; Fisher & Brown, 1988; Hall, 1993). This is one reason why those within the programme have often emphasised that the cheapest concession which can be made is to show that you are actively listening to what is being said. There are actually two sides to this. First, it is important to be able to see the negotiation as others see it, because, if you want to influence them, it is important to see the appeal *for them* of *their* point of view. Second, it is important to communicate that understanding to members of the other side. Otherwise, when you try to say something, they will not be listening. They will, instead, be using their limited processing capacity to complete a different task. To be specific, they will be considering how to rephrase their argument so that this time you will understand it (Fisher & Ury, 1983).

For similar reasons, a good rule seems to be: 'Present your proposals as solutions to problems. State the problem before you give your answer.' If you begin with your own proposal you may find that the other side will stop paying attention. They will not be listening to what you have to say. Instead, they will devote their mental resources to the task of working out their own responses (Fisher & Ury, 1983).

Evaluation

Information-processing approaches give negotiators the respect they are due as intelligent social actors. They force us to consider aspects of complexity in negotiation which other theories ignore. They show that skilled negotiators are skilled perceivers. Negotiators have well-organised and well-schooled systems of evaluative beliefs which allow them quickly to see what less skilled negotiators may never see at all. They avoid the problem that they may see only what they expect to see by making active attempts to root out ideas which are plausible, but false or incomplete. Studies which have compared the performance of effective and less effective negotiators, using techniques of behaviour analysis, are consistent with Welford's (1980) theory that skill is the use of effective strategies which match the capacities of performers to the demands of their task. The best of the 'how to negotiate' texts include practical advice which follows from the application of information-processing perspectives.

THE CHARACTERISTICS OF EFFECTIVE NEGOTIATORS

It is commonplace to find that those who write about the psychology of negotiation include checklists of negotiation skills. Much of the literature is anecdotal, but some is based on questionnaire studies which ask experienced negotiators to identify the personal characteristics which make negotiators effective. If this is done in a very general way, it is likely that results will do little more than reflect some of the central characteristics of the negotiation task, or respondents' general theories about the nature of negotiation.

In this literature, one study stands out: that of Williams (1993). His sample was limited to legal attorneys in civil cases, but he *compared negotiators identified as effective, average, or ineffective* by Q-sort techniques. The main contrast was between cooperative and competitive approaches. Each kind of negotiator wanted to get the best for his or her client. The cooperative negotiators were more constrained by ethical considerations and wanted to reach agreements that were fair. The competitive negotiators were more concerned to make a profit for themselves and to outdo or to outwit their opponents. Williams was able persuasively to suggest that the two kinds of negotiators do not understand one another because they have quite different ideologies. One is problem solving; the other is aggressive.

The cooperative negotiators had some traits in common, regardless of their level of effectiveness. They were all seen as trustworthy, ethical, fair, courteous, personable, tactful, and sincere. The effective negotiators within the cooperative group were seen as fair-minded, with realistic opening positions. They did not use threats, were willing to share information, and actively explored their opponents' positions. In contrast, ineffective negotiators within the cooperative group were seen as trustful, gentle, obliging, patient, forgiving, intelligent, dignified, and self-controlled.

In some ways, the contrast between effective and ineffective negotiators was even more marked when negotiators were competitive. The effective negotiators were dominant, forceful, and attacking. Their strategy was simple: to push their opponents as far as they would go. To do this, they were willing to stretch the facts, take unrealistic opening positions, and withhold information. The ineffective negotiators were seen as irritating, argumentative, quarrelsome, aggressive, rigid, egotistical, headstrong, arrogant, intolerant, and hostile. They had not learned to cope with the 'negative side of efficiency' (see Morley, 1981).

According to Williams, the combination of cooperator and competitor causes the majority of the psychological problems in negotiation. This is too strong a claim, but there is little doubt that each may misinterpret the intentions and actions of the other. Williams has shown that both strategies can be effective, and argues that skilled negotiators should be able to use both. This is important if negotiations cycle through competitive and collaborative stages, and if the difference between the stages is more marked in those negotiations which end in success (see Stephenson, 1981). It seems likely that ineffective negotiators will find it extremely difficult to switch from one stance to the other as the situation demands.

Even so, we may have to recognise that negotiating style has much less impact on effectiveness than personal characteristics such as being prepared (on the facts and on the law), being self-controlled, observing the manners of the Bar, and taking satisfaction in using legal skills. Such conclusions are supported by the more recent research of Lynch and Evans (2002), and to some extent extended into the domain of criminal law, via consideration of plea bargaining. In addition, Lynch and Evans made an attempt to see how such effective negotiators were perceived in terms of the 'Big Five' dimensions of personality. They concluded that it did not matter whether negotiators were extrovert or introvert, nor whether they were aggressive. What mattered, apparently, was whether they were 'emotionally stable, and to a lesser degree creative, conscientious, and likeable' (p. 395). This research is interesting and potentially important, but is limited because the authors did not collect comparative data about average or ineffective negotiators.

Evaluation

Questionnaire studies of the personal characteristics of effective negotiators have to be treated with care (Morley, 1981, 1996). Nevertheless, studies such as those of Raiffa (1982) and Williams (1993) reinforce the argument that there is much more to negotiation than a process of bid and counter-bid. The top five characteristics reported by Raiffa (1982) were, in order of importance: preparation and planning skill, knowledge of the relevant subject matter, ability to think quickly and clearly despite pressure and uncertainty, ability to express thoughts verbally, and listening skill. Williams' evidence suggests that there is no one ideal negotiation style, but that skilled negotiators need to be able to switch from a competitive to cooperative stance as the situation demands. (This is consistent with behavioural studies of real-life negotiations outlined earlier.) Williams' work has also helped to increase our understanding of the dynamics which occur when someone with a cooperative stance negotiates against someone with a competitive stance. Much of the other research that falls within this category needs to be treated with a very great deal of care.

DISCURSIVE MODELS

It has been argued that, as negotiations become more complex, there needs to be a shift from a concern with strategy and tactics to a concern with messages and meanings (Putnam, 1985); a shift from talk about manipulation to talk about what makes sense in particular historical contexts (Morley et al., 1988; Hosking & Morley, 1991). Discursive models rely on some sort of language-action perspective. They are concerned with those collective processes by which participants make sense of change (the 'language' part) and decide how to act, given that something has to be done and commitments have to be made (the 'action' part). The model I set out here relies heavily on what has been said in Morley et al. (1988), Morley (1992), and Morley and Hosking (2003).

One of the main concerns of Morley et al. (1988) was to link talk about negotiation with talk about *narrative decision making*. The central idea was that talk about stories or scripts functioned to identify paradigm cases of threats and opportunities and how they might be handled. It was admitted – indeed insisted – that endorsement of a paradigm case by a particular group of people depended on a series of arguments in which different people tried out different arguments and commitments to different lines of action. What I have tried to show is that the kind of reasoning involved is both 'partisan and highly stylised: dramatising what has happened in the past and what will happen in the future' (Morley et al., 1988). It is this kind of reasoning that instantiates how negotiators *collectively struggle over intellectual problems* (what to count as facts, and how to interpret what is going on) and over *political* problems (what to do, and why). Hence, the attraction of some sort of language-action approach (Morley & Ormerod, 1996; Morley & Hosking, 2003) to be distinguished from some sort of approach based on individual information processing (instantiated in most of cognitive psychology). There are a number of such approaches. The one described here is probably the most general.

There were a number of immediate consequences of applying some such perspective:

1   Bargaining within groups was seen as similar in kind to bargaining between groups.
2   Judicial or quasi-judicial procedures involve much more than the presentation and examination of facts. Arbitrators, like negotiators, 'create order by reconstructing a story from reports which are partisan and incomplete.[5] They use this story as a basis for making a judgment'[6] (Morley et al., 1988, p. 124).
3   There is more to negotiation than bargaining. Negotiators do not reach bargains, nor do they resolve conflicts. Rather they *struggle* to reach agreements that *manage* conflicts – because to manage a conflict is to show that what has happened in the past may be used to justify what should happen in the future.

Let us take this last point seriously. It implies that negotiation is a process in which people meet to define the terms of their relationship, or that of reference groups they represent. The participants are concerned to establish whether certain changes are possible and, if so, at what cost (Hosking & Morley, 1991). The outcome of their deliberations is a set of rules, defining the terms on which the persons, or parties, will do business in the future. This is why negotiators have been described as writing social history (Morley, 1986; Morley, Webb & Stephenson, 1988; Hosking & Morley, 1991).

The writing part of the metaphor is used to remind us that negotiations are conducted in the context of existing rules, and that the effect of an agreement is to change those rules. The social part of the metaphor is used to make the point that, in formal negotiation, the changes have to be explained to other people and accepted by them. This is why one of the major tasks of negotiation is to find a formula, linking what is happening now to what has happened in the past, and to what will happen in the future (Zartman, 1977). The formula provides a rationale showing that people have developed lines of action which make sense in particular social and historical contexts (Harré, 1979). Without such a rationale, negotiation is likely to be prolonged or to break down. Unless the rationale is accepted by those not at the negotiation table, the rules will be broken when attempts are made to put the agreements into effect.

From this perspective the central problem in negotiation is to forge collective commitments that make sense within and between groups. This will require participants to build close relationships with opponents, whether it involves information exchange, collusion (Batstone et al., 1979), or 'appreciative moves' (Kolb, 2004). Kolb's concept of *appreciative moves* is perhaps one way of thinking about what Walton and McKersie (1965) call *attitudinal structuring*. As she says, appreciation includes 'recognizing' O's 'concerns' and giving O 'space' to talk, by retailing 'stories or histories' and 'doing the invisible work of connecting and trust building' (p. 43). It also requires leadership to enable participants to handle cognitive and political dilemmas that are inherent in the process of negotiation. I shall consider each of these three problems in turn.

Forging collective commitments that make sense

Those processes by which we make sense of our world are regarded, pre-eminently, as the province of cognitive psychology (see above: 'Information-processing models'). But there are two crucial elements missing from such models. The first is that our cognitive beliefs are socially 'tuned', because 'What we learn, and how we express that learning, is very much affected by those we meet, where we meet them, and by our relationships with them' (Hosking & Morley, 1991, p. 26). The second is that cognitive psychology has failed to realise the crucial significance of disputation and change in the intellectual and political aspects of our social lives (Harré, 1979; Harré & Gillett, 1994; Morley & Hosking, 2003). Language-action perspectives have the merit that they bring such issues to the fore.

Negotiators have to describe change, or the possibility of change, and *reach a working consensus*, within each party, *that the changes are changes of a certain kind*. Because of this, they face an intellectual struggle. Equally, they face a political struggle because people with different levels of investment in the issues, different sources of power, and different levels of skill, have to forge commitments based on those descriptions, and show that they make sense. This means that negotiators will attempt to find arguments which make sense of what they are doing, and disseminate them to others. It is no accident that successful teams send more information to members of their reference groups, and take greater pains to put that information in an appropriate context (Winham & Bovis, 1978).

From a discursive point of view, one of the most interesting recent developments has been a growth in commentaries by participants from each of the sides in industrial and international negotiations (followed by debate between them). With respect to industrial negotiations, the key text is still that of Friedman and Meredeen (1980).

Each was a major participant in the Ford sewing machinists' strike for equal pay at the Dagenham River Plant (UK, 1968). The power of the analysis came from what might be called a 'thick-textured' analysis of the process of disputation and change, partly through negotiation and partly through action external to negotiations (grievance procedures, working to rule, and strikes). In part, we read an account re-enacting the central themes of the negotiation, explaining what each side wanted, and revealing major problems of internal adjustment (intraorganisational bargaining) within each side. We are given an insight into the kinds of rhetorical argument that were effective and the kinds that were not. We are also given major insights into the ways in which the success of proposals may depend on the way in which claims may be linked to other claims or to bureaucratic procedures (also see Morley et al., 1988). In many respects, what we see is discursive psychology at work – from particular and partisan points of view.

It is easy to see that more research is needed, and that we will have to treat it with caution. So we shall. But there are signs that there is much to be gained from serious and systematic analyses of such debates between participants, as seen in a recent issue of the *Negotiation Journal* (Bar-Zion, 2004; Dajani, 2004).

Building close relationships

Kanter (1984) has argued that the basic commodities of organisational power are the abilities to build relationships based on the exchange of information, resources, and support. This implies that those negotiators who put more effort into building relationships with other people are more likely to be successful, although much of the literature emphasises the size of the network rather than the quality of relationships with focal persons (Hosking & Morley, 1991).

There are two aspects to this. It is important to be in contact with a sufficient number of people to triangulate the different points of view of those people close to the action, because this is how to gain authentic information. At the same time, one reason why some people are more influential than others is that they are linked into networks of relationships through which arguments may be tested or promoted (Batstone, Boraston & Frenkel, 1977; Huff, 1984). Thus, networking serves two functions: that of collecting organisational intelligence and that of building commitments to particular lines of action.

Negotiators may sometimes develop close bargaining relationships with members of opposing teams (Brown, 1973; Batstone, Boraston & Frenkel, 1977; Batstone, 1979). There is an exchange of information which gives participants increased understanding of what is happening, and what is likely to happen, and why. If Kolb (2004) is correct, such understanding has a narrative structure and functions to help negotiators decide how they are willing to negotiate. It is this understanding which makes them credible as negotiators. It means that agreements reached are more likely to stick because they are realistic politically, or otherwise make sense. There may also be a concomitant exchange of support so that each helps the other to work out how goals can be achieved and legitimised in terms of previous agreements, or rules of custom and practice.

Dilemmas in the process of negotiation

Dilemmas arise when negotiators search for acceptable ways of handling issues, whether within or between groups or both. They may all be described under a general rubric of judgements of balance with respect to intellectual or political concerns (Friend & Hickling, 1987; Hosking & Morley, 1991; Morley & Hosking, 2003). All concern structure in the process of negotiation: sometimes at the sociological end of social psychology and sometimes at the psychological end. The more sociological concerns are evident in contrasts such as that between leader and delegate roles (Warr, 1973) or between that of the need for leadership and the need for democracy (Hartley, Kelly & Nicholson, 1983). It is axiomatic in certain versions of folk psychology that unanimity is hard to achieve, but majority rule is not without its problems, especially if the rule is a simple majority rule (more than 50% of the franchise). The more psychological concerns are evident in judgements about whether to make the scope of negotiations more focused or more synoptic; whether to make the treatment of complexity simpler or more elaborate; whether to be more proactive or more reactive; whether to try to reduce uncertainty or to increase uncertainty; and whether to explore options or to close them down (see Friend & Hickling, 1987).

A careful reading of case studies of negotiation will reveal examples of each kind of dilemma, and illustrate some of the ways in which they shaped the process and outcomes concerned (see, for example: Elcock, 1972; Warr, 1973; Morley, 1982, 1992; Meredeen, 1988; Hosking & Morley, 1991).

One example, taken from Morley (1992), may illustrate the potential power of the analysis. It concerns the treatment of progress. The dilemma arises because internal and external negotiations may be seen as the planning and action stages of a single process (Marsh, 1974; Morley, 1982). The balance of strategic judgement is between: (1) a view of an ideal planning process as one in which people become increasingly committed to plans as they narrow the options from broad lines of development to specific proposals (see Levin, 1976); and (2) a recognition that it may be costly to delay too long because it may allow other people to articulate their own definitions of the situation, and seek support for partisan positions, perhaps narrowly defined (see Huff, 1984). There is a clear example of a failure to make a balanced strategic judgement of this kind in the pay and productivity negotiations described by Warr (1973).

Case studies show that many problems follow when teams lack an experienced leader, so that they are unable to cope with cognitive and the political aspects of the negotiation task (Hosking & Morley, 1991; Morley, 1992). Negotiation, whether internal or external, needs to be properly organised. Leaders have a clear responsibility to organise a process in which participants build shared interpretations of what is going on, and why – and of what can be negotiated, and how, and when (Morley, 1992; Morley & Hosking, 2003).

Evaluation

Pruitt and Carnevale (1993) have been generous enough to suggest that the language-action perspective may eventually lead to a fundamental shift in the way we think about negotiation. Certainly, it draws attention to aspects of negotiation which are not given sufficient attention in other models. One aspect concerns the shift from talk about strategy and tactics to talk about messages and meanings; a second aspect concerns the metaphor that negotiators write social history; a third aspect concerns the axioms which underlie a discursive psychology; a fourth aspect concerns negotiation considered as a form of joint decision making. Overall, the effect is to insist that studies of the skills of negotiation need to locate negotiation within its socio-historical context.

OVERVIEW

The analytic approach has the merit of assuming that negotiation involves mixed motives and indicates some intellectually sophisticated ways of looking at some of the skills of negotiation. Unfortunately, and despite some honourable exceptions, such as Walton and McKersie (1965) and Snyder and Diesing (1977), most of those who work within this 'paradigm' seem to assume that there is little more to the process of negotiation than the exchange of bid and counter-bid. Because of this, most behavioural studies are equally impoverished: while some deliver some important conclusions, most do not. Behavioural studies of real-life negotiations help us to discover some of the skills involved in negotiations between representatives of groups, but suffer from limitations of sample size. Information-processing models take seriously the proposition that 'as negotiations become more complex participants may find it increasingly difficult to work out what is going on, and why', so that questions of strategy (how to outwit an opponent) increasingly become subordinated to questions of structure (how to work out what is going on, and why). Both information-processing models and models of the personal characteristics of negotiators help us to show why this may be so. They also help us to elucidate some of the skills employed by the participants. Discursive models show how, and why, negotiators may be described as writing social history. At the moment, the most useful framework theory for describing the skills of negotiation seems to be some sort of language-action approach. I regard this as one form of social constructionism. It has the merit that it treats both the intellectual and political skills of negotiators seriously, and shows some of the ways in which they may be related. The model of skill that is articulated follows from the work of Welford (1980), and helps us to understand those individual and collective processes by which negotiators relate their intellectual capacities to the many demands of the negotiation task.

REFERENCES

Anthony, P. D. (1977). *The conduct of industrial relations*. London: Institute of Personnel Management.

Bacharach, S. B. & Lawler, E. J. (1981). *Bargaining: power, tactics, and outcomes.* San Francisco, CA: Jossey-Bass.

Bales, R. F. (1950). *Interaction process analysis: a method for the study of small groups.* Chicago: University of Chicago Press.

Baron, R. S. & Kerr, N. L. (2003). *Group process, group decision, group action,* 2nd edn. Buckingham: Open University Press.

Bar-Zion, B. (2004). Understanding barriers to peace: reflecting on Israeli-Palestinian economic negotiations. *Negotiation Journal, July,* 383–400.

Batstone, E. (1979). The organization of conflict. In G. M. Stephenson & C. J. Brotherton (Eds), *Industrial relations: a social psychological approach.* Chichester: Wiley.

Batstone, E., Boraston, I. & Frenkel, S. (1977). *Shop stewards in action.* Oxford: Blackwell.

Bazerman, M. H., Magliozzi, T. & Neale, M. A. (1985). Integrative bargaining in a competitive market. *Organizational Behavior and Human Decision Processes, 35,* 294–313.

Bazerman, M. H., Mannix, E. A., Sondak, H. & Thompson, L. (1990). Negotiator behavior and decision processes in dyads, groups, and markets. In J. S. Carroll (Ed.), *Applied social psychology in organizational settings.* Hillsdale, NJ: Lawrence Erlbaum.

Bazerman, M. H., Curhan, J. R., Moore, D. A. & Valley, K. L. (2000). Negotiation. *Annual Review of Psychology, 51,* 279–234.

Braithwaite, R. B. (1955). *Theory of games as a tool for the moral philosopher.* Cambridge: Cambridge University Press.

Brown, W. (1973). *Piecework bargaining.* London: Heinemann Educational.

Carnevale, P. J. & Isen, A. M. (1986). The influence of positive affect and visual access on the discovery of integrative solutions in bilateral negotiation. *Organizational Behavior and Human Decision Processes, 37,* 1–13.

Carnevale, P. J. & Keenan, P. A. (1992). The resolution of conflict: negotiation and third party intervention. In J. Hartley & G. M. Stephenson (Eds), *Employment relations: the psychology of influence and control at work.* Oxford: Blackwell.

Coddington, A. (1968). *Theories of the bargaining process.* London: George Allen & Unwin.

Colman, A. (1982). *Game theory and experimental games: the study of strategic interaction.* Oxford: Pergamon Press.

Dajani, O. M. (2004). Understanding barriers to peace: a Palestinian response. *Negotiation Journal, July,* 401–408.

Douglas, A. (1962). *Industrial peacemaking.* New York: Columbia University Press.

Druckman, D. (Ed.) (1977). *Negotiations: social psychological perspectives.* Beverly Hills, CA: Sage.

Druckman, D. (2001). Turning points in international negotiation: a comparative analysis. *Journal of Conflict Resolution, 34,* 519–544.

Druckman, D. (2004). Departures in negotiation: extensions and new directions. *Negotiation Journal, April,* 185–204.

Elcock, H. (1972). *Portrait of a decision: the Council of Four and the Treaty of Versailles.* London: Eyre Methuen.

Fisher, R. & Ury, W. (1981). *Getting to YES: negotiating agreement without giving in.* Boston, MA: Houghton Mifflin.

Fisher, R. & Ury, W. (1983). *Getting to yes*. London: Hutchinson.

Fisher, R. & Brown, S. (1988). *Getting together: building a relationship that gets to YES*. Boston, MA: Houghton Mifflin.

Friedman, H. & Meredeen, S. (1980). *The dynamics of industrial conflict*. London: Croom Helm.

Friend, J. K. & Hickling, A. (1987). *Planning under pressure: the strategic choice approach*. Oxford: Pergamon Press.

Fry, W. R., Firestone, I. J. & Williams, D. L. (1989). Negotiation process and outcome of stranger dyads and dating couples: do lovers lose? *Basic and Applied Psychology, 4*, 1–16.

George, A. L. (1969). The operational code: a neglected approach to the study of political leaders and decision-making. *International Studies Quarterly, 13*, 190–222.

Hall, L. (Ed.) (1993). *Negotiation: strategies for mutual gain: the basic seminar of the Harvard program on negotiation*. Newbury Park, CA: Sage.

Harré, R. M. (1979). *Social being*. Oxford: Basil Blackwell.

Harré, R. M. & Gillett, G. (1994). *The discursive mind*. Thousand Oaks, CA: Sage.

Hartley, J., Kelly, J. & Nicholson, N. (1983). *Steel strike*. London: Batsford Academic.

Holsti, O. (1970). The 'operational code' approach to the study of political leaders. John Foster Dulles: philosophical and instrumental beliefs. *Canadian Journal of Political Science, 3*, 123–157.

Hosking, D.-M. & Morley, I. E. (1991). *A social psychology of organizing: people, processes, and contexts*. London: Harvester Wheatsheaf.

Huff, A. S. (1984). Situation interpretation, leader behaviour, and effectiveness. In J. G. Hunt, D.-M. Hosking, C. A. Schriesheim & R. Stewart (Eds), *Leaders and managers: international perspectives on managerial behaviour and leadership*. Oxford: Pergamon Press.

Jervis, R. (1970). *The logic of images in international relations*. Princeton, NJ: Princeton University Press.

Jervis, R. (1976). *Perception and misperception in international politics*. Princeton, NJ: Princeton University Press.

Johnson, R. A. (1993). *Negotiation basics: concepts, skills, and exercises*. Newbury Park, CA: Sage.

Kanter, R. M. (1984). *The change masters: corporate entrepreneurs at work*. London: George Allen and Unwin.

Kolb, D. M. (2004). The shadow negotiation and the interest-based approach at Kaiser Permanente. *Negotiation Journal, **January***, 37–46.

Kramer, R. M. (1995). In dubious battle: heightened accountability, dysphoric cognition, and self-defeating bargaining behaviour. In R. M. Kramer & D. M. Messick (Eds), *Negotiation as a social process*. Thousand Oaks, CA: Sage.

Kramer, R. M. & Messick, D. M. (Eds) (1995). *Negotiation as a social process*. Thousand Oaks, CA: Sage.

Landsberger, H. A. (1955). Interaction process analysis of the mediation of labor–management disputes. *Journal of Abnormal Social Psychology, 51*, 552–558.

Lax, D. A. & Sebenius, J. K. (2002). Dealcrafting: the substance of three-dimensional negotiations. *Negotiation Journal, **January***, 5–28.

Levin, P. H. (1976). *Government and the planning process*. London: George Allen & Unwin.

Lockhart, C. (1979). *Bargaining in international conflicts*. New York: Columbia University Press.

Lynch, D. R. & Evans, T. D. (2002). Attributes of highly effective criminal defense negotiators. *Journal of Criminal Justice, 30*, 387–396.

Mannix, E. A., Thompson, L. L. & Bazerman, M. H. (1989). Negotiation in small groups. *Journal of Applied Psychology, 74*, 508–517.

Marengo, F. D. (1979). *The code of British trade union behaviour*. London: Saxon House.

Marsh, P. D. V. (1974). *Contract negotiation handbook*. Epping: Gower Press.

Meredeen, S. (1988). *Managing industrial conflict: seven major disputes*. London: Hutchinson.

Miron, M. S. & Goldstein, A. P. (1979). *Hostage*. Oxford: Pergamon Press.

Morgenstern, O. (1949). The theory of games. *Scientific American, May*, 86–89.

Morley, I. E. (1981). Negotiation and bargaining. In M. Argyle (Ed.), *Social skills and work*. London: Methuen.

Morley, I. E. (1982). Preparation for negotiation: conflict, commitment, and choice. In H. Brandstätter, J. H. Davis & G. Stocker-Kreichgauer (Eds), *Group decision making*. New York: Academic Press.

Morley, I. E. (1984). Bargaining and negotiation. In C. Cooper & P. Makin (Eds), *Psychology for managers*. London: Macmillan and British Psychological Society.

Morley, I. E. (1986). Negotiating and bargaining. In O. Hargie (Ed.), *A handbook of communication skills*. London: Croom Helm.

Morley, I. E. (1992). Intra-organizational bargaining. In J. Hartley & G. M. Stephenson (Eds), *Employment relations: the psychology of influence and control at work*. Oxford: Blackwell.

Morley, I. E. (1996). Negotiation and bargaining. In O. Hargie (Ed.), *A handbook of communication skills*, 2nd edn. London: Routledge.

Morley, I. E. & Ormerod, R. (1966). A language-action approach to operational research. *Journal of the Operational Research Society, 47*, 731–740.

Morley, I. E. & Stephenson, G. M. (1977). *The social psychology of bargaining*. London: George, Allen & Unwin.

Morley, I. E. & Hosking, D.-M. (2003). Leadership, learning and negotiation in a social psychology of organizing. In N. Bennett & L. Anderson (Eds), *Rethinking educational leadership*. London: Sage.

Morley, I. E., Webb, J. & Stephenson, G. M. (1988). Bargaining and arbitration in the resolution of conflict. In W. Stroebe, A. W. Kruglanski, D. Bar-Tal & M. Hewstone (Eds), *The social psychology of intergroup conflict*. Berlin: Springer-Verlag.

Nash, J. F. (1950). The bargaining problem. *Econometrica, 18*, 155–162.

Neisser, U. (1986). *Cognition and reality: principles and implications of cognitive psychology*. San Francisco, CA: Freeman.

Pruitt, D. (1981). *Negotiation behavior*. New York: Academic Press.

Pruitt, D. G. & Carnevale, P. J. (1993). *Negotiation in social conflict*. Buckingham: Open University Press.

Putnam, L. L. (1985). Collective bargaining as organizational communication. In P. K. Tomkins & R. McPhee (Eds), *Organizational communication: traditional themes and new directions*. Beverly Hills, CA: Sage.

Putnam, L. L. (2004). Transformations and critical moments in negotiation. *Negotiation Journal, April*, 275–294.

Putnam, L. L. & Jones, T. S. (1982). Reciprocity in negotiations: an analysis of bargaining interaction. *Communication Monographs, 49*, 171–191.

Putnam, L. L. & Geist, P. (1985). Argument in bargaining: an analysis of the reasoning process. *Southern Speech Communication Journal, 50*, 225–245.

Rackham, N. & Carlisle, J. (1978a). The effective negotiator. I. The behaviour of successful negotiators. *Journal of European Industrial Training, 2*, 6–10.

Rackham, N. & Carlisle, J. (1978b). The effective negotiator. II. Planning for negotiations. *Journal of European Industrial Training, 2*, 2–5.

Raiffa, H. (1982). *The art and science of negotiation.* Cambridge, MA: Harvard University Press.

Rubin, J. Z. & Brown, B. (1975). *The social psychology of bargaining and negotiations.* New York: Academic Press.

Snyder, G. H. & Diesing, P. (1977). *Conflict among nations: bargaining, decision making, and system structure in international crises.* Princeton, NJ: Princeton University Press.

Stephenson, G. M. (1981). Intergroup bargaining and negotiation. In J. C. Turner & H. Giles (Eds), *Intergroup behaviour.* Oxford: Blackwell.

Thompson, L. (1998). *The mind and heart of the negotiator.* Upper Saddle River, NJ: Prentice-Hall.

Thompson, L. L., Mannix, E. A. & Bazerman, M. H. (1988). Group negotiation: effects of decision rule, agenda, and aspiration. *Journal of Personality and Social Psychology, 54*, 86–89.

Toulmin, S., Rieke, R. & Janik, A. (1979). *An introduction to reasoning.* New York: Macmillan.

Tracy, L. & Peterson, R. B. (1986). A behavioural theory of labor negotiations – how well has it fared? *Negotiation Journal, 2*, 93–108.

Tversky, A. & Kahneman, D. (1981). The framing of decisions and the rationality of choice. *Science, 211*, 453–458.

Walton, R. E. & McKersie, R. B. (1965). *A behavioral theory of labor negotiations: an analysis of a social interaction system.* New York: McGraw-Hill.

Warr, P. B. (1973). *Psychology and collective bargaining.* London: Hutchinson.

Welford, A. T. (1980). The concept of social skill and its application to social performance. In W. T. Singleton, P. Spurgeon & R. Stammers (Eds), *The analysis of social skill.* London: Plenum.

Williams, G. R. (1993). Style and effectiveness in negotiation. In L. Hall (Ed.), *Negotiation: strategies for mutual gain: the basic seminar of the Harvard program on negotiation.* Newbury Park, CA: Sage.

Winham, G. R. (1977). Complexity in international negotiation. In D. Druckman (Ed.), *Negotiations: social-psychological perspectives.* Beverly Hills, CA: Sage.

Winham, G. R. & Bovis, H. E. (1978). Agreement and breakdown in negotiation: report on a State Department training simulation. *Journal of Peace Research, 15*, 285–303.

Zartman, I. W. (1977). Negotiation as a joint decision-making process. In I. W. Zartman (Ed.), *The negotiation process: theories and applications.* Beverly Hills, CA: Sage.

NOTES

1   In Morley (1996), I followed Lockhart (1979) and described such models as synthetic. With hindsight, I think that the term 'analytic' is much clearer.

2   Mostly, this has been the proposition, or a simple subject-predicated sentence, or some such equivalent, such as a complete thought phrase. Each coding scheme gives rules for analysing more complex units into such simple units. It is normal for such schemes to insist that one and only one code is applied to each unit. In other cases, the unit is larger and consists of all those sentences of the same type, regardless of length. Each kind of scheme has distinctive strengths and weaknesses.

3   Although every effort is made to specify the rules as precisely as possible, most of the rules involve what is called high inference coding, so that, for each of the schemes, considerable training may be required if two people are reliably to use the scheme in the same way. It is not at all clear that different people trained in different laboratories use the same schemes in entirely the same way.

4   Is one reason for the 'crisis' in social psychology that academics have (mostly) ignored this observation?

5   The language part.

6   The action part.

Chapter 15

Relational communication

Megan K. Foley and Steve Duck

ALTHOUGH SUCH CHAPTERS AS this routinely begin with a justification suggesting that relationships are an important part of life, the fact is really quite self-evident. Relationships define who we are and they are a fundamental and undeniably integrative force in our existence (Hargie & Tourish, 1997). Relationships create and develop our sense of self (Kelley et al., 1983), offer social support in times of need (Sarason & Duck, 2001), provide subtle bases for interpersonal persuasion (Carl & Duck, 2004), and create bulwarks of defence against the intrusions of daily hassles and unforeseen emergencies (Heller & Rook, 2001). The existence of good-quality relationships enhances people's social identity (Weiss, 1974), health prospects (Lyons et al., 1996), likelihood of surviving major life events (Badr et al., 2001), expectations of leading a satisfying life (Freedman, 1978), and ability to endure horrible experiences (Kaniasty & Norris, 2001). Relationships therefore can nowadays be taken for granted as a major influence in life. In short, relationships matter and we all *know* that they do.

It is nevertheless surprisingly difficult to define what 'relating' involves and hence a fortiori very hard to define what can be good or bad or skilful or unskilful about it. In order to set up a consideration of the nature of relationship skill, it is therefore first necessary to give some thought to the nature of the goals or purposes of relating. Once that is established, it is then possible to consider what might be done to achieve those goals and purposes in a 'better' or 'skilled' way.

SOME GOALS AND PURPOSES OF RELATIONSHIPS

The first issue concerns the purposes for which people might enter relationships, such that one can then assess whether their goals are achieved. Without such an assessment, one cannot set standards by which successful or skilful achievement of those purposes could be known or measured.

Weiss (1974) laid out some principles for judging the needs that are satisfied in relationships in the West. He proposed that there are seven provisions of relationships and one could assume that the ability to serve these goals would count as skilled. This should be so not only from the point of view of self fulfilment but also, more subtly, as the sense of fulfilment is judged by others, an important issue for assessments of skill, which can be viewed as an inherent characteristic or else as an attribution made by others (Spitzberg & Cupach, 1985). Such judgements can come from the outside observers as well as being made from the inside as persons assess their satisfaction of cultural norms and so qualify themselves for successful and skilled performance of their relationships in their own eyes.

Weiss (1974) proposed the following seven provisions:

1   *Belonging and a sense of reliable alliance.* The sense that others are available to support one in times of need is an important feeling for people, and it creates a sense of membership in a stable context. To the degree that such a sense of belonging is established and conveyed in relationships, the person has been skilful in fulfilling this need. Many studies have used the extent and depth of a person's membership in a community as a measure of the person's skill in relating (see Sarason et al., 1997, for example).

2   *Emotional integration and stability.* Derived in part from Festinger's (1954) considerations about social comparison, this provision asserts that people seek a sounding board for their emotional responses to life's eventualities, and that the commentary provided by others is a needed addition to their own personal reactions. In assessing skill in relation to this provision, therefore, some expressiveness of emotions is presumed.

3   *Opportunities for communication about self.* Weiss (1974) supposed that people have a desire to talk about themselves and expose elements of their experience and condition. A skilled relater should be one who does this in appropriate ways, neither too much nor too little (see Chapter 8 for further discussion of self-disclosure).

4   *Provision of assistance and physical support.* Given that most models of social support unequivocally suppose that physical and emotional support are requirements of relationships, it is not surprising that Weiss placed emphasis on this self-evident provision of relationships. It might be possible to assess a person's abilities in relationships according to the extent to which the person is successful in eliciting delivery of such support.

5   *Reassurance of worth and value.* Weiss assumes that people have a desire to evaluate themselves positively and to be reassured that they are valuable members of the community in which they exist. Again, this sort of provision could be readily assessed as a measure of the success of a relationship. Indeed, the

skills of establishing it help to develop personal wholeness or stability of self-esteem, and increase trust (Hargie & Tourish, 1996).

6   *Opportunity to help others*. Weiss regards this as a separate provision but it might also be seen as a subcomponent of many of the other components. For example, provision of assistance and physical support can be a way of satisfying a need to help others and thereby maintain one's own and others' views of a person as helpful. However, the voluntary expression of support for others and the provision of help are known to be a rewarding and self-fulfilling experience for both recipient and donor (Hobfoll et al., 1991; Hobfoll, 1996) and are clearly more readily available to the extent that the person has skilfully sustained a network of relationships.

7   *Personality support*. Seen in terms of traditional views of personality, this provision simply means that actions of friendship and closeness represent the supporting of a person's personality needs and values, an assumption that has been foundational in relationship research for several decades (Byrne, 1961, 1971, 1997; Tharp, 1963; Levinger, 1964). Personality support is distinct from reassurance of worth and value in that personality support is accomplished through *verification* of one's existing identity, while the reassurance of worth and value is based on the *enhancement* of that identity (Hargie & Tourish, 1997).

Such individual provisions are fundamental explanations for the existence of relationships, and each offers a way to assess the success or skill of an individual in relating. Yet, as Simmel (1950) noted, any couple tends to judge its satisfaction and performance not only relative to satisfaction of the internal feelings that the participants have about their own relationship but also against cultural and normative standards against which their success or failure may be assessed. Couples from the nineteenth century might judge their personal relationship as satisfying in ways that would horrify couples in the twenty-first century, giving preference to the dominance of the husband over the wife and to an assessment that the judgement of the husband about the relationship amounted to a final truth about it status.

Although a couple may be satisfied with the internal dynamics of their relationship, therefore, some reference of their outcomes to social norms might be expected as a legitimate judgement of the skill of their performance. The modern 'Cosmo questions' about the relative performances in their relationship compared to norms of '10 essential behaviours in relationships' or '15 things your relationship needs' might contribute to a couple's overall satisfaction with their relationship. Indeed, many couples now compare their sexual performance and experience with such standards before judging that they are sexually normal (Sprecher et al., 2005). Such activities and feelings suffice to indicate that the individual analysis of one's own performance is not an adequate measure of the satisfaction in the relationship and hence that the judgement of skill in a relationship does not rest with the couple alone but also with their performance relative to some societal norms. Likewise, an individual's behaviour may be judged skilful or unskilful from different vantage points.

Weiss's provisions, then, may apply only in the ideal but they are a recognisable standard that is used by (and which is derived from) Western standards for skill and performance levels. In the West, the satisfaction within a relationship is judged partly in relation to such norms, and so skill in relationship must also be measured against the existence of norms within a particular society rather than judged simply in terms of the claims of relational participants. As Montgomery (1988) teaches us, then, the communicative standards applied to assessments of 'quality' in relationships have their roots in a society's assumptions about 'personality' and the role of relationships in fulfilling self in relation to communicative standards. Moreover, outsiders may apply socially relevant norms of assessment to the behaviours observed in relationships, and, as Davis (1983) has powerfully noted, even the sexual behaviours in an intimate partnership are subject to the evaluative commentary of others at times. Hence, the issue of the relationships between judgements of 'skill' and actual relationship behaviours is somewhat complex even if one can properly acknowledge the limits on the categories of behaviours to be included.

In order to advance our case, therefore, it is necessary to know something about the behaviours regarded as basic to relating in order to set standards for their skilled performance.

BEHAVIOURS, THOUGHTS, AND RELATING

Some have sought to define relationships in terms of the underlying patterns of behaviour that occur between interactants. For example, Hinde (1981) defined a relationship as 'a series of interactions between two individuals known to each other' (p. 2). Hinde used the following set of eight criteria for describing relationships and distinguished them from otherwise unconnected interaction series:

1   *Content of interactions*: the things that the partners do together.
2   *Diversity of interactions*: those relationships that are multiplex are more likely to be closer and more intimate than those which involve only one type of activity, such as customer–server relationships.
3   *Qualities of interactions*: involving such assessments as intensity of interaction, content of discourse, and sensitivity of one partner to the behaviours of the other.
4   *Relative frequency and patterning of interactions*: for example, the sequencing of negative and positive responses to a partner.
5   *Reciprocity versus complementarity*: relationships are different if an action evokes a similar, reciprocal response, such as 'Hi' to a previous 'Hi', rather than a different but supplementary, complementary one, such as an answer to a question. Some interactions require reciprocity, as in the courteous greeting rituals that are a mark of skill in most superficially polite interactions, whereas others require complementarity, and people are not skilful unless they recognise and use this difference.
6   *Intimacy*: different sorts of relationships differ in the amounts of touch and verbal intrusion into the other's psychological space that are appropriate.
7   *Interpersonal perception*: individuals in different sorts of relationships differ in degree of balance between their perceptions of each other. Satisfying relationships occur successfully only when the perceptions of one partner with another are appropriately meshed.
8   *Commitment*: degrees of commitment not only to the relationship and to

the partner but to the likelihood of future interactions can differentiate relationships.

It is clear from the delineation of these categories that there is a host of ways in which they could be relevant to consideration of skill in relating, and we will consider them more closely below. At this point, it is sufficient to note that variation within these categories – and difference in performance from the expectations associated with each of them – could be critical in the determination that a person is a skilled relater. Inappropriate levels of commitment, intimacy, or sought frequency of interaction could register someone as over-intrusive rather than intimate, or as inappropriately distant rather than friendly and open.

It rapidly becomes apparent, however, that patterning of interaction is a necessary but not a sufficient condition for labelling action as 'relating'. Some form of psychological interdependence is clearly necessary as an adjunct to behavioural interdependence, whether measured in terms of perceived common fate or mutual interest or concern over the outcomes of the other (for example, whether they are equitable and satisfying). Some scholars have noted that relationships exist in the absence of repeated or frequent interaction, whether through the influence of long distance (Rohlfing, 1995; Sahlstein, 2006) or because of estrangement of some sort (as between parent and errant children) or through death (Mikulincer et al., 2003). Some have argued that relationships are partly mentalistic concepts and that the difference between a string of interactions and a relationship is what the parties think about those interactions (Duck, 1980). Indeed, some have pointed to the negative consequences of people's mere thoughts about relationships, such that they could lead to charges of harassment or stalking when one person believes that the relationship exists in a form that the other partner does not see or agree to (Cupach et al., 2001; Spitzberg & Cupach, 2003).

Sigman (1991) noted that people exercise various means to continue the mental element of their relationship in the face of absence or lack of interaction, since: 'Relationships are "larger" than the physical presence or interactional accessibility of the participants' (Sigman, 1991, p. 108). Sigman thus successfully explains how relationships may be continuous despite periods of separation. The discontinuous aspects of social relationships are managed by using relational continuity constructional units (RCCUs) – behaviours that partners use before, during, or after an absence and which function to construct the continuity of the relationship during periods of absence.

Sigman divides RCCUs into three types:

1   *Prospective units* are those behaviours that relationship partners perform before physical separation and 'define the meaning and duration of the impending separation and of the likely return' (Sigman, 1991, p. 112). Examples are farewells, setting agenda for future meetings, and the use of tie signs or tokens of relationships, such as the offer of engagement rings, or 'spoors' (objects left behind and which indicate a likely return, such as a toothbrush in one's lover's bathroom).

2   *Introspective units* represent the relationship's continuity during periods of absence and are exemplified by photographs of the partner on a desk at work, or a greeting card pinned to a personal space.

3   *Retrospective units* mark the ending of a period of relational separation and can be seen in conversations that allow the partners to 'catch-up' on what happened to each other during the period of absence, such as end of day debriefing or catch-up conversations.

In this context, then, it is notable that skilled behaviours in relationships are not necessarily connected to the present alone, and so it becomes critical to Hinde's definition that relational communication is joint discourse that points to *past* and *potential* interaction. In this definition, a relationship emerges from interaction, but is not reducible to it. In other words, relationship is created on the basis of a combination of behavioural skills, but this synthesis exceeds those behaviours. This excess is what renders communication relational: relational communication. Skilled performance is likewise tied not only to the present performance but also to management of future expectations. Thus, relational communication is behaviour that not only develops interactors' shared history but also suggests future interaction. In the following section, we will review various types of relational communication and discuss the value of viewing these behaviours as skills, given the need to consider management not only of behaviour but also of expectations and continuity. The distinction between behavioural and psychological factors points us to the difference that might be made in assessments between outsiders (limited to the behavioural and to inference about the psychological) and insiders (who have access to the psychological as well as to the behavioural) in assessing skill as a performance or as an attribute.

SKILLS AND THE QUALITY OF RELATIONSHIPS

The New Webster's Dictionary defines skill as 'the ability to do something well' (see Chapter 1 for a full discussion of definitional issues in the concept of skill). A chapter on relational communication for a book on communication skills therefore must include discussion of relationship behaviours (doing something), the bases of communicative quality (well), and the relation between the two, since not all relational skills are necessarily intentionally communicative. This chapter will identify some skilled behaviours reckoned to be fundamental to successful social relationships and will then consider some themes that have historically been understood as quality communication in the relationships literature and discuss the basis for these understandings. There is both a performance element (based perhaps on skilful application of relevant rules) and an experiential element here (since satisfaction must imply some skilled ability to extract outcomes desired by the individual reporter). Overlaying both, however, is a strategic element indicating that the ability to make choices between competing or inconsistent rules itself amounts to a skill.

Skills and rules

The first focus must be on whether the very communication of the existence of relationships is a first sign of skill. It is a truism of Western culture that the number of friends that a person can claim is seen as a measure of social success and the implicit rule to *demonstrate* connectedness is a powerful one. Liberace once sent out invitations to 5000 of his closest and dearest personal friends (Duck, 1991). The very ability to 'attract' others is treated as significant and a measure of skill and one's social value. In like manner, the ending of relationships is treated with pity and negativity such that there are no 'successful divorces' but only 'failed marriages' (Rollie & Duck, 2006). Ending of close relationships is stigmatic for their participants and is generally treated with remorse and disapprobation. Hence, existence of numbers of relationships is not sufficient to apply a label of skill but rather the implicit rule requires a *demonstrated* capacity to work and sustain those relationships. Accordingly, the emphasis in the literature taking this line has fallen on the microbehaviours that are used skilfully to demonstrate warmth and openness in relationships, beginning with the non-verbal and later extending to strategic success in the long term.

A skilled relational performance is first connected with needs and provisions that we outlined earlier, as well as with the ability to fulfil the requirements of social prototypes of relating. Davis and Todd (1985) listed the paradigm case features of friendship and noted that such performances as acceptance, respect, trust, and spontaneity were prerequisites of friendship, such that their absence disqualified the relationship as an instance of friendship. Hence, the ability to perform the behaviours associated with such features is a necessary skill and raises the question of the means by which such features are communicated.

The catalogue of behaviours that are counted as skilled here is quite large and covers a considerable range of activities, some of which are clearly 'relational' and some of which are less clearly connected to relationship activity and more obviously associated with smooth but simple social interaction. Argyle (1967) originally observed many skills of social interaction that essentially convey attention, warmth, and friendliness, and without whose presence the continuance of a relationship may be jeopardised. Familiar examples are eye contact, gaze, smiles, nods, and open postures (Argyle, 1967), but the contribution of these behaviours to the establishment and growth of relationships seems to be 'hygienic' rather than substantial. Herzberg (1966) differentiated hygienic factors in organisational contexts from motivational factors. Motivational factors make workers work harder; hygienic factors do not, but their absence makes people work less hard (examples are such things as adequate heating and lighting, whereas motivational factors are pay and respect from supervisors). In like fashion, some of the above non-verbal behaviours seem destined to have effects only in the breach, and to damage the prospects for intimacy when they are absent without substantially increasing them when present (Keeley & Hart, 1994). Nonetheless, the ability to perform such behaviours at all will count as skilled, and hence as a prerequisite of skilled relational behaviour in the above senses.

In addition to such microbehaviours, a larger issue is connected with strategic skills of recognition of the rules of certain situations, and Argyle's later work attended to the designation of social situations and the appropriateness of attendance to the prerequisites of such designation. For example, a skilful relationship with a friend requires recognition of the rule to tell the truth and be open about one's emotional state, so that one expresses warmth or affection and provides emotional support (Argyle & Henderson, 1984). Argyle and Henderson (1985) later broadened the notion of rules to relationships in general and concluded: 'Rules are a very useful guide to many aspects of socially skilled behaviour. We have taken as one criterion of

433

relationship rules whether or not [the breaking of them] results in disruption of a relationship. Social skills are commonly identified by a comparison of the performances of successful and unsuccessful practitioners. The concepts of rules and skill thus have a good deal of overlap' (Argyle & Henderson, 1985, p. 82). It is, however, also apparent that some relationships can survive rule breaking. Furthermore, there are important variations in rules depending on the specific relationship involved, not only across cultures but also within groups, as a function of the needs that are supposed to be fulfilled by the relationships in each case. For example, family life and work relationships are expected in Japan to fulfil some of the needs fulfilled by friendship in the West (Argyle & Henderson, 1985).

Given the strengths and relevance of the rules approach to skill in relationships, one must ask a number of questions in order to position the problems raised by the above comments in relation to the general value of a rules approach to skills. It is clear that there can be different layers of rules, some of which prescribe specific actions in particular circumstances (e.g. smile when you greet someone) and yet others which are of a higher and more abstract order ('be tolerant of friends'). It is also clear that judgements are required about the sets of rules to apply in particular circumstances, and whether it is, for example, more important to expect a smile from friends at each new encounter or to tolerate their bad moods. Such judgements indicate that a skill rests not only on the application of specific rules but in the ability to make wise assessments of the relative importance of applying the rule and ignoring it or supplanting it with some other rule. In short, knowledge of the rules is necessary but not sufficient to warrant a judgement of skilled relational communication, and perception of situational awareness/parsing of situations or even an awareness of cultural and situational norms is an asset that has power only when used with strategic good sense. Larger goals of relating can supplant the microperformances that would otherwise be regarded as skilful, just as social norms about relational conduct within an organisation could be different from those available in a culture more broadly or in society outside the organisation.

Such larger skills of relating might indicate successful affective management on top of the microbehaviours, and there is sometimes a tension between relating effectively (for example, assertively) and relating skilfully (for example, politely). Clearly, integration of goals and needs is a big issue in skill, and the ability to deploy specific tactical skills in a situation is a lower-order analysis. Some critics have therefore asked whether skill resides in the ability to adjust and adapt to situations or in the recognition that a specific rule applies to the relationship presently under consideration.

Spitzberg (1993) noted that the ability to adapt to rules is itself a skill and indicates that competence may be understood as an ability (to perform well) or a quality (an attribution made by observers). Competence has three roles in relationships. First, it has a direct role that facilitates development and management of relationships (skill = success of outcomes). Second, competence mediates how others respond to the actor's behaviour, so managing the appearance of competence is important. (This is the reason why we hear so much about spin doctors these days). Third, competence is a self-inference that affects motivation. Important theoretical and practical issues flow from these observations. If competence is an ability to make choices between options, then there is a dialectics of *motives* (for example, politeness versus assertiveness; communality versus instrumentality; adaptation versus control – the issue of when to adapt to situation and when to be self – attention to short-term versus long-term objectives; the decision to show openness versus closedness/privacy). If competence is an attribution by observers, then there is a dialectics of *attributions* (context-facilitated versus context-impaired; self-deception versus alter-deception; predictability versus novelty; success versus obsolescence – where one can have too much of a good thing or where repetition of a behaviour becomes adaptively unskilled).

Judging relationship skill

Montgomery (1988) argues that our judgements about relational quality are based on ideal standards for relational communication. These standards are located in particular contexts: they can be based on cultural ideologies, shared relational meanings, or individual idiosyncrasies. While not universal, these ideals do have an a priori nature in that these cultural, relational, and personal interactional codes form the basis for particular social behaviour. That is, our judgements about the skilfulness of a relational behaviour are based on its correspondence with ideal relational standards, or scripts.

In actual interaction, the criteria for judging quality communication are pluralistic; cultural, social, and individual criteria all bear on the assessment of communicative quality. For example, Oswald (2000) demonstrated that the ritual performance of the wedding ceremony (cultural), interactions with other wedding guests (social), and personal understandings about commitment (individual) all contributed to the quality of lesbian, bisexual, and gay family members' experiences at weddings. In their discussion of inappropriate relationships, Duck and VanderVoort (2002) presented the negotiation of cultural and relational codes for 'competent' but 'inappropriate' relational behaviour along a continuum from unconventional, notable, and scandalous, to forbidden. This scheme suggests that when criteria for quality relationships conflict, relational behaviour is based on the relative weight that relational partners give to cultural and relational standards.

While standards for the quality of relational communication serve as yardsticks to measure the valence of relationships, scholars also attest that these standards render social relations recognisable and meaningful in a more global sense. Surra and Bohman (1993) assert that people understand their relationships (and judge their quality) by comparing them to relational norms. Fletcher and Simpson (2000) echo that ideal standards for close relationships serve these interpretive and evaluative functions for relationship members, adding that they also serve an adaptive function: when relational scripts do not match the relationship itself, they serve as guidelines for change. Furthermore, Holmberg and MacKenzie (2002) propose that in romantic relationships when partners' personal scripts for enacting and interpreting romantic relationships correspond to normative scripts, couples experience greater relational well-being. These studies suggest that because we understand our relationships on the basis of ideal standards, our understanding of relationships is inextricably bound to our perceptions of their quality.

To deal with such questions, one must reflect on the matter of judgement of quality within a culture. This requires us to explore relationships at the macrolevel and consider how they knock against larger social structures that unobtrusively influence daily existence (Elias, 1977) or deal with the innumerable ways in which everyday social encounters make our experience for us (Wood & Duck, 2005). In different ways, theorists have focused on the means by which social relationships reflect larger social forces and so embody the ways in which 'society' is experienced at the mundane level of experience. If society has a face, it is in the face that attends our daily interactions with each other and constrains or empowers certain forms of social action and experience. Relationships in everyday life therefore embody and manage our connection with 'society' as a larger concept.

Communicative standards

Montgomery (1988) identifies three values implicit in relationships literature that serve as standards for quality and hence obliquely as bases for judgements of skill: positiveness, intimacy, and control. These assumptions remain implicit in the majority of relationship studies. Montgomery goes on to note that *competence* in relationships is judged in terms of the same criteria of positiveness, intimacy, and control. They must of course be understood as having a number of components, stressing the positive in relationships and the elicitation of positive experiences from others, but also being grounded in general psychological tendencies (in the West at least) to achieve self-fulfilment through relationships.

Positivity

The relationships literature demonstrates an overwhelming prosocial bias mostly indicated through the sorts of literature with which we opened this chapter and which regards positivity as the main signal of relational engagement (Acitelli et al., 2000). There is a growing literature on the importance of positive relationships at work (Dutton & Ragins, 2004), but there is also a growing literature on the 'dark side' of relationships (Cupach & Spitzberg, 1994; Duck & Wood, 1995; Spitzberg & Cupach, 1998), which demonstrates an increasing turn from the field's predominant focus on the prosocial nature of relationships. While these studies increasingly represent the negative side of relationships, they serve to reinforce the relational ideal of positiveness. On the other hand, Baxter and Montgomery (2000) have made compelling arguments for the importance of both centrifugal and centripetal relational forces, suggesting that centrifugal forces, such as closedness (privacy), change, and autonomy (independence), also have value for relationships.

All the same, the recognition that there are two sides to relationships that are always present together in experience simply shifts the focus of discussions of 'relational skill' from the performance of those behaviours that are rated positively and toward the issue of the *management* of the competing negative and positive forces that can be guaranteed to be present in all relationships. Rather than focusing on positivity, then, the important development of recent literature is to note the importance of the daily management of the different elements of relationships as well as the contribution of different forms of 'community' in which the management can be practised and held to account (Carl & Duck, 2004; Fritz Harden & Omdahl, 2006).

Intimacy

As is evident from the literature reviewed so far, and from many other sources (e.g. Hendrick & Hendrick, 2001), the assumption is that successful and skilled enactment of relationships revolves around the establishment, increase, and maintenance of intimacy (Sias et al., 2004). Indeed, the title of the Hendrick sourcebook is *Close Relationships*. It appears to be heretical to suggest that skilled relational communication could involve successful maintenance of distance or non-intimacy, despite Delia's (1980) telling observation that by far the majority of our interpersonal relationships not only are distant but persistently remain so. Kirkpatrick, Duck, and Foley (2006) note that relationships at work can embody several different and competing goals; the relational goal of intimacy may be unadvisable in a context dedicated primarily to achieving extrarelational tasks. Here, team-playing can be seen as an important criterion of skill which would not be similarly applied to long-term relationships based on intimacy. The bias in assessments of relationship skill in terms of an intimacy assumption must nevertheless be acknowledged.

Power/control

Most assessments of relationships assume that self-control and power over others are desirable features of relational life (Lovaglia & Lucas, 2006). Dominance is a trait preferred to submission, and authority is preferred to subservience. Problems in relationships at work are assumed to exist when equality of power shifts in friendly roles, with, for example, the promotion of one friend over the other (Zorn, 1995).

As Montgomery (1988) has argued, then, any judgement of the goodness, skill, or quality of a relationship is not a neutrally founded judgement but essentially holds relational activity up against a cultural or contextual standard through which 'quality' of relationships is established. There are no inherently good ways to conduct a relationship, and indeed cultures and contexts differ widely on the performances that are judged to be appropriate and skilled (Argyle & Henderson, 1985; Montgomery, 1988). Hence, any discussion of the 'skilled' performance of relationships necessarily nods toward the existence of cultural and situational norms and standards that apply in one's assessment of relationships and which might not apply to assessment of relationship quality in other cultural or situational contexts. Skill at work or in organisational settings where hierarchies of power are formally operated (Lovaglia & Lucas, 2006) does not necessarily equate to skill in interpersonal relationships within the family, for example. Brisk and authoritative behaviour in one setting may be 'skilled' where soft, warm, and intimate behaviours would be judged 'skilful' in the other (Lovaglia & Lucas, 2006). Hence, judgements about the skilled conduct of relationships must be tempered by the recognition that such judgements are embedded in the acceptance of a cultural and contextual standard for judging both the nature of the

437

relationship between participants and the performance of relationally relevant activities, as well as the outcomes from relationships that are regarded as positive or appropriate in the circumstances.

Ultimately, the reduction of relationships to a set of performable skills is both useful and misleading. Is the 'skill' to be found in a list of performable behaviours or is it found in the ability to adapt and to act in ways not obviously predicted and forced by the situation? Is the truly skilled performer one who follows the rules, or one who shows ability to adapt, change, and modify those general rules? More significantly for our following discussion, can one person ever be judged as 'skilled' in the absence of knowledge about the interaction partner and his or her behaviour? For the entirety of its existence, the research literature on relationships has been criticised for attending to the actions, feelings and reports of only one person in the relationship (Levinger, 1964; Byrne, 1971; Hinde, 1981; Perlman & Duck, 2005). In like manner, it seems absurd to focus on the mechanical behaviours of only one person in a pair and to judge the person as 'skilled' or 'unskilled' without making any assessment of the appropriateness of their activities with respect to the attitudes, feelings, and responses of the other person present.

SKILL AND THE STRUCTURALIST PARADIGM

The claim that we enact and interpret relationships on the basis of ideal standards rests on a structuralist paradigm. Here, relationships are treated as parallel to Saussure's (1910/1993) explanation of language: parole, or speech, is an enacted, performed instantiation of langue, an abstract and a priori system of signs (for example, 'grammar'). Analogously, in the relational structure paradigm, our relational behaviour is an instantiation of a system of relationship standards. As such, relating is understood as synchronic; that is, it takes a 'snapshot' of relational skill at a single point in time, rather than understanding standards for skilled relational behaviour as unfolding over time. According to the relational structure paradigm, social practices that fail to meet the system of relational standards fail to be legitimated as 'good', 'quality', or 'skilled'. If no social practice outside the system of relational standards can be understood as legitimate, alternative social practices lack the force to transform the system of relational standards. Thus, while the concept of ideal standards (whether cultural, relational, or personal) is useful, it is insufficient to explain relational skill. By itself, this perspective does not account for a mechanism that allows for change in the fundamental structure of relational values (Argyle & Henderson, 1985).

The relationships literature shows that our understanding of relationships does indeed change on the basis of social practice. While this does take place on the levels of cultural ideologies and individual idiosyncrasies, the relationships literature most clearly illustrates the transformative power of social practice at the relational level. Bochner, Ellis, and Tillman-Healy (1997) explain that relational partners' accounts of their behaviour serve not only to legitimate it, but also to construct the terms by which relational behaviour can be legitimated. Duck (2002) explains:

> Engagement in interpersonal communication [re]calls forth speakers' daily lives to other people for evaluation (whether appreciation, accountability, or rebuke).

By the same conversational means, people are able to evaluate their rhetorical visions of life, of other people, of themselves, and of a host of other things that have been variously called personality, meaning systems, or culture.

Following this view, we argue for an adjusted conception of relational structure. Relationships are not judged in comparison to static, unchanging abstract and standard structures; instead, relational practices in the living everyday world – the relational paroles as it were – create the basis for their own evaluation. In other words, relational practices are self-structuring. Elias (1977) suggests that the monolithic but abstract conception of social structure is illusory. He argues that social structure comes down to figurations of everyday social relationships; the abstract notion of 'society' is really something substantial that is enacted in a set of relationships between people and their associates. Volosinov (1929/1986) similarly argues that the structure that guides social practices emerges from those social practices themselves. He declares that the structure of the utterance is sociological; that is, it 'obtains between speakers'. Simmel (1950) similarly positions structure as contingent on sociation, or social interaction. For Simmel, 'the content – the materials, so to speak – of sociation [is] everything that is immediately present in individuals', while social forms are abstractions 'through which, or in the shape of which, that content attains social reality' (pp. 107–108). While Simmel maintains a conceptual distinction between social content and social forms, he explains that in sociation the two 'constitute one reality' (p. 107). It is important to note that we are not proposing a mere reversal of the binary between social structure and behaviour. We are not arguing that instead of social structure guiding behaviour, behaviour guides social structure. We introduce relational co-performance, the interstice between behaviour and structure, as a third term that evades the binarism on which the relational structure paradigm relies. In short, we advocate performance as an alternative to structure as the basis for relational signification. Hence, we advocate co-performance as an alternative to skill as the basis for relational signification. In other words, we claim that the notion of skill in relating has fallen prey to the same flaw present in the relational literature as a whole – reliance on the reports and examination of the responses of one person in the dyad.

By focusing on co-performance, we emphasise the fact that relationships and all forms of social behaviour are founded on the notion of (at least) two interactants. Accordingly, it is necessary to be aware of things other than the feelings of one person that are 'present' in any interaction that is located relationally – that is, in a flow of history (Duck, 2002).

Unlike the synchronic skill paradigm, co-performance is rooted in a diachronic conceptualisation of relationships that accounts for both their historicity and their generativity. Our earlier discussion of Hinde (1981) indicated that relational communication is joint discourse that points to *past* and *potential* interaction. In this definition, relationship emerges from past co-performance (history), but is not reducible to it (generativity). As link between past and future, co-performance can be understood as a limen, or threshold, of becoming (Turner, 1982). Relationships are continually recreated through this process of play, where the old and new collide and collude. Any jointly performed discourse is both generative and historical.

First, co-performance is generative: it resignifies the shared history of a relationship by performing new contextual frameworks for interpretation. Bauman and Briggs (1990) argue that participants contextualise their performance (e.g. produce interpretive frameworks) through the contextualisation cues in the performance itself: 'textual details . . . illuminate the manner in which participants are collectively constructing the world around them' (p. 69). This contextualisation of voice is constructive, rendering relational meanings new, though contingent on their historical grounding. Likewise, Duck (2002) notes that the behaviours and talk of two relational partners with each other are both grounded in the partners' awareness of past interaction between themselves. The interpretation of an instant remark depends to some degree on the location of that remark in the relational history between the two interactants and the interaction sequencing as well as in the personality and past record of the speaker. The more one knows of the speaker's history, the more subtly one can interpret the significance of a particular comment.

However, the co-performance not only serves to transform (contextualise), but also to preserve (*en*textualise) existing voices. By calling attention to the form by which the performance is organised, the performance takes itself as its own object, rendering it extractable from its interactional setting. While contextualisation cues can be understood as an emergent structure that organises and situates discourse, contextualisation cues are also markers that call attention to that organising form. Thus, the same performative features account for both (a) the contextualisation or transformation of relational meaning and (b) entextualisation or reification of relational meaning. Thus, relational meanings are always in generative flux, yet at the same time rely on and promote an understanding of shared relationship history.

While we suggest that the structuralist underpinnings of the term 'skill' are problematic for a conception of relationships as processual, the literature overwhelmingly demonstrates that the valence of relational practices is significant. Studies consistently show that relational satisfaction is a meaningful way in which social actors understand their relationships (Davis & Todd, 1985). In addition to this personal experience of relational value, we also recognise the importance of identifying the ethical value of relationships. The literature on intimate partner violence demonstrates the importance of avoiding a relativistic stance where judgements of good and bad have no place (Wood, 2001). In proposing co-performance as an alternative to competence, we are not claiming that relationships cannot or should not be evaluated. Instead, we take issue with the *means by which* relationships are understood to be evaluated in rule-based constructions of skill, in which relational evaluation takes place on the basis of ideal standards. The alternative of co-performance advocates judging relational performances by the criteria the performances themselves construct, rather than against a priori criteria. Because relational performances are historical and generative, they can be judged on the basis of their appropriation of the past to create new performances.

Rather than positioning relational standards as some ideal structure separate from performance, the conditions for evaluating relational behaviour exist within those behaviours themselves. Each utterance contains a palimpset, a trace of previous actions against which that utterance can be judged. Duck (2002) applies the metaphor of hypertext, explaining that relational history is indexed within social interaction, 'linking' the past to the present. We evaluate our relationships on the basis of the indexed past, or present constructions of the past. It is not unusual to claim that relaters continually renegotiate their relational histories, arguments over the usefulness of retrospective data (Duck, 2002) being an excellent example of the entailments of reformulating the past. We further argue, however, that the relational past unveils itself only insofar as it is indexed in interaction. This presentation of the past, which may masquerade as the invocation of a given structure of relational standards, is the basis for determining the value of relational behaviour. In other words, we do not judge a behaviour's value on the basis of extant relational ideals, but in the idealisations that emerge from that behaviour itself.

Locating the criteria for relational skill in the ongoing flux of conversation disrupts the understanding of a behaviour as 'skilled' or 'unskilled', or an individual as 'competent' or 'incompetent'. Incompetence is not just the lack of competence: there is more going on when that label is applied. An attribution of lack of skill is a way of pointing to deficiencies in performance as judged from the cultural, contextual, and situational embedding of the relationship. To label someone as incompetent is to refer to a contextualised speech situation, not a quality of the individual in isolation. Kirkpatrick et al. (2006) suggest that those who are often construed as 'difficult' people are not difficult in themselves, but in relation to others; relational difficulty sits instead in the multiple competing roles that individuals enact. Incompetence, then, is not a matter of personal or performative *deficiency*, but instead a problem of performative *excess*. That is, it is difficult to navigate continually shifting criteria for skill as they emerge through interaction. For example, as individuals are rewarded in relationships, they come to expect increasing rewards (Thibaut & Kelley, 1959). Because criteria for skilled performance are realised within those performances themselves, skilfulness is a moving target. Incompetence is not the lack of competence, but a function of the generativity of relational skill.

OVERVIEW AND IDEAS FOR FUTURE CONSIDERATION

The above concerns bring us back to some issues noted at the beginning and focused on the matter of whether skill is appropriately sited in microbehaviours or macro-action. In other words, do our assessments of 'skill' properly attach to short-term or long-term elements of relational communication? Equally relevant is the issue of whether relationships (especially long-term relationships) are to be seen as inherent or instrumental, such that skill should be assessed relative to 'warm and fuzzy' qualities or to specific outcomes. A third issue of relevance to judgements of skill focuses on the strategic versus the routine aspects of relating. Much has recently been made of the non-strategic mundane and ordinary behaviours of relationships (Dainton, 2000; Wood & Duck, 2005), and the removal of emphasis on strategic activity renders the consideration of pedestrian and apparently insignificant (even phatic) activity much more relevant to judgements of skill. A fourth consideration is whether relational skill can be taught, and a final issue concerns the definition of incompetence and its impact on the health status of the person in ways relevant to the conditions with which we opened the chapter. We will now take these in turn.

Long-term or short-term relating as the basis for assessing skill?

Given that *personal* norms of creditable performance are not sufficient to judge the success of a relationship and that *social* norms about skill may be differently applied, one must make a further distinction between types of relationships for which an assessment of skill or lack of skill may be applied: the long-term versus short-term distinction. It is important to note that the goals of (and hence measures of satisfaction with skill in) long-term and short-term relationships are different. Short-term relationships are judged successful when there is an easy rapport, when first impressions are favourable, and when liking is evoked from someone who did not have any reason to feel it before, being a stranger (Argyle, 1967). Long-term relationships require more than this and are found to require deep similarity and management of established intimacy and of long-term commitment as well as development of significant trust in a variety of contexts and relative to a range of concerns, as well as other things (Hinde, 1981). The distinction in the literature between short-term and long-term relationships readily suggests, therefore, that different skills and criteria for skilfulness apply in each case. We have already considered the specific case of long-term strategic overlay (Spitzberg, 1993) on the dialectics of (in)competence, for example, but there are many other cases where the confusion of short- and long-term goals – and hence of short- and long-term criteria for skilfulness – are quite markedly different. For example, a person who is shy but capable of intimacy might be judged incompetent in one sort of relationship, but not in another (Burgoon & Koper, 1984; Bradshaw, 2006). Hence, the notion of skill is not a simple reference to personal ability but to a person–situation interaction at the very least (see Chapter 2).

The issue of skill also implies an ability of two kinds of observers, both external reviewers and participants, to differentiate the goals and requirements of short- and long-term relationships. The literature on long-term relationships suggests strongly that an underlay of similarity of attitudes is a prerequisite of successful long-term relationships and that different skills might underlie short-term relationships (Duck & Pond, 1989; Perlman & Duck, 2005). Such similarity may be judged differently by insiders and outsiders (Duck & Sants, 1983; Kenny & Acitelli, 1994) because they have available to them different sorts of information about internal states. One obvious difference lies in the knowledge of private relational history and the fact that whereas similarity of underlying 'rhetorical vision' (personal view of the world) is essential to the success of the relationships on the enduring future (Duck & Pond, 1989), in short-term relationships, the basis of the relationship may be independent of such history and could depend only on the fulfilment of instrumental needs and goals which are specific and perhaps even time-limited (Hargie & Tourish, 1996).

What is the parallelism between long-term and short-term relationships? Perhaps short-term relationships work best if they mimic the goals and styles of long-term ones, but, given that they most often have time-limited objectives and are strictly performative in character, this mimicry may not matter. 'Uses' of long-term relationships as an analogy for deciding what short relationships should be offering might point to the errors in too simple a conclusion about the extension of one type of relationship skill to another. It could be argued that short-term relationships are successful to the extent that they may be able to mimic the effects and styles of long-term relationships, but this is actually questionable and the two sorts may better be seen as related but independent forms. Thus, for example, the fact (Davis & Todd, 1985) that long-term relationships are based on trust and intimacy might be heard as a clarion call for all those seeking successful short-term relationships to imitate such features, but it is also apparent that short-term relationships can be quite successful without such features being present (Argyle & Henderson, 1984).

Hence, a primary restriction on the notion of relationships as skilled performances relates to the distinction between long-term and short-term relationships. In the workplace or organisational context, one can see relationships as closer in form to short-term than to long-term relationships, and so different criteria for skill and success in outcome should be applied (Kirkpatrick et al., 2006).

Are relationships intrinsic or instrumental in purpose?

One difference between long- and short-term relationships is that the former are normally expected to fluctuate in outcomes, whereas the emphasis in the latter is immediate and expectant homogeneity. Where a short-term partner may leave the relationship if rewards are not immediately positively balanced against costs, a long-term partner might be more willing to sustain the relationship in the face of (temporary) difficulty, on the grounds that the immediate rewards are not the point. The larger questions, then, are whether relationships are inherent/intrinsic or instrumental and how the answer to this first question affects the idea of skill. It has long been argued in the relationship field that relationships should not be reduced to a calculus of profits and losses but have instead some inherent and intrinsic self-referent qualities that make them desirable in and of themselves (Wright, 1985). Although some wiseacre once said, 'Sincerity is the key to successful relationships and if you can fake sincerity then you have got it made', the emphasis falls here on such an instrumental use of the features of long-term relationships that the claim makes us instantly aware of the merits of Wright's point.

Drawing from Duck (1994), the ability to create and sustain shared meaning systems is the basis for relationship maintenance in the long term and so should be accounted in the assessment of 'skilled performance' in any longer-term association whether strategically or routinely sustained (see next section). In this case, the situation may be complicated in that it is not only that competent communicative performance creates and sustains relationships, but also that relational communication allows us to create shared ideals about relationships and relationshipping. This allows us to maintain the same conceptual scheme, but flip from an outcome-based to a process-based model of competent relationships.

An emphasis on skilled performance for relationships suggests an instrumentality that may not apply successfully to long-term relationships. The ability to achieve goals and to derive specific satisfaction from relationships may be more valuable as a perspective from which to understand short-term relationships where goals are more specific and limited than is true of long-term relationships whose strategic maintenance may require the forgoing of a specific instrumental personal goal at this moment in order to sustain the relationship in the long term in intrinsic form.

Routine versus strategic aspects of maintenance and relating

Throughout the chapter, we have followed the predominant emphasis of the relationship literature in stressing the importance of cognition, awareness, and strategic action in relationships. However, more recent research has focused also on the everyday routine and mundane performances that surround relationships (Duck et al., 1991; Dainton, 2000). The issue that arises in assessing skill, then, is whether the relationship is constituted by the skills or whether skills are necessary but not sufficient for relationship formation and maintenance. The matter is complicated by the fact that performance of relationships requires certain necessary mechanical skills, such as the performance of warmth, acceptance, and friendliness (Argyle, 1967) and, in some cases, intimacy, exclusivity, and trust (Davis & Todd, 1985), but that these are not necessarily skills that are transferable from relationship to relationship or situation to situation. In intimate or romantic long-term relationships, exclusivity is more relevant and important than in short-term business relationships or in friendship, for example, and so the features that characterise skilled performance of exclusivity cannot be readily generalised from one relationship form to another.

Furthermore, communication is not skill-based alone – at least not as 'skill' is normally understood and represented – and cannot be essentialised to different relationship forms, but is more naturally routinised in the activities of daily life that make up particular relationship forms. Everyday conduct of conversation can itself be skilled but does not typically register in the literature because the focus of research is basically on the unfamiliar and extraordinary cases of intimacy growth rather than on the everyday patterns that matter in continuing relationships.

Relationships can be skilled in the short term, but that is not their essence for long-term relationships. In short-term relationships, by contrast, a person can be 'skilled' by reason of the person's ability to complete relevant tasks and to sustain whatever basis of familiarity is necessary for that to be accomplished, but in long-term relationships a strategy devoted to the long-term maintenance of the relations despite short-term cost could be more important and hence more skilled. Moreover, given the variable nature of long-term experience of any kind, the skills of discretion weighed against valour, for example, may make a person better able to handle the inevitable instabilities and ups and downs of relationships (Wood & Duck, 1995) even over and above any skills necessary to handle actual conflict.

Translations from maintenance of long-term to maintenance of short-term relationships are therefore not easy because the implied, and in some cases the explicit, goals are different. The maintenance of a successful short-term business relationship may be different from the goals that confront people in long-term relationships. Even in organisations and business relationships, these goals could be specified in different ways. Hence, the ways in which 'skill' might be characterised in short- and long-term relationships could be quite radically different, depending on whether one sees the maintenance of the relationship as a goal or not, relative to other tasks.

Can relational skill be taught?

Underlying most considerations of 'skill' is the implicit question of whether skilled conduct of relationships can be taught (Argyle, 1967). Yet, in common language, the notion of 'relating' runs counter to any sense of strategic management or, worse, manipulation. The essence of common-sense notions of relating is in genuineness and spontaneity rather than manipulative or strategically managed actions. In short, the goals of it are perceived to be more in line with those of longer-term relationships and there is some suspicion about people who are able to produce immediate or decon-textualised disclosures and openness, particularly where there are power differences between speaker and listener (Cline, 1989).

A further twist on this dilemma is provided by the observation that some of the mechanical 'social skills' are taken to be a barrier to the authenticity and 'true communication' that are preferred in this society, since the mechanical production of smiles, nods and other encouragements or signals of interest is presumed to mask an underlying lack of interest in the comments of the speaker, and hence to fail the test of authenticity. Although, clearly, this is not always the case, the fact that psychotherapists are taught to manage these cues to warmth and intimacy as part of their professional training can be seen to show that the point cuts both ways (Mallinckrodt, 2001). It does indeed mask professional distance but simultaneously has the effect of encouraging the speaker to continue to disclose and explore experiences within the safety of a therapeutic context. Hence an appearance of warmth in the listener can, even if masking some other feelings, lead to benefits for the speaker and to a sense of being accepted (cf. Weiss' provisions discussed earlier). However, it is probable that the sense of acceptance is tested against things other than the immediate non-verbal behaviours associated with one short interaction; hence, the standard for assessing skill is once more a long-term one. It is insufficiently clear at this point whether these long-term skills can be trained in the ways in which short-term ones may be.

If we know 'skill', then what is incompetence?

As we have suggested above, incompetence is not just the lack of competence: there is more going on when that label is applied. The obvious point is that an attribution of lack of skill is a way of pointing to deficiencies in performance as judged from the cultural, contextual, and situational performance of the relationship as it is normally embodied in the culture. However, our points above also suggest that the context for assessment provides different outcomes of judgements depending on whether the relationship is seen as primarily instrumental, short term, and routine, for instance. To label someone as unskilled is to refer to a cultural and situational context as well as to denounce them in some way.

In a broader context, Kirkpatrick et al. (2006) have noted that many terms that appear to characterise someone actually make attributions: that is to say, they do not identify an inherent personal characteristic so much as they place a person in a social category whose operation cannot be understood apart from the social context. For example, a 'shy' person cannot be shy in the absence of other people and a 'difficult' one does not demonstrate difficulty alone. Thus, difficulty and lack of relational skill are essentially terms that require the incorporation or imagining of other people. The perception of a person as a 'difficult person' is based on a set of assumptions about the ultimate goal of a work relationship (namely, the achievement of extra-relational tasks).

In conclusion, the consequences of skilled and unskilled performance are therefore hard to pin down until one decides what level of skill (in the sense of what domain of skill) one is interested in. The ability to sustain long-term relationships that are genuine and open is probably the aspect of relating that is tied to the long-term health issues noted in the opening paragraph of this chapter, although, of course, people who are lonely and isolated may lack the short-term skills that bring them to relationships in the first place. Whatever the health implications of relationships, the basic skills of connection of individuals to society are central to both health and social success.

REFERENCES

Acitelli, L. K., Duck, S. W. & West, L. (2000). Embracing the social in personal relationships and research. In W. Ickes & S. W. Duck (Eds), *Social psychology and personal relationships*. Chichester: Wiley.

Argyle, M. (1967). *The psychology of interpersonal behaviour*. Harmondsworth: Penguin.

Argyle, M. & Henderson, M. (1984). The rules of friendship. *Journal of Social and Personal Relationships*, *1*, 211–237.

Argyle, M. & Henderson, M. (1985). *The rules of relationships*. In S. W. Duck & D. Perlman (Eds), *Understanding personal relationships: an interdisciplinary approach*. London: Sage.

Badr, H., Acitelli, L. K., Duck, S. W. & Carl, W. J. (2001). Weaving social support and relationships together. In B. R. Sarason & S. W. Duck (Eds), *Personal relationships: implications for clinical and community psychology*. Chichester: Wiley.

Bauman, R. & Briggs, C. (1990). Poetics and performance as critical perspectives on language and social life. *Annual Review of Anthropology*, *19*, 59–88.

Baxter, L. A. & Montgomery, B. M. (2000). Rethinking communication in personal relationships from a dialectical perspective. In K. Dindia & S. W. Duck (Eds), *Communication and personal relationships*. Chichester: Wiley.

Bochner, A. P., Ellis, C. & Tillman-Healy, L. P. (1997). Relationships as stories. In S. W. Duck (Ed.), *Handbook of personal relationships*, 2nd edn. Chichester: Wiley.

Bradshaw, S. (2006). Shyness and difficult relationships: formation is just the beginning. In D. C. Kirkpatrick, S. Duck & M. K. Foley (Eds), *Relating difficulty: the processes of constructing and managing difficult interaction*. Mahwah, NJ: Lawrence Erlbaum Associates.

Burgoon, J. K. & Koper, R. J. (1984). Nonverbal and relational communication associated with reticence. *Human Communication Research*, *10*, 601–626.

Byrne, D. (1961). Interpersonal attraction and attitude similarity. *Journal of Abnormal and Social Psychology 62*, 713–715.

Byrne, D. (1971). *The attraction paradigm*. New York: Academic Press.

Byrne, D. (1997). An overview (and underview) of research and theory within the attraction paradigm. *Journal of Social and Personal Relationships*, *14*, 417–431.

Carl, W. J. & Duck, S. W. (2004). How to do things with relationships. In P. Kalbfleisch (Ed.), *Communication yearbook 28*. Thousand Oaks, CA: Sage.

Cline, R. J. W. (1989). The politics of intimacy: costs and benefits determining disclosure intimacy in male–female dyads. *Journal of Social and Personal Relationships*, *6*, 5–20.

Cupach, W. R. & Spitzberg, B. H. (Eds) (1994). *The dark side of interpersonal communication*. Hillsdale, NJ: Lawrence Erlbaum.

Cupach, W. R., Spitzberg, B. H. & Carson, C. L. (2001). Toward a theory of obsessive relational intrusion and stalking. In K. Dindia & S. W. Duck (Eds), *Communication and personal relationships*. Chichester: Wiley.

Dainton, M. (2000). Maintenance behaviors, expectations for maintenance, and satisfaction: linking comparison levels to relational maintenance strategies. *Journal of Social and Personal Relationships*, *17*, 827–842.

Davis, K. E. & Todd, M. J. (1985). Assessing friendship: prototypes, paradigm cases and relationship description. In S. W. Duck & D. Perlman (Eds), *Understanding personal relationships*. London: Sage.

Davis, M. S. (1983). *SMUT: erotic reality/obscene ideology*. Chicago: University of Chicago Press.

Delia, J. G. (1980). Some tentative thoughts concerning the study of interpersonal relationships and their development. *Western Journal of Speech Communication*, *44*, 97–103.

Duck, S. W. (1980). Personal relationships research in the 1980s: towards an understanding of complex human sociality. *Western Journal of Speech Communication*, *44*, 114–119.

Duck, S. W. (1991). *Friends, for life*, 2nd edn, in UK [*Understanding personal relationships*, in USA]. Hemel Hempstead/New York: Harvester Wheatsheaf/Guilford.

Duck, S. W. (1994). *Meaningful relationships: talking, sense, and relating*. Thousand Oaks, CA: Sage.

Duck, S. W. (2002). Hypertext in the key of G: three types of 'history' as influences on conversational structure and flow. *Communication Theory*, *12*, 41–62.

Duck, S. W. & Sants, H. K. A. (1983). On the origin of the specious: are personal relationships really interpersonal states? *Journal of Social and Clinical Psychology*, *1*, 27–41.

Duck, S. W. & Pond, K. (1989). Friends, romans, countrymen; lend me your retrospective data: rhetoric and reality in personal relationships. In C. Hendrick (Ed.), *Close relationships* (vol. 10). Newbury Park, CA: Sage.

Duck, S. W. & Wood, J. T. (Eds) (1995). *Confronting relationship challenges*. Understanding relationship processes, vol. 5. Newbury Park, CA: Sage.

Duck, S. W. & VanderVoort, L. A. (2002). Scarlet letters and whited sepulchres: the social marking of relationships as 'inappropriate'. In R. Goodwin & D. Cramer (Eds), *Inappropriate relationships: the unconventional, the disapproved, and the forbidden*. Mahwah, NJ: Lawrence Erlbaum.

Duck, S. W., Rutt, D. J., Hurst, M. & Strejc, H. (1991). Some evident truths about conversations in everyday relationships: all communication is not created equal. *Human Communication Research*, *18*, 228–267.

Dutton, J. & Ragins, B. (Eds) (2004). *Exploring positive relationships at work*. Mahwah, NJ: Lawrence Erlbaum.

Elias, N. (1977). Towards a theory of social processes. *Zeitschrift für Soziologie*, *6*, 127–149.

Festinger, L. (1954). A theory of social comparison processes. *Human Relations 7*, 117–140.

Fletcher, G. J. O. & Simpson, J. A. (2000). Ideal standards in close relationships: their structure and functions. *Current Directions in Psychological Science*, *9*, 102–105.

Freedman, J. (1978). *Happy people*. New York: Harcourt Brace Jovanovich.

Fritz Harden, J. & Omdahl, B. (Eds) (2006). *Problematic relationships in the workplace*. New York: Peter Lang Publications.

Hargie, O. & Tourish, D. (1996). Auditing communication practices to improve the management of human resources: an inter-organizational study. *Health Services Management Research*, *9*, 209–222.

Hargie, C. & Tourish, D. (1997). Relational communication. In O. Hargie, (Ed.), *The handbook of communication skills*, 2nd edn. London: Routledge.

Hazan, C. & Shaver, P. (1987). Romantic love conceptualized as an attachment process. *Journal of Personality and Social Psychology*, *52*, 511–524.

Heller, K. & Rook, K. S. (2001). Distinguishing the theoretical functions of social ties: implications of support interventions. In B. R. Sarason & S. W. Duck (Eds), *Personal relationships: implications for clinical and community psychology*. Chichester: Wiley.

Hendrick, C. & Hendrick, S. S. (Eds) (2001). *Close relationships: a sourcebook*. Thousand Oaks, CA: Sage.

Herzberg, F. (1966). *Work and the nature of man*. Cleveland, OH: World Publishing.

Hinde, R. A. (1981). The bases of a science of interpersonal relationships. In S. W. Duck & R. Gilmour (Eds), *Personal relationships 1: studying personal relationships*. London: Academic Press.

Hobfoll, S. E. (1996). Social support: will you be there when I need you? In N. Vanzetti & S. W. Duck (Eds), *A lifetime of relationships*. Monterey, CA.: Brooks/Cole.

Hobfoll, S. E., Shoham, S. B. & Ritter, C. (1991). Women's satisfaction with social support and their receipt of aid. *Journal of Personality and Social Psychology*, *61*, 332–341.

Holmberg, D. & MacKenzie, J. (2002). So far, so good: scripts for romantic relationship development as predictors of relational well-being. *Journal of Social and Personal Relationships*, *19*, 777–797.

Kaniasty, K. & Norris, F. H. (2001). Social support dynamics in adjustment to disasters. In B. Sarason & S. W. Duck (Eds), *Clinical psychology and personal relationships*. Chichester: Wiley.

Keeley, M. & Hart, A. (1994). Nonverbal behavior in dyadic interaction. In S. W. Duck (Ed.), *Dynamics of relationships*. Understanding relationships vol. 4. Thousand Oaks, CA: Sage.

Kelley, H. H., Berscheid, E., Christensen, A., Harvey, J., Huston, T. L., Levinger, G. et al. (1983). *Close relationships*. San Francisco, CA: Freeman.

Kenny, D. A. & Acitelli, L. K. (1994). Measuring similarity in couples. *Journal of Family Psychology*, **8**, 417–431.

Kirkpatrick, D. C., Duck, S. & Foley, M. K. (Eds) (2006). *Relating difficulty: the processes of constructing and managing difficult interaction*. Mahwah, NJ: Lawrence Erlbaum Associates.

Levinger, G. (1964). Note on need complementarity in marriage. *Psychological Bulletin*, **51**, 153–157.

Lovaglia, M. J. & Lucas, J. W. (2006). Leadership as the management of power in organizations. In D. C. Kirkpatrick, S. Duck & M. K. Foley (Eds), *Relating difficulty: the processes of constructing and managing difficult interactions*. Mahwah, NJ: Lawrence Erlbaum Associates.

Lyons, R. F., Sullivan, M. J. L. & Ritvo, P. G. (1996). *Relationships in chronic illness and disability*. Thousand Oaks, CA: Sage.

Mallinckrodt, B. (2001). Interpersonal processes, attachment and the development of social competencies in individual and group psychotherapy. In B. R. Sarason & S. W. Duck (Eds), *Personal relationships: implications for clinical and community psychology*. Chichester: Wiley.

Mead, G. H. (1934). *Mind, self, and society*. Chicago: Chicago University Press.

Mikulincer, M., Florian, V. & Hirschberger, G. (2003). The existential functions of close relationships: introducing death into the science of love. *Personality and Social Psychology Review*, **1**, 20–40.

Montgomery, B. M. (1988). Quality communication in personal relationships. In S. W. Duck (Ed.), *Handbook of personal relationships*. Chichester: Wiley.

Oswald, R. F. (2000). A member of the wedding? Heterosexism and family ritual. *Journal of Social and Personal Relationships*, **17**, 349–368.

Perlman, D. & Duck, S. W. (2005). The seven seas: from 'the thousand islands' to interconnected waterways. In A. Vangelisti & D. Perlman (Eds), *Handbook on personal relationships*. Cambridge: Cambridge University Press.

Rohlfing, M. (1995). 'Doesn't anybody stay in one place any more?' An exploration of the understudied phenomenon of long-distance relationships. In J. T. Wood & S. W. Duck (Eds), *Under-studied relationships: off the beaten track* Understanding relationship processes, vol. 6. Newbury Park, CA: Sage.

Rollie, S. S. & Duck, S. W. (2006). Stage theories of marital breakdown. In J. H. Harvey & M. A. Fine (Eds), *Handbook of divorce and relationship dissolution* (pp. 176–193). Mahwah, NJ: Lawrence Erlbaum Associates.

Sahlstein, E. M. (2006). The trouble with distance. In D. C. Kirkpatrick, S. Duck & M. K. Foley (Eds), *Relating difficulty: the processes of constructing and managing difficult interaction*. Mahwah, NJ: Lawrence Erlbaum Associates.

Sarason, B. R. & Duck, S. W. (Eds) (2001). *Personal relationships: implications for clinical and community psychology*. Chichester: Wiley.

Sarason, B. R., Sarason, I. G. & Gurung, R. A. R. (1997). Close personal relationships and health outcomes: a key to the role of social support. In S. W. Duck (Ed.), *Handbook of personal relationships*, 2nd edn. Chichester: Wiley.

Saussure, F. (1910/1993). *Saussure's third course of lectures on general linguistics (1910–1911)*. London: Pergamon.

Sias, P. M., Heath, R. G., Perry, T., Silva, D. & Fix, B. (2004). Narratives of workplace friendship deterioration. *Journal of Social and Personal Relationships*, **21**, 321–340.

Sigman, S. J. (1991). Handling the discontinuous aspects of continuous social relationships: toward research on the persistence of social forms. *Communication Theory*, **1**, 106–127.

Simmel, G. (1950). *The sociology of Georg Simmel*. New York: Free Press.

Spitzberg, B. H. (1993). The dialectics of (in)competence. *Journal of Social and Personal Relationships*, **10**, 137–158.

Spitzberg, B. H. & Cupach, W. R. (1985). *Interpersonal communication competence*. Newbury Park, CA: Sage.

Spitzberg, B. H. & W. R. Cupach (Eds) (1998). *The dark side of close relationships*. New York: Lawrence Erlbaum.

Sprecher, S., Christopher, F. S. & Cate, R. (2005). Sexuality in close relationships. In A. Vangelisti & D. Perlman (Eds), *Handbook on personal relationships*. Cambridge: Cambridge University Press.

Surra, C. A. & Bohman, T. (1993). The development of close relationships: a cognitive perspective. In W. H. Jones & D. Perlman (Eds), *Advances in personal relationships*. London: Jessica Kingsley.

Tharp, R. G. (1963). Psychological patterning in marriage. *Psychological Bulletin*, **60**, 97–117.

Thibaut, J. W. & Kelley, H. H. (1959). *The social psychology of groups*. New York: Wiley.

Turner, V. (1982). *From ritual to theatre: the human seriousness of play*. New York: PAJ Publications.

Volosinov, V. N. (1929/1986). *Marxism and the philosophy of language* (L. Matejks & I. R. Titunik, Trans.). Cambridge Philosophy of Language. Cambridge, MA: Harvard University Press.

Weiss, R. S. (1974). The provisions of social relationships. In Z. Rubin (Ed.), *Doing unto others* (pp. 17–26). Englewood Cliffs, NJ: Prentice-Hall.

Wood, J. T. (2001). The normalization of violence in heterosexual romantic relationships: women's narratives of love and violence. *Journal of Social and Personal Relationships*, **18**, 239–262.

Wood, J. T. & Duck, S. W. (Eds) (2005). *Composing relationships: communication in everyday life*. Belmont, CA: Wadsworth.

Wright, P. H. (1985). Self referent motivation and the intrinsic quality of friendship. *Journal of Social and Personal Relationships*, **1**, 114–130.

Zorn, T. (1995). Bosses and buddies: constructing and performing simultaneously hierarchical and close friendship relationships. In J. T. Wood & S. W. Duck (Eds), *Under-studied relationships: off the beaten track*. Understanding relationship processes, vol. 6. Thousand Oaks, CA: Sage.

Part IV

Interviewing contexts

Chapter 16

The employment interview

Rob Millar and Anne Tracey

DESPITE CONSIDERABLE CRITICISM OVER the past half-century, the use of the interview as a central element in the employment selection and recruitment process remains popular. Given that effective selection and recruitment are vital for the fitness and future survival of an organisation (Latham & Sue-Chan, 1998) and the common usage of the interview method, it seems imperative that effective employment interviewing develops from a base of sound understanding and competent deployment of strategies and skills.

Before embarking on our exploration, it will be helpful to set out briefly what is meant by the term 'employment interview'. McDaniel et al. (1994, p. 599) defined it as 'a selection procedure designed to predict future job performance on the basis of applicants' oral responses to oral enquiries'. In similar fashion, a slightly more comprehensive definition was provided by Wiesner and Cronshaw (1988, p. 276): 'The employment interview is an interpersonal interaction of limited duration between one or more interviewers and a job-seeker for the purpose of identifying interviewee knowledge, skills, abilities and behaviours that may be predictive of success in subsequent employment.' In addition, emphasis has been placed on the importance of the recruiting function whereby prospective applicants need to be attracted to, or persuaded to join, the organisation by providing accurate job-relevant information and by encouraging them to take up offers of employment (Rynes & Barber, 1990; Smith & Robertson, 1993; Kohn & Dipboye, 1998).

The main features of these definitions emphasise the social, inter-personal nature of the employment interview, specify the participants and the main goals and indicate the nature of the information required from interviewees. Implicit within these definitions, and a possible reason for their popularity, is the belief that employers have to meet potential employees face-to-face and that this meeting will enable them to make valid assessments of their suitability for the position (Smith & George, 1992) and the organisation, in what is now becoming known as person–organisation fit (Kristoff, 1996; Cable & Judge, 1997). However, Barber et al. (1994) suggest that clarity of purpose be retained, noting that where attempts are made to meet both selection and recruitment objectives within a single interview the latter function is poorly achieved.

Employment interviewing, as a means of carrying out recruitment and selection functions, is essentially different from other main techniques primarily because of the substantial dependence on interpersonal communication skills. It follows that the employment interview, being viewed as a particular type of social interaction, may be better understood through the application of social interaction models (e.g. Millar et al., 1992) or social process models (e.g. Dipboye, 1992), or in terms of key interpersonal skills (Hargie & Dickson, 2003) relevant to the employment interview context. Of course, interpersonal skills and strategies contribute to the goal attainment of interviewers *and* applicants who are engaged in a reciprocal social relationship; hence, each perspective warrants consideration.

THE INTERVIEWER'S PERSPECTIVE

In terms of the definitions previously cited, interviewers, by way of social interaction, attempt to achieve their identified goals: that is, to make successful predictions of job/organisation suitability across a range of applicants and to ensure that sought-after applicants take up offers to join the organisation. It is incumbent upon interviewers to make considered choices pertaining to the type of interview(s) to be employed and the use of appropriate interpersonal skills, which together enhance the likelihood of the employment interview achieving its selection and/or recruitment objectives.

Analysing employment interviews as social encounters, Stevens (1998) confirmed that they can be viewed as moving through a number of sequential scenes, originally labelled by Tullar (1989) as greeting and establishing rapport, interviewer questioning, applicant questioning, and disengagement. The precise nature of the communication skills required is dictated by the type of interview format adopted, and, as a consequence, the amount of freedom and discretion afforded the interviewer varies.

Interview structure

One of the major dimensions along which interviews can be differentiated relates to their degree of structure. Millar et al. (1992, p. 111) suggested that the main structuring criteria 'relate to the degree of interviewer flexibility with respect to the content of the interview, what is included, how it is sampled, in what sequence and how much freedom is offered to interviewees with respect to their answers (i.e. open ended or multiple choice formats)'. Campion et al. (1997, p. 656) defined structure very broadly as 'any enhancement of the interview that is intended to increase psychometric properties by increasing standardization or otherwise assisting the interviewer in determining what questions to ask and how to evaluate responses'. As a consequence of their extensive literature review, Campion et al. (1997) identified 15 components of structure representative of two main categories: the actual content of the interview and evaluation of the content. In a relatively sophisticated approach, each component can reflect a degree of structure, which ranges from highly structured to completely unstructured, and for any individual interview the permutations are considerable. Nevertheless, adopting a categorical approach may serve to structure a discussion of types of employment interview.

Unstructured interviews as a selection tool

The unstructured interview format has been reported as a very popular approach for personnel selection (Terpstra & Rozell, 1997; Van Der Zee et al., 2002). The unstructured interview tends to devolve considerable power and freedom to interviewers to make important procedural decisions concerning the conduct of the interview itself and subsequent evaluations of information communicated.

One of the more central aspects of interview conduct concerns the role of interviewer-led questions (Stevens, 1998). According to Campion et al. (1997), the derivation of questions employed in typical unstructured interviews is likely to be focused on personality traits or self-descriptions, traditional open-ended questions inviting candidates to talk about themselves and their strengths and weaknesses or indeed about anything the interviewer deems relevant, based on intuition or 'gut feelings' (Harris & Eder, 1999, p. 390). Van Der Zee et al. (2002) found that 34.5% of interviewers said they were free to ask anything they wanted to, and a further 49% selected questions flexibly from a prepared list of topics.

Unstructured interviews specify no standardisation of questioning sequence but rather delegate such control to the interviewer's discretion. It is usual for interviewers to be given complete freedom to decide whether follow-up, probing, or elaboration-type questions are required or not (Campion et al., 1997). Stevens (1998) reported that 55% of interviewers' questions were categorised as 'secondary follow-up probes', and Van Der Zee et al. (2002) found that non-standardised follow-up questioning was employed by 78.2% of interviewers. Given that follow-ups are intended to clarify initial responses by candidates to interviewer questions (Hargie & Dickson, 2003), their use in the employment interview may serve a very important function in removing confusion and developing greater understanding. To this end, the employment of so-called neutral probes and elaborations, such as 'Go on', 'Could you say a bit more about that?', or 'Could you give me an example of . . . ?' (Campion et al., 1997), may reduce information deficiencies yet not introduce irrelevant material.

As indicated earlier, interviewers working within an unstructured format are free to ask whatever questions they *think* are relevant to the purpose of the interview. Often questions are focused on seeking opinions, attitudes, goals, aspirations, self-descriptions, and self-evaluations. In general, such questions tend to be somewhat ambiguous and not always clearly related to purpose, although they are commonly employed (Stevens, 1998). However, they do afford candidates ample opportunity to express themselves, present their credentials, and argue their case to the full, by what Kohn and Dipboye (1998) call giving candidates 'voice'.

Turning to the process of evaluating the responses elicited, unstructured interviews typically conclude with overall or global impressions being recorded. Van Der Zee et al. (2002) reported that 89% of their interviewers did not utilise any rating scales for evaluating responses, and an overall global rating approach was adopted by 64%. According to Ganzach et al. (2000), such a procedure is less accurate than employing rating scales and some form of structured combination.

When considering the effectiveness of unstructured interviews in the selection process, the literature reports inferior validity to more highly structured formats (Conway et al., 1995; Pulakos & Schmitt, 1995; Cortina et al., 2000; Judge et al., 2000; Huffcutt et al., 2001). There are a number of reasons for the poorer psychometric properties of unstructured interview formats as a means of selecting job applicants. The inconsistent use and variable sequencing of primary questions and follow-ups about topics, which may not be job-relevant, conspire to reduce both reliability and validity of the procedure. Assessments made by unstructured techniques are more likely to focus on general mental ability, background credentials (educational and work histories), personality traits (such as agreeableness), social and communication skills, and physical attributes, some of which are poor predictors of job performance (Huffcutt et al., 2001; Posthuma et al., 2002). However, interviewers using low structure formats do make trait assessments (for example, conscientiousness and emotional stability), and these subjective assessments are related to their evaluations of applicant suitability (Van Dam, 2003). Interviewers need to be acutely aware of the immense difficulties in making accurate assessments of candidate personality, and of the pitfalls in making subsequent inferences from trait judgements to job performance (Barrick et al., 2000; Van Dam, 2003). Moreover, interviewers may reach different conclusions based on similar applicant responses by applying varying judgement standards or by viewing the salience of specific traits differentially (Latham et al., 1980; Pulakos et al., 1996; Van Dam, 2003). It is by no means clear whether job-related personality traits can be accurately assessed by unstructured interview formats, a fact which in turn reduces the predictive validity of this type of interview as a means of making selection decisions (Barrick et al., 2000).

Taking a slightly different approach to personality assessment, Blackman and Funder (2002) have focused attention away from the assessment of personality traits regarded as predictive of effective job performance and onto those traits that they termed 'counterproductive'. Rather than focusing on those attributes of knowledge and skills that are very specific to a particular job, attention is turned to a range of behaviours and attitudes that are largely unwanted in potential employees irrespective of the job in question. For example, most employers would prefer their employees to be careful rather than careless in their work, and not to engage in theft, harassment, and even violence in the workplace. Early results from Blackman and Funder (2002) suggest that estimates of such unwanted traits and behaviours are better accomplished in unstructured interviews where the context facilitates a greater expression of quality information by the candidate.

A major consequence of using unstructured interview formats, which also may help to explain their poor psychometric properties, is the increased likelihood of introducing errors or what Campion et al. (1997) describe as 'contamination'. Stevens (1981) identified six main types of selection error that serve to contaminate the content of information elicited in interviews and the evaluations made of it by interviewers.

1   *halo effect*, whereby interviewers tend to rate applicants highly on every dimension because they scored highly on one
2   *central tendency*, whereby interviewers rate all applicants as average and fail to use the whole of the scale
3   *leniency*, whereby interviewers rate all applicants favourably, again failing to discriminate effectively
4   *strictness*, whereby interviewers rate all applicants unfavourably
5   *contrast effect*, whereby the rating of applicants is influenced by how they compare to a previous applicant
6   *stereotyping*, whereby interviewers rely on initial impressions or schemas, set about confirming these impressions, and subsequently rate on this basis.

Unstructured interviews as recruitment tools

According to Posthuma et al. (2002), there is growing acknowledgement that the interview serves a recruitment as well as a selection function. The evidence to date suggests that interviews with less structure seem to be more suited to achieving the recruitment function (Kohn & Dipboye, 1998; Chapman & Rowe, 2001, 2002). When unstructured interview formats are employed, applicants tend to rate the organisation and the interviewer more positively and indicate a greater willingness to accept any job offers that may ensue. It is possible that the more free-flowing conversational nature of unstructured interview formats creates a reaction in applicants that provides them with a greater sense of having had a chance to 'sell' themselves, of having been listened to, and determines a more positive reaction to the experience (Kohn & Dipboye, 1998). Favourable impressions may have important outcomes such as enhancing the organisation's reputation, attracting more future applicants, and reducing the likelihood of lawsuits (Powell, 1991, 1996; Smither et al., 1993; Goltz & Giannantonio, 1995; Posthuma et al., 2002). Therefore, in considering the psychometric qualities of interviews in the employment context, it seems crucial to do so with clarity of purpose to the fore.

Investigations into the social processes involved in employment interviews have revealed a range of psychometric weakness related to poor reliability and low content and predictive validity, especially with respect to the selection function. As a result of these findings, research has focused on reducing the 'human' errors by developing alternative approaches to the unstructured interview. The direction of these developments has witnessed the introduction of increasing amounts of structure, and to varying degrees, the reduction of human discretion in the process.

Structured interviews as selection tools

The development of the structured selection interview emanated from attempts to design an interview in such a way as to reduce the possible influence of individual biases and errors on interviewer decisions. All major reviews have reported significant increases in both the reliability and validity of more highly structured approaches (Wiesner & Cronshaw, 1988; Wright et al., 1989; Motowidlo et al., 1992;

Campion et al., 1994; Conway et al., 1995; Pulakos & Schmitt, 1995; Latham & Sue-Chan, 1999; Judge et al., 2000; Huffcutt et al., 2001).

As stated earlier, structuring may take many forms. A number are specifically related to the question content of the interview. It is commonly agreed that all questions should be derived from a current job analysis, making all questions highly job-related (Campion et al., 1994; Pulakos & Schmitt, 1995). Gollub-Williamson et al. (1997, p. 901) purport that this leads to 'increased content validity and reduces reliance on idiosyncratic beliefs about job requirements and reduces the likelihood of bias'. Furthermore, all job-related questions should be presented in a completely standardised manner and asked of all candidates in the same wording and invariant sequence. Campion et al. (1997) suggest that adopting standardised procedures serves to increase interview reliability (both internal consistency and interrater) and might ease the comparison between candidates and therefore improve validity. The reliance on highly job-related questions may further reduce the intrusion of irrelevant information and minimise the likelihood of interviewer biases adversely influencing selection decisions (Campion et al., 1997).

In the highly structured format, interviewers are prohibited from engaging in any prompting, probing, or elaboration questioning, but are simply required to present the primary questions and may, if necessary, only repeat the question for the candidate. However, Van Der Zee et al. (2002) found only a minority of their interviewers (20%) engaged in no follow-up questioning, and the majority (78%) largely omitted standardisation of follow-up questioning. With structured interviews, it is possible to relax the degree of control and to permit a limited but agreed number of preplanned follow-ups worded in the same manner; for example, 'Is there anything else you would like to tell us?'

Considerable effort has been expended on developing particular types of questions for use in the highly structured selection interview context. As a result, two main types of questions have been developed, those that focus on past experience and those that orient the candidate toward the future. Each is hypothesised to possess predictive qualities, as the former is based on the assumption that past behaviour is the best predictor of future behaviour, and the latter is based on the assumption that goals or intentions are the best predictor of future behaviour (Campion et al., 1994). The two main question types have been characteristic of two related, structured-interviewing approaches, namely, the future-based 'situational interview' (Latham et al., 1980; Latham, 1989) and the past-based 'patterned behaviour description interview' (Janz, 1989). However, both approaches base the interview on a series of questions derived from job analyses and therefore the level of job-relatedness of the question content is high, possibly contributing to enhanced face, content, and predictive validity, and perceptions of fairness (Day & Carroll, 2003). In essence, the two approaches ask candidates to state either what they did do or what they would do when presented with predetermined work scenarios. Van Der Zee et al. (2002) found that interviewers reported employing hypothetical type questions least often, closely followed by past behaviour-oriented questions. Both types were included much less frequently than questions that focused on motivation, goals, ambitions, and previous work experience.

It may be useful to be selective in terms of choosing which approach to adopt, partly on the basis of the type of applicant being considered. If an applicant has little or no past work experience to draw upon, it might be more appropriate to use the situational interview approach, whereas, in the converse situation, the interviews that use reflection back to previous work experience and speculation forward to hypothetical scenarios are both possible (Campion et al., 1997; Gilliland & Steiner, 1999).

Within the highly structured approach, interviewers are required to employ highly structured rating procedures, facilitated by the use of specially designed rating scales provided for each interview question (Campion et al., 1994). Gollub-Williamson et al. (1997) include the provision of objective, specific evaluation criteria as one of their structuring enhancements, and this is a feature of well-constructed situational interviews, although not always present (Latham & Sue-Chan, 1999). The rating scales constructed to 'score' the applicants' responses should be anchored scales with the anchor points identified through discussion with personnel and job experts. Completing specific rating scales for each question may serve to reduce the cognitive overload demanded of interviewers. The gains for reliability by using multiple ratings are strongly endorsed by Conway et al. (1995).

The evidence to date provides strong support for the validity of both types of structured interview in the selection process (Wiesner & Cronshaw, 1988; Wright et al., 1989; Campion et al., 1994; McDaniel et al. 1994; Latham & Skarlicki, 1995; Pulakos & Schmitt, 1995; Huffcutt et al., 1996; Latham & Sue-Chan, 1999; Day & Carroll, 2003). Much of the research fails to find any significant differences between the approaches in terms of predictive validity, although Latham and Sue-Chan (1999) argue that if the question types for the situational interview are properly constructed (that is, contain within them a work-related dilemma) and rating scales are utilised for evaluation, this approach demonstrates superior psychometric properties. Structured approaches were developed primarily to reduce subjectivity and inconsistency, to increase reliability and validity, and to guard against infringing legal guidelines pertaining to fair employment practice and reduce the likelihood of litigation (Gollub-Williamson et al., 1997).

Structured interviews as recruiting tools

Although, as indicated above, structured approaches have demonstrated superior levels of reliability and validity with respect to selection decisions, there are some disadvantages associated with their use. As Goodale (1989, p. 320) observed, 'Highly structured interviews can appear to the applicant a bit like an interrogation, and may place too much emphasis on the *selection* objective at the expense of the *attraction* objective.' There is a growing body of evidence to suggest that highly structured approaches tend to decrease the attractiveness of organisations for candidates (Kohn & Dipboye, 1998; Chapman & Rowe, 2001, 2002). According to Kohn and Dipboye (1998, p. 838), candidates may 'perceive an interview that is job-relevant and highly standardized as overly narrow' and incapable of enabling them to reveal their unique characteristics or to present fully their case for employment.

The belief that using highly structured interview formats may harm an organisation's ability to recruit has been one of the reasons offered by personnel for resisting their inclusion (Van Der Zee et al., 2002). Given the prevalent preference for recruiters to base applicant evaluation on 'intuition', 'feelings', 'experience', or 'body language' (Taylor et al., 1993), and to retain freedom and control over important decision-making and communication processes, the use of structured interviews may also create difficulties for these types of interviewers. They may not, according to Daniel and Valencia (1991, p. 131), wish to be viewed as 'a robot, an impersonal unfeeling scientific instrument', but prefer to be viewed as warm, attentive, likeable, and socially perceptive (Kohn & Dipboye, 1998).

Employment interviews as selection and recruitment tools

The extent to which employment interviews are able to meet both selection and recruitment functions seems more complex and somewhat conflicting. The drive toward greater psychometric qualities through higher levels of structuring serves the selection function admirably but may influence the recruitment function in a quite contrary manner. However, there have been some suggestions that highly structured interviews do not assess all pertinent constructs in the selection process. For example, estimates of counter-productive work-relevant traits seem better achieved by adopting less structured interview formats (Blackman & Funder, 2002). Similarly, accurate assessment of person–environment fit constructs has been viewed as more likely if less structured interview formats are used (Cable & Judge, 1997; Judge et al., 2000).

The selection versus recruitment dilemma has been widely studied (e.g. Kohn & Dipboye, 1998; Gilliland & Steiner, 1999; Chapman & Rowe, 2001; Posthuma et al., 2002). What seems to be the case is that choosing to adopt either a highly structured or an unstructured interview format will fail to meet some of the objectives of employment interviewing. In order to offer the best compromise, where predictive validity for selection can be adequate and applicant reactions mainly positive, greater flexibility of approach is necessary. As Kohn and Dipboye (1998, p. 839) observe, 'Some balance is needed between concerns about the psychometric integrity of interviewer assessments and providing applicants the opportunity to present fully their qualifications.' In general, there are two major possibilities.

The first is to modify the degree of structure within a single interview. Here the rigid standardisation of administration is reduced, thereby allowing candidates more opportunity to 'sell themselves'. This includes encouraging interviewees to ask more questions (Kohn & Dipboye, 1998; Gilliland & Steiner, 1999), by, for example, incorporating a less formal and more interpersonal discussion stage at the end of the interview (Chapman & Rowe, 2001). Campion et al. (1997, p. 670) suggest, 'In practice, it is not likely that the sole use of just one question type is desirable. As long as different types have adequate validity, a range of questions offer variety for both the candidate and interviewer.' These modifications may soften the impression of rigid structuring, increase perceptions of fairness, and reduce negative candidate (and interviewer) reactions (Kohn & Dipboye, 1998; Gilliland & Steiner, 1999; Posthuma et al., 2002).

The second major alternative is to carry out more than one interview, each with its own specific purpose. Even with selection in mind, there may be a case for at least two interviews, each carried out for different purposes (Kohn & Dipboye, 1998; Chapman & Rowe, 2001; Blackman & Funder, 2002). For example, Blackman and

Funder (2002) suggest that employers should initially screen applicants by a more structured interview format to predict future job performance and, for those who are successful at this stage, to add a second unstructured interview to estimate their job-related personality attributes, including counter-productive traits.

There have also been suggestions to separate the selection and recruitment functions and offer two employment interviews, each adopting differing levels of interview structure (Kohn & Dipboye, 1998; Chapman & Rowe, 2001). Kohn and Dipboye (1998, p. 839) suggest using two interviews, 'one designed strictly for prediction and the other designed to allow an informal question-and-answer session to meet the needs of applicants'.

Whatever type of interview format has been utilised, it is always important to consider the disengagement scene (Stevens, 1998) or closure of the interview. The nature of selection interviews, where decisions have not yet been formally taken about the suitability of the candidate for the job, requires a cautious closure. It would seem important that this phase of the interview should acknowledge the effort invested and participation by the interviewee in the interview, yet this must be achieved in a 'neutral' way so as not to raise expectations (Dipboye, 1992). Conventional practice typically allows applicants the opportunity to ask questions at this stage, although highly structured approaches recommend that this be carried out in a separate interview with a personnel representative to ensure that only job-related information is considered for the purposes of reaching a selection decision (Campion et al., 1988). In somewhat less structured methods, applicant questions may be regarded as an important source of information and exert a positive influence on candidate impressions (Burns & Moorehead, 1991).

In summary, the role of selection interviewers requires them to assume substantial responsibility for convening and conducting the interview. Therefore, it is vital that they are knowledgeable about interview tactics and skilled in the utilisation of interpersonal communication skills. Indeed, less structured interview formats often consist of what Kohn and Dipboye (1998, p. 821) call 'free-flowing exchanges between the interviewer and applicant'. Effective interviewers need to focus attention on both the technical qualities of their procedures and on the social context in which candidate recruitment and selection takes place. The extent to which objectives are attained is not simply a function of interviewer competence but is also influenced by the effectiveness of applicants in playing their role. It is to this aspect that we now turn.

THE APPLICANT'S PERSPECTIVE

Given that the employment interview remains the most widely used recruitment tool (Silvester & Chapman, 1996; Howard & Ferris, 1996), it is, for applicants, an inescapable part of the route to future employment. As a result of the information gained during personal interaction with each applicant, interviewers make decisions about the person best suited to the available post (Shannon & Stark, 2003). It has been shown that what applicants do and say in an interview has an impact on interviewer's ratings (Stevens & Kristof, 1995; Young & Kacmar, 1998). Therefore, it is understandable that individuals will want to use the opportunity and the time allotted to them in the interview to create as positive an impression as possible. Here, the applicant's role in impression management is reviewed.

Impression management in the employment interview

Impression management has been defined as 'the conscious or unconscious attempt to construct and portray a particular image by controlling the information available to others (i.e. targets) so that they will view the actor as he or she intended' (Kacmar & Carlson, 1994, p. 688). According to Ralston and Kirkwood (1999, p. 191), 'Whenever we attempt to influence how others see us, we are engaging in impression management.' Nowhere are self-presentation or impression-management strategies more prevalent than in the employment interview (Ellis et al., 2002).

Impression-management strategies

Many factors contribute to candidates' attempts to shape and control the image they project in the interview context. Both verbal and non-verbal impression-management tactics can be crucial to success or failure in the employment interview. Impression management may indeed be a necessary part of employment interviews; if applicants are to ensure that their subjective qualifications are perceived positively, 'impression management techniques play an even greater role in the interview process than previously suspected' (Wade & Kinicki, 1997, p. 37).

In general, there appear to be two main categories of self-presentation behaviour, namely, assertive and defensive (Kacmar et al., 1992). The terms 'offensive' and 'defensive' were adopted by Liden and Parsons (1986) to reflect a similar dichotomy. Assertive tactics can be either self-focused, whereby attention is focused on the interviewee, or other-focused, whereby attention is focused on the interviewer (Kacmar & Carlson, 1999).

In terms of assertive, self-focused tactics, those who wish to embellish their qualifications and minimise their weaknesses will use:

- *self-promotion*: engaging in positive self-descriptions about skills, knowledge, and abilities
- *entitlements*: exaggerating responsibility for positive life experiences and achievements
- *enhancements*: giving an event pronounced value or significance to enhance its importance (Delery & Kacmar, 1998).

Other-focused assertive strategies described by Ellis et al. (2002) include ingratiation tactics utilised by applicants when they wish to cultivate interpersonal liking and attraction between themselves and the interviewer. These include *opinion conformity* (expressing opinions, beliefs, or values that are thought to match those of the interviewer) and *other enhancement* (praising or flattering the interviewer in order to raise their self-esteem). Referring to defensive tactics, Ellis et al. (2002) outlined three that are designed to save face or bolster an individual's image. That is, when they find their image under threat from the interviewer, interviewees will offer *excuses* (claim no responsibility for a negative outcome), *justifications* (accept responsibility but diminish the negative aspects), or *apologies* (accept responsibility and acknowledge the need for restitution).

According to Millar and Gallagher (1997), the advantage in adopting self-focused tactics is that 'applicants can focus the direction of their interviews' content on areas which will allow them to excel, hence creating as positive an impression as possible' (p. 399). Perhaps this explains Stevens and Kristof's (1995) finding that applicants use positive self-focused tactics (self-promotion) more frequently than other impression-management tactics, and supports the assertion by Gilmore and Ferris (1989) and Kacmar et al. (1992) that self-promotion produces positive outcomes in the interview situation. For example, Kristof-Brown et al. (2002) found that self-promoting behaviours led interviewers to see applicants as a good fit and potentially more hireable. Given that interviewers attempt to assess the degree of fit between the applicant and the organisation (Wade & Kinicki, 1997), applicants who cultivate the perception that there is congruence between their values and that of the organisation are more likely to receive job offers (Cable & Judge, 1997).

The impression-management tactics selected by applicants in the interview situation are influenced by a range of personal determinants, such as personality traits (Kristof-Brown et al., 2002), verbal aggressiveness (Lamunde et al., 2003), self-esteem (Delery & Kacmar, 1998), gender (DuBrin, 1994; Kacmar & Carlson, 1994), and cultural background (Sarangi, 1994). For example, while extroverted and agreeable candidates will engage in strategies of self-promotion and positive non-verbal cues (Kristof-Brown et al., 2002), verbally aggressive candidates utilise self-enhancement or entitlement tactics (Lamunde et al., 2003). Entitlements, however, are less likely to be utilised by candidates with higher self-esteem (Delery & Kacmar, 1998).

In addition, Ellis et al. (2002) show that the type of question posed by the interviewer influences the type of impression-management tactic selected. For example, the use of self-promotion is more likely in response to experience-based questions (e.g. 'Tell us about a time . . .') than situational-based questions (e.g. 'Suppose you were . . . How would you address this situation?'). In this case, situational-based questions incurred more ingratiation tactics, particularly opinion conformity (Ellis et al., 2002).

Candidates should be aware that the overuse of self-promotion tactics can backfire. The evidence indicates that interviewers may regard those who over-indulge in such tactics as disingenuous (Eder & Harris, 1999; Gilmore, Stevens, Harrell-Cook & Ferris, 1999). In particular, Kacmar and Carlson (1999) warn applicants against the use of other-focused impression-management tactics, because such tactics receive lower ratings than self-focused tactics in the interview situation. Highlighting the importance of what is said in the interview, Silvester (1997) found that successful candidates were those who made stable and personal attributions for previous negative events, whereas less successful candidates used defensive tactics in the same situation.

The impact of impression management on fairness in the employment interview

Consideration needs to be given to whether successful execution of impression-management tactics could lead to unfairness in employment interview outcomes. Commenting on the harmful consequences of impression management, Ralston and Kirkwood (1999) argued that deceitful or inaccurate information that is intended to mislead interviewers can undermine the value of the interview. On one hand, self-promoting behaviours could be regarded as harmless and positive when they represent a true picture of the applicant's nature and character. At the other end of the continuum, attempts to create an impression through deceit will have negative consequences. For example, feigning motivation, other-directedness, or interpersonal attraction, unless spotted by the interviewer, will lead to error in the selection process (Ralston & Kirkwood, 1999). While they may not be setting out to deceive, by engaging in these tactics, applicants portray the appropriate image for the post, and if they are appointed on the basis of their performance, the behaviour may lead to an error in interviewer judgement (Anderson, 1991). In order to increase fairness in employment interviews, Rosenfeld (1997, p. 804) suggested that impression-management tactics that are 'deceptive, manipulative and insincere' need to be 'detected, minimized and discounted'. The paradox is that, while image building is an inherent part of the interview process and is to some extent a requirement for success, it is necessary for interviewers to be sensitive to self-presentation tactics if they are to make sound judgements about candidates who attend for interview.

MEDIATORS AND INFLUENCES ON THE EMPLOYMENT INTERVIEW AND EMPLOYMENT DECISIONS

The employment interview as a method of selection and recruitment provides applicants with the opportunity to interact personally with a potential employer and, based on their experience of the interview, make decisions about the company. However, many factors affect this experience and can have an influence on the process and outcome for the interviewee. These include personal characteristics such as personality (e.g. Cook et al., 2000), physical appearance (e.g. Polinko & Popovich, 2001; Seiter & Sandry, 2003), and speech style (e.g. Ayres et al., 1998; Cargile, 1997, 2000; Parton et al., 2002). The impact of each of these factors on applicants' experiences in employment interviews is now considered.

Personal characteristics

Before candidates present themselves for interview, recruiters already have established a 'picture' of the individual from the information available to them, usually by way of the application form and/or curriculum vitae. The interview itself is the opportunity for candidates to present themselves in person to the recruiter. Many personal factors of the candidate are then 'visible' and under the scrutiny of the interviewer. It is these factors and their influence on the employment interview that we now turn to, including personality, physical appearance, speech style and confident communication.

Personality

Turning first to the influence of personality, Cook et al. (2000, p. 880) stated that the 'personality characteristics of the interviewee play an important role in the evaluation of the interviewee's performance and the outcomes of the interview'. For example, personality characteristics such as type A/achievement, extroversion, and internal locus of control are associated with positive interview performance and outcome (Cook et al., 2000). Likewise, Anderson et al. (1999) found that interviewer ratings of candidate personality in graduate recruitment interviews have an influence on outcome decisions. Examining the relationship between personality and success in interviewing, Caldwell and Burger (1998) utilised the 'Big Five' personality markers (neuroticism, extroversion, openness, agreeableness, and conscientiousness) and found a link between personality and the likelihood of being employed. Firstly, inferences are drawn about an applicant's personality from how they behave in the interview. Secondly, research supports the notion that the personality of candidates influences how they prepare for an interview, and 'this preparation was related to interview success' (Caldwell & Burger, 1998, p. 131).

Applicants perform better when interviewers exhibit a 'warm personality' (Liden et al., 1993). That is, as a consequence of positive non-verbal interviewer behaviour (head nods, smiling), applicants make a better impression and receive higher ratings. Similarly, the findings of Papadopoulou et al. (1996) indicated that applicants perceived interviewers who were willing to provide information as 'warm and thoughtful'. In turn, it was the provision of information about the job and the company that influenced applicants' decisions to take up a job offer.

Physical appearance

Physical appearance has an impact on hiring decisions (Seiter & Sandry, 2003; Shannon & Stark, 2003), in that recruiters make decisions about candidates based on appearance. In this respect, two aspects, body decoration and obesity factors, seem to be important.

Attempts to portray a particular image can have negative consequences for the individual. Shepperd and Kwavnick (1999) pointed out that body piercing (and tattoos) may be viewed as symbols of rebellion or recklessness. Even the most trivial of cues (a small piece of jewellery, such as an earring) or body piercing (especially noserings) may disadvantage candidates through their being rated as less sociable, trustworthy, and hireable (Seiter & Sandry, 2003). Furthermore, perceptions of men with jewellery may be more negative than those of women (Workman & Johnson, 1994).

It seems that how an applicant's image is regarded and evaluated depends on the attitude of the recruiter. Referring to non-work-related factors (e.g. personal appearance) that are evaluated in the interview, Shannon and Stark (2003, p. 614) stated: 'If the interviewer has any previously acquired dispositions to evaluate certain characteristics with a positive or negative bias, these acquired dispositions, or attitudes, could influence the interviewer's overall evaluation of the applicant.' Perhaps the increasing popularity of piercings will lead to more acceptability in the workplace, and applicants choosing certain image markers will be less disadvantaged since, as expressed by Gorham et al. (1999, p. 282): 'Fashion changes over time as do attire rules and expectations.' It could be argued that employers who do not revise their policies on personal image and dress codes may risk losing potentially excellent employees. Meanwhile, the indications are that candidates in the process of seeking employment should be aware of the expectations of recruiters in terms of dress code and appearance in order to avoid the negative consequences of lower ratings in the interview – or make choices about which firms to apply to.

The belief or perception that overweight or obese people are responsible for their condition (De Jong, 1980) could help to explain why overweight applicants are often rejected for jobs. Pingitore et al. (1994) found that interview ratings for obese (versus non-obese) applicants were more likely to be unfavourable, particularly if interviewers (male or female) were conscious of their own body. Polinko and Popovich (2001, p. 906) suggested, 'Obesity discrimination may occur, first, from the lack of fit between the expectation of an overweight individual's abilities and second, the perceived reality of the job's requirements in terms of skills and abilities.' However, the findings overall indicate a positive shift in discrimination against hiring overweight applicants, despite more negative work-related attributes being attributed to them (e.g. lazy, unattractive). This may be due to a greater awareness of legislation relating to discrimination in employment interviews.

Speech style and communication apprehension (CA)

In the highly evaluative conditions of the employment interview, competence in communicating has a bearing on how applicants are perceived by the interviewer. Specifically, perceptions of communication ability are influenced by factors such as non-standard accents, and style and confidence levels of the candidate. In relation to non-standard accents, Cargile (2000, p. 172) stated: 'Language attitudes research has consistently demonstrated that individuals with non-standard accents are judged to be less suitable for high-status jobs and more suitable for low-status jobs.' Despite this expectation, Cargile (1997, 2000) found that Chinese-accented and Anglo-American speakers were rated equally suitable for a (technical) job, and the lack of discrimination was particularly evident for one high-status job in particular – information systems trainee. However, Chinese-accented speakers were judged to be less suitable for posts in human resources.

In terms of speech style, powerful versus powerless speech was examined by Parton et al. (2002). Professional (and undergraduate) respondents evaluated interviewees' dynamism, social attractiveness, superiority, control over self, control over others, and employability. Evidence suggested that those with a powerful speech style were rated more favourably (competent and employable), particularly by professionals. Parton et al. (2002, p. 154) argued that, as 'impression formation is vital to interview success', interviewees should receive training in verbal presentation including powerful speech.

Such training may also be helpful to those who have difficulty in communicating due to anxiety. In the interview situation, characteristics that are rated highly include confidence, fluency, controlled energy, and body language (Ayres et al., 1998). Applicants who are unable to demonstrate these characteristics, that is, those with high communication apprehension (CA), may be disadvantaged in the employment interview (Ayres et al., 1998). High CAs employ verbal and non-verbal avoidant behaviour (talk less, have reduced eye contact, are less fluent, and ask fewer questions) compared to low CAs; hence, they may be judged as ineffective communicators and consequently unsuitable for the job. If, as Ayres et al. (1998) found, high CAs think about and prepare differently for interviews from their low-CA counterparts, perhaps training for high CAs would help to minimise the impact of CA in critical situations such as the employment interview and help applicants to strengthen their communication skills.

THE EXPERIENCES OF SPECIFIC GROUPS IN THE EMPLOYMENT INTERVIEW

Research in employment interviews has addressed the experiences of specific groups, such as candidates with disabilities and applicants from various racial and ethnic backgrounds. Consideration of such groups is warranted here as research findings relating to interview outcomes are inconsistent.

Applicants with disabilities

Difficulties in employment interviews still persist for people with disabilities (Duckett, 2000; Bell & Klein, 2001). While some research has shown that those with a disability are viewed as less employable than those without a disability (e.g. Gouvier et al., 1991; Ravaud et al., 1992; Bricout & Bentley, 2000), others have found that disabled applicants have been rated equal or better than their non-disabled counterparts (e.g. Marchioro & Bartels, 1994; Nordstrom et al., 1998; Bell & Klein, 2001). For example, Bordieri et al. (1997) demonstrated that, regardless of being equally qualified, an employee with depression would be less likely to be recommended for promotion, while Rumrill et al. (1998) found that applicants with insulin-dependent diabetes would be rated similar to other applicants when rated by rehabilitation counsellors.

Examining the factors that led to interviewers' hiring decisions for applicants with and without disabilities, Hayes and Macan (1997) found that similar factors were used to determine outcomes with both groups (i.e. preinterview impression, attractiveness, likeability, qualifications, self-presentation, employability). In particular, employability seemed important in decision making about both sets of applicants. However, for the disabled group, preinterview impressions were significantly related to perceptions of self-presentation in the interview. That is, how disabled persons present themselves on paper and in person in the interview relates to interviewers' post-interview evaluations. For instance, Wright and Multon (1995) identified the positive influence of candidate non-verbal communication skills for ratings of traits related to employability, such as assertiveness.

The phenomenon of positive bias toward those with disabilities has been explained in a number of ways. For example, Marchioro and Bartels (1994) qualified their finding that no differences were found in attitudes to disabled or non-disabled job interviewees, in terms of social appropriateness. That is, in their desire to provide socially acceptable answers, participants may have 'overcompensated' for negative attitudes toward disabled candidates by giving higher ratings. Similarly, Bell and Klein (2001) suggested that the 'norm to be kind' theory could explain the positively biased outcome for disabled applicants. As they stated: 'This norm suggests that one should never do anything that would be unpleasant to persons with a disability' (p. 238).

That little has changed for the disabled applicant in terms of discrimination was confirmed by Duckett (2000): 'discrimination in employment interviews is very much apparent in the experiences of disabled people' (p. 1034). When he interviewed disabled applicants about their experiences of employment interviews, he found that they described the process in terms of a 'struggle' or 'battle' with the 'odds stacked against them'. Therefore, the indications are that neither the positive bias toward people with disabilities highlighted by research nor the introduction of legislation, as for example in the USA (American with Disabilities Act, 1990 [ADA]) and the UK (Disability Discrimination Act, 1995 [DDA]) to protect the rights of disabled people, has yet to affect the experiences of disabled applicants in search of a career.

In competing for jobs, candidates with disabilities may be tempted to withhold information that they perceive as potentially damaging to their chances of success in an employment interview. However, discussing disabilities during the interview could contribute to relationship building and hence lead to more positive impressions (Dipboye, 1992), and improve the likelihood of being selected for the post (Macan & Hayes, 1995). Therefore, educating an interviewer about the nature of a disability through open and honest discussion may be more beneficial than non-disclosure. In the light of this, the indications by Arvonio et al. (1997) that applicants are likely to provide information about their disability in job applications and during job interviews is a step in the right direction and may improve the selection process for both interviewers and interviewees.

Race and ethnicity

The findings of studies investigating the experiences of racial groups in employment interviews are varied. For example, in a meta-analysis of 31 studies, Huffcutt and Roth (1998) found ratings for both black and Hispanic applicants to be only marginally lower than those for white applicants. Additionally, the more highly structured the interview, the lower the group differences. Similarly, Collins and Gleaves (1998) found no differences for blacks and whites on measures of personality structure and mean scores on agreeableness and conscientiousness. While studies show a lack of racial bias in hiring decisions, prejudice against minority groups still exists (Frazer & Wiersma, 2001). In a previous study assessing promotion potential across race and gender, Landau (1995) found blacks and Asians to be rated lower than whites, and females to be rated lower than males. Hence, interviewer/interviewee racial similarity influences interview outcomes. In addition, Goldberg (2003) showed racial similarity (but not age or gender) to have a significant effect on applicants' evaluations of the recruiters.

INTERVIEWER TRAINING

Given that the recruiter plays a critical role in the process and outcomes in employment interviews, it is important that human-resource managers or those involved in selecting or promoting should be trained for the role. Interviewing is a cognitively demanding process requiring interviewers to self-regulate (monitor thoughts and actions) (Nordstrom, 1996). Therefore, it would seem likely that the more prepared interviewers are for the task, the better they will execute it. Training can have a positive effect on recruiters' perceptions of their interpersonal effectiveness (Connerley, 1997) and on analyses of their conduct (Stevens, 1998).

The power and influence of recruiter behaviour on applicants' perceptions has been demonstrated. Recruiter behaviour affects perceptions of the organisation and attractiveness of the job (Turban et al., 1998; Larsen & Phillips, 2002), and on decisions about whether to accept a job offer (Goltz & Giannantonio, 1995). However, more than any other aspect of the interview (e.g. structure or focus), recruiter behaviour influences applicants' perceptions of the employer (Turban & Dougherty, 1992; Ralston & Brady, 1994). Training could ensure that recruiters are aware of the impact of their behaviour on job applicants and perhaps help them to become more fully informed about procedures and issues pertinent to employment interviews, including impression management, discrimination, and legislation.

It has been suggested that providing interviewers with training may contribute to enhanced interview validity, because trained interviewers tend to make better use of their interview time by asking more relevant and discerning, and less irrelevant, tangential, or potentially discriminatory questions, and this in turn elicits more high-quality information upon which more sound judgements can be based (Gollub-Williamson et al., 1997; Stevens, 1998). In addition, it seems important that interviewers learn to utilise selection and recruitment procedures and methods correctly, whatever system is adopted (Huffcutt & Woehr, 1999).

Looking at impression management, Harris and Eder (1999, p. 385) suggest that 'Even intelligent, critical interviewers can be duly influenced by applicants who display impression management behaviour.' However, Howard and Ferris (1996) support the notion that training could help interviewers to distinguish between insincere and genuine applicants. Perhaps Rosenfeld's (1997) suggestion of interviewer training in 'tactical and strategic impression management' would help achieve this goal. That is, if interviewers placed more emphasis on strategic impression management (i.e. candidate's work history, abilities, and achievements that relate to characteristics such as credibility, competence, and trustworthiness) than on the instant, short-term tactics used by candidates to create a positive image (smiling, eye contact, etc.), it would help recruiters to make fairer decisions. Therefore, if the interview focused on applicants' accounts of themselves to determine their suitability for the job, interviewers' decisions would be less distorted. Additionally, it has been suggested that job-related questions and probes about past and future performance may help to create a balance and help interviewers to overcome applicants' overzealous use of impression-management tactics (Buckley & Weitzel, 1989).

Training could also address Rosenfeld's (1997) call for interviewers to re-evaluate their attitudes to impression management. Such a re-evaluation would help interviewers to see an applicant's ability to employ tactics as a skill rather than an obstacle

469

and that it might be an indication of their ability to do the job. From this perspective, an applicant's self-presentation behaviours could be a reflection of future performance in the working environment (Stevens & Kristof, 1995).

Duckett (2000) suggests that in terms of making judgements about applicants with disabilities, interviewers require training that would help to increase their knowledge of disabilities and disability legislation. Training could also help to develop positive attitudes toward applicants with disabilities and help interviewers' comfort levels with disabled people, given that perceived interviewer discomfort has been found to exacerbate anxiety and nervousness on the part of disabled people (Duckett, 2000). It is important also that training should address interviewers' 'acquired dispositions' or 'attitudes' (as highlighted by Shannon & Stark, 2003) that affect interview outcomes.

LEGAL AND ETHICAL ISSUES

Finally, comment is required on legal and ethical issues as they relate to employment interviewing.

Legal issues

Considerable and increasing focus has been placed on the extent to which recruitment and selection procedures have complied with legal requirements. Issues appear to be related to two aspects of employment interviewing. First, the extent to which candidates are treated the same as all other applicants, with no discriminatory intent or disparate treatment. Second, the extent to which applicants are regarded similarly to other comparison groups with no disparate impact (Arvey & Campion, 1982; Gollub-Williamson et al., 1997). Although specific findings are sparse, Gollub-Williamson et al. (1997) have indicated that interview procedures that display characteristics of a structured approach tend to be more related to successful court rulings in favour of employers. In keeping with procedural justice literature, those aspects of employment interviewing that increase the chances of defeating a legal challenge are principally to do with its job-relatedness, objectivity, question type and structure (preferably situational or behaviour description), rating criteria and response scales, and use of trained interviewers. Second, standardisation and consistency of the administration processes, which provides strong guidelines and minimal discretion to interviewers, is also significant in the eyes of judges (Gilliland, 1993; Gollub-Williamson et al., 1997). In conclusion, Gollub-Williamson et al. (1997, p. 908) state: 'Empirical findings together with the conceptual analysis suggest that structuring the interview might enhance the ability to withstand legal challenge.'

Ethical issues

Despite the drive to enhance validity related to the selection function and improve the chances of successful defence against litigation, the employment interview as experienced by applicants also requires attention from an ethical point of view. Issues of openness, self-disclosure, and invasion of privacy constitute important sources of ethical questions. A major function of interviewers is to collect as much relevant applicant information as possible prior to making selection decisions. However, what comprises relevant and non-discriminatory information must be carefully considered lest interviewers infringe not only the individual rights of applicants but also the law. It is here that careful structuring approaches, described earlier, may be invaluable in focusing on job-related domains and preventing interviewers from straying into highly subjective and potentially biasing areas.

However, according to Poteet (1984) and Wilson (1991), the use of illegal questioning persists and indeed may be widespread, the most common topic areas being criminal record, age, and disabilities. Less common areas are related to marital/family status, religion, sex, national origin, and race. Wilson (1991) also noted that many candidates are unaware that certain questions are illegal and generally acceded to the interviewers' requests for information. If applicants perceive such questions as relevant and receive a favourable interview outcome, the request for such information is less likely to be regarded as an invasion of privacy (Fletcher, 1992). For applicants unhappy about the use of certain illegal and potentially discriminatory questions, Wilson (1991, p. 45) set out a number of possible applicant strategies, all but one of which seeks to do 'the least damage to the interviewee's candidacy'. The choice of strategy depends on the perceived use of the information, the importance of revealing the information to the interviewer, and the desire to secure the job, and ranges from terminating the interview or directly refusing to answer, to expressing concern about the question and then responding to the question itself.

The extent to which applicants assert themselves and feel that they have provided what they regard as salient personal information may also be crucially dependent on the power relationships in the situation. Generally speaking, the distribution of power in selection interviews is not equal, the greater power residing with the interviewer. This may be particularly evident where highly structured procedures are employed, whereby applicants are required to respond to interviewer-initiated questions, to choose from interviewer-provided response alternatives, and never to put any personal questions to the interviewer. As Fletcher (1992) noted, 'Inevitably, where there is power there lies the potential for its abuse and hence for unethical behaviour that violates the rights of the individual.' Interviewers who, inadvertently or not, treat applicants in ways that would be detrimental to their performance by inducing states of discomfort, lowered self-esteem, stress, or anger are behaving unethically. This, ultimately, will prove to be counter-productive in the sense that applicants will be unable to display their potential qualities, will be unimpressed with the organisation's representative, and may be less likely to accept offers of employment.

OVERVIEW

This chapter presented research pertaining to the employment interview as a specific example of a complex social interaction governed by a number of rules and regulations to which participants are expected to conform, and which seeks to serve the dual purpose of recruitment and selection. The focus of the material initially dealt with the employment interview from the interviewer's perspective, setting out the issues relating to the various approaches found to be relevant for practice. This was followed by a similar focus on the role played by the applicant in the employment interview, particularly the influence of impression management. Finally, a brief consideration was given to additional influential factors, the issue of training, and selected legal and ethical issues as they relate to the employment interview context.

REFERENCES

Anderson, N. R. (1991). Decision making in the graduate selection interview: an experimental investigation. *Human Relations, 44*, 403–417.

Anderson, N. R., Silvester, J., Cunningham-Snell, N. & Haddleton, E. (1999). Relationships between candidate self-monitoring, perceived personality, and selection interview outcomes. *Human Relations, 52*, 1115–1131.

Arvey, R. D. & Campion, J. E. (1982). The employment interview: a summary and review of recent research. *Personnel Psychology, 35*, 281–322.

Arvonio, L., Cull, I. & Marini, I. (1997). Employment interview perceptions of persons with visible disabilities. *International Journal of Rehabilitation Research, 20*, 413–416.

Ayres, J., Keereetaweep, T., Chen, P.-E. & Edwards, P. A. (1998). Communication apprehension and employment interviews. *Communication Education, 47*, 1–17.

Barber, A. E., Hollenbeck, J. R., Tower, S. L. & Phillips, J. M. (1994). The effects of interview focus on recruitment effectiveness – a field experiment. *Journal of Applied Psychology, 79*, 886–896.

Barrick, M. R., Patton, G. K. & Haugland, S. N. (2000). Accuracy of interviewer judgements of job applicant personality traits. *Personnel Psychology, 53*, 925–951.

Bell, B. S. & Klein, K. J. (2001). Effects of disability, gender, and job level on ratings of job applicants. *Rehabilitation Psychology, 46*, 229–246.

Blackman, M. C. & Funder, D. C. (2002). Effective interview practices for accurately assessing counterproductive traits. *International Journal of Selection and Assessment, 10*, 109–116.

Bordieri, J. E. Drehmer, D. E. & Taylor, D. W. (1997). Work life for employees with disabilities: recommendations for promotion. *Rehabilitation Counselling Bulletin, 40*, 181–191.

Bricout, J. C. & Bentley, K. J. (2000). Disability status and perceptions of employability by employers. *Social Work Research, 24*, 87–95.

Buckley, M. R. & Weitzel, W. (1989). Comment on the research methodologies used in interview research. In R. W. Eder & G. R. Ferris (Eds), *The employment interview: theory, research and practice* (pp. 204–306). Newbury Park, CA: Sage.

Burns, C. L. & Moorehead, M. A. (1991). Interviews – a candidate's questions can be enlightening. *American Secondary Education, 20*, 25–27.

Cable, D. M. & Judge, T. A. (1997). Interviewers' perceptions of person-organisation fit and organisational selection decisions. *Journal of Applied Psychology, 82*, 546–561.

Caldwell, D. F. & Burger, J. M. (1998). Personality characteristics of job applicants and success in screening interviews. *Personnel Psychology*, *51*, 119–136.

Campion, M. A., Pursell, E. D. & Brown, B. K. (1988). Structured interviewing: raising the psychometric properties of the employment interview. *Personnel Psychology*, *41*, 25–42.

Campion, M. A., Campion, J. E. & Hudson, J. P. (1994). Structured interviewing – a note on incremental validity and alternative question types. *Journal of Applied Psychology*, *79*, 998–1002.

Campion, M. A., Palmer, D. K. & Campion, J. E. (1997). A review of structure in the selection interview. *Personnel Psychology*, *50*, 655–702.

Cargile, A. C. (1997). Attitudes toward Chinese-accented speech. An investigation in two contexts. *Journal of Language and Social Psychology*, *16*, 434–443.

Cargile, A. C. (2000). Evaluations of employment suitability: does accent always matter? *Journal of Employment Counselling*, *37*, 165–177.

Chapman, D. S. & Rowe, P. M. (2001). The impact of videoconference technology, interview structure, and interviewer gender on interviewer evaluations in the employment interview: a field experiment. *Journal of Occupational and Organisational Psychology*, *74*, 279–298.

Chapman, D. S. & Rowe, P. M. (2002). The influence of videoconference technology and interview structure on the recruiting function of the employment interview: a field experiment. *International Journal of Selection and Assessment*, *10*, 185–197.

Collins, J. M. & Gleaves, D. H. (1998). Race, job applicants, and the five-factor model of personality: implications for black psychology, industrial/organisational psychology, and the five-factor theory. *Journal of Applied Psychology*, *83*, 531–544.

Connerley, M. L. (1997). The influence of training on perceptions of recruiters' interpersonal skills and effectiveness. *Journal of Occupational and Organisational Psychology*, *70*, 259–272.

Conway, J. M., Kako, R. A. & Goodman, D. E. (1995). A meta-analysis of interrater and internal consistency reliability of selection interviews. *Journal of Applied Psychology*, *80*, 565–579.

Cook, K. W., Vance, C. A. & Spector, P. E. (2000). The relation of candidate personality with selection-interview outcomes. *Journal of Applied Social Psychology*, *30*, 867–885.

Cortina, J. M., Goldstein, N. B., Payne, S. C., Davison, H. K. & Gilliland, S. W. (2000). The incremental validity of interview scores over and above cognitive ability and conscientiousness scores. *Personnel Psychology*, *53*, 325–351.

Daniel, C. & Valencia, S. (1991). Structured interviewing simplified. *Public Personnel Management*, *20*, 127–134.

Day, A. L. & Carroll, S. A. (2003). Situational and patterned behavior description interviews: a comparison of their validity, correlates, and perceived fairness. *Human Performance*, *16*, 25–47.

De Jong, W. (1980). The stigma of obesity: the consequences of naïve assumptions concerning the cause of physical deviance. *Journal of Health and Social Behaviour*, *21*, 75–87.

Delery, J. E. & Kacmar, K. E. (1998). The influence of applicant and interviewer characteristics on the use of impression management. *Journal of Applied Social Psychology*, *28*, 1649–1669.

Dipboye, R. L. (1992). *Selection interviews: process perspectives*. Cincinnati, OH: South-Western Publishing.

DuBrin, A. J. (1994). Sex differences in the use and effectiveness of tactics of impression management. *Psychological Reports*, *74*, 531–544.

Duckett, P. S. (2000). Disabling employment interviews: warfare to work. *Disability and Society*, *15*, 1019–1039.

Eder, R. W. & Harris, M. M. (Eds) (1999). *The employment interview handbook*. Thousand Oaks, CA: Sage.

Ellis, A. P. J., West, B. J., Ryan, A. M. & DeShon, R. P. (2002). The use of impression management tactics in structured interviews. a function of question type? *Journal of Applied Psychology*, *87*, 1200–1208.

Fletcher, C. (1992). Ethical issues in the selection interview. *Journal of Business Ethics*, *11*, 361–367.

Frazer, R. A. & Wiersma, U. J. (2001). Prejudice versus discrimination in the employment interview: we may hire equally, but our memories harbour prejudice. *Human Relations*, *54*, 173–191.

Ganzach, Y., Kluger, A. N. & Klayman, N. (2000). Making decisions from an interview: expert measurement and mechanical combination. *Personnel Psychology*, *53*, 1–20.

Gilliland, S. W. (1993). The perceived fairness of selection systems: an organizational justice perspective. *Academy of Management Review*, *18*, 694–734.

Gilliland, S. W. & Steiner, D. D. (1999). Applicant reactions. In R. W. Eder & M. M. Harris (Eds), *The employment interview handbook* (pp. 69–82). Thousand Oaks, CA: Sage.

Gilmore, D. C. & Ferris, G. R. (1989). The effects of applicant impression management tactics on interviewer judgments. *Journal of Management*, *15*, 557–564.

Gilmore, D. C., Stevens, C. K., Harrell-Cook, G. & Ferris, G. R. (1999). Impression management tactics. In R. W. Eder & M. M. Harris (Eds), *The employment interview handbook*, (pp. 321–336). Thousand Oaks, CA: Sage.

Goldberg, C. B. (2003). Applicant reaction to the employment interview. A look at demographic similarity and social identity theory. *Journal of Business Research*, *56*, 561–571.

Gollub-Williamson, L. G., Campion, J. E., Malos, S. B., Roehling, M. V. & Campion, M. A. (1997). Employment interview on trial: linking interview structure with litigation outcomes. *Journal of Applied Psychology*, *82*, 900–912.

Goltz, S. M. & Giannantonio, C. M. (1995). Recruiter friendliness and attraction to the job: the mediating role of inferences about the organization. *Journal of Vocational Behavior*, *46*, 109–118.

Goodale, J. G. (1989). Effective employment interviewing. In R. W. Eder & G. R. Ferris (Eds), *The employment interview: theory, research and practice* (pp. 307–323). Newbury Park, CA: Sage.

Gorham, J., Cohen, S. H. & Morris, T. L. (1999). Fashion in the classroom. III. Effects of instructor attire and immediacy in natural classroom interactions. *Communication Quarterly*, *47*, 281–299.

Gouvier, W. D., Steiner, D. D., Jackson, W. T., Schlater, D. & Rain, J. S. (1991). Employment discrimination against handicapped job candidates: an analog study of the effects of neurological causation, visibility of handicap, and public contact. *Rehabilitation Psychology*, *36*, 121–129.

Hargie, O. & Dickson, D. (2003). *Skilled interpersonal communication: research, theory and practice*, 4th edn. London: Routledge.

Harris, M. M. & Eder, R. W. (1999). The state of employment interview practice. In R. W. Eder & M. M. Harris (Eds), *The employment interview handbook* (pp. 369–398). Thousand Oaks, CA: Sage.

Hayes, T. L. & Macan, T. H. (1997). Comparison of the factors influencing interviewer hiring decisions for applicants with those without disabilities. *Journal of Business and Psychology*, *11*, 357–371.

Howard, J. L. & Ferris, G. R. (1996). The employment interview context: social and situational influences on interviewer decisions. *Journal of Applied Social Psychology*, *26*, 112–136.

Huffcutt, A. I. & Roth, P. L. (1998). Racial group differences in employment interview evaluations. *Journal of Applied Psychology*, *83*, 179–189.

Huffcutt, A. I. & Woehr, D. J. (1999). Further analysis of employment interview validity: a quantitative evaluation of interviewer-related structuring methods. *Journal of Organizational Behavior*, *20*, 549–560.

Huffcutt, A. I., Roth, P. L. & McDaniel, M. A. (1996). A meta-analytic investigation of cognitive ability in employment interview evaluations: moderating characteristics and implications for incremental validity. *Journal of Applied Psychology*, *81*, 459–473.

Huffcutt, A. I., Conway, J. M., Roth, P. L. & Stone, N. J. (2001). Identification and meta-analytic assessment of psychological constructs measured in employment interviews. *Journal of Applied Psychology*, *86*, 897–913.

Janz, T. (1989). The patterned behavior description interview: the best prophet of the future is the past. In R. W. Eder & G. R. Ferris (Eds), *The employment interview: theory, research and practice* (pp. 158–168). Newbury Park, CA: Sage.

Judge, T. A., Higgins, C. A. & Cable, D. M. (2000). The employment interview: a review of recent research and recommendations for future research. *Human Resource Management Review*, *10*, 383–406.

Kacmar, K. M. (1999). Effectiveness of impression management tactics across human resource situations. *Journal of Applied Social Psychology*, *29*, 1293–1315.

Kacmar, K. M. & Carlson, D. S. (1994). Using impression management in women's job search processes. *American Behavioral Scientist*, *37*, 682–696.

Kacmar, K. M., Delery, J. E. & Ferris, G. R. (1992). Differential effectiveness of applicant impression management tactics on employment interview decisions. *Journal of Applied Social Psychology*, *22*, 1250–1272.

Kohn, L. S. & Dipboye, R. L. (1998). The effects of interview structure on recruiting outcomes. *Journal of Applied Social Psychology*, *28*, 821–843.

Kristoff, A. L. (1996). Person-organization fit: an integrative review of its conceptualisations, measurement, and implications. *Personnel Psychology*, *49*, 1–49.

Kristof-Brown, A., Barrick, M. R. & Franke, M. (2002). Applicant impression management: dispositional influences and consequences for recruiter perceptions of fit and similarity. *Journal of Management*, *28*, 27–46.

Lamunde, K. G., Scudder, J. & Simmons, D. (2003). The influence of applicant characteristics on use of verbal impression management tactics in the employment selection interview. *Communication Research Reports*, *20*, 299–307.

Landau, J. (1995). The relationship of race and gender to managers' ratings of promotion potential. *Journal of Organisational Behaviour*, *16*, 391–400.

Larsen, D. A. & Phillips, J. I. (2002). Effect of recruiter on attraction to the firm: implications of the elaboration likelihood model. *Journal of Business and Psychology*, *16*, 347–364.

Latham, G. P. (1989). The reliability, validity, and practicality of the situational interview. In R. W. Eder & G. R. Ferris (Eds), *The employment interview: theory, research and practice* (pp. 169–182). Newbury Park, CA: Sage.

Latham, G. P. (1999). A meta-analysis of the situational interview: an enumerative review of reasons for its validity. *Canadian Psychology*, *40*, 56–67.

Latham, G. P. & Skarlicki, D. P. (1995). Criterion-related validity of the situational and patterned behavior description interviews with organizational citizenship behavior. *Human Performance*, *8*, 67–80.

Latham, G. P. & Sue-Chan, C. (1998). Selecting employees in the 21st century: predicting the contribution of I-O psychology to Canada. *Canadian Psychology*, *39*, 14–22.

Latham, G. P. & Sue-Chan, C. (1999). A meta-analysis of the situational interview: an enumerative review of reasons for its validity. *Canadian Psychology*, *40*, 56–67.

Latham, G. P., Saari, L. M., Pursell, E. D. & Campion, M. A. (1980). The situational interview. *Journal of Applied Psychology*, *65*, 422–427.

Liden, R. C. & Parsons, C. K. (1986). A field study of job applicant interview perceptions, alternative opportunities and demographic characteristics. *Personnel Psychology*, *39*, 109–122.

Liden, R. C., Martin, C. L. & Parsons, C. K. (1993). Interviewer and applicant behaviors in employment interviews. *Academy of Management Journal*, *36*, 372–386.

Macan, T. H. & Hayes, T. L. (1995). Both sides of the employment interview interaction: perceptions of interviewers and applicants with disabilities. *Rehabilitation Psychology*, *40*, 261–278.

Marchioro, C. A. & Bartels, L. K. (1994). Perceptions of a job interviewee with a disability. *Journal of Social Behavior and Personality*, *9*, 383–392.

McDaniel, M. A., Whetzel, D. L., Schmidt, F. L. & Maurer, S. D. (1994). The validity of employment interviews: a comprehensive review and meta-analysis. *Journal of Applied Psychology*, *79*, 599–616.

Millar, R. & Gallagher, M. (1997). The Selection Interview. In O. D. W. Hargie (Ed.), *The handbook of communication skills* (pp. 385–408). London: Routledge.

Millar, R., Crute, V. & Hargie, O. (1992). *Professional interviewing*. London: Routledge.

Motowidlo, S. J., Carter, G. W., Dunnette, M. D., Tippins, N., Werner, S., Burnett, J. R. & Vaughan, M. J. (1992). Studies of the structured behavioral interview. *Journal of Applied Psychology*, *77*, 571–587.

Nordstrom, C. R. (1996). The impact of self-regulatory processes on interview evaluations. *Journal of Social Behaviour and Personality*, *11*, 713–728.

Nordstrom, C. R., Huffaker, B. J. & Williams, K. B. (1998). When physical disabilities are not liabilities: the role of applicant and interviewer characteristics on employment interview outcomes. *Journal of Applied Social Psychology*, *28*, 283–306.

Papadopoulou, A., Ineson, E. & Williams, D. (1996). The graduate management trainee preselection interview. Candidates' perceptions of the influence of interpersonal and communication factors on the interview outcomes. *Personnel Review, 25*, 21–37.

Parton, S. R., Siltanen, S. A., Hosman, L. A. & Langenderfer, J. (2002). Employment interviews outcomes and speech style effects. *Journal of Language and Social Psychology, 21*, 144–161.

Pingitore, R., Dugoni, B. L., Tindale, R. S. & Spring, B. (1994). Bias against overweight job applicants in a simulated employment interview. *Journal of Applied Psychology, 79*, 909–917.

Polinko, N. K. & Popovich, P. M. (2001). Evil thoughts but angelic actions: responses to overweight job applicants. *Journal of Applied Social Psychology, 31*, 905–924.

Posthuma, R. A., Morgeson, F. P. & Campion, M. A. (2002). Beyond employment interview validity: a comprehensive narrative review of recent research and trends over time. *Personnel Psychology, 55*, 1–81.

Poteet, G. W. (1984). The employment interview. Avoiding discriminatory questioning. *Journal of Nursing Administration, 14*, 38–42.

Powell, G. N. (1991). Applicant reactions to the initial employment interview: exploring theoretical and methodological issues. *Personnel Psychology, 44*, 67–83.

Powell, G. N. (1996). Recruiters' and applicants' awareness of the other party's postinterview evaluations. *Psychological Reports, 73*, 1363–1369.

Pulakos, E. D. & Schmitt, N. (1995). Experience-based and situational interview questions: studies of validity. *Personnel Psychology, 48*, 289–308.

Pulakos, E. D., Schmitt, N., Whitney, D. & Smith, M. (1996). Individual differences in interviewer ratings: the impact of standardization, consensus discussion, and sampling error on the validity of a structured interview. *Personnel Psychology, 49*, 85–102.

Ralston, S. M. & Brady, R. (1994). The relative influence of the interview communication satisfaction on applicants' recruitment interview decisions. *Journal of Business Communication, 31*, 61–77.

Ralston, S. M. & Kirkwood, W. G. (1999). The trouble with applicant impression management. *Journal of Business and Technical Communication, 13*, 190–207.

Ravaud, J.-F., Madiot, B. & Ville, I. (1992). Discrimination toward disabled people seeking employment. *Social Sciences and Medicine, 35*, 951–958.

Rosenfeld, P. (1997). Impression management, fairness and the employment interview. *Journal of Business Ethics, 16*, 801–808.

Rumrill, P. D., Millington, M. J., Webb, J. M. & Cook, B. G. (1998). Employment expectations as a differential indicator of attitudes toward people with insulin-dependent diabetes mellitus. *Journal of Vocational Rehabilitation, 10*, 271–280.

Rynes, S. L. & Barber, A. E. (1990). Applicant attraction strategies: an organizational perspective. *Academy of Management Review, 15*, 286–310.

Sarangi, S. (1994). Accounting for mismatches in intercultural selection interviews. *Multilingual, 13*, 163–194.

Seiter, J. S. & Sandry, A. (2003). Pierced for success?: the effects of ear and nose piercing on perceptions of job candidates' credibility, attractiveness, and hirability. *Communication Research Reports, 20*, 287–298.

Shannon, M. L. & Stark, C. P. (2003). The influence of physical appearance on personnel selection. *Social Behaviour and Personality, 31*, 613–624.

Shepperd, J. A. & Kwavnick, K. D. (1999). Maladaptive image maintenance. In R. M. Kowalski & M. R. Leary (Eds), *The social psychology of emotional and behavioural problems: interfaces of social and clinical psychology* (pp. 249–277). Washington, DC: American Psychological Society.

Silvester, J. (1997). Spoken attributions and candidate success in graduate recruitment interviews. *Journal of Occupational and Organisational Psychology, 70*, 61–73.

Silvester, J. & Chapman, A. J. (1996). Unfair discrimination in the selection interview: an attributional account. *International Journal of Selection and Assessment, 4*, 63–70.

Smith, M. & George, D. (1992). Selection Methods. *International Review of Industrial and Organizational Psychology, 7*, 55–97.

Smith, M. & Robertson, I. T. (1993). *The theory and practice of systematic personnel selection*, 2nd edn. London: Macmillan.

Smither, J. W., Reilly, R. R., Millsap, R. E., Pearlman, K. & Stoffey, R. W. (1993). Applicant reactions to selection procedures. *Personnel Psychology, 46*, 49–76.

Stevens, C. K. (1998). Antecedents of interview interactions, interviewers' ratings, and applicants' reactions. *Personnel Psychology, 51*, 55–85.

Stevens, C. K. & Kristof, A. L. (1995). Making the right impression. A field study of applicant impression management during job interviews. *Journal of Applied Psychology, 80*, 587–606.

Stevens, G. E. (1981). Faking the chance out of selection interviewing. *Journal of College Placement, 49*, 44–48.

Taylor, P, Mills, A. & O'Driscoll, M. (1993). Personnel selection methods used by New Zealand organisations and personnel consulting firms. *New Zealand Journal of Psychology, 22*, 19–31.

Terpstra, D. E. & Rozell, E. J. (1997). Why some potentially effective staffing practices are seldom used. *Public Personnel Management, 26*, 483–495.

Tullar, W. L. (1989). The employment interview as a cognitive performing script. In R. W. Eder & G. R. Ferris (Eds), *The employment interview: theory, research and practice*, (pp. 233–245). Newbury Park, CA: Sage.

Turban, D. B. & Dougherty, T. M. (1992). Influences of campus recruiting on applicant attraction to firms. *Academy of Management Journal, 35*, 739–765.

Turban, D. B., Forret, M. L. & Hendrickson, C. L. (1998). Applicant attraction to firms: influences of organisation reputation, job and organisational attributes, and recruiter behaviours. *Journal of Vocational Behaviour, 52*, 24–44.

Van Dam, K. (2003). Trait perception in the employment interview: a five-factor model perspective. *International Journal of Selection and Assessment, 11*, 43–55.

Van Der Zee, K. I., Bakker, A. B. & Bakker, P. (2002). Why are structured interviews so rarely used in personnel selection? *Journal of Applied Psychology, 87*, 176–184.

Wade, K. J. & Kinicki, A. J. (1997). Subjective applicant qualifications and interpersonal attraction as mediators within a process model of interview selection decisions. *Journal of Vocational Behavior, 50*, 23–40.

Wiesner, W. H. & Cronshaw, S. F. (1988). A meta-analytic investigation of the impact of interview format and degree of structure on the validity of the employment interview. *Journal of Occupational Psychology, 61*, 275–290.

Wilson, G. L. (1991). Preparing students for responding to illegal selection interview questions. *Bulletin of the Association* for *Business Communication, 54*, 44–49.

Workman, J. E. & Johnson, K. K. P. (1994). Effects of conformity and nonconformity to gender-role expectations for dress: teachers versus students. *Adolescence*, **29**, 207–223.

Wright, G. E. & Multon, K. D. (1995). Employer's perceptions of nonverbal communication in job interviews for persons with physical disabilities. *Journal of Vocational Behavior*, **47**, 214–227.

Wright, P. M., Lichtenfels, P. A. & Pursell, E. D. (1989). The structured interview: additional studies and a meta-analysis. *Journal of Occupational Psychology*, **62**, 191–199.

Young, A. M. & Kacmar, K. M. (1998). ABCs of the interview: the role of affective, behavioural, and cognitive responses by applicants in the employment interview. *International Journal of Selection and Assessment*, **6**, 211–221.

Chapter 17

The helping interview: Developmental counselling and therapy

Sandra A. Rigazio-DiGilio and
Allen E. Ivey

HELPING PEOPLE TO TALK about their thoughts, feelings, and behaviours in relation to important issues and to develop the knowledge and skills necessary to work through these issues is a natural part of everyday life. Whether we are called upon to listen empathically to a friend who has lost a loved one or to assist our young nephew to understand his math lessons, we are often engaged in helping relationships. The skills we use to handle these interactions (e.g. effective listening, conflict management, multiple-perspective taking, problem-solving) are developed and reinforced over our lifetime. Although some of us are well endowed with such attributes, we may not be consistent in how we apply these skills and we may not always attend to the reactions triggered in those we are attempting to help.

Everyone can benefit from obtaining familiarity with the knowledge and practice of counselling skills. In this chapter, we systemically apply a specific set of communication skills that can be used in the service of helping others. Our particular focus is on how to integrate communication theory, psychological research, and developmental perspectives to construct a cognitive-emotional developmental model of helping that can be used in the immediacy of any interview. This model helps us to access the cognitive, emotional, and behavioural aspects of an individual's world, and to expand options for more empowered functioning in these three areas.

At some time in their career, most people will find themselves engaged in a helping encounter. It is our belief that knowledge about communication and developmental theories and approaches can assist professionals to make helping interviews more client-centred. Specifically, the model presented in this chapter provides ways for eliciting and organising the information individuals share with you when they seek help. By learning how to understand the unique ways these individuals perceive and work through their issues, you can develop helping strategies that are in tune with how they already operate in their lives. In this way, you enter their world and engage them in a co-constructive process of expanding their cognitive, affective, and behavioural options for change. This is in contrast to the types of helping models that tend to impose a particular way of thinking, feeling, and acting on clients seeking help.

The skills presented here are drawn from developmental counselling and therapy (DCT), an alternative model of helping that integrates traditional counselling theories and approaches, and presents new concepts for effective interviewing and counselling practice. Further information on DCT as a model of helping, and as a comprehensive framework for organising the multitude of theories and approaches at our disposal, can be found in the writings of Ivey (1987, 1993, 2000); Ivey and Gonçalves (1988); Ivey et al. (1989); Rigazio-DiGilio and Ivey (1991, 1993); Rigazio-DiGilio (1994a); Rigazio-DiGilio and Ivey (1995); Ivey and Ivey (2003); Ivey, Ivey, Myers, and Sweeney (2005). What we focus upon in this chapter are the basic developmental skills, which can be effectively integrated into practice whether in the helping field, the business field, or a service-related occupation.

DEVELOPMENTAL COUNSELLING AND THERAPY (DCT)

DCT, along with its extension to partners and families (systemic cognitive-developmental therapy [SCDT]) (Rigazio-DiGilio & Ivey, 1991, 1993; Rigazio-DiGilio, 1993, 2000; Kunkler & Rigazio-DiGilio, 1994) and to larger social and organisational groups (DCT/SCDT) (Rigazio-DiGilio, 1994a, 1994b, 2002; Ivey, 2000), offers a conceptually coherent developmental framework that is easily learned and directly applicable to interviewing, counselling, and therapy (Borders, 1994; Marszalek & Cashwell, 1998; Strehorn, 1999; Capuzzi & Gross, 2002; Myers, Shoffner & Briggs, 2002). DCT provides highly specific, yet flexible assessment and helping strategies that helpers can use to understand how clients make sense of their world, in general, and the issues that prompt them to seek help, in particular.

DCT as a helping model and a classification system

DCT represents an *alternative approach* to the helping relationship that is holistic and non-pathological. It is focused on the client's world-view and how the client makes meaning of daily existence. By focusing on the unique story and the client's expressive modes of communication, counsellors can identify the specific cognitive-emotional developmental style preferred by the client. DCT combines the descriptive and analytic power of developmental constructs with the interactive precision of skilful interpersonal communication theory. Additionally, the model offers a larger, *integrative classification system* that can be used to organise familiar counselling and interviewing approaches within a developmental framework. As such, DCT provides ways to:

1   use specific types of questioning strategies and attending skills that help the interviewer understand the unique ways clients make sense of and work on their issues

2   organise helping interventions from various counselling models that are tailored to the developmental and cultural needs of these clients and that assist them to obtain wider perspectives on their issues and broader alternatives for change.

The philosophical foundation underlying DCT

DCT is based on a synthesis of neo-Platonic philosophies, developmental theories (Piaget, 1955; Hill & Rodgers, 1964; Gilligan, 1982; Jankowski, 1998), and constructivist thought (Kelly, 1955; Watzlawick, 1984; Vygotsky, 1986; Gergen, 2000; Mahoney, 2003). This synthesis allows for a reinterpretation of how people construct their world-views over time and in relation to their surrounding socio-cultural environment.

The theoretical assumptions underlying DCT

The *primary theoretical assumption* underlying DCT suggests that development is a spherical and recursive process. As such, DCT rejects the traditional notion that development represents linear and hierarchical movement toward increasing levels of cognitive complexity. Rather, maturity is equated with cognitive, affective, and behavioural flexibility, wherein individuals have access to a wide range of intellectual and emotional resources. Helping expand the client's skills in accessing a greater range of perspectives can facilitate development and change.

Within this holistic perspective, DCT metaphorically transforms Piaget's idea that individuals sequentially move through stage-specific, cognitive-developmental levels over their lifespan. DCT instead proposes that human growth and adaptation require a more fluid and repetitive movement within and between the various cognitive-emotional styles as individuals face new developmental or situational tasks. The term *style* is used to express the idea that individuals repeatedly move through various cognitive-emotional developmental ways of viewing the world as they try to make sense of their experience, construct meaning, and act. The four styles identified by DCT are sensorimotor (experiencing), concrete (doing), formal (reflecting), and dialectic/systemic (analysing).

A *second theoretical assumption* undergirding DCT suggests that development is a *co-constructive* phenomenon. Within this postmodern perspective, human development occurs as a function of a dialectic relationship among individuals, relationships, and wider environments. In other words, development and adaptation are considered to occur within a person–environment dialectic transaction. Within this view, individuals, and significant others in their social network, such as partners, families, social organisations, employers, supervisors, co-workers, teachers, and counsellors, interact within a collective environment (Rigazio-DiGilio, Ivey, Kunkler-Peck & Grady, 2005). As such, any portion of the environment can be influenced by, or influence, any other part. This wider view of the client's life space provides numerous perspectives and points of intervention. It also identifies how certain communications within this social network reinforce restraining or enhancing forces and influence the construction of the client's world-view.

The conceptual implications embedded in the constructs of *styles* and *co-constructivism* provide the framework for the application of developmental and communication theories to the helping interview. Again, these ideas provide a framework that interviewers can use to:

1   ask specific questioning strategies that elicit a client's cognitive-emotional style within the natural language of the helping relationship
2   plan various helping strategies that are tailored to facilitate client growth within and between different styles.

As indicated in Box 17.1, research evidence supports these conceptual elements of DCT.

Box 17.1 Research supporting DCT constructs and assumptions

Empirical research has been conducted to determine whether the cognitive-emotional developmental style upon which DCT is based can be reliably identified in the natural language of the interview. Additionally, the predictive validity of the DCT questioning strategies has been investigated, as well as the claim that cognitive flexibility – using several styles to understand and act in the world – is a healthy response to growth and adaptation. Four of these studies relate to the work discussed in this chapter.

1   Rigazio-DiGilio and Ivey (1990) determined that independent raters could indeed classify the predominant cognitive-emotional developmental style used by in-patient depressed clients as they explained the issues that promoted treatment. These raters could identify a client's primary style with a high degree of reliability (0.98; kappa = 0.87). Additionally, this same investigation determined that questions designed to elicit explorations within particular developmental style actually did elicit such explorations. In effect, both short- and long-term depressives responded to questions consistent with the theory (98% of all responses).
2   Heesacker et al. (1995) conducted a factor analytic study of DCT constructs with 1700 subjects. The factor structure for the four cognitive-emotional developmental styles was substantiated. Further, it was found that subjects who were able to access resources within several of the cognitive-emotional styles showed more positive indicators of physical and emotional health than individuals who primarily functioned within one.
3   Strehorn (1999) applied DCT to work with post-secondary students identified with learning disabilities and found that the cognitive-emotional styles could be used to match academic interventions with a student's developmental style.
4   Myers, Shoffner, and Briggs (2002) used the DCT model to assess and treat a child working through her developmental blocks. They found the model to be an effective strategy that may be applied with a variety of clients. The model allowed for the selection of new interventions matched to the developmental style of the client over the course of the treatment.

Identifying DCT developmental styles

DCT posits that, while individuals may use a variety of cognitive-emotional styles, reflective of the interactive nature of their world-view, to interpret and act in their world, most rely significantly on one or two styles (Rigazio-DiGilio & Ivey, 1990). An individual's *predominant style* is the major frame through which the person experiences, interprets, and interacts within the world. Research conducted to test this primary hypothesis confirms that, by attending to clients' natural language during the helping interview, their predominant style can be identified with a high degree of reliability. The predominant style provides interviewers with clues as to how clients organise their world and make meaning of their life tasks, as well as how they think, feel, and act in relation to themselves, other people, and various situations.

The first step in a successful interview is for the helping interviewer to apply effective communication skills to determine the predominant cognitive-emotional style of the client. Knowing this style enables the interviewer to employ receptive and expressive interpersonal skills that mirror the linguistic and cognitive-emotional frames of reference used by the client. The idea of matching our language style to that of the client is important (Gregorc, 1985; Anderson, 1987). For example, clients who talk in concrete specifics and tell linear stories may have trouble understanding the formal abstractions and reflective orientation often associated with interviewing and counselling. The concrete client may have difficulty seeing repeating patterns of behaviour and reflecting on the role of self or the similarities across situations. Therefore, if interviewers can identify their clients' constructions and match their own language style to these constructions, they will have maximum opportunity to join with their clients and to help them learn expanded or alternative ways of thinking, feeling, and behaving (Rigazio-DiGilio, 2002).

The four major cognitive-emotional styles considered by DCT are briefly defined below, along with a corresponding illustration. Additionally, Box 17.2 presents an in-depth description of each style.

The sensorimotor/elemental style

Clients relying on this style tend not to separate cognition and emotion. They are able to experience the 'here and now' directly and immediately. You may find them a bit random in their presentation of issues and concerns. They are often able to experience situations and feelings deeply and at times may be overcome by emotion.

Example client statement dealing with death and dying

(*In tears and overwhelmed*) 'I'm so confused. It was AIDS. I feel lonely and lost. I don't know what to do now.'

485

Box 17.2 The four cognitive-emotional styles

When clients can work within several styles, they can access the resources inherent in each to assist them to experience, understand, and act in their world. When clients rely on one style at the sacrifice of all others, they can be constrained within the limits of that style. Clients who haphazardly fluctuate among the styles appear also to be constrained by ineffective processing. Each style is described below, along with corresponding types of affect, cognitions, and behaviours.

The sensorimotor style
AFFECT Clients who work within this style are dominated by sensory stimuli and affect, seeing minimal distinction between sensory input, cognitions, and emotions. Emotions are sensory based and reactive. These clients can easily experience the immediacy of their emotions in the here-and-now.
COGNITION These clients show minimal capacity to coordinate sensory-based data into an organised understanding or Gestalt. They offer interpretations that, no matter how sophisticated, are illusional or irrational.
BEHAVIOUR Behaviourally, these clients are unable to take effective action based on their beliefs or experiences.

The concrete style
AFFECT Clients working within this style can name and describe emotions within themselves and others from one perspective, and with minimal differentiation. They express emotions outwardly and are unlikely to recognise obvious emotions in others unless clearly made available to them, verbally or non-verbally.
COGNITION These clients focus primarily on a factual description of the details evident in a situation – seeing these details only from their own perspective. There is minimal emphasis on evaluation or analysis. These clients can demonstrate if/then linear thinking, emphasising causality and predictability from a single perspective.
BEHAVIOUR These clients are able to control and describe broad-based, undifferentiated, outwardly focused affect. They are able to find ways to act predictably in their worlds.

The formal style
AFFECT Clients who primarily operate within this style demonstrate an awareness of the complexity of their feelings and are able to separate self from feelings to reflect on their emotions. They can analyse patterns of feelings. However, they have difficulty in experiencing their emotions directly.
COGNITION These clients can describe repeating patterns of affect, thoughts, and behaviours in themselves, in others, and across situations. They can engage in an analysis of the self and the situations they are involved in. However, they have difficulty seeing the constraints in these patterns.
BEHAVIOUR These clients are able to generalise their behaviours to adapt to novel situations. However, they have difficult in determining new behaviours outside their own patterns.

The dialectic/systemic style

AFFECT Clients who primarily use this style can offer a wide range of emotions and can recognise that their emotions can change in relation to their context. These clients, however, have difficult in experiencing their emotions directly, in the immediacy of the here and now.

COGNITION These clients can operate on systems of knowledge and can reflect on how they arrive at their ways of thinking. They are aware that their evolving cognitions are co-constructed over time and in response to differing contexts. They also can challenge their own assumptions and integrations. At times, because they see flaws in virtually all reasoning processes, they involve themselves in deconstructions and reconstructions, without being able to stay within a predictable frame of reference for any period of time.

BEHAVIOUR These clients can interact in their environment, accessing resources and influences within many contextual realms. Those who depend on this style, at the expense of using others, may become lost in their thought process, and find it difficult to interact predictably.

The concrete/situational style

These clients are good storytellers. They can tell you in detail what happened to them and who said what to whom. Many clients relying on this style will want to tell you detailed stories about their lives and specific events and circumstances.

Example client statement

'My partner died last week of AIDS. The funeral was held last Friday at Jones Funeral Home over in the south end of town. There were over 100 people there. I was glad so many people came.'

The formal/reflective style

These clients usually prefer to talk in abstractions and think about or reflect on what happened to them. Often, they will avoid concrete storytelling and direct sensorimotor experiencing. They are likely to be good at defining repeating patterns in themselves and others. They are good at analysis and examination of self, especially on an intellectual level.

Example client statement

'My partner and I had a perfect relationship. We had learned how to live with AIDS and still enjoy one another. I am the type of person who cares a lot for the one I am with. Generally speaking, I was able to deal positively with this whole situation.'

The dialectic/systemic/integrative style

Like formal clients, these clients are good at analysis. In addition they are interested in contextual issues, such as how the wider socio-political environment affects their sense of themselves or how they are part of historical and intergenerational legacies. Women who seek to discover how their personal issues relate to sexism, and minority groups who wish to explore issues of systemic discrimination are using a dialectic/ systemic style to understand and operate within their world. You will also find that clients who focus on multiple perspectives of themselves and the world tend toward this style

Example client statement

'My partner's death can be seen from several perspectives. First, I hurt a lot, but, on the other hand, the last several months were so awful that I'm glad the pain is over – we were able to part in dignity and love. I was both shocked and not surprised at all by my family's reaction to this time of crisis. Some of my aunts and uncles seemed to be afraid of me. I understand that our culture still does not openly embrace homosexuality, but I cannot condone their behaviour at all. Aren't they aware of the messages they're sending to my younger cousins?'

No matter what the issue – coping with AIDS, depression, performance anxiety, vocational decisions, poverty, or any other issue, no two clients will talk about their concerns in the same way. Our task is to assess how our clients are predominantly processing their experience and to match their language with appropriate cognitive, emotional, and behavioural questions, strategies, and tasks. The objective is to help them explore their issues *where they are*. For example, when clients experience emotional catharsis, it is best to support them within the sensorimotor style. If a client needs to tell a concrete story, listen and paraphrase instead of interpreting and reflecting. Using strategies matched to the client's predominant style, interviewers can accelerate the formation of the therapeutic alliance.

Implicit in DCT is the ability to help interviewers to use a full repertoire of familiar communication strategies corresponding to each of the four cognitive-emotional developmental styles so that they can:

1   demonstrate empathy and make a strong connection with clients within their predominant style
2   assist clients to expand the resources available within their predominant style
3   introduce clients to resources available within other, less utilised styles, helping them master these alternative resources.

Generally, clients ask for assistance when they are depending on resources within their predominant style that are not in sync with developmental or environmental demands. Once you join with them in their primary style, you can assist them to expand their use of the resources within it. For example, a client may know how to use problem-solving skills (concrete) to deal with a simple demand, but may be unable to access a more comprehensive problem-solving repertoire for more complicated demands. Assisting such a client to expand the use of problem-solving skills would promote an expanded use of familiar resources.

Moreover, once clients fully explore their issues from the vantage point of their predominant style, they may want you to help them explore their issues from the various frames of reference that are associated with styles which they access less frequently. For example, a battered woman may need to tell you several stories of what has happened in her life (concrete), and also may need assistance to reorganise her life away from the batterer (concrete). Once the stories are told and a safe environment is established, she may want help in exploring the deep emotions associated with her experiences (sensorimotor). She may also benefit from a dialogue in which she can analyse the ways the wider environment assists or ignores the problems of the battered woman and how it either did attend or failed to attend to her needs and her continued safety (dialectic/systemic). Finally, it may be appropriate to work with her regarding how the trauma experience relates to her own self-concept and self-esteem (formal).

Note in the preceding paragraph that a comprehensive treatment programme may require you to be able to work with clients within all styles. There is no 'higher' form of cognition or emotion in the DCT model. The primary goal is to expand the depth and breadth of understanding within each of the cognitive-emotional developmental styles.

FACILITATING COGNITIVE, EMOTIONAL, AND BEHAVIOURAL DEVELOPMENT

DCT identifies two directions which development can follow – horizontal and vertical. *Horizontal development* occurs when we encourage a client to experience life in more depth within one of the four styles. For example, clients often need to grieve their losses emotionally, whether it is a failed examination, the loss of a job, the departure of their child to college, or a divorce. Emotional grieving can occur within all four styles, but may be experienced most fully within the sensorimotor style. Horizontal development can be facilitated by using skilful communication tools to phrase carefully and make statements within this sensorimotor style, thereby ensuring learning within a safe helping environment.

Vertical development occurs when clients shift their style. For example, you may work with clients who are very effective at discussing issues within the formal or dialectic/systemic styles. You may note, however, that their abstract discussions are sometimes used to protect themselves from sensorimotor experiencing or from taking concrete action to change their circumstances. Your task as a helper may be to encourage and linguistically support these clients to move vertically by phrasing questions and comments that help them to consider their issues from more concrete or sensorimotor vantage points.

Many clients come for help during times of developmental transition – points at which they must separate from old ways and move on to the new. These include many of life's milestones – birth of a child, high school and college graduation, the first job, a big promotion, the loss of a job, birth of a grandchild, establishing or dissolving a relationship, the death of loved ones, reaching a particular age, retiring, and facing death or illness. As these changes happen, the individual may need counselling and help to cope with new ways of living.

The use of DCT questioning strategies

DCT offers a set of systemic questioning strategies that are used to:

1   access and assess a client's predominant cognitive-emotional style
2   access and assess a client's ability to move within and between the other three styles
3   promote horizontal and vertical development.

These questioning strategies are presented in Box 17.3.

Box 17.3 The DCT questioning sequence* (abbreviated)

1 Opening presentation of issue

a   Could you tell me what you would like to focus on today?
b   Could you tell me what occurs for you when you focus on the issues that prompted you to seek assistance?

GOAL   Obtain the client's story. Identify the cognitive-emotional style predominantly used by the client.

TECHNIQUES   Use encouraging statements, paraphrasing, and reflection of feeling to bring out data, but try to influence the client's story minimally. Get the story as the client constructs it. Summarise key facts and feelings about what the client has said before moving on.

2 Sensorimotor style

a   Could you think of one visual image that occurs to you when you think of the issue that prompted you to seek help?
b   What are you seeing? Hearing? Feeling? It will be helpful to locate the feeling in your body.

GOAL   Elicit one example and then ask what is being seen/heard/felt. Aim for here-and-now experiencing. Accept randomness.

TECHNIQUES   Summarise at the end of the segment. You may want to ask 'What one thing stands out for you from this?'

3 Concrete style
a   Could you give me a specific example of the situation/issue/problem?
b   Can you describe your feelings in the situation?

GOAL   Obtain a linear description of the event. Look for if/then, causal reasoning.

TECHNIQUES   Ask 'What did he or she do? Say? What happened before? What happened next? What happened after?' Possibly pose the question 'If he or she did X, then what happened?' Summarise before moving on.

4 Formal style

a   Does this happen in other situations? Is this a pattern for you?
b   Do you feel that way in other situations? Are those feelings a pattern for you?

GOAL   Talk about repeating patterns and situations and/or talk about self.

TECHNIQUES   Ask 'What were you saying to yourself when that happened? Have you felt like that in other situations?' Again, reflect feelings and paraphrase as appropriate. Summarise key facts and feelings carefully before moving on.

5 Dialectic/systemic style

a   How do you put together/organise all that you told me? What one thing stands out for you most?
b   How many different ways could you describe your feelings and how they change?

GOALS   To obtain an integrated summary of what has been said. To enable the client to see how reality is co-constructed versus developed from a single view. To obtain different perspectives on the same situation and be aware that each is just one perspective. To note flaws in the present construction, co-construction, or perspective, and move to action.

TECHNIQUES   As we move toward more complex reasoning, several options are open. Before using any of these, summarise what the client has been saying over the entire series of questions.

INTEGRATION   How do you put together/organise all that you told me? What one thing stands out for you most?

CO-CONSTRUCTION   What rule were you (they) operating under? Where did that rule come from? How might someone else (perhaps another family member) describe the situation? (Feelings can be examined using the same types of questions.)

MULTIPLE PERSPECTIVES   How could we describe this from the point of view of some other person or in another theoretical framework or language system? How else might we put it together in another framework?

DECONSTRUCTION AND ACTION   Can you see some flaws in the reasoning or in the patterns of feelings above? How might you change the rules? Given these possibilities, what action might you take?

* This box is modified from Ivey (1993), *Developmental strategies for helpers*.

Example interview

The following is an illustrative interview (the interview is copyright 2003 by A. E. Ivey and M. B. Ivey, and is used here with their permission) designed to show how the DCT framework, along with the use of *basic attending skills* (Ivey & Ivey, 2003) (e.g. paraphrasing, reflection of feelings, summation), can facilitate client growth and understanding (see Chapter 6 for further discussion of reflecting skills). A mother comes for help because she is having many fights with her teenage daughter, who is about to leave home and enter college. This is a common occurrence in many Western cultures – often daughters and mothers work out their need to separate by fighting rather than expressing the sadness of loss. The following actual session is abbreviated for clarity. Identifying data have been disguised to ensure confidentiality.

Interviewer: Lisa what would you like to talk about today?
  [*The interviewer poses an open-ended question to determine the primary cognitive-emotional style being used by the client to understand the issue promoting treatment.*]
Lisa: My daughter Christine and I have been having an immense number of fights lately. We always seem to argue and I find myself becoming really upset. It's her final year in school and she will be leaving home soon. I wanted us to separate smoothly and to remain close to each other.
  [*Lisa presents her issues within the formal styles. She talks about patterns between herself and her daughter. She reflects on herself and her own feelings.*]
Interviewer: So you have been fighting a lot and you feel angry at yourself. What you really want is to remain close. What is the pattern you see emerging that is troubling you?
  [*The interviewer reflects Lisa's feelings, paraphrases, and follows with a question posed within the formal style to join further with her.*]
Lisa: Ever since last summer we just seem to be on two different tracks. Before then, we have really been able to talk about anything and even enjoyed lots of things in common. Now it's just bicker, bicker, bicker.
Interviewer: You are noticing a big shift in the way you and Christine relate. Can you give me some specific examples of the type of arguments you are having with one another?
  [*The interviewer is moving Lisa from a formal perspective to a concrete style in order to examine the details of the situation.*]
Lisa: Sure, just last week we really had a big argument. She was going to the college admissions office and came down dressed up in jeans and a T-shirt. She looked awful.
Interviewer: She was in jeans and you didn't like it?
  [*Interviewer paraphrases Lisa's comments within the concrete style.*]
Lisa: Right. Then I said to her, 'You can't go to an admissions interview dressed like that. You look terrible.' I guess I was too critical. Then she said that she was tired of me telling her what to do all the time. So we argued a bit and felt terrible.
  [*Lisa offers the concrete, descriptive details of the fight. The statement, 'I guess I was too critical' is an indication that Lisa has shifted the concrete conversation to*

a formal self-reflection. Most clients will discuss their issues from multiple devel-opmental perspectives, although usually one style will be primary.]

Interviewer: You felt terrible because of the argument?

[*Interviewer reflects Lisa's feeling, expanding the story horizontally by remaining within the concrete style. The question mark at the end indicates a raised tone of voice and an implied perception check.*]

Lisa: Yes, but then she went upstairs and changed. She looked a lot better. But as she walked out, her eyes were flashing and angry.

Interviewer: Is that the type of thing that happens a lot? Is that typical of the pattern you spoke about before?

[*These are formal operational questions and, if successful, will lead Lisa to talk about the difficulty she is experiencing within the formal style. The movement back to formal, after gathering some concrete details, will help make the pattern analysis more meaningful.*]

Lisa: Yes, exactly. We have been having these little tiffs for about a year now. I just know that the situation makes me feel terrible and I can see that Christine feels badly as well. We have always been so close until this last year. Now she makes me so angry that sometimes I just want her to go and leave.

[*Although Lisa notes her angry feelings, she is not directly experiencing the emotion at this time. Instead, she is commenting on the change in her relationship with Christine, so her comments actually represent a formal (examining) style.*]

Interviewer: I can sense your frustration and hurt. You want something to be different. Do you want to try an exercise in imagery and see what happens? These types of exercises have been helpful before in understanding complex situations.

[*The interviewer provides a summation, followed by a closed-ended question with information. DCT seeks to have the client join in the process of deciding which intervention to use in the session in the belief that clients should have as much say as possible in the path of their own interview.*]

Lisa: OK, let's try one of these exercises again.

Interviewer: Lisa, I'd like you to sit back and relax (*pauses while Lisa closes her eyes*). Now, you said you were feeling hurt by your constant fights with Christine. Could you focus on that feeling of hurt? (*Pause*) Can you locate that hurt in your body in some specific place? (*Lisa points to her heart.*) Now, Lisa, start with that feeling in your body and let your mind wander to whatever comes. (*Pause*) Can you get an image in your mind? What are you seeing?

[*The interviewer is using a basic sensorimotor imaging exercise which we have found is useful in helping clients discover their deeper feelings. As such techniques are often surprisingly powerful, use these carefully and with a full sense of ethics.*]

Lisa: I am seeing Christine when she was two (*tears*) and remembering (*pause*) what she was like when she was an infant (*more tears*).

Interviewer: You seem to be feeling that sensation very deeply right now. What else are you aware of?

[*The interviewer reflects Lisa's feelings and provides an open invitation for Lisa to go where she needs to.*]

Lisa: I really do care for her a lot – in fact, so very much. I think maybe she cares for me too in much the same way. Could it be that we care so much that it's hard for us to separate?

[*Lisa moves away from the sensorimotor experience to formal reflection. With some clients it may be important to help them stay focused within the sensorimotor perspective, but Lisa seems to have gotten a new insight which may be helpful for her to process within her primary formal style. Having returned to sensorimotor experience, she recalls and relearns how important the relationship between her and Christine is. With that awareness, she may be ready to take new action and find new behaviours that will better serve her and her daughter.*]

Interviewer: So, you feel that your caring for one another shows itself in the arguments you are having?

[*The interviewer reflects Lisa's meaning. Lisa is finding that deeper meanings and feelings underlie the surface of the fights she is having with her daughter. The discussion has moved further into the more abstract formal style.*]

Lisa: I guess so. It seems strange to fight when one is close, but I guess that happens.

Interviewer: Let's go a bit further. Could you tell me a bit about what happened for you when you were Christine's age and you left home for college?

[*The interviewer introduces an open-ended question to examine possible parallels between the two situations. At one level this is concrete, as the interviewer is asking for specifics, but at another level it is formal and possibly even dialectic/ systemic, as here she is searching for patterns of patterns and possible intergenerational family issues.*]

Lisa: Well, it was different for me. My mum and I were close, but not so close as Christine and I. I guess being a single parent makes the two of us even closer.

[*Lisa responds within the formal style, noting the differences in meaning between the two situations. Comparisons and contrasts between situations are usually associated with formal reasoning. In addition, Lisa brings up the issue of single parenthood.*]

Interviewer: So, the two situations are different. You feel closer to Christine than perhaps you did to your own mother. Could you go a bit further with that?

[*The interviewer reflects Lisa's meaning with an invitation to expand her analysis via an open-ended question.*]

Lisa: One thing occurs to me. My mum always said, 'Healthy birds fly away.' I wonder if I've been hanging on too much and maybe I'm more of the problem than I thought I was.

[*Lisa is now beginning to draw on strengths from within her intergenerational family history. This represents a transition point between the formal and dialectic/ systemic styles.*]

Interviewer: So, in your family of origin, health is represented by the saying, 'Healthy birds fly away.' What meaning do you make of that? How do family factors relate to what's going on between you and Christine?

[*The focus has changed from the individual to the family, an indicator of a shift to dialectic/systemic questioning.*]

Lisa: I've got it. Christine and I really bonded after the divorce. Sometimes I depended on her too much. But, as mum said, it is the healthy ones who are able to leave home. I should be glad for my successes and maybe let go more easily.

[*Lisa is thinking now using a dialectic/systemic frame of reference. She is beginning to see how the concrete difficulties she is experiencing with her daughter were influenced by the family's developmental history – the divorce. Simultaneously, she*] *is discovering how learnings from her family of origin may be of help to her and her daughter during their own separation process.*]

Interviewer: That is great. It sounds like the situation is making more sense to you now. And perhaps you can draw on the strengths of your mum's legacy to move nearer to beginning the steps toward resolution with your daughter.

Comments on the interview: the importance and power of the sensorimotor and dialectic/systemic styles

The excerpt above illustrates several issues. Let us consider two of these and the implications from a communication perspective.

Images and sensorimotor experiencing

First, you may have noted that imaging was particularly important in discovering the deeper emotions underlying the issues between Lisa and her daughter. Imaging, especially when based on bodily sensations, can be particularly powerful, thus emphasising the influential role of non-verbal communication in the interview process. Often, clients will be rapidly moved to tears or other deep emotions. This type of work should not be done with a client unless the client knows beforehand what to expect and what the interviewer will likely be doing. In the example above, note that Lisa had gone through a similar process before.

DCT stresses the importance of egalitarian relationships in the interview. If the interviewer had simply started the sensorimotor imagery exercise without preparation and consent, it might have been equally powerful, and yet, potentially more threatening and mysterious to the client. DCT emphasises the importance of sharing in advance what is to happen with clients rather than surprising them. We argue strongly against using powerful techniques unless the client is fully informed. We have found the client's direct involvement in the selection and application of techniques has a positive effect on the quantity and quality of self-disclosure, motivation, and commitment during the interview process.

If sensorimotor work of this type is new to you, practise it first with an informed volunteer and utilise it in your work only with appropriate supervision. Even after sufficient practice, you must be prepared to deal with the intensity of the emotions that these types of techniques can trigger in a client. Imagine that, even with informed consent, you and/or the client begin to feel uncomfortable with the depth of emotion expressed. What do you need to do? First, you need to validate whatever experience the client shares with you, for each person experiences deep emotion in a different way. Several additional options for dealing with deep sensorimotor affect are presented in Box 17.4. These ideas can assist you to help clients express more emotion or to help them cope with more emotion than either you or they feel able to at the moment.

Box 17.4 Options for dealing with sensorimotor affect*

1 Observe non-verbal processes
Breathing directly reflects emotional content. Rapid or frozen breathing signals contact with intense emotion. Other cues include facial flushing, pupil contraction/dilation, and body tension.

2 Pace clients and lead them to more expression of affect
Many people get right to the edge of a feeling, and then back away with a joke, a change of subject, or an intellectual analysis. In such instances, you could:

a Say the person looks like they are close to *something important*. 'Would you like to go back and try again?'
b Discuss some positive aspect of the situation. This could free them to face the negative. Anchoring a positive emotion in the body can be a useful resource for clients which you can use from time to time. You as the helper also represent a positive asset yourself.
c Use here-and-now sensorimotor techniques and questioning strategies. Using the present tense (e.g. 'What are you seeing/hearing/feeling?') is particularly helpful. Gestalt exercises also are useful, or other such interventions that help clients become more aware of body feeling. Use the word 'do' if you find yourself uncomfortable with emotion (e.g. 'What do you feel?' or 'What did you feel then?'). Such questions begin to move clients away from the intensity of here-and-now experiencing.

3 Be prepared to deal with tears, rage, despair, joy, or exhilaration
Your own comfort with emotional expression will affect how clients face emotion when in a helping relationship. If you are not comfortable with a particular emotion – yours or your client's – your client is likely to avoid this emotion, or you may handle it less effectively than other emotions.

A balance of being very present, being aware of your own breathing, providing culturally appropriate and supportive eye contact, and, still allowing room to sob, yell, or shake is important.

Keep emotional expression within a fixed time. Ten minutes is a long time when you are crying, and helping the person to reorient also is important.

* This box is adapted from a presentation by Leslie Brain at the University of Massachusetts in 1988.

The dialectic/systemic style

Most helping interviewers operate within the concrete and formal styles. DCT argues that these styles are important, but that the field needs more emphasis on the deeper feelings associated with sensory experience and the complex issues which arise when we view life from the perspectives provided by dialectic/systemic emotion and reasoning. The dialectic/systemic style was only beginning to be explored in the interview example. Lisa starts to realise that the context of her daughter leaving and the history of her divorce are important parts of the concrete, specific fights she and her daughter have been experiencing. This is perhaps, at best, a beginning. Among the many systemic issues which may relate to mother–daughter relationships are gender roles, the impact of cultural expectations, economic issues, and broader social support issues such as the extended family and community.

A conceptual model for matching and expanding client style

A helping interviewer must be able to establish an environment that first responds to a client's primary style and then helps this person explore issues from other cognitive-emotional perspectives. In this way, the interviewer must be able to engage in a co-constructive process – developing helping environments, with clients, that are in sync with the styles being explored. DCT posits four basic therapeutic styles, each one corresponding to one of the four styles. These are illustrated in Figure 17.1 and further explained below.

Style 1: environmental structuring for the sensorimotor style

The interviewer directs the session, extensively using communication skills. Examples of clients who predominantly rely on this style are individuals seen in in-patient psychiatric settings, correctional settings, and traditional one-to-one instructional or teaching settings. It is also true, however, that many other clients often work within the sensorimotor style, for it is here that deeper emotional experience may be reached.

A number of environmental-structuring therapies and techniques are highly useful to clients needing to explore or master resources within this style. Directive psychiatry and counselling are characteristic. In these cases, the helping interviewer 'takes over' for the client and makes necessary decisions. In cases of trauma, such as rape or child abuse, the interviewer has the responsibility of taking action to help the individual. When helping children and families in crisis, the interviewer may be required to take such direct action. With clients who have less severe problems, direct-ive techniques such as relaxation training, structuring an environment for behaviour (for example, working with a hyperactive child), and body-oriented therapies, such as dance and movement therapy, may be appropriate.

Style 2: coaching for the concrete style

To create this environment, the interviewer balances attending and influencing skills and works with the client in a participative manner. The interviewer knows things that the client does not, and is willing to share them. Examples are vocational decision making around a specific issue, assertiveness training, many behavioural techniques, and reality therapy. Here, the helper takes the present developmental capabilities of the client and helps the client enhance, expand, and practise them.

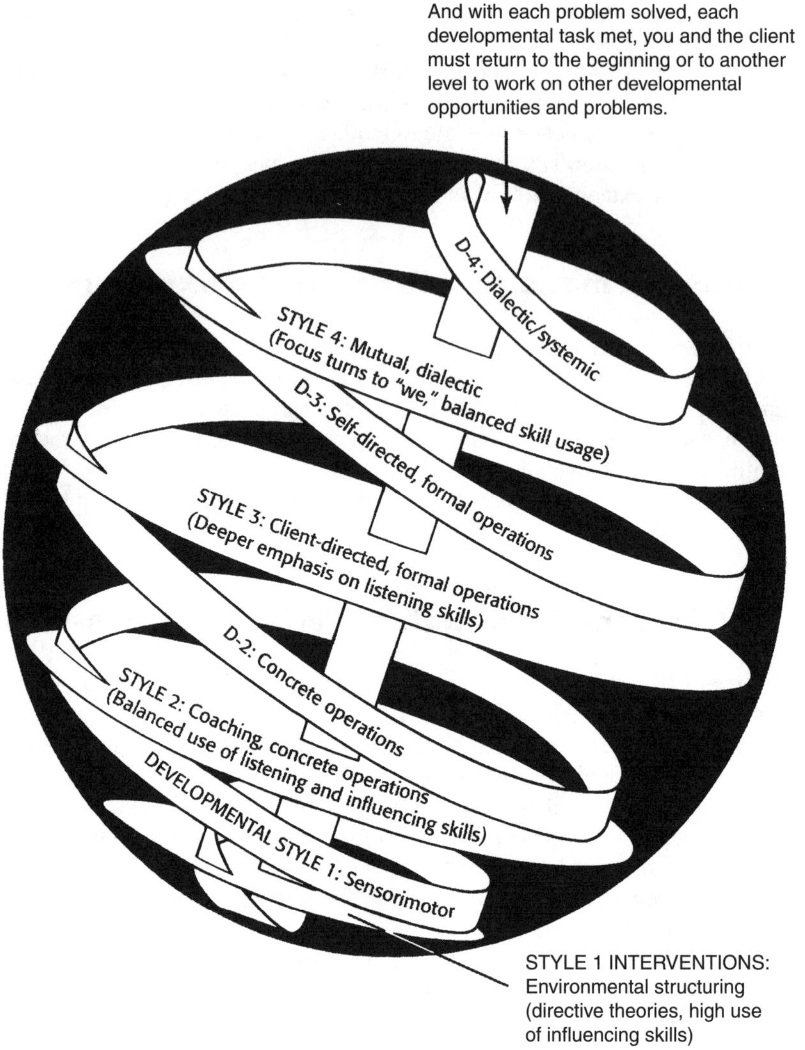

And with each problem solved, each developmental task met, you and the client must return to the beginning or to another level to work on other developmental opportunities and problems.

D-4: Dialectic/systemic

STYLE 4: Mutual, dialectic
(Focus turns to "we," balanced skill usage)

D-3: Self-directed, formal operations

STYLE 3: Client-directed, formal operations
(Deeper emphasis on listening skills)

D-2: Concrete operations

STYLE 2: Coaching, concrete operations
(Balanced use of listening and influencing skills)

DEVELOPMENTAL STYLE 1: Sensorimotor

STYLE 1 INTERVENTIONS:
Environmental structuring
(directive theories, high use
of influencing skills)

Example theories/applications:

Style 1: Body-oriented therapies (medication, meditation, exercise, yoga) and here-and-now strategies (imagery, Gestalt empty chair, focusing)

Style 2: Concrete narratives/storytelling, assertiveness training, thought stopping, automatic thoughts inventory, skills training

Style 3: Reflection on any of the above, person-centred theory, psychodynamic theories, cognitive work

Style 4: Multicultural counselling and therapy, feminist therapy, intergenerational family therapy, social action in community

Figure 17.1 The developmental sphere*
* Reprinted by permission of Lois T. Grady

Style 3: client-directed consulting for formal style

To create this environment, the helper supports the client's reflective search primarily through the use of attending skills and posing reflective questions. Non-directive and classic Rogerian counselling styles typify this approach. Within the formal style, techniques of Frankl's logotherapy, psychoanalytic methods, and the narrative models of therapy may be used. Interpretations and reframes which help the client to examine patterns of self and situations also are germane within this style.

Style 4: mutual collaboration for dialectic/systemic style

Here, the helper promotes self-starters to develop their own goals and methods. Feminist counselling, multicultural counselling, and systemic counselling are prime examples of the type of helping offered within this style. For example, the feminist therapist's emphasis on working with the client as a co-equal typifies this mutual, collaborative style of helping. At times, a therapist using a feminist approach may provide strong direction (style 1), assertiveness training (style 2), or listening (style 3); but ultimately the goal is a co-constructed (style 4) view of the world in which client and therapist learn together.

The sphere illustrated in Figure 17.1 indicates the need to match a helper's style with a client's predominant cognitive-emotional style in order to understand and discuss the primary issues at hand. Some clients are well grounded in the perceptual frames and methods of interpretation which their preferred perspective provides. Some of these people may be so comfortable with using only the resources of one style that they may have significant difficulty in shifting to a new perspective within an alternative style (rigid movement within and among cognitive-emotional styles). Conversely, some clients are not well grounded in any of the four styles and use resources associated with all four, but in a rather haphazard manner (diffuse or chaotic movement within and among cognitive-emotional styles). Finally, some clients have a strong mastery of the perceptual and communication skills found within each style and are cognisant of how and why they choose a particular strategy to interpret events (flexible movement within and among cognitive-emotional styles). This latter type of client typifies the goal of DCT – to help clients knowingly access a variety of perspectives in order to experience, interpret, discuss, and act on their issues. It is because of the variety of client styles and the stated goal of DCT that the helper must be comfortable operating within all four of the styles.

While the three types of clients described above (i.e. rigid, diffuse, flexible) are common, most do not simply operate within one style An example of a client operating within multiple styles may illustrate the complexity of many clients. An older woman entering the job market for the first time may be operating within a confused sensorimotor style vocationally, and not have even the most elementary job-seeking skills. At the same time, she may have had a wide range of experience in volunteer work and may be a successful parent and 'counsellor' to her children and to the neighbourhood families. In these areas of her life, she may be thinking within a formal or even dialectic/systemic frame of reference. She may need concrete skills training as she practises for job interviews and prepares her résumé.

Thus, in a single interview, it may be necessary to move through several different interviewing/counselling styles, depending on the issue being discussed. In relation to this woman, for the purposes of her vocational issues, it may be best to begin by using a structured style, to assist her in navigating through unfamiliar territory. It may also be necessary, however, to assist her in formal reflection in order to facilitate her understanding of the job or career choices she wishes to pursue. It may also be necessary to assist her with the concrete skills of job searching and interviewing. As this client develops more confidence, knowledge, and experience, successful counselling may help her to examine her vocational identity from other styles. She may need to look at herself and her patterns of experience (formal) and then analyse possible job discrimination for older women (dialectic/systemic). It would probably also be helpful to enable her to explore emotional experience within the sensorimotor style.

A note about helper flexibility

You will find you can change your counselling style as your clients grow. The cycle suggested here starts with attending to find out where the client is developmentally, then moves to solidify the psychological and interpersonal resources available within the client's predominant style before shifting to an alternative perspective. Again, the ultimate DCT goal is to help clients effectively access resources from within several of the styles so that they develop a multitude of resources that they can later access along their developmental journey.

Many helpers, however, try to 'hang on' to an old style that worked with the client, and fail to alter flexibly the helping environment as the client moves and grows. If you find, through observation and other types of client feedback, that your interviewing style is no longer working as it did before, shift your style to meet the new developmental needs of your client. Remember: interviewing and counselling are for the client, not for the helper. Quality use of communication skills and developmental theory can provide clients with an optimum range of helping environments that change in conjunction with their growth.

Using DCT within a multicultural perspective

Where does the socio-cultural context end and the individual begin? This question is at the heart of the multiculturalism controversy, evident in literature on helping and interviewing. In the past, it was assumed that a helper, regardless of ethnic background, gender, sexual orientation, and economic class, was objective and minimally biased. Helping was viewed as a neutral interaction and helpers were trained to discount their cultural preconceptions and to attend to the mastery of counselling theory and practice. Unfortunately, this emphasis on the 'technical' aspects of the helping profession minimised the human/cultural aspects of our work. At best, it produced well-intentioned professionals who accepted that they were probably ineffective when working with clients of differing cultural backgrounds. At worst, it continued a type of cultural imperialism that further led to the alienation of many diverse client populations (Rigazio-DiGilio & Ivey, 1995; Ivey et al., 2005).

Many recent models of helping are based on the knowledge that counselling is a multicultural exchange process (Sue, Ivey & Pedersen, 1996; Ponterotto, Casas, Suzuki & Alexander, 2001). These models subordinate the technical skills of helping (i.e. communication skills, empathy skills, awareness of the knowledge base) to understanding the importance of the socio-cultural forces operating on the interview process. Implicit in this awareness is the need to recognise how our own cultural backgrounds enter the helping relationship and interact, with all biases intact, with the cultural backgrounds of our clients.

DCT posits that all counselling takes place in a cultural context. Our model of helping values the *client's own language*, including all the culturally bound assumptions, frames of reference, and unique perspectives that clients use to make meaning of their world. Conversely, our own helping language is extremely important. By posing questions and comments at specific styles we can help clients to examine issues from multiple perspectives while still maintaining a firm sense of self, rather than pushing clients into styles that they are not developmentally ready to enter. As we are given verbal and non-verbal cues that clients are experiencing difficulty within a particular style, the developmentally appropriate response is to return to a style with which they are more comfortable.

DCT questioning strategies and sensitivity to the natural language clients use to process and communicate their feelings, thoughts, and interaction intentionally stress the importance of cultural heritage and the role it plays in a client's construction of the world. By allowing cultural influences to be accepted and used as elements of the interview process, DCT helps make meaning of the individual's family, community, socio-cultural, and political context. Helping individuals learn to perceive social, political, and economic contradictions and to take action against the oppressive elements of reality should be one of our primary goals as helpers (Appleby, Colon & Hamilton, 2001).

OVERVIEW

The effectiveness of the DCT model of helping is based on the careful application of a wide range of communication skills. By integrating developmental theory with interviewing skills, counsellors can fine-tune treatment plans that address the natural changes clients experience over the course of their development and during the counselling relationship. Developmental skills can be an important and useful addition to your practice as a helper. It does little good to speak of complex and abstract ideas with a client working through a divorce who is tearful and confused and needs sensorimotor direction, support, and, later, concrete problem-solving skills.

At the heart of the ideas presented here is the importance of noting where your client 'is at'. How are they thinking and feeling and how are they making sense of the world? Your ability to note whether your client is presenting within the sensorimotor, concrete, formal, and/or dialectic/systemic styles will enable you to match your style and language to the client's idiosyncratic needs.

The DCT questioning strategies presented here can enable you to help clients expand their thinking and emotion within each style or move to another style for further growth. The developmental framework reminds us that different clients need to work within different styles throughout the course of an interview process and that the most helpful interventions will be geared to a style the client is comfortable working within. If your first counselling style does not work, shift your style to another cognitive-emotional style that is aligned to the client's mode of making sense of and operating in the world.

Finally, DCT provides a helping model that recognises the importance of cultural influences operating within the interview and seeks to maximise the value of these influences. The linguistic processes and multicultural sensitivity of DCT allow clients to explore their issues through their natural language and to maximise the cognitive, affective, and behavioural resources each cognitive-emotional style has to offer. This is the ultimate goal of DCT – to empower clients to be able eventually to help themselves (Ivey, 2001).

REFERENCES

Anderson, T. (1987). *Style-shift counseling and developmental therapy with the style-shift indicator*. North Amherst, MA: Microtraining Associates.

Appleby, G. A., Colon, E. & Hamilton, J. (2001). *Diversity, oppression, and social functioning*. Boston, MA: Allyn & Bacon.

Borders, L. D. (1994). Potential for *DCT/SCDT* in addressing two elusive themes of mental health counselling. *Journal of Mental Health Counselling*, *16*, 75–78.

Capuzzi, D. & Gross, D. R. (2002). *Counseling and psychotherapy: theories and interventions*, 3rd edn. New York: Prentice-Hall.

Gergen, K. (2000). *The saturated self: dilemmas of identity in contemporary life*. New York: Basic Books.

Gilligan, C. (1982). *In a different voice*. Cambridge, MA: Harvard University Press.

Gregorc, A. (1985). *Inside styles: beyond the basics*. Columbia, CT: Gabriel Systems.

Heesacker, M., Prichard, S., Rigazio-DiGilio, S. & Ivey, A. (1995). Development of a paper and pencil measure on cognitive-developmental orientations. Unpublished report, Department of Psychology, University of Florida, Gainesville.

Hill, R. & Rogers, R. H. (1964). The developmental approach. In H. Christensen (Ed.), *Handbook of marriage and family therapy* (pp. 171–209). Chicago: Rand McNally.

Ivey, A. (1987). *Developmental therapy: theory into practice*. San Francisco, CA: Jossey-Bass.

Ivey, A. (1993). *Developmental strategies for helpers*. North Amherst, MA: Microtraining.

Ivey, A. E. (2001). Psychotherapy as liberation. In J. Ponterotto, J. Casas, L. Suzuki & C. Alexander (Eds), *Handbook of multicultural counseling*, 2nd edn. Thousand Oaks, CA: Sage.

Ivey, A. E. & Gonçalves, O. (1988). Developmental therapy: integrating developmental processes into the clinical practice. *Journal of Counseling and Development*, *66*, 406–413.

Ivey, A. E. & Ivey, M. B. (2003). *Intentional interviewing and counseling*. Pacific Grove, CA: Brooks/Cole–Thomson Learning.

Ivey, A. E., Gonçalves, O. F. & Ivey, M. B. (1989). Developmental therapy: theory and practice. In O. F. Gonçalves (Ed.), *Advances in the cognitive therapies: the constructive-developmental approach*. Porto, Portugal: APPORT.

Ivey, A. E., Ivey, M. B., Myers, J. E. & Sweeney, T. J. (2005). *Developmental counseling and therapy: promoting wellness over the lifespan*. Boston, MA: Lahaska Press/ Houghton Mifflin.

Jankowski, P. J. (1998). A developmental-constructivist framework for narrative therapy. *Family Therapy*, *25*, 111–120.

Kelly, G. (1955). *The psychology of personal construct*, vol I. New York: W.W. Norton.

Kunkler, K. P. & Rigazio-DiGilio, S. A. (1994). Systemic cognitive-developmental therapy: organizing structured activities to facilitate family development. *Simulation and Gaming: An International Journal of Theory, Design, and Research*, *25*, 75–87.

Mahoney, M. (2003). *Constructivist psychotherapy: a practical guide*. New York: Guilford Press.

Marszalek, J. & Cashwell, C. (1998). The gay and lesbian affirmative development (GLAD) model. Applying Ivey's developmental counseling therapy model to Cass' gay and lesbian identity development model. *Journal of Adult Development and Aging: Theory and Research*, *1*, 13–31.

Myers, J. E., Shoffner, M., Briggs, M. (2002). Developmental counseling and therapy: an effective tool for understanding and counseling children. *The Professional School Counselor*, *5*, 194–202.

Piaget, J. (1955 [1923]). *The language and thought of the child*. New York: New American Library.

Ponterotto, J., Casas, J., Suzuki, L. & Alexander, C. (Eds) (2001). *Handbook of multicultural counseling*, 2nd edn. Thousand Oaks, CA: Sage.

Rigazio-DiGilio, S. A. (1993). Family counselling and therapy: theoretical foundations and issues of practice. In A. Ivey, M. Ivey & L. Simek-Morgan (Eds), *Counselling and psychotherapy: a multicultural perspective*, 3rd edn (pp. 333–358). Needham Heights, MA: Allyn and Bacon.

Rigazio-DiGilio, S. A. (1994a). A co-constructive developmental approach to ecosystemic treatment. *Journal of Mental Health Counselling*, *16*, 43–74.

Rigazio-DiGilio, S. A. (1994b). Beyond paradigms: the multiple implications of a co-constructive-developmental model. *Journal of Mental Health Counselling*, *16*, 205–211.

Rigazio-DiGilio, S. A. (2000). Reconstructing psychological distress and disorder from a relational perspective: a systemic, coconstructive-developmental framework. In R. Neimeyer & J. Raskin (Eds), *Constructions of disorder* (pp. 309–332). Washington, DC: American Psychological Association.

Rigazio-DiGilio, S. A. (2002). Postmodern theories of counseling. In D. C. Locke, J. E. Myers & E. L. Herr (Eds), *The handbook of counseling and psychotherapy*. Thousand Oaks, CA: Sage.

Rigazio-DiGilio, S. A. & Ivey, A. E. (1990). Developmental therapy and depressive disorders: measuring cognitive levels through patient natural language. *Professional Psychology: Research and Practice*, *21*, 470–475.

Rigazio-DiGilio, S. A. & Ivey, A. E. (1991). Developmental counselling and therapy: a framework for individual and family treatment. *Counselling and Human Development*, *24*, 1–20.

Rigazio-DiGilio, S. A. & Ivey, A. E. (1993). Systemic cognitive-developmental therapy:

an integrative framework. *The Family Journal: Counselling and Therapy for Couples and Families*, *1*, 208–219.

Rigazio-DiGilio, S. A. & Ivey, A. E. (1995). Individual and family issues in intercultural counselling and therapy: a culturally-centered perspective. *Canadian Journal of Counselling*, *29*, 244–261.

Rigazio-DiGilio, S. A., Gonçalves, O. & Ivey, A. E. (1994). Developmental counselling and therapy: a model for individual and family treatment. In D. Capuzzi & D. Gross (Eds), *Counselling and psychotherapy: theories and interventions* (pp. 471–513). Columbus, OH: Macmillan/Merill.

Rigazio-DiGilio, S. A., Ivey, A. E., Kunkler-Peck, K. & Grady, L. (2005). *Community genograms: using individual, family and cultural narratives with clients*. New York: Teacher's College Press, Columbia University.

Strehorn, K. C. (1999). Examining services to postsecondary students with learning disabilities through the use of Ivey's developmental counseling and therapy (DCT) model. *Dissertation Abstracts International: Section A. Humanities and Social Sciences*, *59*(7-A), 2367.

Sue, D. W., Ivey, A. & Pedersen, P. (1996). *A theory of multicultural counseling and therapy*. Pacific Grove, CA: Brooks/Cole.

Vygotsky, L. (1986 [1934]). *Thought and language*. Cambridge, MA: MIT Press.

Watzlawick, P. (Ed.) (1984). *The invented reality*. New York: W. W. Norton.

Chapter 18

The appraisal interview reappraised

Dennis Tourish

T HE APPRAISAL INTERVIEW IS one of the most ubiquitous features of life in organisations. It is also one of the most ridiculed. Evidence mounts each year that most such interviews are poorly managed, fail to improve organisational performance, demoralise employees, and subject the managers who administer them to intolerable levels of stress. No wonder that one researcher, unkindly but accurately, has described them as 'the annual fiasco' (Pickett, 2003, p. 237). It is typical of the data that a conference of human-resources professionals found over 90% of those present declaring that, if given the chance, they would modify, revise, or even eliminate the performance appraisal system currently used in their organisations (HR Focus, 2000). Thus, appraisal interviews are governed by some seemingly impregnable assumptions that research nevertheless suggests may be invalid – such as that organisations are rational entities, administrative systems are highly reliable, and most people can be trained to be unbiased and candid in their assessments of others (McCauley, 1997). Some have even argued that traditional appraisals are so inherently dysfunctional that they need to be abolished (e.g. Coens & Jenkins, 2000). Their continuing popularity represents another instance of hope triumphing over experience.

This chapter therefore offers a different perspective from that often found in the literature, particularly practitioner guides that instruct on 'how to'. Firstly, I define appraisal interviews and outline the range of roles they are expected to play. Flowing from this, the voluminous evidence that indicates why appraisals generally fail to work is reviewed. It would be tempting to outline a series of steps and skills that appear to avoid these problems, as many texts do (e.g. Bacal, 2003; Sandler &

Keefe, 2003). However, the conclusion offered here is that such piecemeal perspectives are more likely to compound the problem than resolve it. In particular, it is argued that most people are inherently poor at receiving criticism. We are so sensitive to it that even if critical feedback forms only a small part of the appraisal process, it is likely to be regarded by the recipient as representative of the entire interview. The evidence clearly suggests that when such perceptions arise they derail the main intended point of the appraisal interview – which is to improve performance. But we are also poor at giving accurate criticism or feedback more generally. For example, managers are inclined to exaggerate the personal contribution that people make to negative outcomes and underestimate the role of systems in producing poor performance (Gray, 2002). There is no compelling reason to believe that training or any other intervention will so improve the attitude of most people to either giving or receiving critical feedback that appraisal interviews will become effective for most people in most organisations in the near future. This chapter therefore outlines a framework to move organisations beyond appraisal interviews, and in the direction of both self-appraisal and counselling interviews that, with sufficient support, are more likely to create a regular celebration of positive performance rather than the annual fiasco mostly endured today.

WHAT APPRAISAL INTERVIEWS ARE INTENDED TO BE

Performance appraisal has been optimistically defined as the process of identifying, observing, measuring, and developing human resources in organisations (Cardy & Dobbins, 1994). It is often sold as a means of promoting two-way communication, showing employees respect by demonstrating that their opinions count, and helping to uncover and resolve conflict (Garavan et al., 1997). Feedback is intended to provide employees with information to improve their personal performance and effectiveness (Baruch, 1996). Thus, historically, appraisal interviews were intended to focus on three areas – development, motivation, and recognition of achievement (Smith & Rupp, 2003). Formal performance appraisal, at its best, has therefore been defined as 'a means for managers to identify and reward positive performance, promote a unified focus on the achievement of business goals and provide support for the personal development needs of employees' (Hargie et al., 2004, p. 374). In practice, organisations tend to have a host of other aspirations for their appraisal systems, including differentiating between employees to establish individual remuneration, the identification of training needs, and assessing suitability for promotion (Rees & Porter, 2003). In fact, this constitutes one of the biggest problems with traditional appraisals – like a truck overloaded with freight, and thus prone to capsize, the range of expectations invested in them has imbalanced the entire enterprise. For example, it is difficult to convince people that an appraisal interview is primarily developmental in purpose if promotion decisions also depend on the outcome. It is therefore unsurprising that Rees and Porter (2003, p. 280) note, 'Unfortunately, the available evidence is that most schemes do not work effectively.'

Traditionally, and in most of the literature, the term 'performance appraisal' has generally come to mean 'the annual interview that takes place between the manager and the employee to discuss the individual's job performance during the previous

12 months and the compilation of action plans to encourage improved performance' (Wilson & Western, 2000, p. 93). It is, at any rate, an innocuous-sounding ambition.

The idea that performance appraisal interviews are valuable remains a seductive notion for many managers. In part, this is because evaluating the performance of others is a pervasive activity in which all people routinely engage during most of their interpersonal interactions. Organisational appraisal systems are often regarded as nothing more than 'an attempt to formalise these activities for the benefit of both the individual and the organisation' (Torrington & Hall, 1991, p. 480). This chapter will shortly appraise the extent to which this hope is realised in practice.

Meanwhile, the scope of appraisal has developed rapidly. A Superboss report (Freemantle, 1994), which surveyed over 120 businesses in the UK, found that 89% had a formal performance appraisal system in place. It has been estimated that over 94% of US companies use some form of formal performance appraisal (Latham & Wexley, 1994). A survey of 280 Midwest companies in the USA found that 25% used annual upward appraisals, 18% peer appraisals, and 12% what are known as 360-degree appraisals, in which people evaluate themselves and then receive feedback from their immediate peers, managers, and subordinates (Antonioni, 1996; Atwater et al., 2002). They have become a global phenomenon. For example, appraisals have been widely used in China since the country initiated a programme of economic reform (Easterby-Smith et al., 1995). Zhu and Dowling (1998) concluded that 74.8% of Chinese firms carried out annual performance appraisals, presumably because they imagined that these had contributed to economic growth in the West. It is a wonder, with so many appraisal interviews being conducted, that anyone finds the time to make sure that the real work of the organisation gets done.

Designed to overpower some of the bugbears associated with traditional appraisals, 360-degree appraisals have also become a huge growth area in recent years (Bates, 2002). It has been argued that they offer multiple benefits, since multisource feedback is assumed to provide better performance information, more reliable ratings than what can be obtained from a single supervisor, and improved satisfaction by appraisees after the process is complete (Becton & Schraeder, 2004). Key companies, such as AT&T, the Bank of America, Caterpillar, GTE, and General Electric, have been pioneers in this latter approach. Given these tendencies, Coens and Jenkins (2000) estimate that appraisal interviews are used in about 80% of organisations – although they also estimate that about 90% of appraisers and appraisees are dissatisfied with them.

APPRAISAL INTERVIEWS – THE CRITIQUE

As already noted, research suggests that appraisal interviews are generally ineffective. Many, probably most, are demotivational, divisive, pseudo-scientific, and counterproductive (Freemantle, 1994). One typical study, investigating performance appraisal in a public sector organisation, found over 40% of staff dissatisfied with the system, including many who received good or outstanding ratings as a result of it (Mani, 2002). Among the most common problems are a lack of strategic focus, too much subjectivity on the part of appraisers, an insufficient level of skills on the part of managers, an accumulation of power by potential tyrants (petty Hitlers), who relish the opportunity to pass judgement on others, and a tendency to deliver criticisms of poor performance too long after the event to have an appreciable impact on outcomes (Gray, 2002). Appraisal interviews also tend to focus on individual performance, despite the fact that more work is now conducted in teams and that responsibility is therefore more widely diffused than in the past (Pfeffer, 2001).

Edmonstone (1996) identifies two other crucial problems with appraisal interviews and systems. Firstly, managers are encouraged to focus on current performance rather than future potential, through an emphasis on short-term results. Secondly, appraisals discourage multiskilling in favour of tight specification and detailed evaluations. In today's business environment, it is necessary for people to demonstrate behaviours consistent with such notions as flexibility, willingness to take charge, and tolerance for uncertainty, beyond their immediate tasks in a job description (Pulakos et al., 2000). It is ironic that managers used to chafe at trade union insistence on rigid demarcations. Appraisals may well reinstate such demarcations, by encouraging people to focus their efforts only on those aspects of performance likely to be recognised and rewarded in appraisal interviews.

A further difficulty lies in determining precisely what employees have done, and hence the extent of their contribution to organisational success or failure. For example, long-distance appraisals in multinational corporations (MNCs) encounter the problem that 'the staff involved at headquarters may have difficulty forging a precise image of the circumstances in which the various subsidiaries have had to operate to achieve their results. Consequently, the context of performance may be lost' (Shen, 2004, p. 548). With the elimination of many middle-management posts over the past few decades and a consequent widening in the numbers of direct reports that most managers are now responsible for, this problem goes beyond MNCs. Put simply, many managers are in no position to deliver cogent, well-informed evaluations of the performance of others. Moreover, it is probable that any attempt to do so undermines the sense of autonomy and intrinsic task motivation that is essential in many modern workplaces.

Given the fact that line managers are often under-prepared to handle the interview process, and are confused about how to give critical feedback, the interview (theoretically, the climax of the appraisal process) is also widely regarded as its Achilles heel (Cook & Crossman, 2004). It is little wonder that 'appraisals have become one of the most avoided experiences in organisational life. Supervisors do not like to give them and employees do not like to receive them' (Ford, 2004, p. 551).

Rating systems and performance-related pay

Appraisal interviews are often linked to evaluation of performance in the form of 'rating systems'. Here, performance is graded on a scale, normally of 1 to 5, with 5 representing excellent performance and 1 representing grounds for dismissal. Problems with this are legion (Kennedy & Dresser, 2001). They include:

- The grave difficulty in accurately assessing the details of someone's performance. Results are frequently a team effort. How do we disentangle the extent of each individual's contribution? What happens if we credit one person with all the achievement, when others may think that they put in the same or greater effort? If ratings are awarded which people think are unfair, the 'unfair rating' will become the issue, rather than necessary improvements in performance. Moreover, such approaches threaten to detract from other team-building efforts that may have been made. It is difficult to reconcile team responsibility and commitments with an emphasis on individual responsibility.

• How does one measure intangible factors such as motivation, creativity, team spirit, responsibility, and loyalty? Subjective impressions of performance on these issues tend to govern the ratings that are awarded. I discuss below many of the biases that illuminate why subjectivity is endemic to appraisal interviews – in my view, inescapably so. Typically, the impossibility of escaping subjective assessments makes the eventual 'grade' appear arbitrary to the person receiving it, and so leads to destructive conflict over the assessment awarded, rather than an emphasis on identifying developmental needs.

• When everyone knows that a grade is at stake, the emphasis of the meeting shifts from an open discussion of performance (in which both strengths and weaknesses can be honestly discussed) toward the optimum presentation of the self, the covering up of errors, and inflated claims for one's own performance. Naturally, this will involve a greater reluctance to accept feedback on areas where performance needs to improve.

The outcome of appraisal interviews has also often been linked to the award of performance-related pay. Many of the points made in opposition to the use of rating schemes also apply here. In the first place, such practices contradict what is known about motivation. *Intrinsic* motivation, which is most closely correlated with superior performance, flows from the satisfaction obtained by performing the task at hand, rather than doing it to obtain rewards *extrinsic* to the task itself (Kohn, 1999). Performance is likely to deteriorate when the emphasis shifts from intrinsic motivation to the gaining of extrinsic rewards. There is, therefore, no evidence that tying performance to pay actually improves performance – rather, the opposite is the case (Gray, 2002; Smith & Rupp, 2003).

Linking appraisal to pay in this manner generally transforms feedback into confrontation. Consider the following. In practice, organisations find it difficult to pay more than a limited proportion of people much more than the budgeted average for any given job. The financial gains on offer from such systems therefore tend to be nominal and/or restricted to a small number of people. The majority of an organisation's employees are more likely to emerge from what almost inevitably becomes an adversarial process nursing wounded egos and bearing feelings of resentment. One reason is that most people do not rate their own performance as either average or below average – in fact, they exaggerate their contribution to organisational success (Rollinson & Broadfield, 2002). The use of performance-related pay as part of the appraisal process means that managers use appraisal interviews to inform the majority of their people that their performance is much weaker than they themselves imagine it to be – an outcome which may also activate a large number of destructive, self-fulfilling prophecies. For these reasons, the evidence suggests that a system of performance-related pay demotivates people, that it does not help organisations to retain high performers, does not encourage poor performers to leave, and creates widespread perceptions of unfairness (Institute of Manpower Studies, 1993). It heightens status differentials between managers and employees, and threatens working relationships. In consequence, and perhaps counter-intuitively, performance-related pay (particularly when linked to appraisal) generally fails to improve organisational effectiveness (Eskew & Heneman, 1996). At the very least, the evidence unambiguously suggests that any discussion of training and development issues should be entirely separate from whatever mechanisms are used to determine remuneration (Wilson & Western, 2000).

An illuminating example of what happens when this research is ignored may be in order. Enron was an organisation that combined both a ranking system and the linking of performance to pay. Its bankruptcy in 2001 stands (at the time of writing) as the biggest in US corporate history. As with many other aspects of its internal culture, its approach to appraisal is a valuable case study in what not to do. An internal performance review committee rated employees twice a year (Gladwell, 2002). They were graded on a scale of 1 to 5, on 10 separate criteria, and then divided into one of three groups – 'A's, who were to be challenged and given large rewards; 'B's, who were to be encouraged and affirmed; and 'C's, who were told to shape up or ship out. Those in the 'A' category were referred to internally as 'water walkers'. The process was known as 'rank and yank'. The company's propensity to disproportionately reward those who were high achievers and risk-takers was widely acclaimed by business gurus (e.g. Hamel, 2000). Faculty from the prestigious Harvard Business School produced 11 case studies, uniformly praising its successes. However, problems multiplied. People chased high rankings because the potential rewards were enormous, while low rankings imperilled both their salaries and eventually their jobs. The appearance of success mattered more than its substance. In addition, internal promotions due to the appraisal system reached 20% a year. This made further evaluation more difficult and inevitably more subjective – how could one honestly rank someone's performance when they did not hold a position long enough to render sound judgement possible? Paradoxically, Enron had a punitive internal regime ('rank and yank') but loose control (those adjudged to be top performers moved on too fast to be pinned down). In this case, ratings and performance pay formed a lethal mix. Internal staff churn and a relentless emphasis on achieving high performance ratings in the interests of obtaining ever-greater personal rewards contributed to the lax ethical atmosphere that precipitated the company's downfall.

Versions of rank and yank have been used by many organisations, including General Electric and IBM. IBM, in the early 1990s, actually required that one out of every 10 employees be allocated a poor rating, and given 3 months to improve or be fired (Gabor, 1992). The research evidence overwhelmingly suggests that such practices produce only defiance, defensiveness, and rage (Kohn, 1999). As Kohn has noted, 'Threatening people can make them anxious about the consequences of doing poorly, but the fear of failure is completely different from the desire to succeed' (1999, p. 136). Praise can be used to emphasise that a culture of retribution belongs to the past, and is therefore much more likely to have a positive impact on performance (Seddon, 2001). It is, however, important that praise is not overdone. If it is, people may begin to perform tasks for the praise involved, and so find that their intrinsic motivation goes down. Its main value is a signal that authoritarian management holds no sway in the organisation concerned. The main enemy of innovation, effort, and achievement in the workplace is fear. In short, there is absolutely no evidence that either threatening to cut people's pay, or offering to increase it significantly, improves the quality, as opposed to possibly the quantity, of what they do.

However, illusions still linger, and some organisations now seek sustenance in technology. It has been argued that new software systems enable companies to monitor individual productivity more accurately (and less subjectively), and so target rewards on genuine top performers (Conlin, 2002). Among the companies taking this route are Hewlett-Packard, General Electric, and DuPont. Moreover, it has been suggested that people experience less evaluation apprehension and less emotion when they receive feedback via a computer system. Such systems can also focus the attention of raters on job-relevant behaviours, thereby reducing interpersonal biases (Fletcher & Perry, 2001). However, it has also been found that self-ratings are more inflated and less accurate in electronic communication than face-to-face interaction (Weisband & Atwater, 1999). Greater objectivity could be at the expense of sensitivity, since it removes the direct opportunity to monitor the reaction of recipients (Fletcher, 2001). Thus, appraisal remains primarily a human issue. People's feelings about it are unlikely to change at the sight of managers brandishing spreadsheets. Technology has yet to overcome the problems associated with rating systems, the linking of performance to pay, and the challenge of providing people with meaningful feedback that enables them to change their behaviour.

BIASES IN INTERPERSONAL PERCEPTION

It can be argued that 'the biggest challenge that impedes an effective performance review is the biases we all have' (Losyk, 2002, p. 8). Biases are so pronounced that their existence alone warrants a reappraisal of traditional practice in appraisal interviews. I review, here, the most important biases that have been identified as problematic in the context of appraisal, from the standpoint of both interviewees and interviewers.

The perspective of the interviewee

There is plentiful evidence to suggest that appraisees are likely to have a different and more optimistic view of their work performance than the person appraising them. Self-efficacy biases predispose us to believe that we personally are better on various positively rated dimensions of social behaviour than most other people (Gioia, 1989; Pfeffer & Cialdini, 1998). Furthermore, we tend to assume that others see us in the same rose-tinted light in which we see ourselves. The phenomenon can be observed in any reality TV show seeking to identify the next pop sensation, and in which tuneless warblers exhibit the conviction that they are destined to be as influential as Elvis or Madonna – whatever the judges say. Positive feedback therefore feels intuitively valid while critical feedback that conflicts with our idealised self-image feels erroneous (Tourish & Hargie, 2004). Perhaps for these reasons, appraisees who receive high evaluations tend to perceive the appraisal evaluation as fairer than those who received a low evaluation (Stoffey & Reilly, 1997). Thus, critical feedback is viewed as threatening. People are therefore likely to reject it, so that the feedback received is more likely to stimulate conflict between appraisee and appraiser than serve as the basis for improvements in performance.

In particular, most of us think that we contribute more to group discussions than the average input of everyone else involved, and that more people agree with our opinions than is actually the case (Sutherland, 1992). A major reason for this may be that we are intrinsically motivated to develop a positive evaluation of ourselves, as a means of shoring up our sense of identity (Wilke & Meertens, 1994). This is easily achieved when we exaggerate our role, general level of influence, and contribution to group discussions (Brown, 2000). Again, it means that people who work in teams tend to have a heightened impression of their role in delivering team successes, and look askance at feedback to the effect that their performance is average, ineffective, or poor.

Attribution processes play a crucial role in heightening such effects. We are inclined to explain the behaviour of the people around us as the result of global (that is, what is true of them in one situation is true of them in all) personality characteristics which are also assumed to be permanent, while we excuse our own behaviour as the result of the situation we find ourselves in (Forsterling, 2001). The tendency to overestimate the role of personality in the behaviour of others while exaggerating the role of situation in our own has been termed 'the fundamental attribution error' (Kreitner et al., 2002). Thus, we attribute our failure to the situation, but our successes to personal factors ('I had a good appraisal because I am bright: I had a poor appraisal because this organisation is terrible'). This also tempts us into a process of *blame realignment*, in which our primary concern is to establish our innocence in the face of organisational problems, while putting complete responsibility for the situation on someone else's shoulders. Truly, failure is an orphan, while success has many fathers. Again, this implies that appraisees are likely to have a very different view of their performance from that of an appraiser, stimulating further conflict.

Thus, people are especially sensitive to negative input – what has been termed *the automatic vigilance effect* (Pratto & John, 1991). Its effects in the workplace have been well documented. For example, a study found that attempts to assist people by pointing out improvement needs in their work were perceived as threatening to employees' self-esteem and resulted in defensive behaviour (De Nisi, 1996). In any event, 75% of people saw the evaluations they received as less favourable than their own self-estimates and therefore regarded appraisal interviews as a deflating experience. Follow-up studies found that those aspects of performance most criticised showed the least improvement. Another experimental study offered people feedback after completing a survey, while withholding feedback from others. It found no significant positive changes in those receiving feedback (Atwater et al., 2000). It is critical to remember that employees who do not trust whatever appraisal information they receive tend to discount its value and usefulness (Dobbins et al., 1993). Discounted feedback cannot serve as a guide to either employee development or improved organisational performance. It seems that, overall, negative feedback creates resentment, places obstacles in the path of personal development, and diminishes rather than enhances organisational effectiveness.

It may be argued by defenders of appraisal interviews that the focus should therefore be on the celebration of positive behaviour, and a discussion of how it can be repeated more often. Thus, many texts recommend that when criticisms have to be made they should focus on specific behaviours, be linked to realistic action plans capable of achieving improvements, and occur in the context of a supportive organisational culture. In any event, the main emphasis should be on positive feedback. This is more likely to create focus, clarity, and a bias in favour of action to secure significant change. Wise as this approach appears, it seems unlikely that it can be accommodated within the framework of traditional approaches to appraisal interviews. The automatic vigilance effect suggests that even modest criticisms will predominate in the mind of the recipient, and come to be regarded as more typical of the interview than may have been the case. Moreover, the biases which also afflict appraisers may create an inbuilt tendency to deliver imbalanced, inaccurate, unfocused, and unhelpful feedback. It is to these biases that I now turn.

The perspective of the interviewer

Most of us have a tendency to slot people into categories based on immediately obvious stereotypical traits, such as the colour of their skin, height, accent, and mode of dress (Leyens et al., 1994). Appraisers also categorise in this manner. This inevitably means that they often perceive people based on their own personal prejudices, rather than as their job performance warrants. In particular, a number of biases have been identified that seem particularly active during traditional appraisal interviews, and which derail most of them. These include the following:

- Appraisers frequently fall victim to *the halo effect* (Furnham, 1997). There is a tendency to assume that a positive attribute or a job-related success in one area automatically implies success in others. Enron, the most analysed case study of failure in business history, serves here also as an excellent example. Its traders were rated mostly on their ability to generate the appearance of high profits from their transactions (Tourish & Vatcha, 2005). It was assumed that this was representative of a wider business acumen of long-term value to the company. In fact, their ability on this front signified a lack of sounder business judgement and a spirit of ethical incontinence that helped bring the organisation to bankruptcy.
- *Personal liking bias* means that when supervisors like subordinates, for whatever reason, they generally give them higher performance ratings, their judgement of subordinates' work performance becomes less accurate, and they show a disinclination to punish or deal with poor performance (Lefkowitz, 2000). As was noted earlier, there has been a significant growth in recent years in 360-degree appraisals since, drawing feedback from multiple sources, it has been assumed that it is less likely to be handicapped by such biases. However, the evidence suggests that this expectation is unlikely to be fulfilled. Interpersonal factors, such as liking and similarity, have been found to be more important in determining ratings in 360-degree appraisals than the technical proficiency of the person being appraised (Bates, 2002). We also now live in an increasingly litigious age. There have been a growing number of lawsuits claiming that poor appraisals relative to those of others were influenced more by the personal biases of managers than by the actual performance of the employee (Goldstein, 2001).

- *The horn effect* arises when a problem in one area is assumed to be representative of defects elsewhere (Hargie et al., 2004). If we see a scratch on the bodywork of a new car it might well be that everything else is perfect, but it is unlikely that we will be able to set aside our initial poor impression. As an old Russian proverb puts it: 'A spoonful of tar spoils a barrelful of honey.' In turn, we feel compelled to focus our attention on such negatives rather than positives. Moreover, we are especially sensitive to negative information. This means that it is difficult to set aside a negative impression, once it is formed. For example, it has been found that negative self-disclosures are regarded by most people as much more informative than positive ones (Hargie & Dickson, 2004). The implications for interviews of all kinds are striking. One study of selection interviewing found that, on average, 8.8 items of favourable information were required to change an initially unfavourable impression, but only 3.8 items of unfavourable information were required to alter an initially favourable impression (Bolster & Springbett, 1981). Moreover, it takes more than twice as much positive as negative information to change an initial impression of a candidate (Judge et al., 2000). Thus, in practice, it proves difficult for people to focus most of their attention on examples of positive behaviour, at least in terms of the judgements they form. One consequence is what has been termed the 10–90 effect, in which 90% of time in an appraisal interview is spent discussing the 10% of the job where the employee is performing badly (Hargie et al., 2004).

- *The consistency error* suggests that we have an exaggerated need to feel consistent in our opinions and judgements, and to assume that people and circumstances are more stable than they actually are (Millar et al., 1992). Thus, when we form an initial impression of someone, it is very difficult to change it (Fiske et al., 1999). This predisposes us to interpret new evidence in the light of our existing assumptions, while ignoring anything that contradicts our most cherished beliefs. We have a tendency to seek out and remember information that confirms our prejudices, while ignoring or forgetting anything that suggests we might be wrong (Tourish, 1999). This has been described as *the confirmatory bias* (Rabin & Schrag, 1999). For example, if we expect someone to be a poor performer in their job, it is likely that we will see only evidence of this when we examine what they do. Furthermore, this perception is communicated to the person concerned by our overall bearing, and the tension created results in actual poor performance. Our expectation has created a self-fulfilling prophecy, which, of course, only confirms our view that what we thought at the beginning was right all along (Manzoni & Barsoux, 2002). These latter authors have dubbed this 'the set up to fail syndrome'.

- *The fundamental attribution error*, discussed above, means that an appraiser tends to attribute poor performance to the personality of the interviewee rather than to the situation. For example, it may be assumed that there is low ability to begin with, perhaps compounded by lack of effort. However, if the employee has successes, managers are likely to conclude that it is their own inspired leadership, judgement, and competency that have caused it (Heneman et al., 1989). The notion that it reflects the talent of the employee is downplayed. Employees, meanwhile, are likely to have exactly the opposite perception.

- *The similarity bias* means that we are attracted to people who look like us, sound like us, and form a convenient echo chamber for our own ideas (Millar et al., 1992). Thus, dissenters in organisations are generally penalised for voicing their views (Kassing, 2001). They are at an obvious disadvantage during appraisal interviews. During appraisals, we therefore often observe a *crony effect*, in which yes-men and -women have a natural advantage in the competition for promotion, *and the doppelgänger effect*, in which appraisal ratings reflect the similarities between the person being appraised and the appraiser.

- *The 'what is evaluated problem'* arises when the behaviours being evaluated differ from those required to obtain organisational goals. For example, Abraham (2001) found that companies often identify a variety of competences as essential for managerial effectiveness, such as communication skills, a propensity for risk taking, and team working. However, they persistently fail to use the identified competencies as criteria for assessing performance during appraisal interviews. Under such conditions, rather than driving improved performance, appraisal institutionalises a disconnection between strategic intention and what is rewarded – and therefore what gets done. Such misalignments frequently derail and incapacitate the whole enterprise.

- Each of these problems is exacerbated by *ingratiation effects*. People with lower status habitually seek to influence those of greater status by exaggerating how much they agree with their opinions, policies, and practices (Rosenfeld et al., 1995), and so ingratiate themselves with the powerful. There is plentiful empirical evidence to suggest that most managers are unaware of the extent to which they personally are at the receiving end of these practices, while they also engage in behaviours (again, often unconsciously) which discourage the transmission of critical feedback (e.g. Tourish & Robson, 2003). The effect is that managers become ever more inclined to surround themselves with those who share their views, ape their mannerisms, and uncritically endorse their opinions. Those of a critical disposition are viewed with suspicion and are less likely to advance in the organisational hierarchy. Similarity and liking biases, already endemic, become ever stronger, making accurate and honest appraisals even more difficult to deliver.

Overall, these perceptual biases suggest that we have a high confidence in our judgements of other people, but that many of these judgements are inaccurate. What can be done to improve them? It is often argued that training must be given to help both managers and other employees with the appraisal process and hence to overcome the problems posed by the biases discussed above (e.g. Rees & Porter, 2003; Ford, 2004). Training may indeed help managers, for example, to focus their feedback on behaviours rather than personalities. However, it is unlikely, in my view, that managers and staff can be trained to overcome the formidable range of obstacles to effective appraisal interviews identified in this chapter. The example of people's inbuilt resistance to critical feedback, and the enormous difficulties this creates in transmitting it, best illustrates the problem. 'Regression to the mean' effects describe the inevitable tendency for behaviour to cluster around a central midpoint of performance on any given variable (Hastie & Dawes, 2001). It suggests that most people will be closer to the average, or mean, level of performance than they are to depart significantly from it. Given that appraisal interviews are designed to be implemented by the majority of a population in any given organisation, it can therefore be assumed that their average level of performance will be closer to the mean than it will be to depart from it – that is, the level of performance is likely to be so weak as to be dysfunctional. For example, one survey of 200 large companies found that 70% of employees said they were more confused than enlightened by the feedback they had received (Meyer, 1991). This suggests that most managers are poor at delivering effective feedback and most employees are poor at receiving it. Thus, it may be unwise to assume that training will substantially move the performance of most people from the mean scores of behaviour likely to be found on these issues.

360-DEGREE APPRAISAL – A NEW WAY FORWARD?

At the beginning of this chapter, I noted that the popularity of 360-degree appraisals has grown enormously. Nearly all the Fortune 500 companies in the USA now utilise them, while a growth trend has also been observed in the UK (Mabey, 2001). The 360-degree appraisal, or multisource feedback, involves people evaluating themselves, and then receiving feedback from an immediate supervisor, peers, and (if the person is a manager) direct reports. It is assumed that appraisals from multiple sources provide a wider range of performance information, useful in identifying employee strengths and weaknesses (Gregurus et al., 2001). They are also assumed to have the capacity to increase perceived fairness, reliability, and ratee acceptance of feedback (Harris & Schaubroeck, 1988), to provide an additional legal defence in the face of feedback (Bernardin & Beatty, 1984), and to be more simple and less expensive to administer (Bates, 2002). In essence, applause or boos from a large audience are thought to deliver a more credible verdict on a performance than those of a single spectator.

However, the evidence is mixed, to say the least – particularly on the extent to which 360-degree appraisal delivers improvements in organisational performance. One investigation found it to be associated with a 10.6% decrease in shareholder value (Pfau et al., 2002). Evidently, many such programmes have arisen as a straightforward imitation of what competitors are doing, and have been hurriedly implemented without sufficient attention to such 'minor' details as how feedback should be managed and delivered, and how the process should support bottom-line organisational goals. For example, one survey discovered that over half the companies that introduced 360-degree appraisal quickly abandoned it, in the face of inflated ratings and hostility from employees (Waldman et al., 1998). Doing something 'because everyone else does it' often turns into a doomed quest to find competitive advantage by emulating the mishaps of one's rivals. Moreover, there is also evidence that managers are inclined to rate subordinates more highly in such exercises than their behaviour warrants, since highly rated subordinates make them look good, while peers also are open to collusion by giving each other positive evaluations (Toegel & Conger, 2003).

There have been many suggestions as to how these problems can be overcome. Box 18.1 summarises some of the best-practice guidelines derived from the relevant research (Peiperl, 2001). However, similar guidelines have often been produced for such appraisals. The evidence is that they have failed to improve practice significantly. This suggests that 'how to' advice on 360-degree appraisals must be viewed with

Box 18.1 Guidelines for effective 360-degree appraisal

- *Keep the process simple.* As with traditional appraisals, the more complex the paperwork and the more overwhelming the feedback, the less likelihood there is of sustained behaviour change.
- *Develop your own instrument.* Many 360-degree instruments are available. However, it is best to design one customised for your own organisation, and that meets its own unique needs. Involve people in this effort, and so generate their involvement, understanding, and support.
- *Provide written feedback.* Research suggests that, when multisource feedback is at stake and thus many people have contributed to their evaluation, most people prefer this as their predominant method of feedback.
- *In addition to written feedback, train people to act as coaches.* Most people need someone with whom they can discuss the results they have obtained. People formally allocated this role can function as coaches. They should be trained in active listening, focused interviewing, dealing with feelings, and goal setting.
- *Ensure that those doing the appraising are afforded anonymity.* People are more likely to offer honest opinions if their identity is protected. This depersonalises the nature of the feedback, and helps focus attention on the behaviour changes that are required.
- *Select peer appraisers on the basis of objective criteria.* If persons being appraised are charged with this responsibility, they are more likely to select people who will give them inflated praise rather than suggest how they can do better.
- *Train appraisers.* This should focus on the objectives of the process and the errors associated with it (such as the halo error), and contain scope for questions and discussion regarding the whole process.
- *Train appraisees.* People need training in how to analyse the data, set improvement targets, deal with feelings associated with receiving negative feedback, discuss summary action plans with appraisers, and set specific goals and action plans. *Research clearly suggests that merely receiving feedback does not improve performance* – rather, it is how this feedback is managed and internalised that determines eventual outcomes.
- *Train people in self-awareness.* When people overrate their own performance relative to the perceptions of others, they are more likely to dismiss corrective feedback. A more balanced approach to self-assessment is necessary. Some research has found that even warning people of the danger of overrating their own performance significantly diminishes the problem.

some caution. It is critical to remember that performance appraisal, upward appraisal, and multisource feedback all share one common characteristic – a person is receiving feedback from others about her or his performance. Therefore, the problems with biases and reactions to feedback that we have discussed earlier in this chapter also apply to 360-degree feedback. Negative feedback, or feedback that departs from the person's own perception of their performance, is unlikely to stimulate positive change (Brett & Atwater, 2001).

APPRAISAL INTERVIEWS – AN ALTERNATIVE PERSPECTIVE

I have suggested that performance appraisal is a mutually anxious and error-prone process. In general, appraisal interviews fail in their intended purpose, damage employee morale and self-esteem, and run counter to many organisational values (Juncaj, 2002). For example, they promote individual rather than collective accountability. However, social networks are increasingly important determinants of organisational success (Cross & Parker, 2004). But an emphasis on individual accountability undermines the team ethos, which is vital for the strengthening of social networks. Moreover, there is no substantial evidence that these problems can be fixed. This chapter therefore argues that a new perspective is required to move interaction between managers and employees in the direction of feedback and counselling interviews (see Chapter 17 for a more detailed discussion of the helping interview), and to make increased use of self-appraisals (or evaluations) rather than traditional appraisal interviews, in which a manager provides feedback on the performance of subordinates. The term 'appraisal' has been so besmirched by its repeated failures in most organisations over prolonged periods of time that it is wisest to drop it altogether from the vocabulary of managers.

A number of fundamental principles emerge from the research literature, which can guide organisations in this new direction. None of these are best realised through appraisal interviews, but can be accommodated by a different approach. They include the following:

- Organisations work better when they have clear business goals, widely disseminated and understood by everyone (Grote, 2000).
- People want to know what to do and how to do it, what is expected of them, how they are progressing, and how they fit into the whole organisation (Pickett, 2003). The main focus of feedback should be on *behaviour* and *results* (Tziner et al., 2000). It should also be a reciprocal process. That is, it should focus on what both employees and managers have done in the past year, the results that were obtained, and the behaviours that are required for the coming year. In this way, interaction between managers and staff ceases to be a sad meditation on missed opportunities, and becomes what has been termed 'performance management' (Cederblom, 2002). The suggestion here is that performance management should have a reciprocal and mutual character more consistent with the empowerment ethos required in today's knowledge-oriented workplaces.
- Managers should regularly sit down with each member of their staff and discuss (a) how well the organisation is doing, (b) how the individual concerned is contributing to the overall effort, and (c) what else the organisation in general and the manager in particular could do to enhance the employee's effort (Hargie et al., 2004). Reciprocation needs to be built into the process.
- These discussions should be frequent. Regular mutual feedback, particularly when it arrives soon after whatever is being discussed, gives employees and managers the opportunity to change their behaviour as they go along (Williams, 1997). Organisational systems then also change in tandem with personal behaviour.
- Regular mutual feedback of the kind suggested here should be overwhelmingly

informal, simple, and free of paperwork. Paperwork is an organisation's cholesterol. Less is best. Again, this is a departure from traditional appraisal interviews, which place heavy emphasis on the preparation of forms and often require the formal signing off by both sides on agreed documentation (e.g. Bacal, 2003).

- Managers are entitled to have opinions about the individual's performance, and can usefully communicate such opinions during these informal discussions. This feedback should focus on behaviours rather than personalities, be highly specific, and emphasise successes which the person has had as well as areas where performance could be improved. In particular, it should focus clearly on the task to be achieved, and then identify behaviours that are conducive to task attainment. Toegel and Conger (2003, p. 308) express the point succinctly: 'The best strategy is to focus feedback on the task, because in this case, people are concerned with narrowing the gap between actual and goal performance. If efforts at this level fail, attention will be focused on the task-learning level. However, a serious problem occurs when attention is shifted to the level of the self, and focal leaders start questioning who they really are. In this case, subsequent performance may well suffer because of strong affective reactions, such as disappointment or despair, that could be produced.' A key principle behind building collaborative, problem-solving relationships is that people must be separated from the problem (Cheney et al., 2004). In short, while one can usefully direct feedback at someone's behaviour, it is counter-productive to direct it at their personality. Most of us are attached to our self-image, and do not take kindly to any suggestion that it is fatally flawed! Training is an obvious prerequisite for the approach described here. Most people do not inherently possess the skills required to make such an approach work effortlessly.

- Consistent with the notion of mutuality and reciprocation, similar opportunities to comment on the manager's performance should be afforded to staff. Securing accurate upward feedback is the biggest single communication problem faced by many organisations (Tourish & Robson, 2003). Critical upward feedback is so often met with a hostile response that most people simply give up. Feedback interviews of the kind suggested here create two-way communication and clear this arterial blockage. Tourish and Hargie (2004) suggest a variety of other approaches to institutionalise regular two-way communication in organisations.

- Informal feedback should focus overwhelmingly on examples of excellent performance. Excellent performance, publicly appreciated, is emulated. Poor performance, publicly upbraided, promotes an atmosphere of defeat, resignation, fear, and resentment. It creates a receptive context for failure. Athletes whose coaches always predict disaster seldom win gold medals. Managers should praise publicly, but criticise privately.

- Poor performance should be discussed with the individuals concerned, privately and at once. The focus should be on agreeing an action plan to prevent its recurrence, rather than securing confessions, convictions, and public floggings.

- A culture of openness, honesty, and trust is essential if feedback schemes are to succeed. Otherwise, public compliance is combined with private defiance.

These principles suggest that organisations should abandon appraisal interviews and instead focus their energies on *the management of two-way feedback*. Such feedback should be unthreatening, action oriented, and supportive. In essence, it should be very different from the appraisal interviews that still predominate in most organisations. The rest of this chapter offers some guidance, derived from the research, on how interviews governed by these principles can be managed most effectively.

GUIDELINES FOR EFFECTIVE FEEDBACK INTERVIEWS

Problem-solving interviews/self-appraisal

The aim here is to use exploratory questions and the skills of active listening to help employees identify their own strengths and weaknesses, and devise appropriate action plans for improvement (Beer, 1997). Chapter 9 discusses listening in-depth, and is a useful reference point on this issue. A focus on listening is consistent with perspectives that see the management role as one of coaching. Evaluation is discouraged, since this would supplant the employee's own analysis of what is required by that of the manager. The approach described here reduces such age-old problems as employee defensiveness, since issues raised will be exclusively those identified by the employee.

Such approaches are particularly appropriate if employees are encouraged to engage in self-appraisals, and then discuss these assessments with their line managers (Rees & Porter, 2004). Discussions between managers and employees based on the latter's self-review have been found to be significantly more constructive and satisfying to both parties than those based on the manager's appraisal (Meyer, 1991). In particular, the dignity and self-respect of employees is enhanced, while managers are placed more in the role of counsellor than judge (Wells & Spinks, 1997).

In addition, employees are also more likely to be committed to whatever plans and goals emerge at the end of the process. The evidence would suggest that any such system should start with a basic assumption that people want to do a good job and are trustworthy. As Edmonstone (1996, p. 11) has noted: 'There is a powerful element of self-fulfilling prophecy in this approach, not least because a system designed to check and double-check performance will not encourage people to give of their best – because someone else will change it.' Unfortunately, too many managers still approach appraisal interviews with the conviction that most employees are underperforming and must be tightly scrutinised in the tasks that they do. They therefore view appraisal as a means of confronting poor performance rather than celebrating the positive. It is a strategy that has many attractions, but which the research suggests suffers from one fundamental flaw – it does not work.

HANDLING FEEDBACK INTERVIEWS

The opening of an interview is its most vital point, and determines the prospects for success or failure. This is because the opening triggers further expectancy effects – we tend to assume that how people behave when we first meet them will be typical of how they behave the rest of the time (Eden, 1993). This forms an expectation which may be positive or negative. Such an expectation then governs our own behaviour, and creates self-fulfilling prophecies that often determine the outcome of the inter-action. Our first concern at the beginning of an interview, especially if we approach it in an anxious frame of mind, is to reduce feelings of uncertainty. This predisposes us all the more to pay attention to the other person's opening behaviours, and use them as a framework within which to organise our perceptions of what is happening. The following approaches will therefore be particularly appropriate at the beginning of a feedback, counselling, or problem-solving interview (Millar et al., 1992; Hargie et al., 2004).

- Arrange for relaxed, informal seating. Avoid sitting behind a desk, imposing a physical barrier between yourself and the interviewee.
- People bring social needs into the interview context with them. A short period of informal chat is appropriate, possibly combined with tea or coffee. If this period becomes too extended, the interview loses focus: it should not become an extended gossip. However, some small talk reinforces the informal and human connection which underlies the staff–manager relationship.
- Review what both of you already know and have agreed about the process – for example, the amount of time available and the key issues that you want to address. Make positive statements such as 'This is a very important discussion for me. I've been looking forward to hearing how well your last project is doing.' Describe the interview, stress its positive purpose, explain how you intend to conduct it, and invite comments from the interviewee. In this way, you are shaping and agreeing an agenda for action.
- Beyond this, the rest of the interview time is spent reviewing the issues agreed in advance. The key here is to ask lots of open questions (see Chapter 4), thereby allowing the interviewee the maximum amount of space and opportunity to raises issues which concern them. If self-appraisal has been agreed, this is an even more indispensable approach.

The emphasis throughout should be on supportive, two-way communication, with the interview regarded as an opportunity not only to give feedback but also to receive it.

Agreeing objectives

A central part of the interview will be the agreeing of objectives for the forthcoming year. Too many objectives create disorientation. One hundred priorities equals no priorities. Therefore, a small number of agreed objectives, which should be restricted to the most important business requirements of the organisation, are sufficient (Hargie et al., 2004).

Offering critical feedback and giving instructions

As stated above, the overwhelming focus of the feedback interview should be on positive feedback and agreeing action for the future. However, in some cases, serious problems will exist which must be addressed. How this is done is crucial. If dealt with well, the underlying relationship can actually be improved, and the person concerned will emerge with a much clearer picture of what needs to be changed. Mishandled, the manager's feedback becomes the issue, rather than the job performance of the employee. With all feedback, the perceived credibility of the person or leader offering it is a critical determinant of whether the feedback will be accepted, internalised, and acted upon (Gabris & Ihrke, 2000). Once a manager's style of communicating feedback becomes the issue, their credibility suffers. In general, therefore, critical feedback should be accompanied by precise instructions designed to solve the underlying problem. The following guidelines should help (Goodworth, 1989; Hargie et al., 2004).

1   *Give employees plenty of opportunity to raise issues themselves.* Most people are well aware of problem areas in their performance, although they may be slow to appreciate their full significance. If managers are always the first to raise such problems, they undermine self-confidence and are viewed as aggressive: the messenger is contaminated by the bad news delivered. However, if employees get the chance to raise problems first, managers will be viewed as coaches engaged in joint problem solving, rather than unpopular oracles of doom. Ask questions such as:

    • are there any difficulties in your job that you wish to discuss?
    • where do you most need help to improve in the year ahead?
    • is there anything that has proved more difficult than you expected in the last year?
    • we certainly had some success with that project. Is there any way that we could have done even better?

2   *When your feedback is critical, let the person know what is wrong in clear and unambiguous language.* Having done this, explain why you think the issue is a problem. This is particularly important if the employee has shown little sign of anticipating the criticism made. You should then summarise and repeat to the person the response to the criticism, so that it is clear their response is being heard. However, you should also reassert the underlying point that is being made.

3   *Focus your criticism on specific behaviours that can be changed, rather than on personality traits, which are more resistant to change.* People perceive negative judgements of their personality as an attack (Rakos, 1991). However, they are likely to see comments on specific behaviours as constructive feedback which they can use to make things better. The key here is to assess feedback in terms of the 'DVD' test. Can the person actually 'see' in their mind's eye the behaviour that you are describing? The statement, 'You are always aggressive', is a judgement on the recipient's personality. It is also hard to 'see'. What exactly does this aggression look like, and what can be done to change it? On the other hand, you could say: 'At yesterday's meeting, you walked out and slammed the door behind you, and that was the second time this week.' Such behaviour can certainly be visualised, and immediate steps taken to avoid its recurrence.

4   *Couple criticism with guidelines to solve the problem.* Criticism by itself changes nothing. People need to know what you now expect them to do, and believe that

what you are suggesting is fair, viable, and possible to implement. The acronym *SMART* is widely used to suggest what objectives should look like – that is, they should be *s*pecific, *m*easurable, *a*greed, *r*ealistic, and *t*ime bounded. Offer guidelines about targets that can be achieved (rather than those which are desirable but impossible), that are within the employee's range of competence, that relate to specific behaviours, and that both parties are committed to reviewing within a specified time frame.

Handling critical feedback

Inevitably, managers will also receive criticism. This will sometimes be emotional, wrong-headed, highly personalised, and aggressive. It will also sometimes be constructive, specific, well intentioned, and accurate. It is vital that managers themselves model effective approaches to handling criticism. Otherwise, it will be even harder for them to offer it to others.

Fundamentally, the normal rules of supportive communication still apply in this context. Critical feedback should be listened to and examined honestly to see whether there is any substance to it. The 'four R method' (Kolt & Donohue, 1992) is one useful means of using criticism to strengthen the relationship, and ensure that the channels of communication remain open in the future. This proposes that we should:

1   *R*eceive the other person's comments without interrupting, denying the validity of the criticism, launching immediate counter-attacks, or engaging in other defensive behaviours. This shows an openness to discussion, and an interest in what the other has to say.
2   *R*epeat what has been said as objectively as possible. This method of reflecting back what the other person has said is a core means of building empathy, and shows that what has been said has been understood (see Chapter 6 for a full discussion of the skill of reflecting).
3   *R*equest the other person's ideas about how the difficulty should be dealt with. This helps escape a spiral of defend/attack, and moves the critic into the constructive position of helping to identify solutions. It also ensures that the discussion deals with specifics rather than generalities.
4   *R*eview at the end the different options available and agree the best way forward.

This is consistent with what is generally regarded as a collaborative style of conflict management, designed to obtain a win-win outcome for all concerned (Cheney et al., 2004). It involves exploring the other person's viewpoint, explaining your own perspective, and then creating a sense of resolution and closure.

Closing the interview

Research suggests that we are inclined to remember very well the beginning of an interaction and its end – but lose most of what occurs in the middle. This has been termed the primacy/recency effect (Brunel & Nelson, 2003). It is therefore imperative that the key points that have been agreed are summarised at the end. It is useful to pause after each point made until the other party involved signifies their agreement.

It has also been shown that when people make a public commitment to a particular course of action, it is more likely that their attitudes will shift to agree that it is indeed appropriate (Cialdini, 2001). In turn, this prepares the way for future actions in line with the agreement reached. Interviews of this kind can therefore close with mutual commitments to action – the more immediate, effortful, and visible the better. These will then help secure significant improvements in work performance, in the ability of the organisation to achieve its goals, and in the relationships between managers and staff.

OVERVIEW

Appraisal has become a staple element of practice in human-resource management (Redman, 2001). As has been noted here, it is rapidly growing to embrace both upward appraisal and 360-degree appraisal. But the widespread adoption of a practice does not by itself prove that it is wise. Indeed, this chapter has fundamentally questioned the wisdom of traditional appraisal interviews. Managers often defend them, despite their manifest failures, on the grounds that 'something must be done' to inform people whether their performance is good, and particularly when it is poor. Several such opinions are cited by Segal (2000). This is a shaky defence. The Hippocratic Oath counsels: 'As to diseases, make a habit of two things – to help, or at least do no harm.' This precept could usefully be applied to the practice of appraisal interviews. When most such interviews harm most people and reduce performance most of the time, it is unsatisfactory to defend their continued use on the basis that 'something must be done', however damaging it is. A different focus is required. For example, it is increasingly clear that the selective hiring of good people is a vital determinant of organisational success (e.g. Collins, 2001). It is equally clear that most organisations accord it insufficient priority. If this issue were attended to more effectively, the need to manage the poor performance of a small number by applying dysfunctional systems to the majority would disappear. Moreover, either good or bad performance can be dealt with as soon as it occurs, informally, without delaying feedback to an annual appraisal interview, when neither side is likely to recollect accurately the behaviours in question.

When a certain kind of ship sinks in fair winds or foul, it is timely to question the integrity of its basic design. In terms of appraisal interviews, the organisational insights derived from research in recent decades have been negligible and the improvements in practice insignificant. As two researchers in the area have commented, 'After decades of research, where is the performance appraisal process today? Have the tools and the processes advanced to the point of accurately and effectively measuring the performance of employees? The answer is "probably not".' (Wiese & Buckley, 1998, p. 246). It therefore seems sensible to contemplate the construction of a more seaworthy vessel, and to set a new course.

Accordingly, I have suggested that managers hone their skills in giving and receiving feedback, informally and frequently, and therefore in conducting problem-solving, counselling, and helping interviews. Such approaches are more consistent with the innovative new management styles that are increasingly required for top-level organisational performance. In the workplace, respect for formal hierarchies has drastically declined, ensuring that employees are ever less inclined simply to accept feedback handed down to them by managers (Toegel & Conger, 2003). In any event, widening spans of control mean that managers are increasingly ill equipped to provide feedback that is informed, accurate, timely, or helpful. The following comment by one senior manager expresses a view from which few would now dissent:

> It's impossible to manage or even know what's going on in the depths of the organization. I mean, each of us can fool ourselves into thinking we're smart and running a tight ship. But really the best we can do is create a context and hope that things emerge in a positive way, and this is tough because you can't really see the impact your decisions have on people. (cited in Cross & Parker, 2004, p. 3)

Although it is rarely noted, this problem also poses significant ethical issues (Kerssens-van Drongelen & Fisscher, 2003). Appraisal interviews permit managers, who know less and less about any individual's work, to determine which aspects of their performance are to be evaluated, as well as to decide the consequences of the measurement, including pay and career progression. Basic questions about the limits of power and people's right to involvement are inescapably posed.

By contrast, it is argued here that feedback should be offered in as supportive a manner as possible. Its main emphasis should be on successful behaviours, which can be praised publicly and thus are perceived as having been rewarded. Where negative behaviours are concerned, it is important that feedback is on specific behaviours which can be changed, follows on rapidly from the behaviours in question, is constructive, is linked to important business goals, is highly specific, and is offered in private. Whatever such approaches might be termed, it is certainly best that the damaged language of appraisal is left behind. A great deal of effort has been invested in tinkering with what is irretrievably damaged and straining after the impossible. It is now time to put appraisal interviews out of our collective misery. Managers should instead recognise that more reciprocal and supportive systems of mutual influence are required for building organisational success in the workplaces of the twenty-first century.

REFERENCES

Abraham, S., Karns, L., Shaw, K. & Mena, M. (2001). Managerial competencies and the managerial performance appraisal process. *Journal of Management Development*, *20*, 842–852.

Antonioni, D. (1996). Designing an effective 360-degree appraisal feedback process. *Organizational Dynamics*, *25*, 24–38.

Atwater, L., Waldman, D. & Brett, J. (2000). The influence of feedback on self and follower ratings of leadership. *Personnel Psychology*, *48*, 35–60.

Atwater, L., Waldman, D. & Brett, J. (2002). Understanding and optimising multisource feedback. *Human Resource Management*, *2*, 193–208.

Bacal, R. (2003). *The manager's guide to performance reviews*. London: McGraw-Hill.

Baruch, Y. (1996). Self performance appraisal vs. direct-manager appraisal: a case of congruence. *Journal of Managerial Psychology, 11*, 50–65.

Bates, R. (2002). Liking and similarity as predictors of multi-source ratings. *Personnel Review, 31*, 540–552.

Becton, J. & Schraeder, M. (2004). Participant input into rater selection: potential effects on the quality and acceptance of ratings in the context of 360-degree feedback. *Public Personnel Management, 33*, 23–32.

Beer, M. (1997). Conducting a performance appraisal interview. *Harvard Business School Note No. 9–497–058*.

Bernardin, H. & Beatty, R. (1984). *Performance appraisal: assessing human behaviour at work*. Boston, MA: Kent Publishing.

Bolster, B. & Springbett, N. (1981). The reaction of interviewers to favourable and unfavourable information. *Journal of Applied Psychology, 45*, 97–103.

Brett, J. & Atwater, L. (2001). 360 degree feedback: accuracy, reactions, and perceptions of usefulness. *Journal of Applied Psychology, 86*, 930–942.

Brown, R. (2000). *Group processes*, 2nd edn. Oxford: Blackwell.

Brunel, F. & Nelson, M. (2003). Message order effects and gender differences in advertising. *Journal of Advertising Research, 43*, 330–341.

Cardy, R. & Dobbins, G. (1994). *Performance appraisal: alternative perspectives*. Cincinnati, OH: South Western.

Cederblom, D. (2002). From performance appraisal to performance management: one agency's experience. *Public Personnel Management, 31*, 131–140.

Cheney, G., Christensen, L., Zorn, T. & Ganesh, S. (2004). *Organizational communication in an age of globalization: issues, reflections, practices*. Prospect Heights, IL: Waveland Press.

Cialdini, R. (2001). *Influence*, 4th edn. New York: HarperCollins.

Coens, T. & Jenkins, M. (2000). *Abolishing performance appraisal – why they backfire and what to do instead*. San Francisco, CA: Barret-Koehler.

Collins, J. (2001). *Good to great*. London: Random House.

Conlin, M. (2002). The software says you're just average. *Business Week*, Issue 3771, 25 February, p. 126.

Cook, J. & Crossman, A. (2004). Satisfaction with performance appraisal systems: a study of role perceptions. *Journal of Managerial Psychology, 19*, 526–541.

Cross, R. & Parker, A. (2004). *The hidden power of social networks*. Boston: MA: Harvard Business School Press.

De Nisi, A. (1996). *A cognitive approach to performance appraisal*. London: Routledge.

Dobbins, G., Platz-Vieno, S. & Houston, J. (1993). Effects of trust in appraisal on appraisal feedback effectiveness: a field study. *Journal of Business and Psychology, 7*, 309–321.

Easterby-Smith, M., Malina, D. & Lu, Y. (1995). How culture sensitive is HRM? a comparative analysis of practice in Chinese and UK companies. *International Journal of Human Resource Management, 6*, 31–59.

Eden, D. (1993). Interpersonal expectations in organisations. In P. Blanck (Ed.), *Interpersonal expectations: theory, research and applications*. Cambridge: Cambridge University Press.

Edmonstone, J. (1996). Appraising the state of performance appraisal. *Health Manpower Management*, *22*, 9–13.

Eskew, D. & Heneman, R. (1996). A survey of merit pay plan effectiveness: end of the line for merit pay or hope for improvement? *Human Resource Planning*, *19*, 12.

Fiske, S., Lin, M. & Neuberg, S. (1999). The continuum model: ten years later. In S. Chaiken & Y. Trope (Eds), *Dual-process theories in social psychology*. New York: Guilford Press.

Fletcher, C. (2001). Performance appraisal and management: the developing research agenda. *Journal of Occupational Psychology*, *74*, 473–487.

Fletcher, C. & Perry, E. (2001). Performance appraisal and feedback: a consideration of national culture and a review of contemporary and future trends. In N. Anderson, D. Ones, H. Sinangil & C. Viswesvaran (Eds), *International handbook of industrial, work and organizational psychology*. Beverly Hills, CA: Sage.

Ford, D. (2004). Development of a performance appraisal training program for the Rehabilitation Institute of Chicago. *Journal of European Industrial Training*, *28*, 550–563.

Forsterling, F. (2001). *Attribution: an introduction to theories research and applications*. Hove: Psychology Press.

Freemantle, D. (1994). *The performance of 'performance appraisal' – an appraisal: a superboss research report*. Berkshire: Superboss, p. 4.

Furnham, A. (1997). *The psychology of behaviour at work*. Hove: Psychology Press.

Gabor, A. (1992). Take this job and love it. *New York Times* (F1), 26 January, p. 6.

Gabris, F. & Ihrke, D. (2000). Improving employee acceptance towards performance appraisal and merit pay systems: the role of leadership credibility. *Review of Public Personnel Administration*, *20*, 21–53.

Garavan, T., Morley, M. & Flynn, M. (1997). 360 degree feedback: its role in employee development. *Journal of Management Development*, *16*, 134–147.

Gioia, D. (1989). Self-serving bias as a self-sense-making strategy: explicit vs. tacit impression management. In R. Giacalone & P. Rosenfeld (Eds), *Impression management in organizations*. Hillsdale, NJ: Lawrence Erlbaum.

Gladwell, M. (2002). The talent myth. *The Times (T2)*, 20 August, pp. 2–4.

Goldstein, H. (2001). Appraising the performance of performance appraisals. *IEEE Spectrum*, *38*, 61–63.

Goodworth, C. (1989). *The secrets of successful staff appraisal and counselling*. Oxford: Heinemann.

Gray, G. (2002). Performance appraisals don't work. *Industrial Management*, *44*, 15–17.

Gregurus, G., Robie, C. & Born, M. (2001). Applying the social relations model to self and peer evaluations. *Journal of Management Development*, *20*, 508–525.

Grote, D. (2000). Performance appraisal reappraised. *Harvard Business Review*, *78*, 21.

Hamel, G. (2000). *Leading the revolution*, Boston, MA: Harvard Business School Press.

Hargie, O. & Dickson, D. (2004). *Skilled interpersonal communication*, 4th edn. London: Routledge.

Hargie, O., Dickson, D. & Tourish, D. (2004). *Communication skills for effective management*. London: Palgrave.

Harris, M. & Schaubroeck, J. (1988). A meta-analysis of self-supervisor, self-peer, and peer-supervisor ratings. *Personnel Psychology*, *41*, 43–62.

Hastie, R. & Dawes, R. (2001). *Rational choice in an uncertain world: an introduction to judgement and decision making.* London: Sage.

Heneman, R., Greenberger, D. & Anonyuo, C. (1989). Attributions and exchanges: the effects of interpersonal factors on the diagnosis of employee performance. *Academy of Management Journal, 32*, 466–476.

HR Focus (2000) HR update: HR execs dissatisfied with their performance appraisal systems. *HR Focus, **January**,* 2.

Institute of Manpower (1993). *Pay and performance – the employee experience.* Studies Report, No. 258. London: Institute of Manpower.

Judge, T., Higgins, C. & Cable, D. (2000). The employment interview: a review of recent research and recommendations for future research. *Human Resource Management Review, 4*, 383–406.

Juncaj, T. (2002). Do performance appraisals work? *Quality Progress, 35*, 45–49.

Kassing. J. (2001). From the look of things: assessing perceptions of organisational dissenters. *Management Communication Quarterly, 14*, 442–470.

Kennedy, P. & Dresser, S. (2001). Appraising and paying for performance: another look at an age-old problem. *Employee Benefits Journal, 26*, 8–14.

Kerssens-van Drongelen, I. & Fisscher, O. (2003). Ethical dilemmas in performance management. *Journal of Business Ethics, 45*, 51–63.

Kohn, A. (1999). *Punished by rewards.* New York: Houghton Mifflin.

Kolt, W. & Donohue, R. (1992). *Managing interpersonal conflict.* London: Sage.

Kreitner, R., Kinicki, A. & Buelens, M. (2002). *Organizational behaviour*, 2nd European edn. London: McGraw-Hill.

Latham, G. & Wexley, K. (1994). *Increasing productivity through performance appraisal*, 2nd edn. Reading, MA: Addison-Wesley.

Lefkowitz, J. (2000). The role of interpersonal affective regard in supervisory performance ratings: a literature review and proposed causal model. *Journal of Occupational and Organizational Psychology, 73*, 67–85.

Leyens, J., Yzerbyt, V. & Schadron, G. (1994). *Stereotypes and social cognition.* London: Sage.

Losyk, B. (2002). How to conduct a performance appraisal. *Public Management, 84*, 8–11.

Mabey, C. (2001). Closing the circle: participant views of a 360 degree feedback programme. *Human Resource Management Journal, 11*, 41–53.

Mani, B. (2002). Performance appraisal systems, productivity, and motivation: a case study. *Public Personnel Management, 31*, 141–159.

Manzoni, J. & Barsoux, J. (2002). *The set-up-to-fail syndrome: how good managers cause great people to fail.* Boston, MA: Harvard Business School Press.

McCauley, C. (1997). On choosing sides: seeing the good in both. In D. Bracken, M. Dalton, R. Jako, C. McCauley & V. Pollman (Eds), *Should 360-degree feedback be used only for developmental purposes?* (pp. 23–36). Greensboro, NC: Centre for Creative Leadership.

Meyer, H. (1991). A solution to the performance appraisal feedback enigma. *Academy of Management Executive, 5*, 68–76.

Millar, R. Hargie, O. & Crute, V. (1992). *Professional interviewing.* London: Routledge.

Peiperl, M. (2001). Getting 360 degree feedback right. *Harvard Business Review, 79*, 142–147.

Pfau, B., Kay, I., Nowack, K. & Ghorpade, J. (2002). Does 360-degree feedback negatively affect company performance? *HR Magazine, 47*, 54–59.

Pfeffer, J. (2001). Fighting the war for talent is injurious to your organisation's health. *Organizational Dynamics, 29*, 248–259.

Pfeffer, J. & Cialdini, R. (1998). Illusions of influence. In R. Kramer & M. Neale (Eds), *Power and influence in organizations*. London: Sage.

Pickett, L. (2003). Transforming the annual fiasco. *Industrial and Commercial Training, 35*, 237–240.

Pratto, F. & John, O. (1991). Automatic vigilance: the attention grabbing power of negative social information. *Journal of Personality and Social Psychology, 51*, 380–391.

Pulakos, E., Arad, S., Donovan, M. & Plamondon, K. (2000). Adaptability in the workplace: development of a taxonomy of adaptive performance. *Journal of Applied Psychology, 85*, 612–624.

Rabin, M. & Schrag, J. (1999). First impressions matter: a model of confirmatory bias. *Quarterly Journal of Economics, 114*, 37–82.

Rakos, R. (1991). *Assertive behaviour: theory, research and practice*. London: Routledge.

Redman, T. (2001). Performance appraisal. In T. Redman & A. Wilkinson (Eds), *Contemporary human resource management*. London: Prentice-Hall.

Rees, W. & Porter, C. (2003). Appraisal pitfalls and the training implications. I. *Industrial and Commercial Training, 35*, 280–284.

Rees, W. & Porter, C. (2004). Appraisal pitfalls and the training implications. II. *Industrial and Commercial Training, 36*, 29–34.

Rollinson, D. & Broadfield, A. (2002). *Organisational behaviour and analysis: an integrated approach*, 2nd edn. Harlow: Prentice-Hall.

Rosenfeld, P., Giacalone, R. & Riordan, C. (1995). *Impression management in organizations*. London: Routledge.

Sandler, C. & Keefe, J. (2003). *Performance appraisal phrase book: effective words, phrases, and techniques for successful evaluations*. Avon, MA: Adams Media.

Seddon, J. (2001). Perform a miracle – praise the workers. *Observer Business Supplement*, 11 March, p. 13.

Segal, J. (2000). 86 your appraisal process? *HR Magazine, October*, 199–206.

Shen, J. (2004). International performance appraisals: policies, practices and determinants in the case of Chinese multinational companies. *International Journal of Manpower, 25*, 547–563.

Smith, A. & Rupp, W. (2003). Knowledge workers: exploring the link among performance rating, pay and motivational aspects. *Journal of Knowledge Management, 7*, 107–124.

Stoffey, R. & Reilly, R. (1997). Training appraisees to participate in appraisal: effects on appraisers and appraisees. *Journal of Business and Psychology, 12*, 219–239.

Sutherland, S. (1992). *Irrationality*. London: Constable.

Toegel, G. & Conger, J. (2003). 360-degree assessment: time for reinvention. *Academy of Management Learning and Education, 2*, 297–311.

Torrington, D. & Hall, L. (1991). *Personnel management – a new approach*. Hemel Hempstead: Prentice-Hall.

Tourish, D. (1999). Communicating beyond individual bias. In A. Long (Ed.), *Advanced interaction for community nursing*. London: Macmillan.

Tourish, D. & Robson, P. (2003). Critical upward feedback in organisations: processes, problems and implications for communication management. *Journal of Communication Management*, *8*, 150–167.

Tourish, D. & Hargie, O. (2004). Motivating critical upward communication: a key challenge for management decision making. In D. Tourish & O. Hargie (Eds), *Key issues in organizational communication*. London: Routledge.

Tourish, D. & Vatcha, N. (2005). Charismatic leadership and corporate cultism at Enron: the elimination of dissent, the promotion of conformity and organizational collapse. *Leadership*, *1*, 455–480.

Tziner, A., Joanis, C. & Murphy, K. (2000). A comparison of three methods of performance appraisal with regard to gaol properties, goal perception and ratee satisfaction. *Group and Organization Management*, *25*, 175–190.

Waldman, D., Atwater, L. & Antonioni, D. (1998). Has 360 feedback gone amok? *Academy of Management Executive*, *12*, 86–94.

Weisband, S. & Atwater, L. (1999). Evaluating self and others in electronic and face to face groups. *Journal of Applied Psychology*, *84*, 632–639.

Wells, B. & Spinks, N. (1997). Counselling employees: an applied communication skill. *Career Development International*, *2*, 93–98.

Wiese, D. & Buckley, M. (1998). The evolution of the performance appraisal process. *Journal of Management History*, *4*, 223–249.

Wilke, H. & Meertens, R. (1994). *Group performance*. London: Routledge.

Williams, M. (1997). Performance appraisal is dead. Long live performance management! *Harvard Management Update No. U9702A*, pp. 1–6.

Wilson, J. & Western, S. (2000). Performance appraisal: an obstacle to training and development? *Career Development International*, *6*, 93–99.

Wynne, B. (1995). *Performance appraisal: a practical guide to appraising the performance of employees*. Hemel Hempstead: Technical Communications.

Zhu, J. & Dowling, P. (1998). Performance appraisal in China. In J. Selmer (Ed.), *International management in China: cross-cultural issues* (pp. 115–136). London: Routledge.

Chapter 19

The cognitive interview

Amina Memon

T HE COGNITIVE INTERVIEW (CI) is one of the most exciting developments in forensic psychology in the last 20 years. The CI comprises a series of memory-retrieval techniques designed to increase the amount of information that can be obtained from an eyewitness. It can therefore help investigators obtain more complete and accurate reports from interviewees. The CI was initially developed by the psychologists Ed Geiselman (University of California, Los Angeles) and Ron Fisher (Florida International University) in 1984 as a response to the many requests they received from police officers and legal professionals for a method of improving witness interviews. It is based upon known psychological principles of remembering and retrieval of information from memory. Police detectives trained to use this technique enabled witnesses to produce over 40% more valid information than detectives using traditional interviewing techniques (see Koehnken, Milne, Memon & Bull, 1999, for a meta-analysis of research). Furthermore, university students using this new procedure obtained more information from witnesses than did experienced police officers that interviewed in their normal way (see Fisher & Geiselman, 1992; Memon & Koehnken, 1992; Koehnken et al., 1999; Memon & Higham, 1999, for reviews).

To date, some 65 studies have been conducted. This includes two studies conducted in the field with real-life witnesses and police officers trained in the CI. This chapter provides a critical review of research on the CI and highlights methodological and theoretical issues. Practical issues and implications for future research will be considered. Before describing the procedure and reviewing the empirical research, it is useful to understand *why* a procedure such as the CI is necessary (see also Wells et al., 2000).

WHAT LED TO THE DEVELOPMENT OF THE CI?

The ability to obtain full and accurate information is critical in an investigation – it may determine whether or not a case is solved, yet the eyewitness literature reveals that such recall is difficult to achieve because of the cognitive and social factors that can influence recall accuracy (for reviews, see Bruck & Ceci, 1999; Memon, Vrij & Bull, 2003). The CI arose out of a need to examine ways of improving witness memory (cognitive factors) as well as addressing some of the social factors that can affect the quality of the report obtained from a witness.

Analysis of the techniques used by untrained police officers in Florida (Fisher et al., 1987) suggested some fundamental problems in the conduct of interviews that were leading to ineffective communication and poor memory performance. Fisher et al. (1987) documented several characteristics of the 'standard police interview', among which were constant interruption (when an eyewitness was giving an account), excessive use of question–answer format, and inappropriate sequencing of questions. George (1991) studied the techniques typically used by untrained officers in London and found a remarkably similar pattern among that group. This led to the characterisation of a 'standard police interview' as one of poor quality and stressed the need for an alternative procedure for interviewing witnesses (see Kebbell, Milne & Wagstaff, 2001, for a more recent analysis of the standard interview). In recent years, guidelines have detailed the procedures that should be followed by professionals who interview witnesses (Wells et al., 2000; Home Office, 2003; Scottish Executive, 2003). However, the focus has tended to be on child interviews while there is much room for improving the quality of investigative interviews with adult witnesses (see Cherryman & Bull, 1995; Clarke & Milne, 2001; Gudjonsson, 2003).

The CI represents the alliance of two fields of study: cognition and communication. The original version drew heavily upon what psychologists know about the way in which we remember things. Revisions of the procedure focused more heavily on the practical considerations for managing a social interaction, and this was led by a desire to improve communication in police interviews and alleviate some of the problems described above. Obviously, the 'cognitive' and 'communication' components work in tandem (see also Memon & Stevenage, 1996; Memon & Higham, 1999). However, for the purposes of describing the procedure as it has been depicted in the published literature, the 'cognitive' and 'communication' components will be outlined separately.

WHAT IS THE CI?

The original procedure: the 'cognitive' components

The 'cognitive' part of the CI relies upon two theoretical principles. The first is that a retrieval cue is effective to the extent that there is an overlap between the encoded information and the retrieval cue (Flexser & Tulving, 1978) and that reinstatement of the original encoding context increases the accessibility of stored information (Tulving & Thomson's encoding specificity hypothesis, 1973). The second theoretical perspective that influenced the development of the CI was the multiple trace theory (Bower, 1967). This suggests that, rather than having memories of discrete and unconnected incidents, we have memories made up of a network of associations, and, consequently, there are several means by which a memory could be cued. It follows from this that information not accessible with one technique may be accessible with another (Tulving, 1974).

Context reinstatement

The first technique is for the interviewee to reconstruct mentally the physical and personal contexts that existed at the time of the crime. Although this is not an easy task, the interviewer can help witnesses by asking them to form an *image* or *impression* of the environmental aspects of the original scene (e.g. the location of objects in a room), to comment on their emotional reactions and feelings (surprise, anger, etc.) at the time, and to describe any sounds, smells, and physical conditions (hot, humid, smoky, etc.) that were present. Geiselman and his colleagues (Saywitz et al., 1992) have suggested that it may be helpful for child witnesses to verbalise aloud when mentally reinstating context; for example, to describe the room as the picture comes to mind, and to describe smells, sounds, and other features of the context. The following is an example of how the instructions to reinstate context were administered in a study where adult witnesses were interviewed about a photography session (Memon et al., 1997c):

Interviewer: First of all I'd like you to think back to that day. Picture the room in your head as if you were back there. . . . Can you see it? (*pause for reply*) Think about who was there (*pause*) How you were feeling (*pause*) What you could see (*pause*) What you could hear (*pause*) If you could smell anything (*pause*). Now I want you to tell me as much as you can about what happened when you came to get your photograph taken.

With child witnesses, the context of the original event can be recreated by explicitly requesting the child to think about the context and by asking specific questions that require them to think about it. The questions are asked slowly and deliberately with pauses. It is important to emphasise to children that they must listen carefully to what the interviewer is saying. The instructions to reinstate context were administered as follows in a study where the witnesses were 8- and 9-year-old children being interviewed about a magic show (Memon et al., 1997a):

Interviewer: Put yourself back to the same place where you saw the magic show. Can you see the room now? (*pause*) Tell me about the room (*pause*). Where were you at the time? (*pause*) Tell me about your feelings (*pause*) Could you hear anything? (*pause*) Could you smell anything? (*pause*).

Report everything

A second technique is to ask the interviewee to *report everything*. This may well facilitate the recall of additional information, perhaps by shifting criteria for reporting information. For instance, witnesses are encouraged to report in full without screening out anything they consider to be irrelevant or for which they have only partial recall (Fisher & Geiselman, 1992). The instruction to 'report everything' was used as follows in a study where the witnesses were 6- and 7-year-olds being interviewed about an eye test (Memon et al., 1993).

Interviewer: Just try and tell me what happened, as much as you can remember. If you cannot remember all of it, just tell me what you can. Even little things are important.
Child: We had this . . . even little things?
Interviewer: Even little things.

In addition to facilitating the recall of additional information, this technique may yield information that may be valuable in putting together details from different witnesses to the same crime (see Memon & Bull, 1991). An eyewitness who provides more details is also judged to be more credible in the courtroom (Bell & Loftus, 1989), although the overall accuracy of these details rather than amount of information that is reported should be the major question. Accuracy of details is of great importance in cases where eyewitness evidence is the main source of evidence that is used to incriminate a suspect (Scheck, Neufeld & Dwyer, 2000). Recent research suggests that the report everything instruction, in combination with context reinstatement, might be the most effective component of the CI (Milne & Bull, 2002).

Change perspective

A third technique is to ask for recall from a variety of perspectives. This technique tries to encourage the witnesses to place themselves in the shoes of the victim (if the witness is not a victim) or of another witness and to report what they saw or would have seen. Again the aim is to increase the *amount* of detail elicited. Geiselman et al. (1990) report that changing perspectives can be particularly helpful for children if the following instructions are given: 'Put yourself in that other person's body and describe what they would have seen.' However, there are several concerns about the use of the change perspective instruction, in particular the possibility that it could lead to fabricated details and confuse the witness, as illustrated by the following example taken from the Memon et al. (1993) child witness interviews about an eye test (see also Boon & Noon, 1994; Roberts & Higham, 2002).

Interviewer: What I'd like you to try and do is imagine that you are the nurse and that you can see the room from where she was standing, by the wall chart. Just tell me what you can see.
Child: Umm . . . Did you see the letters, can you see the letters good? and I said yes, and that's all she said to me.

Evidence obtained with this particular technique may not be easily accepted in legal procedures, where it is likely to be seen as encouraging speculation (see Memon & Koehnken, 1992). Moreover, police officers who use the CI have tended not to use the change perspective instruction and fear that a witness could be misled when this instruction is applied (Kebbell & Wagstaff, 1996). There is also evidence that the instruction does not increase recall more than instruction to 'try harder' (Milne & Bull, 2002).

Reverse order

The fourth technique instructs interviewees to make multiple retrieval attempts from different starting points. Interviewees generally feel they have to start at the beginning and are usually asked to do so. However, the CI encourages more focused and extensive retrieval by encouraging witnesses to recall in a variety of orders from the end, or the middle or the most memorable event. Geiselman and Callot (1990) found that it was more effective to recall in forward order once followed by reverse order than to make two attempts to recall from the beginning. There is some doubt that young children can effectively use this technique, as illustrated by the following example from Memon et al., 1993.

Interviewer: OK. What we are going to do now is tell the whole story backwards. Now the very last thing that you did is you went back up to your classroom.
Child: Well, I just walked back and nothing happened.
Interviewer: So what happened before you left the room to go back to your classroom?
Child: I'm not quite sure.

REVISIONS OF THE CI: IMPROVING COMMUNICATION AND RETRIEVAL

The original version of the CI resulted in substantial gains (35%) in the amount of correct information that was elicited from eyewitnesses without any apparent increase in errors (e.g. Geiselman et al., 1985). However, for effective implementation of the 'cognitive' components of the CI, it is necessary to provide interviewers with the necessary social skills and communication strategies to build rapport. As indicated earlier, research with police officers suggested that this was something they lacked. The revised version of the CI (see Geiselman & Fisher, 1997) therefore included the following techniques.

Rapport building

This is an attempt to get to know the witness a bit, clarify what the expectations are, and generally put the person at ease. An important component of rapport building is for the interviewer explicitly to 'transfer control' by making it clear to interviewees that they are the ones in control because they are the ones having to work at remembering. Part of transferring control is to give the witness time to think and respond.

Focused retrieval

The interviewer facilitates eyewitnesses by *focused* memory techniques (to concentrate on mental images of the various parts of the event such as the suspect's face, and use these images to guide recall). Fisher and Geiselman (1992) draw a distinction between conceptual image codes (an image stored as a concept or dictionary definition) and pictorial codes (the mental representation of an image). The notion is that images create dual codes or more meaningful elaborations (Paivio, 1971). The 'imaging' part of the CI usually occurs in the questioning phase of the interview and assumes that the witness has effectively recreated the context in which an event occurred. The instruction could take the following form: 'concentrate on the picture you have in your mind of the suspect, focus on the face and describe it.' To engage the interviewee effectively in focused retrieval, the interviewer needs to speak slowly and clearly, pausing at appropriate points to allow the interviewee time to create an image and respond.

Interviewee compatible questioning

Finally, the timing of the interviewer's questions is critical (deemed interviewee compatible questioning). Questions should be guided by the interviewee's pattern of recall rather than adhering to a rigid protocol. For example, if an interviewee is describing a suspect's clothing, the interviewer should not switch the line of questioning to the actions of the suspect.

TESTING THE CI: AN EFFECTIVE CONTROL GROUP

From a practical perspective, it is important to show that the CI is more effective than the techniques currently in use by police officers and others. From a theoretical perspective, an experimental control is needed to demonstrate that the techniques themselves are causing the effects and not some aspect related to training such as motivation, quality of questioning, or rapport-building skills. The use of the term 'standard' in earlier studies itself implies inferiority. The issue of experimental control has become even more important in testing the revised version of the CI, since it combines the cognitive techniques with some general strategies for improving communication. What evidence is there that the gains in information elicited are not merely due to the improved communication?

More recent tests of the CI have addressed this question by comparing the CI with a procedure known as the structured interview (SI), in which the quality of training in communication and questioning techniques is comparable to the CI. The training of the structured group follows a procedure that is recommended to professionals who interview children (Home Office, 2003; Scottish Executive, 2003). The essence of the Home Office guidance is to treat the interview as a procedure in which a variety of interviewing techniques are deployed in relatively discrete phases, proceeding from general to open, to specific, closed-form questions. Rapport building, through open questions and active listening, is also an important component.

Guenter Koehnken and colleagues (Koehnken et al., 1994, 1995; Mantwill et al., 1995) were the first to demonstrate the superiority of the CI to the SI. The SI group in their studies received training of comparable quality and length to the CI group in basic communication skills. This included instruction on rapport building and use of various types of questioning. The training of the cognitive group also involved the use of the various cognitive techniques. The cognitive and structured interviewers received a sample of written questions and interview transcripts, and the trainers critically evaluated the questions and retrieval aids used by the interviewer (CI group). The SI group focused on the questioning strategy, and not the retrieval aids. The interviewers then watched a videotaped interview. Finally, each interviewer took part in a role play and received feedback on their performance. The training session lasted 4–5 hours.

In the Koehnken et al. (1994) study, the participants (interviewees) and interviewers were non-psychology students without experience in investigative interviewing. The to-be-remembered event was a videotape showing a blood donation. Participants were tested a week after viewing the event. Each interviewer conducted one interview (n=30). The CI significantly increased the amount of correctly recalled information over the SI without increasing the number of errors and confabulated (made-up) details. The interviewers' memory was also tested by asking them to provide, from their memory, written accounts of the event. The superiority of the CI was noted in the interviewer accounts with an average of 42% more correct details than the SI group.

Koehnken et al. (1995) conducted a similar study. The interviews were conducted by psychology students, and adults served as interviewees. Again, there was an increase in correct details with the enhanced CI, although this time a small increase in confabulated details was also noted. However, the overall accuracy (proportion of correct details relative to the total number of details reported) was almost identical in both interview conditions (see also Koehnken et al., 1999).

In the Mantwill et al. (1995) study, a sample of 58 interviewees was drawn from a variety of professional groups and were selected on the basis of their having experience of a blood donation (the to-be-remembered event) or having no experience. The interviewers were non-psychologists of various professions, none of whom had knowledge of blood donation. The number of details elicited in the CI and SI were compared. The enhanced CI yielded 25% more correct information without any differences in errors and confabulations. The performance of experienced and inexperienced participants did not differ significantly.

So far, the evidence suggests that the enhanced CI effects are due to the use of the cognitive techniques rather than merely a result of enhanced communication. However, this does not fit with the results of a series of studies conducted in England as part of a project funded by the Economic and Social Research Council in the UK (Memon et al., 1996a, 1996b, 1997a, 1997b). Memon and colleagues directly examined whether the source of the CI advantage was due to facilitated communication arising from the use of the 'communication' components of the enhanced CI (namely, rapport building and transfer of control), or was the result of the 'cognitive' components of the enhanced CI (context, imagery, reverse order, and reporting in detail). The SI in the Memon et al. studies therefore resembled the enhanced CI more closely than the SI used in the Koehnken studies due to a greater emphasis on 'transfer of control'. As in the Koehnken research, cognitive and structured interviewers received a similar quality of training. The interviewers were psychology students who had no previous experience of interviewing. Both groups were led to believe they were using the superior interview technique. They were trained separately over a period of 2 days in basic communication techniques such as building rapport, and in types of questions to ask, and had the opportunity to conduct role-plays and receive feedback on practice interviews. Finally, Memon et al. introduced a 'second retrieval (SR) phase' in their cognitive/structured interviews. In the SR phase of the CI, participants were instructed to go through the event again in reverse order. The SI group were simply asked to try one more time. The purpose of this SR was directly to test the hypothesis that the various CI techniques merely increase the number of recall attempts, and that this accounts for the gains in new information (reminiscence), a well-documented effect (see Payne, 1987, for a review). These effects could be a result of retrieval practice (Roediger & Thorpe, 1978) or stimulus sampling, whereby repeated attempts to access a memory result in different samples drawn from a population of encoded details.

The studies conducted by Memon and colleagues showed that the CI is a highly complex procedure and that the advantage gained from it may be restricted to a rather narrow set of conditions. When these conditions are violated, the CI appears no better than an effectively matched control group (Memon & Stevenage, 1996). This will be illustrated by considering the results obtained in the Memon et al. research in some detail.

In the Memon et al. (1997a) study in which the interviewees were 8- and 9-year-old children, the CI was found significantly to increase correct and incorrect (errors) details about a live event (interview 2 days after the event) while accuracy was unaffected. More recent studies using young adults and older adults have also reported that the CI increases correct details as well as incorrect details (e.g. Mello & Fisher, 1996). One interpretation of the increase in errors with the CI is that the use of specific instructions, such as 'report everything', affects report criterion (Memon & Higham, 1999). A similar argument has been made about techniques such as hypnosis, where it has been argued the use of a more liberal response criterion is likely to increase errors (see Roberts & Higham, 2002). One way to monitor this source of error is to collect confidence ratings from participants (see Roberts & Higham, 2002, for further details). The practical implications of an increase in errors will be considered later in this chapter.

Memon et al. (1997a) compared the CI and SI as described above with an untrained control group. The interviewers were postgraduate students, and the interviewees (college students) viewed a videotaped event of a sequence in which a child is murdered. In this study, the CI and SI interviewers did not differ in terms of the overall amount recalled, the accuracy of recall, the number of errors, or the number of confabulations (made-up details). Both trained groups elicited more in the way of overall information and amount of correct information than an untrained group. However, this was offset by their producing a significantly higher number of errors and confabulations than the untrained group. These findings are important in themselves, but they also raise the question of what is the appropriate control group. Clearly, if the cognitive interviewers are compared to an untrained group, they show some advantages. However, if the cognitive interviewers are compared to a group matched for everything but the cognitive techniques (namely, the SI), the advantage of the CI disappears.

This finding is at odds with the studies conducted in Germany, and suggests that the effects of the CI depend on the standard of comparison that is used. It is not clear where there is a discrepancy, but it could be due to sampling differences and interviewer differences (Memon's interviewers were psychology graduates and were possibly more motivated). It should be pointed out that while the SI interviewers in the Memon et al. (1997b) study were behaving like CI interviewers they did not use any of the CI techniques. Of course, this does not rule out the possibility that the interviewers were spontaneously using CI techniques. Memon et al. (1997c) found that college students frequently report the use of context reinstatement and imagery as aids to recall. Indeed, such techniques are also reported to be used by older participants drawn from the general population (Harris, 1980). In a recent study of the role of visual imagery in the enhanced CI, Davis, McMahon, and Greenwood (2004) found that Vividness of Visual Imagery scores were unrelated to the amount of information correctly recalled. The authors concluded that the rapport building components of the CI and the SI may evoke spontaneous imagery that is comparable to the explicit instruction to image in a CI. This supports the finding of Memon et al. (1997b).

It appears from the work of Memon and colleagues that the primary effect of the CI is to enhance communication. The 'transfer of control' instruction could be the most effective component of the CI. Transfer of control is achieved in three main ways. Firstly, the interviewers explicitly tell the interviewee that they do not have knowledge of the event and that it is the interviewee that holds all the relevant information. This confers power and status to the interviewee. Secondly, the interviewers ensure that the interviewee is not interrupted when speaking, and pause after interviewees have spoken in case they have more to add. This also conveys to the interviewee that what *they* have to say is important. Finally, whenever possible, the interviewers use open-ended questions, so that it is the interviewee who does most of the talking. The effect of transfer of control may not only be improved rapport but also a more fruitful memory search (e.g. due to interviewers not interrupting) and possibly more effective use of context reinstatement. This explanation could account for the lack of a significant difference between CI and SI groups in the Memon et al. (1997b) study.

It should be noted that in the Memon et al. (1997b) study and in earlier studies (e.g. Memon et al., 1997a) there was considerable variability in interviewer performance. The untrained interviewers in particular adopted quite different styles of questioning; they varied in how persistent they were and how frequently they interrupted interviewees. This has to be taken into consideration in interpreting the results, and suggests that future studies should use more representative samples and collect qualitative data on how interviewer background and motivation may influence their performance (see also Memon et al., 1994b; Memon, Bull & Smith, 1995).

Field tests of the CI

To date, there have been only two field tests of the CI. The first was a project that enlisted the assistance of police detectives in Miami, Florida (Fisher et al., 1989). The second was a study involving the Hertfordshire police in the UK (George, 1991; Clifford & George, 1996).

The aim of the Fisher et al. (1989) field study was to examine the use of the enhanced CI by trained and 'control' police detectives when questioning real-life victims and interviewees. The pretraining phase of the study involved the collection of tape recordings of interviews from a sample of detectives using their usual, standard techniques. Half of the group underwent enhanced CI training over four 60-minute sessions. During this time, they were given an overview of the procedure and the general psychological principles of cognition, training in specific interviewing techniques and communication techniques, and advice on the temporal sequencing of the CI. After the fourth training session, each detective tape recorded a practice interview in the field and received individual feedback from the psychologists on the quality of the interview. The detectives then followed the enhanced CI procedure or 'standard interview' procedure (as defined earlier) during the course of their interviews with real interviewees over a period of time. Two measures of the effects of training were taken. Firstly, number of facts elicited before training (i.e. the tapes from the pilot phase) as compared with after training (thus a within-participants comparison). Secondly, facts elicited by trained and untrained officers after some had undergone the training programme (between-participants). The tapes were transcribed by trained research assistants, who recorded all the relevant details. Opinionated and irrelevant statements were ignored. The statements included physical descriptions, actions, and clothing.

The CI was found to be effective in the before/after comparisons (the within-participants factor) and in the trained/untrained (between-participants) comparison. The trained detectives elicited 47% more information after training and significantly more information than detectives not trained in CI. Baseline measures showed there were no differences between the groups prior to training. In order to examine the impact of CI on the amount of incorrect information recalled, it was necessary to examine corroboration rates. (In real crimes, of course, corroborating information is not always easily available.) When the corroborating source was another interviewee/victim, the corroborating interview was always conducted by someone other than the original detective (usually a uniformed officer). Some 94% of the statements from the interviews in this study were corroborated, and there was no difference in the corroboration rates of pre- and post-training interviews.

The results of the CI field study are promising. Six of the seven detectives who were trained improved significantly. However, given the relatively small sample size, the question of how representative the trained group were remains open. The officers were selected for training rather than being randomly assigned to conditions, and this is of some concern, especially in light of evidence that police officers may not be so open to the use of new techniques (Memon et al., 1994b; 1995). Finally, there was no trained control group in this field study, and data were not provided on the techniques used by interviewers (see Memon & Stevenage, 1996).

Clifford and George (1991, 1996) detail a field evaluation of training in three methods of investigative interviewing. The study involved 28 experienced British police officers, who were randomly assigned to one of four conditions: CI; conversation management; CI and conversation management; and a no-training control group. Conversation management is a procedure that resembles the SI described earlier and includes training in planning the interview, listening skills, conversational styles, question types, and summarising. Prior to training, each participant provided a tape recording of an interview they had conducted with a real-life interviewee or victim. After training, each police officer tape-recorded three more interviews with victims or interviewees of street crimes. The tape recordings were transcribed and evaluated, among other things, for the amount of information provided by the interviewee. The results showed that the CI elicited significantly more information than the standard police interview (14% more than the no-training control group). A before- and after-training comparison showed an increase of 55%. There were no significant differences between conversation management and the untrained control; in fact, the conversation management group fared worse.

At this point, it is necessary to point out two things. Firstly, the success of the CI depends upon adequate training of interviewers in the techniques described above. It is not clear how much training is needed. Some studies report effects with relatively brief training. Fisher et al. (1989) report benefits after four 60-minute sessions, while George (1991) trained officers over 2 days. Memon et al., (1994b) trained officers over a more limited period of time (4 hours) and found this was insufficient to motivate officers to use the new techniques, while Turtle (1995) has evaluated several 1-week training courses on the CI for Canadian police officers and found that training has relatively little effect on the use of CI techniques. Clearly, the effects of training are complex and depend not only on length of training, but quality of training, background of interviewer, attitudes toward training, and so forth. A survey of police officers (Kebbell, Milne & Wagstaff, 1999) suggests that relatively few officers use the full CI in practice, and one reason for this may be that they do not feel they are sufficiently trained in its use.

Secondly, it should be noted that the CI relies upon a cooperative interviewee. It has not as yet been established how useful the CI would be in the case of an interviewee who does not wish to remember (e.g. in the case of a traumatised interviewee) or an interviewee who does not wish to communicate information to the interviewer (e.g. one that is likely to be a suspect). There is also no evidence that the CI is a reliable procedure for eliciting memories from adult clients of childhood events (Memon, 1995). It is therefore of some concern that the CI is mentioned in the British Psychological Society guidelines on good practice when working with recovered memories (Frankland & Cohen, 1999).

So far, the review of evidence has focused largely on studies using adult interviewees (with the exception of the Memon et al. ESRC research). An important question is, to what extent can the CI be effectively used with child interviewees?

The CI and child interviewees

Research has consistently shown that younger children (ages 6–7) will often recall *less* information than older children (ages 10–11) (for reviews, see Westcott, Davies & Bull, 2002; Memon et al., 2003). Given that the primary aim of CI is to increase the *amount* of information retrieved, it may be a most effective procedure to use with young children.

In one of the earliest studies of the CI using children, Saywitz et al. (1992) refined the procedure for children (7–8-year-olds and 10–11-year-olds), using a live event. The to-be-remembered event was a game in which children dressed up, and interacted with and were photographed by a stranger. The CI significantly increased correct facts recalled across both age groups by 26%. In a second study, a 'practice session' was included, the aims of which were to familiarise the children with the CI techniques and to give feedback on their performance. The interviewers were experienced police officers who received written instructions and a 2-hour training session, during which they were informed about child-appropriate language, rapport building, interview preparation, and procedure. The CI group received additional information on the use of the four original CI techniques. The standard interview group were instructed to use the techniques they would normally use. The CI led to more correct details being recalled than did the standard interview (20% increase for the 8–9-year-olds and 44% for the 11–12-year-olds). Furthermore, collapsing across age levels, a practice CI prior to the main interview improved performance by an additional 25%. No increase in the amount of incorrect or confabulated details was observed. Thus, it may help to familiarise children with the CI before they are questioned about the event. Interestingly, it was the older children whose performance improved most with a practice interview, a finding that is the opposite to what we would expect from our understanding of children's development of memory strategy (Ornstein et al., 1985). An analysis was conducted to look at the frequency with which interviewers used the four CI techniques. It was apparent that the student interviewers were more likely to use each of the four techniques than the experienced detectives. For example, only half of the detectives used the 'change perspective' instruction as compared to 94% of the student interviewers. George (1991) in the British field study and Turtle (1995) also found police officers did not use this technique even though they had been trained to do so.

The Saywitz et al. study provides a powerful demonstration of the effectiveness of the CI with children over the age of 8 years. There are, however, several concerns. Firstly, the CI groups received training while the standard group did not. This may affect the motivation of the CI interviewers (Memon et al., 1994b). Secondly, while the authors of this study did attempt to correlate use of each CI technique with overall memory scores, we have no information about the types of details elicited with the various CI techniques. A related point is that the details about errors are not provided. Thirdly, while the CI practice group had an opportunity to practise and become familiar with the task of retrieval, the control group did not. In more recent research, Koehnken et al. (1992) investigated the effectiveness of the enhanced CI with 51 9–10-year-old children who had been shown a short film. After a delay of 3–5 days, they were questioned by trained psychology students about the film, using either the enhanced CI or the SI. In this study, great care was taken to ensure that the SI interviewers were trained in the same way as CI interviewers save for using the special CI techniques. The enhanced CI produced a 93% increase in the amount of correct information recalled compared to the SI. The number of confabulations (the reporting of details not present in the event) increased, however, and this has been found in several studies where the CI had been used with child interviewees (e.g. Mantwill et al., 1995).

Memon et al. (1993) interviewed 32 6–7-year-olds about an eye test. The effectiveness of the CI, comprising the usual four mnemonic techniques, was compared with that of the SI. The latter, like the CI, was a good interview procedure and one in which the interviewers used open-ended questions and did not interrupt the interviewees when speaking. Children's recall of the event was tested 1 week after the event and again 6 weeks later. As illustrated earlier, children had difficulty in understanding interviewer instructions to change perspective and to recall in reverse order, and became confused about what was expected of them. This may have worked against the CI. Indeed, there were no significant differences in the types of information elicited between each type of interview with the exception of information about locations of objects and people, which was significantly greater with the CI. This increase in location information was possibly a result of the language used to fulfil the context instructions (e.g. 'describe the room') rather than a direct product of memory improvement (one of the problems of the CI research has been the difficulty in separating the two).

Memon and colleagues have attempted to isolate the effects of the individual components of the original CI (Memon et al., 1994a) and have tested the effectiveness of the CI with younger children (aged 6–7 years). Each of the four mnemonic techniques of the CI (context, report in detail, change order, and change perspective) was compared with an instruction to 'try harder'. Prior to each interview, there was a practice session in which each child described a familiar activity, using one of the four CI techniques, such as context reinstatement. There were no significant differences in correct recall or errors as a function of instruction condition, and this suggested that the 'try harder' instruction could be as effective as each of the CI techniques. There were a number of interesting differences between the age groups, most notably that the younger children (5-year-olds) performed less well under the CI 'context reinstatement' and 'change perspective' conditions than the 8-year-olds in the same conditions. A qualitative analysis of the interview transcripts suggested that the children did not fully understand all the techniques and had difficulty in using the 'change perspective' instruction. As Ornstein (1991) points out, a good interviewer should tailor the interview to take into consideration the cognitive and linguistic capabilities of the individual child.

A more recent componential analysis of the CI was undertaken by Milne and Bull (2002). They examined the relative effectiveness of each of four original components of the CI mnemonics in three age groups: 5–6-year-olds, 8–9-year-olds, and adults. The children were shown a video of an accident and 48 hours later the participants were interviewed with one of the following six techniques: context reinstatement, change order, change perspective, report everything, context and report everything, or a control 'try-harder' instruction. The only condition which elicited more recall than the control instruction was a combination of context and report everything. Consistent with Memon et al. (1994a), none of the other CI techniques differed in the amount of recall elicited as compared to the try-harder instruction. Surprisingly, there was no effect of age group on the amount of recall elicited with the different instructions. In a study on the accuracy and forensic relevance of information obtained with the CI in adults, Roberts and Higham (2002) found that the mental reinstatement of context and report-everything instruction used in the free narrative was associated with the most correct and relevant details. This supports the results of Milne and Bull (2002) with children.

Limitations of the use of CI with child interviewees

Several problems in applying the CI with children have been identified. Firstly, younger children (6–7 years of age) have difficulty in understanding the CI techniques in the form developed for adults, although more recent studies report that even 4-year-olds can effectively use a modified version of the CI (see below). Secondly, the CI can on occasion increase errors with children (Memon et al., 1995a; Milne et al., 1995) and confabulations (Koehnken et al., 1992). Thirdly, the CI procedure may also increase demand characteristics in that children respond in a way they think may please the interviewer. This is illustrated in the following transcript taken from the Memon et al. (1993) child interviewee study.

Interviewer: OK, but what about the day the nurse came? Can you tell me about that? I know you've told me already, but I need to find out more.
Child: Yes, just in case I am saying the right things.
Interviewer: Well no, not exactly, but just in case you remember any more.
Child: Yes, some different things that I forgot to say at all.
Interviewer: Yes. The best thing to do is to start again and tell me everything again.
Child: Well, I can't tell you the same things.

The use of CI with special populations

This section briefly considers recent research on whether the CI can aid the recall of vulnerable witnesses, namely, very young children, senior citizens, and adults and children with learning disability.

To date, there have been only two published studies of the efficacy of the CI when the witnesses are older adults. Mello and Fisher (1996) found that the CI led to similar increases in correct recall when the participants were older adults (mean age = 72 years), but Searcy, Bartlett, Memon, and Swanson (2001) found no differences in correct identification (recognition) of a culprit when witnesses (aged 62–79 years) were interviewed with an interview procedure resembling the CI. The failure to find an effect of CI on recognition (in this case, identification of a culprit) is consistent with earlier studies (see Geiselman & Fisher, 1997, for a review). It may be that the CI is more effective in the earlier phases of an investigation when a witness is having to retrieve information from memory in the absence of cues.

Holliday (2003a) has recently reported that children as young as 4–5 years can use the CI instructions (context reinstatement, report everything, and reverse order) and generate more details in free recall when the CI techniques are used. Furthermore, with the same age group, Holliday and Albon (2004) report that a CI given after misinformation reduced children's reporting of misinformation at interview (see also Holliday, 2003b). The latter finding is consistent with Memon, Wark, Holley, Bull, and Koehnken (1996a), who studied 8–9-year-olds, but is at odds with that of Hayes and Delamothe (1997), who found that susceptibility to misinformation in children (aged 5–7 and 9–11 years) was unaffected by interview type.

There is some evidence that the CI can aid the recall of adults (Milne, Clare & Bull, 1999) and children (Milne & Bull, 1996) with mild learning disabilities, although further research is required with this population, using larger sample sizes and people with a broader range of learning difficulties.

Interviewer differences

It is generally accepted that interviewee performance varies with the quality of the interviewer and vice versa. There is evidence that interviewer performance varies with interviewer expectations and with level of training (see Memon et al., 1994b, 1995, 1996b) for details. It is possible that extensive training and practice may iron out some of these differences and also make interviewers more flexible when it comes to adapting the procedure to suit the needs of particular interviewees such as young children.

The CI and delay

Witnesses may not be questioned by the police until some time after they have experienced an event, and there may be further delays from the first interview to any subsequent interview. It is therefore important to establish whether the benefits of the CI can be seen over a delay longer than a week.

Memon, Wark, Bull, and Koehnken (1997a) asked children (aged 8–9 years) to view a magic show and interviewed them after a short delay of 2 days (time 1) and/or a longer delay of 12 days (time 2). At time 1, the CI produced a significantly greater amount of correct recall than did the SI. However, at time 1, the CI also produced significantly more recall errors. At time 2, no differences occurred between CI and SI recall. There was, however, a significant hypermnesia effect (a net increase in amount recalled over time), which might account for the lack of CI effect at time 2.

Larsson, Granhag, and Spjut (2003) were interested in whether the positive effects of the CI hold over time (6 months). In their study, 10–11-year-olds viewed a film and were interviewed either 7 days or 6 months later by CI or SI. Larsson et al. found that children in the CI condition recalled significantly more correct details at both retention intervals, although children interviewed after 7 days were more accurate.

Akehurst, Milne, and Koehnken (2003) examined whether the enhanced CI would aid recall with children aged 8–9 and 11–12 years when there was a 6-day delay. Children viewed a video of a shoplifting incident and were interviewed 4 hours or 6 days later. The CI led to an increase in correct recall with no increases in errors. There were no interactions involving age group or delay.

OVERVIEW

The CI emerges as probably the most exciting development in the field of eyewitness testimony in the last 20 years. It is presented as a technique to facilitate recall, and initial tests show consistent gains in the amount of information that can be gathered from an interviewee with the CI. Over the years, studies of the CI have improved in design in that they have shown that the CI can yield more correct information than interviews that contain the same structure and rapport building. The only concern that remains is that the CI can occasionally increase errors, particularly when the witnesses are young. Obviously, the benefits of any innovative technique need to be carefully weighed against any costs. In a forensic investigation, an increase in number of details could be especially helpful at the information-gathering stage in providing new clues that could lead to a successful conviction. On the other hand, what if investigators are led up the wrong path? Thus, research which helps us understand precisely when and why the CI will be effective and yield forensically relevant information is valuable (see Roberts & Higham, 2002, for a recent example).

Until recently, the recommendation was that the CI should be used only with older children (over the ages of 7 years). However, recent research suggests that developmentally modified versions of the CI can elicit twice as many correct details as control interviews in 4- and 5-year-olds (Holliday & Albon, 2004).

Further research is required on how the quality of the interviewer and the effectiveness of CI training affect the quality of evidence. Training should be monitored over a reasonable period of time in order to assess the effects of feedback and experience in use of the CI techniques on interviewer performance. Furthermore, it is essential that researchers consider the effects of interviewer variables either by including interviewers as factors in the design of experimenters or by collecting baseline data on interviewer performance prior to training. Practitioners are advised that a full training programme in CI, together with follow-up training sessions, should be devised before the techniques are used in the field.

REFERENCES

Akehurst, L., Milne, R. & Koehnken, G. (2003). The effects of children's age and delay on recall in a cognitive or structured interview. *Psychology, Crime and Law*, *9*, 97–107.

Bell, B. & Loftus, E. F. (1989). Trivial persuasion in the courtroom: the power of a few minor details. *Journal of Personality and Social Psychology*, *56*, 669–679.

Boon, J. & Noon, E. (1994). Changing perspectives in cognitive interviewing. *Psychology, Crime and Law*, *1*, 59–69.

Bower, G. (1967). A multicomponent theory of memory trace. In K. W. Spence & J. T. Spence (Eds), *The Psychology of Learning and Motivation*, vol. 1. New York: Academic Press.

Bruck, M. & Ceci, S. J. (1999). The suggestibility of children's memory. *Annual Review of Psychology* *50*, 419–439.

Cherryman, J. & Bull, R. (1995). Investigative interviewing. In F. Leishman, B. Loveday & S. Savage (Eds), *Core issues in policing*. London: Longman.

Clarke, C. & Milne, R. (2001). *National evaluation of the PEACE investigative interviewing course. Police Research Award Scheme*. Report No. PRAS/149. Institute of Criminal Justice Studies, University of Portsmouth.

Clifford, B. R. & George, R. (1996). A field evaluation of training in three methods of witness and victim investigative interviewing. *Psychology, Crime and Law*, *2*, 231–248.

Davis, M., McMahon, M. & Greenwood, K. (2004). The role of visual imagery in the enhanced cognitive interview: guided questioning techniques and individual differences. *Journal of Investigative Psychology and Offender Profiling*, *1*, 33–51.

Fisher, R. P. & Geiselman, R. E. (1992). *Memory enhancing techniques for investigative interviewing: the cognitive interview*. Springfield, IL: Charles C. Thomas.

Fisher, R. P., Geiselman, R. E. & Raymond, D. S. (1987). Critical analysis of police interviewing techniques. *Journal of Police Science and Administration*, *15*, 177–185.

Fisher, R. P., Geiselman, R. E. & Amador, M. (1989). Field test of the cognitive interview: enhancing the recollection of actual victims and interviewees of crime. *Journal of Applied Psychology, 74*, 722–727.

Flexser, A. & Tulving, E. (1978). Retrieval independence in recognition and recall. *Psychological Review, 85*, 153–171.

Frankland, A. & Cohen, L. (1999). Working with recovered memories: draft guidelines for good practice. *The Psychologist, 12*, no. 2.

Geiselman, R. E. & Callot, R. (1990). Reverse versus forward recall of script-based texts. *Applied Cognitive Psychology, 4*, 141–144.

Geiselman, R. E. & Fisher, R. P. (1997). Ten years of cognitive interviewing. In D. Payne & F. Conrad (Eds), *Intersections in basic and applied research* (pp. 291–310). Mahwah, NJ: Lawrence Erlbaum.

Geiselman, R. E., Saywitz, K. J. & Bornstein, G. K. (1990). Cognitive interviewing techniques for child interviewees and interviewees of crime. Report to the State Justice Institute. Mahwah, NJ.

Geiselman, R. E., Fisher, R. P., MacKinnon, D. P. & Holland, H. L. (1985). Eyewitness memory enhancement in the police interview: cognitive retrieval mnemonics versus hypnosis. *Journal of Applied Psychology, 70*, 401–412.

George, R. (1991). A field evaluation of the cognitive interview. Unpublished masters thesis, Polytechnic of East London.

George, R. C. & Clifford, B. (1991). A field comparison of the cognitive interview and conversation management. Paper presented at the British Psychological Society Annual Conference, Bournemouth, UK.

Gudjonsson, G. H. (2003). *The psychology of interrogations and confessions: a handbook.* Chichester: Wiley.

Harris, J. E. (1980). Memory aids people use: two interview studies. *Memory and Cognition, 8*, 31–38.

Hayes, B. & Delamothe, K. (1997). Cognitive interviewing procedures and suggestibility in children's recall. *Journal of Applied Psychology, 4*, 562–577.

Holliday, R. E. (2003a). Reducing misinformation effects in children with cognitive interviews: dissociating recollection and familiarity. *Child Development, 74*, 728–751.

Holliday, R. E. (2003b). The effect of a prior cognitive interview on children's acceptance of misinformation. *Applied Cognitive Psychology, 17*, 443–457.

Holliday, R. E. & Albon, A. J. (2004). Minimising misinformation effects in young children with cognitive interview mnemonics. *Applied Cognitive Psychology, 18*, 263–281.

Home Office (2003). *Achieving best evidence in criminal proceedings*. London: Home Office.

Kebbell, M. & Wagstaff, C. (1996). Enhancing the practicality of the cognitive interview in forensic situations. *Psycoloquy, 7* (16), witness-memory.3.kebbell.

Kebbell, M. R., Milne, R. & Wagstaff, G. F. (1999). The cognitive interview: a survey of its forensic effectiveness. *Psychology, Crime and Law, 5*, 101–115.

Kebbell, M. R., Milne, R. & Wagstaff, G. (2001). The cognitive interview in forensic investigations: a review. In G. B. Traverso & L. Bagnoli (Eds), *Psychology and law in a changing world*. Reading: Harwood.

Koehnken, G., Thurer, C. & Zorberbier, D. (1994). The cognitive interview: are interviewers memories enhanced too? *Applied Cognitive Psychology, 8*, 13–24.

Koehnken, G., Schimmossek, E., Aschermann, E. & Höfer, E. (1995). The cognitive interview and the assessment of the credibility of adults' statements. *Journal of Applied Psychology*, *80*, 671–684.

Koehnken, G., Milne, R., Memon, A. & Bull, R. (1999). A meta-analysis on the effects of the cognitive interview. *Psychology, Crime and Law* (special issue), *5*, 3–27.

Koehnken, G., Finger, M., Nitschke, N., Hofer, E. & Aschermann, E. (1992). Does a cognitive interview interfere with a subsequent statement validity analysis? Paper presented at the Conference of the American Psychology–Law Society, San Diego, CA.

Larsson, A. L., Granhag, P. & Spjut, E. (2003). Children's recall and the cognitive interview: do positive effects hold over time? *Applied Cognitive Psychology*, *17*, 203–214.

Mantwill, M., Koehnken, G. & Aschermann, E. (1995). Effects of the cognitive interview on the recall of familiar and unfamiliar events. *Journal of Applied Psychology*, *80*, 68–78.

Mello, E. W. & Fisher, R. P. (1996). Enhancing older adult eyewitness memory with the cognitive interview. *Applied Cognitive Psychology*, *10*, 403–418.

Memon, A. (1995). The British Psychological Society report on recovered memories. *Expert Evidence*, *3*, 155–158.

Memon, A. & Bull, R. (1991). The cognitive interview: its origins, empirical support, evaluation and practical implications. *Journal of Community and Applied Social Psychology*, *1*, 291–307.

Memon, A. & Koehnken, G. (1992). Helping interviewees to remember more: the cognitive interview. *Expert Evidence: The International Digest of Human Behaviour, Science and Law*, *1*, 39–48.

Memon, A. & Stevenage, S. V. (1996). Interviewing witnesses: what works and what doesn't? *Psycoloquy*, *7* (6), psyc. 96.7.06. witness memory.1.memon.

Memon, A. & Higham, P. (1999). A review of the cognitive interview. *Psychology, Crime and Law* (special issue), *5*, 177–196.

Memon, A., Bull, R. & Smith, M. (1995). Improving the quality of the police interview: can training in the use of cognitive techniques help? *Policing and Society*, *5*, 53–68.

Memon, A., Vrij, A. & Bull, R. (2003). *Psychology and law: truthfulness, accuracy and credibility of victims, witnesses and suspects*, 2nd edn. Chichester: Wiley.

Memon, A., Cronin, Ó., Eaves, R. & Bull, R. (1993). The cognitive interview and child interviewees. In G. M. Stephenson & N. K. Clark (Eds), *Children, evidence and procedure*. Issues in Criminological and Legal Psychology, No. 20. British Psychological Society, Leicester, UK.

Memon, A., Cronin, Ó., Eaves, R. & Bull, R. (1994a). An empirical test of the mnemonic components of the cognitive interview. In G. M. Davies, S. Lloyd-Bostock, M. McMurran & C. Wilson (Eds), *Psychology and law: advances in research*. Berlin: De Gruyter.

Memon, A. Wark, L., Bull, R. & Koehnken, G. (1997a). Isolating the effects of the cognitive interview techniques. *British Journal of Psychology*, *88*, 179–198.

Memon, A., Milne, R., Holley, A., Bull, R. & Koehnken, G. (1994b). Towards understanding the effects of interviewer training in evaluating the cognitive interview. *Applied Cognitive Psychology*, *8*, 641–659.

Memon, A., Wark, L., Holley, A., Bull, R. & Koehnken, G. (1996a). Reducing suggestibility in child witness interviews. *Applied Cognitive Psychology*, *10*, 503–518.

Memon, A., Wark, L., Holley, A., Koehnken, G. & Bull, R. (1996b). Interviewer behaviour in structured and cognitive interviews. *Psychology, Crime and Law*, *3*, 181–201.

Memon, A., Wark, L., Holley, A., Bull, R. & Koehnken, G. (1997b). Eyewitness performance in cognitive and structured interviews. *Memory*, *5*, 639–655.

Memon, A., Wark, L., Holley, A., Koehnken, G. & Bull, R. (1997c). Context effects and event memory: how powerful are the effects? In D. Payne & F. Conrad (Eds), *Intersections in basic and applied memory research* (pp. 175–191). Mahwah, NJ: Lawrence Erlbaum.

Milne, R. & Bull, R. (1996). Interviewing children with mild learning disability with a cognitive interview. In N. K. Clark & G. M. Stephenson (Eds), *Investigative and forensic decision making*. Issues in Criminological Psychology, No. 26. Leicester: British Psychological Society.

Milne, R. & Bull, R. (2002). Back to basics: a componential analysis of the original cognitive interview mnemonics with three age groups. *Applied Cognitive Psychology*, *16*, 1–11.

Milne, R. & Bull, R. (2003). Does the cognitive interview help children to resist the effects of suggestive questioning? *Legal and Criminological Psychology*, *8*, 21–38.

Milne, R., Clare, I. C. H. & Bull, R. (1999). Using the cognitive interview with adults with mild learning disabilities. *Psychology, Crime and Law*, *5*, 81–100.

Milne, R., Bull, R., Koehnken, G. & Memon, A. (1995). The cognitive interview and suggestibility. In G. M. Stephenson & N. K. Clark (Eds), *Criminal behaviour: perceptions, attributions and rationality*. Division of Criminological and Legal Psychology Occasional Papers, No. 22. Leicester: British Psychological Society.

Ornstein, P. A. (1991). Putting interviewing in context. In J. Doris (Ed.), *The suggestibility of children's recollections: implications for eyewitness testimony*. Washington, DC: American Psychological Association.

Ornstein, P. A., Stone, B. P., Medlin, R. G. & Naus, M. J. (1985). Retrieving for rehearsal: an analysis of active rehearsal in children's memory. *Developmental Psychology*, *21*, 633–641.

Paivio, A. (1971). *Imagery and verbal processes*. New York: Holt, Rinehart & Winston.

Payne, D. G. (1987). Hypermnesia and reminiscence in recall: a historical and empirical review. *Psychological Bulletin*, *101*, 5–27.

Roberts, W. T. & Higham, P. A. (2002). Selecting accurate statements from the cognitive interview using confidence ratings. *Journal of Experimental Psychology: Applied*, *8*, 33–43.

Roediger, H. L. & Thorpe, L. A. (1978). The role of recall time in producing hypermnesia. *Memory and Cognition*, *6*, 296–305.

Saywitz, K. J., Geiselman, R. E. & Bornstein, G. K. (1992). Effects of cognitive interviewing and practice on children's recall performance. *Journal of Applied Psychology*, *77*, 744–756.

Scheck, B., Neufeld, P. & Dwyer, J. (2000). *Actual innocence*. New York: Random House.

Scottish Executive (2003). *Supporting child witness guidance pack*. Edinburgh: Scottish Executive.

Searcy, J. H., Bartlett, J. C., Memon, A. & Swanson, K. (2001). Aging and lineup performance at long retention intervals: effects of metamemory and context reinstatement. *Journal of Applied Psychology*, **86**, 207–214.

Tulving, E. (1974). Cue-dependent forgetting. *American Scientist*, **62**, 74–82.

Tulving, E. & Thomson, D. M. (1973). Encoding specificity and retrieval processes in episodic memory. *Psychological Review*, **80**, 353–370.

Turtle, J. (1995). Officers: what do they want? what have they got? Paper presented at the first biennial meeting of the Society for Applied Research in Memory and Cognition, University of British Columbia (July).

Wells, G., Malpass, R., Lindsay, R., Fisher, R. P., Turtle, J. & Fulero, S. (2000). From the lab to the police station: a successful application of eyewitness research. *American Psychologist*, **55**, 581–598.

Westcott, H. L., Davies, G. M. & Bull, R. H. C. (2002). Children's testimony: a handbook of psychological research and forensic practice. Wiley Series in the Psychology of Crime, Policing and Law. Chichester: Wiley.

Part V

The training context

Chapter 20

Training in communication skills: Research, theory and practice

Owen Hargie

T HIS BOOK HAS INCORPORATED a detailed analysis of a wide range of communication skills. In total, it proffers a comprehensive language with which to analyse and evaluate interpersonal interaction. Without the necessary linguistic terminology to guide cognitive processes, it is not possible to conceptualise and deal effectively with complex problems. Since social interaction is undoubtedly a complex process, it is essential to have a language with which to describe, analyse, and attempt to understand this milieu. Thus, the reader should be familiar with a wide glossary of interactional terms, pertaining to verbal and non-verbal communication in group and dyadic contexts, which can be employed when observing, describing, and evaluating interpersonal communication.

An increased knowledge of the nature of communication should be followed by an increase in social competence. This competence encompasses both an ability to perceive and interpret accurately the cues being emitted by others, and a capacity to behave skilfully in response to others. Therefore, it is vital that the information contained in this book be *used* by the reader, who should be prepared to experiment with various social techniques until the most effective response repertoire is developed in any particular situation. It is anticipated that such experimentation will, for many professionals, occur in the context of a skills-training programme. For this reason, it is useful to examine the rationale for the skills approach to training, and some of the criticisms which have been levelled at this approach.

TRAINING IN SOCIAL SKILLS

In his overview of the skills approach, Argyle (1999, p. 142) noted: 'One of the implications of looking at social behaviour as a social skill was the likelihood that it could be trained in the way that manual skills are trained.' This in fact proved to be the case. As discussed in the Introduction to this book, many professionals now undergo some form of specialised training in interpersonal communication as a preparation for practical experience. The most widely utilised method of training for professionals is the microtraining approach, which can be traced back to the development of microteaching in teacher education. Microteaching was first introduced at Stanford University, California, in 1963, when a number of educationists there decided that existing techniques for training teachers 'how to teach' needed to be revised. In recognising the many and manifold nuances involved in classroom teaching, the Stanford team felt that any attempt to train teachers should take place in a simplified situation (Allen & Ryan, 1969). Attention was turned to the methods of training used in other fields, where complicated skills were taught by being 'broken down' into simpler skill areas, and training often occurred in a simulated situation, rather than in the real environment.

Thus, prior to the presentation of a play, actors engage in rehearsals when various scenes are practised in isolation until judged to be satisfactory. Tennis players in training concentrate on specific aspects, such as the serve, smash, lob, volley, and backhand, in order to improve their overall game. Similarly, the learner driver learns to use various controls separately before taking the car on the road. The rationale in all of these instances is to analyse the overall complex act in terms of simpler component parts, train the individual to identify and utilise the parts separately, and then combine the parts until the complete act is assimilated.

At Stanford, this approach was applied to the training of teachers in a programme which comprised learning a number of teaching skills in a scaled-down teaching encounter termed 'microteaching'. In microteaching, the trainee taught a small group of pupils (5–10) for a short period of time (5–10 minutes), during which time the focus was on one particular skill of teaching, such as using questions. This 'microlesson', which took place in college with actual pupils being bussed in, was video-recorded, and the trainee then received feedback on the skill under review (e.g. effectiveness of the questioning techniques used), in the form of a video replay coupled with tutorial guidance. This procedure was repeated for a number of teaching skills, and was designed to prepare students more systematically for actual classroom teaching practice.

Research in microteaching found this to be an effective method for training teachers (Hargie & Maidment, 1979; McGarvey & Swallow, 1986). As a result, this training method was adapted by trainers in other fields to meet their own particular training requirements (Hayes, 2002). This eventually resulted in the introduction of the term 'microtraining', to describe the approach wherein the core skills involved in professional interaction are identified separately, and trainees are provided with the opportunity to acquire these in a safe training environment. More recently, the term 'communication skills training' (CST) has been employed to describe this microtraining method.

Hargie and Saunders (1983) identified three distinct phases in this form of CST, namely, preparation, training, and evaluation. At the preparation stage, the skills necessary for effective professional communication are identified (for a review of skill identification methods, see Caves, 1988). Although most of the skills presented in this book are relevant to all professions, there are important differences in focus and emphasis. For example, teachers use a much larger volume of questions during lessons than counsellors in helping sessions, and the main types of questions used also differ (see Chapter 4). Thus, the application of skills to contexts is an important task during preparation.

The second stage is the implementation of training. The first part of training is devoted to what Dickson et al. (1997) referred to as the sensitisation phase, during which trainees learn to identify and label the communication skills. This involves guided reading, lectures, seminars, and the use of video models of skills in action. Sensitisation is followed by practice, when trainees are given an opportunity to try out the skills, usually in a simulated encounter such as role-play. This practice is normally video recorded and is then followed by the phase when trainees receive feedback on their performance in the form of comments from tutor and peers, together with discussion and analysis of the video replay.

The final element is the evaluation of the programme. This includes ascertaining the attitudes of trainees to the CST programme itself, charting changes in the performance of trainees and their ability to interact successfully in the professional situation, and monitoring the impact of the programme upon relevant client groups. Although a large amount of formal evaluation has been conducted in this field, trainers also should evaluate their programmes informally, in terms of feedback from trainees, other tutors, and fieldwork supervisors. Such information can then be used to guide future training approaches.

The CST paradigm is clearly based on a 'reductionist' strategy for the study of social interaction. As was discussed in Chapters 1 and 2, this approach to the analysis of social skill evolved from work carried out in the field of motor skill, where a similar modus operandi had proved to be successful. Thus, it was argued, just as a motor sequence, such as driving a car or operating a machine, can be broken down into component actions, so, too, can a social sequence, such as interviewing or teaching, be broken down into component skills.

CRITICISMS OF THE SKILLS APPROACH

This reductionist methodology to the study of interpersonal communication has met with some opposition from adherents of other theoretical perspectives. The opposition falls into two main areas. First, it is argued that the analysis of communication in terms of skills simply does not make sense, since the study of such component skills is totally different from the study of the whole communication. Second, there is the view that by analysing social interaction in terms of skilled behaviour the spontaneity and genuineness of human interaction is lost. It is useful to examine each of these criticisms separately.

The whole and the parts

Advocates of Gestalt psychology reject the notion that it is meaningful to isolate small segments of an overall sequence, and study these in isolation from the whole. Gestalt psychology (the psychology of form) originated in Germany in the early twentieth century, and emphasised the concept of structure. A central tenet of Gestaltism is that the whole is greater than the sum of the parts. Once an overall structure is broken down into smaller units, it is argued, the original meaning or form is changed accordingly, since the study of each of the units in isolation is not equivalent to the study of the whole. For example, a triangle comprises three intersecting straight lines, yet the study of each of the lines in isolation is patently different from the study of the overall triangle.

Within Gestalt literature, however, there is confusion as to the nature of the relationship of component elements to the whole from which they are derived. Murphy and Kovach (1972) illustrated how, on the one hand, some Gestaltists argued that the component parts need to be studied in terms of their interrelationships in order to understand the whole structure. On the other hand, however, there is the view that there are no component parts with separate attributes, and that structures can be studied meaningfully only as total entities. Taking this latter, more extreme interpretation, social interaction could be likened to a beautiful piece of pottery. The beauty and meaning of the pottery lie in its wholeness, and if the piece of pottery is smashed into smaller parts this beauty and meaning are lost forever. It does not make sense to study each of the smaller parts separately in order to understand the whole, and even if the parts are carefully put back together again the original beauty is lost.

But is social interaction broken down in this sense in CST? Proponents of CST would argue that the answer to this question is 'no'. Rather, social interaction is analysed in terms of clearly identifiable behaviours that are, at the same time, interrelated. Although emphasis is placed on one particular skill sequence of behaviours at a time during training, others will be present. Thus, for instance, while the focus may be on the skill of questioning, it is recognised that skills such as listening or reinforcing are also operative when questions are being employed. No one skill is used in total isolation, and in this sense the 'parts' of social interaction differ from the 'parts' of a broken piece of pottery. Indeed, it can be argued that the piece of pottery as an entity represents only one component and that the analogy to interaction is therefore spurious. To take a different example, in studying a motor car, it is essential to understand the workings of the various elements which comprise the more complex whole in order to diagnose breakdown, effect repair, or improve performance. In similar vein, social interaction is a multifarious process that necessitates careful examination to ensure understanding. Just as it is possible to drive a car without understanding the mechanics of its operation, so it is possible to interact socially without being able to analyse the key dimensions involved in the process. However, to achieve greater comprehension and insight, identify areas of communication weakness, or train people to improve their social repertoire, a much more systematic and greater depth of analysis is required.

Obviously, each of the interpersonal skills studied can exist only in a social context. Social interaction, by definition, can never occur in a vacuum and this is recognised within the skills model which underpins the 'micro' approach to the analysis of interpersonal interaction (see Chapter 2, for a discussion of this model). In practice, the CST method can be described as one of homing in and honing up, in which one aspect of social interaction is focused upon at a time, and trainees are encouraged to develop and refine their use of this particular aspect. Once the trainee has acquired a working knowledge of a number of skills of social interaction, the ultimate goal is to encourage the appropriate use of these skills in an integrated fashion.

It is also emphasised within the skills model that the overall process of social interaction is affected by a large number of both situational and personal factors, which may be operative at any given moment (see Chapter 2). The study of skills per se is undertaken in order to provide some insight into this overall process of communication. It is recognised that not only should these elements be studied separately, but also that consideration should be given to the interrelationship between elements. This line of thought is consistent with the view of those Gestaltists who hold that the study of parts should be undertaken in terms of their interrelationships, in order to understand the overall structure.

Artificiality

Another objection that has been raised in opposition to CST is that, by teaching interpersonal skills, social interaction will eventually lose its natural beauty and become artificial and stilted. Everyone will become so aware of their own actions, and the actions and reactions of others, that this knowledge will inhibit their natural behaviour. In the final analysis, people will all end up behaving in the same fashion, and individuality will be lost for ever. This line of argument raises several important issues concerning the skills approach to training in communication.

During CST, those undergoing instruction will become aware of the nature and function of social behaviour – indeed, the development of such awareness is one of the main objectives of training. As a result of such awareness, social actions will become more conscious and at times may even seem artificial. This also occurs during the learning of motor skills. For example, the learner driver will be conscious of the component skills necessary to perform the act of driving, namely, depressing clutch, engaging gear, releasing clutch, depressing accelerator, and so on. When one is completely conscious of all of these motor skills, the overall act becomes less fluent – thus, the learner driver may experience 'kangaroo petrol syndrome'! With practice and experience, however, the motor skills involved in driving a car become less conscious, and eventually the individual performs the actions automatically. It is at this stage that the person is said to be skilled.

A similar phenomenon occurs in CST. Once the individual receives instruction in the use of a particular skill, the cognitive processes involved in the performing of this skill become conscious. At this stage, a 'training dip' may occur, where the awareness of the skill actually interferes with its implementation and performance suffers accordingly. This is not a particularly surprising phenomenon and occurs not just with trainees undergoing programmes of CST, but with all students involved in the academic study of human behaviour, where, as noted by Mulholland (1994, p. xiv), there can be 'a period of awkwardness and self-consciousness, but once that stage has passed people would be left with an increase in knowledge about the communicative practices of their daily lives, and an enhanced potential to communicate successfully.' After the training period, the use of skills will again become spontaneous, and the individual will lose this self-consciousness. However, if an interaction becomes strained, we are more likely to become more aware of and focus upon actual behaviour. At such times, prior training in communication skills should bear fruit, allowing us to reflect quickly on the likely consequences of certain courses of action, in relation to the probable reactions of the others involved.

Training dips are also encountered in the learning of motor skills. Thus, someone being coached in tennis may find that having to focus on the component elements of, and practise separately, the serve, lob, smash, or volley actually interferes with the overall performance. It is only when the tennis player has a chance to 'put it all together' that performance begins to improve. Ivey et al. (2002), in pointing out that 'Awareness of the many components involved in learning a skill can interfere with coordination' (p. 429), used the analogy of the Japanese samurai to illustrate this aspect of skill learning. Samurai learn the complex process of sword handling through an intensive programme in which the component skills are broken down and studied separately. Once the skills have been fully acquired, the samurai go to a mountain to meditate and deliberately 'forget' what has been learned. When they return and find they do not have to think about the skills, but can implement them 'naturally', they have become samurai.

The initial emphasis in CST has been on identifying social behaviours, and grouping these behaviours into skills in order to facilitate the training process. In this respect, CST has been successful and, as illustrated in this book, advances have been made in the identification and classification of a large number of skills in terms of their behavioural determinants. Once the behaviours have been mastered by the trainee, the categorisation, by the individual, of these behaviours into more global skill concepts seems to facilitate their utilisation during social interaction. As discussed in Chapter 1, such larger skill concepts are assimilated into the cognitive schemata employed by the individual during social encounters. These are then used to guide responses in that they provide various strategies for the individual to employ in the course of any interaction sequence (e.g. ask *questions* to get information, provide *rewards* to encourage participation, be *assertive* to ensure that one's rights are respected, introduce *humour* to make the interaction more enjoyable). Just as the tennis player combines the separate motor skills, once these social skill concepts have been fully assimilated, they, too, are 'put together' in the overall social performance. Behaviour then becomes smoother and fully coordinated, with the individual employing the concepts subconsciously. In other words, the person becomes more socially skilled.

As mentioned earlier, the study of communication skills provides the individual with a language for interpreting social interaction. This is of vital import, since without such a language it would be extremely difficult to analyse or evaluate social behaviour. By studying interaction in terms of skills, it is possible to discuss the nuances of interpersonal communication, and give and receive feedback on performance. It also facilitates reflection on previous encounters, and the conceptualisation of these in terms of the appropriateness of the skills employed, and how these could be developed or refined. Indeed, this process of self-analysis is one of the most important long-term benefits of CST.

The argument that providing professionals with the opportunity to engage in CST will result in them all behaving in exactly the same way can also be countered. This is analogous to arguing that by teaching everyone to talk we will all eventually end up saying exactly the same things. Just as the latter state of affairs has not prevailed, there is absolutely no reason to believe that the former state of affairs would either. Individual differences will always influence the ways in which people behave socially. One's personality, home background, attitudes, values, and so on invariably affect one's goals in any given situation, and this, in turn, accordingly affects how one behaves. Different professionals develop different styles of behaviour in different contexts, and this is a desirable state of affairs. There is no evidence to suggest that, after instruction in interpersonal skills, everyone will conform to a set pattern of behaviour in any given situation. Rather, it is hoped that the individual will become more aware of the consequences of particular actions in given situations and will be able to choose those deemed most suitable.

The emphasis during CST is on the development of understanding of social interaction, in terms of the effects of behaviour. Any controls on this behaviour should come from within the individual, who is always the decision maker in terms of choice of responses. It is intended that the individual will become freer as a result of such training, possessing a greater behavioural repertoire from which to choose. This is, in fact, evidenced by the finding that CST serves to increase the confidence of trainees in the professional situation.

The function of training

In terms of wider social and cultural concerns, another criticism of the CST approach pertains to the reason for offering this training, the actual purpose of the programme itself, and the meanings imbued in the process. For example, Elmes and Costello (1992) criticised CST in the business sphere, on the basis that it is an inherently manipulative means of strengthening management control within organisations. They argued that CST uses covert methods of control by creating emotional indebtedness (employees may conceive attendance as a form of paid vacation and so have their loyalty to the company increased), by transforming the training experience into a sophisticated type of social drama conducted by charismatic trainers in such a way as to create a form of mystification, and by changing the views of trainees about what constitutes effective communication. It should be noted that such criticisms could be applied to any form of communicaton training in the business sphere, and not just to CST. However, the criticisms of CST made by Elmes and Costello (1992) were based primarily upon observations at one workshop, and have been countered by Hargie and Tourish (1994).

The 'time-off from work' argument could be levelled at any form of in-service training away from the workplace wherein trainees are allowed to participate during working hours. The CST programme discussed by Elmes and Costello took place away from participants' workplace, in a rather plush environment, and was undertaken by trainers wearing expensive apparel. But this would not be typical. While it is likely that in-service training can be best facilitated if people are away from the day-to-day pressures of work, little research exists to validate the exact location of training programmes. Yet, removing employees from their work environment can also be viewed as mystification and manipulation – the interpretation proffered by Elmes and Costello (1992). However, if it is accepted that training is necessary, decisions then have to be taken about its location. Training can, and does, occur in-house run by staff in the organisation's own training department and using the firm's facilities. Where these do not exist, external consultants can be employed, and such training normally occurs in modest hotels or conference-type locations. Typically, training is conducted by staff in normal business attire. In all of these senses, the CST course experienced by Elmes and Costello, with its palatial surroundings, is not typical. At the pre-service level, of course, CST normally occurs in college, conducted by far from mystifying lecturing staff, within a less grandiose setting!

Elmes and Costello did, however, raise the more important issue of CST being conducted primarily for the benefit of trainees. Of course, this can also lead to bene-fits for the employer in relation to job performance of employees. For instance, if a hospital pharmacist attends a training programme on the skills of interviewing, it would be reasonable for the employing authority to expect benefits to accrue, both for the pharmacist, in terms of greater knowledge, awareness, insight, and job satisfac-tion, and for patients, in terms of how they are dealt with during actual interviews. However, some of the central concerns highlighted by Elmes and Costello (1992) were in fact detailed by Pawlak et al. (1982), who, in recognising the tensions that may be inherent between the goals of organisations and those of trainees, pointed out that CST trainers 'may have to confront management with the incongruence if it is marked and likely to lead to low trainee motivation or dissatisfaction. In extreme circum-stances, they may even have to refuse to offer the training program' (p. 379).

In their analysis of CST as manipulation, Elmes and Costello failed to dis-tinguish between the *acquisition* of skill and how it is *exercised*. Certainly, all skills are open to abuse. Children taught to write may later use the skill of writing to spray obscenities on walls or send poison pen letters, but this does not mean that they should not be taught to be literate. Likewise, people may use interpersonal skills learned during CST for devious, Machiavellian purposes. However, the possibility of such abuse does not *ipso facto* mean that people should be denied training in how to function effectively with others. What is clear is that ethical issues in CST should form an integral part of the training package, and this would include how the knowledge learned should be used. For instance, Elmes and Costello contended that it is unethical to attempt behavioural change without individuals being aware such an attempt is being made. This is true, and so the aims and objectives of CST should be fully itemised by trainers at the outset of the programme, and discussed with trainees. The main ethical dimensions of communication – honesty, openness, justice, respect for others, and non-maleficence – should also be covered (see Hargie, Dickson & Tourish, 2004).

What Elmes and Costello did identify was that the wider phenomenological concerns regarding the backdrop within which training occurs have not been charted (although, again, this is true of most forms of training, not just CST). The social meaning of the process for trainer and trainee has not been a central area of focus. While recognising the importance of situational context, skills theorists have not grappled with the issue of how trainees conceptualise their involvement in training and what meanings are construed therein. Trainees probably bring a range of inter-pretations to the training process, some of which will be more positive than others.

Training does not occur in a vacuum, and research into CST should consider the wider ramifications of the methodological and social dimensions which underpin this approach. For example, an organisation may wish employees to undergo CST simply to produce greater profits as a result of increased sales or influencing skills on their part. This would be an example of CST deployed as management control rather than for the personal development of the trainee. An ethical consideration of these issues would suggest that a CST programme should seek to address both the wider needs of the organisation and the individual needs of the trainee.

THE EFFECTIVENESS OF CST

A vast volume of research has been conducted into the effectiveness of the microtrain-ing approach to CST. Part of the problem with comparisons of research in this field is that CST is not a unitary phenomenon. Rather, there are wide variations in approach within this paradigm, in terms of number of skills covered, time spent on each phase of training, nature and use of model tapes, type and length of practical sessions, numbers of trainees involved, total training time, and so on. Indeed, Dickson et al. (1997) illustrated how CST has been widely adapted to meet the specific needs of a variety of diverse groups. For example, it has been shown to be highly effective in clinical contexts (Emmers-Sommer, Allen, Bourhis, Sahlstein et al., 2004). Indeed, in this latter realm, Segrin and Givertz (2003, p. 167) concluded: 'The evidence accumu-lated thus far suggests that social skills training has great promise for improving the condition of people who are dealing with an amazingly vast array of challenges in life.'

More generally, the main conclusion to be reached from an analysis of research investigations is that this system of training offers significant benefits. In an early review, these were summarised by Ellis and Whittington (1981, pp. 195–196) as follows:

1   Short-term effects are consistently reported.
2   Trainees' attitudes toward the experience are positive.
3   Results (short- and long-term) are at least as positive as most comparable interventions.
4   It engenders debate among theorists, practitioners and trainees about the nature and contexts of interaction.
5   It is a relatively short, inexpensive intervention strategy which proved viable across a wide range of trainees and settings.
6   The face-validity of the exercise is high. Other activities with similar face-validity are far more expensive and, to date, lack any comparably rigorous evaluation.

In a slightly later review, Hargie and Saunders (1983, p. 163) likewise concluded: 'The general outcome from this research has been to demonstrate that microtraining is an effective method for improving the communicative competence of trainees; that it is often more effective than alternative training approaches; and that it is well received by both trainers and trainees alike.'

These findings have been confirmed in a whole host of studies across a variety of professional contexts, as detailed by, among others, Baker and Daniels (1989), Baker et al. (1990), Cronin and Glenn (1991), Papa and Graham (1991), Irving (1995), Tourish and Hargie (1995), Dickson et al. (1997), Ostell et al. (1998), and Ivey, D'Andrea, Ivey, and Simek-Morgan (2002). For example, Dickson et al. (1997), in relation to CST with health professionals, concluded that 'skills training is effective in improving communication performance, clinical practice and patient satisfaction' (p. 48). Likewise, the conclusion reached by Baker and Daniels (1989) in relation to counsellor training was that 'the microcounseling paradigm, as it has been used thus far, is an effective educational program' (p. 218). In an evaluation of CST in the business field, Papa and Graham (1991) found that 'Managers participating in communication skills training received significantly higher performance ratings on interpersonal skills, problem-solving ability and productivity' (p. 368) than those receiving no such training. Similarly, Cronin and Glenn (1991), in their analysis of the effects of CST on the communicative competence of students in the higher education context, concluded that 'this approach holds significant promise for curricular development and improvement of student communication skills' (p. 356). It should be realised, of course, that if a communication-training programme is not well designed, or does not fully meet the requirements of the situation for which the trainee is being prepared, it will be less effective (see Roloff, Putnam & Anastasiou, 2003), or even harmful (see Hajek & Giles, 2003). The prerequisites for effective training were aptly delineated by Street (2003, p. 926):

> The programs that have been most successful (a) are intensive and delivered over an extended period of time, (b) provide opportunities for practice and feedback on performance, (c) present role models, (d) provide follow-up assessments and review, and, importantly, (e) have institutional support and incentives promoting the value of effective communication.

Thus, there is overwhelming evidence that, when used in a systematic, coordinated and informed fashion, CST is indeed an effective training medium. As summarised by Ivey (1994, p. 17), 'a general conclusion is warranted that considerable validation of the microtraining model is found in the research literature'.

OVERVIEW

This book has presented a comprehensive analysis and evaluation of effective interpersonal communication, in terms of providing an understanding of many of the nuances of social interaction, highlighting the importance of an awareness of one's own behaviour and of its effect upon others, interpreting and making sense of the responses of others, and generally contributing to increased social awareness and interpersonal competence. The importance of effective communication skills cannot be overemphasised. As summarised by Rogers and Escudero (2004, p. 3), 'Social relationships lie at the heart of our humanness, and in turn, communication lies at the heart of our relationships.' We now know that socially skilled individuals tend to be happier and more resistant to stress and psychosocial problems, and to achieve more in academic and professional contexts. Given these potential benefits, it is important for us to analyse and attempt to understand the processes involved in skill acquisition and development.

The theoretical perspectives discussed in Part I are essential in that they provide an underlying rationale for the analytic approach to communication adopted in the remaining chapters of the book. The core communication skills covered in Part II are of direct application to all professionals. Likewise, in most occupations, people spend a considerable proportion of their time working in groups, being assertive, negotiating, and ensuring effective relationships are maintained with others, and so knowledge of these specialised aspects, as covered in Part III, is of vital import. Finally, the dimensions of interviewing included in Part IV are of relevance to most professionals, who will be involved to a greater or lesser degree in selecting, appraising, helping, or using a cognitive approach to eliciting information.

Overall, therefore, this text should be a useful handbook for many professionals, both pre-service and practising. Ideally, it can be employed as a course reader during training programmes in communication, thereby facilitating the learning by trainees of interpersonal skills and dimensions. However, it can also be employed solely as a reference text by the interested, experienced professional. Either way, the coverage represents the most comprehensive review to date of communication skills. At the same time, it should be recognised that this is a rapidly developing field of study and, as knowledge increases, further skills and dimensions will be identified, and awareness of interpersonal communication expanded accordingly.

REFERENCES

Allen, D. & Ryan, K. (1969). *Microteaching*. Reading, MA: Addison-Wesley.

Argyle, M. (1999). Why I study social skills. *The Psychologist*, *12*, 142.

Baker, S. & Daniels, T. (1989). Integrating research on the microcounseling paradigm: a meta-analysis. *Journal of Counseling Psychology*, *36*, 213–222.

Baker, S., Daniels, T. & Greeley, A. (1990). Systematic training of graduate level counselors: narrative and meta-analytic reviews of three major programs. *Counseling Psychologist*, *18*, 355–421.

Caves, R. (1988). Consultative methods for extracting expert knowledge about professional competence. In R. Ellis (Ed.), *Professional competence and quality assurance in the caring professions*. London: Croom Helm.

Cronin, M. & Glenn, P. (1991). Oral communication across the curriculum in higher education: the state of the art. *Communication Education*, *40*, 356–367.

Dickson, D., Hargie, O. & Morrow, N. (1997). *Communication skills training for health professionals*, 2nd edn. London: Chapman & Hall.

Ellis, R. & Whittington, D. (1981). *A guide to social skill training*. London: Croom Helm.

Elmes, M. & Costello, M. (1992). Mystification and social drama: the hidden side of communication skills training. *Human Relations*, *45*, 427–445.

Emmers-Sommer, T., Allen, M., Bourhis, J., Sahlstein, E., Laskowski, K., Falato, W., Ackerman, J., Erian, M., Barringer, D., Weiner, J., Corey, J., Kreiger, J., Moramba, G.

& Cashman, L. (2004). A meta-analysis of the relationship between social skills and sexual offenders. *Communication Reports*, *17*, 1–10.

Hajek, C. & Giles, H. (2003). New directions in intercultural communication competence: the process model. In J. Greene & B. Burleson (Eds), *Handbook of communication and social interaction skills*. Mahwah, NJ: Lawrence Erlbaum.

Hargie, O. (1980). An evaluation of a microteaching programme. D.Phil. thesis, University of Ulster, Jordanstown.

Hargie, O. & Maidment, P. (1979). *Microteaching in perspective*. Belfast: Blackstaff Press.

Hargie, O. & Saunders, C. (1983). Training professional skills. In P. Dowrick & S. Biggs (Eds), *Using video*. London: Wiley.

Hargie, O. & Tourish, D. (1994). Communication skills training: management manipulation or personal development? *Human Relations*, *47*, 1377–1389.

Hargie, O. Dickson, D. & Tourish, D. (2004). *Communication skills for effective management*. Basingstoke: Macmillan.

Hayes, J. (2002). *Interpersonal skills at work*, 2nd edn. London: Routledge.

Irving, P. (1995). A reconceptualisation of Rogerian core conditions of facilitative communication: implications for training. D.Phil. thesis, University of Ulster, Jordanstown.

Ivey, A. (1994). *Intentional interviewing and counseling: facilitating client development in a multicultural society*, 3rd edn. Pacific Grove, CA: Brooks/Cole.

Ivey, A., D'Andrea, M., Ivey, M. & Simek-Morgan, L. (2002). *Theories of counseling and psychotherapy: a multicultural perspective*, 5th edn. Boston, MA: Allyn and Bacon.

McGarvey, B. & Swallow, D. (1986). *Microteaching in teacher education and training*. London: Croom Helm.

Mulholland, J. (1994). *Handbook of persuasive tactics. A practical language guide*. London: Routledge.

Murphy, G. & Kovach, J. (1972). *Historical introduction to modern psychology*. London: Routledge & Kegan Paul.

Ostell, A., Baverstock, S. & Wright, P. (1998). Interpersonal skills of managing emotion at work. *The Psychologist*, *12*, 30–34.

Papa, M. & Graham, E. (1991). The impact of diagnosing skill deficiencies and assessment-based communication training on managerial performance. *Communication Education*, *40*, 368–384.

Pawlak, E., Way, I. & Thompson, D. (1982). Assessing factors that influence skills training in organizations. In E. K. Marshall & P. D. Kurtz (Eds), *Interpersonal helping skills*. San Francisco, CA: Jossey-Bass.

Rogers, L. & Escudero, V. (2004). Theoretical foundations. In L. Rogers & V. Escudero (Eds), *Relational communication: an international perspective to the study of process and form*. Mahwah, NJ: Lawrence Erlbaum.

Roloff, M., Putnam, L. & Anastasiou, L. (2003). Negotiation skills. In J. Greene & B. Burleson (Eds), *Handbook of communication and social interaction skills*. Mahwah, NJ: Lawrence Erlbaum.

Segrin, C. & Givertz, M. (2003). Methods of social skills training and development. In J. Greene & B. Burleson (Eds), *Handbook of communication and social interaction skills*. Mahwah, NJ: Lawrence Erlbaum.

Street, R. (2003). Interpersonal communication skills in health care contexts. In J. Greene & B. Burleson (Eds), *Handbook of communication and social interaction skills*. Mahwah, NJ: Lawrence Erlbaum.

Tourish, D. & Hargie, C. (1995). Preparing students for selection interviews: a template for training and curriculum development. *Innovation and Learning in Education, 1*, 22–27.

Name index

Subject index

10-year rule for learning complex
skills 11
theory of planned behaviour 15, 327–8
theory of reasoned action 15
theory of reasoned action 326–7
theory of self-regulation 15
theory of trying 15
touch 47, 57, 80, 87, 88, 89, 93, 94, 104,
129, 430
tough-mindedness 56
track-checking behaviour 51
training in communication skills:
background to 553–5; criticisms of
555–9; effectiveness of 561–2;
functions of 559–61; phases of 555

trait theorists 56
trust 27, 132, 165, 173, 182, 186, 212–3,
220, 230, 232, 234, 236, 239, 241, 249,
252, 315, 346, 397–9, 414, 417, 429,
433, 442–4, 465, 469, 512, 519, 520
trust-attraction hypothesis 236
type A and type B personalities
typewriting skills 8, 27

uncertainty reduction 42, 237
upshot formulations 180

wh-questions 128

zone of proximal development 155